Nibbāna
The Mind Stilled

Venerable
Bhikkhu Katukurunde Ñāṇananda

Study Edition

Theravada Tipitaka Press

Free Publication – Printed at cost level for private reference only. No commercial value. Free ebook version available online.

Nibbāna Meditation Association

www.nibbānam.com

Visit our website at *books.nibbanam.com* where you can download a free digital copy of this printed edition.

Or contact the editor via nibbanam@gmail.com

Printed in the United States of America

First Printing: May 2010

ISBN- 9781453713006

Dedicated to My Upajjhāya,

The late Venerable

Matara Sri Ñāṇārāma Mahāthera

of Meetirigala Nissarana Vanaya

Forest Hermitage,

Sri Lanka

About Nibbāna – The Mind Stilled

"Bikkhu Katukurunde Nanananda is one of Sri Lanka's foremost meditative monks. He aparently lives in a little rock 'kuti' with a little rock bed like the arahanths of the past in Sri Lanka. He entertains guests very little and spends most of his time in seclusion. He does give meditation instructions for those who are serious and I know monks and nuns from all over Sri Lanka who visit him for instructions. He spent many years in quiet seclusion until one day his teacher invited him to talk on nibbana. This was followed by the 'nibbana' sermons which blew everyone away. He has another series known as the 'pahankanuwa sermons' denoting the place they were delivered from. He is the epitome of monkhood for his practice, renunciation, humbleness, faith and wisdom."

www.dhammawheel.com

"...out in the jungle living beneath a huge boulder in a tin corrugated hut with a skeleton and a few bookcases of dhamma books was Nanananda. I can say of all the monks I met in Sri Lanka he made the greatest impression, in his devotion to practice, his command of Pali (which he was a lecturer in), and his very modern ... views of Dhamma. Truly a remarkable man following the path... I encountered a monk capable of imparting the power and complexity of the dhamma simply and succintly."

E.Spellman

"...profound, comprehensive and enlightening. no other series of Dhamma talks in Sri Lanka had (and still has) such an influence on Buddhists and Vipassana practioners as this series of 33 Dhamma talks given by the Venerable Katukurunde Nyanananda, one of Sri Lanka's most renowned Dhamma teachers. Sparked by the improper understanding of high ranking Buddhist monks on key Buddhist concepts and insights, the Venerable Nyanananda, with his unmatched knowledge of the Tipitaka worked him and his audience through - as it seems - all dark, difficult and mysterious explanations of the Buddha leaving only clarity, understanding and wisdom behind - a clear roadmap to what insight meditation is all about, what the Buddha's Dhamma tries to achieve and how the goal itself, Nibbana, is to be properly understood."

Bhikkhu Isidatta,
www.nibbanam.com

About the Author

The venerable author of this compendium of sermons on Nibbāna was born in 1940. He graduated from the University of Peradeniya in 1962 and served as an Assistant Lecturer in Pāli at the same University for a brief period. Impelled by a deep understanding of the teachings of the Buddha, he renounced his post in 1967 to enter the Order of Buddhist monks under the name Katukurunde Ñāṇananda in the forest monastic tradition of Sri Lanka.

The 33 sermons on Nibbāna, of which the 25 are translated into English and are presented in this edition, were originally delivered by the venerable author to his fellow monks at the behest of his revered preceptor, the late venerable Matara Sri Ñāṇārāma Mahāthera, the chief incumbent of Meetirigala Hermitage (Meetirigala Nissarana Vanaya) and an illustrious exponent of Insight Meditation in Sri Lanka. The meeting of these two eminent disciples of the Buddha in a teacher–pupil relationship for nearly two decades, led to an outstanding seminal contribution to the understanding of the Dhamma in its correct perspective.

The reader of these pages will no doubt find unmistakable evidence of the author's exposure to the methods of critical examination in the understanding of exegetical treatises during his university days. The mode of presentation, however, reveals a penetrative understanding of the deeper aspects of the Buddha's teaching blossoming into a harmonious blend of academic erudition with practical application of that intensive learning process afforded by the contemplative life of a forest monk.

Readers familiar with the author's *Concept and Reality*, *Ideal Solitude*, and *Magic of the Mind* will find that the present set of sermons draws upon some of the doctrinal points outlined in those books for deeper analysis. Indeed these sermons exhibit a salutary orientation towards the practical aspects of the Buddha's teaching – a tendency already evident in the author's *Towards Calm and Insight*, and *Seeing Through*.

—Mr. G.T. Bandara
The Settler, D.G.M.B
Royal Institute, 191, Havelock Road,
Colombo – 05.
Sri Lanka

Contents

About the Author 5
Contents 7
Abbreviations 9
Introduction 11
Nibbāna Sermon 1 15
Nibbāna Sermon 2 41
Nibbāna Sermon 3 69
Nibbāna Sermon 4 99
Nibbāna Sermon 5 125
Nibbāna Sermon 6 151
Nibbāna Sermon 7 177
Nibbāna Sermon 8 203
Nibbāna Sermon 9 233
Nibbāna Sermon 10 263
Nibbāna Sermon 11 289
Nibbāna Sermon 12 313
Nibbāna Sermon 13 337
Nibbāna Sermon 14 363
Nibbāna Sermon 15 389
Nibbāna Sermon 16 415
Nibbāna Sermon 17 441
Nibbāna Sermon 18 467
Nibbāna Sermon 19 491

Abbreviations

A	Aṅguttara Nikāya
Abhidh-av	Abhidhammāvatāra
Abhidh-s	Abhidhammatthasaṅgaha
As	Atthasālinī (Comy on the Dhammasaṅgaṇī)
It	Itivuttaka
Ud	Udāna
Ud-a	Paramatthadīpanī (Comy on the Udāna)
Ja	Jātaka
Th	Theragāthā
Th-a	Theragāthā Aṭṭhakathā
Thī	Therīgāthā
D	Dīgha Nikāya
Dhp	Dhammapada
Dhp-a	Dhammapada Aṭṭhakathā
Khp	Khuddhakapāṭha
Nett	Nettippakaraṇa
Nid I	Mahāniddesa
Nid II	Cūḷaniddesa
Paṭis	Paṭisambhidāmagga
Peṭ	Peṭakopadesa
Pj I	Paramatthajotikā (comy on Khp)
Pj II	Paramatthajotikā (comy on Sn)
Ps	Papañcasūdani (comy on M)
M	Majjhima Nikāya
Mil	Milindapañha
Mp	Manorathapūraṇī (Comy on A)
Vibh-a	Sammohavinodanī (Comy on Vibhaṅga)
Vin	Vinaya
Vism	Visuddhimagga
S	Saṃyutta Nikāya
Sn	Sutta Nipāta
Spk	Sāratthappakāsinī (Comy on S)
Sp-t	Sāratthadīpanī (Subcomy on Vin)
Sv	Sumaṅgalavilāsinī (Comy on D)
Sv-pṭ	Sumaṅgalavilāsinī-purāṇa-ṭikā (Subcomy on D)

Introduction

"Nibbāna" – the ultimate goal of the Buddhist, has been variously understood and interpreted in the history of Buddhist thought. One who earnestly takes up the practice of the Noble Eightfold Path for the attainment of this goal, might sometimes be dismayed to find this medley of views confronting him. Right View, as the first factor of that path, has always to be in the vanguard in one's practice. In the interest of this Right View, which one has to progressively 'straighten-up,' a need for clarification before purification might sometimes be strongly felt. It was in such a context that the present series of 33 sermons on Nibbāna came to be delivered.

The invitation for this series of sermons came from my revered teacher, the late Venerable Matara Sri Ñāṇārāma Mahāthera, who was the resident meditation teacher of Meetirigala Nissaran Vanaya Meditation Center. Under his inspiring patronage these sermons were delivered once every fortnight before the group of resident monks of Nissarana Vanaya, during the period of Dec. 12th 1988–Jan. 30th, 1991. The sermons, which were originally circulated on cassettes, began issuing in book form only in 1997, when the first volume of the Sinhala series titled *Nivane Niveema* came out, published by the Dharma Grantha Mudrana Bhāraya or 'Dhamma Publication Trust' set up for the purpose in the Department of Public Trustee, Sri Lanka. The series is scheduled to comprise eleven volumes of which 9 have come out.[1] The entire series is for free distribution as Dhammadāna – 'the gift of truth that excels all

1 This introduction is from the Venerable Ñāṇananda's first print of the Nibbāna sermons. This current edition contains 25 of the 33 sermons currently available in English.

other gifts.' The sister series to come out in English will comprise 7 volumes in 5 sermons each, which will likewise be strictly for free distribution since Dhamma is priceless.[2]

In these sermons I have attempted to trace the original meaning and significance of the Pāli term Nibbāna (Skt. Nirvāna) based on the evidence from the discourses of the Pāli Canon. This led to a detailed analysis and a re-appraisal of some of the most controversial suttas on Nibbāna often quoted by scholars in support of their interpretations. The findings, however, were not presented as dry scholastic exposition of mere academic interest. Since the sermons were addressed to a meditative audience keen on *realizing* Nibbāna, edifying similes, metaphors and illustrations had their place in the discussion. The gamut of 33 sermons afforded sufficient scope for dealing with almost all the salient teachings in Buddhism from a practical point of view.

The present translation, in so far as it is faithful to the original, will reflect the same pragmatic outlook. While the findings could be of interest even to the scholar bent on theorizing Nibbāna, it is hoped that the mode of presentation will have a special appeal for those who are keen on *realizing* it.

I would like to follow up these few prefatory remarks with due acknowledgments to all those who gave their help and encouragement for bringing out this translation:

To the venerable Anālayo of Lewella Meditation Centre, Kandy, for the meticulous care and patience with which he traced the parallel footnote references from English Editions and for many helpful suggestions on presentation and formatting.

To Mr. U. Mapa, presently the Ambassador of Sri Lanka in Myanmar, for his yeoman service in taking the necessary steps to

2 Please note the copyfree notice on the first page of this book. This book is not for commercial resale.

establish the Dhamma Publications Trust in his former capacity as the Public Trustee of Sri Lanka.

To Mr. G.T. Bandara, Director, Royal Institute, for taking the lead in this Dhammadāna movement with his initial donation and for his devoted services as the Settler of the Trust.

To Mrs. Yukie Sirimane for making available this translation as well as our other publications to the world through the Internet under her website, www.beyondthenet.net.

And last but not least to Mr. Hideo Chihashi, Director, Green Hill Meditation Institute, Tokyo, Japan and his group of relatives, friends and pupils for their munificence in sponsoring the publication of the first volume of *Nibbāna – The Mind Stilled.*

Nibbānam paramam sukham
Nibbāna is the supreme bliss.

—Bhikkhu K. Ñāṇananda
Potgulgal Aranya
'Pahankanuwa'
Kandegedara
Dewalegama
Sri Lanka

August 2002 (B.E. 2548)

Nibbāna Sermon 1

Namo tassa Bhagavato Arahato Sammāsambuddhassa
Namo tassa Bhagavato Arahato Sammāsambuddhassa
Namo tassa Bhagavato Arahato Sammāsambuddhassa

Etaṃ santaṃ, etaṃ paṇītaṃ, yadidaṃ sabbasaṅkhārasamatho sabbūpadhipaṭinissaggo taṇhakkhayo virāgo nirodho nibbānaṃ.[1]

"This is peaceful, this is excellent, namely the stilling of all preparations, the relinquishment of all assets, the destruction of craving, detachment, cessation, extinction."

With the permission of the Most Venerable Great Preceptor and the assembly of the venerable meditative monks.

Recently we have had an occasion to listen to a series of sermons on *Nibbāna* and there have been differences of opinion regarding the interpretation of some deep *suttas* on *Nibbāna* in those sermons. And so the venerable Great Preceptor suggested to me that it would be useful to this group if I would give a set of sermons on *Nibbāna*, touching on those controversial points.

At first, for many reasons, I hesitated to accept this invitation for a serious task, but then, as the venerable Great Preceptor repeatedly encouraged me on this, I gave some thought as to how best I could set about doing it. And it occurred to me that it would be best if I could address these sermons directly to the task before us in this Nissarana Vanaya, and that is meditative attention, rather

1 M I 436, *MahāMālunkyasutta*.

than dealing with those deep controversial *suttas* in academic isolation. And that is why I have selected the above quotation as the theme for the entire set of sermons, hoping that it would help create the correct atmosphere of meditative attention.

Etaṃ santaṃ etaṃ paṇītaṃ, yadidaṃ sabbasaṅkhārasamatho sabbūpadhipaṭinissaggo taṇhakkhayo virāgo nirodho nibbānaṃ. "This is peaceful, this is excellent, namely the stilling of all preparations, the relinquishment of all assets, the destruction of craving, detachment, cessation, extinction."

This in fact is a meditation subject in itself, a *kammaṭṭhāna*. This is the reflection on the peace of *Nibbāna, upasamānussati*. So if we can successfully make use of this as both the heading and the theme of these sermons, we would be in a position to understand those six qualities of the *Dhamma*. We are told that the *Dhamma* is *svākkhāta*, that it is well-proclaimed, *sandiṭṭhika*, can be seen here and now, *akālika*, timeless, *ehipassika*, inviting one to come and see, *opanayika*, leading one onwards, *paccattaṃ veditabbo viññūhi*, that it can be understood by the wise each one by himself.[2]

This set of sermons would have fulfilled its purpose if it drives home the true significance of these six qualities of the *Dhamma*.

Now at the very outset I would like to say a few things by way of preparing the background and I do hope that this assembly would bear with me for saying certain things that I will be compelled to say in this concern. By way of background something has to be said as to why there are so many complications with regard to the meaning of some of the deep *suttas* on *Nibbāna*.

There is a popular belief that the commentaries are finally traceable to a miscellany of the Buddha word scattered here and there, as *pakiṇṇakadesanā*. But the true state of affairs seems to be rather different. Very often the commentaries are unable to say something conclusive regarding the meaning of deep *suttas*. So

---

[2] D II 93, *MahāParinibbānasutta*.

they simply give some possible interpretations and the reader finds himself at a loss to choose the correct one. Sometimes the commentaries go at a tangent and miss the correct interpretation. Why the commentaries are silent on some deep *suttas* is also a problem to modern day scholars. There are some historical reasons leading to this state of affairs in the commentaries.

In the *Āṇisutta* of the *Nidānavagga* in the *Saṃyutta Nikāya* we find the Buddha making certain prophetic utterances regarding the dangers that will befall the *Sāsana* in the future. It is said that in times to come, monks will lose interest in those deep *suttas* which deal with matters transcendental, that they would not listen to those *suttas* that have to do with the idea of emptiness, *suññatā*. They would not think it even worthwhile learning or pondering over the meanings of those *suttas*:

> *Ye te suttantā tathāgatabhāsitā gambhīrā gambhīratthā lokuttarā suññatappaṭisaṃyuttā, tesu bhaññamānesu na sussūssisanti na sotaṃ odahissanti na aññā cittaṃ upaṭṭhāpessanti na te dhamme uggahetabbaṃ pariyāpuṇitabbaṃ maññissanti.*[3]

There is also another historical reason that can be adduced. An idea got deeply rooted at a certain stage in the *Sāsana* history that what is contained in the *Sutta Piṭaka* is simply the conventional teaching and so it came to imply that there is nothing so deep in these *suttas*. This notion also had its share in the present lack of interest in these *suttas*. According to *Manorathapūraṇī*, the *Aṅguttara* commentary, already at an early stage in the *Sāsana* history of Sri Lanka, there had been a debate between those who upheld the precept and those who stood for realization.[4] And it is said that those who upheld the precept won the day. The final

---

[3] S II 267, *Āṇisutta*.

[4] Mp I 92.

conclusion was that, for the continuity of the *Sāsana*, precept itself is enough, not so much the realization.

Of course the efforts of the reciter monks of old for the preservation of the precept in the midst of droughts and famines and other calamitous situations are certainly praiseworthy. But the unfortunate thing about it was this: the basket of the Buddha word came to be passed on from hand to hand in the dark, so much so that there was the risk of some valuable things slipping out in the process.

Also there have been certain semantic developments in the commentarial period, and this will be obvious to anyone searching for the genuine *Dhamma*. It seems that there had been a tendency in the commentarial period to elaborate even on some lucid words in the *suttas*, simply as a commentarial requirement, and this led to the inclusion of many complicated ideas. By too much over drawing in the commentaries, the deeper meanings of the *Dhamma* got obscured. As a matter of fact, the depth of the *Dhamma* has to be seen through lucidity, just as much as one sees the bottom of a tank only when the water is lucid.

> *Dve nāma kiṃ?*
> *Nāmañca rūpañca.*[5]
>
> "What is the 'two'?"
> "Name and form."

This is the second out of the ten questions Buddha had put to the Venerable *sāmanera* Sopāka who had attained *Arahant*-ship at the age of seven. It is like asking a child: "Can you count up to ten?" All the ten questions were deep, the tenth being on *Arahant*-ship. But of course Venerable Sopāka gave the right answer each time. Now it is the second question and its answer that we are concerned

---

[5] Khp 2.

with here: *nāmañca rūpañca*. In fact, this is a basic teaching in insight training.

It is obvious that *nāma* means 'name,' and in the *suttas* also, *nāma*, when used by itself, means 'name.' However when we come to the commentaries we find some kind of hesitation to recognize this obvious meaning. Even in the present context, the commentary, *Paramatthajotikā*, explains the word 'name' so as to mean 'bending.' It says that all immaterial states are called *nāma*, in the sense that they bend towards their respective objects and also because the mind has the nature of inclination: *Ārammaṇābhimukhaṃ namanato, cittassa ca natihetuto sabbampi arūpaṃ 'nāman'ti vuccati.*[6]

And this is the standard definition of *nāma* in *Abhidhamma* compendiums and commentaries. The idea of bending towards an object is brought in to explain the word *nāma*. It may be that they thought it too simple an interpretation to explain *nāma* with reference to 'name,' particularly because it is a term that has to do with deep insight. However as far as the teachings in the *suttas* are concerned, *nāma* still has a great depth even when it is understood in the sense of 'name.'

Nāmaṃ sabbaṃ anvabhavi,
nāmā bhiyyo na vijjati,
nāmassa ekadhammassa,
sabbeva vasam anvagū.[7]

"Name has conquered everything,
There is nothing greater than name,
All have gone under the sway
Of this one thing called name."

---

[6] Pj I 78.

[7] S I 39, *Nāmasutta*.

Also there is another verse of the same type, but unfortunately its original meaning is often ignored by the present day commentators:

> *Akkheyyasaññino sattā,*
> *akkheyyasmiṃ patiṭṭhitā,*
> *akkheyyaṃ apariññāya,*
> *yogam āyanti maccuno.*[8]

> "Beings are conscious of what can be named,
> They are established on the nameable,
> By not comprehending the nameable things,
> They come under the yoke of death."

All this shows that the word *nāma* has a deep significance even when it is taken in the sense of 'name.'

But now let us see whether there is something wrong in rendering *nāma* by 'name' in the case of the term *nāma-rūpa*. To begin with, let us turn to the definition of *nāma-rūpa* as given by the Venerable Sāriputta in the *Sammādiṭṭhisutta* of the *Majjhima Nikāya*:

> *Vedanā, saññā, cetanā, phasso, manasikāro – idaṃ vuccatāvuso, nāmaṃ; cattāri ca mahābhūtāni, catunnañca mahābhūtānaṃ upādāyarūpaṃ – idaṃ vuccatāvuso, rūpaṃ. Iti idañca nāmaṃ idañca rūpaṃ – idam vuccatāvuso nāmarūpaṃ.*[9]

> "Feeling, perception, intention, contact, attention – this, friend, is called 'name.' The four great primaries and form dependent on the four great primaries – this, friend, is

[8] S I 11, *Samiddhisutta.*

[9] M I 53, *Sammādiṭṭhisutta.*

> called 'form.' So this is 'name' and this is 'form' – this, friend, is called 'name-and-form.'"

Well, this seems lucid enough as a definition but let us see, whether there is any justification for regarding feeling, perception, intention, contact and attention as 'name.' Suppose there is a little child, a toddler, who is still unable to speak or understand language. Someone gives him a rubber ball and the child has seen it for the first time. If the child is told that it is a rubber ball, he might not understand it. How does he get to know that object? He smells it, feels it, and tries to eat it, and finally rolls it on the floor. At last he understands that it is a plaything. Now the child has recognized the rubber ball not by the name that the world has given it, but by those factors included under 'name' in *nāma-rūpa*, namely feeling, perception, intention, contact and attention.

This shows that the definition of *nāma* in *nāma-rūpa* takes us back to the most fundamental notion of 'name,' to something like its prototype. The world gives a name to an object for purposes of easy communication. When it gets the sanction of others, it becomes a convention.

While commenting on the verse just quoted, the commentator also brings in a bright idea. As an illustration of the sweeping power of name, he points out that if any tree happens to have no name attached to it by the world, it would at least be known as the 'nameless tree.'[10] Now as for the child, even such a usage is not possible. So it gets to know an object by the aforesaid method. And the factors involved there, are the most elementary constituents of name.

Now it is this elementary name-and-form world that a meditator also has to understand, however much he may be conversant with the conventional world. But if a meditator wants to understand this name-and-form world, he has to come back to the state of a child,

---

10 Spk I 95 commenting on S I 39.

at least from one point of view. Of course in this case the equanimity should be accompanied by knowledge and not by ignorance. And that is why a meditator makes use of mindfulness and full awareness, *satisam pajañña*, in his attempt to understand name-and-form.

Even though he is able to recognize objects by their conventional names, for the purpose of comprehending name-and-form, a meditator makes use of those factors that are included under 'name': feeling, perception, intention, contact and attention. All these have a specific value to each individual and that is why the *Dhamma* has to be understood each one by himself – *paccattaṃ veditabbo*. This *Dhamma* has to be realized by oneself. One has to understand one's own world of name-and-form by oneself. No one else can do it for him. Nor can it be defined or denoted by technical terms.

Now it is in this world of name-and-form that suffering is found. According to the Buddha, suffering is not out there in the conventional world of worldly philosophers. It is to be found in this very name-and-form world. So the ultimate aim of a meditator is to cut off the craving in this name-and-form. As it is said: *acchecchi taṇhaṃ idha nāmarūpe*.[11]

Now if we are to bring in a simile to clarify this point, the Buddha is called the incomparable surgeon, *sallakatto anuttaro*.[12] Also he is sometimes called *taṇhāsallassa hantāraṃ*, one who re moves the dart of craving.[13] So the Buddha is the incomparable surgeon who pulls out the poison-tipped arrow of craving.

We may say therefore that, according to the *Dhamma*, *nāmarūpa*, or name-and-form, is like the wound in which the arrow is embedded. When one is wounded by a poison-tipped arrow, the bandage has to be put, not on the archer or on his bowstring, but

---

[11] S I 12, *Samiddhisutta*.

[12] Sn 560, *Selasutta*.

[13] S I 192, *Pavāraṇāsutta*.

on the wound itself. First of all the wound has to be well located and cleaned up. Similarly, the comprehension of name-and-form is the preliminary step in the treatment of the wound caused by the poison-tipped arrow of craving.

And it is for that purpose that a meditator has to pay special attention to those basic components of 'name' – feeling, perception, intention, contact and attention – however much he may be proficient in words found in worldly usage. It may even appear as a process of unlearning down to childlike simplicity. But of course, the equanimity implied there, is not based on ignorance but on knowledge.

We find ourselves in a similar situation with regard to the significance of *rūpa* in *nāma-rūpa*. Here too we have something deep, but many take *nāma-rūpa* to mean 'mind and matter.' Like materialists, they think there is a contrast between mind and matter. But according to the *Dhamma* there is no such rigid distinction. It is a pair that is interrelated and taken together it forms an important link in the chain of *paṭicca samuppāda*.

Rūpa exists in relation to 'name' and that is to say that form is known with the help of 'name.' As we saw above, that child got a firsthand knowledge of the rubber ball with the help of contact, feeling, perception, intention and attention. Now in the definition of 'form' as *cattāri ca mahābhūtāni, catunnañca mahābhūtānaṃ upādāya rūpaṃ* the four great primaries are mentioned because they constitute the most primary notion of 'form.' Just as much as feeling, perception, intention, contact and attention represent the most primary notion of 'name,' conventionally so called, even so the four great primaries form the basis for the primary notion of 'form,' as the world understands it.

It is not an easy matter to recognize these primaries. They are evasive like ghosts. But out of their interplay we get the perception of form, *rūpasaññā*. In fact what is called *rūpa* in this context is *rūpasaññā*. It is with reference to the behaviour of the four great elements that the world builds up its concept of form. Its perception, recognition and designation of form is in terms of that behaviour. And that behaviour can be known with the help of those members representing name.

The earth element is recognized through the qualities of hardness and softness, the water element through the qualities of cohesiveness and dissolution, the fire element through hotness and coolness, and the wind element through motion and inflation. In this way one gets acquainted with the nature of the four great primaries. And the perception of form, *rūpasaññā*, that one has at the back of one's mind, is the net result of that acquaintance. So this is *nāma-rūpa*. This is one's world. The relationship between *rūpa* and *rūpasaññā* will be clear from the following verse:

Yattha nāmañca rūpañca,
asesaṃ uparujjhati,
paṭighaṃ rūpasaññā ca,
etthesā chijjate jaṭā.

This is a verse found in the *Jaṭāsutta* of the *Saṃyutta Nikāya*.[14] In that *sutta* we find a deity putting a riddle before the Buddha for solution:

Anto jaṭā bahi jaṭā,
jaṭāya jaṭitā pajā,
taṃ taṃ Gotama pucchāmi,
ko imaṃ vijaṭaye jaṭaṃ.

"There is a tangle within, and a tangle without,
The world is entangled with a tangle.
About that, oh Gotama, I ask you,
Who can disentangle this tangle?"

---

[14] S I 13, *Jaṭāsutta*.

The Buddha answers the riddle in three verses, the first of which is fairly well known, because it happens to be the opening verse of the *Visuddhimagga*:

> *Sīle patiṭṭhāya naro sapañño,*
> *cittaṃ paññañca bhāvayaṃ,*
> *ātāpī nipako bhikkhu,*
> *so imaṃ vijaṭaye jaṭaṃ.*

This means that a wise monk, established in virtue, developing concentration and wisdom, being ardent and prudent, is able to disentangle this tangle. Now this is the second verse:

> *Yesaṃ rāgo ca doso ca,*
> *avijjā ca virājitā,*
> *khīṇāsavā arahanto,*
> *tesaṃ vijaṭitā jaṭā.*

> "In whom lust, hate
> And ignorance have faded away,
> Those influx-free *Arahants*,
> It is in them that the tangle is disentangled."

It is the third verse that is relevant to our topic:

> *Yattha nāmañca rūpañca,*
> *asesaṃ uparujjhati,*
> *paṭighaṃ rūpasaññā ca,*
> *etthesā chijjate jaṭā.*

> "Where name and form
> As well as resistance and the perception of form
> Are completely cut off,
> It is there that the tangle gets snapped."

The reference here is to *Nibbāna*. It is there that the tangle is disentangled.

The coupling of name-and-form with *paṭigha* and *rūpasaññā* in this context, is significant. Here *paṭigha* does not mean 'repugnance,' but 'resistance.' It is the resistance which comes as a reaction to inert matter. For instance, when one knocks against something in passing, one turns back to recognize it. Sense reaction is something like that.

The Buddha has said that the worldling is blind until at least the *Dhamma*-eye arises in him. So the blind worldling recognizes an object by the very resistance he experiences in knocking against that object.

Paṭigha and *rūpasaññā* form a pair. *Paṭigha* is that experience of resistance which comes by the knocking against an object, and *rūpasaññā*, as perception of form, is the resulting recognition of that object. The perception is in terms of what is hard, soft, hot or cold. Out of such perceptions common to the blind worldlings, arises the conventional reality, the basis of which is the world.

Knowledge and understanding are very often associated with words and concepts, so much so that if one knows the name of a thing, one is supposed to know it. Because of this misconception the world is in a tangle. Names and concepts, particularly the nouns, perpetuate the ignorance in the world. Therefore insight is the only path of release. And that is why a meditator practically comes down to the level of a child in order to understand name and form. He may even have to pretend to be a patient in slowing down his movements for the sake of developing mindfulness and full awareness.

So we see that there is something really deep in *nāma-rūpa*, even if we render it as 'name-and-form.' There is an implicit connection with 'name' as conventionally so called, but unfortunately this connection is ignored in the commentaries, when they bring in the idea of 'bending' to explain the word 'name.' So we need not hesitate to render *nāma-rūpa* by 'name-and-form.' Simple as it may appear, it goes deeper than the worldly concepts of name and form.

Now if we are to summarise all what we have said in this connection, we may say: 'name' in 'name-and-form' is a **formal** name. It is an apparent name. 'Form' in 'name-and-form' is a **nominal** form. It is a form only in name.

We have to make a similar comment on the meaning of the word *Nibbāna*. Here too one can see some unusual semantic developments in the commentarial period. It is very common these days to explain the etymology of the word *Nibbāna* with the help of a phrase like: *Vānasaṅkhātāya taṇhāya nikkhantattā.*[15] And that is to say that *Nibbāna* is so called because it is an exit from craving which is a form of weaving.

To take the element *vāna* in the word to mean a form of weaving is as good as taking *nāma* in *nāma-rūpa* as some kind of bending. It is said that craving is a kind of weaving in the sense that it connects up one form of existence with another and the prefix *ni* is said to signify the exit from that weaving.

But nowhere in the *suttas* do we get this sort of etymology and interpretation. On the other hand it is obvious that the *suttas* use the word *Nibbāna* in the sense of 'extinguishing' or 'extinction.' In fact this is the sense that brings out the true essence of the *Dhamma*.

For instance the *Ratanasutta*, which is so often chanted as a *paritta*, says that the *Arahants* go out like a lamp: *Nibbanti dhīrā yathāyaṃ padīpo.*[16] "Those wise ones get extinguished even like this lamp."

The simile of a lamp getting extinguished is also found in the *Dhātuvibhaṅgasutta* of the *Majjhima Nikāya.*[17] Sometimes it is the figure of a torch going out: *Pajjotass'eva nibbānaṃ, vi mokho*

---

15 Abhidh-s VI í 30.

16 Sn 235, *Ratanasutta*.

17 M III 245, *Dhātuvibhaṅgasutta*.

cetaso ahu, "the mind's release was like the extinguishing of a torch."[18]

The simile of the extinction of a fire is very often brought in as an illustration of *Nibbāna* and in the *Aggivacchagottasutta* of the *Majjhima Nikāya* we find the Buddha presenting it as a sustained simile, giving it a deeper philosophical dimension.[19] Now when a fire burns, it does so with the help of firewood. When a fire is burning, if someone were to ask us: "What is burning?" – what shall we say as a reply? Is it the wood that is burning or the fire that is burning? The truth of the matter is that the wood burns because of the fire and the fire burns because of the wood. So it seems we already have here a case of relatedness of this to that, *idappaccayatā.* This itself shows that there is a very deep significance in the fire simile.

Nibbāna as a term for the ultimate aim of this *Dhamma* is equally significant because of its allusion to the going out of a fire. In the *Asaṅkhatasaṃyutta* of the *Saṃyutta Nikāya* as many as thirty-three terms are listed to denote this ultimate aim.[20] But out of all these epithets, *Nibbāna* became the most widely used, probably because of its significant allusion to the fire. The fire simile holds the answer to many questions relating to the ultimate goal.

The wandering ascetic Vacchagotta, as well as many others, accused the Buddha of teaching a doctrine of annihilation: *Sato sattassa ucchedaṃ vināsaṃ vibhavaṃ paññāpeti.*[21] Their accusation was that the Buddha proclaims the annihilation, destruction and nonexistence of a being that is existent. And the Buddha answered them fairly and squarely with the fire simile.

"Now if a fire is burning in front of you dependent on grass and twigs as fuel, you would know that it is burning dependently and

---

[18] D II 157, *MahāParinibbānasutta.*

[19] M I 487, *Aggivacchagottasutta.*

[20] S IV 368-373.

[21] M I 140, *Alagaddūpamasutta.*

not independently, that there is no fire in the abstract. And when the fire goes out, with the exhaustion of that fuel, you would know that it has gone out because the conditions for its existence are no more."

As a sidelight to the depth of this argument it may be mentioned that the *Pāli* word *upādāna* used in such contexts has the sense of both 'fuel' as well as 'grasping,' and in fact, fuel is something that the fire grasps for its burning. *Upādānapaccayā bhavo*, "dependent on grasping is existence."[22] These are two very important links in the doctrine of dependent arising, *paṭicca samuppāda*.

The eternalists, overcome by the craving for existence, thought that there is some permanent essence in existence as a reality. But what had the Buddha to say about existence? He said that what is true for the fire is true for existence as well. That is to say that existence is dependent on grasping. So long as there is a grasping, there is an existence. As we saw above, the firewood is called *upādāna* because it catches fire. The fire catches hold of the wood, and the wood catches hold of the fire. And so we call it firewood. This is a case of a relation of this to that, *idappaccayatā*. Now it is the same with what is called 'existence,' which is not an absolute reality.

Even in the *Vedic* period there was the dilemma between 'being' and 'non-being.' They wondered whether being came out of non-being, or non-being came out of being. *Katham asataḥ sat jāyeta*, "How could being come out of non-being?"[23] In the face of this dilemma regarding the first beginnings, they were sometimes forced to conclude that there was neither non-being nor being at the start, *nāsadāsīt no sadāsīt tadānīm*.[24] Or else in the confusion they would sometimes leave the matter unsolved, saying that perhaps only the creator knew about it.

---

22 D II 57, *MahāNidānasutta*.

23 *Chāndogya-Upaniṣad* 6.2.1,2.

24 *Ṛgveda* X.129, *Nāsadīya Sūkta*.

All this shows what a lot of confusion these two words *sat* and *asat*, being and non-being, had created for the philosophers. It was only the Buddha who presented a perfect solution, after a complete reappraisal of the whole problem of existence. He pointed out that existence is a fire kept up by the fuel of grasping, so much so that, when grasping ceases, existence ceases as well.

In fact the fire simile holds the answer to the tetralemma included among the ten unexplained points very often found mentioned in the *suttas*. It concerns the state of the *Tathāgata* after death, whether he exists, does not exist, both or neither. The presumption of the questioner is that one or the other of these four must be and could be answered in the affirmative.

The Buddha solves or dissolves this presumptuous tetralemma by bringing in the fire simile. He points out that when a fire goes out with the exhaustion of the fuel, it is absurd to ask in which direction the fire has gone. All that one can say about it, is that the fire has gone out: *Nibbuto tveva saṅkhaṃ gacchati*, "It comes to be reckoned as 'gone out.'"[25]

It is just a reckoning, an idiom, a worldly usage, which is not to be taken too literally. So this illustration through the fire simile drives home to the worldling the absurdity of his presumptuous tetralemma of the *Tathāgata*.

In the *Upasīvasutta* of the *Pārāyaṇavagga* of the *Sutta Nipāta* we find the lines:

Accī yathā vātavegena khitto,
atthaṃ paleti na upeti saṅkhaṃ,

"Like the flame thrown out by the force of the wind
Reaches its end, it cannot be reckoned."[26]

---

[25] M I 487, *Aggivacchagottasutta*.

[26] 1074, *Upasīvamāṇavapucchā*.

Here the reckoning is to be understood in terms of the four propositions of the tetralemma. Such reckonings are based on a total misconception of the phenomenon of fire.

It seems that the deeper connotations of the word *Nibbāna* in the context of *paṭicca samuppāda* were not fully appreciated by the commentators. And that is why they went in search of a new etymology. They were too shy of the implications of the word 'extinction.' Probably to avoid the charge of nihilism they felt compelled to reinterpret certain key passages on *Nibbāna*. They conceived *Nibbāna* as something existing out there in its own right. They would not say where, but sometimes they would even say that it is everywhere. With an undue grammatical emphasis they would say that it is on coming to that *Nibbāna* that lust and other defilements are abandoned: *Nibbānaṃ āgamma rāgādayo khīṇāti ekameva nibbānaṃ rāgakkhayo dosakkhayo mohakkhayo ti vuccati.*[27]

But what do we find in the joyous utterances of the *theras* and *therīs* who had realized *Nibbāna*? As recorded in such texts as *Thera-* and *Therī-gāthā* they would say: *Sītibhūto'smi nibbuto*, "I am grown cool, extinguished as I am."[28] The words *sītibhūta* and *nibbuta* had a cooling effect even to the listener, though later scholars found them inadequate.

Extinction is something that occurs within an individual and it brings with it a unique bliss of appeasement. As the *Ratanasutta* says: *Laddhā mudhā nibbutiṃ bhuñjamānā*, "They experience the bliss of appeasement, won free of charge."[29] Normally, appeasement is won at a cost, but here we have an appeasement that comes gratis.

From the worldly point of view 'extinction' means annihilation. It has connotations of a precipice that is much dreaded. That is

---

27 Vibh-a 53.

28 Th 298, *Rāhula Thera*.

29 Sn 228, *Ratanasutta*.

why the commentators conceived of it as something out there, on reaching which the defilements are abandoned, *nibbānaṃ āgamma rāgādayo khīṇāti*. Sometimes they would say that it is on seeing *Nibbāna* that craving is destroyed.

There seems to be some contradiction in the commentarial definitions of *Nibbāna*. On the one hand we have the definition of *Nibbāna* as the exit from craving, which is called a 'weaving.' And on the other it is said that it is on seeing *Nibbāna* that craving is destroyed. To project *Nibbāna* into a distance and to hope that craving will be destroyed only on seeing it, is something like trying to build a staircase to a palace one cannot yet see. In fact this is a simile which the Buddha had used in his criticism of the Brahmin's point of view.[30]

In the *Dhammacakkappavattanasutta* we have a very clear statement of the third noble truth. Having first said that the second noble truth is craving, the Buddha goes on to define the third noble truth in these words: *Tassāyeva taṇhāya asesavirāganirodho cāgo paṭinissaggo mutti anālayo*.[31]

This is to say that the third noble truth is the complete fading away, cessation, giving up, relinquishment of that very craving. That it is the release from and non-attachment to that very craving. In other words it is the destruction of this very mass of suffering which is just before us.

In the *suttas* the term *taṇhakkhayo*, the destruction of craving, is very often used as a term for *Nibbāna*.[32] But the commentator says that destruction alone is not *Nibbāna*: *Khayamattaṃ na nibbānaṃ*.[33] But the destruction of craving itself is called the highest bliss in the following verse of the *Udāna*:

---

30 E.g. at D I 194, *Poṭṭhapādasutta*.

31 E.g. at S V 421, *Dhammacakkappavattanasutta*.

32 E.g. at It 88, *Aggappasàdasutta*.

33 Abhidh-av 138.

Yañca kāmasukhaṃ loke,
yaṃ c'idaṃ diviyaṃ sukhaṃ,
taṇhakkhaya sukhass'ete,
kalaṃ n'agghanti soḷasiṃ.[34]

"Whatever bliss from sense-desires there is in the
world,
Whatever divine bliss there is,
All these are not worth one-sixteenth
Of the bliss of the destruction of craving."

Many of the verses found in the *Udāna* are extremely deep and this is understandable, since *udāna* means a 'joyous utterance.' Generally a joyous utterance comes from the very depths of one's heart, like a sigh of relief. As a matter of fact one often finds that the concluding verse goes far deeper in its implications than the narrative concerned. For instance, in the *Udapāna sutta*, we get the following joyous utterance, coming from the Buddha himself:

Kiṃ kayirā udapānena,
āpā ce sabbadā siyuṃ,
taṇhāya mūlato chetvā,
kissa pariyesanaṃ care.[35]

"What is the use of a well,
If water is there all the time,
Having cut craving at the root,
In search of what should one wander?"

This shows that the destruction of craving is not a mere destruction.

---

34 Ud 11, *Rājasutta*.

35 Ud 79, *Udapānasutta*.

Craving is a form of thirst and that is why *Nibbāna* is sometimes called *pipāsavinayo*, the dispelling of the thirst.[36] To think that the destruction of craving is not sufficient is like trying to give water to one who has already quenched his thirst. But the destruction of craving has been called the highest bliss. One who has quenched his thirst for good, is aware of that blissful experience. When he sees the world running here and there in search of water, he looks within and sees the wellspring of his bliss.

However to most of our scholars the term *taṇhakkhaya* appeared totally negative and that is why they hesitated to recognize its value. In such conventional usages as *Nibbānaṃ āgamma* they found a grammatical excuse to separate that term from *Nibbāna*.

According to the Buddha the cessation of existence is *Nibbāna* and that means *Nibbāna* is the realization of the cessation of existence. Existence is said to be an eleven-fold fire. So the entire existence is a raging fire. Lust, hate, delusion – all these are fires. Therefore *Nibbāna* may be best rendered by the word 'extinction.' When once the fires are extinguished, what more is needed?

But unfortunately Venerable Buddhaghosa was not prepared to appreciate this point of view. In his *Visuddhimagga* as well as in the commentaries *Sāratthappakāsinī* and *Sammohavinodanī*, he gives a long discussion on *Nibbāna* in the form of an argument with an imaginary heretic.[37] Some of his arguments are not in keeping with either the letter or the spirit of the *Dhamma*.

First of all he gets the heretic to put forward the idea that the destruction of lust, hate and delusion is *Nibbāna*. Actually the heretic is simply quoting the Buddha's word, for in the *Nibbāna sutta* of the *Asaṅkhatasaṃyutta* the destruction of lust, hate and delusion is called *Nibbāna*: *Rāgakkhayo, dosakkhayo, mohakkhayo – idaṃ vuccati nibbānaṃ*.[38]

---

[36] A II 34, *Aggappasādasutta*.

[37] Vism 508; Spk III 88; Vibh-a 51.

[38] S IV 371, *Nibbānasutta*.

The words *rāgakkhaya, dosakkhaya* and *mohakkhaya* together form a synonym of *Nibbāna*, but the commentator interprets it as three synonyms. Then he argues out with the imaginary heretic that if *Nibbāna* is the extinguishing of lust it is something common even to the animals, for they also extinguish their fires of lust through enjoyment of the corresponding objects of sense.[39] This argument ignores the deeper sense of the word extinction, as it is found in the *Dhamma*.

In the *Māgaṇḍiyasutta* of the *Majjhima Nikāya* the Buddha gives the simile of a man with a skin disease sitting beside a pit of hot embers to explain the position of lustful beings in the world.[40] That man is simply trying to assuage his pains by the heat of the fire. It is an attempt to warm up, not to cool down. Similarly what the lustful beings in the world are doing in the face of the fires of lust is a warming up. It can in no way be compared to the extinction and the cooling down of the *Arahants*.

As the phrase *nibbutiṃ bhuñjamānā* implies, that extinction is a blissful experience for the *Arahants*. It leaves a permanent effect on the *Arahant*, so much so that upon reflection he sees that his influxes are extinct, just as a man with his hands and feet cut off, knows upon reflection that his limbs are gone.[41] It seems that the deeper implications of the word *Nibbāna* have been obscured by a set of arguments which are rather misleading.

In fact I came forward to give these sermons for three reasons: Firstly because the venerable Great Preceptor invited me to do so. Secondly in the hope that it will be of some benefit to my co-dwellers in the *Dhamma*. And thirdly because I myself felt rather concerned about the inadequacy of the existing interpretations.

What we have said so far is just about the word *Nibbāna* as such. Quite a number of *suttas* on *Nibbāna* will be taken up for

---

39 Vibh-a 53.

40 M I 507, *Māgaṇḍiyasutta*.

41 M I 523, *Sandakasutta*.

discussion. This is just a preamble to show that the word *Nibbāna* in the sense of 'extinction' has a deeper dimension, which has some relevance to the law of dependent arising, *paṭicca samuppāda*.

By bringing in an etymology based on the element *vāna*, much of the original significance of the word *Nibbāna* came to be undermined. On quite a number of occasions the Buddha has declared that the cessation of suffering is *Nibbāna*, or else that the destruction of craving is *Nibbāna*. Terms like *dukkhanirodho* and *taṇhakkhayo* have been used as synonyms. If they are synonyms, there is no need to make any discrimination with regard to some of them, by insisting on a periphrastic usage like *āgamma*.

Yet another important aspect of the problem is the relation of *Nibbāna* to the holy life or *brahmacariya*. It is said that when the holy life is lived out to the full, it culminates in *Nibbāna*.

In the *Rādhasaṃyutta* of the *Saṃyutta Nikāya* we find the Venerable Rādha putting a series of questions to the Buddha to get an explanation.[42] First of all he asks: *Sammādassanaṃ pana, bhante, kimatthiyaṃ?* "For what purpose is right vision?" And the Buddha gives the answer: *Sammādassanaṃ kho, Rādha, nibbidatthaṃ*, "Rādha, right vision is for purposes of disgust or dejection." And that is to say, disgust for *saṃsāra*.

The next question is: for what purpose is disgust? And the Buddha answers: disgust is for dispassion. What is the purpose of dispassion? The purpose of dispassion is release. What is the purpose of release? The purpose of release is *Nibbāna*. Last of all Venerable Rādha puts the question:

Nibbānaṃ pana, bhante, kimatthiyaṃ? "For what purpose is *Nibbāna*?" And the Buddha gives this answer: *Accasarā, Rādha, pañhaṃ, nāsakkhi pañhassa pariyantaṃ gahetuṃ. Nibbānogadhañhi, Rādha, brahmacariyaṃ vussati, nibbānaparāyanaṃ nibbānapariyosānaṃ*. "Rādha, you have gone beyond the scope of

---

[42] S III 189, *Mārasutta*.

your questions, you are unable to grasp the limit of your questions. For, Rādha, the holy life is merged in *Nibbāna*, its consummation is *Nibbāna*, its culmination is *Nibbāna*."

This shows that the holy life gets merged in *Nibbāna*, just as rivers get merged in the sea. In other words, where the holy life is lived out to the full, *Nibbāna* is right there. That is why Venerable Nanda, who earnestly took up the holy life encouraged by the Buddha's promise of heavenly nymphs, attained *Arahant*-hood almost in spite of himself. At last he approached the Buddha and begged to relieve him of the onus of his promise. This shows that when one completes the training in the Holy Life, one is already in *Nibbāna*. Only when the training is incomplete, can one go to heaven.

Here, then, is a result which comes of its own accord. So there is no justification for a periphrastic usage like, "on reaching *Nibbāna*." No glimpse of a distant object is necessary. At whatever moment the Noble Eightfold Path is perfected, one attains *Nibbāna* then and there. Now, in the case of an examination, after answering the question paper, one has to wait for the results – to get a pass.

Here it is different. As soon as you have answered the paper correctly, you have passed immediately and the certificate is already there. This is the significance of the term *aññā* used in such contexts. *Aññā* stands for full certitude of the experience of *Nibbāna*.

The experience of the fruit of *Arahant*-ship gives him the final certificate of his attainment, *aññāphalo*.[43] That is why *Nibbāna* is called something to be realized. One gets the certitude that birth is extinct and that the holy life is lived out to the full, *khīṇā jāti, vusitaṃ brahmacariyaṃ*.[44]

---

[43] The term *aññāphalo* occurs at A IV 428, *Ānandasutta*.

[44] E.g. at D I 84, *Sāmaññaphalasutta*.

Of course there are some who still go on asking: what is the purpose of *Nibbāna*? And it is to answer this type of question that many scholars go on hair splitting. Normally in the world, whatever one does has some purpose or other. All occupations, all trades and businesses, are for gain and profit. Thieves and burglars also have some purpose in mind. But what is the purpose of trying to attain *Nibbāna*? What is the purpose of *Nibbāna*? Why should one attain *Nibbāna*?

It is to give an answer to this question that scholars brought in such phrases as *Nibbānaṃ pana āgamma*, 'on reaching *Nibbāna.*' They would say that 'on reaching *Nibbāna,*' craving would be destroyed. On closer analysis it would appear that there is some fallacy in this question. For if there is any aim or purpose in attaining *Nibbāna*, *Nibbāna* would not be the ultimate aim. In other words, if *Nibbāna* is the ultimate aim, there should be no aim in attaining *Nibbāna*. Though it may well sound a tautology, one has to say that *Nibbāna* is the ultimate aim for the simple reason that there is no aim beyond it.

However, this might need more explanation. Now as far as craving is concerned, it has the nature of projection or inclination. It is something bent forward, with a forward view, and that is why it is called *bhavanetti*, the leader in becoming.[45] It leads one on and on in existence, like the carrot before the donkey. So that is why all objects presented by craving have some object or purpose as a projection. Craving is an inclination.

But what is the position if one makes the destruction of craving itself one's object? Now craving because of its inclining nature is always bent forward, so much so that we get an infinite progression. This is for that, and that is for the other. As the phrase *taṇhā ponobhavikā* implies, craving brings up existence again and again.[46]

---

[45] D II 90, *MahāParinibbānasutta*.

[46] E.g. at S V 421, *Dhammacakkappavattanasutta*.

But this is not the case when one makes the destruction of craving one's aim. When that aim is attained, there is nothing more to be done. So this brings us to the conclusion that the term *taṇhakkhayo*, destruction of craving, is a full-fledged synonym of *Nibbāna*.

Well, this much is enough for today. Time permitting and life permitting, I hope to continue with these sermons. I suppose the most Venerable Great Preceptor made this invitation with the idea of seeing one of his children at play. For good or for bad, I have taken up the invitation. Let the future of the *Sāsana* be the final judge of its merits.

Nibbāna Sermon 2

Namo tassa Bhagavato Arahato Sammāsambuddhassa
Namo tassa Bhagavato Arahato Sammāsambuddhassa
Namo tassa Bhagavato Arahato Sammāsambuddhassa

Etaṃ santaṃ, etaṃ paṇītaṃ, yadidaṃ sabbasaṅkhārasamatho sabbūpadhipaṭinissaggo taṇhakkhayo virāgo nirodho nibbānaṃ.[1]

"This is peaceful, this is excellent, namely the stilling of all preparations, the relinquishment of all assets, the destruction of craving, detachment, cessation, extinction."

With the permission of the Most Venerable Great Preceptor and the assembly of the venerable meditative monks.

The second sermon on *Nibbāna* has come up for today. Towards the end of our sermon the other day we raised the point: Why is it improper to ask such questions as: 'What is the purpose of *Nibbāna*? Why should one attain *Nibbāna*?'[2] Our explanation was that since the holy life or the Noble Eightfold Path has *Nibbāna* as its ultimate aim, since it gets merged in *Nibbāna*, any questions as to the ultimate purpose of *Nibbāna* would be inappropriate.

In fact at some places in the canon we find the phrase *anuttara brahmacariyapariyosāna* used with reference to *Nibbāna*.[3] It

---

1 M I 436, *MahāMālunkyasutta*.

2 See sermon 1.

3 D I 203, *Poṭṭhapādasutta*.

means that *Nibbāna* is the supreme consummation of the holy life. The following standard phrase announcing a new *Arahant* is very often found in the *suttas*:

> *Yassatthāya kulaputtā sammadeva agārasmā anagāriyaṃ pabbajanti, tadanuttaraṃ brahmcariyapariyosānaṃ diṭṭheva dhamme sayaṃ abhiññā sacchikatvā upasampajja vihāsi.*[4]
>
> "In this very life he realized by his own higher knowledge and attained to that supreme consummation of the holy life for the purpose of which clansmen of good family rightly go forth from home to homelessness."

Now what is the justification for saying that one attains to *Nibbāna* by the very completion of the holy life? This Noble Eightfold Path is a straight path: *Ujuko nāma so maggo, abhayā nāma sā disā.*[5] "This path is called the 'straight' and the direction it goes is called the 'fearless.'" In the *Itivuttaka* we come across a verse which expresses this idea more vividly:

> *Sekhassa sikkha mānassa,*
> *ujumaggānusārino,*
> *khayasmiṃ paṭhamaṃ ñāṇaṃ,*
> *tato aññā anantarā.*[6]
>
> "To the learner, learning
> In pursuit of the straight path,
> First comes the knowledge of destruction
> And then immediately the certitude."

---

[4] D I 177, *Kassapasīhanādasutta.*

[5] S I 33, *Accharāsutta.*

[6] It 53, *Indriyasutta.*

It is the fruit of *Arahant*-ship which gives him the certitude of the attainment of *Nibbāna*.

Here the word *anantarā* has been used. That concentration proper to the fruit of *Arahant*-ship is called *ānantarikā samādhi*.[7] This means that the attainment of the fruit is immediate.

Though it may be so in the case of the *Arahant*, what about the stream-winner, the *sotāpanna*, one may ask. There is a general belief that in the case of a *sotāpanna* the vision of *Nibbāna* is like a glimpse of a distant lamp on a road with many bends and the *sotāpanna* has just negotiated the first bend.

But in accordance with the *Dhamma* it may be said that the norm of immediacy is applicable even to the knowledge of the first path. One who attains to the fruit of stream-winning may be a beggar, an illiterate person, or a seven year old child. It may be that he has heard the *Dhamma* for the first time. All the same, a long line of epithets is used with reference to him in the *suttas* as his qualifications: *Diṭṭhadhammo pattadhammo viditadhammo pariyogāḷhadhammo tiṇṇavicikiccho vigatakathaṃkatho vesārajjappatto aparappaccayo satthusāsane*.[8]

Diṭṭhadhammo, he is one who has seen the *Dhamma*, the truth of *Nibbāna*. It is said in the *Ratanasutta* that along with the vision of the first path, three fetters are abandoned, namely *sakkāyadiṭṭhi*, the self-hood view, *vicikicchā*, sceptical doubt, and *sīlabbataparāmāsa*, attachment to holy vows and ascetic practices.[9] Some might argue that only these fetters are abandoned at this stage, because it is a glimpse of *Nibbāna* from a distance. But then there is this second epithet, *pattadhammo*, which means that he has reached the *Dhamma*, that he has arrived at *Nibbāna*. Not only that, he is *viditadhammo*, he is one who has understood the *Dhamma*, which is *Nibbāna*. He is *pariyogāḷhadhammo*, he has

---

[7] Peṭ 188.

[8] D I 110, *Ambaṭṭhasutta*.

[9] Sn 231, *Ratanasutta*.

plunged into the *Dhamma*, he has dived into the *Dhamma*, which is *Nibbāna*. He is *tiṇṇavicikiccho*, he has crossed over doubts. *Vigatakathaṃkatho*, his waverings are gone. *Vesārajjappatto*, he has attained to proficiency. *Aparappaccayo satthusāsane*, in regard to the dispensation of the teacher he is not dependent on others. And that is to say that he could attain to *Nibbāna* even without another's help, though of course with the teacher's help he would attain it sooner.

So this string of epithets testifies to the efficacy of the realization by the first path. It is not a mere glimpse of *Nibbāna* from a distance. It is a reaching, an arrival or a plunge into *Nibbāna*. For purposes of illustration we may bring in a legend connected with the history of Sri Lanka. It is said that when King Gajabāhu invaded India, one of his soldiers, Nīla, who had Herculean strength, parted the seawater with a huge iron bar in order to make way for the king and the army. Now when the supramundane path arises in the mind the power of thought is as mighty as the blow of Nīla with his iron bar. Even with the first blow the seawater parted, so that one could see the bottom. Similarly the sweeping influxes are parted for a moment when the transcendental path arises in a mind, enabling one to see the very bottom – *Nibbāna*. In other words, all preparations (*saṅkhāras*) are stilled for a moment, enabling one to see the cessation of preparations.

We have just given a simile by way of illustration, but incidentally there is a *Dhammapada* verse which comes closer to it:

> *Chinda sotaṃ parakkamma,*
> *kāme panuda brāhmaṇa,*
> *saṅkhārānaṃ khayaṃ ñatvā,*
> *akataññū'si brāhmaṇa.*[10]

> "Strive forth and cut off the stream,
> Discard, oh Brahmin, sense-desires,

[10] Dhp 383, *Brāhmaṇavagga*.

> Having known the destruction of preparations, oh
> Brahmin,
> Become a knower of the un-made."

So this verse clearly indicates what the knowledge of the path does when it arises. Just as one leaps forward and cuts off a stream of water, so it cuts off, even for a moment, the preparations connected with craving. Thereby one realizes the destruction of preparations – *saṅkhārānaṃ khayaṃ ñatvā.*

Like the sea water parted by the blow of the iron bar, preparations part for a moment to reveal the very bottom which is 'unprepared,' the *asaṅkhata. Akata*, or the un-made, is the same as *asaṅkhata*, the unprepared. So one has had a momentary vision of the sea bottom, which is free from preparations. Of course, after that experience, influxes flow in again. But one kind of influxes, namely *diṭṭhāsavā*, influxes of views, is gone for good and will never flow in again.

Now how was it that some with keen wisdom like Bāhiya attained *Arahant*-ship even while listening to a short sermon from the Buddha? They had dealt four powerful blows in quick succession with the iron bar of the path-knowledge to clear away all possible influxes.

What is called *akata* or *asaṅkhata*, the un-made or the unprepared, is not something out there in a distance, as an object of thought. It is not a sign to be grasped by one who wants to attain *Nibbāna*.

Language encourages us to think in terms of signs. Very often we find it difficult to get rid of this habit. The worldlings with their defilements have to communicate with each other and the structure of the language has to answer their needs. So the subject-object relationship has become a very significant feature in a language. It always carries the implication that there is a thing to be grasped and that there is someone who grasps, that there is a doer and a thing done. So it is almost impossible to avoid such usages as: 'I want to see *Nibbāna*, I want to attain *Nibbāna*.' We are made to think in terms of getting and attaining.

However sometimes the Buddha reminds us that this is only a conventional usage and that these worldly usages are not to be taken too seriously. We come across such an instance in the *Sagāthavagga* of the *Saṃyutta Nikāya* where the Buddha retorts to some questions put by a certain deity.[11] The deity named Kakudha asks the Buddha: "Do you rejoice, oh recluse?" And the Buddha retorts: "On getting what, friend?" Then the deity asks: "Then, recluse, do you grieve?" And the Buddha quips back: "On losing what, friend?" So the deity concludes: "Well then, recluse, you neither rejoice nor grieve!" And the Buddha replies: "That is so, friend."

It seems, then, that though we say we 'attain' *Nibbāna* there is nothing to gain and nothing to lose. If anything – **what is lost is an ignorance that there is something, and a craving that there is not enough** – and that is all one loses.

Now there are quite a number of synonyms for *Nibbāna*, such as *akata* and *asaṅkhata*. As already mentioned, there is even a list of thirty-three such epithets, out of which one is *dīpa*.[12] Now *dīpa* means an island. When we are told that *Nibbāna* is an island, we tend to imagine some sort of existence in a beautiful island. But in the *Pārāyanavagga* of the *Sutta Nipāta* the Buddha gives a good corrective to that kind of imagining in his reply to a question put by the Brahmin youth Kappa, a pupil of Bāvarī. Kappa puts his question in the following impressive verse:

Majjhe sarasmiṃ tiṭṭhataṃ,
oghe jāte mahabbhaye,
jarāmaccuparetānaṃ,
dīpaṃ pabrūhi mārisa,
tvañca me dīpam akkhāhi,
yathayidaṃ nāparaṃ siyā.[13]

---

[11] S I 54, *Kakudhosutta*.

[12] S IV 372.

[13] Sn 1092, *Kappamāṇavapucchā*.

"Unto them that stand midstream,
When the frightful floods flow forth,
To them in decay-and-death forlorn,
An island, sire, may you proclaim.
An island which none else excels,
Yea, such an isle, pray tell me sire."

And the Buddha gives his answer in two inspiring verses:

Majjhe sarasmiṃ tiṭṭhataṃ,
oghe jāte mahabbhaye,
jarāmaccuparetānaṃ,
dīpaṃ pabrūmi Kappa te.

Akiñcanaṃ anādānaṃ,
etaṃ dīpaṃ anāparaṃ,
nibbānaṃ iti naṃ brūmi,
jarāmaccuparikkhayaṃ.

"Unto them that stand midstream,
When the frightful floods flow forth,
To them in decay-and-death forlorn,
An island, Kappa, I shall proclaim.

"Owning naught, grasping naught,
The isle is this, none else besides.
Nibbāna, that is how I call that isle,
Wherein is decay decayed and death is dead."

Akiñcanaṃ means 'owning nothing,' *anādānaṃ* means 'grasping nothing.' *Etaṃ dīpaṃ anāparaṃ*, this is the island, nothing else. *Nibbānaṃ iti naṃ brūmi, jarāmaccuparikkhayaṃ*, "and that I call *Nibbāna*, which is the extinction of decay-and-death."

From this also we can infer that words like *akata*, *asaṅkhata* and *sabba-saṅkhārā-samatha* are full fledged synonyms of *Nibbāna*. *Nibbāna* is not some mysterious state quite apart from them. It is not something to be projected into a distance.

Some are in the habit of getting down to a discussion on *Nibbāna* by putting *saṅkhata* on one side and *asaṅkhata* on the other side. They start by saying that *saṅkhata*, or the 'prepared,' is *anicca*, or impermanent. If *saṅkhata* is *anicca*, they conclude that *asaṅkhata* must be *nicca*, that is the unprepared must be permanent. Following the same line of argument they argue that since *saṅkhata* is *dukkha*, *asaṅkhata* must be *sukha*. But when they come to the third step, they get into difficulties. If *saṅkhata* is *anattā*, or not-self, then surely *asaṅkhata* must be *attā*, or self. At this point they have to admit that their argument is too facile and so they end up by saying that after all *Nibbāna* is something to be realized.

All this confusion arises due to a lack of understanding of the law of Dependent Arising, *paṭicca samuppāda*. Therefore, first of all, we have to say something about the doctrine of *paṭicca samuppāda*.

According to the *Ariyapariyesanasutta* of the *Majjhima Nikāya*, the Buddha, soon after his enlightenment, reflected on the profundity of the *Dhamma* and was rather disinclined to preach it. He saw two points in the doctrine that are difficult for the world to see or grasp. One was *paṭicca samuppāda*: *Duddasaṃ idaṃ ṭhānaṃ yadidaṃ idappaccayatā paṭiccasamuppādo.*[14] "Hard to see is this point, namely dependent arising which is a relatedness of this to that."

And the second point was *Nibbāna*: *Idampi kho ṭhānaṃ duddasaṃ yadidaṃ sabbasaṅkhārasamatho sabbūpadhipaṭinissaggo taṇhakkhayo virāgo nirodho nibbānaṃ.* "And this point, too, is difficult to see, namely the stilling of all preparations, the relinquishment of all assets, the destruction of craving, detachment, cessation, extinction."

From this context we can gather that if there is any term we can use to define *paṭicca samuppāda*, a term that comes closer to it in

---

[14] M I 167, *Ariyapariyesanasutta*.

meaning, it is *idappaccayatā*. The Buddha himself has described *paṭicca samuppāda* in this context as a relatedness of this to that, *idappaccayatā*. As a matter of fact the basic principle which forms the noble norm of this doctrine of dependent arising is this *idappaccayatā*. Let us now try to get at its meaning by examining the doctrine of *paṭicca samuppāda*.

In quite a number of contexts, such as the *Bahudhātukasutta* of the *Majjhima Nikāya* and the *Bodhivagga* of the *Udāna* the law of *paṭicca samuppāda* is set out in the following manner:

> *Iti imasmiṃ sati idaṃ hoti,*
> *imassuppādā idaṃ uppajjati*
> *imasmiṃ asati idaṃ na hoti,*
> *imassa nirodhā idaṃ nirujjhati –*

> *yadidaṃ avijjāpaccayā saṅkhārā, saṅkhārapaccayā viññāṇaṃ, viññāṇapaccayā nāmarūpaṃ, nāmarūpapaccayā saḷāyatanaṃ, saḷāyatanapaccayā phasso, phassapaccayā vedanā, vedanāpaccayā taṇhā, taṇhāpaccayā upādānaṃ, upādānapaccayā bhavo, bhavapaccayā jāti, jātipaccayā jarāmaraṇaṃ sokaparidevadukkhadomanassūpāyāsā sambhavanti. Evametassa kevalassa dukkhakkhandhassa samudayo hoti.*

> *Avijjāyatveva asesavirāganirodhā saṅkhāranirodho, saṅkhāranirodhā viññāṇanirodho, viññāṇanirodhā nāmarūpanirodho, nāmarūpanirodhā saḷāyatananirodho, saḷāyatananirodhā phassanirodho, phassanirodhā vedanānirodho, vedanānirodhā taṇhānirodho, taṇhānirodhā upādānanirodho, upādānanirodhā bhavanirodho, bhavanirodhā jātinirodho, jātinirodhā jarāmaraṇaṃ*

sokaparidevadukkhadomanassūpāyāsā nirujjhanti. Evametassa kevalassa dukkhakkhandhassa nirodho hoti.[15]

"Thus: This being – this comes to be,
With the arising of this – this arises.
This not being – this does not come to be,
With the cessation of this – this ceases.

"That is to say, dependent on ignorance, preparations come to be; dependent on preparations, consciousness; dependent on consciousness, name-and-form; dependent on name-and-form, the six sense-bases; dependent on the six sense-bases, contact; dependent on contact, feeling; dependent on feeling, craving; dependent on craving, grasping; dependent on grasping, becoming; dependent on becoming, birth; dependent on birth, decay-and-death, sorrow, lamentation, pain, grief and despair come to be. Thus is the arising of this entire mass of suffering.

"But with the complete fading away and cessation of ignorance, comes the cessation of preparations; with the cessation of preparations, the cessation of consciousness; with the cessation of consciousness, the cessation of name-and-form; with the cessation of name-and-form, the cessation of the six sense-bases; with the cessation of the six sense-bases, the cessation of contact; with the cessation of contact, the cessation of feeling; with the cessation of feeling, the cessation of craving; with the cessation of craving, the cessation of grasping; with the cessation of grasping, the cessation of becoming; with the cessation of becoming, the cessation of birth; with the cessation of birth, the cessation of decay-and-death, sorrow, lamentation, pain, grief

[15] M III 63, *Bahudhātukasutta*, and Ud 1, the *Bodhisuttas*.

and despair cease to be. Thus is the cessation of this entire mass of suffering."

This is the thematic statement of the law of *paṭicca samuppāda*. It is set out here in the form of a fundamental principle. *Imasmiṃ sati idaṃ hoti*, "This being, this comes to be." *Imassuppādā idaṃ uppajjati,* "With the arising of this, this arises." *Imasmiṃ asati idaṃ na hoti*, "This not being, this does not come to be." *Imassa nirodhā idaṃ nirujjhati*, "With the cessation of this, this ceases." It resembles an algebraical formula.

And then we have the conjunctive *yadidaṃ*, which means "namely this" or "that is to say." This shows that the foregoing statement is axiomatic and implies that what follows is an illustration. So the twelve linked formula beginning with the words *avijjāpaccayā saṅkhārā* is that illustration. No doubt the twelve-linked formula is impressive enough. But the important thing here is the basic principle involved, and that is the fourfold statement beginning with *imasmiṃ sati*.

This fact is very clearly brought out in a certain *sutta* in the *Nidānavagga* of the *Saṃyutta Nikāya*. There the Buddha addresses the monks and says: *Paṭiccasamuppādañca vo, bhikkhave, desessāmi paṭiccasamuppanne ca dhamme.*[16] "Monks, I will teach you dependent arising and things that are dependently arisen."

In this particular context the Buddha makes a distinction between dependent arising and things that are dependently arisen. In order to explain what is meant by dependent arising, or *paṭicca samuppāda*, he takes up the last two links in the formula, in the words: *jātipaccayā, bhikkhave, jarāmaraṇaṃ*, "Monks, dependent on birth is decay-and-death." Then he draws attention to the importance of the basic principle involved: *Uppādā vā Tathāgatānaṃ anuppādā vā Tathāgatānaṃ, ṭhitā va sā dhātu*

---

16 S II 25, *Paccayasutta*.

dhammaṭṭhitatā dhammaniyāmatā idappaccayatā. (Etc.) Out of the long exhortation given there, this is the part relevant to us here.

Jātipaccayā, bhikkhave, jarāmaraṇaṃ, "Dependent on birth, oh monks, is decay-and-death," and that is to say that decay-and-death has birth as its condition. *Uppādā vā Tathāgatānaṃ anuppādā vā Tathāgatānaṃ*, "Whether there be an arising of the *Tathāgatās* or whether there be no such arising." *Ṭhitā va sā dhātu dhammaṭṭhitatā dhammaniyāmatā idappaccayatā*, "That elementary nature, that orderliness of the *Dhamma*, that norm of the *Dhamma*, the relatedness of this to that does stand as it is."

So from this it is clear that the underlying principle could be understood even with the help of a couple of links. But the commentary seems to have ignored this fact in its definition of the term *idappaccayatā*. It says: *Imesaṃ jarāmaraṇādīnaṃ paccayā idappaccayā, idappaccayāva idappaccayatā.*[17] The word *imesaṃ* is in the plural and this indicates that the commentator has taken the dependence in a collective sense. But it is because of the fact that even two links are sufficient to illustrate the law, that the Buddha follows it up with the declaration that this is the *paṭicca samuppāda*. And then he goes on to explain what is meant by 'things dependently arisen':

Katame ca, bhikkhave, paṭiccasamuppannā dhammā? Jarāmaraṇaṃ, bhikkhave, aniccaṃ saṅkhataṃ paṭiccasamuppannaṃ khayadhammaṃ vayadhammaṃ virāgadhammaṃ nirodhadhammaṃ.

"What, monks, are things dependently arisen?" And then, taking up just one of the last links, he declares: "Decay-and-death, monks, is impermanent, prepared, dependently arisen, of a nature to get destroyed, to pass away, fade away and cease."

By the way, the word *virāga* usually means detachment or dispassion. But in such contexts as *avijjāvirāgā* and *pītiyā ca virāgā* one has to render it by words like 'fading away.' So that *avij-*

---

[17] Spk II 40.

jāvirāga could be rendered as: 'by the fading away of ignorance,' and *pītiyā virāgā* would mean 'by the fading away of joy.'

It seems, then, that decay-and-death themselves are impermanent, that they are prepared or made up, that they are dependently arisen. Decay-and-death themselves can get destroyed and pass away. Decay as well as death can fade away and cease.

Then the Buddha takes up the preceding link *jāti*, or birth. And that too is given the same qualifications. In the same manner he takes up each of the preceding links up to and including ignorance, *avijjā*, and applies to them the above qualifications. It is significant that every one of the twelve links, even ignorance, is said to be dependently arisen.

Let us try to understand how, for instance, decay-and-death themselves can get destroyed or pass away. Taking the *idappaccayatā* formula as a paradigm, we can illustrate the relationship between the two links birth and decay-and-death. Instead of saying: this being, that comes to be (and so forth), now we have to say: birth being, decay-and-death comes to be. With the arising of birth, decay-and-death arises. Birth not being, decay-and-death does not come to be. With the cessation of birth, decay-and-death ceases.

Now birth itself is an arising. But here we can't help saying that birth 'arises.' It is like saying that birth is born. How can birth get born? Similarly death is a passing away. But here we have to say that death itself 'passes away.' How can death pass away? Perhaps, as we proceed, we might get the answers to these questions.

Now at this point let us take up for discussion a certain significant passage in the *MahāNidānasutta* of the *Dīgha Nikāya*. In the course of an exposition of the law of *paṭicca samuppāda*, addressed to Venerable Ānanda, the Buddha makes the following statement:

> *Ettāvatā kho, Ānanda, jāyetha vā jīyetha vā mīyetha vā cavetha vā upapajjetha vā. Ettāvatā adhivacanapatho, ettāvatā niruttipatho, ettāvatā paññattipatho, ettāvatā*

> *paññāvacaraṃ, ettāvatā vaṭṭaṃ vattati itthattaṃ paññāpanāya yadidaṃ nāmarūpaṃ saha viññāṇena.*[18]

> "In so far only, Ānanda, can one be born, or grow old, or die, or pass away, or reappear, in so far only is there any pathway for verbal expression, in so far only is there any pathway for terminology, in so far only is there any pathway for designation, in so far only is the range of wisdom, in so far only is the round kept going for there to be a designation as the this-ness, that is to say: name-and-form together with consciousness."

We have rendered the term *itthatta* by 'this-ness,' and what it means will become clear as we go on. In the above quotation the word *ettāvatā*, which means 'in so far only,' has as its point of reference the concluding phrase *yadidaṃ nāmarūpaṃ saha viññāṇena*, "that is to say: name-and-form together with consciousness." So the statement, as it is, expresses a complete idea. But some editions have an additional phrase: *aññamañña-paccayatā pavattati*, "exists in a mutual relationship." This phrase is obviously superfluous and is probably a commentarial addition.

What is meant by the Buddha's statement is that name-and-form together with consciousness is the rallying point for all concepts of birth, decay, death and rebirth. All pathways for verbal expression, terminology and designation converge on name-and-form together with consciousness. The range of wisdom extends only up to the relationship between these two. And it is between these two that there is a whirling round so that one may point out a this-ness. In short, the secret of the entire *saṃsāric* existence is to be found in this whirlpool.

Vaṭṭa and *āvaṭṭa* are words used for a whirlpool. We shall be bringing up quotations in support of that meaning. It seems,

---

[18] D II 63, *MahāNidānasutta.*

however, that this meaning has got obscured in the course of time. In the commentaries and in some modern translations there is quite a lot of confusion with regard to the meaning of the phrase *vaṭṭaṃ vattati*. In fact one Sinhala translation renders it as '*saṃsāric* rain.' What rain has to do with *saṃsāra* is a matter for conjecture. What is actually meant by *vaṭṭaṃ vattati* is a whirling round, and *saṃsāra*, even literally, is that. Here we are told that there is a whirling round between name-and-form and consciousness, and this is the *saṃsāric* whirlpool to which all the aforesaid things are traceable.

Already in the first sermon we tried to show that name in name-and-form has to do with names and concepts. Now from this context it becomes clear that all pathways for verbal expression, terminology and designation converge on this whirlpool between name-and-form and consciousness.

Now that we have attached so much significance to a whirlpool, let us try to understand how a whirlpool is formed. Let us try to get at the natural laws underlying its formation. How does a whirlpool come to be?

Suppose a river is flowing downward. To flow downward is in the nature of a river. But a certain current of water thinks: "I can and must move upstream." And so it pushes on against the main stream. But at a certain point its progress is checked by the main stream and is thrust aside, only to come round and make a fresh attempt, again and again. All these obstinate and unsuccessful attempts gradually lead to a whirling round. As time goes on, the run-away current understands, as it were, that it cannot move forward. But it does not give up. It finds an alternative aim in moving towards the bottom. So it spirals downward, funnel-like, digging deeper and deeper towards the bottom, until an abyss is formed. Here then we have a whirlpool.

While all this is going on, there is a crying need to fill up the chasm, and the whirlpool develops the necessary force of attraction to cater to it. It attracts and grasps everything that comes within its reach and sends it whirling down, funnel like, into the chasm. The whirling goes on at a tremendous speed, while the circumference grows larger and larger. At last the whirlpool becomes a centre of a tremendous amount of activity.

While this kind of activity is going on in a river or a sea, there is a possibility for us to point it out as 'that place' or 'this place.' Why? Because there is an activity going on. Usually, in the world, the place where an activity is going on is known as a 'unit,' a 'centre,' or an 'institution.' Since the whirlpool is also a centre of activity, we may designate it as a 'here' or 'there.' We may even personify it. With reference to it, we can open up pathways for verbal expression, terminology and designation.

But if we are to consider the form of activity that is going on here, what is it after all? It is only a perversion. That obstinate current thought to itself, out of delusion and ignorance: I can and must move upstream. And so it tried and failed, but turned round only to make the same vain attempt again and again. Ironically enough, even its **progress** towards the bottom is a **stagnation**.

So here we have ignorance on one side and craving on the other, as a result of the abyss formed by the whirlpool. In order to satisfy this craving there is that power of attraction: grasping. Where there is **grasping**, there is **existence**, or ***bhava***. The entire whirlpool now appears as a centre of activity.

Now the basic principle underlying this whirlpool is to be found in our bodies. What we call 'breathing' is a continuous process of emptying and filling up. So even the so-called 'life-principle' is not much different from the activity of a whirlpool. The functioning of the lungs and the heart is based on the same principle and the blood circulation is in fact a whirling round. This kind of activity is very often known as 'automatic,' a word which has connotations of **self**-sufficiency. But at the root of it there is a perversion, as we saw in the case of the whirlpool. All these activities are based on a conflict between two opposite forces.

In fact existence in its entirety is not much different from the conflict of that obstinate current of water with the main stream. This characteristic of conflict is so pervasive that it can be seen even in the basic laws governing the existence of a society. In our social life, rights and responsibilities go hand in hand. We can enjoy certain privileges, provided we fulfill our duties. So here too we have a tangle within and a tangle without.[19]

Now this is about the existence of the society as such. And what about the field of economics? There too the basic principles show the same weakness. Production is governed by laws of supply and demand. There will be a supply so long as there is a demand. Between them there is a conflict. It leads to many complications. The price mechanism is on a precarious balance and that is why some wealthy countries are forced to the ridiculous position of dumping their surplus into the sea.

All this shows that existence is basically in a precarious position. To illustrate this, let us take the case of two snakes of the same size, trying to swallow up each other. Each of them tries to swallow up the other from the tail upwards and when they are half way through the meal, what do we find? A **snake cycle**. This snake cycle goes round and round, trying to swallow up each other. But will it ever be successful?

The precarious position illustrated by the snake cycle, we find in our own bodies in the form of respiration, blood circulation and so forth. What appears as the stability in the society and in the economy, is similarly precarious. It is because of this conflict, this unsatisfactoriness, that the Buddha concluded that the whole of existence is suffering.

When the arising aspect is taken too seriously, to the neglect of the cessation aspect, instead of a conflict or an unsatisfactoriness one tends to see something automatic everywhere. This body as well as machines such as water pumps and electrical appliances seem to work on an automatic principle. But in truth there is only a conflict between two opposing forces. When one comes to think of it, there is no '**auto**'-ness even in the automatic.

All that is there, is a bearing up with difficulty. And this in fact is the meaning of the word *dukkha*. *Duḥ* stands for 'difficulty' and

---

[19] S I 13, *Jaṭāsutta*.

kha for 'bearing up.' **Even with difficulty one bears it up, and though one bears it up, it is difficult**.

Now regarding the question of existence we happened to mention that because of a whirlpool's activity, one can point out a '**here**' with reference to it. We can now come back to the word *itthattaṃ*, which we left out without comment in the quotation *ettāvatā vaṭṭaṃ vattati itthattaṃ paññāpanāya*, "in so far only does the whirlpool whirl for the designation of an *itthatta.*" Now what is this *itthatta*? *Ittha* means 'this,' so *itthattaṃ* would mean 'this-ness.' The whirling of a whirlpool qualifies itself for a designation as a 'this.'

There are a couple of verses in the *Dvayatānupassanāsutta* of the *Sutta Nipāta* which bring out the meaning of this word more clearly:

> *Jāti maraṇa saṃsāraṃ,*
> *ye vajanti punappunaṃ,*
> *itthabhāvaññathābhāvaṃ,*
> *avijjāyeva sā gati.*[20]

> *Taṇhā dutiyo puriso,*
> *dīgham addhāna saṃsāraṃ,*
> *itthabhāvaññathābhāvaṃ,*
> *saṃsāraṃ nātivattati.*[21]

Ye jāti maraṇa saṃsāraṃ punappunaṃ vajanti, "they that go on again and again the round of birth and death." *Itthabhāvaññathābhāvaṃ,* "which is a this-ness and an otherwise-ness," or "which is an alternation between a this-ness and an otherwise-ness." *Sā gati avijjāya eva*, "that going of them, that faring of them, is only a journey of ignorance." *Taṇhā dutiyo puriso*, "the man with craving

---

[20] Sn 729, *Dvayatānupassanāsutta*.

[21] Sn 740, *Dvayatānupassanāsutta*.

as his second," (or his companion). *Dīgham addhāna saṃsāraṃ*, "faring on for a long time in *saṃsāra*." *Itthabhāvaññathābhāvaṃ, saṃsāraṃ nātivattati*, "does not get away from the round which is a this-ness and an otherwise-ness," or "which is an alternation between a this-ness and an otherwise-ness." What is meant by it, is the transcendence of *saṃsāra*.

We saw above how the concept of a 'here' arose with the birth of a whirlpool. In fact one's birth is at the same time the birth of a 'here' or 'this place.' And that is what is meant by *itthabhāva* in the two verses quoted above. *Itthabhāva* and *itthatta* both mean 'this-ness.' In both verses this 'this-ness' is coupled with an otherwise-ness, *aññathābhāva*. Here too we see a conflict between two things, this-ness and otherwise-ness. The cycle of *saṃsāra*, represented by birth and death, *jāti maraṇa saṃsāraṃ*, is equivalent to an alternation between this-ness and otherwise-ness, *itthabhāvaññathābhāva*. And as the first verse says, this recurrent alternation between this-ness and otherwise-ness is nothing but a journey of ignorance itself.

Though we have given so much significance to the two terms *itthabhāva* and *aññathābhāva*, the commentary to the *Sutta Nipāta* treats them lightly. It explains *itthabhāvaṃ* as *imaṃ manussabhāvaṃ*, which means "this state as a human being," and *aññathābhāvaṃ* as *ito avasesa aññanikāyabhāvaṃ*, "any state of being other than this."[22] This explanation misses the deeper significance of the word *itthatta*.

In support of this we may refer to the *Pāṭikasutta* of the *Dīgha Nikāya*. There we are told that when the world system gets destroyed at the end of an aeon, some being or other gets reborn in an empty Brahma mansion, and after being there for a long time, thinks, out of a feeling of loneliness: *Aho vata aññepi sattā itthattaṃ āgaccheyyuṃ*.[23] "How nice it would be if other beings

---

[22] Pj II 505.

[23] D III 29, *Pāṭikasutta*.

also come to this state." In this context the word *itthatta* refers to the Brahma world and not the human world. From the point of view of the Brahmas, *itthatta* refers to the Brahma world and only for us here, it means the human world.

However this is just a narrow meaning of the word *itthatta*. When the reference is to the entire round of existence or *saṃsāra*, *itthatta* does not necessarily mean 'this human world.' The two terms have a generic sense, because they represent some basic principle. As in the case of a whirlpool, this-ness is to be seen together with an otherwise-ness. This illustrates the conflict characteristic of existence. Wherever a this-ness arises, a possibility for an otherwise-ness comes in. *Itthabhāva* and *aññathābhāva* go together.

Aniccatā, or impermanence, is very often explained with the help of the phrase *vipariṇāmaññathābhāva*.[24] Now here too we have the word *aññathābhāva*. Here the word preceding it, gives a clue to its true significance. *Vipariṇāma* is quite suggestive of a process of evolution. Strictly speaking, *pariṇāma* is evolution, and *pariṇata* is the fully evolved or mature stage. The prefix *vi* stands for the anti-climax. The evolution is over, now it is becoming other. Ironically enough, this state of 'becoming-other' is known as otherwise-ness, *aññathābhāva*. And so this twin, *itthabhāva* and *aññathābhāva*, tell us the nature of the world. Between them, they explain for us the law of impermanence.

In the section of the Threes in the *Aṅguttara Nikāya* the three characteristics of a *saṅkhata* are explained in this order: *Uppādo paññāyati, vayo paññāyati, ṭhitassa aññathattaṃ paññāyati*,[25] "An arising is manifest, a passing away is manifest and an otherwise-ness in the persisting is manifest."

This implies that the persistence is only apparent and that is why it is mentioned last. There is an otherwise-ness even in this

---

[24] E.g. at M II 110, *Piyajātikasutta*.

[25] A I 152, *Saṅkhatalakkhaṇasutta*.

apparently persistent. But later scholars preferred to speak of three stages as*uppāda, ṭhiti, bhaṅga*,[26] "arising, persistence, and breaking up." However the law of impermanence could be sufficiently understood even with the help of two words, *itthabhāva* and *aññathābhāva*, this-ness and otherwise-ness. Very often we find the Buddha summing up the law of impermanence in the two words *samudaya* and *vaya*, "arising" and "passing away."[27]

There is an apparent contradiction in the phrase *ṭhitassa aññathatta*, but it reminds us of the fact that what the world takes as static or persisting is actually not so. The so-called 'static' is from beginning to end an otherwise-ness. Now if we are to relate this to the two links *jāti* and *jarāmaraṇaṃ* in *paṭicca samuppāda*, we may say that as soon as one is born the process of otherwise-ness sets in. Wherever there is birth, there is death. One of the traditional *Pāli* verses on the reflections on death has the following meaningful lines:

Uppattiyā sahevedaṃ, maraṇam āgataṃ sadā,[28] "Always death has come, even with the birth itself." Just as in a conjoined pair, when one is drawn the other follows, even so when birth is drawn in, decay-and-death follow as a matter of course.

Before the advent of the Buddha, the world believed in the possibility of a birth devoid of decay-and-death. It believed in a form of existence devoid of grasping. Because of its ignorance of the pair-wise relatedness of this-to-that, *idappaccayatā*, it went on with its deluded search. And that was the reason for all the conflict in the world.

According to the teaching of the Buddha, the concept of birth is equivalent to the concept of a 'here.' As a matter of fact, this birth of a 'here' is like the first peg driven for the measurement of a

---

26 E.g. at Ps IV 88.

27 E.g. at M I 56, *Satipaṭṭhānasutta*.

28 This is found in the set of verses on *maraṇasati* among the *caturārakkhāgāthā* (four protective *kamaṭṭhānas*) in standard *Paritta* books.

world. Because of the pair-wise relationship, the very first '**birth-day-present**' that one gets as soon as one is born, is – **death**. The inevitable death that he is entitled to. This way we can understand the deeper significance of the two words *itthabhāva* and *aññathābhāva*, this-ness and otherwise-ness.

We have to say the same thing with regard to the whirlpool. Apparently it has the power to control, to hold sway. Seen from a distance, the whirlpool is a centre of activity with some controlling power. Now, one of the basic meanings of the concept of self is the ability to control, to hold sway. And a whirlpool too, as seen from a distance, seems to have this ability. Just as it appears automatic, so also it seems to have some power to control.

But on deeper analysis it reveals its **not-self** nature. What we have here is simply the conflict between the main stream and a run-away current. It is the outcome of the conflict between two forces and not the work of just one force. It is a case of relatedness of this-to-that, *idappaccayatā*. As one verse in the *Bālavagga* of the *Dhammapada* puts it: *Attā hi attano natthi*,[29] "Even oneself is not one's own."

So even a whirlpool is not its own, there is nothing really automatic about it. This then is the *dukkha*, the suffering, the conflict, the unsatisfactoriness. What the world holds on to as existence is just a process of otherwise-ness, as the Buddha vividly portrays for us in the following verses of the *Nandavagga* of the *Udāna*.

Ayaṃ loko santāpajāto, phassapareto
rogaṃ vadati attato,
yena yena hi maññati,
tato taṃ hoti aññathā.
Aññathābhāvī bhavasatto loko,
bhavapareto bhavam evābhinandati,

---

[29] Dhp 62, *Bālavagga*.

yad'abhinandati taṃ bhayaṃ,
yassa bhāyati taṃ dukkhaṃ,
bhava vippahānāya kho panidaṃ
brahmacariyaṃ vussati.[30]

"This anguished world, fully given
to contact,
Speaks of a disease as self.
In whatever terms it conceives of,
Even thereby it turns otherwise.
The world, attached to becoming,
Given fully to becoming,
Though becoming otherwise,
Yet delights in becoming.
What it delights in is a fear
What it fears from
Is a suffering.
But then this holy life is lived for the
abandoning of that very becoming."

Just a few lines – but how deep they go! The world is in anguish and is enslaved by contact. What it calls self is nothing but a disease. *Maññati* is a word of deeper significance. *Maññanā* is conceiving under the influence of craving, conceit and views. Whatever becomes an object of that conceiving, by that very conception it becomes otherwise. That is to say that an opportunity arises for an otherwise-ness, even as 'death' has come together with 'birth.'

So conceiving, or conception, is itself the reason for otherwise-ness. Before a '**thing**' becomes '**otherwise**,' it has to become a '**thing**.' And it becomes a 'thing' only when attention is focused on it under the influence of craving, conceit and views and it is

---

30 Ud 32, *Lokasutta*.

separated from the whole world and grasped as a '**thing.**' And that is why it is said:

> *Yaṃ yañhi lokasmim upādiyanti,*
> *teneva Māro anveti jantuṃ.*[31]

> "Whatever one grasps in the world,
> By that itself *Māra* pursues a being."

The world is attached to becoming and is fully given to becoming. Therefore its very nature is otherwise-ness, *aññathābhāvī.* And then the Buddha declares the inevitable outcome of this contradictory position: *yad abhinandati taṃ bhayaṃ*, whatever one delights in, that is a fear, that is a danger. What one delights in, is 'becoming' and that is a source of fear. And *yassa bhāyati taṃ dukkhaṃ*, what one fears, or is afraid of, that is suffering. And of what is one afraid? One is afraid of the otherwise-ness of the thing that one holds on to as existing. So the otherwise-ness is the suffering and the thing grasped is a source of fear.

For instance, when one is walking through a town with one's pockets full of gems, one is afraid because of the valuables in one's pockets. Even so, the existence that one delights in is a source of fear. What one fears is change or otherwise-ness, and that is suffering. Therefore it is that this holy life is lived for the abandonment of that very becoming or existence.

So from this quotation it becomes clear that the nature of existence is 'otherwise-ness.' It is the insight into this nature that is basic in the understanding of *idappaccayatā*. What is known as the arising of the *Dhamma*-eye is the understanding of this predicament in worldly existence. But that *Dhamma*-eye arises together with a solution for this predicament: *Yaṃ kiñci samudaya-*

---

[31] Sn 1103, *Bhadrāvudhamāṇavapucchā.*

dhammaṃ sabbaṃ taṃ nirodhadhammaṃ.[32] "Whatever is of a nature to arise, all that is of a nature to cease."

As far as the arising aspect is concerned, this whirlpool is formed due to the grasping through craving, conceit and views. Once this *saṃsāric* whirlpool is formed, it keeps on attracting all that is in the world, all that is within its reach, in the form of craving and grasping. But there is a cessation to this process. It is possible to make it cease. Why? Because it is something arisen due to causes and conditions. Because it is a process based on two things, without a self to hold sway. That is why we have mentioned at the very outset that every thing is impermanent, prepared and dependently arisen, *aniccaṃ, saṅkhataṃ, paṭicca samuppannaṃ.*

Everyone of the twelve links in the formula, including ignorance, is dependently arisen. They are all arisen due to causes and conditions, they are not permanent, *aniccaṃ*. They are only made up or prepared, *saṅkhataṃ*. The word *saṅkhataṃ* is explained in various ways. But in short it means something that is made up, prepared, or concocted by way of intention. *Paṭicca samuppannaṃ* means conditionally arisen and therefore it is of a nature to get destroyed, *khayadhamma*. It is of a nature to pass away, *vayadhamma*. It is of a nature to fade away, *virāgadhamma*. It is of a nature to cease, *nirodhadhamma*.

It seems that even the colour or shade of decay-and-death can fade away and that is why we have pointed out their relevance to the question of concepts. This nature of fading away is understood by one who has had an insight into the law of arising and cessation.

Saṃsāra is a whirlpool as far as the ordinary beings caught up in it are concerned. Now what about the *Arahants*? How is the idea of this whirlpool presented in the case of the *Arahants*? It is simply said that for them there is no whirling round for there to be

---

32 S V 423, *Dhammacakkapavattanasutta*.

a designation: *vaṭṭaṃ tesaṃ natthi paññāpanāya.*[33] So in their case, there is no whirling round to justify a designation.

This, then, is something deeper than the whirlpool itself. The whirlpool can be pointed out because of its activity. But not so easily the emancipated ones and that is why there is so much controversy regarding the nature of the *Tathāgatha*. The image of the whirlpool in its relation to the emancipated ones is beautifully presented in the following verse from the *Cūḷavagga* of the *Udāna*:

Acchecchi vaṭṭaṃ byagā nirāsaṃ,
visukkhā saritā na sandati,
chinnaṃ vaṭṭaṃ na vattati,
es' ev' anto dukkhassa.[34]

"He has cut off the whirlpool
And reached desirelessness,
The stream dried up now no longer flows.
The whirlpool cut off whirls no more.
This, even this, is suffering's end."

What has the *Arahant* done? He has cut off the whirlpool. He has breached it and has reached the desireless state. The stream of craving is dried up and flows no more. The whirlpool cut off at the root, no more whirls. And this is the end of suffering. The cutting off of the whirlpool is the realization of cessation, which is *Arahant*-hood.

It is because of the accent on the arising aspect that the current tries to move against the main stream. When that attempt is given up, the rest happens as a matter of course. This idea is even more clearly brought out by the following two verses in the *Sagātha-*

---

33 M I 141, *Alagaddūpamasutta*.

34 Ud 75, *DutiyaLakuṇḍakabhaddiyasutta*.

vagga of the *Saṃyutta Nikāya*. They are in the form of a dialogue between a deity and the Buddha. The deity asks:

Kuto sarā nivattanti,
kattha vaṭṭaṃ na vattati,
kattha nāmañca rūpañca
asesaṃ uparujjhati?[35]

"From where do currents turn back,
Where whirls no more the whirlpool,
Where is it that name-and-form
Is held in check in a way complete?"

The Buddha gives the answer in the following verse:

Yattha āpo ca paṭhavī,
tejo vāyo na gādhati,
ato sarā nivattanti,
ettha vaṭṭaṃ na vattati,
ettha nāmañca rūpañca,
asesaṃ uparujjhati.

"Where earth and water, fire and wind no
footing find,
From there it is that currents turn back.
There the whirlpool whirls no more
And there it is that name-and-form
Is held in check in a way complete."

The reference here is to *Nibbāna*. Whether it is called *sabbasaṅkhārasamatha*, the stilling of all preparations, or *asaṅkhatadhātu*, the unprepared element, it means the state of cessation. And when

[35] S I 15, *Sarasutta*.

the *Arahant*'s mind is in that state, the four elements, which are like ghosts, do not haunt him. They do not get a '**footing**' in that consciousness. When they fade away, due to detachment, those currents do not flow and the whirlpool whirls no more. Name and form are fully held in check there.

Now as far as the meaning of *rūpa* in *nāma-rūpa* in this reference is concerned, its definition as *cattāri ca mahābhūtāni, catunnañca mahābhūtānaṃ upādāyarūpaṃ* is quite significant.[36] It draws attention to the fact that the four great primaries underlie the concept of form. This is something unique, since before the advent of the Buddha the world thought that in order to get away from *rūpa* one has to grasp *arūpa*. But the irony of the situation is that, even in *arūpa*, *rūpa* is implicit in a subtle form. Or in other words, *arūpa* takes *rūpa* for granted.

Supposing someone, walking in the darkness of the night, has a hallucination of a devil and runs away to escape from it. He thinks he is running away from the devil, but he is taking the devil with him. The devil is in his mind, it is something imagined. Similarly, until the Buddha came into the scene, the worldlings grasped *arūpa* in order to get away from *rūpa*. But because of the dichotomy between *rūpa* and *arūpa*, even when they swung as far as the highest formless realms, they were still in bondage to *saṅkhāras*, or preparations. As soon as the momentum of their swing of *saṅkhāras* got fully spent, they swung back to *rūpa*. So here too we see the question of duality and dichotomy.

This sermon has served its purpose if it has drawn attention to the importance of the questions of duality, dichotomy and the relatedness of this to that, *idappaccayatā*. So this is enough for today.

---

[36] M I 53, *Sammādiṭṭhisutta*.

Nibbāna Sermon 3

Namo tassa Bhagavato Arahato Sammāsambuddhassa
Namo tassa Bhagavato Arahato Sammāsambuddhassa
Namo tassa Bhagavato Arahato Sammāsambuddhassa

Etaṃ santaṃ, etaṃ paṇītaṃ, yadidaṃ sabbasaṅkhārasamatho sabbūpadhipaṭinissaggo taṇhakkhayo virāgo nirodho nibbānaṃ.[1]

"This is peaceful, this is excellent, namely the stilling of all preparations, the relinquishment of all assets, the destruction of craving, detachment, cessation, extinction."

With the permission of the Most Venerable Great Preceptor and the assembly of the venerable meditative monks.

Today we have before us the third sermon on *Nibbāna*. The other day, with the help of the simile of a whirlpool, we attempted an explanation of the terms *saṃsāra* on the one hand, and *Nibbāna* on the other, that is to say 'going round,' or *saṃsaraṇa*, and 'going out,' or *nissaraṇa*.[2] We also cited *suttas* to illustrate both the arising (*samudaya*) and cessation (*nirodha*) aspects of the law of dependent arising.

As regards this whirlpool, to show a parallel development with the links of the law of dependent arising, by way of a sustained simile, we may say that the ignorance in presuming that it is possible to go against the main stream of the three signata –

---

1 M I 436, *MahāMālunkyasutta*.

2 See sermon 2.

impermanence, suffering and not-self – is the place of its origin. That heap of preparations impelled by ignorance, which takes the current forward, may be regarded as *saṅkhāras*. And where the current in its progress clashes with the main stream to become a whirlpool, that pushing forward against the main stream is *viññāṇa* or consciousness.

The outcome of the clash is *nāma-rūpa*, or name-and-form, with its formal name and nominal form. That link in the formula of dependent arising called *saḷāyatana*, or six sense-bases, could be regarded as the outgrowth of this name-and-form. We can understand that link, too, in relation to the simile of the whirlpool. As the whirlpool goes on for a long time, an abyss is formed, the functioning of which could be compared to the six sense-bases.

As a matter of fact, bodily pains are comparable to an abyss. In a certain *sutta* in the *Saṃyutta Nikāya* the Buddha says: *Sārīrikānaṃ kho etaṃ bhikkhave dukkhānaṃ vedanānaṃ adhivacanaṃ, yadidaṃ pātālo'ti.*[3] "Monks, abyss is a synonym for painful bodily feelings."

When one comes to think about that statement, it would appear that the thirst of craving arises in beings in various forms of existence because of painful feeling. The *Sallattenasutta* adds to this by stating that the uninstructed worldling, on being touched by painful feeling, delights in sense pleasures, because he knows no way out of painful feeling other than the sense pleasures.[4]

In the light of that statement it seems that the abyss is the endless barrage of painful feelings. The force of attraction that arises from the abyss is like the thirst to quell those painful feelings. The grasping that follows is the functioning of the same force of attraction. It attracts all the flotsam and jetsam around it, as things organically appropriated, *upādinna*, to put up a show of existence, or *bhava*. That is, a spot that can be pointed out with the help of

---

[3] S IV 206, *Pātālasutta*.

[4] S IV 208, *Sallattenasutta*.

things thus grasped by the whirlpool. So this whirlpool or vortex simile gives us some idea of the law of dependent arising.

The insight into the basic principle of dependent arising, is in fact regarded as the arising of the 'eye of *Dhamma*.' About the stream-winner it is said that the dustless stainless eye of *Dhamma* has arisen in him. The following phrase, which sums up the significance of that *Dhamma*-eye, comes up quite often in the discourses: *Yaṃ kiñci samudayadhammaṃ sabbaṃ taṃ nirodhadhammaṃ.*[5] "Whatever is of a nature to arise, all that is of a nature to cease."

Sometimes it is briefly alluded to with the couple of terms *samudaya* and *nirodha*, as *samudayo samudayo* and *nirodho nirodho.*[6] It is as if the experience of that insight has found expression as an exclamation: "Arising, arising! Ceasing, ceasing!" The above phrase only connects up the two aspects of that experience.

It seems then that what is called the '*Dhamma*-eye,' is the ability to see the *Nibbānic* solution in the very vortex of the *samsāric* problem. That way of analysis which puts *samsāra* and *Nibbāna* far apart, into two watertight compartments, as it were, gives rise to interminable problems. But here we see that, just as much as one could realize *Nibbāna* by discovering the cause of suffering and following the path to its cessation, which in effect is the understanding of the four noble truths, one could also put an end to this vortex by understanding its cause and applying the correct means for its cessation.

In the previous sermon we happened to quote some Canonical verses, which declared that the vortex does not exist for an *arahant.*[7] Now as regards the condition after the cessation of the

---

[5] D I 110, D I 148, D II 41, D II 288, M I 380, M I 501, M II 145, M III 280, S IV 47, S IV 107, S IV 192, S V 423, A IV 186, A IV 210, A IV 213, Ud 49.

[6] D II 33, S II 7, S II 105.

[7] See sermon 2.

vortex, if someone asks where the vortex or the whirlpool has gone, what sort of answer can we give? It is the same difficulty that comes up in answering the question: "Where has the fire gone after it has gone out?" Because here too, what we call the whirlpool is that current of water which went against the main stream. It also consists of water, like the body of water outside it. So we cannot say that they united, nor can we say that it went and hid somewhere.

Here we find ourselves in a queer situation. All we can say in fairness to truth is that there had been a certain form of activity, a certain state of unrest, due to certain causes and conditions. Because of that activity that was going on there, it was possible to designate it, to give it a name. By worldly convention one could refer to it as "that place" or "this place."

The entire field of activity was called a whirlpool by worldly convention. But now, the so-called whirlpool is no more. The worldly convention is no more applicable as in the case of an extinguished fire. The word "fire" was introduced, the concept of "fire" was created, to designate a certain state of affairs that arose due to causes and conditions, due to graspings. So from this also we can see that it is in concepts that ignorance finds a camouflage.

Being unaware of it the world goes on amassing concepts and even expects to see them in *Nibbāna*. There are some who fondly hope to get a vision of their lists of concepts when they realize *Nibbāna*. But that wisdom penetrates through even the concepts and that is why it is called *udayatthagāminī paññā ariyā nibbedhikā*,[8] "the *ariyan* penetrative wisdom that sees the rise and fall."

The idea of penetration is already implicit in the phrase *yaṃ kiñci samudayadhammaṃ sabbaṃ taṃ nirodhadhammaṃ*, "whatever is of a nature to arise, all that is of a nature to cease." If anything has the nature to arise, by that very nature it is bound to come to its end. And that is why the wandering ascetic Upatissa,

---

[8] E.g. at D III 237, *Saṅgītisutta*.

who was to become Venerable Sāriputta later, attained the fruit of a stream-winner even on hearing the first two lines of the verse uttered by Venerable *Assaji*:

Ye dhammā hetuppabhavā,
tesaṃ hetuṃ tathāgato āha.[9]

"Of things that arise from a cause,
their cause the *Tathāgata* has told."

When a wise man hears that something has arisen due to causes and conditions, he immediately understands that it could be made to cease by the removal of those conditions, even with out further explanation. It is the dustless stainless *Dhamma*-eye that enables one to see the *Nibbānic* solution in the very structure of the *saṃsāric* problem.

In our quotation from the *MahāNidānasutta* it was said that all pathways for verbal expression, terminology and designation exist so long as the vortex of *saṃsāra* is kept going.[10] The implication, therefore, is that they have no existence beyond it. This is the significance of the word *ettāvatā*, "in so far only."

Ettāvatā jāyetha vā jīyetha vā mīyetha vā cavetha vā upapajjetha vā.[11] "In so far only can one be born, or grow old, or die, or pass away, or reappear."

So the concepts of birth, decay-and-death, passing away and reappearing, are meaningful only in the context of the *saṃsāric* vortex between consciousness and name-and-form. If somehow or other this interrelation could be broken, this *saṃsāric* vortex, the whirlpool, could be stopped, then, after that, nothing remains to be

9 Vin I 40.

10 See sermon 2.

11 D II 63, *MahāNidānasutta*.

said, nothing remains to be predicated. And as it is said in the *Upasīvasutta* of the *Sutta Nipāta*:

Yena naṃ vajju, taṃ tassa natthi,[12] "That by which they would speak of him, that for him exists not."

There are a number of Canonical passages that show us the relevance of this vortex simile to the understanding of the doctrine of *paṭicca samuppāda*. In the *MahāPadānasutta* of the *Dīgha Nikāya* we find a lengthy description of the manner in which the *bodhisatta* Vipassī got an insight into *paṭicca samuppāda*. We are told that his mode of approach was one of radical reflection, or *yoniso manasikāra*, literally: "attention by way of the matrix." One might as well say that it is an attention by way of the vortex. It is as if a man with keen vision, sitting under a tree by a river, were to watch how a fallen leaf gets carried away by the water current, only to get whirled up and disappear in a vortex.

It is clearly stated in the case of Vipassī *bodhisatta* that his understanding through wisdom came as a result of 'radical reflection,' *yoniso manasikārā ahu paññāya abhisamayo*.[13] So his insight into *paṭicca samuppāda* was definitely not due to recollection of past lives. *Yoni* means the 'matrix,' or the 'place of origin.' So in *yoniso manasikāra* always the attention has to turn towards the place of origin.

So, true to this method, we find the *bodhisatta* Vipassī starting his reasoning from the very end of the *paṭicca samuppāda* formula: *Kimhi nu kho sati jarāmaraṇaṃ hoti, kiṃ paccayā jarāmaraṇaṃ?* "Given what, does decay-and-death come to be, from which condition comes decay-and-death?" And to this question, the following answer occurred to him:

Jātiyā kho sati jarāmaraṇaṃ hoti, jātipaccayā jarāmaraṇaṃ. "Given birth, does decay-and-death come to be, from birth as condition comes decay-and-death." In the same manner, taking

---

[12] Sn 1076, *Upasīvamāṇavapucchā*.

[13] D II 31, *MahāPadānasutta*.

pair by pair, he went on reasoning progressively. For instance his next question was:

Kimhi nu kho sati jāti hoti, kiṃ paccayā jāti? "Given what, does birth come to be, from which condition comes birth?" And the answer to it was:

Bhave kho sati jāti hoti, bhavapaccayā jāti. "Given becoming, birth comes to be, from becoming as condition comes birth." He went on reasoning like this up to and including name-and-form. But when he came to consciousness, he had to turn back. When he searched for the condition of consciousness, he found that name-and-form itself is the condition, whereby he understood their interdependence, and then he gave expression to the significance of this discovery in the following words:

> *Paccudāvattati kho idaṃ viññāṇaṃ nāmarūpamhā, nāparaṃ gacchati. Ettāvatā jāyetha vā jīyetha vā mīyetha vā cavetha vā upapajjetha vā, yadidaṃ nāmarūpapaccayā viññāṇaṃ, viññāṇapaccayā nāmarūpaṃ, nāmarūpapaccayā saḷāyatanaṃ, saḷāyatanapaccayā phasso, phassapaccayā vedanā, vedanāpaccayā taṇhā, taṇhāpaccayā upādānaṃ, upādānapaccayā bhavo, bhavapaccayā jāti, jātipaccayā jarāmaraṇaṃ sokaparidevadukkhadomanassūpāyāsā sambhavanti. Evametassa kevalassa dukkhakkhandhassa samudayo hoti.*

By means of radical reflection the *bodhisatta* Vipassī understood that all concepts of birth, decay-and-death converge on the relationship between consciousness and name-and-form:

> "This consciousness turns back from name-and-form, it does not go beyond. In so far can one be born, or grow old, or die, or pass away, or reappear, in so far as this is, namely: consciousness is dependent on name-and-form, and name-and-form on consciousness; dependent on name-and-form, the six sense-bases; dependent on the six sense-bases, contact; dependent on contact, feeling;

> dependent on feeling, craving; dependent on craving, grasping; dependent on grasping, becoming; dependent on becoming, birth; and dependent on birth, decay-and-death, sorrow, lamentation, pain, grief and despair come to be. Thus is the arising of this entire mass of suffering."

The fact that this understanding of *paṭicca samuppāda* signified the arising of the *Dhamma*-eye in Vipassī *bodhisatta* is stated in the following words:

> *Samudayo samudayo'ti kho, bhikkhave, Vipassissa bodhisattassa pubbe ananussutesu dhammesu cakkhum udapādi, ñāṇaṃ udapādi, paññā udapādi, vijjā udapādi, āloko udapādi.*

> "'Arising, arising,' thus, O! monks, in regard to things unheard of before, there arose in the *bodhisatta* Vipassī the eye, the knowledge, the wisdom, the science, the light."

In the same way, it is said that the *bodhisatta* clarified for himself the cessation aspect through radical reflection:

Kimhi nu kho asati jarāmaraṇaṃ na hoti, kissa nirodhā jarāmaraṇaṃ nirodho? "In the absence of what, will decay-and-death not be, with the cessation of what, is the cessation of decay-and-death?" And as the answer to it, the following thought occurred to him:

Jātiyā kho asati jarāmaraṇaṃ na hoti, jātinirodhā jarāmaraṇaṃnirodho. "In the absence of birth, there is no decay-and-death, with the cessation of birth is the cessation of decay-and-death." Likewise he went on reflecting progressively, until he reached the link between name-and-form and consciousness, and then it occurred to him:

Nāmarūpanirodhā viññāṇanirodho, viññāṇanirodhā nāmarūpanirodho. "From the cessation of name-and-form comes the cessation of consciousness, from the cessation of consciousness comes the cessation of name-and-form."

Once this vital link is broken, that is, when consciousness ceases with the cessation of name-and-form, and name-and-form ceases with the cessation of consciousness, then all the other links following name-and-form, such as the six sense-bases, contact and feeling, come to cease immediately.

The *MahāPadānasutta* goes on to say that the *bodhisatta* Vipassī continued to dwell seeing the arising and passing away of the five grasping groups and that before long his mind was fully emancipated from the influxes and that he attained to full enlightenment. It is also said in the *sutta* in this connection that the *bodhisatta* followed this mode of reflection, because he understood that it is the way of insight leading to awakening: *Adhigato kho myāyaṃ vipassanā maggo bodhāya.* "I have found this path of insight to awakening, to enlightenment."

And as we saw above the most important point, the pivotal point, in this path of insight, is the relationship between name-and-form and consciousness. The commentary raises the question, why the *bodhisatta* Vipassī makes no mention of the first two links, *avijjā* and *saṅkhārā*, and gives the explanation that he could not see them, as they belong to the past.[14]

But this is not the reason. The very ignorance regarding the relationship between name-and-form and consciousness – is *avijjā*. And what accounts for the continuity of this relationship – is *saṅkhārā*. It is because of these preparations that the vortical interplay between consciousness and name-and-form is kept going.

Simply because the first two links are not mentioned in the *sutta*, the commentators give the explanation that they belong to the past. But it should be clear that the *bodhisatta* Vipassī could not have aroused the *Dhamma*-eye without those two links. Why they are not specially mentioned here is because they are in the background. It is true that there is a mode of exposition, in which

[14] Sv II 459.

avijjā, or ignorance, takes precedence. But what we have here is a different mode of exposition, according to which one has to stop short at the interrelation between consciousness and name-and-form.

As to the cause of this mutual relationship, we have to go back to the vortex simile. Usually, the progress of a current of water is visible at some distance away from the vortex. In this case, the current of water forgets its own impermanent, suffering and not-self nature, and goes ahead in search of a permanent, pleasurable and self nature. And this itself – is *avijjā*, or ignorance. This very tendency of the narrow water current to push on against the main body of water, is itself what is called consciousness.

Similarly, in the context of the *saṃsāric* individual, what forms the background for the interplay between consciousness and name-and-form, is the non-understanding that the net result of the interplay is suffering, that it only leads to suffering. In other words, it is the tendency to go ahead in search of a state of permanence, pleasure and self, ignoring the three characteristics of impermanence, suffering and not-self.

The heap of preparations or efforts arising out of that tendency are the *saṅkhārās*. It is on these very preparations or efforts that consciousness depends, and then we have name-and-form existing in relation to it. On the side of name-and-form, or beyond it, we have all the other links of the *paṭicca samuppāda*. So in this way we can form a mental picture of the formula of *paṭicca samuppāda* by some sort of a pictorial explanation. It seems, then, that this discourse is further proof of the statements found in the *MahāNidānasutta*.

There is yet another discourse, one preached by Venerable Sāriputta, which supports our conclusions. It is found in the *Nidānasaṃyutta* of the *Saṃyutta Nikāya*. There Venerable Sāriputta brings out a simile that is even simpler than the vortex simile. He compares consciousness and name-and-form to two bundles of reeds. When two bundles of reeds stand, one supporting the other, if one of those is drawn out, the other would fall down. And if the latter is drawn out, the former will fall down: *Ekaṃ ākaḍḍheyya, ekā papateyya, aparaṃ ce ākaḍḍheyya, aparā papateyya.*[15]

The mutual interrelation between consciousness and name-and-form is like that of two bundles of reeds, mutually supporting each other. Having given this simile, Venerable Sāriputta goes on to mention the other links of the *paṭicca samuppāda* formula, as in the case of the *bodhisatta* Vipassī's insight. It runs: "Dependent on name-and-form, the six sense-bases; dependent on the six sense-bases, contact; dependent on contact, feelings" (and so on). And then the cessation aspect of these links is also given.

By way of illustration, let us suppose that the consciousness bundle of reeds is standing on the left side, and the name-and-form bundle is on the right. Then we have a number of other bundles, such as the six sense-bases, contact and feeling, all leaning on to the name-and-form bundle of reeds. These are all dependent on the name-and-form bundle.

Now, as soon as the consciousness bundle is drawn out, all the others on the right side fall down immediately. There is no interval. True to the qualities of the *Dhamma*, summed up in the terms *sandiṭṭhika*, *akālika* and *ehipassika*, that is, to be seen here and now, not involving time, and inviting to come and see, the entire mass of *saṃsāric* suffering ceases immediately. So, this discourse is further proof of the fact that we have here quite a different state of affairs, than what is commonly believed to be the significance of the *paṭicca samuppāda* formula.

That is why we have pointed out that the concepts of birth, decay-and-death are of the nature of fading away. That is also why decay-and-death have been described as impermanent, made up, dependently arisen, of a nature to wither away, pass away, fade away and cease: *Aniccaṃ saṅkhataṃ paṭiccasamuppannaṃ khayadhammaṃ vayadhammaṃ virāgadhammaṃ nirodhadhammaṃ.*[16]

---

15 S II 114, *Naḷakalāpīsutta*.

16 S II 26, *Paccayasutta*.

When one comes to think of it, one may find it difficult to understand why decay-and-death are called impermanent and withering or decaying. But the reason is that all concepts, in so far as they are leaning on to the name-and-form bundle, have to fall down when the opposite bundle of reeds is drawn out. That is to say that the entire mass of *saṃsāric* suffering ceases immediately, and the whirlpool of *saṃsāra* comes to an end.

This, then, seems to be the most plausible conclusion. According to the interpretation we have adopted, in the *MahāHatthipadopamasutta* of the *Majjhima Nikāya* Venerable Sāriputta brings out as a quotation a certain statement of the Buddha on *paṭicca samuppāda*. It runs:

Yo paṭiccasamuppādaṃ passati so dhammaṃ passati; yo dhammaṃ passati so paṭiccasamuppādaṃ passati.[17] "He who sees the law of dependent arising, sees the *Dhamma*; he who sees the *Dhamma*, sees the law of dependent arising."

This shows that the quintessence of the *Dhamma* is in fact the law of dependent arising itself. Now there are these six qualities of the *Dhamma*, summed up in the well known formula, which every Buddhist believes in. This *Dhamma* is well-preached, *svākkhāto*. It can be seen here and now, *sandiṭṭhiko*, that is, one can see it by oneself here in this very world. It is timeless, *akāliko*. It invites one to come and see, *ehipassiko*. It leads one on, *opanayiko*. It can be realized by the wise each one by him self, *paccattaṃ veditabbo viññūhi.*[18]

Though we all have faith in these qualities of the *Dhamma*, let us see whether the traditionally accepted interpretation of *paṭicca samuppāda* is faithful to these qualities, particularly to the two qualities *sandiṭṭhiko* and *akāliko*.

According to that accepted interpretation, presented by the venerable author of the *Visuddhimagga*, the first two links of the

---

[17] M I 190, *MahāHatthipadopamasutta*.

[18] D II 93, *MahāParinibbānasutta*.

formula belong to the past, and the last two links belong to the future. The remaining eight links in the middle are taken to represent the present.[19] That means, we have here the three periods of time. So it is not – timeless.

And that is why they explained that the *bodhisatta* Vipassī did not see the first two links. Perhaps, the presumption is, that since these two links belong to the past, they can be seen only by the knowledge of the recollection of past lives. But on the other hand, the *suttas* tell us that even the stream-winner has a clear understanding of *paṭicca samuppāda*: *Ariyo c'assa ñāyo paññāya sudiṭṭho hoti suppaṭividdho.*[20] "By him the Noble Norm is well seen and well penetrated through with wisdom."

The 'noble norm' is none other than the law of dependent arising, and the stream-winner has seen it well, penetrated into it well with wisdom. The prefix *su-* implies the clarity of that vision. The question, then, is how a stream-winner, who has no knowledge of the recollection of past lives, can get this insight.

Whatever it may be, the accepted interpretation, as already mentioned, puts the first two links into the past. That is to say, ignorance and preparations are referred to the past. Birth, decay-and-death are referred to the future. The eight links in between are explained with reference to the present. Thus the formula is divided into three periods.

Not only that, in the attempt to interpret the formula as referring to three stages in the *saṃsāric* journey of an individual, additional links had to be interposed to prop up the interpretation.[21] Ignorance, preparations, craving, grasping and becoming are regarded as the past causes. Depending on these past causes, consciousness, name-and-form, six sense-bases, contact and feeling are said to arise as results in the present. And again, with ignorance, prepara-

---

19 Vism 578.

20 S II 68, *Pañcaverabhayāsutta*.

21 Paṭis I 52, Vism 579.

tions, craving, grasping and becoming as present causes, consciousness, name-and-form, six sense-bases, contact and feeling arise as results in the future.

This kind of interpretation is also advanced. But this interpretation in terms of pentads violates the interrelatedness between the twelve links in the formula. We have already drawn attention to the fact of interrelation between the two links in each pair. In fact, that itself has to be taken as the law of dependent arising. That is the basic principle itself: Because of one, the other arises. With its cessation, the other ceases. There is this mode of analysis, but then it is disrupted by the attempt to smuggle in additional links into the formula.

Furthermore, according to this accepted commentarial exegesis, even the term *bhava*, or becoming, is given a twofold interpretation. As *kamma*-process-becoming and rebirth-process-becoming. In the context *upādānapaccaya bhavo*, dependent on grasping is becoming, it is explained as rebirth-process-becoming, while in the case of the other context, *bhavapaccaya jāti*, dependent on becoming is birth, it is taken to mean *kamma*-process-becoming. So the same term is explained in two ways. Similarly, the term *jāti*, which generally means birth, is said to imply rebirth in the context of the formula of dependent arising.

There are many such weak points in the accepted interpretation. Quite a number of authoritative modern scholars have pointed this out. Now all these short-comings could be side-tracked, if we grant the fact, as already mentioned, that the secret of the entire *saṃsāric* vortex is traceable to the two links consciousness and name-and-form. As a matter of fact, the purpose of the formula of dependent arising is to show the way of arising and cessation of the entire mass of suffering, and not to illustrate three stages in the *saṃsaric* journey of an individual.

The distinctive feature of this law of dependent arising is its demonstrability in the present, as suggested by the terms 'to be seen here and now' and 'timeless,' even as the *bodhisatta* Vipassī discovered it, through radical reflection itself. The salient characteristic of the teaching of the Buddha is its visibility here and now and timelessness. This fact is well revealed by the *Hemakasutta* of the *Sutta Nipāta*. The brahmin youth Hemaka sings praise of the Buddha in the following verses:

> *Ye me pubbe viyākaṃsu,*
> *huraṃ Gotamasāsanā,*
> *iccāsi iti bhavissati,*
> *sabbaṃ taṃ itihītihaṃ,*
> *sabbaṃ taṃ takkavaḍḍhanaṃ,*
> *nāhaṃ tattha abhiramiṃ.*
> *Tvañca me dhammam akkhāhi,*
> *taṇhā nigghātanaṃ muni,*
> *yaṃ viditvā sato caraṃ,*
> *tare loke visattikaṃ.*[22]

> "Those who explained to me before,
> Outside the dispensation of Gotama,
> All of them said: 'so it was, and so it will be,'
> But all that is 'so and so' talk,
> All that is productive of logic,
> I did not delight therein.
> But now to me, O! sage,
> Proclaim your *Dhamma*,
> That is destructive of craving,
> By knowing which and mindfully faring along,
> One might get beyond the world's viscosity."

Now, to paraphrase: Whatever teachers explained to me their teachings outside your dispensation, used to bring in the past and the future in their explanations, saying: "So it was, and so it will be." That is, they were always referring to a past and a future. But all that can be summed up as 'so and so' talk.

---

[22] Sn 1084-1085, *Hemakamāṇavapucchā*.

By the way, the term *itihītiha* had already become a technical term for 'hearsay' among the ascetics. Such teachings based on hearsay were productive of logic, as for instance testified by the *Sabbāsavasutta* of the *Majjhima Nikāya*: "Was I in the past, was I not in the past? What was I in the past? How was I in the past? Having been what, what did I become in the past? Shall I be in the future? Shall I not be in the future? What shall I be in the future? How shall I be in the future? Having been what, what shall I become in the future?" (And so on.)[23]

"But, I was not pleased with such teachings," says Hemaka, "It is only you, O! sage, who teaches the *Dhamma* that destroys the craving in the present, understanding which, and mindfully following it accordingly, one could go beyond the sticky craving in the world." Hemaka's praise of the Buddha was inspired by this most distinctive feature in the *Dhamma*.

We have already stated that by '*Dhamma*' is meant the law of dependent arising. This is further proof that the basic principle underlying the formula of dependent arising could be traced to the constant relationship between consciousness and name-and-form, already present in one's mental continuum, without running into the past or leaping towards the future.

We know that, in order to ascertain whether a banana trunk is pith-less, it is not necessary to go on removing its bark, layer after layer, from top to bottom. We only have to take a sharp sword and cut the trunk in the middle, so that the cross-section will reveal to us its pith-less nature. Similarly, if we cut in the middle the banana trunk of preparations with the sharp sword of wisdom, *paññāmayaṃ tikhiṇamasiṃ gahetvā*,[24] its internal structure as revealed by the cross-section will convince us of the essence-less nature of the group of preparations.

---

[23] M I 8, *Sabbāsavasutta*.

[24] Th 1094, *Tālapuṭa Thera*.

Whatever existence there was in the past, that too had the same essence-less nature. And whatever existence there will be in the future, will have this same essencelessness. And I see it now, in my own mental continuum, as something visible here and now, not involving time. It is with such a conviction that the noble disciple utters the words: "Arising, arising! Cessation, cessation!" That is how he arrives at the realization summed up in the phrase: *Yaṃ kiñci samudayadhammaṃ, sabbaṃ taṃ nirodhadhammaṃ.*[25] "Whatever is of the nature to arise, all that is of the nature to cease." All this goes to show that the accepted interpretation has certain short-comings.

To take up another simile, we have already alluded to the fact that the Buddha has been compared to a physician.[26] Though this might well sound a modernism, we may say that a specialist doctor today needs only a drop of blood or blood tissue for a full diagnosis of a patient's disease. When seen under the microscope, that blood tissue reveals the pathological condition of the patient. Even the patient himself could be invited to see for him self the result of the blood test.

But once the disease has been cured, the doctor could invite the patient again to undergo a blood test, if he likes to assure himself of the fact that that disease has been effectively treated. The Buddha's teaching has a similar 'here and now' and timeless quality. What is noteworthy is that this quality is found in the law of dependent arising.

Then there is another question that crops up out of this traditional interpretation of the formula of dependent arising. That is, the reason why the two links, ignorance and preparations, are referred to the past.

In some discourses, like the *MahāNidānasutta*, there is a discussion about a descent of consciousness into a mother's womb.[27]

---

25 See above footnote 4.

26 See sermon 1.

27 D II 63, *MahāNidānasutta*.

Simply because there is such a discussion, one might think that the law of dependent arising has reference to a period beyond one's conception in a mother's womb.

But if we carefully examine the trend of this discussion and analyse its purpose, such a conclusion will appear to be groundless. The point which the Buddha was trying to drive home into Venerable Ānanda by his catechism, is that the constant interrelation that exists between consciousness and name-and-form is present even during one's life in the mother's womb. This catechism can be analysed into four parts. The first question is:

Viññāṇaṃ va hi, Ānanda, mātukucchismiṃ na okkamissatha, api nu kho nāmarūpaṃ mātukucchismiṃ samuccissatha? And Venerable Ānanda's answer is: *No h'etaṃ, bhante.* "If, Ānanda, consciousness were not to descend into a mother's womb, would name-and-form remain there?" "It would not, Lord."

The Buddha is asking whether name-and-form can persist in remaining inside the mother's womb, if consciousness refuses to descend into it, so to say. The word *samuccissatha* presents a difficulty as regards etymology. But it is quite likely that it has to do with the idea of remaining, as it has an affinity to the word *ucciṭṭha*, leftover, remnant.

So the point raised here is that, in the event of a non-descent of consciousness into the mother's womb, name-and-form will not be left remaining there. Name-and-form has to have the support of consciousness. However, in this interrelation, it is consciousness that decides the issue. If consciousness does not descend, name-and-form will not remain there.

So even if, at the moment of death, one has a thought of some mother's womb, if consciousness does not descend in the proper manner, name-and-form cannot stay there. Name-and-form has always to be understood in relation to consciousness. It is not something that is to be found in trees and rocks. It always goes hand in hand with consciousness. So, the upshot of the above discussion is that name-and-form will not remain there without the support of consciousness.

Venerable Ānanda's response to the first question, then, is: "That indeed is not the case, O! Lord." Then the Buddha asks: *Viññāṇaṃ va hi, Ānanda, mātukucchismiṃ okkamitvā vokkamissatha, api nu kho nāmarūpaṃ itthattāya abhinibbattissatha?* "If, Ānanda, consciousness, having descended into the mother's womb, were to slip out of it, would name-and-form be born into this state of existence?" Venerable Ānanda's reply to it is again: "That indeed is not the case, Lord."

Now the question is: Ānanda, if for some reason or other, consciousness, having descended into the mother's womb, slips out of it, will name-and-form secure birth as a this-ness, or *itthatta*. We have mentioned above that *itthatta* is a term with some special significance.[28] That is, how a 'there' becomes a 'here,' when a person takes birth in a particular form of existence. In short, what it implies, is that a person comes to be born.

In other words, if consciousness, having descended into the mother's womb, slips out of it, that name-and-form will not mature into a this-ness and be born into a this-ness. There is no possibility of the this-ness coming into being. For there to be a this-ness, both consciousness and name-and-form must be there. We can understand, then, why Venerable Ānanda replied in the negative.

The next question the Buddha puts, is this: *Viññāṇaṃ va hi, Ānanda, daharasseva sato vocchijjissatha kumārakassa vā kumārikāya vā, api nu kho nāmarūpaṃ vuddhiṃ virūḷhiṃ vepullaṃ āpajjissatha?* "If, Ānanda, the consciousness of a boy or a girl were cut off when he or she is still young, will name-and-form come to growth and maturity?" To that question too, Venerable Ānanda replies: "That indeed is not the case, Lord."

Now that the preliminary questions have been correctly answered, the Buddha then comes out with the following conclusion, since the necessary premises are complete:

---

28 See sermon 2.

Tasmātih' Ānanda, es' eva hetu etaṃ nidānaṃ esa samudayo esa paccayo nāmarūpassa, yadidaṃ viññāṇaṃ. "Therefore, Ānanda, this itself is the cause, this is the reason, origin and condition for name-and-form, namely consciousness."

What is emphasized here, is the importance of consciousness. Out of the two, namely consciousness and name-and-form, what carries more weight with it, is consciousness, even if there be a trace of name-and-form. What the above questionnaire makes clear, is that name-and-form arises in a mother's womb because of consciousness. But that name-and-form will not remain there, if consciousness does not properly descend into the womb.

Also, if consciousness, after its descent, were to slip out, name-and-form will not reach the state of a this-ness. So much so that, even after one's birth as a boy or girl, if consciousness gets cut off in some way or other, name-and-form will not reach growth and maturity. So from all this, it is clear that consciousness is an essential condition for there to be name-and-form. Then the Buddha introduces the fourth step:

Viññāṇaṃ va hi, Ānanda, nāmarūpe patiṭṭhaṃ na labhissatha, api no kho āyatiṃ jātijarāmaraṇaṃ dukkhasamudayasambhavo paññāyetha? "If, Ānanda, consciousness were not to find a footing, or get established in, name-and-form, would there be an arising or origin of birth, decay, death and suffering in the future?" "No indeed, Lord," says Venerable Ānanda.

Now this fourth point is extremely important. What it implies is that, though the aforesaid is the normal state of affairs in *saṃsāra*, if for some reason or other consciousness does not get established on name-and-form, if at all such a contrivance were possible, there will not be any *saṃsāric* suffering again. And this position, too, Venerable Ānanda grants.

So from this discussion, too, it is obvious that, simply because there is a reference to a mother's womb in it, we cannot conclude that ignorance and preparations are past causes. It only highlights the mutual relationship between consciousness and name-and-form.

Now the question that comes up next is: "How does consciousness not get established on name-and-form? In what respects does it not get established, and how?"

The consciousness of a *saṃsāric* individual is always an established consciousness. It is in the nature of this consciousness to find a footing on name-and-form. These two go together. That is why in the *Sampasādanīyasutta* of the *Dīgha Nikāya* it is mentioned in the discussion on the attainments to vision, *dassanasamāpatti*, that a person with such an attainment sees a man's stream of consciousness that is not cut off on either side, established in this world and in the next: *Purisassa ca viññāṇasotaṃ pajānāti, ubhayato abbocchinnaṃ idha loke patiṭṭhitañca para loke patiṭṭhitañca.*[29] What is implied here is the established nature of consciousness. The consciousness of a *saṃsāric* individual is established both in this world and in the next.

Another attainment of vision, mentioned in the *sutta*, concerns the seeing of a man's stream of consciousness not cut off on either side, and not established in this world or in the next. And that is a reference to the consciousness of an *arahant*. So an *arahant*'s consciousness is an unestablished consciousness, whereas the consciousness of the *saṃsāric* individual is an established consciousness.

That is precisely why in the *Sagāthavagga* of the *Saṃyutta Nikāya* and in the *Sāratthapakāsinī*, where the episode of Venerable Godhika's suicide is mentioned, it is said that, though he cut his own neck intending to commit suicide, he was able to attain *parinibbāna* as an *arahant* by radically attending to the deadly pain.[30] But *Māra* took him to be an ordinary person and hovered around in search of his consciousness – in vain. The Buddha, on the other hand, declared that Venerable Godhika passed away with an unestablished consciousness:

---

29 D III 105, *Sampasādanīyasutta*.

30 Spk I 183 commenting on S I 121.

Appatiṭṭhitena ca, bhikkhave, viññāṇena Godhiko kulaputto parinibbuto.[31] "O! monks, the clansman Godhika passed away with an unestablished consciousness."

The consciousness of an ordinary *saṃsāric* individual is always established. The above mentioned relationship is always there. Because of this we can say that there is always a knot in the consciousness of the *saṃsāric* individual. For him, this world and the next world are tied together in a knot. In this case, what is needed, is only the untying of the knot. There is no need of a fresh tying up, as the knot is already there.

But the term *paṭisandhi viññāṇa*, or rebirth-linking-consciousness, is now so widely used that we cannot help making use of it, even in relating a *Jātaka* story. The idea is that, after the death-consciousness, there occurs a rebirth-linking-consciousness. However, some scholars even raise the question, why a term considered so important is not to be found in the discourses. On many an occasion the Buddha speaks about the descent into a womb. But apart from using such terms as *okkanti*,[32] descent, *gabbhassa avakkanti*,[33] descent into a womb, and *uppatti*,[34] arising, he does not seem to have used the term *paṭisandhi*.

What is meant by this term *paṭisandhi*? It seems to imply a tying up of two existences. After death there is a 'relinking.' We have mentioned above, in connection with the simile of the bundles of reeds that, when the consciousness bundle of reeds is drawn, the name-and-form bundle of reeds falls. And when the name-and-form bundle of reeds is drawn, the consciousness bundle of reeds falls. And that there is a relationship of mutuality condition between them.

---

[31] S I 122, *Godhikasutta*.

[32] D II 305, M I 50, M I 62, M III 249, S II 3.

[33] M II 156, *Ghoṭamukhasutta*.

[34] A II 133, *Saṃyojanasutta*.

The question, then, is why a tying up is brought in, while granting the relationship by mutuality condition. Because, going by the same simile, it would be tantamount to saying that rebirth-linking-consciousness straightens up when death-consciousness falls, as if, when one bundle of reeds is drawn, the other straightens up. This contradicts the nature of mutuality condition. There is no timelessness here. Therefore *paṭisandhi* is a term that needs critical scrutiny.

The mental continuum of a *saṃsāric* being is always knotted with a tangle within and a tangle without.[35] And it is already implicit in the relationship between consciousness and name-and-form. What happens at the dying moment is usually posed as a deep problem. But if we carefully examine the situation in the light of Canonical discourses, we could see here an illustration of the law of dependent arising itself.

Now as far as this established consciousness and the unestablished consciousness are concerned, we have already drawn attention to the relationship between a 'here' and a 'there.' We came across the term *itthatta*, otherwise called *itthabhāva*. As a rendering for it, we have used the term 'this-ness.' And then we have already pointed out that this *itthabhāva*, or this-ness, goes hand in hand with *aññatthābhāva*, or otherwise-ness. That is to say, wherever a this-ness arises, wherever a concept of a something arises, as a rule that itself is the setting in of transformation or change.

This-ness and otherwise-ness are therefore to be found in a pairwise combination. Wherever there is a this-ness, there itself is an otherwise-ness. So in this way, because of the fact that, due to this this-ness itself, wherever this-ness arises, otherwise-ness arises, together with it, wherever there is a 'there,' there is always a 'here.' This, then, is how the consciousness of the *saṃsāric* being functions.

---

35 S I 13, *Jaṭāsutta*, see sermon 1.

As far as one's everyday life is concerned, what is called the conscious body, is the body with consciousness. Generally we regard this body as something really our own. Not only that, we can also objectify things outside us, beyond our range of vision, things that are objects of thought or are imagined. That is what is meant by the Canonical phrase:

Imasmiñca saviññāṇake kāye bahiddhā ca sabbanimittesu ahaṃkāra mamaṃkāra mānānusayā na honti.[36] "There are no latencies to conceit by way of I-making and mine-making regarding this conscious body and all outside signs."

What it implies, is that one can have latencies to conceit by way of I-making and mine-making regarding this conscious body as well as all outside signs. Now, if we consider the deeper implications of this statement, we can get at some new perspective for understanding the nature of the relationship between consciousness and name-and-form.

If someone, deeply attached to a person who is not near him, but living somewhere far far away, is heavily immersed in some deep thought, then, even if there is some painful contact, such as the prick of a fly, or the bite of a mosquito, or even if another comes and shakes him by the shoulder, he might not feel it, because he is so immersed in the thought.

Now, why is that? Normally, the rightful place for consciousness is this body. But what has happened now, is that it has gone away temporarily and united with the name-and-form out side, with that object far away. But it can be awakened. This is the way the mind travels.

It is due to a lack of clear understanding about the journey of the mind, that the concept of a relinking-consciousness was found to be necessary. The way the mind travels is quite different from the way the body travels. The journey of the body is a case of leaving one place to go to another. But the mind's journey is not

---

[36] M III 18, *MahāPuṇṇamasutta*.

like that. It is a sort of whirling or turning round, as in the case of a whirlpool or a vortex.

That is to say, just as in the case of a rubber-band which could be stretched lengthwise or crosswise, there is a certain whirling round going on between consciousness and name-and-form. It is because of that whirling motion, which could either be circular or oval shaped, that consciousness and name-and-form could either get drawn apart, or drawn in, as they go round and round in a kind of vortical interplay.

So in a situation like the one mentioned above, for that person, the distant has become near. At the start, when he fell to thinking, it was a 'there' for him. Then it became a 'here.' And the here became a 'there.' This brings out, in a subtle way, the relevance of these concepts to the question of understanding such teachings as the law of dependent arising.

Concepts of a here and a there are in a way relative. They presuppose each other. *Itthabhāva*, this-ness, and *aññathābhāva*, otherwise-ness, referred to above, mean the same thing. *Itthabhāva* goes hand in hand with *aññathābhāva*. They are bound in a pairwise combination. When you drag in one, the other follows of necessity. It is the same in the case of the relationship between birth on the one hand, and decay-and-death on the other, as already mentioned.

Also, consciousness and name-and-form always move in an orbit. It is not something like the journey of the body. Thought goes, but it rests on consciousness, it gravitates towards consciousness. It is because consciousness also has gone there that we say someone is 'immersed' or 'engrossed' in some thought. It is consciousness that carries more weight.

This is sufficiently clear even from the *Dhamma* discussion of the Buddha, quoted above. If consciousness does not descend into a mother's womb, name-and-form will not remain there. If consciousness does not join in to provide the opportunity, it will not grow. This is the nature of the relationship between them.

Though not well authenticated, cases have been reported of persons, on the verge of death, going through such unusual experiences as visualizing their own body from some outside standpoint. Taking into consideration the above mentioned relationship, this is quite understandable. That external standpoint might not be a place which has the ability to sustain that consciousness, or which is capable of creating a new body out of the four primary elements. All the same, it temporarily escapes and goes there and is now wavering to decide, whether or not to come back to the body, as it were. It is on such occasions that one visualizes one's own body from outside.

So here we have the norm of the mind's behaviour. Seen in this way, there is no need for a fresh tying up, or relinking, because it is the same vortex that is going on all the time. In the context of this *saṃsāric* vortex, the 'there' becomes a 'here,' and a 'here' becomes a 'there.' The distant becomes a near, and a near becomes a distant.

It is owing to this state of affairs that the consciousness of the *saṃsāric* individual is said to be always established. There is a certain twin character about it. Whenever consciousness leaves this body for good, it goes and rests on a name-and-form object which it had already taken up. In other words, this is why the Buddha did not find it necessary to coin a new term to express the idea of conception in some mother's womb.

Consciousness has as its object name-and-form. It is precisely because of consciousness that one can speak of it as a name-and-form. It is like the shadow that falls on consciousness. Name-and-form is like an image.

Now in taking a photograph, there is a similar turn of events. Even if one does not pose for the photograph with so much make-up, even if one turns one's back to the camera, at least a shade of his shape will be photographed as an image, if not his form. Similarly, in the case of the *saṃsāric* individual, even if he does not entertain an intention or thought construct, if he has at least the latency, *anusaya*, that is enough for him to be reborn in some form of existence or other.

That is why the Buddha has preached such an important discourse as the *Cetanāsutta* of the *Nidāna Saṃyutta* in the *Saṃyutta Nikāya*. It runs:

> *Yañca, bhikkhave, ceteti yañca pakappeti yañca anuseti, ārammaṇam etaṃ hoti viññāṇassa ṭhitiyā. Ārammaṇe sati patiṭṭhā viññāṇassa hoti. Tasmiṃ patiṭṭhite viññāṇe virūḷhe nāmarūpassa avakkanti hoti. Nāmarūpapaccayā saḷāyatanaṃ, saḷāyatanapaccayā phasso, phassapaccayā vedanā, vedanāpaccayā taṇhā, taṇhāpaccayā upādānaṃ, upādānapaccayā bhavo, bhavapaccayā jāti, jātipaccayā jarāmaraṇaṃ sokaparidevadukkhadomanassūpāyāsā sambhavanti. Evametassa kevalassa dukkhakkhandhassa samudayo hoti.*[37]

> "Monks, whatever one intends, whatever one mentally constructs, whatever lies latent, that becomes an object for the stationing of consciousness. There being an object, there comes to be an establishment of consciousness. When that consciousness is established and grown, there is the descent of name-and-form. Dependent on name-and-form the six sense-bases come to be; dependent on the six sense-bases arises contact; and dependent on contact arises feeling; dependent on feeling, craving; dependent on craving, grasping; dependent on grasping, becoming; dependent on becoming, birth; dependent on birth, decay-and-death, sorrow, lamentation, pain, grief and despair come to be. Such is the arising of this entire mass of suffering."

Then comes the second instance:

---

[37] II 66, *Cetanāsutta*.

> *No ce, bhikkhave, ceteti no ce pakappeti, atha ce anuseti, ārammaṇam etaṃ hoti viññāṇassa ṭhitiyā. Ārammaṇe sati patiṭṭhā viññāṇassa hoti. Tasmiṃ patiṭṭhite viññāṇe virūḷhe nāmarūpassa avakkanti hoti. Nāmarūpapaccayā saḷāyatanaṃ, saḷāyatanapaccayā phasso, phassapaccayā vedanā, vedanāpaccayā taṇhā, taṇhāpaccayā upādānaṃ, upādānapaccayā bhavo, bhavapaccayā jāti, jātipaccayā jarāmaraṇaṃ sokaparidevadukkhadomanassūpāyāsā sambhavanti. Evametassa kevalassa dukkhakkhandhassa samudayo hoti.*

> "Monks, even if one does not intend or construct mentally, but has a latency, that becomes an object for the stationing of consciousness. There being an object, there comes to be the establishment of consciousness. When that consciousness is established and grown, there is the descent of name-and-form. Dependent on name-and-form the six sense-bases come to be; dependent on the six sense-bases arises contact; and dependent on contact, feeling; dependent on feeling, craving; dependent on craving, grasping; dependent on grasping, becoming; dependent on becoming, birth; dependent on birth, decay-and-death, sorrow, lamentation, pain, grief and despair come to be. Such is the arising of this entire mass of suffering."

The significance of this second paragraph is that it speaks of a person who, at the time of death, has no intentions or thought constructs as such. But he has the latency. This itself is sufficient as an object for the stationing of consciousness. It is as if he has turned his back to the camera, but got photographed all the same, due to his very presence there. Now comes the third instance:

> *Yato ca kho, bhikkhave, no ceva ceteti no ca pakappeti no ca anuseti, ārammaṇam etaṃ na hoti viññāṇassa ṭhitiyā. Ārammaṇe asati patiṭṭhā viññāṇassa na hoti. Tadappatiṭṭhite viññāṇe avirūḷhe nāmarūpassa avakkanti na hoti.*

> *Nāmarūpanirodhā saḷāyatananirodho, saḷāyatananirodhā phassanirodho, phassanirodhā vedanānirodho, vedanānirodhā taṇhānirodho, taṇhānirodhā upādānanirodho, upādānanirodhā bhavanirodho, bhavanirodhā jātinirodho, jātinirodhā jarāmaraṇaṃ sokaparidevadukkhadomanassūpāyāsā nirujjhanti. Evametassa kevalassa dukkhakkhandhassa nirodho hoti.*

> "But, monks, when one neither intends, nor constructs mentally, and has no latency either, then there is not that object for the stationing of consciousness. There being no object, there is no establishment of consciousness. When consciousness is not established and not grown up, there is no descent of name-and-form, and with the cessation of name-and-form, there comes to be the cessation of the six sense-bases; with the cessation of the six sense-bases, the cessation of contact; with the cessation of contact, the cessation of feeling; with the cessation of feeling, the cessation of craving; with the cessation of craving, the cessation of grasping; with the cessation of grasping, the cessation of becoming; with the cessation of becoming, the cessation of birth; with the cessation of birth, the cessation of decay-and-death, sorrow, lamentation, pain, grief and despair come to cease. Thus is the cessation of this entire mass of suffering."

This third instance is the most significant. In the first instance, there were the intentions, thought constructs and latency. In the second instance, that person had no intentions or thought constructs, but only latency was there. In this third instances, there is neither an intention, nor a thought construct, and not even a latency.

It is then that there comes to be no object for the stationing of consciousness. There being no object, there is no establishment of consciousness, and when consciousness is unestablished and not grown, there is no descent of name-and-form. Where there is no descent of name-and-form, there at last comes to be that cessation of name-and-form with which the six sense-bases, and all the rest of it, down to the entire mass of *saṃsāric* suffering, cease altogether then and there.

Nibbāna Sermon 4

Namo tassa Bhagavato Arahato Sammāsambuddhassa
Namo tassa Bhagavato Arahato Sammāsambuddhassa
Namo tassa Bhagavato Arahato Sammāsambuddhassa

Etaṃ santaṃ, etaṃ paṇītaṃ, yadidaṃ sabbasaṅkhārasamatho sabbūpadhipaṭinissaggo taṇhakkhayo virāgo nirodho nibbānaṃ.[1]

"This is peaceful, this is excellent, namely the stilling of all preparations, the relinquishment of all assets, the destruction of craving, detachment, cessation, extinction."

With the permission of the Most Venerable Great Preceptor and the assembly of the venerable meditative monks.

Towards the end of the last sermon, we were trying to explain how the process of the *saṃsāric* journey of beings could be understood even with the couple of terms *itthabhāva* and *aññatthābhāva*, or this-ness and otherwise-ness.[2] On an earlier occasion, we happened to quote the following verse in the *Sutta Nipāta*:

> *Taṇhā dutiyo puriso,*
> *dīghamaddhāna saṃsāraṃ,*
> *itthabhāvaññathābhāvaṃ,*
> *saṃsāraṃ nātivattati.*[3]

---

1 M I 436, *Mahāmālunkyasutta*.

2 See sermon 3.

3 Sn 740, *Dvayatānupassanāsutta*; (see sermon 2, footnote 22).

It means: "The man with craving as his second," (or 'as his companion,') "faring on for a long time in *saṃsāra*, does not transcend the round, which is of the nature of a this-ness and an otherwise-ness."

This is further proof that the two terms imply a circuit. It is a circuit between a 'here' and a 'there,' or a 'this-ness' and an 'otherwise-ness.' It is a turning round, an alternation or a circuitous journey. It is like a rotation on the spot. It is an ambivalence between a here and a there.

It is the relationship between this this-ness and otherwise-ness that we tried to illustrate with quotations from the *suttas*. We mentioned in particular that consciousness, when it leaves this body and gets well established on a preconceived object, which in fact is its name-and-form object, that name-and-form attains growth and maturity there itself.[4] Obviously, therefore, name-and-form is a necessary condition for the sustenance and growth of consciousness in a mother's womb.

It should be clearly understood that the passage of consciousness from here to a mother's womb is not a movement from one place to another, as in the case of the body. In reality, it is only a difference of point of view, and not a transmigration of a soul. In other words, when consciousness leaves this body and comes to stay in a mother's womb, when it is fully established there, 'that' place becomes a 'this' place. From the point of view of that consciousness, the 'there' becomes a 'here.' Consequently, from the new point of view, what was earlier a 'here,' becomes a 'there.' What was formerly 'that place' has now become 'this place' and vice versa. That way, what actually is involved here, is a change of point of view. So it does not mean completely leaving one place and going to another, as is usually meant by the journey of an individual.

---

[4] See sermon 3.

The process, then, is a sort of going round and round. This is all the more clear by the Buddha's statement that even consciousness is dependently arisen. There are instances in which the view that this selfsame consciousness fares on in *saṃsāra* by itself, *tadevidaṃ viññāṇaṃ sandhāvati saṃsarati, anaññaṃ*, is refuted as a wrong view.[5]

On the one hand, for the sustenance and growth of name-and-form in a mother's womb, consciousness is necessary. On the other hand, consciousness necessarily requires an object for its stability. It could be sometimes an intention, or else a thought construct. In the least, it needs a trace of latency, or *anusaya*. This fact is clear enough from the *sutta* quotations we brought up towards the end of the previous sermon. From the *Cetanāsutta*, we happened to quote on an earlier occasion, it is obvious that at least a trace of latency is necessary for the sustenance of consciousness.[6]

When consciousness gets established in a mother's womb, with this condition in the least, name-and-form begins to grow. It grows, at it were, with a flush of branches, in the form of the six sense bases, to produce a fresh tree of suffering. It is this idea that is voiced by the following well known verse in the *Dhammapada*:

Yathāpi mūle anupaddave daḷhe
chinno pi rukkho punareva rūhati
evam pi taṇhānusaye anūhate
nibbattati dukkham idaṃ punappunaṃ.[7]

"Just as a tree, so long as its root is unharmed and firm,
Though once cut down, will none the less grow up
again,

5 M I 256, *Mahātaṇhāsaṅkhayasutta*.

6 See sermon 3.

7 Dhp 338, *Taṇhāvagga*.

Even so, when craving's latency is not yet rooted out,
This suffering gets reborn again and again."

It is clear from this verse too that the latency to craving holds a very significant place in the context of the *saṃsāric* journey of a being. In the *Aṅguttara Nikāya* one comes across the following statement by the Buddha: *Kammaṃ khettaṃ, viññāṇaṃ bījaṃ, taṇhā sineho.*[8] "*Kamma* is the field, consciousness is the seed, craving is the moisture." This, in effect, means that consciousness grows in the field of *kamma* with craving as the moisture.

It is in accordance with this idea and in the context of this particular simile that we have to interpret the reply of Selā *Therī* to a question raised by *Māra*. In the *Sagātha Vagga* of the *Saṃyutta Nikāya* one comes across the following riddle put by *Māra* to the *arahant* nun Selā:

Ken'idaṃ pakataṃ bimbaṃ,
ko nu bimbassa kārako,
kvannu bimbaṃ samuppannaṃ,
kvannu bimbaṃ nirujjhati?[9]

"By whom was this image wrought,
Who is the maker of this image,
Where has this image arisen,
And where does the image cease?"

The image meant here is one's body, or one's outward appearance which, for the conventional world, is name-and-form. Selā *Therī* gives her answer in three verses:

Nayidaṃ attakataṃ bimbaṃ,
nayidaṃ parakataṃ aghaṃ,

---

[8] A I 223, *Paṭhamabhavasutta*.

[9] S I 134, *Selāsutta*.

hetuṃ paṭicca sambhūtaṃ,
hetubhaṅgā nirujjhati.

Yathā aññataraṃ bījaṃ,
khette vuttaṃ virūhati,
pathavīrasañcāgamma,
sinehañca tadūbhayaṃ.

Evaṃ khandhā ca dhātuyo,
cha ca āyatanā ime,
hetuṃ paṭicca sambhūtā,
hetubhaṅgā nirujjhare.

"Neither self-wrought is this image,
Nor yet other-wrought is this misery,
By reason of a cause, it came to be,
By breaking up the cause, it ceases to be.

"Just as in the case of a certain seed,
Which when sown on the field would feed
On the taste of the earth and moisture,
And by these two would grow.

"Even so, all these aggregates
Elements and bases six,
By reason of a cause have come to be,
By breaking up the cause will cease to be."

The first verse negates the idea of creation and expresses the conditionally arisen nature of this body. The simile given in the second verse illustrates this law of dependent arising. It may be pointed out that this simile is not one chosen at random. It echoes the idea behind the Buddha's statement already quoted, *kammaṃ khettaṃ, viññāṇaṃ bījaṃ, taṇhā sineho. Kamma* is the field, consciousness the seed, and craving the moisture.

Here the venerable *Therī* is replying from the point of view of *Dhamma*, which takes into account the mental aspect as well. It is not simply the outward visible image, as commonly understood by *nāma-rūpa*, but that image which falls on consciousness as its object. The reason for the arising and growth of *nāma-rūpa* is therefore the seed of consciousness. That consciousness seed grows in the field of *kamma*, with craving as the moisture. The outgrowth is in terms of aggregates, elements and bases. The cessation of consciousness is none other than *Nibbāna*.

Some seem to think that the cessation of consciousness occurs in an *arahant* only at the moment of his *parinibbāna*, at the end of his lifespan. But this is not the case. Very often, the deeper meanings of important *suttas* have been obliterated by the tendency to interpret the references to consciousness in such contexts as the final occurrence of consciousness in an *arahant*'s life – *carimaka viññāṇa*.[10]

What is called the cessation of consciousness has a deeper sense here. It means the cessation of the specifically prepared consciousness, *abhisaṅkhata viññāṇa*. An *arahant*'s experience of the cessation of consciousness is at the same time the experience of the cessation of name-and-form. Therefore, we can attribute a deeper significance to the above verses.

In support of this interpretation, we can quote the following verse in the *Munisutta* of the *Sutta Nipāta*:

> *Saṅkhāya vatthūni pamāya bījaṃ,*
> *sineham assa nānuppavecche,*
> *sa ve munī jātikhayantadassī,*
> *takkaṃ pahāya na upeti saṅkhaṃ.*[11]

> "Having surveyed the field and measured the seed,
> He waters it not for moisture,
> That sage in full view of birth's end,
> Lets go of logic and comes not within reckoning."

---

[10] E.g. at Sv-pṭ I 513.

[11] Sn 209, *Munisutta*.

By virtue of his masterly knowledge of the fields and his estimate of the seed of consciousness, he does not moisten it with craving. Thereby he sees the end of birth and transcends logic and worldly convention. This too shows that the deeper implications of the *MahāNidānasutta*, concerning the descent of consciousness into the mother's womb, have not been sufficiently appreciated so far.

Anusaya, or latency, is a word of special significance. What is responsible for rebirth, or *punabbhava*, is craving, which very often has the epithet *ponobhavikā* attached to it. The latency to craving is particularly instrumental in giving one yet another birth to fare on in *saṃsāra*. There is also a tendency to ignorance, which forms the basis of the latency to craving. It is the tendency to get attached to worldly concepts, without understanding them for what they are. That tendency is a result of ignorance in the worldlings and it is in itself a latency. In the *sutta* terminology the word *nissaya* is often used to denote it. The cognate word *nissita* is also used alongside. It means 'one who associates something,' while *nissaya* means 'association.'

As a matter of fact, here it does not have the same sense as the word has in its common usage. It goes deeper, to convey the idea of 'leaning on' something. Leaning on is also a form of association. Worldlings have a tendency to tenaciously grasp the concepts in worldly usage, to cling to them dogmatically and lean on them. They believe that the words they use have a reality of their own, that they are categorically true in their own right. Their attitude towards concepts is tinctured by craving, conceit and views.

We come across this word *nissita* in quite a number of important *suttas*. It almost sounds like a topic of meditation. In the *Channovādasutta* of the *Majjhima Nikāya* there is a cryptic passage, which at a glance looks more or less like a riddle:

> *Nissitassa calitaṃ, anissitassa calitaṃ natthi. Calite asati passaddhi, passaddhiyā sati nati na hoti, natiyā asati āgatigati na hoti, āgatigatiyā asati cutūpapāto na hoti,*

> *cutūpapāte asati nev'idha na huraṃ na ubhayamantare. Es' ev' anto dukhassa.*[12]

> "To the one attached, there is wavering. To the unattached one, there is no wavering. When there is no wavering, there is calm. When there is calm, there is no inclination. When there is no inclination, there is no coming and going. When there is no coming and going, there is no death and birth. When there is no death and birth, there is neither a 'here' nor a 'there' nor a 'between the two.' This itself is the end of suffering."

It looks as if the ending of suffering is easy enough. On the face of it, the passage seems to convey this much. To the one who leans on something, there is wavering or movement. He is perturbable. Though the first sentence speaks about the one attached, the rest of the passage is about the unattached one. That is to say, the one released. So here we see the distinction between the two. The one attached is movable, whereas the unattached one is not. When there is no wavering or perturbation, there is calm. When there is calm, there is no inclination. The word *nati* usually means 'bending.' So when there is calm, there is no bending or inclination. When there is no bending or inclination, there is no coming and going. When there is no coming and going, there is no passing away or reappearing. When there is neither a passing away nor a reappearing, there is neither a 'here,' nor a 'there,' nor any position in between. This itself is the end of suffering.

The *sutta* passage, at a glance, appears like a jumble of words. It starts by saying something about the one attached, *nissita*. It is limited to just one sentence: 'To one attached, there is wavering.' But we can infer that, due to his wavering and unsteadiness or restlessness, there is inclination, *nati*. The key word of the passage

---

12 M III 266, *Channovādasutta*.

is *nati*. Because of that inclination or bent, there is a coming and going. Given the twin concept of coming and going, there is the dichotomy between passing away and reappearing, *cuti/uppatti*. When these two are there, the two concepts 'here' and 'there' also come in. And there is a 'between the two' as well. Wherever there are two ends, there is also a middle. So it seems that in this particular context the word *nati* has a special significance.

The person who is attached is quite unlike the released person. Because he is not released, he always has a forward bent or inclination. In fact, this is the nature of craving. It bends one forward. In some *suttas* dealing with the question of rebirth, such as the *Kutūhalasālāsutta*, craving itself is sometimes called the grasping, *upādāna*.[13] So it is due to this very inclination or bent that the two concepts of coming and going, come in. Then, in accordance with them, the two concepts of passing away and reappearing, fall into place.

The idea of a journey, when viewed in the context of *saṃsāra*, gives rise to the idea of passing away and reappearing. Going and coming are similar to passing away and reappearing. So then, there is the implication of two places, all this indicates an attachment. There is a certain dichotomy about the terms here and there, and passing away and reappearing. Due to that dichotomous nature of the concepts, which beings tenaciously hold on to, the journeying in *saṃsāra* takes place in accordance with craving. As we have mentioned above, an alternation or transition occurs.

As for the released person, about whom the passage is specially concerned, his mind is free from all those conditions. To the unattached, there is no wavering. Since he has no wavering or unsteadiness, he has no inclination. As he has no inclination, there is no coming and going for him. As there is no coming and going, he has no passing away or reappearing. There being no passing

---

13 S IV 400, *Kuthūhalasālāsutta*: '*taṇhupādāna*.'

away or reappearing, there is neither a here, nor a there, nor any in between. That itself is the end of suffering.

The *Udāna* version of the above passage has something significant about it. There the entire *sutta* consists of these few sentences. But the introductory part of it says that the Buddha was instructing, inciting and gladdening the monks with a *Dhamma* talk connected with *Nibbāna*: *Tena kho pana samayena Bhagavā bhikkhū nibbānapaṭisaṃyuttāya dhammiyā kathāya sandasseti samādapeti samuttejeti sampahaṃseti.*[14] This is a pointer to the fact that this sermon is on *Nibbāna*. So the implication is that in *Nibbāna* the *arahant*'s mind is free from any attachments.

There is a discourse in the *Nidāna* section of the *Saṃyutta Nikāya*, which affords us a deeper insight into the meaning of the word *nissaya*. It is the *Kaccāyanagottasutta*, which is also significant for its deeper analysis of right view. This is how the Buddha introduces the sermon:

> *Dvayanissito khvāyaṃ, Kaccāyana, loko yebhuyyena: atthitañceva natthitañca. Lokasamudayaṃ kho, Kaccāyana, yathābhūtaṃ sammappaññāya passato yā loke natthitā sā na hoti. Lokanirodhaṃ kho, Kaccāyana, yathābhūtaṃ sammappaññāya passato yā loke atthitā sā na hoti.*[15]

> "This world, Kaccāyana, for the most part, bases its views on two things: on existence and non-existence. Now, Kaccāyana, to one who with right wisdom sees the arising of the world as it is, the view of non-existence regarding the world does not occur. And to one who with right wisdom sees the cessation of the world as it really is, the view of existence regarding the world does not occur."

---

[14] Ud 81, *Catutthanibbānapaṭisaṃyuttasutta.*

[15] S II 17, *Kaccāyanagottasutta.*

The Buddha comes out with this discourse in answer to the following question raised by the brahmin Kaccāyana: *Sammā diṭṭhi, sammā diṭṭhī'ti, bhante, vuccati. Kittāvatā nu kho, bhante, sammā diṭṭhi hoti?* "Lord, 'right view,' 'right view,' they say. But how far, Lord, is there 'right view?'"

In his answer, the Buddha first points out that the worldlings mostly base themselves on a duality, the two conflicting views of existence and non-existence, or 'is' and 'is not.' They would either hold on to the dogmatic view of eternalism, or would cling to nihilism. Now as to the right view of the noble disciple, it takes into account the process of arising as well as the process of cessation, and thereby avoids both extremes. This is the insight that illuminates the middle path.

Then the Buddha goes on to give a more detailed explanation of right view:

> *Upayupādānābhinivesavinibandho khvāyaṃ, Kaccāyana, loko yebhuyyena. Tañcāyaṃ upayupādānaṃ cetaso adhiṭṭhānaṃ abhinivesānusayaṃ na upeti na upādiyati nādhiṭṭhāti: 'attā me'ti. 'Dukkham eva uppajjamānaṃ uppajjati, dukkhaṃ nirujjhamānaṃ nirujjhatī'ti na kaṅkhati na vicikicchati aparapaccayā ñāṇam ev' assa ettha hoti. Ettāvatā kho, Kaccāyana, sammā diṭṭhi hoti.*

> "The world, Kaccāyana, for the most part, is given to approaching, grasping, entering into and getting entangled as regards views. Whoever does not approach, grasp, and take his stand upon that proclivity towards approaching and grasping, that mental standpoint, namely the idea: 'This is my soul,' he knows that what arises is just suffering and what ceases is just suffering. Thus, he is not in doubt, is not perplexed, and herein he has the knowledge that is not dependent on another. Thus far, Kaccāyana, he has right view."

The passage starts with a string of terms which has a deep philosophical significance. *Upaya* means 'approaching,' *upādāna* is 'grasping,' *abhinivesa* is 'entering into,' and *vinibandha* is the consequent entanglement. The implication is that the worldling is prone to dogmatic involvement in concepts through the stages mentioned above in an ascending order.

The attitude of the noble disciple is then outlined in contrast to the above dogmatic approach, and what follows after it. As for him, he does not approach, grasp, or take up the standpoint of a self. The word *anusaya*, latency or 'lying dormant,' is also brought in here to show that even the proclivity towards such a dogmatic involvement with a soul or self, is not there in the noble disciple. But what, then, is his point of view? What arises and ceases is nothing but suffering. There is no soul or self to lose, it is only a question of arising and ceasing of suffering. This, then, is the right view.

Thereafter the Buddha summarizes the discourse and brings it to a climax with an impressive declaration of his *via media*, the middle path based on the formula of dependent arising:

> *'Sabbam atthī'ti kho, Kaccāyana, ayam eko anto. 'Sabbaṃ natthī'ti ayaṃ dutiyo anto. Ete te, Kaccāyana, ubho ante anupagamma majjhena Tathāgato Dhammaṃ deseti:*
>
> *Avijjāpaccayā saṅkhārā, saṅkhārapaccayā viññāṇaṃ, viññāṇapaccayā nāmarūpaṃ, nāmarūpapaccayā saḷāyatanaṃ, saḷāyatanapaccayā phasso, phassapaccayā vedanā, vedanāpaccayā taṇhā, taṇhāpaccayā upādānaṃ, upādānapaccayā bhavo, bhavapaccayā jāti, jātipaccayā jarāmaraṇaṃ sokaparidevadukkhadomanassūpāyāsā sambhavanti. Evametassa kevalassa dukkhakkhandhassa samudayo hoti.*
>
> *Avijjāya tveva asesavirāganirodhā saṅkhāranirodho, saṅkharanirodhā viññāṇanirodho, viññāṇanirodhā nāmarūpanirodho, nāmarūpanirodhā saḷāyatananirodho,*

saḷāyatananirodhā phassanirodho, phassanirodhā vedanānirodho, vedanānirodhā taṇhānirodho, taṇhānirodhā upādānanirodho, upādānanirodhā bhavanirodho, bhavanirodhā jātinirodho, jātinirodhā jarāmaraṇaṃ sokaparidevadukkhadomanassūpāyāsā nirujjhanti. Evametassa kevalassa dukkhakkhandhassa nirodho hoti.

"'Everything exists,' Kaccāyana, is one extreme. 'Nothing exists' is the other extreme. Not approaching either of those extremes, Kaccāyana, the *Tathāgata* teaches the *Dhamma* by the middle way:

"From ignorance as condition, preparations come to be; from preparations as condition, consciousness comes to be; from consciousness as condition, name-and-form comes to be; from name-and-form as condition, the six sense-bases come to be; from the six sense-bases as condition, contact comes to be; from contact as condition, feeling comes to be; from feeling as condition, craving comes to be; from craving as condition, grasping comes to be; from grasping as condition, becoming comes to be; from becoming as condition, birth comes to be; and from birth as condition, decay-and-death, sorrow, lamentation, pain, grief and despair come to be. Such is the arising of this entire mass of suffering.

"From the complete fading away and cessation of that very ignorance, there comes to be the cessation of preparations; from the cessation of preparations, there comes to be the cessation of consciousness; from the cessation of consciousness, there comes to be the cessation of name-and-form; from the cessation of name-and-form, there comes to be the cessation of the six sense-bases; from the cessation of the six sense-bases, there comes to be the cessation of contact; from the cessation of contact, there comes to be the cessation of feeling; from the cessation of

> feeling, there comes to be the cessation of craving; from the cessation of craving, there comes to be the cessation of grasping; from the cessation of grasping, there comes to be the cessation of becoming; from the cessation of becoming, there comes to be the cessation of birth; and from the cessation of birth, there comes to be the cessation of decay-and-death, sorrow, lamentation, pain, grief and despair. Such is the cessation of this entire mass of suffering."

It is clear from this declaration that in this context the law of dependent arising itself is called the middle path. Some prefer to call this the Buddha's metaphysical middle path, as it avoids both extremes of 'is' and 'is not.' The philosophical implications of the above passage lead to the conclusion that the law of dependent arising enshrines a certain pragmatic principle, which dissolves the antinomian conflict in the world.

It is the insight into this principle that basically distinguishes the noble disciple, who sums it up in the two words *samudayo*, arising, and *nirodho*, ceasing. The arising and ceasing of the world is for him a fact of experience, a knowledge. It is in this light that we have to understand the phrase *aparappaccayā ñāṇam ev'assa ettha hoti*, "herein he has a knowledge that is not dependent on another." In other words, he is not believing in it out of faith in someone, but has understood it experientially. The noble disciple sees the arising and the cessation of the world through his own six sense bases.

In the *Saṃyutta Nikāya* there is a verse which presents this idea in a striking manner:

> *Chasu loko samuppanno,*
> *chasu kubbati santhavaṃ,*

channam eva upādāya,
chasu loko vihaññati.[16]

"In the six the world arose,
In the six it holds concourse,
On the six themselves depending,
In the six it has its woes."

The verse seems to say that the world has arisen in the six, that it has associations in the six, and that depending on those very six, the world comes to grief. Though the commentators advance an interpretation of this six, it does not seem to get the sanction of the *sutta* as it is. According to them, the first line speaks of the six internal sense bases, such as the eye, ear and nose.[17] The world is said to arise in these six internal sense bases. The second line is supposed to refer to the six external sense bases. Again the third line is interpreted with reference to the six internal sense bases, and the fourth line is said to refer to the six external sense bases. In other words, the implication is that the world arises in the six internal sense bases and associates with the six external sense bases, and that it holds on to the six internal sense bases and comes to grief in the six external sense bases.

This interpretation seems to miss the point. Even the grammar does not allow it, for if it is a case of associating 'with' the external sense bases, the instrumental case would have been used instead of the locative case, that is, *chahi* instead of *chasu*. On the other hand, the locative *chasu* occurs in all the three lines in question. This makes it implausible that the first two lines are referring to two different groups of sixes. It is more plausible to conclude that the reference is to the six sense bases of contact, *phassāyatana*, which include both the internal and the external. In

16 S I 41, *Lokasutta*.

17 Spk I 96.

fact, at least two are necessary for something to be dependently arisen. The world does not arise in the six internal bases in isolation. It is precisely in this fact that the depth of this *Dhamma* is to be seen.

In the *Samudayasutta* of the *Saḷāyatana* section in the *Saṃyutta Nikāya* this aspect of dependent arising is clearly brought out:

> *Cakkhuñca paṭicca rūpe ca uppajjati cakkhuviññāṇaṃ, tiṇṇaṃ saṅgati phasso, phassapaccayā vedanā, vedanāpaccayā taṇhā, taṇhāpaccayā upādānaṃ, upādānapaccayā bhavo, bhavapaccayā jāti, jātipaccayā jarāmaraṇaṃ sokaparidevadukkhadomanassūpāyāsā sambhavanti. Evametassa kevalassa dukkhakkhandhassa samudayo hoti.*[18]

> "Dependent on the eye and forms arises eye consciousness; the coming together of the three is contact; with contact as condition, arises feeling; conditioned by feeling, craving; conditioned by craving, grasping; conditioned by grasping, becoming; conditioned by becoming, birth; and conditioned by birth, decay-and-death, sorrow, lamentation, pain, grief and despair. Thus is the arising of this entire mass of suffering."

Here the *sutta* starts with the arising of contact and branches off towards the standard formula of *paṭicca samuppāda*. Eye consciousness arises dependent on, *paṭicca*, two things, namely eye and forms. And the concurrence of the three is contact. This shows that two are necessary for a thing to be dependently arisen.

So in fairness to the *sutta* version, we have to conclude that the reference in all the four lines is to the bases of contact, comprising both the internal and the external. That is to say, we cannot discriminate between them and assert that the first line refers to

---

[18] S IV 86, *Dukkhasutta*.

one set of six, and the second line refers to another. We are forced to such a conclusion in fairness to the *sutta*.

So from this verse also we can see that according to the usage of the noble ones the world arises in the six sense bases. This fact is quite often expressed by the phrase *ariyassa vinaye loko*, the world in the noble one's discipline.[19] According to this noble usage, the world is always defined in terms of the six sense bases, as if the world arises because of these six sense bases. This is a very deep idea. All other teachings in this *Dhamma* will get obscured, if one fails to understand this basic fact, namely how the concept of the world is defined in this mode of noble usage.

This noble usage reveals to us the implications of the expression *udayatthagāminī paññā*, the wisdom that sees the rise and fall. About the noble disciple it is said that he is endowed with the noble penetrative wisdom of seeing the rise and fall, *udayatthagāminiyā paññāya sammanāgato ariyāya nibbhedikāya*.[20] The implication is that this noble wisdom has a penetrative quality about it. This penetration is through the rigidly grasped almost impenetrable encrustation of the two dogmatic views in the world, existence and non-existence.

Now, how does that penetration come about? As already stated in the above quoted *Kaccāyanasutta*, when one sees the arising aspect of the world, one finds it impossible to hold the view that nothing exists in the world. His mind does not incline towards a dogmatic involvement with that view. Similarly, when he sees the cessation of the world through his own six sense bases, he sees no possibility to go to the other extreme view in the world: 'Everything exists.'

The most basic feature of this principle of dependent arising, with its penetrative quality, is the breaking down of the power of the above concepts. It is the very inability to grasp these views

---

19 S IV 95, *Lokakāmaguṇasutta*.

20 E.g. at D III 237, *Saṅgītisutta*.

dogmatically that is spoken of as the abandonment of the personality view, *sakkāyadiṭṭhi*. The ordinary worldling is under the impression that things exist in truth and fact, but the noble disciple, because of his insight into the norm of arising and cessation, understands the arising and ceasing nature of concepts and their essencelessness or insubstantiality.

Another aspect of the same thing, in addition to what has already been said about *nissaya*, is the understanding of the relatedness of this to that, *idappaccayatā*, implicit in the law of dependent arising. In fact, we began our discussion by highlighting the significance of the term *idappaccayatā*.[21] The basic principle involved, is itself often called *paṭicca samuppāda*. "This being, this comes to be, with the arising of this, this arises. This not being, this does not come to be. With the cessation of this, this ceases."

This insight penetrates through those extreme views. It resolves the conflict between them. But how? By removing the very premise on which it rested, and that is that there are two things. Though logicians might come out with the law of identity and the like, according to right view, the very bifurcation itself is the outcome of a wrong view. That is to say, this is only a conjoined pair. In other words, it resolves that conflict by accepting the worldly norm.

Now this is a point well worth considering. In the case of the twelve links of the formula of dependent arising, discovered by the Buddha, there is a relatedness of this to that, *idappaccayatā*. As for instance already illustrated above by the two links birth and decay-and-death.[22] When birth is there, decay-and-death come to be, with the arising of birth, decay-and-death arise (and so on). The fact that this relatedness itself is the eternal law, is clearly

---

[21] See sermon 1.

[22] See sermon 3.

revealed by the following statement of the Buddha in the *Nidānasaṃyutta* of the *Saṃyutta Nikāya*:

> *Avijjāpaccayā, bhikkhave, saṅkhārā. Ya tatra tathatā avitathatā anaññathatā idappaccayatā, ayaṃ vuccati, bhikkhave, paṭiccasamuppādo.*[23]
>
> "From ignorance as condition, preparations come to be. That suchness therein, the invariability, the not-otherwiseness, the relatedness of this to that, this, monks, is called dependent arising."

Here the first two links have been taken up to illustrate the principle governing their direct relation. Now let us examine the meaning of the terms used to express that relation. *Tathā* means 'such' or 'thus,' and is suggestive of the term *yathābhūta-ñāṇadassana*, the knowledge and vision of things as they are. The correlatives *yathā* and *tathā* express between them the idea of faithfulness to the nature of the world. So *tathatā* asserts the validity of the law of dependent arising, as a norm in accordance with nature. *Avitathatā*, with its double negative, reaffirms that validity to the degree of invariability. *Anaññathatā*, or not-otherwiseness, makes it unchallengeable, as it were. It is a norm beyond contradiction.

When a conjoined pair is accepted as such, there is no conflict between the two. But since this idea can well appear as some sort of a puzzle, we shall try to illustrate it with a simile. Suppose two bulls, a black one and a white one, are bound together at the neck and allowed to graze in the field as a pair. This is sometimes done to prevent them from straying far afield. Now out of the pair, if the white bull pulls towards the stream, while the black one is pulling towards the field, there is a conflict. The conflict is not due to the

---

23 S II 26, *Paccayasutta*.

bondage, at least not necessarily due to the bondage. It is because the two are pulling in two directions. Supposing the two bulls, somehow, accept the fact that they are in bondage and behave amicably. When then the white bull pulls towards the stream, the black one keeps him company with equanimity, though he is not in need of a drink. And when the black bull is grazing, the white bull follows him along with equanimity, though he is not inclined to eat.

Similarly, in this case too, the conflict is resolved by accepting the pair-wise combination as a conjoined pair. That is how the Buddha solved this problem. But still the point of this simile might not be clear enough. So let us come back to the two links, birth and decay-and-death, which we so often dragged in for purposes of clarification. So long as one does not accept the fact that these two links, birth and decay-and-death, are a conjoined pair, one would see between them a conflict. Why? Because one grasps birth as one end, and tries to remove the other end, which one does not like, namely decay-and-death. One is trying to separate birth from decay-and-death. But this happens to be a conjoined pair. "Conditioned by birth, monks, is decay-and-death." This is the word of the Buddha. Birth and decay-and-death are related to each other.

The word *jarā*, or decay, on analysis would make this clear. Usually by *jarā* we mean old age. The word has connotations of senility and decrepitude, but the word implies both growth and decay, as it sets in from the moment of one's birth itself. Only, there is a possible distinction according to the standpoint taken. This question of a standpoint or a point of view is very important at this juncture. This is something one should assimilate with a meditative attention. Let us bring up a simile to make this clear.

Now, for instance, there could be a person who makes his living by selling the leaves of a particular kind of tree. Suppose another man sells the flowers of the same tree, to make his living. And yet another sells the fruits, while a fourth sells the timber. If we line them up and put to them the question, pointing to that tree: 'Is this tree mature enough?,' we might sometimes get different answers.

Why? Each would voice his own commercial point of view regarding the degree of maturity of the tree. For instance, one who sells flowers would say that the tree is too old, if the flowering stage of the tree is past.

Similarly, the concept of decay or old age can change according to the standpoint taken up. From beginning to end, it is a process of decay. But we create an artificial boundary between youth and old age. This again shows that the two are a pair mutually conjoined. Generally, the worldlings are engaged in an attempt to separate the two in this conjoined pair. Before the Buddha came into the scene, all religious teachers were trying to hold on to birth, while rejecting decay-and-death. But it was a vain struggle. It is like the attempt of the miserly millionaire Kosiya to eat rice-cakes alone, to cite another simile.

According to that instructive story, the millionaire Kosiya, an extreme miser, once developed a strong desire to eat rice-cakes.[24] As he did not wish to share them with anyone else, he climbed up to the topmost story of his mansion with his wife and got her to cook rice-cakes for him. To teach him a lesson, Venerable MahāMoggallāna, who excelled in psychic powers, went through the air and appeared at the window as if he is on his alms round. Kosiya, wishing to dismiss this intruder with a tiny rice-cake, asked his wife to put a little bit of cake dough into the pan. She did so, but it became a big rice-cake through the venerable *Thera*'s psychic power. Further attempts to make tinier rice-cakes ended up in producing ever bigger and bigger ones. In the end, Kosiya thought of dismissing the monk with just one cake, but to his utter dismay, all the cakes got joined to each other to form a string of cakes. The couple then started pulling this string of cakes in either direction with all their might, to separate just one from it. But without success. At last they decided to let go and give up, and offered the entire string of cakes to the venerable *Thera*.

---

[24] Dhp-a I 367.

The Buddha's solution to the above problem is a similar let go-ism and giving up. It is a case of giving up all assets, *sabbūpadhipaṭinissagga*. You cannot separate these links from one another. Birth and decay-and-death are intertwined. This is a conjoined pair. So the solution here, is to let go. All those problems are due to taking up a standpoint. Therefore the kind of view sanctioned in this case, is one that leads to detachment and dispassion, one that goes against the tendency to grasp and hold on. It is by grasping and holding on that one comes into conflict with *Māra*.

Now going by the story of the millionaire Kosiya, one might think that the Buddha was defeated by *Māra*. But the truth of the matter is that it is *Māra* who suffered defeat by this sort of giving up. It is a very subtle point. *Māra*'s forte lies in seizing and grabbing. He is always out to challenge. Sometimes he takes delight in hiding himself to take one by surprise, to drive terror and cause horripilation. So when *Māra* comes round to grab, if we can find some means of foiling his attempt, or make it impossible for him to grab, then *Māra* will have to accept defeat.

Now let us examine the Buddha's solution to this question. There are in the world various means of preventing others from grabbing something we possess. We can either hide our property in an inaccessible place, or adopt security measures, or else we can come to terms and sign a treaty with the enemy. But all these measures can sometimes fail. However, there is one unfailing method, which in principle is bound to succeed. A method that prevents all possibilities of grabbing. And that is – letting go, giving up. When one lets go, there is nothing to grab. In a tug-of-war, when someone is pulling at one end with all his might, if the other suddenly lets go of its hold, one can well imagine the extent of the former's discomfiture, let alone victory. It was such a discomfiture that fell to *Māra*'s lot, when the Buddha applied this extraordinary solution. All this goes to show the importance of such terms as *nissaya* and *idappaccayatā* in understanding this *Dhamma*.

We have already taken up the word *nissaya* for comment. Another aspect of its significance is revealed by the *Satipaṭṭhāna-*

sutta. Some parts of this *sutta*, though well known, are wonderfully deep. There is a certain thematic paragraph, which occurs at the end of each subsection in the *Satipaṭṭhānasutta*. For instance, in the section on the contemplation relating to body, *kāyānupasssanā*, we find the following paragraph:

> *Iti ajjhattaṃ vā kāye kāyānupassī viharati, bahiddhā vā kāye kāyānupassī viharati, ajjhattabahiddhā vā kāye kāyānupassī viharati; samudayadhammānupassī vā kāyasmiṃ viharati, vayadhammānupassī vā kāyasmiṃ viharati, samudayavayadhammānupassī vā kāyasmiṃ viharati; 'atthi kāyo'ti vā pan'assa sati paccupaṭṭhitā hoti, yāvadeva ñāṇamattāya paṭissatimattāya; anissito ca viharati, na ca kiñci loke upādiyati.*[25]

> "In this way he abides contemplating the body as a body internally, or he abides contemplating the body as a body externally, or he abides contemplating the body as a body internally and externally. Or else he abides contemplating the arising nature in the body, or he abides contemplating the dissolving nature in the body, or he abides contemplating the arising and dissolving nature in the body. Or else the mindfulness that 'there is a body' is established in him only to the extent necessary for just knowledge and further mindfulness. And he abides independent and does not cling to anything in the world."

A similar paragraph occurs throughout the *sutta* under all the four contemplations, body, feeling, mind and mind objects. As a matter of fact, it is this paragraph that is called *satipaṭṭhāna bhāvanā*, or meditation on the foundation of mindfulness.[26] The preamble to

---

[25] M I 56, *Satipaṭṭhānasutta*.

[26] S V 183, *Vibhaṅgasutta*.

this paragraph introduces the foundation itself, or the setting up of mindfulness as such. The above paragraph, on the other hand, deals with what pertains to insight. It is the field of insight proper. If we examine this paragraph, here too we will find a set of conjoined or twin terms:

"In this way he abides contemplating the body as a body internally, or he abides contemplating the body externally," and then: "he abides contemplating the body both internally and externally." Similarly: "He abides contemplating the arising nature in the body, or he abides contemplating the dissolving nature in the body," and then: "he abides contemplating both the arising and dissolving nature in the body."

"Or else the mindfulness that 'there is a body' is established in him only to the extent necessary for knowledge and remembrance." This means that for the meditator even the idea 'there is a body,' that remembrance, is there just for the purpose of further development of knowledge and mindfulness.

"And he abides independent and does not cling to anything in the world." Here too, the word used is *anissita*, independent, or not leaning towards anything. He does not cling to anything in the world. The word *nissaya* says something more than grasping. It means 'leaning on' or 'associating.'

This particular thematic paragraph in the *Satipaṭṭhānasutta* is of paramount importance for insight meditation. Here, too, there is the mention of internal, *ajjhatta*, and external, *bahiddhā*. When one directs one's attention to one's own body and another's body separately, one might sometimes take these two concepts, internal and external, too seriously with a dogmatic attitude. One might think that there is actually something that could be called one's own or another's. But then the mode of attention next mentioned unifies the two, as internal-external, *ajjhattabahiddhā*, and presents them like the conjoined pair of bulls. And what does it signify? These two are not to be viewed as two extremes, they are related to each other.

Now let us go a little deeper into this interrelation. The farthest limit of the internal is the nearest limit of the external. The farthest limit of the external is the nearest limit of the internal. More strictly rendered, *ajjhatta* means inward and *bahiddhā* means outward. So here we have the duality of an inside and an outside. One might think that the word *ajjhattika* refers to whatever is organic. Nowadays many people take in artificial parts into their bodies. But once acquired, they too become internal. That is why, in this context *ajjhattika* has a deeper significance than its usual rendering as 'one's own.'

Whatever it may be, the farthest limit of the *ajjhatta* remains the nearest limit of the *bahiddhā*. Whatever portion one demarcates as one's own, just adjoining it and at its very gate is *bahiddhā*. And from the point of view of *bahiddhā*, its farthest limit and at its periphery is *ajjhatta*. This is a conjoined pair. These two are interrelated. So the implication is that these two are not op posed to each other. That is why, by attending to them both together, as *ajjhattabahiddhā*, that dogmatic involvement with a view is abandoned. Here we have an element of reconciliation, which prevents adherence to a view. This is what fosters the attitude of *anissita*, unattached.

So the two, *ajjhatta* and *bahiddhā*, are neighbours. Inside and outside as concepts are neighbours to each other. It is the same as in the case of arising and ceasing, mentioned above. This fact has already been revealed to some extent by the *Kaccāyanagottasutta*.

Now if we go for an illustration, we have the word *udaya* at hand in *samudaya*. Quite often this word is contrasted with *atthagama*, going down, in the expression *udayatthagaminī paññā*, the wisdom that sees the rise and fall. We can regard these two as words borrowed from everyday life. *Udaya* means sunrise, and *atthagama* is sunset. If we take this itself as an illustration, the farthest limit of the forenoon is the nearest limit of the afternoon. The farthest limit of the afternoon is the nearest limit of the forenoon. And here again we see a case of neighbourhood. When one understands the neighbourly nature of the terms *udaya* and *atthagama*, or *samudaya* and *vaya*, and regards them as interrelated by the principle of *idappaccayatā*, one penetrates them both by that mode of contemplating the rise and fall of the body together, *samudayavayadhammānupassī vā kāyasmiṃ viharati*, and develops a penetrative insight.

What comes next in the *satipaṭṭhāna* passage, is the outcome or net result of that insight. "The mindfulness that 'there is a body' is established in him only to the extent necessary for pure knowledge and further mindfulness," *atthi kāyo'ti vā pan'assa sati pacupaṭṭhitā hoti, yāvadeva ñāṇamattāya paṭissatimattāya.* At that moment one does not take even the concept of body seriously. Even the mindfulness that 'there is a body' is established in that meditator only for the sake of *yavadeva*, clarity of knowledge and accomplishment of mindfulness. The last sentence brings out the net result of that way of developing insight: "He abides independent and does not cling to anything in the world."

Not only in the section on the contemplation of the body, but also in the sections on feelings, mind, and mind objects in the *Satipaṭṭhānasutta*, we find this mode of insight development. None of the objects, taken up for the foundation of mindfulness, is to be grasped tenaciously. Only their rise and fall is discerned. So it seems that, what is found in the *Satipaṭṭhānasutta*, is a group of concepts. These concepts serve only as a scaffolding for the systematic development of mindfulness and knowledge. The Buddha often compared his *Dhamma* to a raft: *nittharaṇatthāya no gahaṇatthāya*, "for crossing over and not for holding on to."[27] Accordingly, what we have here are so many scaffoldings for the up-building of mindfulness and knowledge.

Probably due to the lack of understanding of this deep philosophy enshrined in the *Satipaṭṭhānasutta*, many sects of Buddhism took up these concepts in a spirit of dogmatic adherence. That dogmatic attitude of clinging on is like the attempt to cling on to the scaffoldings and to live on in them. So with reference to the *Satipaṭṭhānasutta* also, we can understand the importance of the term *nissaya*.

---

[27] M I 134, *Alagaddūpamasutta*.

Nibbāna Sermon 5

Namo tassa Bhagavato Arahato Sammāsambuddhassa
Namo tassa Bhagavato Arahato Sammāsambuddhassa
Namo tassa Bhagavato Arahato Sammāsambuddhassa

Etaṃ santaṃ, etaṃ paṇītaṃ, yadidaṃ sabbasaṅkhārasamatho sabbūpadhipaṭinissaggo taṇhakkhayo virāgo nirodho nibbānaṃ.[1]

"This is peaceful, this is excellent, namely the stilling of all preparations, the relinquishment of all assets, the destruction of craving, detachment, cessation, extinction."

With the permission of the Most Venerable Great Preceptor and the assembly of the venerable meditative monks.

Towards the end of our last sermon, we discussed, to some extent, a special mode of attention, regarding the four objects of contemplation in the *Satipaṭṭhānasutta* – body, feelings, mind, and mind-objects.[2] That discussion might have revealed a certain middle path indicated by the Buddha.

We drew attention to a thematic paragraph, occurring through out the *Satipaṭṭhānasutta*, which outlines a method of using objects and concepts for *satipaṭṭhāna* meditation without dogmatic involvement. This leads the meditator to a particular kind of attitude, summed up by the concluding phrase: "He abides

---

1 M I 436, *MahāMālunkyasutta*.

2 See sermon 4.

independent and does not cling to anything in the world," *anissito ca viharati, na ca kiñci loke upādiyati.*[3]

By way of clarification, we brought in the simile of a scaffolding for a building, that here the concepts only serve as a scaffolding for building up mindfulness and knowledge.[4] Talking about the scaffolding, we are reminded of two different attitudes, namely, the attitude of leaning onto and dwelling in the scaffolding itself, and the enlightened attitude of merely utilizing it for the purpose of erecting a building.

For further explanation of this technique, we may take up the two terms *parāmasana* and *sammasana*. It might be better to distinguish the meanings of these two terms also with the help of a simile. As for a simile, let us take up the razor, which is such a useful requisite in our meditative life. There is a certain special way in sharpening a razor. With the idea of sharpening the razor, if one grabs it tightly and rubs it on the sharpening stone, it will only become blunt. *Parāmasana*, grasping, grabbing, is something like that.

What then is the alternative? A more refined and softer approach is required as meant by the term *sammasana*. There is a proper mode of doing it. One has to hold the razor in a relaxed way, as if one is going to throw it away. One holds it lightly, ready to let go of it at any time. But, of course, with mindfulness. The wrist, also, is not rigid, but relaxed. Hand is supple at the joints and easy to swing. Then with that readiness, one sharpens the razor, sliding it smoothly on the stone. First: up, up, up, then: down, down, down, and then: up down, up down, up down. The third combined movement ensures that those parts of the blade still untouched by the stone will also get duly sharpened.

It is in the same manner that the razor of insight wisdom has to be whetted on the sharpening stone of the *Satipaṭṭhānasutta.*

---

[3] M I 56, *Satipaṭṭhānasutta*.

[4] See sermon 4.

Inward, inward, inward – outward, outward, outward – inward outward, inward outward. Or else: arising, arising, arising – ceasing, ceasing, ceasing – arising ceasing, arising ceasing.

This is an illustration for the method of reflection, or *sammasana*, introduced by the Buddha in the *Satipaṭṭhānasutta*. Words and concepts have to be made use of, for attaining *Nibbāna*. But here the aim is only the up-building of mindfulness and knowledge. Once their purpose is served, they can be dismantled without being a bother to the mind. This is the significance of the concluding phrase "He abides independent and does not cling to anything in the world."[5]

There is another *sutta* in which the Buddha has touched upon this same point in particular. It is the *Samudayasutta* in the *Satipaṭṭhānasaṃyutta* of the *Saṃyutta Nikāya*.[6] In that *sutta*, the Buddha has proclaimed the arising and the going down of the four foundations of mindfulness. He begins by saying: "Monks, I shall teach you the arising and the going down of the four foundations of mindfulness." *Catunnaṃ, bhikkhave, satipaṭṭhānānaṃ samudayañca atthagamañca desessāmi.*

He goes on to say: "What, monks, is the arising of the body? With the arising of nutriment is the arising of the body and with the cessation of the nutriment is the going down of the body." *Ko ca, bhikkhave, kāyassa samudayo? Āhārasamudayā kāyassa samudayo, āhāranirodhā kāyassa atthagamo.*

Similarly: "With the arising of contact is the arising of feeling, and with the cessation of contact is the going down of feeling." *Phassasamudayā vedanānaṃ samudayo, phassanirodhā vedanānaṃ atthagamo.*

And then: "With the arising of name-and-form is the arising of the mind, and with the cessation of name-and-form is the going

---

[5] M I 56, *Satipaṭṭhānasutta.*

[6] S V 184, *Samudayasutta.*

down of the mind." *Nāmarūpasamudayā cittassa samudayo, nāmarūpanirodhā cittassa atthagamo.*

And lastly: "With the arising of attention is the arising of mind-objects, and with the ceasing of attention is the going down of mind-objects." *Manasikārasamudayā dhammānaṃ samudayo, manasikāranirodhā dhammānaṃ atthagamo.*

This, too, is an important discourse, well worth remembering, because here the Buddha is dealing with the arising and cessation, or arising and going down, of the four objects used for establishing mindfulness.

As we know, the concept of nutriment in this *Dhamma* is much broader than the worldly concept of food. It does not imply merely the ordinary food, for which the term used is *kabaliṅkārāhāra*, or material food. Taken in a deeper sense, it includes the other three kinds of nutriment as well, namely *phassa*, or contact, *mano-sañcetanā*, or volition, and *viññāṇa*, or consciousness. These four together account for the concept of body as such. Therefore, due to these four there comes to be a body, and with their cessation the body ends. So also in the case of feeling. We all know that the arising of feeling is due to contact.

The reference to name-and-form in this context might not be clear enough at once, due to various definitions of name-and-form, or *nāma-rūpa*. Here, the reason for the arising of the mind is said to be name-and-form. Mind is said to arise because of name-and-form, and it is supposed to go down with the cessation of name-and-form.

The fact that the mind-objects arise due to attention is note worthy. All the mind-objects mentioned in the fourth section of contemplation arise when there is attention. And they go down when attention is not there. In other words, attending makes objects out of them. This way, we are reminded that, apart from making use of these words and concepts for the purpose of attaining *Nibbāna*, there is nothing worth holding on to or clinging to dogmatically. So if a meditator works with this aim in mind, he will be assured of a state of mind that is independent and clinging-free, *anissita, anupādāna*.

One marvelous quality of the Buddha's teaching emerges from this discussion. A mind-object is something that the mind hangs on to as the connotations of the word *ārammaṇa* (cp. *ālambhana*) suggest. But because of the mode of insight wisdom outlined here, because of the middle path approach, even the tendency to 'hang-on' is finally done away with and the object is penetrated through. Despite the above connotations of 'hanging on' (*ārammaṇa*), the object is transcended. Transcendence in its highest sense is not a case of surpassing, as is ordinarily understood. Instead of leaving behind, it penetrates through. Here then, we have a transcendence that is in itself a penetration.

So the terms *anissita* and *anupādāna* seem to have a significance of their own. More of it comes to light in quite a number of other *suttas*. Particularly in the *Dvayatānupassanāsutta* of the *Sutta Nipāta* we come across the following two verses, which throw more light on these two terms:

Anissito na calati,
nissito ca upādiyaṃ,
itthabhāvaññathābhāvaṃ,
saṃsāraṃ nātivattati.

Etam ādīnavaṃ ñatvā,
nissayesu mahabbhayaṃ,
anissito anupādāno,
sato bhikkhu paribbaje.[7]

"The unattached one wavers not, but the one attached, clinging on, does not get beyond *saṃsāra*, which is an alternation between a this-ness and an otherwise-ness (*itthabhāvaññathābhāva*).

[7] Sn 752-753, *Dvayatānupassanāsutta*.

> "Knowing this peril, the great danger, in attachments or supports (*nissayesu*), let the monk fare along mindfully, resting on nothing, clinging to nothing."

Caught up in the dichotomy of *saṃsāric* existence, which alternates between this-ness and otherwise-ness, one is unable to transcend it, so long as there is attachment and clinging. *Nissayas* are the supports that encourage clinging in the form of dogmatic adherence to views. Seeing the peril and the danger in them, a mindful monk has no recourse to them. This gives one an idea of the attitude of an *arahant*. His mind is free from enslavement to the conjoined pairs of relative concepts.

This fact is borne out by certain Canonical statements, which at first sight might appear as riddles. The two last sections of the *Sutta Nipāta*, the *Aṭṭhakavagga* and the *Pārāyanavagga* in particular, contain verses which are extremely deep. In the *Aṭṭhakavagga*, one often comes across apparently contradictory pairs of terms, side by side. About the *arahant* it is said that: "He neither grasps nor gives up," *nādeti na nirassati*.[8] "There is nothing taken up or rejected by him," *attaṃ nirattaṃ na hi tassa atthi*.[9]

By the way, the word *attaṃ* in this context is derived from *ādātta* (*ā* + *dā*), by syncopation. It should not be mistaken as a reference to *attā*, or soul. Similarly, *niratta* is from *as*, to throw, *nirasta*, conveying the idea of giving up or putting down.

There is nothing taken up or given up by the *arahant*. Other such references to the *arahant*'s attitude are: *Na rāgarāgī na virāgaratto*, "He is neither attached to attachment, nor attached to

---

[8] Sn 954, *Attadaṇḍasutta*.

[9] Sn 787, *Duṭṭhaṭṭhakasutta*.

detachment."[10] *Na hi so rajjati no virajjati*, "He is neither attached nor detached."[11]

It is in order to explain why such references are used that we took all this trouble to discuss at length the significance of such terms as *nissaya*.[12] Probably due to a lack of understanding in this respect, the deeper meanings of such *suttas* have got obscured. Not only that, even textual corruption through distorted variant readings has set in, because they appeared like riddles. However, the deeper sense of these *suttas* sometimes emerges from certain strikingly strange statements like the following found in the *Khajjanīyasutta* of the *Saṃyutta Nikāya*. The reference here is to the *arahant*:

> *Ayaṃ vuccati, bhikkhave, bhikkhu neva ācināti na apacināti, apacinitvā ṭhito neva pajahati na upādiyati, pajahitvā ṭhito neva viseneti na usseneti, visenetvā ṭhito neva vidhūpeti na sandhūpeti.*[13]

> "Monks, such a monk is called one who neither amasses nor diminishes; already diminished as he is, he neither gives up nor grasps; already given up as he is, he neither disbands nor binds together; already disbanded as he is, he neither exorcizes nor proficiates."

Even to one who does not understand the language, the above quotation would sound enigmatic. Even the rendering of the terms used here is not an easy matter, because of the nuances they seem to convey. We could perhaps say that such a monk neither amasses or accumulates, nor diminishes. Since he is already diminished,

---

[10] Sn 795, *Suddhaṭṭhakasutta*.

[11] Sn 813, *Jarāsutta*.

[12] See sermon 4.

[13] S III 90, *Khajjaniyasutta*.

presumably as regards the five aggregates, he neither abandons nor grasps anew. Since the giving up is complete, he neither binds together or enlists (note the word *sena,* army), nor disbands. Disbanding (if not 'disarmament'), being complete, there is neither exorcizing or smoking out, nor proficiating or inviting. The coupling of these terms and their peculiar employment is suggestive of the *arahant*'s freedom from the dichotomy.

In the *Brāhmaṇavagga* of the *Dhammapada* too, we come across a similar enigmatic verse:

Yassa pāraṃ apāraṃ vā,
pārāpāraṃ na vijjati,
vītaddaraṃ visaṃyuttaṃ,
tam ahaṃ brūmi brāhmaṇaṃ.[14]

"For whom there is neither a farther shore,
Nor a hither shore, nor both,
Who is undistressed and unfettered,
Him I call a Brahmin."

In this context the word *brāhmaṇa* refers to the *arahant*. Here too, it is said that the *arahant* has neither a farther shore, nor a hither shore, nor both. This might sometimes appear as a problem. Our usual concept of an *arahant* is of one who has crossed over the ocean of *saṃsāra* and is standing on the other shore. But here is something enigmatic.

We come across a similar *sutta* in the *Sutta Nipāta* also, namely its very first, the *Uragasutta*. The extraordinary feature of this *sutta* is the recurrence of the same refrain throughout its seventeen verses. The refrain is:

---

[14] Dhp 385, *Brāhmaṇavagga*.

So bhikkhu jahāti orapāraṃ,
urago jiṇṇamiva tacaṃ purāṇaṃ.[15]

"That monk forsakes the hither and the tither,
Like a snake its slough that doth wither."

This simile of the slough, or the worn-out skin of the snake, is highly significant. To quote one instance:

Yo nājjhagamā bhavesu sāraṃ,
vicinaṃ pupphamiva udumbaresu,
so bhikkhu jahāti orapāraṃ,
urago jiṇṇamiva tacaṃ purāṇaṃ.[16]

"That monk who sees no essence in existence,
Like one seeking flowers in *Udumbara* trees,
Will give up the hither as well as the thither,
Like the snake its slough that doth wither."

The *arahant* has abandoned his attachment to existence. As such, he is free from the bondage of those conjoined terms in worldly usage. So the *arahant* looks at the worldly usage in the same way as a snake would turn back and look at the worn-out skin he has sloughed off. Sometimes we see a snake moving about with a remnant of its slough hanging on. We might even think that the snake is carrying its slough around. It is the same in the case of the *arahants*.

Now there is this term *sa-upādisesa Nibbānadhātu*. Taking the term at its face value, some might think that the clinging is not yet over for the *arahants* – that there is still a little bit left. The *arahant*, though he has attained release and realized *Nibbāna*, so

---

15 Sn 1-17 , *Uragasutta.*

16 Sn 5, *Uragasutta.*

long as he is living in the world, has to relate to the external objects in the world somehow through his five senses, making use of them. Seeing it, some might conclude that it is because of some residual clinging. But we have to understand this in the light of the simile of the worn-out skin. In the case of the *arahant*, too, the sloughed off skin is still hanging on.

As a sidelight we may cite a remark of Venerable Sāriputta: *Iminā pūtikāyena aṭṭiyāmi harāyāmi jigucchāmi*,[17] "I am harassed and repelled by this body, I am ashamed of it." This is because the body is for him something already abandoned. All this goes to show that the *arahant* has an unattached, unclinging attitude.

Linguistic usage, which is a special feature of existence, is enlivened by the cravings, conceits, and views with which it is grasped. Worldlings thrive on it, whereas the *arahants* are free from it. This is the upshot of the above discussion on the terms *anusaya* and *nissaya*.[18]

Yet another important term that should receive attention in any discussion on *Nibbāna* is *āsava*. This is because the *arahant* is often called a *khīṇāsava*, one whose *āsavas* are extinct.[19] *Āsavakkhayo*, extinction of *āsavas*, is an epithet of *Nibbāna*.[20] So the distinct feature of an *arahant* is his extinction of *āsavas*.

Now, what does *āsava* mean? In ordinary life, this word is used to denote fermentation or liquor that has got fermented for a long time.[21] If there is even a dreg of ferment in a vessel, it is enough to cause fermentation for any suitable raw material put into it. So also are the *āsavas*. They are like the residual dregs of the ebullient mass of defilements in beings, which have under gone fermentation for a long, long time in *saṃsāra*.

---

[17] A IV 377, *Sīhanādasutta*.

[18] See sermon 4.

[19] E.g. at D III 83, *Aggaññasutta*.

[20] E.g. at Dhp 253, *Malavagga*.

[21] E.g. the *pupphāsava, phalāsava, madhvāsava, guḷāsava* at Sv III 944.

Very often, *āsavas* are said to be of three kinds, as *kāmāsavā, bhavāsavā*, and *avijjāsavā*. The term *āsava* in this context is usually rendered as 'influxes.' We may understand them as certain intoxicating influences, which create a world of sense-desires, a stupor that gives a notion of existence and leads to ignorance. These influxes are often said to have the nature of infiltrating into the mind. Some times a fourth type of influxes, *diṭṭhāsavā*, is also mentioned. But this can conveniently be subsumed under *avijjāsavā*.

The extinction of influxes becomes a distinctive characteristic of an *arahant*, as it ensures complete freedom. One could be said to have attained complete freedom only if one's mind is free from these influxes. It is because these influxes are capable of creating intoxication again and again.

The immense importance of the extinction of influxes, and how it accounts for the worthiness of an *arahant*, is sometimes clearly brought out. The ultimate aim of the Buddha's teaching is one that in other systems of thought is generally regarded as attainable only after death. The Buddha, on the other hand, showed a way to its realization here and now.

As a matter of fact, even brahmins like Pokkharasāti went about saying that it is impossible for a human being to attain something supramundane: *Katham'hi nāma manussabhūto uttarimanussadhammā alamariyañāṇadassanavisesaṃ ñassati vā dakkhati vā sacchi vā karissati?*[22] "How can one as a human being know or see or realize a supramundane state, an extraordinary knowledge and vision befitting the noble ones?" They thought that such a realization is possible only after death. Immortality, in other systems of thought, is always an after death experience.

Now the realization of the extinction of influxes, on the other hand, gives a certain assurance about the future. It is by this extinction of influxes that one wins to the certitude that there is no

---

22 M II 200, *Subhasutta*.

more birth after this. *Khīṇā jāti,*[23] extinct is birth! Certitude about something comes only with realization. In fact, the term *sacchikiriya* implies a seeing with one's own eyes, as the word for eye, *akśi*, is implicit in it.

However, everything cannot be verified by seeing with one's own eyes. The Buddha has pointed out that there are four ways of realization or verification:

> *Cattāro me, bhikkhave, sacchikaraṇīyā dhammā. Katame cattaro? Atthi, bhikkhave, dhammā kāyena sacchikaraṇīyā; atthi, bhikkhave, dhammā satiyā sacchikaraṇīyā; atthi, bhikkhave, dhammā cakkhunā sacchikaraṇīyā; atthi, bhikkhave, dhammā paññāya sacchikaraṇīyā.*[24]
>
> "Monks, there are these four realizable things. What four? There are things, monks, that are realizable through the body; there are things, monks, that are realizable through memory; there are things, monks, that are realizable through the eye; there are things, monks, that are realizable through wisdom."

By way of explanation, the Buddha says that the things realizable through the body are the eight deliverances, the things realizable through memory are one's former habitations, the things realizable through the eye are the death and rebirth of beings, and what is realizable through wisdom, is the extinction of influxes.

One's former lives cannot be seen with one's own eyes by running into the past. It is possible only by purifying one's memory and directing it backwards. Similarly, the death and rebirth of beings can be seen, as if with one's fleshly eye, by the divine eye, by those who have developed it. So also the fact of extirpating all

---

[23] E.g. at D I 84, *Sāmaññaphalasutta*.

[24] A II 182, *Sacchikaraṇīyasutta*.

influxes is to be realized by wisdom, and not by any other means. The fact that the influxes of sensuality, existence, ignorance, and views, will not flow in again, can be verified only by wisdom. That is why special mention is made of *Nibbāna* as something realizable.[25]

Because *Nibbāna* is said to be something realizable, some are of the opinion that nothing should be predicated about it. What is the reason for this special emphasis on its realizability? It is to bring into sharp relief the point of divergence, since the Buddha taught a way of realizing here and now something that in other religions was considered impossible.

What was it that they regarded impossible to be realized? The cessation of existence, or *bhavanirodha*. How can one be certain here and now that this existence has ceased? This might sometimes appear as a big puzzle. But all the same, the *arahant* experiences the cessation of existence as a realization. That is why he even gives expression to it as: *Bhavanirodho Nibbānaṃ*,[26] "cessation of existence is *Nibbāna*."

It comes about by this extinction of influxes. The very existence of 'existence' is especially due to the flowing in of influxes of existence. What is called 'existence' is not the apparent process of existing visible to others. It is something that pertains to one's own mental continuum.

For instance, when it is said that some person is in the world of sense desires, one might sometimes imagine it as living surrounded by objects of sense pleasure. But that is not always the case. It is the existence in a world of sense desires, built up by sensuous thoughts. It is the same with the realms of form and formless realms. Even those realms can be experienced and attained while living in this world itself.

---

25 A I 159, *Nibbutasutta*.

26 A V 9, *Sāriputtasutta*.

Similarly, it is possible for one to realize the complete cessation of this existence while living in this very world. It is accomplished by winning to the realization that the influxes of sense desires, existence, and ignorance, no longer influence one's mind.

So all this goes to show the high degree of importance attached to the word *āsava*. The *Sammādiṭṭhisutta* of the *Majjhima Nikāya* seems to pose a problem regarding the significance of this term. At one place in the *sutta* it is said that the arising of ignorance is due to the arising of influxes and that the cessation of ignorance is due to the cessation of influxes: *Āsavasamudayā avijjāsamudayo, āsavanirodhā avijjānirodho.*[27]

If the *sutta* says only this much, it will not be such a problem, because it appears as a puzzle to many nowadays, why ignorance is placed first. Various reasons are adduced and arguments put forward as to why it is stated first out of the twelve factors. The fact that there is still something to precede it could therefore be some consolation.

But then, a little way off, in the selfsame *sutta*, we read: *Avijjāsamudayā āsavasamudayo, avijjanirodhā āsavanirodho,*[28] "With the arising of ignorance is the arising of influxes, with the cessation of ignorance is the cessation of influxes." Apparently this contradicts the previous statement. The preacher of this discourse, Venerable Sāriputta, is not one who contradicts himself. So most probably there is some deep reason behind this.

Another problem crops up, since ignorance is also counted among the different kinds of influxes. This makes our puzzle all the more deep. But this state of affairs could best be understood with the help of an illustration. It is in order to explain a certain fascinating behaviour of the mind that even *arahants* of great wisdom had to make seemingly contradictory statements.

---

[27] M I 54, *Sammādiṭṭhisutta*.

[28] M I 55, *Sammādiṭṭhisutta*.

We have to draw in at this juncture a very important discourse in the *Saṃyutta Nikāya*, which is a marvel in itself. It comes in the section on the aggregates, *Khandhasaṃyutta*, as the second *Gaddulasutta*. Here the Buddha makes the following impressive declaration:

> *'Diṭṭhaṃ vo, bhikkhave, caraṇaṃ nāma cittan'ti?' 'Evaṃ, bhante.' 'Tampi kho, bhikkhave, caraṇaṃ nāma cittaṃ citteneva cintitaṃ. Tenapi kho, bhikkhave, caraṇena cittena cittaññeva cittataraṃ. Tasmātiha, bhikkhave, abhikkhaṇaṃ sakaṃ cittaṃ paccavekkhitabbaṃ: Dīgharattam idaṃ cittaṃ saṃkiliṭṭhaṃ rāgena dosena mohenā'ti. Cittasaṃkilesā, bhikkhave, sattā saṃkilissanti, cittavodānā sattā visujjhanti.*
>
> *'Nāhaṃ, bhikkhave, aññaṃ ekanikāyampi samanupassāmi evaṃ cittaṃ, yathayidaṃ, bhikkhave, tiracchānagatā pāṇā. Tepi kho, bhikkhave, tiracchānagatā pāṇā citteneva cintitā. Tehipi kho, bhikkhave, tiracchānagatehi pāṇehi cittaññeva cittataraṃ. Tasmātiha, bhikkhave, bhikkhunā abhikkhaṇaṃ sakaṃ cittaṃ paccavekkhitabbaṃ: Dīgharattam idaṃ cittaṃ saṃkiliṭṭhaṃ rāgena dosena mohenā'ti. Cittasaṃkilesā, bhikkhave, sattā saṃkilissanti, cittavodānā sattā visujjhanti.'*[29]
>
> "'Monks, have you seen a picture called a movie (*caraṇa*)?' 'Yes, Lord.' 'Monks, even that picture called a movie is something thought out by the mind. But this mind, monks, is more picturesque than that picture called a movie. Therefore, monks, you should reflect moment to moment on your own mind with the thought: For a long time has this mind been defiled by lust, hate, and delusion.

---

[29] S III 151, *Gaddulasutta*.

By the defilement of the mind, monks, are beings defiled. By the purification of the mind, are beings purified.

"'Monks, I do not see any other class of beings as picturesque as beings in the animal realm. But those beings in the animal realm, monks, are also thought out by the mind. And the mind, monks, is far more picturesque than those beings in the animal realm. Therefore, monks, should a monk reflect moment to moment on one's own mind with the thought: For a long time has this mind been defiled by lust, hate, and delusion. By the defilement of the mind, monks, are beings defiled. By the purification of the mind, are beings purified.'"

Here the Buddha gives two illustrations to show how marvelous this mind is. First he asks the monks whether they have seen a picture called *caraṇa*. Though the word may be rendered by movie, it is not a motion picture of the sort we have today. According to the commentary, it is some kind of variegated painting done on a mobile canvas-chamber, illustrative of the results of good and evil karma.[30] Whatever it may be, it seems to have been something marvelous. But far more marvelous, according to the Buddha, is this mind. The reason given is that even such a picture is something thought out by the mind.

Then, by way of an advice to the monks, says the Buddha: 'Therefore, monks, you should reflect on your mind moment to moment with the thought: For a long time this mind has been defiled by lust, hate, and delusion.' The moral drawn is that beings are defiled by the defilement of their minds and that they are purified by the purification of their minds. This is the illustration by the simile of the picture.

---

[30] Spk II 327.

And then the Buddha goes on to make another significant declaration: 'Monks, I do not see any other class of beings as picturesque as beings in the animal realm.' But since those beings also are thought out by the mind, he declares that the mind is far more picturesque than them. Based on this conclusion, he repeats the same advice as before.

At first sight the *sutta*, when it refers to a picture, seems to be speaking about the man who drew it. But there is something deeper than that. When the Buddha says that the picture called *caraṇa* is also something thought out by the mind, he is not simply stating the fact that the artist drew it after thinking it out with his mind. The reference is rather to the mind of the one who sees it. He, who sees it, regards it as something marvelous. He creates a picture out of it. He imagines something picturesque in it.

In fact, the allusion is not to the artist's mind, but to the spectator's mind. It is on account of the three defilements lust, hate, and delusion, nurtured in his mind for a long time, that he is able to appreciate and enjoy that picture. Such is the nature of those influxes.

That is why the Buddha declared that this mind is far more picturesque than the picture in question. So if one turns back to look at one's own mind, in accordance with the Buddha's advice, it will be a wonderful experience, like watching a movie. Why? Because reflection reveals the most marvelous sight in the world.

But usually one does not like to reflect, because one has to turn back to do so. One is generally inclined to look at the thing in front. However, the Buddha advises us to turn back and look at one's own mind every moment. Why? Because the mind is more marvelous than that picture called *caraṇa*, or movie.

It is the same declaration that he makes with reference to the beings in the animal realm. When one comes to think about it, there is even less room for doubt here, than in the case of the picture. First of all, the Buddha declares that there is no class of beings more picturesque than those in the animal realm. But he follows it up with the statement that even those beings are thought out by the mind, to draw the conclusion that as such the mind is more picturesque than those beings of the animal realm.

Let us try to sort out the point of this declaration. Generally, we may agree that beings in the animal realm are the most picturesque. We sometimes say that the butterfly is beautiful. But we might hesitate to call a blue fly beautiful. The tiger is fierce, but the cat is not. Here one's personal attitude accounts much for the concepts of beauty, ugliness, fierceness, and innocence of animals. It is because of the defiling influence of influxes, such as ignorance, that the world around us appears so picturesque.

Based on this particular *sutta*, with its reference to the *caraṇa* picture as a prototype, we may take a peep at the modern day's movie film, by way of an analogy. It might facilitate the understanding of the teachings on *paṭicca samuppāda* and *Nibbāna* in a way that is closer to our everyday life. The principles governing the film and the drama are part and parcel of the life outside cinema and the theatre. But since it is generally difficult to grasp them in the context of the life outside, we shall now try to elucidate them with reference to the cinema and the theatre.

Usually a film or a drama is shown at night. The reason for it is the presence of darkness. This darkness helps to bring out the darkness of ignorance that dwells in the minds of beings. So the film as well as the drama is presented to the public within a framework of darkness. If a film is shown at day time, as a matinee show, it necessitates closed windows and dark curtains. In this way, films and dramas are shown within a curtained enclosure.

There is another strange thing about these films and dramas. One goes to the cinema or the theatre saying: "I am going to see a film show, I am going to see a drama." And one returns saying: "I have seen a film show, I have seen a drama." But while the film show or the drama is going on, one forgets that one is seeing a show or a drama.

Such a strange spell of delusion takes over. This is due to the intoxicating influence of influxes. If one wishes to enjoy a film show or a drama, one should be prepared to get intoxicated by it. Otherwise it will cease to be a film show or a drama for him.

What do the film producers and dramatists do? They prepare the background for eliciting the influxes of ignorance, latent in the minds of the audience. That is why such shows and performances are held at night, or else dark curtains are employed. They have an intricate job to do. Within the framework of darkness, they have to create a delusion in the minds of their audience, so as to enact some story in a realistic manner.

To be successful, a film or a drama has to be given a touch of realism. Though fictitious, it should be apparently real for the audience. There is an element of deception involved, a hoodwink. For this touch of realism, quite a lot of make-up on the part of actors and actresses is necessary. As a matter of fact, in the ancient Indian society, one of the primary senses of the word *saṅkhāra* was the make-up done by actors and actresses.

Now in the present context, *saṅkhāra* can include not only this make-up in personal appearance, but also the acting itself, the delineation of character, stage-craft, etc. In this way, the film producers and dramatists create a suitable environment, making use of the darkness and the make-up contrivances. These are the *saṅkhāras*, or the 'preparations.'

However, to be more precise, it is the audience that make preparations, in the last analysis. Here too, as before, we are compelled to make a statement that might appear strange: So far not a single cinema has held a film show and not a single theatre has staged a drama.

And yet, those who had gone to the cinema and the theatre had seen film shows and dramas. Now, how can that be? Usually, we think that it is the film producer who produced the film and that it is the dramatist who made the drama.

But if we are to understand the deeper implications of what the Buddha declared, with reference to the picture *caraṇa*, a film show or drama is produced, in the last analysis, by the spectator himself. When he goes to the cinema and the theatre, he takes with him the spices needed to concoct a film or a drama, and that is: the influxes, or *āsavas*. Whatever technical defects and shortcomings there are in them, he makes good with his influxes.

As we know, in a drama there is a certain interval between two scenes. But the average audience is able to appreciate even such a drama, because they are influenced by the influxes of sense desire, existence, and ignorance.

With the progress in science and technology, scenes are made to fall on the screen with extreme rapidity. All the same, the element of delusion is still there. The purpose is to create the necessary environment for arousing delusion in the minds of the audience. Whatever preparations others may make, if the audience does not respond with their own preparations along the same lines, the drama will not be a success. But in general, the worldlings have a tendency to prepare and concoct, so they would make up for any shortcomings in the film or the drama with their own preparations and enjoy them.

Now, for instance, let us think of an occasion when a film show is going on within the framework of darkness. In the case of a matinee show, doors and windows will have to be closed. Supposing the doors are suddenly flung open, while a vivid technicolour scene is flashing on the screen, what happens then? The spectators will find themselves suddenly thrown out of the cinema world they had created for themselves. Why? Because the scene in technicolour has now lost its colour. It has faded away. The result is dejection, disenchantment. The film show loses its significance.

That film show owed its existence to the dark framework of ignorance and the force of preparations. But now that the framework has broken down, such a vast change has come over, resulting in a disenchantment. Now the word *rāga* has a nuance suggestive of colour, so *virāga*, dispassion, can also literally mean a fading away or a decolouration. Here we have a possible instance of *nibbidā virāga*, disenchantment, dispassion, at least in a limited sense.

A door suddenly flung open can push aside the delusion, at least temporarily. Let us consider the implications of this little event. The film show, in this case, ceases to be a film show because of a flash of light coming from outside. Now, what would have happened if this flash of light had come from within – from within one's mind? Then also something similar would have happened. If the light of wisdom dawns on one's mind while watching a film show or a drama, one would even wonder whether it is actually a film or a drama, while others are enjoying it.

Speaking about the film show, we mentioned above that the spectator has entered into a world of his own creation. If we are to analyse this situation according to the law of dependent origination, we may add that in fact he has a consciousness and a name-and-form in line with the events of the story, based on the preparations in the midst of the darkness of ignorance. With all his experiences in seeing the film show, he is building up his five aggregates.

Therefore, when the light of wisdom comes and dispels the darkness of ignorance, a similar event can occur. One will come out of that plane of existence. One will step out of the world of sense desires, at least temporarily.

Now, with regard to the *arahants*, too, the same trend of events holds good. When their ignorance ceases, leaving no residue, *avijjāya tveva asesavirāganirodhā*, exhausting the influxes as well, preparations also cease. Why? Because the preparations owe their existence to ignorance. They have the ability to prepare so long as there is ignorance. *Saṅkhāra* generally means preparations. It is the make-up and the make-believe which accounted for the delusion. The darkness of ignorance provided the setting for it. If somehow or other, the light of wisdom enters the scene, those preparations, *saṅkhāra*, became no-preparations, *visaṅkhāra*, and the prepared, *saṅkhata*, becomes a non-prepared, *asaṅkhata*.

So what was true with regard to the film show, is also true, in a deeper sense, with regard to the events leading up to the attainment of *arahant*-hood. With the dawn of that light of wisdom, the preparations, or *saṅkhāra*, lose their significance and become *visaṅkhāra*.

Though for the world outside they appear as preparations, for the *arahant* they are not preparations, because they do not prepare a *bhava*, or existence, for him. They are made ineffective. Similarly, the prepared or the made-up, when it is understood as something prepared or made-up, becomes an un-prepared or an un-made. There is a subtle principle of un-doing involved in this.

Sometimes, this might be regarded as a modernistic interpretation. But there is Canonical evidence in support of such an interpretation. For instance, in the *Dvayatānupassanāsutta* of the *Sutta Nipāta*, we come across the following verse:

Nivutānaṃ tamo hoti,
andhakāro apassataṃ,
satañca vivaṭaṃ hoti,
āloko passatāmiva,
santike na vijānanti,
magā dhammassa akovidā.[31]

"Murk it is to those enveloped,
As darkness unto the undiscerning,
But to the good wide ope' it is,
As light is unto those discerning,
So near, and yet they know not,
Fools, unskilled in the Norm."

It is all murky to those enveloped by the hindrance of ignorance, like the darkness for those who are unable to see. But for the noble ones, it is visible like an open space, even as the light to those with vision. Though it is near at hand, fools, inexpert in the *Dhamma*, do not understand. This same impression of the Buddha comes up again in the following verse in the *Udāna*:

Mohasambandhano loko,
bhabbarūpo va dissati,

[31] Sn 763, *Dvayatānupassanāsutta*.

upadhibandhano bālo,
tamasā parivārito,
sassatoriva khāyati,
passato n'atthi kiñcanaṃ.[32]

"The world, enfettered to delusion,
Feigns a promising mien,
The fool, to his assets bound,
Sees only darkness around,
It looks as though it would last,
But to him who sees there is naught."

The world appears as real to one who is fettered to delusion. He imagines it to be reliable. And so the fool, relying on his assets, is encompassed by the darkness. To him the world appears as eternal. But the one who has the right vision, knows that in reality there is nothing.

All this goes to show that the life outside is not much different from what goes on within the four walls of the cinema and the theatre. Just as, in the latter case, an enjoyable story is created out of a multitude of scenes, relayed at varying degrees of rapidity, backed by the delusive make-up of actors and actresses, so that one may lose oneself in a world of fantasy, even so, according to the point of view of *Dhamma*, the lifestyle outside is something made up and concocted.

However, the darkness within is much thicker than the darkness outside. The darkness outside may be dispelled even by a door flung open, as we saw above. But not so easily the darkness within. That is why, in the psalms of the *Theras* and *Therīs*, it is said that they split or burst asunder the mass of delusion,

32 Ud 79, *Udenasutta*.

tamokkhandhaṃ padāliya, tamokkhandhaṃ padālayiṃ.[33] The pitchy black darkness of ignorance in the world is one that is thick enough to be split up and burst asunder. So it seems, the darkness within is almost tangibly thick. But the first incision on this thick curtain of darkness is made by the path knowledge of the Stream-winner.

As a side-light, we may cite an episode from the lives of the Venerables Sāriputta and *Mahā* Moggalāna, the two chief disciples of the Buddha. Formerly, as brahmin youths, they were known as Upatissa and Kolita. These two young men once went to see a hilltop festival, called *giraggasamajja.*[34] Since by then, their discerning wisdom was already matured, they suddenly developed a dejection about the entertainment going on. The hilltop festival, as it were, lost its festivity for them. They understood the vanity of it and could no longer enjoy it as before.

They may have already had a distant glimpse of the similarity between the two levels of experience, mentioned above. But they on their own could not get at the principles underlying the delusion involved.

Much later, as a wandering ascetic, when Upatissa met the Venerable Assaji *Thera* on his alms-round, he begged the latter to preach the *Dhamma* to him. Venerable Assaji said: "I know only a little." Upatissa also assured him: "I need only a little." Venerable Assaji preached 'a little' and Upatissa, too, heard 'a little,' but since there was much in it, the latter attained the Fruit of Stream-winning even on hearing the first two lines of the following verse:

Ye dhammā hetuppabhavā,
tesam hetuṃ Tathāgato āha,

---

[33] Th 627, *Sunīto Thero*; Thī 3, *Puṇṇā Therī*; Thī 28, *Cittā Therī*; Thī 44, *Uttamā Therī*; Thī 120, *Tiṃsamattā Therī*; Thī 173-174, *Vijayā Therī*; Thī 180, *Uttarā Therī*.

[34] Dhp-a I 88.

tesañca yo nirodho,
evaṃ vādi mahāsamaṇo.[35]

"Of things that proceed from a cause,
Their cause the *Tathāgata* has told,
And also their cessation,
Thus teaches the great ascetic."

The verse gives in a nutshell the law of dependent arising. From it, Upatissa got the clue to his riddle of life.

Some interpret the word *hetu*, cause, in this verse, as *avijjā*, or ignorance, the first link. But that is not the case. It refers to the basic principle known as *idappaccayatā*, the relatedness of this to that.[36] *Hetuppabhavā dhammā* is a reference to things dependently arisen. In point of fact, it is said about a Stream-winner that he has seen well the cause as well as the things arisen from a cause: *Hetu ca sudiṭṭho, hetusamuppanā ca dhammā.*[37] That means that he has seen the law of dependent arising as also the dependently arisen phenomena.

We have already discussed the significance of these two terms.[38] What is called *paṭicca samuppāda* is the basic principle itself. It is said that the wandering ascetic Upatissa was able to arouse the path of Stream-winning on hearing just the first two lines,[39] and these state the basic principle as such.

The word *tesaṃ*, plural, clearly implies that the reference is to all the twelve factors, inclusive of ignorance. The cessation, also, is of those twelve, as for instance it is said in the *Udāna*: *Khayaṃ*

---

35 Vin I 40.

36 *Idappaccayatā* is discussed in detail above, see sermon 2.

37 A III 440, *CatutthaAbhabbaṭṭhānasutta.*

38 See sermon 2.

39 Sp-ṭ III 226 (Burmese ed.)

paccayānaṃ avedi,[40] "understood the cessation of conditions," since all the twelve are conditions.

To sum up: Whatever phenomena that arise from a cause, their cause is *idappaccayatā*, or the law of relatedness of this to that.

> This being, this exists,
> With the arising of this, this arises.
> This not being, this does not exist,
> With the cessation of this, this ceases.

And then the cessation of things arisen from a cause is ultimately *Nibbāna* itself. That is the implication of the oft recurrent phrase *avijjāya tveva asesavirāganirodhā,*[41] "with the complete fading away and cessation of that very ignorance."

So then, from this discussion it should be clear that our illustration with the help of the simile of the cinema and the theatre is of much relevance to an understanding of the law of dependent arising. With this much, we shall wind up today.

---

[40] Ud 2, *DutiyaBodhisutta.*

[41] M I 263, *MahāTaṇhāsaṅkhayasutta.*

Nibbāna Sermon 6

Namo tassa Bhagavato Arahato Sammāsambuddhassa
Namo tassa Bhagavato Arahato Sammāsambuddhassa
Namo tassa Bhagavato Arahato Sammāsambuddhassa

Etaṃ santaṃ, etaṃ paṇītaṃ, yadidaṃ sabbasaṅkhārasamatho sabbūpadhipaṭinissaggo taṇhakkhayo virāgo nirodho nibbānaṃ.[1]

"This is peaceful, this is excellent, namely the stilling of all preparations, the relinquishment of all assets, the destruction of craving, detachment, cessation, extinction."

With the permission of the Most Venerable Great Preceptor and the assembly of the venerable meditative monks.

In our last sermon, we happened to discuss how the concept of existence built up with the help of ignorance and influxes, comes to cease with the cessation of ignorance and influxes.[2] We explained it by means of similes and illustrations, based on the film show and the drama. As the starting point, we took up the simile of the picture called *caraṇa*, which the Buddha had made use of in the *Gaddulasutta* of the *Saṃyutta Nikāya*.[3] With reference to a picture called *caraṇa*, popular in contemporary India, the Buddha has declared that the mind is more picturesque than that *caraṇa* picture. As an adaptation of that *caraṇa* picture for the modern

---

1 M I 436, *MahāMālunkyasutta*.

2 See sermon 5.

3 S III 151, see sermon 5.

day, we referred to the movie film and the drama in connection with our discussion of *saṅkhāras* in particular and *paṭicca samuppāda* in general. Today, let us try to move a little forward in the same direction.

In the latter part of the same *Gaddulasutta* of the *Saṃyutta Nikāya*, *Khandhasaṃyutta*, the Buddha gives a simile of a painter.[4] Translated it would read as follows: "Just as a dyer or a painter would fashion the likeness of a woman or of a man, complete in all its major and minor parts, on a well planed board, or a wall, or on a strip of cloth, with dye or lac or turmeric or indigo or madder, even so the untaught worldling creates, as it were, his own form, feelings, perceptions, preparations, and consciousness."

What the Buddha wants to convey to us by this comparison of the five grasping groups to an artefact done by a painter, is the insubstantiality and the vanity of those five groups. It brings out their compound and made-up nature. This essencelessness and emptiness is more clearly expressed in the *Pheṇapiṇḍūpamasutta* of the *Khandhasaṃyutta*. The summary verse at the end of that discourse would suffice for the present:

> *Pheṇapiṇḍūpamaṃ rūpaṃ,*
> *vedanā bubbuḷūpamā,*
> *marīcikūpamā saññā,*
> *saṅkhārā kadalūpamā,*
> *māyūpamañca viññāṇaṃ,*
> *dīpitādiccabandhunā.*[5]

It says that the Buddha, the kinsman of the sun, has compared form to a mass of foam, feeling to a water bubble, perception to a mirage, preparations to a banana trunk, and consciousness to a magic show. These five similes bring out the insubstantiality of the

---

[4] S III 152, *Gaddulasutta*.

[5] S III 142, *Pheṇapiṇḍūpamasutta*.

five grasping groups. Their simulating and deceptive nature is indicated by the similes. Not only the magic show, but even the other similes, like the mass of foam, are suggestive of simulation, in giving a false notion of compactness. They all convey the idea of insubstantiality and deceptiveness. Consciousness in particular, is described in that context as a conjurer's trick.

In the course of our discussion we happened to touch upon the significance of *saṅkhāras*, or preparations. As far as their relevance to films and dramas is concerned, they impart an appearance of reality to 'parts' and 'acts' which make up a film or a drama. Realism, in the context of art and drama, amounts to an apparent reality. It connotes the skill in deceiving the audience. It is, in fact, only a show of reality. The successful drama is one that effectively hoodwinks an audience. So realism, in that context, means appearing as real. It therefore has a nuance of deception.

Now what supports this deceptive and delusive quality of preparations is ignorance. All this 'acting' that is going on in the world is kept up by ignorance, which provides the background for it. Just as, in a drama, such preparations as change of dress, make-up contrivances, character portrayal, and stage-craft, create an atmosphere of delusion, so also are the *saṅkhāras*, or preparations, instrumental in building up these five grasping groups. So all this goes to show that the term *saṇkhāra* has the sense of preparing or producing. The realistic appearance of a film or a drama is capable of creating a delusion in an audience. Similarly, the apparent reality of the animate and inanimate objects in the world, creates delusion in the worldlings.

Now to hark back to two lines of a verse we had quoted earlier, *mohasambandhano loko, bhabbarūpo va dissati*,[6] "The world appears as real to one who is fettered to delusion." This means that the world has an apparent reality, that it merely gives the impression of something real to one who is deluded. It is clear, therefore,

---

6 Ud 79, *Udenasutta*, see sermon 5.

that *saṅkhāras* are responsible for some sort of preparation or concoction. What serves as the background for it, is the darkness of ignorance. This preparation, this concoction goes on, behind the veil of ignorance.

We come across a discourse in the *Saṃyutta Nikāya*, in which this primary sense of preparation in the word *saṅkhāra* is explicitly stated, namely the *Khajjanīyasutta*. In that discourse, each of the five grasping groups is defined, and the term *saṅkhāra* is defined as follows:

> *Kiñca, bhikkhave, saṅkhāre vadetha? Saṅkhatam abhisaṅkharontī'ti kho, bhikkhave, tasmā 'saṅkhārā'ti vuccanti. Kiñca saṅkhatam abhisaṅkharonti? Rūpaṃ rūpattāya saṅkhatam abhisaṅkharonti, vedanaṃ vedanattāya saṅkhatam abhisaṅkharonti, saññaṃ saññattāya saṅkhatam abhisaṅkharonti, saṅkhāre saṅkhārattāya saṅkhatam abhisaṅkharonti, viññāṇaṃ viññāṇattāya saṅkhatam abhisaṅkharonti. Saṅkhatam abhisaṅkharontī'ti kho, bhikkhave, tasmā 'saṅkhārā'ti vuccanti.*[7]

> "And what, monks, would you say are 'preparations?' They prepare the prepared – that, monks, is why they are called preparations. And what is the prepared that they prepare? They prepare, as a prepared, form into the state of form, they prepare, as a prepared, feeling into the state of feeling, they prepare, as a prepared, perception into the state of perception, they prepare, as a prepared, preparations into the state of preparations, they prepare, as a prepared, consciousness into the state of consciousness. They prepare the prepared, so, that is why, monks, they are called preparations."

---

[7] S III 87, *Khajjanīyasutta*.

This explains why *saṅkhāras* are so called. That is to say, the sense in which they are called *saṅkhāras*. They prepare the prepared, *saṅkhata*, into that state. And the prepared is form, feeling, perception, preparations, and consciousness. *Saṅkhāras* are therefore instrumental in building up each of these grasping groups. The most intriguing statement is that even the *saṅkhāras* are built up by *saṅkhāras*. They play the part of preparing a sort of make-believe activity. In this sense it is associated with the idea of intention, as being produced by intention.

The two terms *abhisaṅkhataṃ abhisañcetayitaṃ* are often found in juxtaposition, as if they are synonymous.[8] *Abhisaṅkhata* means 'specially prepared,' and *abhisañcetayitaṃ* means 'thought out' or 'intended.' Here we see the relationship of *saṅkhāras* to intention. The preparation is done by means of intentions. The two words *ceteti pakappeti* are also found used together.[9] Intention and imagination play their part in this matter of preparation. So in the last analysis, it is something constructed by imagination. All of these five groups are thought-constructs. As suggested by the similes of the picture and the painter, these five groups, in the final reckoning, turn out to be the products of imagination.

As far as the nature of these preparations is concerned, there are these three kinds of preparations mentioned in the *Dhamma*, namely *kāyasaṅkhāra, vacīsaṅkhāra*, and *manosaṅkhāra*, bodily preparations, verbal preparations, and mental preparations.[10] These terms have to do with merit and demerit. They are cited in connection with *kamma*, implying that beings accumulate *kamma* by means of body, word and mind.

What supports this heaping up of preparations is ignorance. Ignorance provides the background, as in the case of the drama and the movie. This relationship between ignorance and prepara-

---

[8] E.g. at M I 350, *Aṭṭhakanāgarasutta*.

[9] E.g. at S II 65, *Cetanāsutta*.

[10] E.g. at A I 122, *Saṅkhārasutta*.

tions is clearly brought out in the *Cetanāsutta* of the *Sañcetaniyavagga* of the *Aṅguttara Nikāya.*[11] According to that *sutta*, the world attributes an activity to something by regarding it as a unit – by perceiving it as a compact unit. In other words, it is the way of the world to superimpose the concept of a unit or self-agency to wherever there appears to be some sort of activity. As we mentioned in connection with the simile of the whirlpool, viewed from a distance, the whirlpool appears as a centre or a base.[12] In the same way, wherever there appears to be some form of activity, we tend to bring in the concept of a unit.

Now it is this very ignorance, this 'ignoring,' that becomes the seed-bed for preparations. The basic presumption of this ignorance is that preparations must originate from a unitary centre. And the Buddha also points out, in the *Cetanāsutta* of the *Sañcetaniya-vagga*, that the root cause of bodily, verbal, and mental preparations, is ignorance.[13] Since the discourse is rather lengthy, we propose to analyse it in three sections, for facility of understanding.

> *Kāye vā, bhikkhave, sati kāyasañcetanāhetu uppajjati ajjhattaṃ sukhadukkhaṃ. Vācāya vā, bhikkhave, sati vācīsañcetanāhetu uppajjati ajjhattaṃ sukhadukkhaṃ. Mane vā, bhikkhave, sati manosañcetanāhetu uppajjati ajjhattaṃ sukhadukkhaṃ avijjāpaccayā va.*

> "Monks, when the body is there, due to bodily intention, there arises inward pleasure and pain. Monks, when speech is there, due to verbal intention, there arises inward pleasure and pain. Monks, when mind is there, due to

---

[11] A II 157, *Cetanāsutta.*

[12] See sermon 2.

[13] A II 157, *Cetanāsutta.*

mental intention, there arises inward pleasure and pain, all conditioned by ignorance."

Now let us take this as the first section and try to get at its meaning. Given the concept of a body, due to intentions based on that concept of a body, there arises inwardly pleasure and pain. That is, when one imagines that there is a body, due to thoughts which take body as their object, one experiences pleasure and pain. What is called 'the body,' is a huge mass of activity, something like a big workshop or a factory. But because of ignorance, if one takes it as one thing, that is as a unit, then there is room for bodily intention to come in. One can objectify the body and arouse thoughts of the body. Thereby one experiences pleasure and pain. This is the implication of the above statement.

Similarly, in the case of speech, it may be said that language is a conglomeration of letters and words. But when speech is taken as a real unit, one can form intentions about speech and inwardly experience pleasure and pain. So also in the case of the mind. It is not an entity by itself, like a soul, as postulated by other religions. It is again only a heap of thoughts. But if one grants that there is a mind, due to that very presumption, one experiences inwardly pleasure and pain with mind as its object. The concluding phrase of that paragraph is particularly significant. It says that all this is conditioned by ignorance.

Let us now take up the second part:

> *Sāmaṃ vā taṃ, bhikkhave, kāyasaṅkhāraṃ abhisaṅkharoti, yaṃ paccayāssa taṃ uppajjati ajjhattaṃ sukhadukkhaṃ. Pare vāssa taṃ, bhikkhave, kāyasaṅkhāraṃ abhisaṅkharonti, yaṃ paccayāssa taṃ uppajjati ajjhattaṃ sukhadukkhaṃ. Sampajāno vā taṃ, bhikkhave, kāyasaṅkhāraṃ abhisaṅkharoti, yaṃ paccayāssa taṃ uppajjati ajjhattaṃ sukhadukkhaṃ. Asampajāno vā taṃ, bhikkhave, kāyasaṅkhāraṃ abhisaṅkharoti, yaṃ paccayāssa taṃ uppajjati ajjhattaṃ sukhadukkhaṃ.*

> "Either he himself prepares that bodily preparation, owing to which there would be that inward pleasure and pain. Or else others prepare for him that bodily preparation, owing to which there would be for him inward pleasure and pain. Either he, being fully aware, prepares that bodily preparation, owing to which there would be for him inward pleasure and pain. Or else he, being fully unaware, prepares that bodily preparation, owing to which there would be for him that inward pleasure and pain."

The substance of this paragraph seems to be that one by oneself prepares the bodily preparation that brings one pleasure or pain inwardly and that others also prepare for him such a bodily preparation. It is also said that the bodily preparation can occur either with or without awareness. About the verbal and mental preparations too, a similar specification is made. This is the summary of the second section.

The third and final section is the most significant:

> *Imesu, bhikkhave, dhammesu avijjā anupatitā. Avijjāya tveva asesavirāganirodhā so kāyo na hoti yaṃ paccayāssa taṃ uppajjati ajjhattaṃ sukhadukkhaṃ, sā vācā na hoti yaṃ paccayāssa taṃ uppajjati ajjhattaṃ sukhadukkhaṃ, so mano na hoti yaṃ paccayāssa taṃ uppajjati ajjhattaṃ sukhadukkhaṃ, khettaṃ taṃ na hoti, vatthum taṃ na hoti, āyatanaṃ taṃ na hoti, adhikaraṇaṃ taṃ na hoti, yaṃ paccayāssa taṃ uppajjati ajjhattaṃ sukhadukkhaṃ.*

> "Monks, in all these cases, ignorance hangs on. But with the remainderless fading away and cessation of ignorance, that body is not there, owing to which there can arise for him inward pleasure or pain, that speech is not there, owing to which there can arise for him inward pleasure and pain, that mind is not there, owing to which there can arise for him inward pleasure and pain. That field is not there, that site is not there, that base is not there, that reason is

> not there, owing to which there can arise for him inward pleasure or pain."

Since all the instances mentioned earlier are accompanied by ignorance, the utter fading away and cessation of that very ignorance prevents, as it were, the crystallization of that body, speech, and mind, due to which inward pleasure and pain can arise. In other words, it removes the field, the ground, the base and the provenance for the arising of inward pleasure and pain.

This shows that, once the existence of a body is granted, with that concept of a body as its object, bodily preparations come to be built up. Or, in other words, given the concept of a body, and due to bodily intention, that is by treating it as a real unit, one experiences inwardly pleasure and pain because of thoughts concerning the body.

So also in regard to speech and mind. It is emphatically stated that all this occurs because of ignorance. What confers on them all the status of a unit, through the perception of the compact, is this very ignorance. As for the second paragraph, what it says is simply that those bodily preparations and the like can be made by oneself as well as by others, and that too either being aware or unaware.

Now all these are related to ignorance. Therefore, at whatever point of time this ignorance ceases completely in someone, then for him there is no consciousness of a body, though from an outside point of view he appears to have a body. He may use words, he may speak, but for him there is nothing substantial in linguistic usage. He seems to be making use of a mind, mind-objects also come up, but he does not regard it as a unit. Therefore, inwardly, no pleasures and pains come up.

With the cessation of ignorance comes the cessation of preparations. Thereby all pleasures and pains cease. This, in other words, is the state of *Nibbāna*. It appears, then, that this discourse gives us a clue to the state of *Nibbāna*. It says something about bodily, verbal, and mental preparations.

If we try to understand its message in relation to the analogy of the film show and the drama, mentioned earlier, we may offer the following explanation: Now in the case of a film show or a drama, the preparations remain as preparations so long as there is that darkness of ignorance. The realism or the realistic appearance of the acting of actors and actresses, or the roles and guises they assume in dress and speech, depends on the veil of ignorance that conceals their true nature.

Similarly, here too, the implication is that it is ignorance which invests these preparations with the realistic appearance. If at any point of time that ignorance happens to cease, then there will be no pleasure or displeasure for the audience, however much make-up and pretension there is.

It is such a situation of non-enjoyment that we happened to mention in the previous sermon with reference to the witnessing of a hilltop festival by Upatissa and Kolita.[14] They had a flash of insight due to the light of wisdom that came from within, not due to any illumination from outside. Because of it, those preparations ceased to be preparations. From this we can understand that the term *saṅkhāra* becomes meaningful only against the background of ignorance.

To move a step further, it is against the background of both ignorance and preparations that all the subsequent links in the formula become meaningful. As far as the interrelation between consciousness and name-and-form is concerned, all what we have said above regarding the reflection of name-and-form on consciousness,[15] becomes meaningful only so long as the reality of preparations is granted, that is, only so far as their deceptive nature is maintained. But that deceptive nature owes its existence to ignorance. This way we can unravel one aspect of the essential significance of the term *saṅkhāra*.

Then there is another point worth considering in this respect. *Saṅkhāra* as the second link in the *paṭicca samuppāda* formula is

---

[14] See sermon 5.

[15] See sermon 1.

defined by the Buddha in the *Vibhaṅgasutta* in the *Nidānasaṃyutta* not in terms of *kāyasaṅkhāra*, *vacīsaṅkhāra*, and *manosaṅkhāra*, but as *kāyasaṅkhāro*, *vacīsaṅkhāro*, and *cittasaṅkhāro*.[16] This might seem rather intriguing. *Katame ca, bhikkhave, saṅkhārā? Tayome, bhikkhave, saṅkhārā – kāyasaṅkhāro, vacīsaṅkhāro, cittasaṅkhāro*. "What, monks, are preparations? Monks, there are these three preparations – body-preparation, speech-preparation, and mind-preparation."

Also, it is noteworthy that here the term is given in the singular. In the majority of instances it is found in the plural number, but here in the definition of the term the singular is used as *kāyasaṅkhāro*, *vacīsaṅkhāro* and *cittasaṅkhāro*. The significance of this usage is explained for us by the *Cūḷavedallasutta*, in the *Dhamma* discussion between the *arahant* nun Dhammadinnā and the lay disciple Visākha. There the venerable *Therī*, in answer to a question raised by the lay disciple, comes out with a definition of these three terms: *Assāsapassāsā kho, āvuso Visākha, kāyikā, ete dhammā kāyappaṭibaddhā, tasmā assāsapassāsā kāyasaṅkhāro.*[17] "Friend Visākha, in-breaths and out-breaths are bodily, these things are bound up with the body, that is why in-breaths and out-breaths are a body-preparation."

According to this interpretation, in-breathing and out-breathing are a body-preparation in the sense that their activity is connected with the body. There is no explicit mention of karma here.

Then the definition of *vacīsaṅkhāro* is as follows: *Pubbe kho, āvuso Visākha, vitakketvā vicāretvā pacchā vācaṃ bhindati, tasmā vitakkavicārā vacīsaṅkhāro.* "Friend Visākha, first having thought and pondered one breaks into speech, that is why thinking and pondering are a speech-preparation." Here *vacīsaṅkhāra* is defined as thinking and pondering, not in terms of karma such as abusive speech and the like.

---

[16] S II 4, *Vibhaṅgasutta*.

[17] M I 301, *Cūḷavedallasutta*.

Then, as the third, *cittasaṅkhāro* is given the following definition: *Saññā ca vedanā ca cetasikā ete dhammā cittappaṭibaddhā, tasmā saññā ca vedanā ca cittasaṅkhāro*. "Perception and feeling are mental, they are bound up with the mind, that is why perception and feeling are a mind-preparation." Perception and feeling are called a mind-preparation because they are mental and have to do with the mind.

According to this definition it appears, then, that what the Buddha had indicated as the second link of the formula of dependent arising, is in-breathing and out-breathing, thinking and pondering, and perception and feeling. The mode of interpretation, we have adopted, shows us that the word *saṅkhāra*, in the context of a drama, for instance, can mean preparations or some sort of preliminary arrangement or fashioning.

Now this sense of preparation is applicable to in-breaths and out-breaths too. As we know, in all our bodily activities, particularly in lifting some weight and the like, or when exerting our selves, we sometimes take a deep breath, almost impulsively. That is to say, the most basic activity of this body is in-breathing and out-breathing.

Moreover, in the definition of *vacīsaṅkhāro* it is clearly stated that one speaks out having first thought out and pondered. This is a clear instance of the role of *saṅkhāra* as a 'preparation' or a preliminary activity. Now the word 'rehearsal' is in common use in the society. Sometimes, the day before a drama is staged for the society, a sort of trial performance is held. Similarly, before breaking out into speech, one thinks and ponders. That is why sometimes we find words issuing out before we can be aware of it. Thinking and pondering is called *vacīsaṅkhāro*, because they 'prepare' speech. The sense of 'preparation' is therefore quite apt.

Then there is perception and feeling, for which the term *cittasaṅkhāro* is used here, instead of *manosaṅkhāra*. The reason for it is that what we reckon as *manosaṅkhāra* is actually the more prominent level represented by intentions and the like. The background for those intentions, the subliminal preparatory stage, is to be found in perception and feeling. It is perception and feeling that give the impetus for the arising of the more prominent stage of intention. They provide the necessary mental condition for doing evil or good deeds. This way, we can get at the subtle nuances of the term *saṅkhāra*. Just as in the case of an iceberg floating in the ocean, the greater part is submerged and only a fraction of it shows above the surface, so also the deeper nuances of this term are rather imperceptible.

Beneath our heap of body actions, verbal actions and mental acts of willing or intentions lies a huge mountain of activities. Breathing in and breathing out is the most basic activity in one's life. It is, in fact, the criterion for judging whether one is alive or dead. For instance, when someone falls in a swoon, we examine him to see whether he is still breathing, whether this basic activity is still there in him. Also, in such a case, we try to see whether he can speak and feel, whether perception and feeling are still there in him. So in this way we can understand how these basic forms of activity decide the criterion for judging whether life is present or extinct in a person.

That activity is something internal. But even at that level, defilements lie dormant, because ignorance is hiding there too. In fact, that is precisely why they are reckoned as *saṅkhāra*. Usually, one thinks in terms of 'I' and 'mine,' as: "I breathe," "I speak," "I see," and "I feel." So, like the submerged portion of an iceberg, these subtler layers of preparations also have ignorance hidden within them. That is why the attempt of pre-Buddhistic ascetics to solve this *saṃsāric* riddle by tranquility alone met with failure.

Pre-Buddhistic ascetics, and even Ālāra Kālāma and Uddaka Rāmaputta, thought that they can get out of this *saṃsāra* by tranquillizing the bodily activities, the verbal activities, and the mental activities. But they did not understand that all these are *saṅkhāras*, or preparations, therefore they were confronted with a certain dilemma. They went on calming down the bodily activities to subtler and subtler levels. They calmed down the in-breaths and out-breaths, they managed to suppress thinking and pondering by concentration exercises, but without proper understanding. It was only a temporary calming down.

However, once they reached the level of neither-perception-nor-non-perception, they had to face a certain problem. In fact, the very designation of that level of attainment betrays the dilemma they were in. It means that one is at a loss to say definitely whether there is some perception or not. The *Pañcattayasutta* clearly reveals this fact. It gives expression to the problem facing those ascetics in the following significant statement:

Saññā rogo saññā gaṇḍo saññā sallaṃ, asaññā sammoho, etaṃ santaṃ etaṃ paṇītaṃ yadidaṃ nevasaññānāsaññaṃ.[18] "Perception is a disease, perception is a boil, perception is a dart, but not to have perception is to be deluded; this is peaceful, this is excellent, that is, neither-perception-nor-non-perception."

They understood to some extent that this perception is a disease, a trouble, a tumour, or a wound, or else a thorn, they wanted to be free from perception. But then, on the other hand, they feared that to be totally free from perception is to be in a deluded state. Therefore they concluded: 'This is peaceful, this is excellent, that is neither-perception-nor-non-perception,' and came to a halt there. That is why the Buddha rejected even Ālāra Kālāma and Uddaka Rāmaputta and went in search of the stilling of all preparations.

So the kind of tranquility meditation followed by the pre-Buddhistic ascetics, through various higher knowledges and meditative attainments, could never bring about a stilling of all preparations. Why? Because the ignorance underlying those preparations were not discernible to their level of wisdom. In the least, they could not even recognize their *saṅkhāra* nature. They thought that these are only states of a soul. Therefore, like the present day Hindu Yogins following the philosophy of the *Upaniśads*, they thought that breathing is just one layer of the self, it is one of the outer rinds of the soul.

---

[18] M II 231, *Pañcattayasutta.*

In fact, the 'kernel' of self was supposed to have around it the four rinds, *annamaya, prāṇamaya, saṃjñamaya,* and *vijñāṇamaya.* That is to say, made out of food, breath, perception, and consciousness, respectively. Apart from treating them as states of a self, they were not able to understand that all these activities are *saṅkhāras* and that ignorance is the spring-board for them.

In view of the fact that *Nibbāna* is called the stilling of all preparations, *sabbasaṅkhārasamatha*, one might sometimes conclude that the attainment of the cessation of perceptions and feeling, *saññāvedayitanirodha*, is in itself *Nibbāna*. But it is on rising from that attainment, which is like a deep freeze, that one makes contact with the three deliverances, the signless, *animitta*, the desireless, *appaṇihita*, and the void, *suññata*.

According to the Buddhist outlook, it is wisdom that decides the issue, and not tranquility. Therefore, in the last analysis, preparations cease to be preparations when the tendency to grasp the sign in the preparations is got rid of and signlessness is experienced. The 'sign' stands for the notion of permanence and it accounts for the deceptive nature of preparations, as in the case of an actor's make-up and stage-craft. It is the sign of permanence that leads to a desire for something, to expectations and aspirations.

So that sign has to leave together with the desire, for the Desireless Deliverance to come about. Then one has to see all this as essenceless and void. It is just because of desire that we regard something as 'essence-tial.' We ask for the purpose of something, when we have desire. Now it is through this unique vision of the Signless, the Desireless, and the Void, that the Buddha arrived at the state of stilling of all preparations.

We resort to the simile of the film show and the drama not out of disregard for the precept concerning abstention from such diversions, but because the Buddha has called dancing a form of mad behaviour. *Ummattakam idaṃ, bhikkhave, ariyassa vinaye yadidaṃ naccaṃ.*[19] "This, monks, is a form of madness according to the noble one's discipline, namely dancing." Now what is the nature of a madman? He is jumpy. From the standpoint of *Dhamma*, dancing is a form of jumpiness. In fact, all preparations are that. It shows a nervous stress as well as a nervous release. It is an endless series of winding and unwinding.

What makes this problem of *saṃsāra* such a knotty one to solve? We go on heaping up karmic actions, but when the time comes to experience their consequences, we do not regard them as mere results of karma, but superimpose an 'I' on that experience. So we act with the notion of an 'I' and react to the consequences again with the notion of an 'I.' Because of that egoistic reaction, we heap up fresh karma. So here is a case of stress and release, of winding and rewinding.

This is like a tangled skein. Sometimes, when an unskilled person tries to disentangle a tangled skein while disentangling one end, the other end gets entangled. So it is, in the case of this *saṃsāric* ball of thread. While doing a karma, one is conscious of it as "I am doing it." And when it is the turn to suffer for it, one does not think it as a result of that karma. Consequently one accumulates fresh karma through various attachments and conflicts arising out of it. Here too we see some sort of a drama.

Now if one can get the opportunity to see either a rehearsal or the backstage preparations for a drama, which however is not usually accessible to the public, one would be able to see through the drama. If one can steal a peep into the backstage make-up contrivances of actors and actresses, one would see how ugly persons can become comely and the wretched can appear regal. One would then see what a 'poor show' it is.

In the same way there is something dramatic in these basic preparations, namely – in-breathing and out-breathing, thinking and pondering, perception and feeling. If one sees these backstage

---

[19] A I 261, *Ruṇṇasutta.*

preparations with wisdom, one would be disenchanted. What tranquility meditation does, is to temporarily calm them down and derive some sort of happiness. That too is necessary from the point of view of concentration, to do away with restlessness and the like, but it does not dispel ignorance. That is why, in insight meditation, one tries to understand preparations for what they are by dispelling ignorance.

The more one sees preparations as preparations, ignorance is dispelled, and the more one dispels ignorance, the preparations lose their significance as preparations. Then one sees the nature of preparations with wisdom as signless, desireless, and void. So much so that, in effect, preparations cease to be preparations.

This is something of a marvel. If we now hark back to the two words 'winding' and 'rewinding,' the entire world, or *saṃsāric* existence in its entirety, is a process of winding and rewinding. Where the winding ends and the rewinding begins is a matter beyond our comprehension. But one thing is clear – all these comes to cease when craving and grasping are abandoned. It is towards such an objective that our minds turn by recognizing preparations for what they are, as a result of a deeper analysis of their nature.

The relation of *saṅkhāras* to ignorance is somewhat similar to the relation a drama has to its backstage preparations. It seems, then, that from the standpoint of *Dhamma* the entire *saṃsāra* is a product of specifically prepared intentions, even like the drama with its backstage preparations.

Let us return to the simile of the cinema again. The average man, when he says that he has seen a film show, what he has actually seen is just one scene flashing on the screen at a time. As we happened to mention in an earlier sermon, people go to the cinema and to the theatre saying: "We are going to see a film show, we are going to see a drama."[20] And they return saying: "We

---

[20] See sermon 5.

have seen a film show, we have seen a drama." But actually, they have neither seen a film nor a drama completely.

What really has happened? How did they see a film show? Just as much as one creates a name-and-form on one's screen of consciousness with the help of preparations, the film-goer has created a story by putting together the series of scenes falling on the screen.

What we mean to say is this: Now supposing the series of consecutive frames, which make up a motion picture, is made to appear on the scene when there is no spectator in the cinema hall – will there be a film at all? While such an experiment is going on, if a film-goer steps in late, halfway through, he would not be able to gather that portion of the film already gone. It is gone, gone, gone forever. Those preparations are irrevocably past.

A film show actually becomes a film show thanks to that glue used by the audience – the glue of craving. The Buddha has preached that this craving has three characteristics, namely: *ponobhavika, nandirāgasahagata*, and *tatratatrābhinandi.*[21] *Ponobhavika* as a characteristic of craving means, in its broader sense, that it leads to re-becoming. One might think that by 're-becoming' only the connecting up of one existence in *saṃsāra* with another is meant. But that is not all. It is craving that connects up one moment of existence with another.

One who is seeing a film show, for instance, connects up the first scene with the second, in order to understand the latter. And that is how one 'sees' a film show and comes back and says: "I have seen a film show." All the scenes do not fall on the screen at once, but a connecting-up goes on. That is the idea behind the term *ponobhavika*. In this connecting up of one scene with another there is an element of re-becoming or re-generation.

Then there is the term *nandirāgasahagata*. This is the other additive which should be there for one to enjoy the film show. It

---

[21] S V 421, *Dhammacakkappavattanasutta*.

means the nature of delighting and getting attached. Craving in particular is like a glue. In fact, a synonym for it is *lepa*, which means a 'glue.'[22] Another synonym is *visattika*, an 'adhesive' or a 'sticky substance.'[23] Even the word *rāga*, or attachment, already conveys this sense. So craving, or desire, glues the scenes together.

Then comes the term *tatratatrābhinandi*, the nature of delighting, in particular now here, now there. It is, in effect, the association of one scene with another in order to make up a story out of it. That is why we made the statement: 'So far not a single cinema has held a film show and not a single theatre has staged a drama.'[24] But all the same, those who went to the cinema and the theatre witnessed a show and a drama. How? They produced them, or prepared them, with their 'sticky' defilements on their own.

Now in the same way, worldly beings create a film show of name-and-form on the screen of consciousness with the help of preparations, or *saṅkhāras*. Name-and-form is a product of imagination. What insight meditators often refer to as reflection on 'name-and-form preparations,' amounts to this. Is there something real in name-and-form? In our very first sermon we happened to say something on this point.[25]

In the *Dvayatānupassanāsutta* of the *Sutta Nipāta* the Buddha gives utterance to the following verse:

> *Anattani attamāniṃ,*
> *passa lokaṃ sadevakaṃ,*
> *niviṭṭhaṃ nāmarūpasmiṃ,*
> *idaṃ saccan'ti maññati.*[26]

---

[22] E.g. at Nid I 54: *taṇhālepo.*

[23] Dhp 335: *taṇhā loke visattikā, (Taṇhāvagga).*

[24] See sermon 5.

[25] See sermon 1.

[26] Sn 756, *Dvayatānupassanāsutta.*

"Just see the world, with all its gods,
Fancying a self where none exists,
Entrenched in name-and-form it holds
The conceit that this is real."

It is as if the Buddha is pinpointing the illusory and deceptive nature of name-and-form. As we mentioned before, scenes fall on the cinema screen only one at a time. Because of the rapidity of the movie film, it is difficult for one to be aware of this fact. Now, in the case of a drama, the curtain goes down between acts and the audience waits for the curtain to go up. But they wait, ready with their glue to connect the previous act with the one to come, to construct a drama. By the time a certain scene falls on the cinema screen, the previous one is gone for good. Scenes to follow have not yet come. Whatever scene falls on the screen, now, will not stay there. So what we have here, is something illusory, a deceptive phenomenon.

Let us now consider an instance like this: Sometimes we see a dog, crossing a plank over a stream, stopping halfway through to gaze at the water below. It wags its tail, or growls, or keeps on looking at and away from the water, again and again. Why does it do so? Seeing its own image in the water, it imagines that to be another dog. So it either wags its tail in a friendly way, or growls angrily, or else it keeps on stealing glances out of curiosity – love, hate, and delusion.

In this case, the dogs thinks that it is looking because it sees a dog. But what is really happening? It is just because it is looking that it sees a dog. If the dog had not looked down, it would not have seen a dog looking up at it from below, that is to say – its own image. Now it is precisely this sort of illusion that is going on with regard to this name-and-form, the preparations, and sense-perception. **Here lies the secret of Dependent Arising**.

As a flash-back to our film show, it may be added that if a film reel is played at a time when there is no spectator, no film show will be registered anywhere, because there is no mind to put together. It merely flashed on the screen. But if someone had been there to receive it, to contact with his sense-bases, that is, to see with his eyes, hear with his ears, and make mental contact with desire, then there comes to be a film show. And so also in the case of a drama.

Film producers and dramatists think that the production of the film and the drama is solely their work. But in the last analysis, it is the audience that gives the film and the drama the finishing touch, to make them finished products. Similarly, we tend to think that every object in the world exists in its own right. But then this is what is called *sakkāyadiṭṭhi*, the 'personality view,' which carries with it the self-bias.

It is such a view that made the dog imagine that there is another dog in the water. It imagined that the dog is there, even when it is not looking. It may have thought: "I am looking because a dog appears there." But the fact is that the dog appears there because it cares to look. Here, then, we have a case of dependent arising, or *paṭicca samuppāda.*

The word *paṭicca* has a very deep meaning. The Buddha borrowed many words from the existing philosophical tradition in India. Sometimes he infused new meanings into them and adopted them to his terminology. But the term *paṭicca samuppāda* is not to be found in any other philosophical system. The special significance of the term lies in the word *paṭicca.*

On a certain occasion, the Buddha himself gave a definition to this term *paṭicca samuppāda*. Now it is fairly well known that the Buddha declared that all this suffering is dependently arisen. What then is to be understood by the word *dukkha*, or 'suffering?' He defines it in terms of the five grasping groups, or the five aggregates of clinging, as it is said: *saṅkhittena pañcupādānakkhandhā dukkhā,*[27] "In short, the five grasping groups are suffering." So then suffering, or the five grasping groups, is something dependently arisen.

---

[27] S V 421, *Dhammacakkappavattanasutta.*

In one discourse in the *Nidānasaṃyutta* of the *Saṃyutta Nikāya* we find the Buddha making the following significant statement: *Paṭiccasamuppannaṃ kho, Upavāṇa, dukkhaṃ vuttaṃ mayā. Kiṃ paṭicca? Phassaṃ paṭicca.*[28] "Upavāṇa, I have declared that suffering is dependently arisen. Dependent on what? **Dependent on contact**." So from this statement, also, it is clear that the five groups of grasping arise because of contact, that is by contacting through the six bases.

Considered in this way, a thing is called dependently arisen because it arises on being touched by the six sense-bases. That is why it is called *anicca*, or impermanent. The film show, for instance, was not something already made, or 'ready made.' It arose due to contact. The phrase *saṅkhataṃ paṭiccasamuppannaṃ,*[29] 'prepared and dependently arisen,' suggests that the prepared nature is also due to that contact. What may be called *abhisaṅkhata viññāṇa,*[30] 'specifically prepared consciousness,' is that sort of consciousness which gets attached to name-and-form.

When one sees a film show, one interprets a scene appearing on the screen according to one's likes and dislikes. It becomes a thing of experience for him. Similarly, by imagining a self in name-and-form, consciousness gets attached to it. It is such a consciousness, which is established on name-and-form, that can be called *abhisaṅkhata viññāṇa*.

Then could there be also a consciousness which does not reflect a name-and-form? Yes, there could be. That is what is known as *anidassana viññāṇa,*[31] or 'non-manifestative consciousness.' This brings us to an extremely abstruse topic in this *Dhamma*.

---

[28] S II 41, *Upavāṇasutta.*

[29] E.g. at M III 299, *Indriyabhāvanāsutta.*

[30] S III 58, *Udānasutta* (cf. *viññāṇaṃ . . . anabhisaṅkhacca vimuttaṃ*).

[31] E.g. at M I 329, *Brahmanimantanikasutta.*

There is a very deep verse occurring at the end of the *Kevaḍḍhasutta* of the *Dīgha Nikāya* which has been variously interpreted by scholars both eastern and western. It runs:

Viññāṇaṃ anidassanaṃ,
anantaṃ sabbato pabhaṃ,
ettha āpo ca paṭhavī,
tejo vāyo na gādhati,
ettha dīghañca rassañca,
aṇuṃ thūlaṃ subhāsubhaṃ,
ettha nāmañca rūpañca,
asesaṃ uparujjhati,
viññāṇassa nirodhena,
etth'etaṃ uparujjhati.[32]

The commentary advances several interpretations to this verse.[33] Being unable to give one definite meaning, it suggests several. However, since we have developed a certain mode of interpretation so far, we propose to give preference to it before getting down to the commentarial interpretation. Now let us see whether our mode of interpretation can make this verse meaningful.

First of all, we have to trace the circumstances which provide the setting for this verse in the *Kevaḍḍhasutta*. The Buddha brings out a past episode, relating to the company of monks. A certain monk conceived the riddle: 'Where do these four great primaries, earth, water, fire, and air, cease altogether?' He did not approach the Buddha with his problem, probably because he thought that somewhere in this world-system those four elements could cease.

So what did he do? As he had psychic powers he went from heaven to heaven and *Brahma* realm to *Brahma* realm, asking the gods and *Brahmas* this question: 'Where do these four primaries

---

[32] D I 223, *Kevaḍḍhasutta*.

[33] Sv II 393.

cease?' None among the gods and *Brahmas* could answer. In the end, *Mahā Brahma* himself asked him, why he took the trouble to come all the way there, when he could have easily consulted the Buddha. Then that monk approached the Buddha and put the riddle to him.

But before answering the riddle, the Buddha recommended a restatement of it, saying: 'Monk, that is not the way you should put it. You should have worded it differently.' Now that means that the question is wrongly put. It is incorrect to ask where the four great primaries cease. There is a particular way of wording it. And this is how the Buddha reformulated that riddle:

Kattha āpo ca paṭhavī,
tejo vāyo na gādhati,
kattha dīghañca rassañca,
aṇuṃ thūlaṃ subhāsubhaṃ,
kattha nāmañca rūpañca,
asesaṃ uparujjhati?

"Where do earth and water,
Fire and wind no footing find,
Where is it that long and short,
Fine and coarse, pleasant, unpleasant,
As well as name-and-form,
Are held in check in a way complete?"

Here the Buddha introduces a phrase of special significance: *na gādhati*, 'does not find a footing.' So the question, as restated, means: "Where do the four primaries not get a footing?" The question, then, is not about a cessation of the four primaries, it is not a question of their cessation somewhere in the world or in the world system. The correct way to put it, is to ask where the four great primaries do not find a footing. The Buddha adds that it may also be asked where long and short, fine and coarse, pleasant and unpleasant, as well as name-and-form are held in check completely. The word *uparujjhati* means 'holding in check.'

Having first reformulated the question, the Buddha gave the answer to it in the verse previously quoted. Let us now try to get at the meaning of this verse. We shall not translate, at the very outset, the first two lines of the verse, *viññāṇaṃ anidassanaṃ, anantaṃ sabbato pabhaṃ*. These two lines convey a very deep meaning. Therefore, to start with, we shall take the expression as it is, and explain its relation to what follows.

It is in this consciousness, which is qualified by the terms *anidassanaṃ, anantaṃ*, and *sabbato pabhaṃ*, that earth, water, fire, and air do not find a footing. Also, it is in this consciousness that long and short, fine and coarse, and pleasant and unpleasant, as well as name-and-form, are kept in check. It is by the cessation of consciousness that all these are held in check.

Nibbāna Sermon 7

Namo tassa Bhagavato Arahato Sammāsambuddhassa
Namo tassa Bhagavato Arahato Sammāsambuddhassa
Namo tassa Bhagavato Arahato Sammāsambuddhassa

Etaṃ santaṃ, etaṃ paṇītaṃ, yadidaṃ sabbasaṅkhārasamatho sabbūpadhipaṭinissaggo taṇhakkhayo virāgo nirodho nibbānaṃ.[1]

"This is peaceful, this is excellent, namely the stilling of all preparations, the relinquishment of all assets, the destruction of craving, detachment, cessation, extinction."

With the permission of the Most Venerable Great Preceptor and the assembly of the venerable meditative monks.

Towards the end of the last sermon we happened to quote a certain verse from the *Kevaḍḍhasutta* of the *Dīgha Nikāya*. The verse runs as follows:

Viññāṇaṃ anidassanaṃ,
anantaṃ sabbato pabhaṃ,
ettha āpo ca paṭhavī,
tejo vāyo na gādhati,
ettha dīghañca rassañca,
aṇuṃ thūlaṃ subhāsubhaṃ,
ettha nāmañca rūpañca,
asesaṃ uparujjhati,

---

1 M I 436, *MahāMālunkyasutta*.

viññāṇassa nirodhena,
etth'etaṃ uparujjhati.[2]

The other day, we could give only a general idea of the meaning of this verse in brief, because of the question of time. Today, we propose to attempt a detailed explanation of it. To start with, we purposely avoid rendering the first two lines, which appear as the crux of the whole verse. Taking those two lines as they are, we could paraphrase the verse as follows:

It is in a consciousness, that is *anidassana, ananta,* and *sabbato pabha*, that earth, water, fire, and air do not find a footing. It is in this consciousness that long and short, fine and coarse, and pleasant and unpleasant, as well as name-and-form, are kept in check. It is by the cessation of consciousness that all these are held in check.

Let us now try to sort out the meaning of the difficult words in the first two lines. First of all, in the expression *viññāṇaṃ anidassanaṃ*, there is the term *anidassana*. The meaning of the word *nidassana* is fairly well known. It means 'illustration.' Something that 'throws light on' or 'makes clear' is called *nidassana*. This is the basic sense.

We find an instance of the use of this word, even in this basic sense, in the first *Kosalasutta* among the Tens of the *Aṅguttara Nikāya*. It is in connection with the description of *abhibhāyatanā*, bases of mastery, where there is a reference to contemplation devices known as *kasiṇa*. It is said that even the flax flower can be used initially as a sign for *kasiṇa* meditation. A flax flower is described in the following words: *Umāpupphaṃ nīlaṃ nīlavaṇṇaṃ nīlanidassanaṃ nīlanibhāsaṃ*,[3] which may be rendered as: "The flax flower, blue, blue-coloured, manifesting blue, shining blue." *Nīlanidassanaṃ* suggests that the flax flower is an illustration of

---

[2] D I 223, *Kevaḍḍhasutta*.

[3] A V 61, *Kosalasutta*.

blue colour, or that it is a manifestation of blue. *Anidassana* could therefore be said to refer to whatever does not manifest anything.

In fact, we have a very good example in support of this suggested sense in the *Kakacūpamasutta* of the *Majjhima Nikāya*. There we find the Buddha putting a certain question to the monks in order to bring out a simile: "Monks, suppose a man comes with crimson, turmeric, indigo, or carmine and says: 'I shall draw pictures and make pictures appear on the sky!' What do you think, monks, could that man draw pictures and make pictures appear there?" Then the monks reply: *Ayañhi, bhante, ākāso arūpī anidassano. Tattha na sukaraṃ rūpaṃ likhituṃ, rūpapātubhāvaṃ kātuṃ.*[4] "This sky, Lord, is immaterial and non-illustrative. It is not easy to draw a picture there or make manifest pictures there."

Here we have the words in support of the above suggested meaning. The sky is said to be *arūpī anidassano*, immaterial and non-illustrative. That is why one cannot draw pictures there or make pictures appear there. There is nothing material in the sky to make manifest pictures. That is, the sense in which it is called *anidassano* in this context.

Let us now see how meaningful that word is, when used with reference to consciousness as *viññāṇaṃ anidassanaṃ*. Why the sky is said to be non-manifestative we could easily understand by the simile. But how can consciousness become non-manifestative? First and foremost we can remind ourselves of the fact that our consciousness has in it the ability to reflect. That ability is called *paccavekkhana*, 'looking back.' Sometimes the Buddha has given the simile of the mirror with reference to this ability, as for instance in the *AmbalatthikāRāhulovādasutta* of the *Majjhima Nikāya*.[5] In the *Ānandasutta* of the *Khandhasaṃyutta*, also, he has used the simile of the mirror.[6] In the former *sutta* preached to

---

4 M I 127, *Kakacūpamasutta*.

5 M I 415, *AmbalatthikāRāhulovādasutta*.

6 S III 105, *Ānandasutta*.

Venerable Rāhula the Buddha uses the simile of the mirror to stress the importance of reflection in regard to bodily, verbal, and mental action.

In our last sermon, we gave a simile of a dog crossing a plank over a stream and looking at its own reflection in the water.[7] That, too, is a kind of reflection. But from that we can deduce a certain principle with regard to the question of reflection, namely, that the word stands for a mode of becoming deluded as well as a mode of getting rid of the delusion. What creates a delusion is the way that dog is repeatedly looking down from his own point of view on the plank to see a dog in the water. That is unwise reflection born of non-radical attention, *ayoniso manasikāra*. Under the influence of the personality view, *sakkāyadiṭṭhi*, it goes on looking at its own image, wagging its tail and growling. But wise reflection born of radical attention, *yoniso manasikāra*, is what is recommended in the *AmbalatthikāRāhulovādasutta* with its thematic repetitive phrase *paccavekkhitvā, paccavekkhitvā*,[8] "reflecting again and again."

Wise reflection inculcates the *Dhamma* point of view. Reflection based on right view, *sammā diṭṭhi*, leads to deliverance. So this is the twin aspect of reflection. But this we mention by the way. The point we wish to stress is that consciousness has in it the nature of reflecting something, like a mirror.

Now *viññāṇaṃ anidassanaṃ* is a reference to the nature of the released consciousness of an *arahant*. It does not reflect anything. To be more precise, it does not reflect a *nāma-rūpa*, or name-and-form. An ordinary individual sees a *nāma-rūpa*, when he reflects, which he calls 'I' and 'mine.' It is like the reflection of that dog, which sees its own delusive reflection in the water. A non-*arahant*, upon reflection, sees name-and-form, which however he mistakes to be his self. With the notion of 'I' and 'mine' he falls

---

[7] See sermon 6.

[8] M I 415, *AmbalatthikāRāhulovādasutta*.

into delusion with regard to it. But the *arahant*'s consciousness is an unestablished consciousness.

We have already mentioned in previous sermons about the established consciousness and the unestablished consciousness.[9] A non-*arahant*'s consciousness is established on name-and-form. The unestablished consciousness is that which is free from name-and-form and is unestablished on name-and-form. The established consciousness, upon reflection, reflects name-and-form, on which it is established, whereas the unestablished consciousness does not find a name-and-form as a reality. The *arahant* has no attachments or entanglements in regard to name-and-form. In short, it is a sort of penetration of name-and-form, without getting entangled in it. This is how we have to unravel the meaning of the expression *anidassana viññāṇa*.

By way of further clarification of this sense of *anidassana*, we may remind ourselves of the fact that manifestation requires something material. That is obvious even from that simile picked up at random from the *Kakacūpamasutta*. As for the consciousness of the *arahant*, the verse in question makes it clear that earth, water, fire, and air do not find a footing there. It is because of these four great primaries that one gets a perception of form. They are said to be the cause and condition for the designation of the aggregate of form: *Cattāro kho, bhikkhu, mahābhūtā hetu, cattāro mahābhūtā paccayo rūpakkhandhassa paññāpanāya*.[10] "The four great primaries, monk, are the cause and condition for the designation of the form group."

Now the *arahant* has freed his mind from these four elements. As it is said in the *Dhātuvibhaṅgasutta*: *Paṭhavīdhātuyā cittaṃ virājeti*,[11] "He makes his mind dispassionate with regard to the earth-element." *Āpodhātuyā cittaṃ virājeti*, "He makes his mind

---

9 See sermon 3 and 4.

10 M III 17, *MahāPuṇṇamasutta*.

11 M III 240, *Dhātuvibhaṅgasutta*.

dispassionate with regard to the water-element." As he has freed his mind from the four elements through disenchantment, which makes them fade away, the *arahant*'s reflection does not engender a perception of form. As the verse in question puts it rather rhetorically, *ettha āpo ca paṭhavī, tejo vāyo na gādhati,* "Herein water and earth, fire and air find no footing."

Here the word *gādhati* is particularly significant. When, for instance, we want to plumb the depth of a deep well, we lower something material as a plumb into the well. Where it comes to stay, we take as the bottom. In the consciousness of the *arahant*, the material elements cannot find such a footing. They cannot manifest themselves in that unplumbed depth of the *arahant*'s consciousness.

> *Viññāṇaṃ anidassanaṃ,*
> *anantaṃ sabbato pabhaṃ,*
> *ettha āpo ca paṭhavī,*
> *tejo vāyo na gādhati.*
>
> "Consciousness, which is non-manifestative,
> Endless and lustrous on all sides,
> It is here that water, earth,
> Fire, and air no footing find."

It is precisely because the material elements cannot make themselves manifest in it, that this consciousness is called 'non-manifestative.' In the same connection we may add that such distinctions as long and short, fine and coarse, and pleasant and unpleasant are not registered in that consciousness, because they pertain to things material. When the consciousness is freed from the four elements, it is also free from the relative distinctions, which are but the standards of measurements proper to those elements.

Let us now consider the implications of the term *anantaṃ* – 'endless,' 'infinite.' We have already said something about the plumbing of the depth of waters. Since the material elements have faded away in that consciousness, they are unable to plumb its depth. They no longer serve as an '**index**' to that consciousness. Therefore, that consciousness is endless or infinite.

It is endless also in another sense. With regard to such distinctions as 'long' and 'short' we used the word '**relative**.' These are relative concepts. We even refer to them as conjoined pairs of terms. In worldly usage they are found conjoined as 'long and short,' 'fine and coarse,' 'pleasant and unpleasant.' There is a dichotomy about these concepts, there is a bifurcation. It is as if they are put within a rigid framework.

When, for instance, we go searching for a piece of wood for some purpose or other, we may say: "This piece of wood is too long." Why do we say so? Because we are in need of a shorter one. Instead of saying that it is not '**sufficiently**' short, we say it is too long. When we say it is too short, what we mean is that it is not sufficiently long. So then, long and short are relevant within one framework. As a matter of fact, all measurements are relative to some scale or other. They are meaningful within some framework of a scale.

In this sense, too, the worldling's way of thinking has a tendency to go to extremes. It goes to one extreme or the other. When it was said that the world, for the most part, rests on a dichotomy, such as that between the two views 'Is' and 'Is not,'[12] this idea of a framework is already implicit. The worldling's ways of thought '**end-up**' in one extreme or the other within this framework. The *arahant* transcends it, his consciousness is, therefore, endless, *ananta*.

There is a verse in the *Pāṭaligāmiyavagga* of the *Udāna*, which clearly brings out this fact. Most of the discourses in that section of the *Udāna* deal with *Nibbāna* – *Nibbānapaṭisaṃyutta* – and the following verse, too, is found in such a discourse:

---

[12] S II 17, *Kaccāyanagottasutta*, see sermon 4.

Duddasaṃ anantaṃ nāma,
na hi saccaṃ sudassanaṃ,
paṭividdhā taṇhā jānato,
passato natthi kiñcanaṃ.[13]

This verse, like many other deep ones, seems to have puzzled the commentators. Let alone the meaning, even the variant readings had posed them a problem, so much so that they end up giving the reader a choice between alternate interpretations. But let us try to get at the general trend of its meaning.

Duddasaṃ anantaṃ nāma, "Hard to see is the endless" – whatever that 'endless' be. *Na hi saccaṃ sudassanaṃ,* "The truth is not easily seen," which in effect is an emphatic assertion of the same idea. One could easily guess that this 'endless' is the truth and that it refers to *Nibbāna*. *Paṭividdhā taṇhā* means that "craving has been penetrated through." This penetration is through knowledge and wisdom, the outcome of which is stated in the last line. *Janato passato natthi kiñcanaṃ*, "to one who know and sees there is NOTHING." The idea is that when craving is penetrated through with knowledge and wisdom, one realizes the voidness of the world. Obviously, the reference here is to *Nibbāna*.

The entire verse may now be rendered as follows:

"Hard to see is the Endless,
Not easy 'tis to see the truth,
Pierced through is craving,
And naught for him who knows and sees."

The commentator, however, is at a loss to determine whether the correct reading is *anataṃ* or *anantaṃ* and leaves the question open. He gives one interpretation in favour of the reading *anataṃ*.[14] To show its justifiability he says that *natā* is a synonym for

[13] Ud 80, *DutiyaNibbānapaṭisaṃyuttasutta*.

[14] Ud-a 393.

taṇhā, or craving, and that *anataṃ* is a term for *Nibbāna*, in the sense that there is no craving in it. It must be pointed out that it is *nati* and not *natā* that is used as a synonym for *taṇhā*.

Anyway, after adducing reasons for the acceptability of the reading *anataṃ*, he goes on to say that there is a variant reading, *anantaṃ*, and gives an interpretation in support of it too. In fact, he interprets the word *anantaṃ* in more than one sense. Firstly, because *Nibbāna* is permanent, it has no end. And secondly it is endless because it is immeasurable, or *appamāṇa*.

In our interpretation of the word *anantaṃ* we have not taken it in the sense of permanence or everlastingness. The word *appamāṇa*, or immeasurable, can have various nuances. But the one we have stressed is the transcendence of relative concepts, limited by their dichotomous nature. We have also alluded to the unplumbed depth of the *arahant*'s consciousness, in which the four elements do not find a footing.

In the *Buddhavagga* of the *Dhammapada* we come across another verse which highlights the extraordinary significance of the word *anantaṃ*:

> *Yassa jālinī visattikā,*
> *taṇhā natthi kuhiñci netave,*
> *taṃ Buddham anantagocaraṃ,*
> *apadaṃ kena padena nessatha?*[15]

Before attempting a translation of this verse, some of the words in it have to be commented upon. *Yassa jālinī visattikā. Jālinī* is a synonym for craving. It means one who has a net or one who goes netting. *Visattikā* refers to the agglutinative character of craving. It keeps worldlings glued to objects of sense. The verse may be rendered as follows:

---

[15] Dhp 180, *Buddhavagga*.

"He who has no craving, with nets in and agglutinates to lead him somewhere – by what track could that Awakened One of infinite range be led – trackless as he is?"

Because the Buddha is of infinite range, he is trackless. His path cannot be traced. Craving wields the net of name-and-form with its glue when it goes ranging. But since the Awakened One has the '**endless**' as his range, there is no track to trace him by.

The term *anantagocaraṃ* means one whose range has no end or limit. If, for instance, one chases a deer, to catch it, one might succeed at least at the end of the pasture. But the Buddha's range is endless and his 'ranging' leaves no track.

The commentators seem to interpret this term as a reference to the Buddha's omniscience – to his ability to attend to an infinite number of objects.[16] But this is not the sense in which we interpret the term here. The very fact that there is '**no object**' makes the Buddha's range endless and untraceable. Had there been an object, craving could have netted him in. In support of this interpretation, we may allude to the following couple of verses in the *Arahanta-vagga* of the *Dhammapada*:

Yesaṃ sannicayo natthi,
ye pariññāta bhojanā,
suññato animitto ca,
vimokkho yesa gocaro,
ākāse va sakuntānaṃ,
gati tesaṃ durannayā.

Yassāsavā parikkhīṇā,
āhāre ca anissito,
suññāto animitto ca,
vimokkho yassa gocaro,

[16] Dhp-a III 197.

ākāse va sakuntānaṃ,
padaṃ tassa durannayaṃ.[17]

Both verses express more or less the same idea. Let us examine the meaning of the first verse. The first two lines are: *Yesaṃ sannicayo natthi, ye pariññāta bhojanā.* "Those who have no accumulation and who have comprehended their food." The words used here are charged with deep meanings. Verses in the *Dhammapada* are very often rich in imagery. The Buddha has on many occasions presented the *Dhamma* through deep similes and metaphors. If the metaphorical sense of a term is ignored, one can easily miss the point.

For instance, the word *sannicaya*, in this context, which we have rendered as 'accumulation,' is suggestive of the heaping up of the five aggregates. The word *upacaya* is sometimes used with reference to this process of heaping up that goes on in the minds of the worldlings.[18] Now this heaping up, as well as the accumulation of *kamma*, is not there in the case of an *arahant*. Also, they have comprehended their food. The comprehension of food does not mean simply the usual reflection on food in terms of elements. Nor does it imply just one kind of food, but all the four nutriments mentioned in the *Dhamma*, namely *kabaḷiṅkārāhāra*, material food, *phassa*, contact, *manosañcetanā*, volition, and *viññāṇa*, consciousness.[19]

The next two lines tell us what the true range or pasture of the *arahants* is. It is an echo of the idea of comprehension of food as well as the absence of accumulation. *Suññato animitto ca, vimokkho yesa gocaro*, "Whose range is the deliverance of the void and the signless." When the *arahants* are in their attainment to the fruit of *arahant*-hood, their minds turn towards the void and

17 Dhp 92 - 93, *Arahantavagga.*

18 E.g. at M III 287, *MahāSaḷāyatanikasutta.*

19 E.g. at S II 101, *Atthirāgasutta.*

the signless. When they are on this feeding-ground, neither *Māra* nor craving can catch them with their nets. They are trackless – hence the last two lines *ākāse va sakuntānaṃ, gati tesa durannayā,* "Their track is hard to trace, like that of birds in the sky."

The word *gati* in this last line is interpreted by the commentators as a reference to the 'whereabouts' of the *arahants* after their *parinibbāna.*[20] It has dubious associations of some place as a destination. But in this context, *gati* does not lend itself to such an interpretation. It only refers to their mental compass, which is untraceable, because of their deliverance trough the void and the signless.

The next verse also bring out this idea. *Yassāsavā parikkhīṇā, āhāre ca anissito,* "Whose influxes are extinct and who is unattached in regard to nutriment." *Suññāto animitto ca, vimokkho yassa gocaro,* "Whose range is the void and the signless." *Ākāse va sakuntānaṃ, padaṃ tassa durannayaṃ,* "His path is hard to trace, like that of birds in the sky." This reminds us of the last line of the verse quoted earlier, *apadaṃ kena padena nessatha*, "By what track could one lead him, who is trackless?"[21] These two verses, then, throw more light on the meaning of the expression *anantagocara* – of infinite range – used as an epithet for the Awakened One.

Let us now get at the meaning of the term *sabbato pabham,* in the context *viññāṇaṃ anidassanaṃ, anantaṃ sabbato pabhaṃ.*[22] In our discussion of the significance of the drama and the cinema we mentioned that it is the darkness in the background which keeps the audience entranced in a way that they identify themselves with the characters and react accordingly.[23] The darkness in

---

[20] Dhp -a II 173.

[21] Dhp 180, *Buddhavagga.*

[22] D I 223, *Kevaḍḍhasutta.*

[23] See sermon 5.

the background throws a spell of delusion. That is what makes for 'enjoyment.'

Of course, there is some sort of light in the cinema hall. But that is very limited. Some times it is only a beam of light, directed on the screen. In a previous sermon we happened to mention that even in the case of a matinee show, dark curtains and closed doors and windows ensure the necessary dark background.[24] Here, in this simile, we have a clue to the meaning *sabbato pabhaṃ*, luminous or lustrous on all sides. Suppose a matinee show is going on and one is enjoying it, entranced and deluded by it. Suddenly doors and windows are flung open and the dark curtains are removed. Then immediately one slips out of the cinema world. The film may go on, but because of the light coming from all sides, the limited illumination on the screen fades away, before the total illumination. The film thereby loses its enjoyable quality.

As far as consciousness, or *viññāṇa*, is concerned, it is not something completely different from wisdom, *paññā*, as it is defined in the *Mahāvedallasutta*. However, there is also a difference between them, *paññā bhāvetabbā, viññāṇaṃ pariññeyyaṃ*, "Wisdom is to be developed, consciousness is to be comprehended."[25] Here it is said that one has to comprehend the nature of consciousness.

Then one may ask: 'We are understanding everything with consciousness, so how can one understand consciousness?' But the Buddha has shown us the way of doing it. Wisdom, when it is developed, enables one to comprehend consciousness. In short, consciousness is as narrow as that beam of light falling on the cinema screen. That is to say, the specifically prepared consciousness, or the consciousness crammed up in name-and-form, as in the case of the non-*arahant*. It is as narrow as the perspective of

---

24 See sermon 5.

25 M I 293, *MahāVedallasutta*.

the audience glued to the screen. The consciousness of the ordinary worldling is likewise limited and committed.

Now what happens when it is fully illuminated on all sides with wisdom? It becomes *sabbato pabhaṃ*, lustrous on all sides. In that lustre, which comes from all sides, the framework of ignorance fades away. It is that released consciousness, free from the dark framework of ignorance, that is called the consciousness which is lustrous on all sides, in that cryptic verse in question. This lustre, associated with wisdom, has a special significance according to the discourses. In the *Catukkanipāta* of the *Aṅguttara Nikāya* we come across the following *sutta*:

> *Catasso imā, bhikkhave, pabhā. Katamā catasso? Candappabhā, suriyappabhā, aggippabhā, paññāpabhā. Imā kho, bhikkhave, catasso pabhā. Etad aggaṃ, bhikkhave, imāsaṃ catunnaṃ pabhānaṃ yadidaṃ paññāpabhā.*[26]

> "Monks, there are these four lustres. Which four? The lustre of the moon, the lustre of the sun, the lustre of fire, and the lustre of wisdom. These, monks, are the four lustres. This, monks, is the highest among these four lustres, namely the lustre of wisdom."

Another important discourse, quoted quite often, though not always correctly interpreted, is the following:

> *Pabhassaram idaṃ, bhikkhave, cittaṃ. Tañca kho āgantukehi upakkilesehi upakkiliṭṭhaṃ. Taṃ assutavā puthujjano yathābhūtaṃ nappajānāti. Tasmā assutavato puthujjanassa citta bhāvanā natthī'ti vadāmi.*

> *Pabhassaram idaṃ, bhikkhave, cittaṃ. Tañca kho āgantukehi upakkilesehi vippamuttaṃ. Taṃ sutavā ari-*

[26] A II 139, *Pabhāsutta*.

> *yasāvako yathābhūtaṃ pajānāti. Tasmā sutavato ariyasāvakassa citta bhāvanā atthī'ti vadāmi.*[27]
>
> "This mind, monks, is luminous, but it is defiled by extraneous defilements. That, the uninstructed ordinary man does not understand as it is. Therefore, there is no mind development for the ordinary man, I declare.
>
> "This mind, monks, is luminous, but it is released from extraneous defilements. That, the instructed noble disciple understands as it is. Therefore, there is mind development for the instructed noble disciple, I declare."

It is sufficiently clear, then, that the allusion is to the luminous mind, the consciousness of the *arahant*, which is non-manifestative, infinite, and all lustrous. To revert to the analogy of the cinema which, at least in a limited sense, helps us to form an idea about it, we have spoken about the stilling of all preparations.[28] Now in the case of the film, too, there is a stilling of preparations. That is to say, the preparations which go to make it a '**movie**' film are '**stilled**.' The multicoloured dresses of actors and actresses become colourless before that illumination, even in the case of a technicolour film. The scenes on the screen get blurred before the light that suddenly envelops them.

And what is the outcome of it? The preparations going on in the minds of the audience, whether induced by the film producers or aroused from within, are calmed down at least temporarily. This symbolizes, in a limited sense, the significance of the phrase *sabbasaṅkhārasamatha*, the stilling of all preparations.

Then what about the relinquishment of all assets, *sabbūpadhipaṭinissagga*? In the context of the film show, it is the bundle of

---

27 A I 10, *Accharāsaṅghātavagga*.

28 See sermon 5.

experiences coming out of one's 'vested-interests' in the marvelous cinema world. These assets are relinquished at least for the moment. Destruction of craving, *taṇhakkhayo*, is momentarily experienced with regard to the blurred scenes on the screen.

As to the term *virāga*, we have already shown that it can be understood in two senses, that is, dispassion as well as the fading away which brings about the dispassion.[29] Now in this case, too, the fading away occurred, not by any other means, but by the very fact that the limited narrow beam of consciousness got superseded by the unlimited light of wisdom.

Nirodha means cessation, and the film has now ceased to be a film, though the machines are still active. We have already mentioned that in the last analysis a film is produced by the audience.[30] So its cessation, too, is a matter for the audience. This, then, is the cessation of the film.

Now comes *Nibbāna*, extinction, or extinguishment. Whatever heated emotions and delirious excitements that arose out of the film show cooled down, at least momentarily, when the illumination takes over. This way we can form some idea, somewhat inferentially, about the meaning and significance of the term *sabbato pabhaṃ*, with the help of this illustration based on the film show.

So now we have tackled most of the difficulties to the interpretation of this verse. In fact, it is the few words occurring in the first two lines that has posed an insoluble problem to scholars both eastern and western. We have not yet given the commentarial interpretation, and that, not out of disrespect for the venerable commentators. It is because their interpretation is rather hazy and inconclusive. However, we shall be presenting that interpretation at the end of this discussion, so as to give the reader an opportunity to compare it with ours.

---

[29] See sermon 5.

[30] See sermon 5.

But for the present, let us proceed to say something about the last two lines as well. *Viññāṇassa nirodhena, etth'etaṃ uparujjhati.* As we saw above, for all practical purposes, name-and-form seem to cease, even like the fading away of the scenes on the cinema screen. Then what is meant by this phrase *viññāṇassa nirodhena*, with the cessation of consciousness? The reference here is to that *abhisaṅkhata viññāṇa*, or the specifically prepared consciousness. It is the cessation of that concocted type of consciousness which was formerly there, like the one directed on the cinema screen by the audience. With the cessation of that specifically prepared consciousness, all constituents of name-and-form are said to be held in check, *uparujjhati*.

Here, too, we have a little problem. Generally, *nirujjhati* and *uparujjhati* are regarded as synonymous. The way these two verbs are used in some *suttas* would even suggest that they mean the same thing. As a matter of fact, even the *CūḷaNiddesa*, which is a very old commentary, paraphrases *uparujjhati* by *nirujjhati*: *uparujjhatī'ti nirujjhati.*[31]

Nevertheless, in the context of this particular verse, there seems to be something deep involved in the distinction between these two verbs. Even at a glance, the two lines in question are suggestive of some distinction between them. *Viññāṇassa nirodhena, etth'etaṃ uparujjhati*, the *nirodha* of consciousness is said to result in the *uparodha* of whatever constitutes name-and-form. This is intriguing enough.

But that is not all. By way of preparing the background for the discussion, we have already made a brief allusion to the circumstances in which the Buddha uttered this verse.[32] What provided the context for its utterance was a riddle that occurred to a certain monk in a moment of fancy. The riddle was: 'Where do these four great primaries cease altogether?' There the verb used is *niruj-*

---

31 Nid II 110.

32 See sermon 6.

jhanti.[33] So in order to find where they cease, he whimsically went from heaven to heaven and from *Brahma*-world to *Brahma*-world. As we mentioned earlier, too, it was when the *Mahā Brahma* directed that monk to the Buddha, saying, "Why 'on earth' did you come all this way when the Buddha is there to ask?," that the Buddha reworded the question. He pointed out that the question was incorrectly worded and revised it as follows, before venturing to answer it:

> *Kattha āpo ca paṭhavī,*
> *tejo vāyo na gādhati,*
> *kattha dīghañca rassañca,*
> *aṇuṃ thūlaṃ subhāsubhaṃ,*
> *kattha nāmañca rūpañca,*
> *asesaṃ uparujjhati?*[34]

The word used by the Buddha in this revised version is *uparujjhati* and not *nirujjhati*. Yet another innovation is the use of the term *na gādhati*. Where do water, earth, fire, and air find no footing? Or where do they not get established? In short, here is a word suggestive of plumbing the depth of a reservoir. We may hark back to the simile given earlier, concerning the plumbing of the consciousness with the perception of form. Where do the four elements not find a footing? Also, where are such relative distinctions as long and short, subtle and gross, pleasant and unpleasant, as well as name-and-form, completely held in check?

In this restatement of the riddle, the Buddha has purposely avoided the use of the verb *nirujjhati*. Instead, he had recourse to such terms as *na gādhati*, 'does not find a footing,' 'does not plumb,' and *uparujjhati*, 'is held in check,' or 'is cut off.' This is evidence enough to infer that there is a subtle distinction between

---

[33] D I 215, *Kevaḍḍhasutta*.

[34] D I 223, *Kevaḍḍhasutta*.

the nuances associated with the two verbs *nirujjhati* and *uparujjhati*.

What is the secret behind this peculiar usage? The problem that occurred to this monk is actually of the type that the materialists of today conceive of. It is, in itself, a fallacy. To say that the four elements **cease** somewhere in the world, or in the universe, is a contradiction in terms. Why? Because the very question: 'Where do they cease?,' presupposes an answer in terms of those elements, by way of defining that place. This is the kind of uncouth question an ordinary materially inclined person would ask.

That is why the Buddha reformulated the question, saying: 'Monk, that is not the way to put the question. You should not ask 'where' the four great primaries cease, but rather where they, as well as the concepts of long and short, subtle and gross, pleasant and unpleasant, and name-and-form, are held in check.' The question proper is not where the four great primaries cease, but where they do not get established and where all their accompaniments are held in check.

Here, then, we see the Buddha relating the concept of matter, which the world takes for granted, to the perception of form arising in the mind. The four great primaries haunt the minds of the worldlings like ghosts, so they have to be exorcised from their minds. It is not a question of expelling them from this world, or from any heavenly realm, or the entire world-system. That exorcism should take place in this very consciousness, so as to put an end to this haunting.

Before the light of wisdom those ghosts, namely the four great primaries, become ineffective. It is in the darkness of ignorance that these ghosts haunt the worldlings with the perception of form. They keep the minds of the worldlings bound, glued, committed and limited. What happens now is that the specifically prepared consciousness, which was bound, glued, commit ted and limited, becomes fully released, due to the light of wisdom, to become non-manifestative, endless, and lustrous on all sides. So, to sum up, we may render the verse in question as follows:

"Consciousness, which is non-manifestative,
Endless, lustrous on all sides,
Here it is that earth and water,
Fire and air no footing find,
Here it is that long and short,
Fine and coarse, pleasant, unpleasant,
And name-and-form,
Are cut off without exception,
When consciousness has surceased,
These are held in check herein."

Though we ventured to translate the verse, we have not yet given the commentarial interpretation of it. Since this might seem a short coming, we shall now present what the commentator has to say on this verse.

Venerable Buddhaghosa, before coming to this verse in his commentary to the *Kevaḍḍhasutta*, gives an explanation as to why the Buddha reformulated the original question of that monk. According to him, the question: 'Where do the four great primaries cease?,' implied both the organic and the inorganic aspects of matter, and in revising it, the Buddha limited its scope to the organic. In other words, Venerable Buddhaghosa presumes that the revised version has to be interpreted with reference to this human body. Hence he explains such words as 'long' and 'short,' occurring in the verse, in a limited sense as referring to the body's stature. How facile this interpretation turns out to be, one can easily discern as we go on.

Venerable Buddhaghosa keeps on reminding the reader that the questions are relevant only to the organic realm, *upādinnaṃ yeva sandhāya pucchati.*[35] So he interprets the terms *dīghañca rassañca*, long and short, as relative distinctions of a person's height, that is tallness and shortness. Similarly, the words *aṇuṃ thūlaṃ,*

---

[35] Sv II 393.

subtle and gross, are said to mean the small and big in the size of the body. Likewise *subha* and *asubhaṃ* are taken to refer to the comely and the ugly in terms of body's appearance.

The explanation given to the phrase *nāmañca rūpañca* is the most astounding of all. *Nāma* is said to be the name of the person and *rūpa* is his form or shape. All this goes to show that the commentator has gone off at a tangent, even in the interpretation of this verse, which is more or less the prologue to such an intricate verse as the one in question. He has blundered at the very outset in limiting the scope of those relative terms to the organic, thereby obscuring the meaning of that deep verse.

The significance of these relative terms, from the linguistic point of view, has been overlooked. Words like *dīghaṃ/rassaṃ* and *aṇuṃ/thūlaṃ* do not refer to the stature and size of some person. What they convey is the dichotomous nature of concepts in the world. All those deeper implications are obscured by the reference to a person's outward appearance. The confusion becomes worse confounded, when *nāmañca rūpañca* is interpreted as the name and the shape of a person. So the stage is already set for a shallow interpretation, even before presenting the verse beginning with *viññāṇaṃ anidassanaṃ*.

It is on such an unsound premise that the commentator bases his interpretation of the verse in question. We shall try to do justice to that exposition, too. It might necessitate a fair amount of quotations, though it is difficult to be comprehensive in this respect.

The commentator begins his exposition with the word *viññāṇaṃ* itself. He comes out with a peculiar etymology: *Viññāṇan'ti tattha viññātabbanti viññāṇaṃ nibbānassa nāmaṃ*, which means that the word *viññāṇa*, or consciousness, is in this context a synonym for *Nibbāna*, in the sense that it is 'to be known,' *viññātabbaṃ*. This forced etymology is far from convincing, since such a usage is not attested elsewhere. Moreover, we come across a long list of epithets for *Nibbāna*, as many as thirty-three, in the

Asaṅkhatasaṃyutta of the *Saṃyutta Nikāya*, but *viññāṇa* is not counted as one.[36] In fact, nowhere in the discourses is *viññāṇa* used as a synonym for *Nibbāna*.

Next, he takes up the word *anidassana*, and makes the following comment: *Tad etaṃ nidassanābhāvato anidassanaṃ*, that *Nibbāna* is called *anidassana* because no illustration for it could be given. The idea is that it has nothing to compare with. Then comes the explanation of the word *anantaṃ*. According to the commentator *Nibbāna* is called *ananta*, endless, because it has neither the arising-end, *uppādanto*, nor the falling-end, *vayanto*, nor the otherwiseness of the persisting-end, *ṭhitassa aññathatta*. Strangely enough, even the last mentioned middle-state is counted as an 'end' in the commentator's concept of three ends. So this is the substance of his commentary to the first three words *viññāṇaṃ, anidassanaṃ, anantaṃ*.

The commentarial interpretation of the term *sabbato pabhaṃ* is even more confusing. The word *pabhā* is explained as a synonym for *papa*, meaning 'ford.' The *bha* element in the word, he explains, is a result of consonantal interchange with the original *pa* in *papa*. *Pakārassa pana bhakāro kato*. The idea is that the original form of this particular term for *Nibbāna* is *sabbato papaṃ*. The meaning attributed to it is 'with fords on all sides.' *Nibbāna* is supposed to be metaphorically conceived as the ocean, to get down into which there are fords on all sides, namely the thirty-eight topics of meditation. This interpretation seems rather far-fetched. It is as if the commentator has resorted to this simile of a ford, because he is already 'in deep waters'! The word *pabhā*, as it is, clearly means light, or radiance, and its association with wisdom is also well attested in the canon.

Though in his commentary to the *Dīgha Nikāya* Venerable Buddhaghosa advances the above interpretation, in his commentary to the *Majjhima Nikāya* he seems to have had second thoughts

---

[36] S IV 359, *Asaṅkhatasaṃyutta*.

on the problem. In the *Brahmanimantanikasutta* of the *Majjhima Nikāya*, also, the first two lines of the verse, *viññāṇaṃ anidassanaṃ, anantaṃ sabbato pabhaṃ,* occur.[37] But here the commentator follows a different line of interpretation. Whereas in his commentary to the *Kevaḍḍhasutta* he explains *anidassanaṃ* as an epithet of *Nibbāna*, in the sense of having nothing to compare with, here he takes it in the sense of not being visible to the eye. *Cakkhuviññāṇassa āpāthaṃ anupagamanato anidassanaṃ nāma,*[38] "It is called *anidassana* because it does not come within the range of eye-consciousness."

In explaining the term *sabbato pabhaṃ*, he suggests several alternative interpretations. In the first interpretation, he takes *pabhā* to mean light, or lustre. *Sabbato pabhan'ti sabbato pabhāsampannaṃ. Nibbānato hi añño dhammo sappabhataro vā jotivantataro vā parisuddhataro vā paṇḍarataro vā natthi.* "*Sabbato pabhaṃ* means more lustrous than anything else. For there is nothing more lustrous or luminous or purer or whiter than *Nibbāna*." In this interpretation *Nibbāna* is even regarded as something white in colour!

The etymology of the term *sabbato pabhaṃ* has been given a twist, for the word *sabbato* is taken in a comparative sense, 'more lustrous than anything.' As we have pointed out, the term actually means 'lustrous on all sides.' Then a second interpretation is given, bringing in the word *pabhū*, 'lord' or 'chief.' *Sabbato vā pabhū*, that is to say more prominent than anything else. In support of it he says: *Asukadisāya nāma nibbānaṃ natthī'ti na vattabbaṃ*, "It should not be said that in such and such a direction *Nibbāna* is not to be found." He says that it is called *pabhū*, or lord, because it is to be found in all directions. Only as the third interpretation he cites his simile of the ford already given in his commentary to the *Kevaḍḍhasutta*.

---

37 M I 329, *Brahmanimantanikasutta*.

38 Ps II 413.

What is the reason for giving so many figurative interpretations as alternatives to such a significant verse? Surely the Buddha would not have intended the verse to convey so many conflicting meanings, when he preached it.

No doubt the commentators have made a great effort to preserve the *Dhamma*, but due to some unfortunate historical circumstances, most of the deep discourses dealing with the subject of *Nibbāna* have been handed down without even a clue to the correct version among variant readings. This has left the commentators nonplussed, so much so that they had to give us several vague and alternative interpretations to choose from. It is up to us to decide, whether we should accept this position as it is, or try to improve on it by exploring any other possible means of explanation.

We had occasion to mention in our very first sermon that the Buddha himself has prophesied that those discourse which deal with voidness would, in time to come, go into disuse, with their deeper meanings obscured.[39] The interpretations just quoted go to show that already the prediction has come true to a great extent.

The phrase we quoted from the *Brahmanimantanikasutta* with its reference to *anidassana viññāṇa* occurs in a context which has a significance of its own. The relevant paragraph, therefore, deserves some attention. It runs as follows:

> *Viññānaṃ anidassanaṃ anantaṃ sabbato pabhaṃ, taṃ paṭhaviyā paṭhavittena ananubhūtaṃ, āpassa āpattena ananubhūtaṃ, tejassa tejattena ananubhūtaṃ, vāyassa vāyattena ananubhūtaṃ, bhūtānaṃ bhūtattena ananubhūtaṃ, devānaṃ devattena ananubhūtaṃ, pajāpatissa pajāpatittena ananubhūtaṃ, brahmānaṃ brahmattena ananubhūtaṃ, ābhassarānaṃ ābhassarattena ananubhūtaṃ, subhakiṇhānaṃ subhakiṇhattena ananubhūtaṃ,*

---

[39] S II 267, *Āṇisutta*; see sermon 1.

> *vehapphalānaṃ vehapphalatte ananubhūtaṃ, abhibhussa abhibhuttena ananubhūtaṃ, sabbassa sabbattena ananubhūtaṃ.*[40]
>
> "Consciousness which makes nothing manifest, infinite and all lustrous, it does not partake of the earthiness of earth, the wateriness of water, the fieriness of fire, the airiness of air, the creature-hood of creatures, the *deva*-hood of *devas*, the *Pajāpati*-hood of *Pajāpati*, the *Brahma*-hood of *Brahma*, the radiance of the Radiant Ones, the *Subhakiṇha*-hood of the *Subhakiṇha Brahmas*, the *Vehapphala*-hood of the *Vehapphala Brahmas*, the overlord-ship of the overlord, and the all-ness of the all."

This peculiar paragraph, listing thirteen concepts, seems to convey something deep about the nature of the non-manifestative consciousness. That consciousness does not partake of the earthiness of earth, the wateriness of water, the fieriness of fire, and the airiness of air. That is to say, the nature of the four elements does not inhere in this consciousness, they do not manifest themselves in it. Similarly, the other concepts, like *deva*-hood, *Brahma*-hood, etc., which the worldlings take seriously as real, have no applicability or validity here.

The special significance of this assertion lies in the context in which the Buddha declared it. It is to dispel a wrong view that Baka the *Brahma* conceived, in regarding his *Brahma* status as permanent, everlasting and eternal, that the Buddha made this declaration before that *Brahma* himself in the *Brahma* world. The whole point of the discourse, then, is to challenge the wrong view of the *Brahma*, by asserting that the non-manifestative consciousness of the *arahant* is above the worldly concepts of elements and divinity and the questionable reality attributed to them. In other

---

[40] M I 329, *Brahmanimantanikasutta.*

words, they do not manifest themselves in it. They are transcended.

Nibbāna Sermon 8

Namo tassa Bhagavato Arahato Sammāsambuddhassa
Namo tassa Bhagavato Arahato Sammāsambuddhassa
Namo tassa Bhagavato Arahato Sammāsambuddhassa

Etaṃ santaṃ, etaṃ paṇītaṃ, yadidaṃ sabbasaṅkhārasamatho sabbūpadhipaṭinissaggo taṇhakkhayo virāgo nirodho nibbānaṃ.[1]

"This is peaceful, this is excellent, namely the stilling of all preparations, the relinquishment of all assets, the destruction of craving, detachment, cessation, extinction."

With the permission of the Most Venerable Great Preceptor and the assembly of the venerable meditative monks.

The other day we ended our sermon by discussing how far the *Brahmanimantanikasutta* of the *Majjhima Nikāya* helps us to understand what *anidassana viññāṇa* is. We quoted a certain paragraph from that discourse as a starting point for our discussion. Let us now remind ourselves of it:

> *Viññānaṃ anidassanaṃ anantaṃ sabbato pabhaṃ, taṃ paṭhaviyā paṭhavittena ananubhūtaṃ, āpassa āpattena ananubhūtaṃ, tejassa tejattena ananubhūtaṃ, vāyassa vāyattena ananubhūtaṃ, bhūtānaṃ bhūtattena ananubhūtaṃ, devānaṃ devattena ananubhūtaṃ, pajāpatissa pajāpatittena ananubhūtaṃ, brahmānaṃ brahmattena*

---

[1] M I 436, *MahāMālunkyasutta*.

> *ananubhūtaṃ, ābhassarānaṃ ābhassarattena ananubhūtaṃ, subhakiṇhānaṃ subhakiṇhattena ananubhūtaṃ, vehapphalānaṃ vehapphalattena ananubhūtaṃ, abhibhussa abhibhuttena ananubhūtaṃ, sabbassa sabbattena ananubhūtaṃ.*[2]

> "Consciousness which makes nothing manifest, infinite and all lustrous. It does not partake of the earthiness of earth, the wateriness of water, the fieriness of fire, the airiness of air, the creature-hood of creatures, the *deva*-hood of *devas*, the *Pajāpati*-hood of *Pajāpati*, the *Brahma*-hood of *Brahma*, the radiance of the Radiant Ones, the *Subhakiṇha*-hood of the *Subhakiṇha Brahmas*, the *Vehapphala*-hood of the *Vehapphala Brahmas*, the overlord-ship of the overlord, and the all-ness of the all."

The gist of this paragraph is that the non-manifestative consciousness which is infinite and all lustrous, is free from the qualities associated with any of the concepts in the list, such as the earthiness of earth and the wateriness of water. That is to say it is not under their influence, it does not partake of them, *ananubhūtaṃ*. Whatever nature the world attributes to these concepts, whatever reality they invest it with, that is not registered in this non-manifestative consciousness. That is why this consciousness is said to be uninfluenced by them.

Usually, the worldlings attribute a certain degree of reality to concepts in everyday usage. These may be reckoned as mind-objects, things that the mind attends to. The word *dhamma* also means 'a thing,' so the worldling thinks that there is some-'thing' in each of these concepts. Or, in other words, they believe that there is something as an inherent nature or essence in these objects of the mind.

---

[2] M I 329, *Brahmanimantanikasutta*.

But the quotation in question seems to imply that this so-called nature is not registered in the *arahant*'s mind. It is extremely necessary for the worldling to think that there is some real nature in these mind-objects. Why? Because in order to think of them as objects they have to have some essence, at least they must be invested with an essence, and so the worldlings do invest them with some sort of an essence, and that is the earthiness of earth, the wateriness of water, etc. Likewise there is a being-hood in beings, a *deva*-hood in *devas*, a *Pajāpati*-hood in *Pajāpati*, a *Brahma*-hood in *Brahma*, so much so that even in the concept of all, there is an all-ness – and this is the worldlings' standpoint.

Attributing a reality to whatever concept that comes up, the worldlings create for themselves perceptions of permanence, perceptions of the beautiful, and perceptions of self. In other words, they objectify these concepts in terms of craving, conceit and views. That objectification takes the form of some inherent nature attributed to them, such as earthiness, *deva*-hood etc.

But as for the non-manifestative consciousness, it is free from the so-called natures that delude the worldlings. In the consciousness of the *arahants*, there is not that infatuation with regard to the mass of concepts which the worldlings imagine as real, in order to keep going this drama of existence. This fact is clearly borne out by another statement in the *Brahmanimantanikasutta*. The Buddha makes the following declaration, to break the conceit of Baka the *Brahma*, who conceived the idea of permanence regarding his status as a *Brahma*:

Paṭhaviṃ kho ahaṃ, brahme, paṭhavito abhiññāya yāvatā paṭhaviyā paṭhavittena ananubhūtaṃ tadabhiññāya paṭhaviṃ nāhosim, paṭhaviyā nāhosiṃ, paṭhavito nāhosiṃ, paṭhaviṃ me'ti nāhosiṃ, paṭhaviṃ nābhivadiṃ.[3]

"Having understood through higher knowledge earth as earth, O Brahma," (that is to say having understood by means of a special

---

[3] ibid.

kind of knowledge, and not by means of the ordinary sense-perception), "and having understood through higher knowledge whatever that does not partake of the earthiness of earth," (the reference here is to that non-manifestative consciousness, which is to be described in the passage to follow), "I did not claim to be earth," *paṭhaviṃ nāhosim*, "I did not claim to be on earth," *paṭhaviyā nāhosiṃ*, "I did not claim to be from earth," *paṭhavito nāhosiṃ*, "I did not claim earth as mine," *paṭhaviṃ me'ti nāhosiṃ*, "I did not assert earth," *paṭhaviṃ nābhivadiṃ*.

The declensional forms given here are also suggestive of the fact that once the worldlings attribute some inherent nature to those concepts in terms of a 'ness,' as in earthy-ness, and make them amenable to their cravings, conceits and views, declensional forms come into usage, a few instances of which have been mentioned here. So, with regard to this earth, one can conceive of it as 'my earth,' or as 'I am on earth,' or 'I who am on the earth,' or 'from the earth.' By holding on tenaciously to these declensional forms of one's own creation, one is only asserting one's ego.

Now, for instance, we all know that what is called 'a flower' is something that can fade away. But when one conceives of it as 'The-flower-I-saw,' and thereby appropriates it into the concept of an I, it gets invested with the nature of permanence, since it can be 're-called.' A perception of permanence which enables one to think about it again, arises out of it. This is the idea behind the above reference.

It is in the nature of the released mind not to take these concepts seriously. It does not have a tenacious grasp on these declensional forms. It is convinced of the fact that they are mere conventions in ordinary usage. Due to that conviction itself, it is not subject to them. "I did not claim to be earth, I did not claim to be on earth, I did not claim to be from earth, I did not claim earth as mine, I did not assert earth," *paṭhaviṃ nābhivadiṃ*.

Here the word *abhivadiṃ* is suggestive of conceit. The three terms *abhinandati*, *abhivadati* and *ajjhosāya tiṭṭhati* are often mentioned together in the discourses.[4] *Abhinandati* means delighting in particular, which is suggestive of craving. *Abhivadati* means an assertion by way of conceit – an assertion which implies 'a taking up' of something. *Ajjhosāya tiṭṭhati* stands for dogmatic involvement regarding views. Thus *abhinandati*, *abhivadati,* and *ajjhosāya tiṭṭhati* correspond to the three terms *taṇhā*, craving, *māna*, conceit, and *diṭṭhi*, views, respectively.

Now out of these, what we find here is *abhivadati* – *paṭhaviṃ nābhivadiṃ*, "I did not assert earth" – I did not make any assertion about earth by way of conceit. From this, too, we can infer that the ordinary man in this world takes his perception of the earth seriously, and by conceiving of it as 'earth is mine,' 'I am on the earth,' etc., invests the concepts with a permanent nature. But this is a kind of device the worldlings adopt in order to perpetuate the drama of existence. However, everyone of these elements is void.

In this particular context, the four elements earth, water, fire and air, are mentioned at the very outset. The Buddha, having understood the emptiness and impermanence of these elements, does not cling to them. The ordinary worldling, on the other hand, clings to the perception of earth in a piece of ice because of its hardness. But as we know, when we heat it up to a certain degree, its watery quality reveals itself. Further heating would bring up its fiery nature. Continuous heating will convert it into vapour, revealing its air quality.

Thus these four great primaries, which the world clings to, also have the nature of impermanence about them. The emancipated one, who rightly understands this impermanence through his higher knowledge, does not get upset by their ghostly configurations. His consciousness is not subject to them. This is the import of the above paragraph.

---

[4] E.g. at M I 266, *MahāTaṇhāsaṅkhayasutta*.

The same holds true with regard to the other concepts. *Saṃsāric* beings have their conventional usages. One might think of oneself as a god among gods. Now Baka the *Brahma* had the conceit 'I am a *Brahma*.' But even his *Brahma*-status gets melted away like that piece of ice, at least after some aeons. So even *Brahma*-hood is subject to 'liquidation,' like an ice-cube.

In this way, the released consciousness of the *arahant* does not register a perception of permanence with regard to the concepts which masquerade as real in the worldling's drama of existence. That is why it is called 'non-manifestative' consciousness. That non-manifestative consciousness is free from those concepts.

By way of further explanation of the nature of this released mind, we may drop a hint through the analogy of the film and the drama, which we have employed throughout. Now, for instance, in order to produce a tragic scene on the screen, the film producers adopt subtle devices and camera tricks. Sometimes an awe-inspiring scene of conflagration or ruthless arson, which drives terror into the hearts of the audience, is produced with the help of cardboard houses. Cardboard houses are set on fire, but the audience is hoodwinked into thinking that a huge mansion is on fire. Similarly, terrific traffic accidents are displayed on the screen with the help of a few toys.

In this drama of existence, too, there are similar tragic scenes. Now, in spite of their tragic quality, if any member of the audience truly understands at that moment that these are cardboard houses and toys toppled from hill tops, he sees something comic in the apparently tragic. Likewise, in this drama of existence, there is a tragic aspect as well as a comic aspect.

As a matter of fact, both these words, tragic and comic, can be accommodated within the highly significant term *saṃvega*, anguish, sense of urgency. In trying to arouse *saṃvega* with regard to *saṅkhāras*, or preparations, we could bring in both these attitudes. The ordinary worldling sees only the tragic side of the drama of existence, and that is because of his ignorance. But the *arahant*, the emancipated one, sees in this drama of existence a comic side as well.

As an illustration we may allude to those occasions in which the Buddha himself and those disciples with psychic powers like Venerable MahāMoggalāna, are said to have shown a faint smile, *situppāda*, on seeing how beings in *saṃsāra* are reborn in high and low realms according to their deeds, as in a puppet show.[5] Of course, that spontaneous smile has nothing sarcastic or unkind about it. But all the same, it gives us a certain hint. This spontaneous smile seems to be the outcome of an insight into the comic aspect of this existential drama. The faint smile is aroused by the conviction of the utter futility and insubstantiality of the existential drama, seeing how beings who enjoyed high positions come down to the level of hungry ghosts, *petas*, or even to lower realms in their very next birth. It is somewhat like the response of one who has correctly understood the impermanence and the illusory nature of things shown on a film screen.

When one comes to think of this drama of existence, *saṃsāric* beings appear like puppets drawn upwards by the five higher fetters, *uddhambhāgiya saṃyojana*, and drawn downwards by the five lower fetters, *orambhāgiya saṃyojana*. They reappear more or less like puppets, manipulated up and down by strings, which are but the results of their own deeds.

The wherewithal for the drama of existence is supplied by the four great primaries – the four basic elements of earth, water, fire and air. In the case of a film or a drama, sometimes the same object can be improvised in a number of ways, to produce various scenes and acts. What in one scene serves as a sitting-stool, could be improvised as a footstool in another scene, and as a table in yet another. Similarly, there is something called double-acting in films. The same actor can delineate two characters and appear in different guises in two scenes.

A similar state of affairs is to be found in this drama of existence. In fact, the Buddha has declared that there is not a single

---

5 M II 45, M II 74, S I 24, S II 254-258, A III 214.

being in *saṃsāra* who has not been one of our relations at some time or other.[6] We are in the habit of putting down such relations to a distant past, in order to avoid a rift in our picture of the world by upsetting social conventions. But when one comes to think of it in accordance with the *Dhamma*, and also on the strength of certain well attested facts, sometimes the male or the female baby cuddled by a mother could turn out to be her own dead father or mother.

Such a strangely ludicrous position is to be found in the acts of this drama of existence. Usually the world is unaware of such happenings. Though ludicrous, the world cannot afford to laugh at it. Rather, it should be regarded as a sufficient reason for arousing an anguished sense of urgency: 'What a pity that we are subject to such a state of affairs! What a pity that we do not understand it because of the power of influxes and latencies and thereby heap up defilements!'

Such an awareness of the emptiness of all this can give rise to anguish. One can get some understanding on the lines of the signless, the unsatisfactory, and the void, by contemplating these facts. One can also contemplate on the four elements, how they are at the beginning of a world period, and how they get destroyed at the end of a world period, in the conflagration at the end of an aeon. Likewise, when one comes to think of the state of persons or beings in general, in accordance with this fact of relationship, there is much room for anguish and a sense of urgency.

It is because of all this that the Buddha sometimes declares, as in the discourse on the rising of seven suns, *Sattasuriyasutta*, that this is "enough to get disenchanted with all preparations, enough to get detached from them, enough to get released from them," *alameva sabbasaṅkhāresu nibbindituṃ alaṃ virajjituṃ alaṃ vimuccituṃ.*[7]

---

[6] S II 189-190, *Anamataggasaṃyutta.*

[7] A IV 100, *Sattasuriyasutta.*

We have been drawing upon a particular nuance of the term *saṅkhāra* throughout, that is, as things comparable to those instruments, temporarily improvised in a dramatic performance just for the purpose of producing various acts on the stage. It is the same with persons, who are like actors playing their parts.

Beings, who are born in accordance with their karma, entertain the conceit 'I am a god,' 'I am a *Brahma*.' Once their karma is spent up, they get destroyed and are reborn somewhere or other. It is the same with those items used in a drama, such as the stool and the footstool. But the intriguing fact is that those in the audience, watching each of those acts, grasp as such whatever objects they see on the stage when they produce their individual dramas.

We have already mentioned at the very outset that the final stage in the production of a drama is a matter for the audience and not for the theatricians. Each member of the audience creates a drama in his own mind, putting together all preparations. What serves as a stool in one act of the drama, may be used as a footstool in the next. In the first instance it sinks into the minds of the audience as a stool, and in the next as a footstool. It is the same in the case of beings and their relationships.

It must have been due to this state of affairs in the drama of existence, which arouses anguish, that the Buddha makes the declaration in quite a number of discourses dealing with the topic of impermanence, including those which describe the destruction of the aeon: 'This is enough, monks, to get disenchanted with all preparations, to get detached from them, to get released from them.'

These preparations are comparable to a film reel, which is the basic requirement for the film of name-and-form shown on the screen of consciousness of beings in this world. As the world is regarded as a sort of stage, trees, beings and objects in our environment are like objects on the stage. But the intriguing fact about it is that the ordinary man in the world is unaware of their 'prepared' nature as a frame work.

When one is watching a film, one becomes unaware of the fact that it is just something shown on the screen. At that moment it appears as something real and life-like. It is about this apparent reality that the Buddha speaks when he utters the following lines in the *Itivuttaka*: *Jātaṃ bhūtaṃ samuppannaṃ, kataṃ saṅkhatamaddhuvaṃ*;[8] "Born, become, arisen, made up, prepared, unstable." Whatever appears as real in this world, is actually made and prepared by *saṅkhāras*. It is their insubstantial nature, their impermanent, unsatisfactory and not-self nature, that is hinted at by these lines.

The term *saṅkhāra* is suggestive of some artificiality about this world. Everything that goes to 'make-it-up' is a *saṅkhāra*. The non-manifestative consciousness, which is aware of its impermanent nature, is therefore free from these preparations. It is free from those concepts which the worldlings cling to. It remains unshaken by their ghostly transfigurations. We come across four wonderful verses in the *Adhimutta Theragāthā* which, though extremely simple, give us a deep insight into this freedom in the *arahant*'s mind.

The story of Venerable Adhimutta is a marvelous one.[9] While going through a forest Venerable Adhimutta got caught to a band of robbers, who were just getting ready to offer a human sacrifice to the gods. So they got hold of this *arahant* as their victim. But the latter showed no consternation. There was no fear or terror in his face. The bandit chief asked him why he is unmoved. Then the Venerable Adhimutta uttered a set of verses in reply. Out of them, we may quote the following four significant verses:

Natthi cetasikaṃ dukkhaṃ,
anapekkhassa gāmani,
atikkantā bhayā sabbe,
khīṇasaṃyojanassa ve.[10]

---

[8] It 37, *Ajātasutta*.

[9] Th-a III 12.

[10] Th 707, *Adhimutta Theragāthā*.

"There is no mental pain
To one with no expectations, oh headman,
All fears have been transcended
By one whose fetters are extinct."

Na me hoti 'ahosin'ti,
'bhavissan'ti na hoti me,
saṅkhārā vibhavissanti,
tattha kā paridevanā?[11]

"It does not occur to me 'I was,'
Nor does it occur to me 'I will be,'
Mere preparations get destroyed,
What is there to lament?"

Suddhaṃ dhammasamuppādaṃ,
suddhaṃ saṅkhārasantatiṃ,
passantassa yathābhūtaṃ,
na bhayaṃ hoti gāmani.[12]

"To one who sees as it is,
The arising of pure *dhammas*
And the sequence of pure preparations,
There is no fear, oh headman."

Tiṇakaṭṭhasamaṃ lokaṃ,
yadā paññāya passati,
mamattaṃ so asaṃvindaṃ,
'natthi me'ti na socati.[13]

---

[11] Th 715, ibid.

[12] Th 716, ibid.

[13] Th 717, ibid.

"When one sees with wisdom,
This world as comparable to grass and twigs,
Not finding anything worthwhile holding on as mine,
One does not grieve: 'O! I have nothing!'"

At least a fraction of the gist of these four verses has already come up in some form or other in the sermons given so far. Now as for the first verse, addressed to the bandit chief, the first two lines say that there is no mental pain to one who has no expectations, cravings, or desire. The next two lines state that one whose fetters are destroyed has transcended fears.

To begin with, let us get at the meaning of this verse. Here it is said that there is no mental pain, *natthi cetasikaṃ dukkhaṃ*. In an earlier sermon based on the *Cetanāsutta* we happened to mention that for one who does not take body, word, and mind as real, there is no inward pleasure and pain, *ajjhattaṃ sukhadukkhaṃ*.[14] The relevant quotation is:

> *Avijjāya tveva asesavirāganirodhā so kāyo na hoti, yaṃ paccayāssa taṃ uppajjati ajjhattaṃ sukhadukkhaṃ . . . sā vācā na hoti . . . so mano na hoti . . . khettaṃ taṃ na hoti, vatthum taṃ na hoti, āyatanaṃ taṃ na hoti, adhikaraṇaṃ taṃ na hoti, yaṃ paccayāssa taṃ uppajjati ajjhattaṃ sukhadukkhaṃ.*[15]

With the complete fading away and cessation of ignorance, the *arahant* has no notion of a body. That is, he does not have a perception of a body, like that of a worldling, who takes it as such, due to his perception of the compact, *ghanasaññā*. Likewise that speech is not there, *sā vācā na hoti*. The basic reason for speech-preparation is the reality attributed to words and linguistic usages.

---

[14] See sermon 6.

[15] A II 158, *Cetanāsutta*.

When, for instance, someone scolds us, we are displeased at it because of the reality given to those words. Similarly, that mind is not there, *so mano na hoti.* It is only the collocation of preparations which arise and cease that is conceived as 'my mind.'

Therefore, whatever field, site, base or reason, owing to which there can arise inward pleasure or pain, is no longer there. If the bandits had actually killed him, he would not have had any mental pain, because he lets go before *Māra* comes to grab. This is the idea expressed in the first verse.

As for the second verse, there too the idea of voidness is well expressed. The thought 'I was,' does not occur to me. The idea 'I am' is not in me. Nor do I entertain the idea 'I will be.' That is to say, it does not occur to me that I had a past or that I will have a future. It only occurs to me that preparations get destroyed. That was what happened in the past and will happen in the future. So what is there to lament?

A very important idea emerges from these verses. Now this series of sermons is on the subject of *Nibbāna*. We thought of giving these sermons because of the existing variety of conflicting views on *Nibbāna*. There is no clear idea even about our goal, not only among non-Buddhists, but even among Buddhists themselves. From these verses we can glean some important facts. Here the reference is to existence. This *arahant* must have had numerous births as *pretas*, *Brahmas*, gods, and human beings. But he is not saying something false here. What is really meant by saying that it does not occur to me 'I was?'

Ordinary worldlings, or even those with higher psychic powers, when they see their past lives think of it as 'I was so and so in such and such a birth.' Sometimes one entertains a conceit at the thought 'I was a god,' 'I was a *Brahma*.' If he had been an animal or a *preta*, he is somewhat displeased. Such is not the case with this *arahant*. He sees that what was in the past is a mere heap of preparations, and what will be in the future is again a heap of preparations. It is like the case of that cinema goer who understands that whatever comes up in the film is artificially got up. It is a state of mind aroused by wisdom. 'So what is there to lament,' is the attitude resulting from it.

On an earlier occasion, we happened to compare these preparations to a heap of windings and unwindings in existence.[16] Now as to this process of winding and unwinding, we may take as an illustration the case of a rope. There is a winding and an unwinding in it. We can form an idea about the nature of this existence even with the help of a simple illustration.

Nibbāna has been defined as the cessation of existence.[17] The Buddha says that when he is preaching about the cessation of existence, some people, particularly the brahmins who cling to a soul theory, bring up the charge of nihilism against him.[18] Not only those brahmins and heretics believing in a soul theory, but even some Buddhist scholars are scared of the term *bhavanirodha*, fearing that it leads to a nihilistic interpretation of *Nibbāna*. That is why they try to mystify *Nibbāna* in various ways. What is the secret behind this attitude? It is simply the lack of a clear understanding of the unique philosophy made known by the Buddha.

Before the advent of the Buddha, the world conceived of existence in terms of a perdurable essence as 'being,' *sat*. So the idea of destroying that essence of being was regarded as annihilationism. It was some state of a soul conceived as 'I' and 'mine.' But according to the law of dependent arising made known by the Buddha, existence is something that depends on grasping, *upādānapaccayā bhavo*. It is due to grasping that there comes to be an existence. This is the pivotal point in this teaching.

In the case of the footstool, referred to earlier, it became a footstool when it was used as such. If in the next act it is used to sit on, it becomes a stool. When it serves as a table, it becomes a table. Similarly in a drama, the same piece of wood, which in one act

---

[16] See sermon 6.

[17] E.g. at S II 117, *Kosambisutta*.

[18] M I 140, *Alagaddūpamasutta*.

serves as a walking stick to lean on, could be seized as a stick to beat with, in the next act.

In the same way, there is no essential thing-hood in the things taken as real by the world. They appear as things due to cravings, conceits and views. They are conditioned by the mind, but these psychological causes are ignored by the world, once concepts and designations are superimposed on them. Then they are treated as real objects and made amenable to grammar and syntax, so as to entertain such conceits and imaginings as, for instance, 'in the chair,' 'on the chair,' 'chair is mine,' and so on.

Such a tendency is not there in the released mind of the *arahant*. He has understood the fact that existence is due to grasping, *upādānapaccayā bhavo*. Generally, in the explanation of the law of dependent arising, the statement 'dependent on grasping, becoming' is supposed to imply that one's next life is due to one's grasping in this life. But this becoming is something that goes on from moment to moment. Now, for instance, what I am now holding in my hand has become a fan because I am using it as a fan. Even if it is made out of some other material, it will still be called a fan. But if it were used for some other purpose, it could become something else. This way we can understand how existence is dependent on grasping.

We began our discussion with the statement that existence is a heap of windings and unwindings. Let us now think of a simple illustration. Suppose a rope or a cord is being made up by winding some strands from either end by two persons. For the strands to gather the necessary tension, the two persons have to go on winding in opposite directions. But for the sake of an illustration, let us imagine a situation in which a third person catches hold of the strands in the middle, just before the other two start their winding. Oddly enough, by mistake, those two start winding in the same direction. Both are unaware of the fact that their winding is at the same time an unwinding. The one in the middle, too, is ignorant that it is his tight grasp in the middle which is the cause of stress and tension.

To all appearance, a cord is being made up which may be taken as two cords on either side of the one who has his hold on the middle. However, viewed from a distance, for all practical purposes it is just one cord that is being winded up.

To introduce a note of discord into this picture, let us suppose that the man in the middle suddenly lets go of his hold with a 'twang.' Now what happens to the cord? The windings in the same direction from both ends, which made it a cord, immediately get neutralized and **the cord ceases to be a cord**! Something like the stilling of all preparations and the abandonment of all assets happens at that moment. One realizes, 'as-it-is,' that no real cord existed at all.

The same state of affairs prevails in this world. The impermanence of this world, according to the Buddha, does not affect us so long as there is no grasping on our part. All windings in this world get unwinded immediately. This is the nature of the world. This is what is meant by *udayabbaya*, or rise and fall.

Now what happens if there is no grasping in the middle while the winding is going on in the same direction from both ends? No cord at all is made up, even if the two at either end go on winding for aeons and aeons. Why? Simply because they are winding in the same direction.

It is the same in the case of the world. The impermanence we see around us in this world does not affect us by itself. We are affected only when we grasp. It is the grasp in the middle that accounts for the cord, or rather, for whatever **has the semblance of a cord**. In fact, this is what the worldlings call 'the world.' This is what they take as **real**. Now what is the consequence of taking it to be real? If it is real and permanent, whatever is contrary to it, is annihilation, the destruction of a real world.

Keeping in mind the meaning of the Buddha's dictum 'dependent on grasping is existence,' *upādānapaccayā bhavo*, if one cares to reflect on this little illustration, one would realize that there is actually nothing real to get destroyed. There is no self or soul at all to get destroyed.

As a matter of fact, the impermanence of the world is a process of momentary arisings and ceasings. Given the grasping in the middle, that is to say, 'dependent on grasping is becoming,' the other links follow suit, namely 'dependent on becoming, birth; dependent on birth, decay-and-death, sorrow, lamentation, pain, grief and despair arise,' *bhavapaccayā jāti, jātipaccayā jarāmaraṇaṃ sokaparidevadukkhadomanassūpāyāsā sambhavanti.*

It is somewhat like the unpleasant tension caused by the winding, in the person who has a grasp at the middle. We have already referred to a short aphorism which sums up the content of the insight of those who realize the fruits of the path, like that of a stream-winner, namely, *yaṃ kiñci samudayadhammaṃ, sabbaṃ taṃ nirodhadhammaṃ*, "Whatever is of a nature to arise, all that is of a nature to cease."[19]

It does not seem to say anything significant, on the face of it. But it succinctly expresses the plainest conviction a stream-winner gets of the innocent process of arising and ceasing in the world. It is as if the one who had his grasp in the middle lets go of his hold for a while, through the power of the path moment.

It is in the nature of the ordinary worldling to hold on, and to hang on. That is why the man who grasped the cord in the middle refuses to let go of his hold in the midst of windings and unwindings, however much hardship he has to undergo in terms of sorrow, lamentation, pain, grief and despair. For him, it is extremely difficult to let go. Until a Buddha arises in the world and proclaims the *Dhamma*, the world stubbornly refuses to let go.

Now if one gives up the tendency to grasp, at least for a short while by developing the noble eightfold path at its supramundane level, and lets go even for one moment, then one understands as one grasps again that now there is less stress and tension. Personality view, doubt and dogmatic adherence to rules and observanc-

---

[19] See sermon 2.

es, *sakkāyadiṭṭhi, vicikicchā, sīlabbataparāmāsa,* are gone. An unwinding has occurred to some extent. The strands of the cord are less taut now.

One also understands, at the moment of arising from that supramundane experience, that one comes back to 'existence' because of grasping, because of the tendency to hold on. That this tendency to hold on persists due to influxes and latencies – due to unabandoned defilements – is also evident to him. This, in effect, is the immediate understanding of the law of dependent arising. It seems, then, that we have here in this simile of the cord, a clue to an understanding of the nature of this existence.

Worldlings in general, whether they call themselves Buddhist or non-Buddhist, conceive of existence in terms of a perdurable essence as 'being,' somewhat along the lines of the view of heretics. *Nibbāna* is something that drives terror into the worldlings, so long as there is no purification of view. The cessation of existence is much dreaded by them.

Even the commentators, when they get down to defining *Nibbāna*, give a wrong interpretation of the word *dhuva*. They sometimes make use of the word *sassata* in defining *Nibbāna*.[20] This is a word that should never be brought in to explain the term *Nibbāna*. According to them, *Nibbāna* is a permanent and eternal state. Only, you must not ask us, what precisely it is. For, if we are more articulate, we would be betraying our proximity to such views as *Brahmanirvāna*.

What is the secret behind this anomalous situation? It is the difficulty in interpreting the term *dhuva*, which the Buddha uses as a synonym for *Nibbāna*.[21] The true significance of this synonym has not been understood. It means stable or immovable. Of course, we do come across this term in such contexts as *niccaṃ, dhuvaṃ,*

---

[20] E.g. at Dhp-a III 320 when explaining *accutaṃ ṭhānaṃ* of Dhp 225.

[21] S IV 370, *Asaṅkhatasaṃyutta*.

sassataṃ, acavanadhammaṃ,[22] "permanent, stable, eternal, not liable to passing away," when *Brahma* gives expression to his conceit of eternal existence. But that is because these terms are more or less related to each other in sense.

Then, in which sense is *Nibbāna* called *dhuva*? In the sense that the experience of *Nibbāna* is irreversible. That is why it is referred to as *acalaṃ sukhaṃ,*[23] "unshakeable bliss." The term *akuppā cetovimutti*, "unshakeable deliverance of the mind," expresses the same idea. Sometimes the Buddha refers to *Nibbāna* as *akuppā cetovimutti.*[24] All other such deliverances are shakeable, or irritable. As the expression *kuppapaṭicca santi*, "peace dependent on irritability,"[25] implies, they are irritable and shakeable.

Even if they are unshaken during one's lifetime, they get shaken up at death. The final winning post is the pain of death. That is the critical moment at which one can judge one's own victory or defeat. Before the pain of death, all other deliverances of the mind fall back defeated. But this deliverance, this unshakeable deliverance with its 'let go' strategy at the approach of death, gets never shaken. It is unshakeable. That is why it is called the bliss unshaken, *acalaṃ sukhaṃ*. That is why it is called stable, *dhuvaṃ*. It seems, then, that some of the terms used by the Buddha as epithets or synonyms of *Nibbāna* have not been correctly understood.

Sometimes the Buddha employs words, used by heretics, in a different sense. In fact, there are many such instances. Now, if one interprets such instances in the same sense as heretics use those words, it will amount to a distortion of the *Dhamma*. Here, too, we have such an instance. Unfortunately the commentators have used the term *sassata* to define *Nibbāna*, taking it to be something eternal.

---

22 E.g. at M I 326, *Brahmanimantanikasutta.*

23 Ud 93, *DutiyaDabbasutta*; Th 264, *Vimala Thera.*

24 M I 197, *MahāSāropamasutta.*

25 Sn 784, *Duṭṭhaṭṭhakasutta.*

The main reason behind this is the misconception regarding existence – that there is an existence in truth and fact. There is this term *asmimāna*, which implies that there is the conceit 'am' in this world. All other religious teachers were concerned with the salvation of a real 'I.' Or, in other words, to confer immortality on this 'I.' The Buddha, on the contrary, declared that what actually '**is**' there, is a conceit – the conceit 'am.' All what is necessary is the dispelling of this conceit. That is why we sometimes come across such references to *Nibbāna* as *sammā mānābhisamayā antam akāsi dukkhassa*,[26] "by rightly understanding conceit, he made an end of suffering," or *asmimānasamugghātaṃ pāpuṇāti diṭṭheva dhamme Nibbānaṃ*,[27] "One arrives at the eradication of the conceit 'am' which in itself is the attainment of *Nibbāna* here and now."

Some seem to think that the eradication of the conceit 'am' is one thing, and *Nibbāna* another. But along with the eradication of the conceit 'am,' comes extinction. Why? Because one has been winding all this time imagining this to be a real cord or rope. One remains ignorant of the true state of affairs, due to one's grasp in the middle. But the moment one lets go, one understands.

It is the insight into this secret that serves as the criterion in designating the *ariyan* according to the number of births he has yet to take in *saṃsāra*. Thus, the stream-winner is called *sattakkhattuparamo*,[28] 'seven-times-at-the-most.' With the sudden unwinding, which reduces the tension, one understands the secret that the noble eightfold path is the way to unwinding.

One hangs on, because one is afraid to let go. One thinks that to let go is to get destroyed. The Buddha declares that the heaviness of one's burden is due to one's grasping.[29] What accounts for its

---

[26] M I 12, *Sabbāsavasutta*.

[27] A IV 353, *Sambodhisutta*.

[28] S II 185, *Puggalasutta*.

[29] S III 25, *Bhārasutta*.

weight is the very tenacity with which one clings to it. This the worldlings do not understand. So they cling on to the rope, for fear of getting destroyed. But if one lets go of one's hold, even for a moment, one would see that the tensed strands will get relaxed at least for that moment – that there is an immediate unwinding. Full understanding of that unwinding will come when one 'lets-go' completely. Then all influxes and latencies are destroyed.

So this little verse gives us a deep insight into the problem. What is there to lament? Because there are no notions like 'I was' or 'I am.' There is only a destruction of preparations.

The term *vibhava* is used in this context in a different sense. It refers here to the destruction of preparations. When using the two terms *bhava* and *vibhava*, some conceive of *bhava*, or existence, as a real perdurable essence, like a soul, and *vibhava* as its destruction. But here the word *vibhava*, in *vibhavissanti*, refers to the destructions of preparations. There is nothing lamentable about it. In the context of a drama, they are the paraphernalia improvised to stage an act, like the stool and the footstool. When one comes to think of individuals, they are no better than a multitude of puppets manipulated by fetters of existence in accordance with karma.

Even in the delivering of this sermon, there is a trace of a puppet show. The sermon is inspired by the audience. If there is no audience, there is no sermon. We are all enacting a drama. Though for us, this particular act of the drama is so important, there might be similar dramatic acts a few meters away from here in the jungle. A swarm of black ants might be busily hauling away an earthworm reeling in pain. That is one act in their own drama of life. All our activities are like that.

It is our unawareness of this framework that constitutes ignorance. If at any time one sees this framework of ignorance, free from influxes and latencies, one gets an unobstructed vision of the world. It is as if the doors of the cinema hall are suddenly flung open. The scene on the screen fades away completely then and there, as we have described above.[30] Let us now come to the third verse:

Suddhaṃ dhammasamuppādaṃ,
suddhaṃ saṅkhārasantatiṃ,
passantassa yathābhūtaṃ,
na bhayaṃ hoti gāmani.[31]

"To one who sees the arising of pure phenomena and the sequence of pure preparations as it is, there is no fear, oh headman." This verse, too, has a depth of meaning, which we shall now try to elucidate.

Why are the phenomena qualified by the word pure, *suddha dhamma*, in this context? Because the mind-objects, which are generally regarded as *dhamma* by the world, are impure. Why are they impure? Because they are 'influenced' by influxes. Now here we have 'un-influenced' or influx-free phenomena. To the *arahant*'s mind the objects of the world occur free of influxes. That is to say, they do not go to build up a prepared, *saṅkhata*. They are quasi-preparations. They do not go to build up a film show.

If, for instance, one who is seeing a film show, has the full awareness of the artificiality of those library-shots which go to depict a tragic scene on the screen, without being carried away by the latency to ignorance, one will not be able to 'enjoy' the film show. In fact, the film show does not exist for him. The film show has 'ceased' for him.

Similarly, the *arahant* sees phenomena as pure phenomena. Those mind-objects arise only to cease, that is all. They are merely a series of preparations, *suddhaṃ saṅkhārasantatiṃ*. 'The film reel is just being played' – that is the way it occurs to him. Therefore, "to one who sees all this, there is no fear, oh headman."

---

[30] See sermon 5.

[31] Th 716, *Adhimutta Theragāthā*.

Let us try to give an illustration for this, too, by way of an analogy. As we know, when a sewing machine goes into action, it sews up two folds of cloth together. But supposing suddenly the shuttle runs out of its load of cotton. What happens then? One might even mistake the folds to be actually sewn up, until one discovers that they are separable. This is because the conditions for a perfect stitch are lacking. For a perfect stitch, the shuttle has to hasten and put a knot every time the needle goes down.

Now, for the *arahant*, the shuttle refuses to put in the knot. For him, preparations, or *saṅkhāras*, are ineffective in producing a prepared, or *saṅkhata*. He has no cravings, conceits and views. For knots of existence to occur, there has to be an attachment in the form of craving, a loop in the form of conceit, and a tightening in the form of views. So, then, the *arahant*'s mind works like a sewing machine with the shuttle run out of its load of cotton. Though referred to as 'functional consciousness,' its function is not to build up a prepared, since it is influx-free. The phenomena merely come up to go down, just like the needle.

Why is ignorance given as the first link in the formula of dependent arising? It is because the entire series is dependent on ignorance. It is not a temporal sequence. It does not involve time. That is why the *Dhamma* is called timeless, *akālika*. It is the stereotype interpretation of the formula of dependent arising in terms of three lives that has undermined the immediate and timeless quality of the *Dhamma*. Since ignorance is the root cause of all other conditions, inclusive of becoming, *bhava*, birth, *jāti*, and decay-and-death, *jarāmaraṇaṃ*, that state of affairs immediately ceases with the cessation of ignorance. This, then, is the reason for the last line, *na bhayaṃ hoti gāmani*, "there is no fear, oh headman."

Deathlessness, *amata*, means the absence of the fear of death. The fear that the world has about death is something obsessional.

It is like the obsessional dread aroused by the sight of an anthill due to its association with a cobra.

As a matter of fact, this body has been compared to an anthill in the *Vammikasutta* of the *Majjhima Nikāya*.[32] This bodily frame, made up of the four elements, procreated by parents and built up with food and drink, is metaphorically conceived as an anthill. The discourse says: "Take the knife, oh wise one, and dig in." The world has the obsession that there is a real cobra of a self inside this anthill. But once it is dug up, what does one find? One discovers an *arahant*, who has realized selflessness, a selfless cobra, worthy of honour. Of course, this might sound as a post-script on *Vammikasutta*, but the metaphor is so pregnant with meaning, that it can well accommodate this interpretation, too.

The world has a 'perception-of-the-compact,' *ghanasaññā*, with regard to this body made up of the four elements. Because of that very perception or notion of compactness, there is a fear of death.

There is birth, because there is existence. Now this might, on analysis, give us an insight into the law of dependent arising. The term *jāti*, or birth, generally calls to mind the form of a child coming out of the mother's womb. But in this context the Buddha uses the term in relation to *bhava*, or existence, which in its turn is related to *upādāna*, or grasping. It is at the time we use something as a foot stool that a footstool is 'born.' When it has ceased to serve that purpose, the footstool is 'dead.'

It is in this sense that all assets, *upadhi*, are said to be of a nature to be born, *jātidhammā hete, bhikkhave, upadhayo*,[33] "All these assets, monks, are of the nature to be born." Not only the animate objects, like wife and children, men and women slaves, etc., but even gold and silver are mentioned there as of a nature to be born. Now let us ponder over this statement. How can gold and silver be born? How can they grow old? They are born because of

---

[32] M I 144, *Vammikasutta*.

[33] M I 162, *Ariyapariyesanasutta*.

craving, conceit and views. They come into existence. They are born. Because of birth, they grow old. Therefore they become objects for sorrow, lamentation and the like to arise.

For one who looks upon them as pure preparations, all those objects do not crystallize into 'things.' The description of the non-manifestative consciousness in the *Brahmanimantanikasutta* looks like a riddle in the form of a jumble of negative terms like *paṭhaviṃ nāhosim, paṭhaviyā nāhosiṃ, paṭhavito nāhosiṃ*, etc., "I did not claim to be earth, I did not claim to be in earth, I did not claim to be from earth."

But what is the general idea conveyed by these expressions? The implication is that the *arahant* looks upon all those concepts, which the worldlings make use of to make up an existence and to assert the reality of this drama of existence, as mere pretensions. He is convinced of their vanity and insubstantiality. As we have already explained with the simile of the sewing machine, an existence does not get stitched up or knitted up. The cessation of existence is experienced then and there.

Some seem to think that the *arahant* experiences the *Nibbānic* bliss only after his death. But the cessation of existence is experienced here and now, *diṭṭheva dhamme*. This is something marvelous and unknown to any other religious system. It is just at the moment that the shuttle of the sewing machine runs out of its load of cotton that the cessation of existence is experienced. It is then that the latencies are uprooted and all influxes are destroyed. Cravings, conceits and views refuse to play their part, with the result that mere preparations come up and go down. This is the ambrosial deathless. It is said that the *arahants* partake of ambrosial deathlessness, *amataṃ paribhuñjanti*.[34]

What actually happened in the case of the Venerable *arahant* Adhimutta was that the bandit chief understood the *Dhamma* and set him free, instead of killing him, and even got ordained under

---

[34] A I 45, *Amatavagga*.

him. But even if he had killed him, Venerable Adhimutta would have passed away, experiencing the ambrosial deathless. Why? Because he can let go before *Māra* comes to grab. He is, therefore, fearless. The obsessional fear of death common to worldlings has vanished. This, then, is the ambrosia. It is not some medicine or delicious drink for the possession of which gods and demons battle with each other. It is that bliss of deliverance, the freedom from the fear of death. Needless to say that it requires no seal of everlastingness.

As we once pointed out, in tune with the two lines of the following canonical verse, *kiṃ kayirā udapānena, āpā ce sabbadā siyuṃ,*[35] "What is the use of a well, if water is there all the time?" Once the thirst is quenched forever, why should one go in search of a well? Let us now take up the next verse.

> *Tiṇakaṭṭhasamaṃ lokaṃ,*
> *yadā paññāya passati,*
> *mamattaṃ so asaṃvindaṃ,*
> *'natthi me'ti na socati.*[36]

Now all these verses are eloquent expressions of voidness, *suññatā*. When one sees with wisdom the entire world, that is both the internal and external world, as comparable to grass and twigs in point of worthlessness, one does not entertain the conceit 'mine' and therefore does not lament, saying: 'Oh, I have nothing.' One is not scared of the term *bhavanirodha*, or cessation of existence. Why? Because all these are worthless things.

Here too, we may add something more by way of explanation, that is as to how things become 'things' in this world – though this may seem obvious enough. Since we have been so concerned with dramas, let us take up a dramatic situation from the world.

---

[35] Ud 79, *Udapānasutta*; see sermon 1.

[36] Th 717, *Adhimutta Theragāthā*.

A man is hastily walking along a jungle path. Suddenly his foot strikes against a stone. 'Oh, it is so painful!' He kicks the stone with a curse. A few more steps, and another stone trips him. This time it is even more painful. He turns round, quietly, picks up the stone, cleans it carefully, looking around, wraps it up in his handkerchief and slips it into his pocket. Both were stones. But why this special treatment? The first one was a mere pebble, but the second one turned out to be a gem!

The world esteems a gem stone as valuable because of craving, conceits and views. So the first accident was a mishap, but the second – a stroke of luck. Now, had all these mishaps and haps been filmed, it would have become something of a comedy. Everything in our environment, even our precious possessions like gold, silver, pearls, and gems, appear like the paraphernalia improvised for a dramatic performance on the world stage. Once they come on the stage, from backstage, they appear as real things. Not only do they appear as real, relative to the acts of the drama, but they get deposited in our minds as such.

It is such 'deposits' that become our aggregates of grasping, or 'assets,' which we take along with us in this *saṃsāra* in the form of likes and dislikes. Loves and hates contracted in the past largely decide our behaviour in the present with some sort of subconscious acquiescence, so much so that we often form attachments and revengeful aversions in accordance with them. When one comes to think of it, there is something dramatic about it. When something serves as a footstool in a particular act, it is 'really' a footstool. When it is improvised to serve as some other thing in the next act, one is unaware of the fact that it is the same object. One is not aware of the hoodwink involved in it. Such a state of affairs prevails over the nature of preparations, *saṅkhāras*.

Being ignorant of the fact that these are purely preparations, the worldlings take concepts too seriously, to come to conclusions such as 'I was so and so in such and such a birth,' thereby clinging on to all the animate and inanimate objects in the world. They are actually comparable to things temporarily improvised to depict a particular scene in a drama or a film show. That is why we compared the four elements to ghosts.[37] Deluded by their ghostly transfigurations, the worldlings create for themselves a perception of form. The verse in question gives us an insight into this particular aspect of the drama of existence.

A meditator can get at least an inkling of the emptiness and insubstantiality of this drama of existence, when he trains himself in keeping the four postures with mindfulness and full awareness. By practising it, he gets an opportunity to witness a monodrama, free of charge. And this is the drama: When walking, he understands: 'I am walking'; when standing, he understands: 'I am standing'; when sitting, he understands: 'I am sitting'; when lying down, he understands: 'I am lying down.'[38] While keeping one's postures in this manner, one sees in outline one's own form as if one were acting in a monodrama.

When the basis of the factors of the form group is removed, those in the name group are reduced to purposeless activations. Earth, water, fire and air constitute the basis of form. When a meditator becomes dispassionate with regard to these four elements, when they begin to fade away for him, the factors in the name group assume a ghostly character. He feels as if he is performing a drama with non-existing objects. He opens a non-existing door, sits on a non-existing chair, and so on.

Now if we try to understand this in terms of an analogy of a drama, as we have been doing throughout, we may compare it to a mime or a dumb show. In a dumb show, one might see such acts as follows: An actor rides a no-bike, climbs a no-hill, meets a no-friend and has a no-chat with him. Or else he may sit on a no-chair by a no-table and writes a no-letter with a no-pen. What we mean by the no-nos here is the fact that on the stage there is neither a bicycle, nor a hill, nor another person, nor any other object like a chair, a table or a pen. All these are merely suggested by his

---

[37] See sermon 1.

[38] M I 57, *Satipaṭṭhānasutta.*

acting. This kind of dumb show has a comic effect on the audience.

An insight meditator, too, goes through a similar experience when he contemplates on name-and-form, seeing the four elements as empty and void of essence, which will give him at least an iota of the conviction that this drama of existence is empty and insubstantial. He will realize that, as in the case of the dumb show, he is involved with things that do not really exist. This amounts to an understanding that the factors of the name group are dependent on the form group, and vice versa.

Seeing the reciprocal relationship between name-and-form, he is disinclined to dabble in concepts or gulp down a dose of prescriptions. If form is dependent on name, and name is dependent on form, both are void of essence. What is essential here, is the very understanding of essencelessness. If one sits down to draw up lists of concepts and prescribe them, it would only lead to a mental constipation. Instead of release there will be entanglement. Such a predicament is not unlikely.

Nibbāna Sermon 9

Namo tassa Bhagavato Arahato Sammāsambuddhassa
Namo tassa Bhagavato Arahato Sammāsambuddhassa
Namo tassa Bhagavato Arahato Sammāsambuddhassa

Etaṃ santaṃ, etaṃ paṇītaṃ, yadidaṃ sabbasaṅkhārasamatho sabbūpadhipaṭinissaggo taṇhakkhayo virāgo nirodho nibbānaṃ.[1]

"This is peaceful, this is excellent, namely the stilling of all preparations, the relinquishment of all assets, the destruction of craving, detachment, cessation, extinction."

With the permission of the Most Venerable Great Preceptor and the assembly of the venerable meditative monks.

This is the ninth sermon in the series of sermons given on the topic of *Nibbāna*. In our last sermon we discussed, to some extent, how the insubstantiality and the vanity of the comic acts enacted by *saṃsāric* beings in this drama of existence gradually become clear to a meditator as he keeps his postures according to the *Satipaṭṭhānasutta*. We mentioned how the fact that name is only a shadow of form is revealed to the meditator when he is attending to his postures seeing the elements constituting the basis of form as empty.

By way of analogy we brought in the simile of a mime or a dumb show. What characterizes that kind of drama is the comic nature of the acts which depict scenes suggestive of animate or

---

1 M I 436, *MahāMālunkyasutta*.

inanimate objects not actually present on the stage. A meditator becomes aware, while attending to his postures, that he is merely enacting a dumb show. He comes to understand how far name is dependent on form, and the four elements appear to him as empty.

In the *Satipaṭṭhānasutta* we find the following instruction in regard to the keeping of postures: *Yathā yathā vā pan'assa kāyo paṇihito hoti tathā tathā naṃ pajānāti,*[2] "In whatever way his body is disposed, so he understands it." This is suggestive of the attempt of a spectator to understand the mimicry of an actor or an actress in a pantomime. While attending to one's postures one feels as if one is watching a one-man dumb show. One gets an opportunity to watch it even more keenly when one comes to the section on full awareness, *sampajaññapabba*, dealing with the minor postures, *khuddaka iriyāpatha.*

The worldlings are in the habit of creating material objects in accordance with the factors on the name side in an extremely subtle manner, by grasping the four elements under the influence of the personality view, *sakkāyadiṭṭhi.* The material objects around us are recognized as such by grasping the four elements. The definition of the form aspect in name-and-form points to such a conclusion: *cattāro ca mahābhūtā catunnañca mahābhūtānaṃ upādāya rūpaṃ,*[3] "the four great primaries and form dependent on those four primaries."

The word *upādāya* in this context has a special connotation of relativity. So in this way, material objects are created with the help of factors in the name group. This reveals a certain principle of relativity. In this relativity one sees the emptiness of both name and form. This same principle of relativity is implicit in some other statements of the Buddha, but they are rather neglected for a lack of recognition of their significance. We come across such a discourse with a high degree of importance in the *Saḷāyatana-*

---

[2] M I 56, *Satipaṭṭhānasutta.*

[3] M I 53, *Sammādiṭṭhisutta.*

vagga of the *Saṃyutta Nikāya*. There the Buddha states that principle of relativity with the help of an illustration:

> *Hatthesu, bhikkhave, sati ādānanikkhepanaṃ paññāyati, pādesu sati abhikkamapaṭikkamo paññāyati, pabbesu sati sammiñjanapasāraṇaṃ paññāyati, kucchismiṃ sati jighacchā pipāsā paññāyati.*[4]

> "When there are hands, monks, a taking up and putting down is apparent; when there are feet, a going forward and coming back is apparent; when there are joints, a bending and stretching is apparent; when there is a belly, hunger and thirst is apparent."

Then the contrary of this situation is also given:

> *Hatthesu, bhikkhave, asati ādānanikkhepanaṃ na paññāyati, pādesu asati abhikkamapaṭikkamo na paññāyati, pabbesu asati sammiñjanapasāraṇaṃ na paññāyati, kucchismiṃ asati jighacchā pipāsā na paññāyati.*

> "When there are no hands, a taking up and putting down is not apparent; when there are no feet, a going forward and coming back is not apparent; when there are no joints, a bending and stretching is not apparent; when there is no belly, hunger and thirst are not apparent."

What is implied by all this is that basic principle of relativity. Some meditators, engaged in *satipaṭṭhāna* meditation, might think that materiality does not really exist and only mentality is there. In other words, there are no hands, only a taking up and putting down is there. There are no feet, only a going and coming is there. That

---

4 S IV 171, *Hatthapādopamasutta*.

way, they might dogmatically take the bare activity as real and subject it to an analysis. But what is important here is the understanding of the relativity between the two, which reveals the emptiness of both. If, on the other hand, one of them is taken too seriously as real, it ends up in a dogmatic standpoint. It will not lead to a deeper understanding of the emptiness of name and form.

Now in the case of a pantomime, as already mentioned, a spectator has to imagine persons and things not found on the stage as if they are present, in order to make sense out of an act. Here too we have a similar situation. Name and form exist in relation to each other. What one sees through this interrelation is the emptiness or insubstantiality of both.

We brought up all these analogies of dramas and film shows just to give an idea of the impermanence of *saṅkhāras*, or preparations. In fact, the term *saṅkhāra*, is very apt in the context of dramas and film shows. It is suggestive of a pretence sustained with some sort of effort. It clearly brings out their false and unreal nature.

The purpose of the perception of impermanence, with regard to this drama of existence, is the dispelling of the perception of permanence about the things that go to make up the drama. With the dispelling of the perception of permanence, the tendency to grasp a sign or catch a theme is removed. It is due to the perception of permanence that one grasps a sign in accordance with perceptual data. When one neither takes a sign nor gets carried away by its details, there is no aspiration, expectation, or objective by way of craving. When there is no aspiration, one cannot see any purpose or essence to aim at.

It is through the three deliverances, the signless, the desireless, and the void, that the drama of existence comes to an end. The perception of impermanence is the main contributory factor for the cessation of this drama. Some of the discourses of the Buddha, concerning the destruction of the world, can be cited as object lessons in the development of the perception of impermanence leading to the signless deliverance.

For instance, in the discourse on the appearance of the seven suns, *Sattasuriyasutta*, mentioned earlier,[5] this world system, which is so full of valuable things like the seven kinds of jewels, gets fully consumed in a holocaust leaving not even a trace of ash or soot, as if some ghee or oil has been burned up. The perception of impermanence, arising out of this description, automatically leads to an understanding of voidness.

If the conviction that not only the various actors and actresses on the world stage, but all the accompanying decorations get fully destroyed together with the stage itself at some point of time grips the mind with sufficient intensity to exhaust the influxes of sensuality, existence and ignorance, emancipation will occur then and there. That may be the reason why some attained *arahant-hood* immediately on listening to that sermon.[6] That way, the perception of impermanence acts as an extremely powerful antidote for defilements.

> *Aniccasaññā, bhikkhave, bhāvitā bahulīkatā sabbaṃ kāmarāgaṃ pariyādiyati, sabbaṃ rūparāgaṃ pariyādiyati, sabbaṃ bhavarāgaṃ pariyādiyati, sabbaṃ avijjaṃ pariyādiyati, sabbaṃ asmimānaṃ pariyādiyati samūhanati.*[7]

> "Monks, the perception of impermanence, when developed and intensively practised, exhausts all attachments to sensuality, exhausts all attachments to form, exhausts all attachments to existence, exhausts all ignorance, exhausts all conceits of an 'am' and eradicates it completely."

---

5 A IV 100, *Sattasuriyasutta*; see sermon 8.

6 Mp IV 52.

7 S III 155, *Aniccasaññāsutta*.

This shows that the perception of impermanence gradually leads to an understanding of voidness, as is clearly stated in the following quotation: *Aniccasaññino, bhikkhave, bhikkhuno anattasaññā saṇṭhāti. Anattasaññī asmimānasamugghātaṃ pāpuṇāti diṭṭheva dhamme nibbānaṃ.*[8]

"Monks, in one who has the perception of impermanence, the perception of not-self gets established. With the perception of not-self, he arrives at the destruction of the conceit 'am,' which is extinction here and now."

Such an assessment of the importance of the perception of impermanence will enable us to make sense out of the seemingly contradictory statements in some of the verses in the *Dhammapada*, such as the following:

Puttā matthi dhanaṃ matthi,
iti bālo vihaññati,
attā hi attano natthi,
kuto puttā kuto dhanaṃ?[9]

"Sons I have, wealth I have,
So the fool is vexed,
Even oneself is not one's self,
Where then are sons, where is wealth?"

The perception of not-self at its highest, gives rise to the idea of voidness, as implied by the dictum *suññam idaṃ attena vā attaniyena vā*,[10] "This is empty of self or anything belonging to a self."

Some are afraid of this term *suññatā*, emptiness, voidness, for various reasons. That is why we mentioned at the very outset,

---

[8] A IV 353, *Sambodhisutta*.

[9] Dhp 62, *Bālavagga*.

[10] E.g. at M I 297, *Mahāvedallasutta*.

already in the first sermon, that gradually the monks themselves showed a lack of interest in those discourses that deal with the idea of voidness.[11] The Buddha had already predicted, as a danger that will befall the *Sāsana* in the future, this lack of regard for such discourses. This prediction reveals the high degree of importance attached to them.

The last two sections of the *Sutta Nipāta*, namely *Aṭṭhakavagga* and *Pārāyanavagga*, abound in extremely deep sermons. In the *Pārāyanavagga*, for instance, we find the Brahmin youth Mogharāja putting the following question to the Buddha: *Kathaṃ lokaṃ avekkhantaṃ, maccurājā na passati?*[12] "By looking upon the world in which manner can one escape the eye of the king of death?" The Buddha gives the answer in the following verse:

Suññato lokaṃ avekkhassu,
Mogharāja sadā sato,
attānudiṭṭhim ūhacca,
evaṃ maccutaro siyā,
evaṃ lokam avekkhantaṃ,
maccurājā na passati.[13]

"Look upon the world as void,
Mogharāja, being mindful at all times,
Uprooting the lingering view of self,
Get well beyond the range of death,
Him who thus looks upon the world,
The king of death gets no chance to see."

From this we can infer that the entire *Dhamma*, even like the world system itself, inclines towards voidness. This fact is borne

---

11 S II 267, *Āṇisutta*; see sermon 1.

12 Sn 1118, *Mogharājamāṇavapucchā*.

13 Sn 1119, ibid.

out by the following significant quotation in the *CūḷaTaṇhā-saṅkhayasutta*, cited by Sakka as an aphorism given by the Buddha himself: *Sabbe dhammā nālaṃ abhinivesāya.*[14] Though we may render it simply as "nothing is worth clinging on to," it has a deeper significance. The word *abhinivesa* is closely associated with the idea of entering into or getting entangled in views of one's own creation. The implication, then, is that not only the views as such, but nothing at all is worth while getting entangled in. This is suggestive of the emptiness of everything.

This brings us to a very important *sutta* among the Eighths of the *Aṅguttara Nikāya*, namely the *Kiṃmūlakasutta*. In this particular *sutta* we find the Buddha asking the monks how they would answer a set of questions which wandering ascetics of other sects might put to them. The questions are as follows:

> *Kiṃ mūlakā, āvuso, sabbe dhammā? Kiṃ sambhavā sabbe dhammā? Kiṃ samudayā sabbe dhammā? Kiṃ samosaraṇā sabbe dhammā? Kiṃ pamukhā sabbe dhammā? Kim adhipateyyā sabbe dhammā? Kim uttarā sabbe dhammā? Kiṃ sārā sabbe dhammā?*[15]

> "What is the root of all things? What is the origin of all things? Where do all things arise? Towards what do all things converge? What is at the head of all things? What dominates all things? What is the point of transcendence of all things? What is the essence of all things?"

The monks confessed that they were unable to answer those questions on their own and begged the Buddha to instruct them. Then the Buddha gave the exact answer to each question in a cut

---

[14] M I 251, *CūḷaTaṇhāsaṅkhayasutta*.

[15] A IV 338, *Kiṃmūlakasutta*.

and dried form, saying, this is the way you should answer if wandering ascetics of other sects raise those questions.

> *Chandamūlakā, āvuso, sabbe dhammā, manasikārasambhavā sabbe dhammā, phassasamudayā sabbe dhammā, vedanāsamosaraṇā sabbe dhammā, samādhipamukhā sabbe dhammā, satādhipateyyā sabbe dhammā, paññuttarā sabbe dhammā, vimuttisārā sabbe dhammā.*

> "Rooted in desire, friends, are all things. Born of attention are all things. Arisen from contact are all things. Converging on feeling are all things. Headed by concentration are all things. Dominated by mindfulness are all things. Surmountable by wisdom are all things. Yielding deliverance as essence are all things."

Before getting down to an analysis of the basic meaning of this discourse, it is worthwhile considering why the Buddha forestalled a possible perplexity among his disciples in the face of a barrage of questions likely to be levelled by other sectarians. Why did he think it fit to prepare the minds of the disciples well in advance of such a situation?

Contemporary ascetics of other sects, notably the brahmins, entertained various views regarding the origin and purpose of 'all things.' Those who subscribed to a soul theory, had different answers to questions concerning thing-hood or the essence of thing. Presumably it was not easy for the monks, with their not-self standpoint, to answer those questions to the satisfaction of other sectarians. That is why those monks confessed their incompetence and begged for guidance.

It was easy for those of other sects to explain away the questions relating to the origin and purpose of things on the basis of their soul theory or divine creation. Everything came out of *Brahma*, and self is the essence of everything. No doubt, such answers were substantial enough to gain acceptance. Even modern philosophers are confronted with the intricate problem of determining the exact criterion of a 'thing.' What precisely accounts for the thing-hood of a thing? What makes it no-thing?

Unfortunately for the *sutta*, its traditional commentators seem to have ignored the deeper philosophical dimensions of the above questionnaire. They have narrowed down the meaning of the set of answers recommended by the Buddha by limiting its application to wholesome mental states.[16] The occurrence of such terms as *chanda, sati, samādhi,* and *paññā*, had probably led them to believe that the entire questionnaire is on the subject of wholesome mental states. But this is a serious underestimation of the import of the entire discourse. It actually goes far deeper in laying bare a basic principle governing both skilful and unskilful mental states.

Now, for instance, the first two verses of the *Dhammapada* bring out a fundamental law of psychology applicable to things both skilful and unskilful: *Manopubbaṅgamā dhammā, manoseṭṭhā manomayā.*[17] Both verses draw upon this fundamental principle. Nowadays, these two lines are variously interpreted, but the basic idea expressed is that "all things have mind as their forerunner, mind is their chief, and they are mind-made." This applies to both skilful and unskilful mental states.

Now the *sutta* in question has also to be interpreted in the same light, taking into account both these aspects. It must be mentioned, in particular, that with the passage of time a certain line of interpretation gained currency, according to which such terms as *chanda* were taken as skilful in an exclusive sense. For instance, the term *sati*, wherever and whenever it occurred, was taken to refer to *sammā sati*.[18] Likewise, *chanda* came to be interpreted as

---

[16] Sv-pṭ I 138.

[17] Dhp 1, 2, *Yamakavagga.*

[18] Cf. the discussion at As 250.

kusalacchanda, desire or interest in the skilful, or *kattukamyatā-chanda*, desire to perform.[19]

But we have to reckon with a special trait in the Buddha's way of preaching. His sermons were designed to lead onward the listeners, gradually, according to their degree of understanding. Sometimes the meaning of a term, as it occurs at the end of a sermon, is different from the meaning it is supposed to have at the beginning of the sermon. Such a technique is also evident.

The term *chanda* is one that has both good and bad connotations. In such contexts as *chandarāga*[20] and *chandajaṃ aghaṃ*,[21] it is suggestive of craving as the cause of all suffering in this world. It refers to that attachment, *rāga*, which the world identifies with craving as such. But in the context *chandaiddhipāda*,[22] where the reference is to a particular base for success, it is reckoned as a skilful mental state. However, that is not a sufficient reason to regard it as something alien to the generic sense of the term.

There is an important *sutta*, which clearly reveals this fact, in the *Saṃyutta Nikāya*. A brahmin named Uṇṇābha once came to Venerable Ānanda with a question that has a relevance to the significance of the term *chanda*. His question was: *Kim atthiyaṃ nu kho, bho Ānanda, samaṇe Gotame brahmacariyaṃ vussati?*[23] "Sir Ānanda, what is the purpose for which the holy life is lived under the recluse Gotama?" Venerable Ānanda promptly gives the following answer: *Chandappahānatthaṃ kho, brāhmaṇa, bhagavati brahmacariyaṃ vussati*. "Brahmin, it is for the abandonment of desire that the holy life is lived under the Exalted One." Then the brahmin asks: *Atthi pana, bho Ānanda, maggo atthi paṭipadā*

19 Vibh-a 289.

20 E.g. at D II 58, *MahāNidānasutta*.

21 S I 22, *Nasantisutta*.

22 E.g. at S V 253, *Iddhipādasaṃyutta*.

23 S V 272, *Uṇṇābhabrāhmaṇasutta*.

etassa chandassa pahānāya? "Is there, sir Ānanda, a way or practice for the abandonment of this desire?" Venerable Ānanda says: "Yes." Now, what is the way he mentions in that context? It is none other than the four bases for success, *iddhipāda*, which are described as follows:

> *Chandasamādhipadhānasaṅkhārasamannāgataṃ iddhipādaṃ bhāveti, viriyasamādhipadhānasaṅkhārasamannāgataṃ iddhipādaṃ bhāveti, cittasamādhipadhānasaṅkhārasamannāgataṃ iddhipādaṃ bhāveti, vīmaṃsāsamādhipadhānasaṅkhārasamannāgataṃ iddhipādaṃ bhāveti.*

1) "One develops the basis for success that has volitional preparations leading to a concentration through desire,"
2) "One develops the basis for success that has volitional preparations leading to a concentration through energy,"
3) "One develops the basis for success that has volitional preparations leading to a concentration by making up the mind,"
4) "One develops the basis for success that has volitional preparations leading to a concentration through investigation."

Venerable Ānanda replies that the way of practice to be followed for the abandonment of desire is the above mentioned four bases pertaining to desire, energy, mind and investigation. The brahmin is puzzled at this reply. He thinks, if that is so, desire is not abandoned, it is still there. And he raises this objection to show that there is an implicit contradiction: *Chandeneva chandaṃ pajahissatī'ti, netaṃ ṭhānaṃ vijjati*, "that one abandons desire by desire itself is an impossibility." Then the Venerable Ānanda brings out a simile to convince the brahmin of the implicit truth in his reply.

"What do you think, brahmin, is it not the case that you earlier had the desire 'I will go to the park,' and after you came here, the appropriate desire subsided?" So this is the logic behind the statement concerning the abandonment of craving. The term *chanda* is used here in the first instance with reference to that type of craving for the purpose of the abandonment of craving.

Desire as a basis for success is developed for the very abandonment of desire. So there is no question about the use of the same word. Here, *chanda* as a base of success still belongs to the *chanda*-family. A desire should be there even for the abandonment of desire. This is a distinctive basic principle underlying the middle path.

Some have a great liking for the word *chanda*, but dislike the word *taṇhā*. So much so that, if one speaks of a craving for attaining *Nibbāna*, it might even be regarded as a blasphemy. In another sermon given by Venerable Ānanda himself, one addressed to a particular sick nun, we find the statement: *Taṇhaṃ nissāya taṇhā pahātabbā*,[24] "Depending on craving one should abandon craving." That again is suggestive of a special application of the middle path technique. But the kind of craving meant here is not something crude. It is specifically explained there that it is the longing arising in one for the attainment of *arahant*-hood on hearing that someone has already attained it. Of course, there is a subtle trace of craving even in that longing, but it is one that is helpful for the abandonment of craving. So one need not fight shy of the implications of these words.

As a matter of fact, even the word *rati*, attachment, is used with reference to *Nibbāna*. When, for instance, it is said that the disciple of the Buddha is attached to the destruction of craving, *taṇhakkhayarato hoti sammāsambuddhasāvako*,[25] it may sound rather odd, because the word *rati* usually stands for lust. However,

---

24 A II 145, *Bhikkuṇīsutta.*

25 Dhp 187, *Buddhavagga.*

according to the Middle Path principle of utilizing one thing to eliminate another, words like *chanda* and *taṇhā* are used with discretion. Sometimes terms like *nekkhamasita domanassa*,[26] unhappiness based on renunciation, are employed to indicate the desire for attaining *Nibbāna*. Therefore the statement *chanda-mūlakā sabbe dhammā* need not be interpreted as referring exclusively to skilful mental states.

With regard to the significance of *sati* and *samādhi*, too, we may mention in passing, that terms like *micchā sati*, wrong mindfulness, and *micchā samādhi*, wrong concentration, do sometimes occur in the discourses.[27] So let us examine whether the set of statements under consideration has any sequential coherence or depth.

"Rooted in desire, friends, are all things." We might as well bring out the meaning of these statements with the help of an illustration. Supposing there is a heap of rubbish and someone approaches it with a basket to collect it and throw it away. Now, about the rubbish heap, he has just a unitary notion. That is to say, he takes it as just one heap of rubbish. But as he bends down and starts collecting it into the basket, he suddenly catches sight of a gem. Now the gem becomes the object of his desire and interest. A gem arose out of what earlier appeared as a rubbish heap. It became the thing for him, and desire was at the root of this phenomenon – true to the dictum "rooted in desire, friends, are all things."

Then what about origination through attention? It is through attention that the gem came into being. One might think that the origin of the gem should be traced to the mine or to some place where it took shape, but the Buddha traces its origin in accordance with the norm *manopubbaṅgamā dhammā*, "mind is the forerunner

---

[26] M III 220, *Saḷāyatanavibhaṅgasutta*.

[27] D II 353, D III 254, 287, 290, 291, M I 118, M III 77, 140, S II 168, S III 109, S V 1, 12, 13, 16, 18-20, 23, 383, A II 220-229, A III 141, A IV 237, A V 212-248.

of all things." So then, the root is desire and the source of origin is attention, the very fact of attending.

Phassasamudayā sabbe dhammā, "All things arise from contact." There was eye-contact with the gem as something special out of all the things in the rubbish heap. So the gem 'arose' from eye-contact. *Vedanāsamosaraṇā sabbe dhammā*, "All things converge on feeling." As soon as the eye spotted the gem, a lot of pleasant feelings about it arose in the mind. Therefore, all things converge on feeling.

Samādhipamukhā sabbe dhammā, "Headed by concentration are all things." Here, in this case, it may be wrong concentration, *micchā samādhi*, but all the same it is some kind of concentration. It is now a concentration on the gem. It is as if his meditation has shifted from the rubbish heap to the gem. *Satādhipateyyā sabbe dhammā*, "Dominated by mindfulness are all things." As to this dominance, undistracted attention is necessary for the maintenance of that thing which has now been singled out. Where there is distraction, attention is drawn to other things as well. That is why mindfulness is said to be dominant. Be it the so-called wrong mindfulness, but nonetheless, it is now directed towards the gem.

Now comes the decisive stage, that is, the 'surmountability by wisdom,' *paññuttarā*. Let us for a moment grant that somehow or other, even though wrongly, *micchā*, some kind of surrogate mindfulness and concentration has developed out of this situation. Now, if one wants to cross over in accordance with the *Dhamma*, that is, if one wants to attain *Nibbāna* with this gem itself as the topic of meditation, one has to follow the hint given by the statement *paññuttarā sabbe dhammā*, "surmountable by wisdom are all things."

What one has to do now is to see through the gem, to penetrate it, by viewing it as impermanent, fraught with suffering, and not-self, thereby arriving at the conviction that, after all, the gem belongs to the rubbish heap itself. The gem is transcended by the wisdom that it is just one item in this rubbish heap that is 'The world' in its entirety. If one wins to the wisdom that this gem is something like a piece of charcoal, to be destroyed in the holocaust at the end of a world period, one has transcended that gem.

So then, the essence of all things is not any self or soul, as postulated by the brahmins. Deliverance is the essence. In such discourses as the *Mahāsāropamasutta*, the essence of this entire *Dhamma* is said to be deliverance.[28] The very emancipation from all this, to be rid of all this, is itself the essence. Some seem to think that the essence is a heaping up of concepts and clinging to them. But that is not the essence of this teaching. It is the ability to penetrate all concepts, thereby transcending them. The deliverance resulting from transcendence is itself the essence.

With the cessation of that concept of a gem as some special thing, a valuable thing, separate from the rest of the world, as well as of the ensuing heap of concepts by way of craving, conceit and views, the gem ceases to exist. That itself is the deliverance. It is the emancipation from the gem. Therefore, *vimuttisārā sabbe dhammā*, "deliverance is the essence of all things."

So then, we have here a very valuable discourse which can even be used as a topic of insight meditation. The essence of any mind object is the very emancipation from it, by seeing it with wisdom. Considered in this light, everything in the world is a meditation object. That is why we find very strange meditation topics mentioned in connection with the attainments of ancient *arahant* monks and nuns. Sometimes, even apparently unsuitable meditation objects have been successfully employed.

Meditation teachers, as a rule, do not approve of certain meditation objects for beginners, with good reasons. For instance, they would not recommend a female form as a meditation object for a male, and a male form for a female. That is because it can arouse lust, since it is mentioned in the *Theragāthā* that lust arose in some monk even on seeing a decayed female corpse in a cemetery.[29] But

---

[28] M I 197, *MahāSāropamasutta*.

[29] Th 315-316, *Rājadatta Thera*.

in the same text one comes across an episode in connection with Venerable Nāgasamāla, which stands in utter contrast to it.

Venerable Nāgasamāla attained *arahant*-hood with the help of a potentially pernicious meditation object, as he describes it, in his words: "Once, on my begging round, I happened to look up to see a dancing woman, beautifully dressed and bedecked, dancing to the rhythm of an orchestra just on the middle of the highway."[30] And, what happened then?

> *Tato me manasikāro,*
> *yoniso udapajjatha,*
> *ādīnavo pāturahu,*
> *nibbidā samatiṭṭhatha,*
> *tato cittaṃ vimucci me,*
> *passa dhammasudhammataṃ.*[31]

> "Just then, radical attention
> Arose from within me,
> The perils were manifest,
> And dejection took place,
> Then my mind got released,
> Behold the goodness of the Norm."

If one wishes to discover the goodness of this norm, one has to interpret the *sutta* in question in a broader perspective, without limiting its application to skilful mental states. If a train of thoughts had got started up about that gem, even through a wrong concentration, and thereby a wrong mindfulness and a wrong concentration had taken shape, at whatever moment radical attention comes on the scene, complete reorientation occurs instantaneously, true to those qualities of the *Dhamma* implied by

---

30 Th 267-268, *Nāgasamāla Thera.*

31 Th 269-270, *Nāgasamāla Thera.*

the terms, *sandiṭṭhika*, visible here and now, *akālika*, not involving time, and *ehipassika*, inviting one to come and see.

Some might wonder, for instance, how those brahmins of old who had practiced their own methods of concentration, attained *arahant*-hood on hearing just one stanza as soon as they came to the Buddha.[32] The usual interpretation is that it is due to the miraculous powers of the Buddha, or else that the persons concerned had an extraordinary stock of merit. The miracle of the *Dhamma*, implicit in such occurrences, is often ignored.

Now as to this miracle of the *Dhamma*, we may take the case of someone keen on seeing a rainbow. He will have to go on looking at the sky indefinitely, waiting for a rainbow to appear. But if he is wise enough, he can see the spectrum of rainbow colours through a dew drop hanging on a leaf of a creeper waving in the morning sun, provided he finds the correct perspective. For him, the dewdrop itself is the meditation object. In the same way, one can sometimes see the entire *Dhamma*, thirty-seven factors of enlightenment and the like, even in a potentially pernicious meditation object.

From an academic point of view, the two terms *yoniso manasikāra*, radical attention, and *ayoniso manasikāra*, non-radical attention, are in utter contrast to each other. There is a world of difference between them. So also between the terms *sammā diṭṭhi*, right view, and *micchā diṭṭhi*, wrong view. But from the point of view of realisation, there is just a little difference.

Now as we know, that spectrum of the sun's rays in the dew drop disappears with a very little shift in one's perspective. It appears only when viewed in a particular perspective. What we find in this *Dhamma* is something similar. This is the intrinsic nature of this *Dhamma* that is to be seen here and now, timeless, leading onward, and realizable by the wise each one by himself.

---

32 Pj II 587.

Our interpretation of this *sutta*, taking the word *sabbe dhammā* to mean 'all things,' is further substantiated by the *Samiddhi Sutta* found in the section on the Nines in the *Aṅguttara Nikāya*. It is a discourse preached by Venerable Sāriputta. To a great extent, it runs parallel to the one we have already analysed. The difference lies only in a few details. In that *sutta* we find Venerable Samiddhi answering the questions put to him by Venerable Sāriputta, like a pupil at a catechism. The following is the gist of questions raised and answers given:

'Kim ārammaṇā, Samiddhi, purisassa saṅkappavitakkā uppajjantī'ti?'
'Nāmarūpārammaṇā, bhante.'

'Te pana, Samiddhi, kva nānattaṃ gacchantī'ti?'
'Dhātūsu, bhante.'

'Te pana, Samiddhi, kiṃ samudayā'ti?'
'Phassasamudayā, bhante.'

'Te pana, Samiddhi, kiṃ samosaraṇā'ti?'
'Vedanāsamosaraṇā, bhante.'

'Te pana, Samiddhi, kiṃ pamukhā'ti?'
'Samādhipamukhā, bhante.'

'Te pana, Samiddhi, kim adhipateyyā'ti?'
'Satādhipateyyā, bhante.'

'Te pana, Samiddhi, kim uttarā'ti?'
'Paññuttarā, bhante.'

'Te pana, Samiddhi kiṃ sārā'ti?'
'Vimuttisārā, bhante.'

'Te pana, Samiddhi, kim ogadhā'ti?'
'Amatogadhā, bhante.'[33]

Except for the first two questions and the last one, the rest is the same as in the questionnaire given by the Buddha. But from this catechism it is extremely clear that Venerable Sāriputta is asking about thoughts and concepts. In the case of the previous *sutta*, one could sometimes doubt whether the word *sabbe dhammā* referred to skilful or unskilful mental states. But here it is clear enough that Venerable Sāriputta's questions are on thoughts and concepts. Let us now try to translate the above catechism:

"With what as objects, Samiddhi, do concepts and thoughts arise in a man?"
"With name-and-form as object, venerable sir."

"But where, Samiddhi, do they assume diversity?"
"In the elements, venerable sir."

"But from what, Samiddhi, do they arise?"
"They arise from contact, venerable sir."

"But on what, Samiddhi, do they converge?"
"They converge on feeling, venerable sir."

"But what, Samiddhi, is at their head?"
"They are headed by concentration, venerable sir."

"But by what, Samiddhi, are they dominated?"
"They are dominated by mindfulness, venerable sir."

---

[33] A IV 385, *Samiddhisutta*.

"But what, Samiddhi, is their highest point?"
"Wisdom is their highest point, venerable sir."

"But what, Samiddhi, is their essence?"
"Deliverance is their essence, venerable sir."

"But in what, Samiddhi, do they get merged?"
"They get merged in the deathless, venerable sir."

Some noteworthy points emerge from this catechism. All concepts and thoughts have name-and-form as their object. The eighteen elements account for their diversity. They arise with contact. They converge on feeling. They are headed by concentration. They are dominated by mindfulness. Their acme or point of transcendence is wisdom. Their essence is deliverance and they get merged in the deathless. Be it noted that the deathless is a term for *Nibbāna.* therefore, as we have stated above, everything has the potentiality to yield the deathless, provided radical attention is ushered in.

It is indubitably clear, from this catechism, that the subject under consideration is concepts and thoughts. All mind objects partake of the character of concepts and thoughts. Therefore the mind objects, according to the Buddha, have to be evaluated on the lines of the above mentioned normative principles, and not on the lines of self essence and divine creation as postulated by soul theories.

In accordance with the dictum 'mind is the forerunner of all things,' *manopubbaṅgamā dhammā,*[34] the course of training advocated by the Buddha, which begins with name-and-form as object, reaches its consummation in seeing through name-and-form, that is, in its penetration. It culminates in the transcendence of name-and-form, by penetrating into its impermanent, suffering-

[34] Dhp 1, *Yamakavagga.*

fraught, and not-self nature. This fact is borne out by the discourses already quoted.

The essence of the teaching is release from name-and-form. When one rightly understands the relation between name and form as well as their emptiness, one is able to see through name-and-form. This penetration is the function of wisdom. So long as wisdom is lacking, consciousness has a tendency to get entangled in name-and-form. This is the insinuation of the following *Dhammapada* verse about the *arahant*:

> *Kodhaṃ jahe vippajaheyya mānaṃ,*
> *saṃyojanaṃ sabbam atikkameyya,*
> *taṃ nāmarūpasmim asajjamānaṃ,*
> *akiñcanaṃ nānupatanti dukkhā.*[35]

> "Let one put wrath away, conceit abandon,
> And get well beyond all fetters as well,
> That one, untrammelled by name-and-form,
> With naught as his own – no pains befall."

The path shown by the Buddha, then, is one that leads to the transcendence of name-and-form by understanding its emptiness. In this connection, the *Brahmajālasutta* of the *Dīgha Nikāya* reveals a very important fact on analysis.[36] What it portrays is how the sixty-two wrong views lose their lustre in the light of wisdom emanating from the non-manifestative consciousness of the Buddha, which is lustrous on all sides, *sabbato pabha.*[37]

As to how a lustre could be superseded, we have already explained with reference to a film show.[38] The film show lost its

---

[35] Dhp 221, *Kodhavagga.*

[36] D I 1-46, *Brahmajālasutta.*

[37] D I 223, *Kevaḍḍhasutta.*

[38] See sermon 5.

lustre when the doors were flung open. The narrow beam of light, directed on the cinema screen, faded away completely before the greater light now coming from outside. Similarly, the sixty-two wrong views in the *Brahmajālasutta* are seen to fade away before the light of wisdom coming from the non-manifestative consciousness of the Buddha. The narrow beams of sixty-two wrong views faded in the broader flood of light that is wisdom.

Those heretics who propounded those wrong views, conceived them by dogmatically hoiding on to name-and-form. They got entangled in name-and-form, and those views were the product of speculative logic based on it. We come across an allusion to this fact in the *MahāViyūhasutta* of the *Sutta Nipāta*. There it is declared that those of other sects are not free from the limitations of name-and-form:

> *Passaṃ naro dakkhiti nāmarūpaṃ,*
> *disvāna vā ñassati tānim eva,*
> *kāmaṃ bahuṃ passatu appakaṃ vā,*
> *na hi tena suddhiṃ kusalā vadanti.*[39]

> "A seeing man will see only name-and-form,
> Having seen he will know just those constituents alone,
> Let him see much or little,
> Experts do not concede purity thereby."

In the *Brahmajālasutta* itself we find some views advanced by those who had higher knowledges. With the help of those higher knowledges, which were still of the mundane type, they would see into their past, sometimes hundreds of thousands of their past lives, and drawing also from their ability to read others' minds, they would construct various views. Many such views are record-

---

[39] Sn 909, *Mahāviyūhasutta.*

ed in the *Brahmajālasutta*, only to be rejected and invalidated. Why so? The reason is given here in this verse.

The man who claims to see with those higher knowledges is seeing only name-and-form, *passaṃ naro dakkhiti nāmarūpaṃ*. Having seen, he takes whatever he sees as real knowledge, *disvāna vā ñassati tānim eva*. Just as someone inside a closed room with tinted windowpanes sees only what is reflected on those dark panes, and not beyond, even so, those 'seers' got enmeshed in name-and-form when they proceeded to speculate on what they saw as their past lives. They took name-and-form itself to be real. That is why the Buddha declared that whether they saw much or little, it is of no use, since experts do not attribute purity to that kind of vision, *kāmaṃ bahuṃ passatu appakaṃ vā, na hi tena suddhiṃ kusalā vadanti*.

Here it is clear enough that those narrow wrong views are based on name-and-form, assuming it to be something real. The Buddha's vision, on the other hand, is one that transcends name-and-form. It is a supramundane vision. This fact is clearly revealed by the implications of the very title of the *Brahmajālasutta*. At the end of the discourse, the Buddha himself compares it to an all-embracing super-net.[40] Just as a clever fisherman would throw a finely woven net well over a small lake, so that all the creatures living there are caught in it as they come up, all the possible views in the world are enmeshed or forestalled by this super-net, or *brahmajāla*.

Let us now pause to consider what the mesh of this net could be. If the *Brahmajālasutta* is a net, what constitutes that fine mesh in this net? There is a word occurring all over the discourse, which gives us a clear answer to this question. It is found in the phrase which the Buddha uses to disqualify every one of those views, namely, *tadapi phassapaccayā, tadapi phassapaccayā*,[41] "and that

---

[40] D I 46, *Brahmajālasutta*.

[41] D I 42, *Brahmajālasutta*.

too is due to contact, and that too is due to contact." So from this we can see that contact is the mesh of this net.

The medley of wrong views, current among those of other sects, is the product of the six sense-bases dependent on contact. The Buddha's vision, on the other hand, seems to be an all-encompassing lustre of wisdom, born of the cessation of the six sense-bases, which in effect, is the vision of *Nibbāna*. This fact is further clarified in the *sutta* by the statement of the Buddha that those who cling to those wrong views, based on name-and-form, keep on whirling within the *saṃsāric* round because of those very views.

> *Sabbe te chahi phassāyatanehi phussa phussa paṭisaṃvedenti, tesaṃ phassapaccayā vedanā, vedanāpaccayā taṇhā, taṇhāpaccayā upādānaṃ, upādānapaccayā bhavo, bhavapaccayā jāti, jātipaccayā jarāmaraṇaṃ sokaparidevadukkhadomanassupāyāsā sambhavanti. Yato kho, bhikkhave, bhikkhu, channaṃ phassāyatanānaṃ samudayañca atthagamañca assādañca ādīnavañca nissara-ṇañca yathābhūtaṃ pajānāti, ayaṃ imehi sabbeheva uttaritaraṃ pajānāti.*[42]

> "They all continue to experience feeling coming into contact again and again with the six sense-bases, and to them dependent on contact there is feeling, dependent on feeling there is craving, dependent on craving there is grasping, dependent on grasping there is becoming, dependent on becoming there is birth, and dependent on birth, decay, death, sorrow, lamentation, pain, grief and despair come to be. But when, monks, a monk knows, as they truly are, the arising, the going down, the satisfaction, the peril and the stepping out concerning the six sense-bases, that monk has

---

[42] D I 45, *Brahmajālasutta.*

a knowledge which is far superior to that of all those dogmatists."

This paragraph clearly brings out the distinction between those who held on to such speculative views and the one who wins to the vision made known by the Buddha. The former were dependent on contact, that is, sensory contact, even if they possessed worldly higher knowledges. Because of contact originating from the six sense-bases there is feeling. Because of feeling they are lured into craving and grasping which make them go round and round in *saṃsāra*.

The emancipated monk who keeps to the right path, on the other hand, wins to that synoptic vision of the six sense-bases, replete in its five aspects. That is what is known as the light of wisdom. To him, all five aspects of the six sense-bases become clear, namely the arising, the going down, the satisfaction, the peril and the stepping out. That light of wisdom is considered the highest knowledge, precisely because it reveals all these five aspects of the six sense-bases.

The reference to the formula of dependent arising in the above passage is highly significant. It is clear proof of the fact that the law of dependent arising is not something to be explained with reference to a past existence. It is a law relevant to the present moment.

This name-and-form is reflected on consciousness. Now as to this consciousness, the *Nidānasaṃyutta* of the *Saṃyutta Nikāya*, which is a section dealing with the law of dependent arising in particular, defines it in a way that includes all the six types of consciousness:

Katamañca, bhikkhave, viññāṇaṃ? Chayime, bhikkhave, viññāṇakāyā – cakkhuviññāṇaṃ, sotaviññāṇaṃ, ghāna-

> *viññāṇaṃ, jivhāviññāṇaṃ, kāyaviññāṇaṃ, manoviññāṇaṃ, idaṃ vuccati, bhikkhave, viññāṇaṃ.*[43]
>
> "And what, monks, is consciousness? There are these six classes of consciousness – eye-consciousness, ear-consciousness, nose-consciousness, tongue-consciousness, body-consciousness and mind-consciousness; this, monks, is called consciousness."

This shows that the consciousness mentioned in the formula of dependent arising is not something like a re-linking consciousness. The reference here is not to just one consciousness. It is in dependence on name-and-form, reflected on all six types of consciousness, that the six sense-bases get established.

The discrimination between an 'internal' and an 'external' is the outcome of the inability to penetrate name-and-form, to see through it. There is an apparent duality: I, as one who sees, and name-and-form, as the objects seen. Between them there is a dichotomy as internal and external. It is on this very dichotomy that the six sense-bases are 'based.' Feeling and all the rest of it come on top of those six sense-bases. Craving and grasping follow suit, as a result of which those dogmatists get caught up in the vicious cycle of dependent arising and keep running round in *saṃsāra* as the Buddha has declared.

So then, it becomes clear from the *Brahmajālasutta* that such a wide variety of wrong views exist in this world due to the dogmatic involvement in name-and-form reflected on consciousness, that is by mistaking the reflection to be one's self. This, in brief, is tantamount to *sakkāyadiṭṭhi*, or personality view.

Now let us take up a parable by way of an illustration of the distinction between the wrong view of the dogmatists, already analysed, and the right view, which is in complete contrast to it. It

---

43 S II 4, *Vibhaṅgasutta*.

is an episode in the *Ummaggajātaka* which more or less looks like a parable to illustrate this point.[44] In the *Ummaggajātaka* one comes across the problem of a gem. In that story there are in fact several such problems concerning gems, and we are taking up just one of them.

The citizens of Mithilā came and informed king Videha that there is a gem in the pond near the city gate. The king commissioned his royal adviser Senaka with the task of taking out the gem. He went and got the people to empty the pond but failed to find the gem there. Even the mud was taken out and the earth dug up in a vain attempt to locate the gem. When he confessed his failure to the king, the latter entrusted the job to *bodhisatta* Mahosadha, the youngest adviser. When he went there and had a look around, he immediately understood that the gem is actually in a crow's nest on a palm tree near the pond. What appeared in the pond is only its reflection. He convinced the king of this fact by getting a man to immerse a bowl of water into the pond, which also reflected the gem. Then the man climbed up the palm tree and found the gem there, as predicted by Mahosadha.

If we take this episode as an illustration, the view of the dogmatists can be compared to Senaka's view. The discovery of the Buddha that name-and-form is a mere reflection is like the solution advanced by *bodhisatta* Mahosadha to the problem of the gem in the pond.

Now what is the role of personality view in this connection? It is said that the Buddha preached the *Dhamma* adopting a *via media* between two extreme views. What are they? The eternalist view and the nihilist view. The eternalist view is like that attachment to the reflection. Sometimes, when one sees one's own image in water, one falls in love with it, imagining it to be someone else, as in the case of the dog on the plank mentioned in an

---

[44] Ja VI 129 (no 546), *Ummaggajātaka*.

earlier sermon.[45] It can sometimes arouse hate as well. Thus there could be both self-love and self-hate.

Inclining towards these two attitudes, the personality view itself leads to the two extreme views known as eternalism and nihilism, or annihilationism. It is like Senaka's attempt to find the gem by emptying the water and digging the bottom of the pond. The Buddha avoids both these extremes by understanding that this name-and-form is a reflection, owing to the reflective nature of this pond of consciousness. It has no essence.

The name in this name-and-form, as we have already stated in an earlier sermon, is merely a formal name, or an apparent name.[46] And the form here is only a nominal form, a form only in name. There is neither an actual name nor a substantial form here. Name is only apparent, and form is only nominal. With this preliminary understanding one has to arouse that wisdom by building up the ability to see through name-and-form, in order to win to freedom from this name-and-form.

So, in this sermon, our special attention has been on name-and-form, on the interrelation between name-and-form and consciousness. All this reveals to us the importance of the first two lines of the problematic verse already quoted, *viññāṇaṃ anidassanaṃ anantaṃ sabbato pabhaṃ*,[47] "Consciousness which is non-manifestative, endless, lustrous on all sides."

According to the Buddha's vision, by fully comprehending the fact that name-and-form is a mere image, or reflection, the non-manifestative consciousness develops the penetrative power to see through it. But those others, who could not understand that it is a reflection, aroused self-love and self-hate. It is as if one is trying to outstrip one's shadow by running towards it out of fun, while the

---

45 See sermon 6.

46 See sermon 1.

47 M I 329, *Brahmanimantanikasutta.*

other is trying to flee from it out of fear. Such is the nature of the two extreme views in this world.

> *Dvīhi, bhikkhave, diṭṭhigatehi pariyuṭṭhitā devamanussā olīyanti eke, atidhāvanti eke, cakkhumanto ca passanti.*[48]

> "Obsessed by two views, monks, are gods and men, some of whom lag behind, while others overreach, only they do see that have eyes to see."

This is how the *Itivuttaka*, the collection of the 'thus said' discourses, sums up the situation in the world. Some fall back and lag behind, while others overstep and overreach. It is only they that see, who have eyes to see.

---

[48] It 43, *Diṭṭhigatasutta*.

Nibbāna Sermon 10

Namo tassa Bhagavato Arahato Sammāsambuddhassa
Namo tassa Bhagavato Arahato Sammāsambuddhassa
Namo tassa Bhagavato Arahato Sammāsambuddhassa

Etaṃ santaṃ, etaṃ paṇītaṃ, yadidaṃ sabbasaṅkhārasamatho sabbūpadhipaṭinissaggo taṇhakkhayo virāgo nirodho nibbānaṃ.[1]

"This is peaceful, this is excellent, namely the stilling of all preparations, the relinquishment of all assets, the destruction of craving, detachment, cessation, extinction."

With the permission of the Most Venerable Great Preceptor and the assembly of the venerable meditative monks.

This is the tenth sermon in the series of sermons on *Nibbāna*. With the help of a parable based on the problem of the gem in the *Ummaggajātaka*, we made an attempt, towards the end of our last sermon, to clarify to some extent how the personality view arises due to the ignorance of the fact that name-and-form is something reflected on consciousness. We mentioned in brief how a certain would-be wise man took the trouble to empty a pond and even dig out the mud under the impression that there is actually a gem in it, simply because there appeared to be a gem in the pond.

Similarly, by taking to be real name-and-form, which is only an image reflected on consciousness leading to a personality view, *sakkāyadiṭṭhi*, both eternalism and nihilism, built on the two views

---

1 M I 436, *MahāMālunkyasutta*.

of existence and non-existence, tended towards two extremes. Under the influence of self love, eternalism took up the view that there is a self, and looked forward to its perpetuation. Prompted by self hate, annihilationism or nihilism cherished the fond hope that the release from this self will occur at death. Both these extreme views confuse the issue by not understanding the reflected image as such.

Now how did the middle path, which the Buddha introduced to the world, avoid these two extremes? It is by offering a knowledge and vision of things as they are, *yathābhūtañāṇadassana*, in place of those two views of existence and non-existence. In other words, he made known to the world the true knowledge and vision that name-and-form is merely an image reflected on consciousness.

There is a special significance in the word *yathābhūta*. In contradistinction to the two words *bhava* and *vibhava*, the word *bhūta* has some peculiarity of its own. In order to clarify the meaning of the term *yathābhūta*, we can draw upon a discourse in the *Itivuttaka*, a few lines of which we had already quoted at the end of the previous sermon. When presented in full, that discourse will make it clear why the Buddha introduced the word *bhūta* in preference to the existing usage in terms of *bhava* and *vibhava*. This is how that discourse proceeds:

> *Dvīhi, bhikkhave, diṭṭhigatehi pariyuṭṭhitā devamanussā olīyanti eke, atidhāvanti eke, cakkhumanto va passanti. Kathañca, bhikkhave, olīyanti eke? Bhavārāmā, bhikkhave, devamanussā bhavaratā bhavasammuditā, tesaṃ bhavanirodhāya dhamme desiyamāne cittaṃ na pakkhandati na pasīdati na santiṭṭhati nādhimuccati. Evaṃ kho, bhikkhave, olīyanti eke.*

> *Kathañca, bhikkhave, atidhāvanti eke? Bhaveneva kho pana eke aṭṭīyamānā harāyamānā jigucchamānā vibhavaṃ abhinandanti – yato kira, bho, ayaṃ attā kāyassa bhedā paraṃ maraṇā ucchijjati vinassati na hoti paraṃ*

maraṇā, etaṃ santaṃ etaṃ paṇītaṃ etaṃ yāthāvanti. Evaṃ kho, bhikkhave, atidhāvanti eke.

Kathañca, bhikkhave, cakkhumanto passanti? Idha bhikkhu bhūtaṃ bhūtato passati, bhūtaṃ bhūtato disvā bhūtassa nibbidāya virāgāya nirodhāya paṭipanno hoti. Evaṃ kho, bhikkhave, cakkhumanto va passantī'ti."[2]

"Obsessed by two views, monks, are gods and men, some of whom lag behind, while others overreach. Only they do see that have eyes to see. How, monks, do some lag behind? Gods and men, monks, delight in existence, they are attached to existence, they rejoice in existence. When *Dhamma* is being preached to them for the cessation of existence, their minds do not reach out towards it, do not get pleased in it, do not get steadied in it, do not rest confident with it. It is thus that some lag behind.

"How, monks, do some overreach? Being troubled, ashamed, and disgusted of existence as such, some delight in non-existence – since this self, at the breaking up of this body after death, will be annihilated and destroyed, this is peace, this is excellent, this is how it should be. Thus, monks do some overreach.

"And how, monks, do those with eyes see? Herein a monk sees the become as become. Having seen the become as become, he is treading the path towards dejection, dispassion and cessation regarding becoming. Thus it is, monks, that those with eyes see."

---

2 It 43, *Diṭṭhigatasutta*.

This passage clearly brings out the extreme nature of those two views of existence and non-existence. The two verses occurring at the end of this *sutta* present the gist of the discourse even more clearly:

Ye bhūtaṃ bhūtato disvā,
bhūtassa ca atikkamaṃ,
yathābhūte vimuccanti,
bhavataṇhā parikkhayā.

Sa ve bhūtapariñño so,
vītataṇho bhavābhave,
bhūtassa vibhavā bhikkhu,
nāgacchati punabbhavaṃ.

"Those who have seen the become as become,
As well as the going beyond of whatever has become,
Are released in regard to things as they are,
By the exhaustion of craving for becoming.

"That monk, who has fully comprehended the become,
Who is devoid of craving for continued becoming,
By the discontinuation of what has become,
Will not come back again to a state of becoming."

Now it is extremely clear, even from the quotation as it stands, that the Buddha has interposed this word *bhūta* between the dichotomous terms *bhava* and *vibhava*. In the contemporary society, these two terms were used to denote the existence and the destruction of a soul. This usage is clearly revealed by some discourses, in which those who held onto similar views expressed them in such terms as*bhavissāmi* and *na bhavissāmi*.[3] These expressions, meaning

---

[3] E.g. at M I 8, *Sabbāsavasutta*; or at M I 135, *Alaggadūpamasutta*.

'I will be' and 'I will not be,' carry with them an implication of a person or a self.

The term *bhūta*, on the other hand, is not amenable to such a usage. It has the passive sense of something that has become. Like that reflection mentioned earlier, it conveys the idea of being produced by causes and conditions. Going by the analogy of the reflected image mentioned above, the eternalist, because of his narcissistic self love, gets attached to his own self image and lags behind. When the Buddha preaches the *Dhamma* for the cessation of existence, he shrinks from fear that it would lead to the destruction of his self. It is like the narcissistic attempt to embrace one's own image in water out of self love.

The annihilationist view leads to an attitude of escapism, like that of one who is obsessed by his own shadow. One cannot outstrip one's own shadow. It is only a vain attempt. So also is the fond hope of the nihilist that by simply negating self one can be free from repeated birth. It turns out to be mere wishful thinking, because simply by virtue of the view 'I shall not be after death' one cannot win deliverance, so long as such defilements like ignorance and craving are there. These were the two extremes towards which those two dogmatic views of eternalism and annihilationism tended.

By introducing the term *bhūta* the Buddha made it known that the five groups are the product of causes and conditions, that they are conditionally arisen. In the *Itivuttaka*, for instance, one comes across the following significant lines: *Jātaṃ bhūtaṃ samuppannaṃ, kataṃ saṅkhatamaddhuvaṃ..*[4] The reference here is to the five groups of grasping. They are "born," "become," "arisen," (that is conditionally arisen), "made up," "prepared," and "unstable." These words are suggestive of some artificiality. The word *addhuvaṃ* brings out their impermanence and insubstantiality. There is no eternal essence, like *sat*, or being. It is merely a self

---

4 It 37, *Ajātasutta*.

image, a reflection. So it seems that the word *bhūta* has connotations of being a product of causes and conditions.

Therefore, in spite of the scare it has aroused in the soul-theorists, *Nibbāna* is not something that destroys a truly existing entity. Though *Nibbāna* is called *bhavanirodha*,[5] cessation of existence, according to the outlook of the Buddha the worldlings have merely a craving for existence, *bhavataṅhā*, and not a real existence. It is only a conceit of existence, the conceit 'am,' *asmimāna*.

In reality it amounts to a craving, and this is the significance of the term *taṅhā ponobhāvikā*, craving which makes for re-becoming. Because of that craving, which is always bent forward, worldlings keep running round in *saṃsāra*. But on analysis a concrete situation always reveals a state of a become, a *bhūta*, as something produced by causes and conditions.

A donkey drags a wagon when a carrot is projected towards it from the wagon. The journey of beings in *saṃsāra* is something like that. So what we have here is not the destruction of some existing essence of being or a soul. From the point of view of the *Dhamma* the cessation of existence, or *bhavanirodha*, amounts to a stopping of the process of becoming, by the removal of the causes leading to it, namely ignorance and craving. It is, in effect, the cessation of suffering itself.

Those who held on to the annihilationist view, entertained the hope that their view itself entitled them to their cherished goal. But it was in vain, because the ignorance, craving, and grasping within them created for them the five groups of grasping, or this mass of suffering, again and again despite their view, *uppajjati dukkham idaṃ punappunaṃ*.

So what we have here is a deep philosophy of things as they are, which follows a certain law of causality. The Buddha's middle

---

[5] E.g. at A V 9, *Sāriputtasutta*.

path is based on this knowledge and vision of things as they are, avoiding both extremes of self indulgence and self mortification.

Let us now consider the question of existence involved in this context. The terms *bhava* and *vibhava* are generally associated with the idea of worlds' existence. Some seem to take *atthi*, or 'is,' as the basic element in the grammatical structure. Very often those upholders of dogmatic views brought up such propositions as 'every-thing exists,' *sabbaṃ atthi*, and 'nothing exists,' *sabbaṃ natthi*, before the Buddha, expecting him to give a categorical answer.[6]

But the Buddha pointed out that *asmi*, or 'am,' is more basic than the usage of 'is' and 'is not.' The most elementary concept is *asmi*, or 'am.' Hence the term *asmimāna*, the conceit 'am.' In the grammatical structure, the pride of place should be given to *asmi*, or 'am.' We sometimes tend to regard *atthi*, or 'is,' as the primary term. But *asmi* deserves pride of place in so far as it is the basic element in the grammatical structure. It is like the central peg from which all measurings and surveyings of the world start, since the word *māna* in *asmimāna* also means 'measuring.' Given *asmi*, or 'am,' everything else comes to be.

Let us take an illustration. If, for instance, we say "there is something," someone will pose the question "where is it?" It should be either here or there or yonder, that is, over there. It can be in one of those three places. Now, if it is here, how does that place become a 'here?' That is where I am. 'There' is where he is, and 'yonder' is where you are.

So we have here the framework of the grammar. Here is the basic lining up for the formation of the grammatical structure, its most elementary pattern. So, then, 'I am,' 'you are,' and 'he is.' In this way we see that one can speak of the existence of something relative to a viewpoint represented by 'am' or 'I am.' That is why the Buddha rejected as extremes the two views of absolute

---

6 E.g. at S II 76, *Jāṇussoṇisutta*.

existence and absolute non-existence, based on 'is,' *atthi*, and 'is not,' *natthi*.

Only when there is an 'I,' can something exist relative to that I. And that something, if it is 'there,' it is where 'I' am not present, or at a distance from me. If it is 'yonder,' or over there, it is before you who are in front of me. And if it is 'here,' it is beside me. From this we can see that this conceit 'am' is, as it were, the origin of the whole world, the origin of the world of grammar.

On a previous occasion, too, while discussing the significance of the two terms *itthabhāva* and *aññathābhāva*, we had to make a similar statement.[7] The Buddha draws our attention to a very important fact in this concern, namely, the fact that the conceit 'am' does not arise without causes and conditions. It is not something uncaused, and unconditioned. If it is uncaused and unconditioned, it can never be made to cease. The notion 'am' arises due to certain causes and conditions. There is a word suggestive of this causal origin, namely *upādāya*.

Now, for instance, we use the term *pañc'upādānakkhandha*. When we speak of the five groups of grasping, the word *upādāna* (*upa* + *ā* + *dā*) is often rendered by grasping. The prefix *upa* is supposed to imply the tenacity of the hold.[8] One can therefore ask whether it is not sufficient to relax the hold on the five groups. Strictly speaking, the prefix *upa* in *upādāna* conveys the sense of proximity or nearness. Sometimes the two words *upeti* and *upādiyati* are found in juxtaposition. *Upeti*, *upa* + *i*, to go, means 'coming near' or 'approaching,' and *upādiyati* has the sense of 'holding on to,' having come close. In other words, we have here not only a case of holding, but of holding 'on to.'

So the totality of existence, from the point of view of *Dhamma*, is dependent on a holding on, or a grasping on. It is not something uncaused and unconditioned. Here we may remind ourselves of

---

[7] See sermon 2.

[8] Vism 569.

the simile of the winding of a rope or a cord which we brought up in a previous sermon.[9] We cannot help going back to the same simile again and again, if we are to deepen our understanding of the *Dhamma*.

In that illustration we spoke of two persons winding up several strands to make a rope or a cord. But both are winding in the same direction from either end. Such an attempt at winding, however long it is continued, does not result in an actual winding, for the simple reason that the winding from one end is continually being unwinded from the other end. But what happens if a third person catches hold of the rope in the middle? Due to that hold on the middle, something like a rope appears to get winded up.

Now existence, too, is something similar. It is because of the hold in the middle that the rope gets wound up. From the point of view of an outsider, the one in the middle is holding on to a rope. But the truth is, that the semblance of a rope is there due to that holding on itself. This, then, is the norm of this world. 'Whatever is of a nature to arise, all that is of a nature to cease, ' *yaṃ kiñci samudayadhammaṃ, sabbaṃ taṃ nirodhadhammaṃ.*[10]

It is in the nature of things that every winding ends up in an unwinding. But because of that hold in the middle, the windings get accumulated. Just because of his hold in the middle, his hand is under stress and strain. Similarly, the stress and strain that is existence is also due to a grasping or a holding on to, *upādāna-paccayā bhavo*.

In fact, we have not given this illustration merely for the sake of a simile. We can adduce reasons for its validity even from the discourses. This word *upādāya* is particularly noteworthy. As we have already shown, *upādāna* does not simply mean grasping, or grasping rigidly, but holding on to something, having come close to it. This holding on creates a certain relationship, which may be

---

9 See sermon 8.

10 S V 423, *Dhammacakkappavattanasutta*.

technically termed a relativity. The two stand relative to each other. For instance, that rope exists relative to the grasping of the person who holds on to it. Now *upādāya* is the absolutive form of *upādāna*, it has the implication of something relative.

There is a discourse in the *Khandhasaṃyutta*, which clearly reveals this fact. It is a sermon preached by Venerable Puṇṇa Mantāṇiputta to Venerable Ānanda. This is the relevant paragraph:

> *Upādāya, āvuso Ānanda, asmīti hoti, no anupādāya. Kiñca upādāya asmīti hoti, no anupādāya? Rūpaṃ upādāya asmīti hoti, no anupādāya; vedanaṃ upādāya asmīti hoti, no anupādāya; saññaṃ upādāya asmīti hoti, no anupādāya; saṅkhāre upādāya asmīti hoti, no anupādāya; viññāṇaṃ upādāya asmīti hoti, no anupādāya. Upādāya, āvuso Ānanda, asmīti hoti, no anupādāya.*
>
> *Seyyathāpi, āvuso Ānanda, itthī vā puriso vā daharo yuvā maṇḍanakajātiko ādāse vā parisuddhe pariyodāte acche vā udakapatte sakaṃ mukhanimittaṃ paccavekkhamāno upādāya passeyya, no anupādāya, evam eva kho, āvuso Ānanda, upādāya asmīti hoti, no anupādāya.*[11]

Let us now try to get at the meaning of this important passage, which should clarify further what we have already attempted to explain through similes.

> "It is with dependence, friend Ānanda, that the notion 'am' occurs, not without dependence. With dependence on what, does the notion 'am' occur, and not without dependence? With dependence on form does the notion 'am' occur, not without dependence; with dependence on feeling does the notion 'am' occur, not without dependence; with

[11] S III 105, *Ānandasutta*.

> dependence on perception does the notion 'am' occur, not without dependence; with dependence on preparations does the notion 'am' occur, not with out dependence; with dependence on consciousness does the notion 'am' occur, not without dependence.
>
> "Just as, friend Ānanda, a woman or a man, youthful and fond of adornment, in looking at her or his facial image in a mirror or in a bowl filled with pure, clear, clean water, would be seeing it with dependence and not without dependence, even so, friend Ānanda, it is with dependence that the notion 'am' occurs, not without dependence."

In fact, it is rather difficult to render the word *upādāya*. It means 'in dependence on' something and has a relative sense. Reinforced with the emphatic double negative, the assertion seems to imply that the notion 'am' is something dependent and not independent, that it arises due to causes and conditions. In the explanation that follows, this dictum is substantiated by bringing in the five groups or aggregates, relative to which one posits an 'am.'

The subsequent illustration serves to bring out the required nuance of the term *upādāya*, which is more often connected with the rather gross idea of grasping. The young woman or the young man is looking at her or his face in a mirror. They can see their own face, or the sign of it, *mukhanimitta*, only with the help of a mirror, that is, as an image reflected on it. They are dependent on a mirror or a similar object for seeing their own face, not independent.

What Venerable Puṇṇa Mantāṇiputta seems to stress, is that the notion 'am' is the result of grasping or holding on to form, feeling, perception, preparations, and consciousness. It is when one looks into a mirror that one suddenly becomes self-conscious. Whether one has a liking or a dislike for what one sees, one gets the notion 'this is me.' So it is by coming close to a mirror which reflects one's facial image that the notion 'am' occurs depending on it.

The word *upādāya* therefore approximates to the idea of coming close and holding on to.

That notion occurs due to a relationship arising from that holding on. Even if one already has no such notion, the moment one looks into a mirror one is suddenly reminded of it, as if to exclaim: "Ah, here I am!" This is the gist of what Venerable Puṇṇa Mantāṇiputta is trying to put across through this discourse.

This shows that the conceit 'am' arises due to the five grasping groups. The absolutive *upādāya*, though akin to *upādāna*, has a deeper significance. It is a word suggestive of a relationship. It does not merely mean a holding on, but also a certain necessary relationship arising out of that holding on. Just as the looking into a mirror or a bowl of water gives rise to a facial image as a reflection, here too the relationship calls forth the deluded reflection "here I am." Given the notion "here I am," there follows the corollary "things that are mine."

So there is supposed to be an 'I' in contradistinction to things that are 'mine.' It is the difficulty to demarcate the area of applicability between these two concepts that has given rise to insoluble problems. 'Who am I and what is mine?' The twenty modes of personality view, *sakkāya diṭṭhi*, portray how one is at one's wit's end to solve this problem.

Let us now see how the twenty modes of personality view are made up. For instance, as regards form, it is four-fold as follows: *Rūpaṃ attato samanupassati, rūpavantaṃ vā attānaṃ, attani vā rūpaṃ, rūpasmiṃ vā attānaṃ.*[12] "He regards form as self, or self as possessing form, or form as in self, or self as in form." It is the same with the other four groups. In this way, the personality view is altogether twenty-fold.

All this comes about due to the ignorance that name-and-form is only a reflection, like that facial image. In grasping this self image of name-and-form one grasps the five groups. Attachment to

---

[12] M I 300, *Cūḷavedallasutta.*

name-and-form amounts to a holding on to these five groups. To many, the relationship between name-and-form and the grasping groups appears as a big puzzle. Wherever one looks, one sees this self image of name-and-form. But when one grasps it, what comes within the grasp is a group of form, feeling, perception, preparations, and consciousness.

The magical illusion created by consciousness is so complete that it is capable of playing a dual role, as in double acting. Be cause it reflects, like a mirror, consciousness itself is grasped, just as one grasps the mirror. Not only the reflection of the mirror, but the mirror itself is grasped. The grasping group of consciousness represents such a predicament.

One can form an idea about the relation between name-and-form and consciousness by going deeper into the implications of this discourse. In the discussion of the interrelation between name and form, the Buddha makes use of two highly significant terms, namely *adhivacanasamphassa* and *paṭighasamphassa.* How contact arises dependent on name-and-form is explained by the Buddha in the *MahāNidānasutta* of the *Dīgha Nikāya.*[13] It is addressed to Venerable Ānanda in the form of a catechism.

Phassa, or contact, is a sort of hybrid, carrying with it the implications of both *adhivacanasamphassa* and *paṭighasamphassa.* That is to say, it partakes of the character of name, *nāma*, as suggested by *adhivacanasamphassa*, as well as that of form, *rūpa*, indicated by *paṭighasamphassa.* This will be clear from the relevant section of the catechism in the *MahāNidānasutta*:

> *'Nāmarūpapaccayā phasso'ti iti kho panetaṃ vuttaṃ, tad'Ānanda, imināpetaṃ pariyāyena veditabbaṃ, yathā nāmarūpapaccayā phasso. Yehi, Ānanda, ākārehi yehi liṅgehi yehi nimittehi yehi uddesehi nāmakāyassa paññatti hoti, tesu ākāresu tesu liṅgesu tesu nimittesu tesu*

[13] D II 62, *MahāNidānasutta.*

uddesesu asati api nu kho rūpakāye adhivacanasamphasso paññāyethā'ti?'

'No hetaṃ, bhante.'

'Yehi, Ānanda, ākārehi yehi liṅgehi yehi nimittehi yehi uddesehi rūpakāyassa paññatti hoti, tesu ākāresu tesu liṅgesu tesu nimittesu tesu uddesesu asati api nu kho nāmakāye paṭighasamphasso paññāyethā'ti?'

'No hetaṃ, bhante.'

'Yehi, Ānanda, ākārehi yehi liṅgehi yehi nimittehi yehi uddesehi nāmakāyassa ca rūpakāyassa ca paññatti hoti, tesu ākāresu tesu liṅgesu tesu nimittesu tesu uddesesu asati api nu kho adhivacanasamphasso vā paṭighasamphasso vā paññāyethā'ti?'

'No hetaṃ, bhante.'

'Yehi, Ānanda, ākārehi yehi liṅgehi yehi nimittehi yehi uddesehi nāmarūpassa paññatti hoti, tesu ākāresu tesu liṅgesu tesu nimittesu tesu uddesesu asati api nu kho phasso paññāyethā'ti?'

'No hetaṃ, bhante.'

'Tasmātih'Ānanda, eseva hetu etaṃ nidānaṃ esa samudayo esa paccayo phassassa, yadidaṃ nāmarūpaṃ.'

"From name-and-form as condition, contact comes to be. Thus it has been said above. And that Ānanda, should be understood in this manner, too, as to how from name-and-form as condition, contact arises. If, Ānanda, all those modes, characteristics, signs and exponents, by which the name-group, *nāma-kāya*, is designated were absent, would there be manifest any verbal impression, *adhivacanasamphassa*, in the form-group, *rūpa-kāya*?"

"There would not, lord."

"If, Ānanda, all those modes, characteristics, signs and exponents, by which the form-group is designated were absent, would there be manifest any resistance-impression, *paṭighasamphasso*, in the name-group?"

"There would not, lord."

"And if, Ānanda, all those modes, characteristics, signs and exponents, by which there is a designation of both name-group and form-group were absent, would there be manifest either any verbal impression or any resistance-impression?"

"There would not, lord."

"And if, Ānanda, all those modes, characteristics, signs and exponents, by which there comes to be a designation of name-and-form were absent, would there be manifest any contact?"

"There would not, lord."

"Wherefore, Ānanda, this itself is the cause, this is the origin, this is the condition for contact, that is to say, name-and-form."

With the help of four words of allied sense, namely *ākāra*, mode, *liṅga*, characteristic, *nimitta*, sign, and *uddesa*, exponent, the Buddha catechetically brings out four conclusions by this disquisition. They are:

1) By whatever modes, characteristics, signs and exponents the name-group, *nāma-kāya*, is designated, in their absence no designation of verbal impression, *adhivacanasamphassa*, in the form-group, *rūpa-kāya*, is possible.

2) By whatever modes, characteristics, signs and exponents the form-group is designated, in their absence no designa-

tion of resistance-impression, *paṭighasamphasso*, in the name-group, *nāmakāya*, is possible.

3) By whatever modes, characteristics, signs and exponents both name-group and form-group are designated, in their absence no designation of verbal impression or resistance-impression is possible.

4) By whatever modes, characteristics, signs and exponents name-and-form is designated, in their absence no designation of contact is possible.

All this may well appear like a riddle, but then let us consider what name-and-form means, to begin with. The definition we gave to *nāma* in our very first sermon happened to be different from the well known definition nowadays given in terms of a bending.[14] We interpreted *nāma* in the sense of a 'naming.' Now this term *adhivacana* also conveys the same idea. *Adhivacana*, synonym, *nirutti*, nomenclature, and *paññatti*, designation, are part and parcel of linguistic usage.

In the *Niruttipathasutta* of the *Khandhasaṃyutta* one comes across three terms, *niruttipatha, adhivacanapatha,* and *paññattipatha*, pathways of nomenclature, pathways of synonyms, and pathways of designation.[15] These three terms are closely allied in meaning, in that they bring out in a sharp relief the three aspects of linguistic usage. *Nirutti* emphasises the explanatory or expository function of language, *adhivacana* its symbolic and metaphorical character, while *paññatti* brings out its dependence on convention.

What we have here is *adhivacanasamphassa*. Its affinity to name is obvious, and this is precisely the meaning we attributed to *nāma*. Therefore, what we have in this concept of *nāmakāya*, or

---

[14] See sermon 1.

[15] S III 71, *Niruttipathasutta*.

name-group, literally 'name-body,' is a set of first principles in linguistic usage pertaining to definition.

The form-group, or *rūpakāya*, literally 'form-body,' on the other hand has something to do with resistance, as suggested by the term *paṭighasamphassa*. *Paṭigha* means 'striking against.' Form, or *rūpa,* has a striking quality, while name, or *nāma,* has a descriptive quality. *Phassa,* or contact, is a hybrid of these two. This is what gives a deeper dimension to the above disquisition.

The point that the Buddha seeks to drive home is the fact that the concept of contact necessarily presupposes both name and form. In other words, name and form are mutually interrelated, as already stated above. There would be no verbal impression in the form-group, if there were no modes, characteristics, etc., proper to name. Likewise there could be no resistant impression in the name-group, if there were no modes, characteristics, etc., proper to form.

At first sight these two may appear as totally opposed to each other. But what is implied is a case of mutual interrelation. The expression peculiar to the name-group is a necessary condition for the form-group, while the resistance peculiar to the form-group is a necessary condition for the name-group. Since here we have something deep, let us go for an illustration for the sake of clarity.

As we have already stated, a verbal impression in regard to the form-group is there because of the constituents of the name-group. Now the form-group consists of the four great primaries earth, water, fire and air. Even to distinguish between them by their qualities of hardness and softness, hotness and coolness, etc., feeling, perception, intention, contact and attention, which are the constituents of the name-group, have to play their part. Thus it is with the help of those members on the name side that the four basic elements associated with form receive recognition.

Metaphor is a figure of speech, common in ornate literary language as well as in technical terminology. Here the inanimate is animated by personification. What is proper to the animate world is superimposed on the inanimate. Now the word *adhivacana* is, even literally, a superimposition, and it is a term with obvious metaphorical associations. Whereas in the literary field it has an ornate value as a figurative expression, in technical usage it serves the purpose of facility of expression by getting the tools to speak for themselves.

For instance, a carpenter might speak of two planks touching each other as if they can actually touch and feel. The concept of touch, even when it is attributed to inanimate objects, is the outcome of attention, in this case the attention of the carpenter. Here, again, we are reminded of the role of attention in the origination of things as stated in the *Kiṃmūlakasutta* and *Samiddhisutta* discussed above.[16] In accordance with the dictum "Mind is the forerunner of all things,"[17] "All things are rooted in interest, they originate with attention and arise out of contact," *chandamūlakā, āvuso, sabbe dhammā, manasikārasambhavā, phassasamudayā*, etc.[18] Wherever the carpenter's interest went, his attention discovered and picked up the thing, and here the thing is the fact of two planks touching each other.

Interest, attention and contact together bring out some deeper implications of the law of dependent arising. Not only with regard to inanimate objects, but even in the case of this conscious body, the question of contact is related to the fact of attention.

If, for instance I ask what I am touching now, one might say that I am touching the palm leaf fan in my hand. This is because we usually associate the idea of touching with the hand that holds. But suppose I put away the fan and ask again what I am touching now, one might find it difficult to answer. It might not be possible for another to guess by mere external observation, since it is essentially subjective. It is dependent on my attention. It could even be my robe that I am touching in the sense of contact, in

---

[16] A IV 385, *Samiddhisutta*; A IV 338, *Kiṃmūlakasutta*; see sermon 9.

[17] Dhp 1, *Yamakavagga*.

[18] A IV 338, *Kiṃmūlakasutta*.

which case I am becoming conscious of my body as apart from the robe I am wearing.

Consciousness follows in the wake of attention. Whatever my attention picks up, of that I am conscious. Though I have in front of me so many apparently visible objects, until my attention is focused, eye-consciousness does not come about. The basic function of this type of consciousness, then, is to distinguish between the eye and the object seen. It is only after the eye has become conscious, that other factors necessary for sense perception fall into place.

The two things born of that basic discrimination, together with the discriminating consciousness itself, that is eye-consciousness, make up the concept of contact. *Cakkhuñca paṭicca rūpe ca uppajjati cakkhuviññāṇaṃ, tiṇṇaṃ saṅgati phasso.*[19] "Dependent on eye and forms, eye-consciousness arises, the concurrence of the three is contact."

The same principle holds good in the case of the two planks touching each other. All this goes to show that it is with the help of the factors in the name-group that we can even metaphorically speak of a contact between inanimate things.

Let us now consider how resistance-impression, *paṭighasamphassa*, comes about. It is said that the factors of the form-group have a part to play in producing resistance-impression on the name-group. We sometimes speak of an idea 'striking us,' as if it were something material. Or else an idea could be 'at the back' of our mind and a word 'on the tip' of our tongue.

The clearest manifestation of contact is that between material objects, where collision is suggestive of resistance, as implied by the word *paṭigha*. This primary sense of striking against or striking together is implicit even in the simile given by the Buddha in the *Dhātuvibhaṅgasutta* of the *Majjhima Nikāya*, and in the *Phassa-*

---

19 M I 111, *Madhupiṇḍikasutta.*

mūlakasutta of the *Saṃyutta Nikāya*, concerning two sticks being rubbed together to kindle a fire.[20]

Though as a gross manifestation contact is primarily associated with the form-group, it is essentially connected with the name-group, as we have already explained with illustrations. It is when both resistance-impression and verbal impression come together that contact arises, dependent on name-and-form, *nāmarūpa-paccayā phasso*.

Another point that needs to be clarified in this connection is the exact significance of the word *rūpa*. This word has been variously interpreted and explained among different Buddhist sects. How did the Buddha define *rūpa*? In ordinary usage it can mean either forms visible to the eye, or whatever is generally spoken of as 'material.' Its exact significance has become a subject of controversy. What precisely do we mean by '*rūpa*'?

The Buddha himself has explained the word, giving the following etymology in the *Khajjanīyasutta* of the *Khandhasaṃyutta* in the *Saṃyutta Nikāya*. While defining the five groups there, he defines the form group as follows:

> *Kiñca, bhikkhave, rūpaṃ vadetha? Ruppatīti kho, bhikkhave, tasmā rūpan'ti vuccati. Kena ruppati? Sītena pi ruppati, uṇhena pi ruppati, jighacchāya pi ruppati, pipāsāya pi ruppati, daṃsamakasavātātapasarīsapasamphassena pi ruppati. Ruppatīti kho, bhikkhave, tasmā rūpan'ti vuccati.*[21]

> "And what, monks, do you call *rūpa*? It is affected, monks, that is why it is called *rūpa*. Affected by what? Affected by cold, affected by heat, affected by hunger, affected by thirst, affected by contact with gadflies, mosqui-

---

[20] M III 242, *Dhātuvibhaṅgasutta*; S IV 215, *Phassamūlakasutta*.

[21] S III 86, *Khajjanīyasutta*.

> toes, wind, sun and serpents. It is affected, monks, that is why it is called *rūpa*."

This definition seems to convey something very deep, so much so that various Buddhist sects came out with various interpretations of this passage. The Buddha departs from the way of approach taken up by the materialistic systems of thought in the world in defining *rūpa* with *ruppati*, 'being affected.' It is not the inanimate trees and rocks in the world that are said to be affected by cold and heat, but this conscious body. So this body is not conceived of as a bundle of atoms to be animated by introducing into it a life faculty, *jīvitindriya*. What is meant by *rūpa* is this same body, this body with form, which, for the meditator, is a fact of experience.

Attempts at interpretation from a scholastic point of view created a lot of complications. But the definition, as it stands, is clear enough. It is directly addressed to experience. The purpose of the entire *Dhamma* preached by the Buddha is not to encourage an academic dabbling in philosophical subtleties with a mere jumble of words. The purpose is utter disenchantment, dispassion and cessation, *ekantanibbidāya, virāgāya, nirodhāya*.[22] Therefore the etymology given here in terms of *ruppati*, 'to be affected,' is in full accord with that purpose. *Rūpa* is so called, because it is affected by cold, heat, and the sting of gadflies, mosquitoes, etc., not because of any atomism in it.

If we are to examine further the meaning of this verb *ruppati*, we can count on the following quotation from the *Piṅgiyasutta* of the *Pārāyanavagga* in the *Sutta Nipāta*. It runs: *ruppanti rūpesu janā pamattā*,[23] "Heedless men are affected in regard to forms." The canonical commentary *Cūḷaniddesa*, commenting on the word, brings out the various nuances connected with it. *Ruppantīti*

---

[22] This expression occurs e.g. at D II 251, *MahāGovindasutta*.

[23] Sn 1121, *Piṅgiyamāṇavapucchā*.

kuppanti pīḷayanti ghaṭṭayanti byādhitā domanassitā honti.[24] "*Ruppanti* means to be adversely affected, to be afflicted, to come into contact with, to be dis-eased and dis-pleased."

Surely it is not the trees and rocks that are affected in this manner. It is this animate body that is subject to all this. The pragmatic purpose of utter detachment, dispassion and cessation is clear enough even from this commentary. What is known as the form-group, *rūpakkhandha*, is one vast wound with nine apertures.[25] This wound is affected when it is touched by cold and heat, when gadflies and mosquitoes land on it. This wound gets irritated by them.

We come across yet another canonical reference in support of these nuances in the following two lines in the *Uṭṭhānasutta* of the *Sutta Nipāta*. *Āturānañhi kā niddā, sallaviddhāna ruppataṃ.*[26] "For what sleep could there be for those who are afflicted, being pierced with a dart."

These two lines stress the need for heedfulness for beings pierced with the arrow of craving. Here, too, the verb *ruppati* has the sense of being affected or afflicted. All this goes to show that the early Buddhist concept of *rūpa* had a striking simplicity about it.

As we have already stated at the very outset, the teachings in the discourses are simple enough. But there is a certain depth in this very simplicity, for it is only when the water is lucid and limpid that one can see the bottom of a pond. But with the passage of time there was a tendency to lose interest in these discourses, because of the general predilection for complexity.

Materialistic philosophers, in particular, were carried away by this trend, whether they were Hindus or Buddhists. Modern day scientists, too, got caught in this trend. They pursued the material-

---

[24] Nidd II 238.

[25] A IV 386, *Gaṇḍasutta*.

[26] Sn 331, *Uṭṭhānasutta*.

istic overtones of the word *rūpa*, without realizing that they are running after a mirage. They went on analysing matter, until they ended up with an atomism and grasped a heap of concepts. The analysis of matter thus precipitated a grasping of a mass of concepts. Whether one grasps a pole or a mole, it is a grasping all the same.

The Buddha's admonitions, on the contrary, point in a different direction. He pointed out that in order to be free from the burden some oppression of form, one has to be free from the perception of form. What is of relevance here is the very perception of form, *rūpasaññā*. From the point of view of *Dhamma*, any attempt at analysis of the materialistic concept of form, or any microscopic analysis of matter, would lead to a pursuit of a mirage.

This fact, the modern day scientist is now in a position to appreciate. He has found that the mind with which he carries on the analysis is influencing his findings at every level. In other words, he has been running after a mirage, due to his ignorance of the mutual interrelation between name and form. One would not be in such a plight, if one understands that the real problem at issue is not that of form, but of the perception of form.

In an earlier sermon we happened to quote a verse which makes it extremely clear. Let us now hark back to that verse, which occurs in the *Jaṭāsutta* of the *Saṃyutta Nikāya*:[27]

Yattha nāmañca rūpañca,
asesaṃ uparujjhati,
paṭighaṃ rūpasaññā ca,
etthesā chijjate jaṭā.

"Where name and form
As well as resistance and perception of form
Are completely cut off,
It is there that the tangle gets snapped."

---

27 S I 13, *Jaṭāsutta*; see sermon 1.

The entire *saṃsāric* problem is solved when the tangle gets snapped. Name and form, resistance and perception of form are completely cut off in that non-manifestative consciousness mentioned in our earlier sermons.[28] That, in effect, is the end of the tangle within and the tangle without.

Our discussion of the law of dependent arising must have made it clear that there is an interrelation between name-and-form and consciousness on the one hand, and between name and form themselves on the other. This, then, is a case of a tangle within and a tangle without. Like the central spot of a whirlpool, the deepest point of the entire formula of *paṭicca samuppāda* is traceable to the interrelation that obtains between name and form on the one hand, and between name-and-form and consciousness on the other.

As far as the significance of perception of form is concerned, the true purpose of the spiritual endeavour, according to the Buddha, is the very freedom from this perception of form. How does perception of form come about? It is due to that 'striking against,' or resistance. Perception of form arises, for instance, when gadflies and mosquitoes land on this body.

As we have already mentioned, even the distinctions of hard and soft, etc., with which we recognize the four elements, is a matter of touching. We are only trying to measure and gauge the four great primaries with this human frame. We can never ever comprehend fully the gamut of these four great primaries. But we are trying to understand them through this human frame in a way that is meaningful to our lives.

All kinds of beings have their own specific experience of 'touch,' in relation to their experience of the four elements. So what we have here is entirely a question of perception of form. The true purpose, then, should be the release of one's mind from this perception of form. It is only when the mind is freed from resistance and the perception of form, as well as from name-and-

---

[28] See sermon 7.

form, that one can win to the deliverance from this problem of the tangle within and the tangle without that is *saṃsāra*.

Yet another fact emerges from the above discussion. The two views of existence and non-existence, *bhava/vibhava*, asserting an absolute existence and an absolute non-existence, seem to have posed an insoluble problem to many philosophers. Concerning the origin of the world, they wondered whether *sat*, or being, came out of *asat*, or non-being, or vice versa.

All these problems arose out of a misunderstanding about form, or material objects, as we may well infer from the following two lines of a verse in the *Kalahavivādasutta* of the *Sutta Nipāta*. *Rūpesu disvā vibhavaṃ bhavañca, vinicchayaṃ kurute jantu loke.*[29] "Having seen the existence and destruction of material forms, a man in this world comes to a conclusion."

What is the conclusion? That there is an absolute existence and an absolute non-existence. One comes to this conclusion drawing an inference from the behaviour of visible objects. For instance, we could presume that this machine before us exists in an absolute sense, ignoring the causes and conditions underlying its existence. The day this machine is destroyed we would say: "It was, but now it is not."

The Buddha has pointed out that such absolute views of existence and non-existence are a result of an incorrect understanding about form. What actually is involved here is the perception of form. Due to a misconception about the perception of form, the world inclines towards the two extreme views of absolute existence and absolute non-existence.

So the whole point of our discussion today has been the clarification of the mutual interrelation between name and form, to show that name-and-form itself is only an image, or a shadow, reflected on consciousness.

---

[29] Sn 867, *Kalahavivādasutta*.

Nibbāna Sermon 11

Namo tassa Bhagavato Arahato Sammāsambuddhassa
Namo tassa Bhagavato Arahato Sammāsambuddhassa
Namo tassa Bhagavato Arahato Sammāsambuddhassa

Etaṃ santaṃ, etaṃ paṇītaṃ, yadidaṃ sabbasaṅkhārasamatho sabbūpadhipaṭinissaggo taṇhakkhayo virāgo nirodho nibbānaṃ.[1]

"This is peaceful, this is excellent, namely the stilling of all preparations, the relinquishment of all assets, the destruction of craving, detachment, cessation, extinction."

With the permission of the Most Venerable Great Preceptor and the assembly of the venerable meditative monks.

This is the eleventh sermon in the series of sermons on *Nibbāna*. In our last sermon, we tried to explain that contact arises dependent on name-and-form, because form gets a verbal impression by the naming quality in name, and name gets a resistance-impression by the striking quality in form. In the context of this *Dhamma*, contact, properly so-called, is a combination of these two, namely verbal impression and resistance-impression.

We also happened to mention the other day a new etymological explanation given by the Buddha to the word *rūpa*, quoting the relevant passage from the *Khajjanīyasutta* of the *Khandhasaṃyutta* in the *Saṃyutta Nikāya*. He has defined the form group with reference to 'affectation': *Ruppatīti kho, bhikkhave, tasmā*

---

1 M I 436, *MahāMālunkyasutta*.

rūpan'ti vuccati.[2] "It is affected, monks, that is why it is called form. By what is it affected? By cold, heat, hunger, thirst, and the sting of gadflies, mosquitoes and the like."

While analysing the implications of this 'being affected,' we mentioned that the form group could be compared to a wound. According to the commentarial exegesis, too, *ruppati* means to be adversely affected, to be afflicted, to come into conflict with, to be diseased and displeased. These are reminiscent of the responses usually associated with the person who has an easy lacerable wound. To say that a *paṭighasamphassa* arises because of this lacerable quality is therefore very apt.

The primary sense of the word *paṭigha* is 'striking against.' Perception of form arises as a result of an attempt to understand through the factors on the name side this particular striking against, which resembles the laceration of a wound. This perception of form, which follows in the wake of the feeling that arises when something strikes against form, is like the groping of a blind man in the dark. Generally, the worldling is in the habit of staring at the form that comes within his grasp, to ascertain its true nature. Likewise, he touches the form he sees with his eyes to verify it. As the saying goes: 'Seeing is believing, but touch is the real thing.'

But both these attempts are like the gropings of a blind man. The worldling is unable to get rid of his delusion completely by either of these methods. It is because he is accustomed to draw conclusions under the influence of his perception of the compact, *ghanasaññā*.

The fact that the two extreme views of existence and non-existence are also the outcome of this perception of the compact in regard to form, is borne out by the following two lines of the verse we quoted from the *Kalahavivādasutta* in our previous sermon. *Rūpesu disvā vibhavaṃ bhavañca, vinicchayaṃ kurute jantu loke.*[3]

---

[2] S III 86, *Khajjanīyasutta.*

[3] Sn 867, *Kalahavivādasutta.*

"Having seen the existence and destruction of material forms, a man in this world comes to a conclusion."

The worldling has the idea that material forms have an absolute existence. This idea is the result of his perception of form. It is a perception arising out of his impression of that 'striking against.' whatever the level of this perception of form be, it is not better than the impression of a blind man. The two extreme views of absolute existence and non-existence in the world are based on this kind of impression.

Various types of views and opinions current in the world regarding material forms and matter in general, are the outcome of the notion that they are absolutely real. There is a tendency in the worldling to presume that what he grasps with his hands and sees with his eyes exists absolutely. So a thing is said to exist for some length of time, before it gets destroyed. The logical conclusion, then, is that all things in the world exist absolutely and that at some point of time they get absolutely destroyed. This is how the two extreme views of absolute existence and absolute non-existence have arisen in this world. This is the outcome of a perception of form, which is tantamount to a pursuit of a mirage. It is an illusion.

The Buddha has declared, in the *Jaṭāsutta*, that where name-and-form as well as resistance and perception of form are cut off and surcease, there the entire *saṃsāric* problem, which amounts to a tangle within and a tangle without, is also conclusively solved.[4] That this is so could be inferred to some extent from what we have discussed so far.

Nāma and *rūpa*, as well as *paṭigha-* and *rūpasaññā*, are highly significant terms. *Paṭigha-* and *rūpasaññā* are equivalent to *paṭighasamphassa* and *adhivacanasamphassa* respectively. Now as to this perception of form, it is basically conditioned by contact.

---

[4] S I 13, *Jaṭāsutta*; cf. volume I sermon 1.

That is why the *Kalahavivādasutta* states that contact is the cause of the two views of existence and non-existence.

In this *Kalahavivādasutta* one finds a series of questions and answers going deeper and deeper into the analysis of contact, step by step. The question *phasso nu lokasmiṃ kutonidāno*, "What is the cause of contact in this world?" gets the answer *nāmañca rūpañca paṭicca phasso*, "dependent on name-and-form is contact."[5] The next question is: *Kismiṃ vibhūte na phussanti phassā*, "In the absence of what, do contacts not bring about contact," or, "touches do not touch?" It gets the answer: *Rūpe vibhūte na phusanti phassā*, "In the absence of form, contacts do not bring about contact."

The question that comes up next, and the answer given, are extremely important. They lead to a deep analysis of the *Dhamma*, so much so that both verses deserve to be quoted in full. The question is:

Kathaṃsametassa vibhoti rūpaṃ,
sukhaṃ dukhaṃ vā pi kathaṃ vibhoti,
etaṃ me pabrūhi yathā vibhoti,
taṃ jāniyāmā iti me mano ahu.[6]

"To one constituted in which manner does form
cease to exist,
Or, how even pleasure and pain cease to exist,
Do tell me how all these become non-existent,
Let us know this, such a thought arose in me."

The answer to this question is couched in this extraordinary verse:

Na saññasaññī na visaññasaññī,
no pi asaññī na vibhūtasaññī,

[5] Sn 871-872, *Kalahavivādasutta.*

[6] Sn 873, *Kalahavivādasutta.*

evaṃ sametassa vibhoti rūpaṃ,
saññānidānā hi papañcasaṅkhā.[7]

What this verse purports to describe is the state of a person for whom form as also pleasure and pain has ceased to exist. He is not one with normal perception, nor is he one with abnormal perception. He is not non-percipient, nor has he rescinded perception. It is to one constituted in this manner that form ceases to exist, for, *papañcasaṅkhā* – whatever they may be – have perception as their source.

The meaning of this verse needs to be clarified further. According to the *MahāNiddesa*, the allusion in this verse is to one who is on the path to the formless realms, having attained the first four absorptions.[8] The commentary is forced to that conclusion, because it takes the phrase *na vibhūtasaññī* as negating formless realms as such. The assumption is that the person referred to is neither conscious with normal perception, nor abnormally unconscious, nor devoid of perception, as in the attainment of cessation, nor in one of the formless attainments. So then, the only possibility seemed to be to identify it with some intermediate state. That is why the *MahāNiddesa* and the other commentaries interpret this problematic state as that of one who is on the path to formless attainments, *arūpamaggasamaṅgi.*[9]

However, considerations of context and presentation would lead to a different conclusion. The extraordinary state alluded to by this verse seems to be a surpamundane one, which goes far deeper than the so-called intermediate state. The transcendence of form, indicated here, is more radical than the transcendence in attaining to formless states. It is a transcendence at a supramundane level, as we may well infer from the last line of the verse, *saññānidānā hi*

---

7 Sn 874, *Kalahavivādasutta.*

8 Nidd I 280.

9 Nidd I 280 and Pj II 553.

papañcasaṅkhā. Papañcasaṅkhā is a term which has a relevance to insight meditation and the denouement of the *sutta* is also suggestive of such a background. The *Kalahavivādasutta*, consisting of sixteen verses, is, from beginning to end, a network of deep questions and answers leading to levels of insight. The opening verse, for instance, states the initial problem as follows:

> *Kuto pahūtā kalahā vivādā,*
> *paridevasokā sahamaccharā ca,*
> *mānātimānā saha pesuṇā ca,*
> *kuto pahūtā te tad iṅgha brūhi.*[10]

> "Whence do spring up contentions and disputes,
> Lamentations, sorrows and envies,
> And arrogance together with slander,
> Whence do they spring up, pray tell me this."

It is in answer to this basic question that this discourse gradually unfolds itself. In accordance with the law of dependent arising, the cause of contentions and disputes is said to be the tendency to hold things dear, *piyappahūtā kalahā vivādā*. Then the question is about the cause of this idea of holding things dear. The cause of it is said to be desire, *chandanidānāni piyāni loke*. Things dear originate from desire. Desire, or interest, makes things 'dear.'

The next question is: What is the origin of desire? Desire is traced to the distinction between the pleasant and the unpleasant. It is in reply to the question regarding the origin of this distinction between the pleasant and the unpleasant that contact is brought in. In fact, it is the question as to the origin of contact, *phasso nu lokasmiṃ kuto nidāno*, which formed the starting point of our discussion. The answer to that question is name-and-form,

---

[10] Sn 862, *Kalahavivādasutta*.

nāmañca rūpañca. So in this chain of causes, the link that comes next to contact is name-and-form.

Now the verse in question beginning with *na saññasaññī* goes deeper than name-and-form. Even the question about contact has a peculiar wording: *Kismiṃ vibhūte na phusanti phassā*, "When what is not there, do touches not touch?" The question, then, is not just the cessation of contact as such. The answer, too, has the same peculiarity. *Rūpe vibhūte na phusanti phassā*, "It is when form is not there that touches do not touch." It is the subsequent question regarding form that brings out the cryptic verse as the answer.

All this goes to show that the verse in question alludes to a supramundane state far transcending the formless or any supposed intermediate stage. The transcendence of pleasure and pain, as well as perception of form, is implied here. The verse beginning with *na saññasaññī* brings the entire analytical disquisition to a climax. It comes as the thirteenth verse in the series. Usually, such a disquisition leads up to a climax, highlighting *Nibbāna*. It is obvious, therefore, that the reference here is to the *Nibbānic* mind.

We have here four negations: *Na saññasaññī – na visaññasaññī – no piasaññī – na vibhūtasaññī.* These four negations insinuate a strange supramundane level of perception. In short, it is an attempt to analyse the crux of the *Dhamma* in terms of perception. As to the provocation for such an approach, we may remind ourselves of the fact that, according to the Buddha, release from materiality amounted to a release from the perception of form. Here, we have something really deep.

As it was stated in the *Jaṭāsutta*, for the disentangling of the tangle, name-and-form, resistance and perception of form, have to be cut off. This last mentioned perception of form, or *rūpasaññā*, is highly significant. Before the advent of the Buddha the general belief, even among ascetics, was that, in order to be free from form, one has to attain to the formless, *arūpa*. But, as we pointed out in an earlier sermon, this kind of approach to the question of freedom from form, is like the attempt of one who, having imagined a ghost in the darkness of the night, runs away to escape it.[11] He is simply taking the fantasy of the ghost with him.

Likewise, perception of form is already implicit in the formless. What has been done is only a pushing away of the perception of form with the help of *saṅkhāras*. It is merely a suppression of form through the power of absorption. It does not amount to a cessation of the perception of form.

What, then, is the message the Buddha gave to the world regarding the abandonment by way of eradication? He pointed out that freedom from form can be won only by comprehending a certain deep normative principle behind perception. Till then, one keeps on going round and round in *saṃsāra*. Even if one breaks away from form to stay for aeons in formless realms, one swings back to form at the end of that period. Why? Because the ghost of form still haunts the formless. It is precisely because of this fact that pre-Buddhistic ascetics could not free themselves from the round of existence.

The *Kalahavivādasutta* as a whole, could be regarded as an extremely deep analysis of the basis of the two views of existence and non-existence. Our departure from the *MahāNiddesa* in regard to the interpretation of this discourse might sometimes be called in question. But let the wise judge its reasonableness on its own merits.

According to our interpretation so far, the thirteenth verse marks the climax of the discourse, with its allusion to *Nibbāna*. This is obvious from the fourteenth verse, in which the questioner confesses: *Yaṃ taṃ apucchimha akittayī no, aññaṃ taṃ pucchāma tad iṅgha brūhi.*[12] "Whatever we have asked you, that you have explained to us. Now we wish to ask you something else, pray, give us an answer to that too."

---

[11] See sermon 7.

[12] Sn 875, *Kalahavivādasutta*.

The question now posed is this: *Ettāvataggaṃ nu vadanti h'eke, yakkhassa suddhiṃ idha paṇḍitāse, udāhu aññam pi vadanti etto?* "Do some, who are reckoned as wise men here, declare the highest purity of the soul with this much alone, or else do they posit something beyond this?" The interlocutor is trying to get the solution restated in terms of the two views of existence and non-existence. The term *yakkha* is used in this context in the sense of an individual soul.[13] It betrays an assumption based on a wrong view. The question concerns the purity of the individual soul. The interlocutor wants to ascertain whether wise men in the world declare this state as the highest purity of the soul, or whether they go beyond this in postulating something more. Here is an attempt to get the answer already given restated in terms of the soul theory, a sort of anti-climax. The two concluding verses that follow, give the lie to this presumptuous question:

Ettāvataggaṃ pi vadanti h'eke
yakkhassa suddhiṃ idha paṇḍitāse,
tesaṃ paneke samayaṃ vadanti
anupādisese kusalā vadānā.

"Some, who are regarded as wise men here,
Call this itself the highest purity of the individual soul,
But there are again some among them, who speak of an annihilation,
Claiming to be experts in the cessation without residue."

Ete ca ñatvā upanissitā ti
ñatvā munī nissaye so vimaṃsī,
ñatvā vimutto na vivādam eti
bhavābhavāya na sameti dhīro.

---

13 Similar connotations recur in the variant reading *paramayakkhavisuddhi* at A V 64, and in the expression *yakkhassa suddhi* at Sn 478.

> "Knowing that they are dependent on speculative views,
> The sage with discernment, with regard to whatever is speculative,
> Emancipated as he is through understanding, does not enter into dispute,
> A truly wise man does not fall back either on existence or on non-existence."

The concluding verse amounts to a refutation of both these extreme views. The truly wise sage, who is released with proper discernment of the nature of dogmatic involvement, has no disputes with those who are at loggerheads with each other on the issue of existence and non-existence. This, in effect, means that *Nibbāna* as a goal avoids both extremes of eternalism and nihilism.

The *Upasīvasutta* in the *Pārāyanavagga* of the *Sutta Nipāta* provides further proof of the plausibility of the above interpretation. There, *Nibbāna* as the cessation of consciousness in the *arahant*, is compared to the extinction of a flame:

> *Accī yathā vātavegena khitto*
> *atthaṃ paleti na upeti saṅkhaṃ*
> *evaṃ munī nāmakāyā vimutto*
> *atthaṃ paleti na upeti saṅkhaṃ.*[14]

> "As flame flung on by force of wind,
> Reaches its end, comes not within reckoning,
> So the sage, released from name-and-form,
> Reaches his end, comes not within reckoning."

---

[14] Sn 1074, *Upasīvamāṇavapucchā*.

When a flame goes out, it cannot be reckoned as having gone in any of the directions, like north, east, south, and west. All what can be said about it, is that it has gone out.[15]

Even after the Buddha has given this reply, the brahmin youth Upasīva, entrenched as he is in the eternalist view, raises a question which is similar to the one already quoted. He, too, is trying to understand it in terms of the two extreme views of existence and non-existence:

Atthaṃgato so uda vā so natthi
udāhu ve sassatiyā arogo,
taṃ me munī sādhu viyākarohi,
tathā hi te vidito esa dhammo.

"Has he reached his end, or is he no more,
Or is he eternally well,
That to me, sage, in full explain,
For this *Dhamma* is well within your ken."

In the discourses we find similar instances of attempts to determine, in terms of those two extreme views, even a conclusive statement of the Buddha on the question of *Nibbāna*. Yet another instance is found in the *Poṭṭhapādasutta* of the *Dīghanikāya*. There the Buddha outlines the path to *Nibbāna* from the point of view of perception. The discourse, therefore, is one that highlights the importance of the term *saññā*. In that discourse, the path of training leading to *Nibbāna* is introduced under the heading *anupubbābhisaññānirodha-sampajāna-samāpatti*, "the attainment, with full awareness, to the gradual cessation of higher levels of perception."[16]

---

15 M I 487, *Aggivacchagottasutta*.

16 D I 184, *Poṭṭhapādasutta*.

What is significant in this particular context, is that the invitation for this exposition came from the ascetics of other sects. In response to their request to enlighten them on the subject of the cessation of higher levels of perception, *abhisaññānirodha*, the Buddha gave quite a long account of the course of training required for it. But at the end of that deep exposition, the wandering ascetic Poṭṭhapāda raises the following question: *Saññā nu kho purisassa attā, udāhu aññā saññā aññā attā?* "Is perception a man's soul, or is perception something and soul another?" This is typical of their bigoted attitude, which prevented them from understanding this *Dhamma*, free from the soul prejudice.

We went so far as to bring out all this evidence, because the point at issue is fairly important. Even the attempt of the *Mahā-Niddesa* to explain the verse beginning with *na saññasaññī* is far from conclusive. It is not at all likely that the ascetics of other sects subscribed to a view that the intermediate stage between the fourth absorption and the first formless absorption is equivalent to the purest state of the soul. Such an interim state is of no account.

As we go on, we might come across further proof of the tenability of this interpretation. The verse beginning with *na saññasaññī* is not easily forgotten, because of its unusual accent on the negative particle. We might have to hark back to it when we come across similar discourses dealing with *Nibbāna*. Till then, let us remind ourselves of two similes we have already given, in order to get a foretaste of the significance of this problematic verse.

Firstly, the Buddha's simile of the magic show as an illustration for consciousness in the *Pheṇapiṇḍūpamasutta – māyūpamañca viññāṇaṃ.*[17] While describing the five groups, he compares consciousness to a magical performance at crossroads, conducted by a magician or his apprentice. A man with the right type of vision, watching this magic show, understands that it is empty,

---

[17] S III 142, *Pheṇapiṇḍūpamasutta.*; cf. also sermon 6.

hollow and void of essence. It is as if he has seen through the tricks and deceptions of the magician.

While watching a magic show, the audience in general reacts to it with gaping mouths and exclamations. But how would a man with radical attention and penetrative wisdom, who is fully aware of the tricks of the magician, watch a magic show? He is simply looking on with a vacant gaze.

This reminds us of the significance of the word *viññāṇaṃ anidassanaṃ anantaṃ sabbato pabhaṃ.*[18] That gaze is 'endless,' *anantaṃ*, in the sense that it does not have the magic show as its object. It goes beyond. It is also 'non-manifestative,' *anidassanaṃ*, since the magic show does not manifest itself, as it has now been penetrated through with wisdom. This wisdom is revealing in its 'all lustrous' nature, *sabbato pabhaṃ*, so much so that the tricks are seen-through.

So this man with discernment is watching with a vacant gaze. Now how would such a person appear to one who is deluded and enchanted by the magic show? The latter might regard the former as an inattentive spectator who misses the magic show. Or else, he might think that the other is out of his senses, or insensate.

What the riddle verse beginning with *na saññasaññī* refers to, is such a vacant gaze. That is to say, the person referred to is not one with the ordinary worldling's perception, which is deluded, nor has he fainted and become unconscious, *na saññasaññī na visaññasaññī*. He is not in a trance, devoid of perception, *no pi asaññī*, nor has he put and end to perception, *na vibhūtasaññī*. What these four negations highlight, is that vacant gaze of the one who is emancipated through wisdom.

Somewhat on the lines of the simile used by the Buddha, we might reintroduce, as a flashback, the simile of the cinema.[19] Though it has a modernistic flavour, it could perhaps be more

---

[18] M I 329, *Brahmanimantanikasutta*; cf. also sermon 8.

[19] See sermons 5, 6 and 7.

easily understood. Let us suppose that a matinee show of a technicolour film is in progress with closed doors and windows. Suddenly, by some technical defect, the doors and windows are flung open. What would be the change of perspective in the spectator now? He, too, would be looking on with a vacant gaze. Though still the show is going on, he is no longer seeing it. A sort of 'cessation' has occurred, at least temporarily.

The theme as well as the objective of all our sermons is expressed in the quotation beginning with "This is peaceful, this is excellent," etc., which forms the rubric, as it were, for each sermon. The change that occurs in the spectator now, is somewhat reminiscent of it. Though not all preparations, at least those preparations connected with the film show are momentarily 'stilled.' Whatever assets in the form of the bundle of experiences on which the film show is evalued, are 'relinquished.' The craving or the desire for the show has gone down. The colourful show has 'faded away,' making way for detachment. The film show has 'ceased' for him. It is also extinct for him, since his burning desire has cooled off now. In this way, we can understand the four puzzling negations in that riddle verse as an attempt to describe the vacant gaze of this spectator, and that man with discernment at the magic show.

Another aspect of special significance in this riddle verse emerges from the last line, *saññānidānā hi papañcasaṅkhā*, which could be tentatively rendered as "for [whatever are termed] *papañcasaṅkhā* have perception as their source." *Papañca* is a term with a deep philosophical dimension in Buddhism. In fact, even the rise of many Buddhist sects could be put down to an insufficient appreciation of its significance. In our own philosophical tradition, too, much of the confusion with regard to the interpretation of *Nibbāna* seems to have come about due to a lack of understanding in this particular field. Therefore we propose to devote sufficient time and attention to clarify the significance of this term *papañca*.

To begin with, we can bring up clear evidence of the fact that the word *papañca* is used in the discourses to convey some deep idea. As a rule, whenever the Buddha presents a set of ideas pertaining to some *Dhamma* topic, the deepest or the most important of them is mentioned last. This feature is quite evident in the *Aṅguttara Nikāya*, where very often a sermon is seen to unfold itself in an ascending order, leading to a climax. In an enumeration of items 'the last but not the least,' happens to be the most important. Granted that this is the general trend, we can trace as many as nine such contexts among the *suttas* in which *papañca* is counted last.[20] This itself is a clue to its importance.

One of the most telling instances is to be found in the Eights of the *Aṅguttara Nikāya*. It is called *Anuruddhamahāvitakkasutta*. There we are told that to Venerable Anuruddha, once meditating in solitude in Pācīnavaṃsa Park, the following seven thoughts occurred, concerning *Dhamma*:

> *Appicchassāyaṃ dhammo, nāyaṃ dhammo mahicchassa; santuṭṭhassāyaṃ dhammo, nāyaṃ dhammo asantuṭṭhassa; pavivittassāyaṃ dhammo, nāyaṃ dhammo saṅgaṇikārāmassa; āraddhaviriyassāyaṃ dhammo, nāyaṃ dhammo kusītassa; upaṭṭhitasatissāyaṃ dhammo, nāyaṃ dhammo muṭṭhassatissa; samāhitassāyaṃ dhammo, nāyaṃ dhammo asamāhitassa; paññavato ayaṃ dhammo, nāyaṃ dhammo duppaññassa.*[21]

> "This *Dhamma* is for one who wants little, not for one who wants much; this *Dhamma* is for one who is contented, not for one who is discontent; this *Dhamma* is for one who is secluded, not for one who is fond of society; this *Dhamma* is for the energetic, not for one who is lazy; this

---

20 D II 276, *Sakkapañhasutta*; D III 287, *Dasuttarasutta*; M I 65, *Cūḷasīhanādasutta*; M I 112 *Madhupiṇḍikasutta*; A III 293, *Bhaddakasutta*; A III 294, *Anutappiyasutta*; A IV 230, *Anuruddhamahāvitakkasutta*; A IV 331, *Parihānasutta*; Sn 874, *Kalahavivādasutta*.

21 A IV 228, *Anuruddhamahāvitakkasutta*.

> *Dhamma* is for one who has set up mindfulness, not for one who is laggard in mindfulness; this *Dhamma* is for one who is composed, not for one who is flustered; this *Dhamma* is for one who is wise, not for one who is unwise."

When these seven thoughts occurred to him, Venerable Anuruddha kept on pondering over them for a long while, probably with some *Dhamma* zest. He might have even felt confident that this is a perfect set of *Dhamma* thoughts, since the number is seven and wisdom comes last. However, the Buddha was monitoring his behaviour of mind from Bhesakaḷāvanae, many leagues away, and found that this set of seven is far from complete. So he appeared before Venerable Anuruddha through his psychic power and, having first commended Venerable Anuruddha for those seven thoughts, calling them 'thoughts of a great man,' *mahāpurisavitakka*, gave him an eighth to add on to them and ponder upon. The eighth thought of a great man is:

Nippapañcārāmassāyaṃ Dhammo nippapañcaratino, nāyaṃ Dhammo papañcārāmassa papañcaratino. "This *Dhamma* is for one who likes and delights in *nippapañca* and not for one who likes and delights in *papañca*."

Following the Buddha's instructions in this concern, Venerable Anuruddha attained *Arahant*-hood, and uttered two verses as a paean of joy. From the two verses it becomes clear that the Buddha's helpful hint regarding *nippapañca* – whatever it may mean – was what triggered off his attainment:

> *Yathā me ahu saṅkappo,*
> *tato uttari desayi,*
> *nippapañcarato Buddho,*
> *nippapañcaṃ adesayi.*
>
> *Tassāhaṃ Dhamma maññāya,*
> *vihāsiṃ sāsane rato,*

tisso vijjā anuppattā,
kataṃ Buddhassa sāsanaṃ.[22]

"Whatever thoughts I had on my own,
Going far beyond them the Lord preached to me,
The Buddha, who delights in *nippapañca*,
Preached *nippapañca* to me.

"Understanding his *Dhamma*,
I dwelt delighting in his admonishment,
The three knowledges are attained,
Done is the Buddha's behest."

The words of Venerable Anuruddha clearly reveal the immense significance attached to the term *papañca* and its relevance to the question of attaining *Nibbāna*. It is noteworthy that a number of *suttas* like *Kalahavivādasutta*, *Sakkapañhasutta*, *Cūḷasīhanāda-sutta*, and *Madhupiṇḍikasutta* give prominence to the term *papañca* by listing it as the last.[23] One of the most important discourses throwing light on the significance of this term *papañca* is the *Madhupiṇḍikasutta* of the *Majjhima Nikāya*. We shall therefore proceed to discuss this particular *sutta* at some length.

The *Madhupiṇḍikasutta* is in fact a discourse that unfolds itself in three stages, like a three act play. It might not be inapt to say something about the title of this discourse by way of introduction, before we get down to an analysis of it. At the conclusion of the discourse, Venerable Ānanda makes the following comment on its significance before the Buddha: "Lord, just as if a man overcome by hunger and exhaustion came upon a honey-ball, and, from whatever side he goes on licking it, he would get a sweet delec-

---

22 A IV 235, *Anuruddhamahāvitakkasutta*.

23 D II 276, *Sakkapañhasutta*; M I 65, *Cūḷasīhanādasutta*; M I 112 *Madhupiṇḍikasutta*; Sn 874, *Kalahavivādasutta*.

table flavour which remains unimpaired, so too, Lord, any nimble witted monk, from whatever angle he examines with wisdom the meaning of this discourse on the *Dhamma*, he would find satisfaction and gladness of mind. What is the name of this discourse, Lord?"[24] It was then that the Buddha gave this name to the discourse, saying: "Well, then, Ānanda, you may remember this discourse on the *Dhamma* as the 'honey-ball discourse.'"

We might not have the ability to assimilate fully the flavour of this discourse, and in any case we might not even have sufficient time for it today. However, if we are to make a start, we may begin with the first act, that is, where we find the Buddha spending his noon-day siesta at *Mahāvana* in Kapilavatthu. The *Sakyan* Daṇḍapāṇi, so called because he used to carry a staff in hand, comes to see the Buddha and puts the following short question to him: *Kiṃvādī samaṇo kimakkhāyi?* "What does the recluse assert, what does he proclaim?"

The Buddha's reply to it is rather long and winding, so much so that it is not easy to render it clear enough:

> *Yathāvādi kho, āvuso, sadevake loke samārake sabrahmake sassamaṇabrāhmaṇiyā pajāya sadevamanussāya na kenaci loke viggayha tiṭṭhati, yathā ca pana kāmehi visaṃyuttaṃ viharantaṃ taṃ brāhmaṇaṃ akathaṃkathiṃ chinnakukkuccaṃ bhavābhave vītataṇhaṃ saññā nānusenti, evaṃvādī kho ahaṃ, āvuso, evamakkhāyī.*

> "According to whatever doctrine, friend, one does not quarrel with anyone in the world with its gods, its *Māras* and *Brahmas*, with the progeny of the world comprising recluses and brahmins, gods and men, and also due to which perceptions no more underlie that brahmin who abides detached from sense pleasures, without perplexity,

---

[24] M I 114, *Madhupiṇḍikasutta.*

> remorse cut off and devoid of craving for any kind of existence, such is my doctrine, friend, thus do I proclaim it."

It must be noted that the word brahmin in this context refers to the *Arahant*. The reply, winding as it is, goes deeper in its insinuations, touching the presumptions of the questioner. That is to say, generally, in the world, if anyone proclaims a doctrine, it is natural that it will come into conflict with other doctrines. Also, in proclaiming that doctrine one has to have latent perceptions relating to it. The Buddha's reply, however, seems to contradict these presumptions. In a nutshell, the reply amounts to this:

Firstly, the Buddha's teaching is such that he does not come into conflict with others. Secondly, perceptions do not lie latent in him.

The occurrence of the term *saññā*, perception, in this context, is also significant. We have already stressed the importance of this term. Perceptions do not lie latent in the Buddha or in the doctrine propounded by him.

Daṇḍapāṇi's response to this reply of the Buddha is also recorded in the *sutta*. It is dramatic enough to substantiate our comparison of the discourse to a three-act play. Daṇḍapāṇi shook his head, wagged his tongue, raised his eyebrows into a three-lined frown on his forehead and departed, leaning on his stick. The Buddha's reply did not arouse any faith in him.

In the next act we find the Buddha seated in the company of the monks in the evening and telling them of his brief encounter with Daṇḍapāṇi. Then one of the monks requested an explanation of the enigmatic reply the Buddha had given to Daṇḍapāṇi. The Buddha's explanation, however, took the form of an even longer statement, no less enigmatic than the former. It runs:

> *Yatonidānaṃ, bhikkhu, purisaṃ papañcasaññāsaṅkhā samudācaranti, ettha ce natthi abhinanditabbaṃ abhivaditabbaṃ ajjhosetabbaṃ, esevanto rāgānusayānaṃ, esevanto paṭighānusayānaṃ, esevanto diṭṭhānusayānaṃ, esevanto vicikicchānusayānaṃ, esevanto mānānusayā-*

> *naṃ, esevanto bhavarāgānusayānaṃ, esevanto avijjānusayānaṃ, esevanto daṇḍādāna-satthādāna-kalaha-viggaha-vivāda-tuvaṃtuvaṃ-pesuñña-musāvādānaṃ, etthete pāpakā akusalā dhammā aparisesā nirujjhanti.*

> "From whatever source *papañcasaññāsaṅkhā* beset a man, if, in regard to that, there is nothing to be delighted in, asserted, or clung to, then this itself is the end of the underlying tendencies to attachment, to aversion, to views, to doubts, to conceit, to attachment towards existence, and to ignorance. This itself is the end of taking rods and weapons, quarrels, disputes, accusations, slander and false speech. Here these evil unskilful states cease without remainder."

After making such a long and winding statement, the Buddha rose from his seat and went into his dwelling, as if it were the end of the second act. One can well imagine the consternation of the monks at this dramatic turn of events. The explanation looked even more astounding than the original statement, because of its elliptical character. So here is a case of a puzzle within a puzzle. It is the first few words that are most puzzling.

Naturally, the monks were so perplexed that they decided to approach Venerable MahāKaccāna and request him to give them a detailed exposition of the Buddha's words, as he had been praised by the Buddha for his skill in this respect. When they went to him and made the request, Venerable MahāKaccāna showed some modest hesitation at first, but finally agreed to it.

Now we come to the third act, in which Venerable Mahā-Kaccāna is giving the exposition:

> *Cakkhuñc'āvuso paṭicca rūpe ca uppajjati cakkhuviññāṇaṃ, tiṇṇaṃ saṅgati phasso, phassapaccayā vedanā, yaṃ vedeti taṃ sañjānāti, yaṃ sañjānāti taṃ vitakketi, yaṃ vitakketi taṃ papañceti, yaṃ papañceti tatonidānaṃ*

purisaṃ papañcasaññāsaṅkhā samudācaranti atītānāgatapaccuppannesu cakkhuviññeyyesu rūpesu.

Not only with regard to eye and forms, but also with reference to all the other sense-faculties, including the mind, together with their respective sense-objects, a similar statement is made. Suffice it to translate the one quoted above as a paradigm:

"Dependent on the eye and forms, brethren, arises eye-consciousness; the concurrence of the three is contact; because of contact, feeling; what one feels, one perceives; what one perceives, one reasons about; what one reasons about, one turns into *papañca*; what one turns into *papañca*, owing to that," (*tatonidānaṃ,* which is the correlative of *yatonidānaṃ* forming the key word in the Buddha's brief summary above), "*papañcasaññāsaṅkhā* beset him who directed his powers of sense-perception. They overwhelm him and subjugate him in respect of forms cognizable by the eye belonging to the past, the future and the present." It is the same with regard to the ear and sounds and the rest. Lastly, even about mind and mind-objects Venerable Mahā-Kaccāna makes a similar statement.

At this point, we are forced to say something about the commentarial explanation of this particular passage. It seems that the commentarial exegesis has failed to bring out the deeper implications of the term *papañcasaññāsaṅkhā*. The main reason for the confusion is the lack of attention on the part of the commentator to the peculiar syntax of the formula in question.

The formula begins on an impersonal note, *cakkhuñc'āvuso paṭicca rūpe ca uppajjati cakkhuviññāṇaṃ.* The word *paṭicca* is reminiscent of the law of dependent arising. *Tiṇṇaṃ saṅgati phasso,* "The concurrence of the three is contact." *Phassapaccayā vedanā,* "Conditioned by contact is feeling." From here onwards the formula takes a different turn. *Yaṃ vedeti taṃ sañjānāti, yaṃ sañjānāti taṃ vitakketi, yaṃ vitakketi taṃ papañceti,* "What one feels, one perceives; what one perceives, one reasons about; what one reasons about, one turns into *papañca*."

In this way, we can distinguish three phases in this description of the process of sense perception in Venerable MahāKaccāna's exposition. It begins with an impersonal note, but at the point of feeling it takes on a personal ending, suggestive of deliberate activity. *Yaṃ vedeti taṃ sañjānāti, yaṃ sañjānāti taṃ vitakketi, yaṃ vitakketi taṃ papañceti,* "What one feels, one perceives; what one perceives, one reasons about; what one reasons about, one turns into *papañca*."

Though we render the formula in this way, the commentary explains it differently. It ignores the significance of the personal ending and interprets the sensory process periphrastically, for example as *saññā sañjānāti*, *vitakko vitakketi*, "perception perceives," "reasoning reasons about," etc.[25] It amounts to saying that, when feeling occurs, perception comes forward and perceives it, then reasoning takes up the task of reasoning about perception. *Papañca* then steps in and converts that reasoning into *papañca*. This is how the commentary explains that formula. It has left out of account the significance of the use of the active voice in this section of the formula.

There is a special purpose in using the active voice in this context. It is in order to explain how a man is overwhelmed by *papañcasaññāsaṅkhā* – whatever it may be – that Venerable MahāKaccāna has introduced this sequence of events in three phases. In fact, he is trying to fill in the gap in the rather elliptical statement of the Buddha, beginning with *yatonidānaṃ, bhikkhu, purisaṃ papañcasaññāsaṅkhā samudācaranti,* "Monk, from whatever source *papañcasaññāsaṅkhā* beset a man." The initial phase is impersonal, but then comes the phase of active participation.

From feeling onwards, the person behind it takes over. What one feels, one perceives; what one perceives, one reasons about; what one reasons about, one turns into *papañca*. The grossest

---

[25] Ps II 77.

phase is the third. Venerable MahāKaccāna's formula shows how the process of sense-perception gradually assumes a gross form. This third phase is implicit in the words *yaṃ papañceti tato-nidānaṃ purisaṃ papañcasaññāsaṅkhā samudācaranti*, "What one turns into *papañca*, owing to that *papañcasaññāsaṅkhā* beset that man." The word *purisaṃ* is in the accusative case here, implying that the person who directed sense-perception is now beset with, or overwhelmed by, *papañcasaññāsaṅkhā*, as a result of which all the evil unskilful mental states come to be. This itself is an index to the importance of the term *papañca*.

The course of events suggested by these three phases may be illustrated with the legend of the three magicians. While journeying through a forest, three men, skilled in magic, came upon a scattered heap of bones of a tiger. To display their skill, one of them converted the bones into a complete skeleton, the second gave it flesh and blood, and the third gave it life. The resurrected tiger devoured all three of them. It is such a predicament that is hinted at by the peculiar syntax of the formula in question.

The comparison of this discourse to a honey-ball is understandable, since it holds the secret of the latent tendencies towards dogmatic views. It also affords a deep insight into the nature of the linguistic medium, and words and concepts in everyday usage.

We haven't yet clarified the meaning of the term *papañca*. It is already found in common parlance as a word suggestive of verbosity and circumlocution. Etymologically, it is traceable to *pra + ŏ pañc*, and it conveys such meanings as 'spreading out,' 'expansion,' 'diffuseness' and 'manifoldness.' Verbosity and circumlocution usually lead to delusion and confusion. However, the word *papañca* is sometimes used to denote a conscious elaboration of what is already expressed in brief. In this particular sense, the cognate term *vipañcitaññū* is used in the context of four types of persons, distinguished according to their levels of understanding, namely *ugghaṭitaññū, vipañcitaññū, neyyo,* and *pa-*

daparamo.[26] Here, *vipañcitaññū* signifies that sort of person to whom comprehension of the doctrine comes when the meaning of what is uttered in brief is analysed in detail.

All in all, *papañca* in linguistic usage has the insinuation of a certain degree of delusion brought about by verbosity and circumlocution. But here the term has a deeper philosophical dimension. Here it is not a case of linguistic usage, but the behaviour of the mind as such, since it concerns sense-perception. The fact that it follows in the wake of *vitakka* is suggestive of its affinity to *vicāra*, or discursive thought, so often quoted as the twin of *vitakka*, that is as *vitakkavicāra*.

The mind has the tendency to wander afar, all alone, *dūraṅgamaṃ ekacaraṃ*,[27] through the medium of thought, or *vitakka*. When *vitakka* breaks loose and runs riot, it creates a certain deluded state of mind, which is *papañca*.

---

[26] A II 135, *Ugghaṭitaññūsutta*.

[27] Dhp 37, *Cittavagga*.

Nibbāna Sermon 12

Namo tassa Bhagavato Arahato Sammāsambuddhassa
Namo tassa Bhagavato Arahato Sammāsambuddhassa
Namo tassa Bhagavato Arahato Sammāsambuddhassa

Etaṃ santaṃ, etaṃ paṇītaṃ, yadidaṃ sabbasaṅkhārasamatho sabbūpadhipaṭinissaggo taṇhakkhayo virāgo nirodho nibbānaṃ.[1]

"This is peaceful, this is excellent, namely the stilling of all preparations, the relinquishment of all assets, the destruction of craving, detachment, cessation, extinction."

With the permission of the Most Venerable Great Preceptor and the assembly of the venerable meditative monks.

This is the twelfth sermon in the series of sermons on *Nibbāna*. At the beginning of our last sermon, we brought up the two terms *papañca* and *nippapañca*, which help us rediscover quite a deep dimension in Buddhist philosophy, hidden under the sense of time. In our attempt to clarify the meaning of these two terms, initially with the help of the *Madhupiṇḍikasutta*, what we could determine so far is the fact that *papañca* signifies a certain gross state in sense-perception.

Though in ordinary linguistic usage *papañca* meant 'elaboration,' 'circumlocution,' and 'verbosity,' the *Madhupiṇḍikasutta* has shown us that in the context of sensory perception it has some special significance. It portrays how a person, who directed sense

---

1 M I 436, *MahāMālunkyasutta*.

perception, is overwhelmed by *papañcasaññāsaṅkhā* with regard to sense-objects relating to the three periods of time, past, present, and future, as a result of his indulging in *papañca* based on reasoning about percepts.

All this goes to show that *papañca* has connotations of some kind of delusion, obsession, and confusion arising in a man's mind due to sense perception. In explaining the meaning of this term, commentators very often make use of words like *pamatta*, 'excessively intoxicated,' 'indolent,' *pamāda*, 'headlessness,' and *madana*, 'intoxication.' For example: *Kenaṭṭhena papañco? Mattapamattākārapāpanaṭṭhena papañco.*[2] "*Papañca* in what sense? In the sense that it leads one on to a state of intoxication and indolence." Sometimes it is commented on as follows: *papañcitā ca honti pamattākārapattā.*[3] "They are subject to *papañca*, that is, they become more or less inebriated or indolent." Or else it is explained as *madanākārasaṇṭhito kilesapapañco.*[4] "*Papañca* of a defiling nature which is of an inebriating character."

On the face of it, *papañca* looks like a term similar in sense to *pamāda*, indolence, heedlessness. But there is a subtle difference in meaning between them. *Pamāda*, even etymologically, conveys the basic idea of 'excessive intoxication.' It has a nuance of inactivity or inefficiency, due to intoxication. The outcome of such a state of affairs is either negligence or heedlessness. But as we have already pointed out, *papañca* has an etymological background suggestive of expansion, elaboration, verbosity and circumlocution. Therefore, it has no connotations of inactivity and inefficiency. On the other hand, it seems to imply an inability to reach the goal due to a deviation from the correct path.

---

[2] Sv III 721.

[3] Spk III 73.

[4] Mp III 348.

Let us try to understand the distinction in meaning between *pamāda* and *papañca* with the help of an illustration. Suppose we ask someone to go on an urgent errant to Colombo. If instead of going to Colombo, he goes to the nearest tavern and gets drunk and sleeps there – that is a case of *pamāda*. If, on the other hand, he takes to a long labyrinthine road, avoiding the shortest cut to Colombo, and finally reaches Kandy instead of Colombo – that is *papañca*.

There is such a subtle difference in the nuances associated with these two terms. Incidentally, there is a couplet among the Sixes of the *Aṅguttara Nikāya*, which sounds like a distant echo of the illustration we have already given:

Yo papañcam anuyutto
papañcābhirato mago,
virādhayī so Nibbānaṃ,
yogakkhemaṃ anuttaraṃ.

Yo ca papañcaṃ hitvāna,
nippapañca pade rato,
ārādhayī so Nibbānaṃ,
yogakkhemaṃ anuttaraṃ.[5]

"The fool who indulges in *papañca*,
Being excessively fond of it,
Has missed the way to *Nibbāna*,
The incomparable freedom from bondage.

"He who, having given up *papañca*,
delights in the path to *nippapañca*,
Is well on the way to *Nibbāna*,
The incomparable freedom from bondage."

---

5 A III 294, *Bhaddakasutta* and *Anutappiyasutta*.

In this way we can understand the difference between the two words *papañca* and *pamāda* in respect of the nuances associated with them.

Commentaries very often explain the term *papañca* simply as a synonym of craving, conceit, and views, *taṇhādiṭṭhimānānam etaṃ adhivacanaṃ.*[6] But this does not amount to a definition of *papañca* as such. It is true that these are instances of *papañca,* for even in the *Madhupiṇḍikasutta* we came across the three expressions *abhinanditabbaṃ, abhivaditabbaṃ,* and *ajjhositabbaṃ,* suggestive of them.[7]

Abhinanditabbaṃ means 'what is worth delighting in,' *abhivaditabbaṃ* means 'what is worth asserting,' *ajjhositabbaṃ* means 'what is worth clinging on to.' These three expressions are very often used in the discourses to denote the three defilements craving, conceit and views. That is to say, 'delighting in' by way of craving with the thought 'this is mine'; 'asserting' by way of conceit with the thought 'this am I'; and 'clinging on to' with the dogmatic view 'this is my soul.'

Therefore the commentarial exegesis on *papañca* in terms of craving, conceit and views is to a great extent justifiable. However, what is particularly significant about the term *papañca* is that it conveys the sense of proliferation and complexity of thought, on the lines of those three basic tendencies. That is why the person concerned is said to be 'overwhelmed by *papañcasaññāsaṅkhā.*'[8]

Here we need to clarify for ourselves the meaning of the word *saṅkhā.* According to the commentary, it means 'parts,' *papañcasaññāsaṅkhā'ti ettha saṅkhā'ti koṭṭhāso,*[9] "'*papañcasaññāsaṅkhā,*' here in '*saṅkhā*' means parts." In that case *papañcasaṅkhā* could

---

6 Ps II 10.

7 M I 109, *Madhupiṇḍikasutta*.

8 M I 112, *Madhupiṇḍikasutta*.

9 Ps II 75.

be rendered as 'parts of *papañca*,' which says nothing significant about *saṅkhā* itself. On the other hand, if one carefully examines the contexts in which the terms *papañcasaññāsaṅkhā* and *papañcasaṅkhā* are used in the discourses, one gets the impression that *saṅkhā* means something deeper than 'part' or 'portion.'

Saṅkhā, samaññā and *paññatti* are more or less synonymous terms. Out of them, *paññatti* is fairly well known as a term for 'designation.' *Saṅkhā* and *samaññā* are associated in sense with *paññatti*. *Saṅkhā* means 'reckoning' and *samaññā* is 'appellation.' These three terms are often used in connection with worldly usage.

We come across quite a significant reference, relevant to this question of *papañca*, in the *Niruttipathasutta* of the *Khandhasaṃyutta* in the *Saṃyutta Nikāya.* It runs:

> *Tayome, bhikkhave, niruttipathā, adhivacanapathā, paññattipathā asaṅkiṇṇā asaṅkiṇṇapubbā, na saṅkīyanti, na saṅkīyissanti, appaṭikuṭṭhā samaṇehi brāhmaṇehi viññūhi. Katame tayo? Yaṃ, bhikkhave, rūpaṃ atītaṃ niruddhaṃ vipariṇataṃ 'ahosī'ti tassa saṅkhā, 'ahosī'ti tassa samaññā, 'ahosī'ti tassa paññatti, na tassa saṅkhā 'atthī'ti, na tassa saṅkhā 'bhavissatī'ti.*[10]

> "Monks, there are these three pathways of linguistic usage, of synonyms and of designation, that are not mixed up, have never been mixed up, that are not doubted and will not be doubted, and are undespised by intelligent recluses and brahmins. What are the three? Whatever form, monks, that is past, ceased, transformed, 'it was' is the reckoning for it, 'it was' is its appellation, 'it was' is its designation, it is not reckoned as 'it is,' it is not reckoned as 'it will be.'"

---

[10] S III 71, *Niruttipathasutta.*

The burden of this discourse, as it proceeds in this way, is the maxim that the three periods of time should never be mixed up or confounded. For instance, with regard to that form that is past, a verb in the past tense is used. One must not imagine what is past to be existing as something present. Nor should one imagine whatever belongs to the future as already existing in the present.

Whatever has been, is past. Whatever is, is present. It is a common mistake to conceive of something that is yet to come as something already present, and to imagine whatever is past also as present. This is the confusion the world is in. That is why those recluses and brahmins, who are wise, do not mix them up.

Just as the above quoted paragraph speaks of whatever is past, so the discourse continues to make similar statements with regard to whatever is present or future. It touches upon all the five aggregates, for instance, whatever form that is present is reckoned as 'it is,' and not as 'it was' or 'it will be.' Similarly, whatever form that is yet to come is reckoned as 'it will be,' and not as 'it was' or 'it is.' This is how the *Niruttipathasutta* lays down the basic principle of not confounding the linguistic usages pertaining to the three periods of time.

Throughout this discourse, the term *saṅkhā* is used in the sense of 'reckoning.' In fact, the three terms *saṅkhā, samaññā* and *paññatti* are used somewhat synonymously in the same way as *nirutti, adhivacana* and *paññatti*. All these are in sense akin to each other in so far as they represent the problem of worldly usage.

This makes it clear that the intriguing term *papañcasaññā-saṅkhā* has a relevance to the question of language and modes of linguistic usages. The term could thus be rendered as 'reckonings born of prolific perceptions.'

If we are to go deeper into the significance of the term *saṅkhā*, we may say that its basic sense in linguistic usage is connected with numerals, since it means 'reckoning.' As a matter of fact, numerals are more primitive than letters, in a language.

To perceive is to grasp a sign of permanence in something. Perception has the characteristic of grasping a sign. It is with the help of signs that one recognizes. Perceptions of forms, perceptions of sounds, perceptions of smells, perceptions of tastes, etc., are so many ways of grasping signs. Just as a party going through a forest would blaze a trail with an axe in order to find their way back with the help of notches on the trees, so does perception catch a sign in order to be able to recognize.

This perception is like the groping of a blind man, fumbling in the dark. There is a tendency in the mind to grasp a sign after whatever is felt. So it gives rise to perceptions of forms, perceptions of sounds, etc. A sign necessarily involves the notion of permanence. That is to say, a sign stands for permanence. A sign has to remain unchanged until one returns to it to recognize it. That is also the secret behind the mirage nature of perception as a whole.[11]

As a matter of fact, the word *saññā*, used to denote perception as such, primarily means the 'sign,' 'symbol,' or 'mark,' with which one recognizes. But recognition alone is not enough. What is recognized has to be made known to the world, to the society at large. That is why *saññā*, or perception, is followed by *saṅkhā*, or reckoning.

The relationship between *saṅkhā, samaññā* and *paññatti* in this connection could also be explained. *Saṅkhā* as 'reckoning' or 'counting' totals up or adds up into groups of, say, five or six. It facilitates our work, particularly in common or communal activities. So the most primitive symbol in a language is the numeral.

Samaññā, or appellation, is a common agreement as to how something should be known. If everyone had its own way of making known, exchange of ideas would be impossible. *Paññatti*, or designation, determines the pattern of whatever is commonly agreed upon. This way we can understand the affinity of meaning between the terms *saṅkhā, samaññā* and *paññatti*.

---

11 *Marīcikūpamā saññā* at S III 142, *Pheṇapiṇḍūpamasutta*.

Among them, *saṅkhā* is the most primitive form of reckoning. It does not simply mean reckoning or adding up in terms of numerals. It is characteristic of language too, as we may infer from the occurrence of the expression *saṅkhaṃ gacchati* in many discourses. There the reckoning meant is a particular linguistic usage. We come across a good illustration of such a linguistic usage in the *MahāHatthipadopamasutta*, where Venerable Sāriputta is addressing his fellow monks:

> *Seyyathāpi, āvuso, kaṭṭhañca paṭicca valliñca paṭicca tiṇañca paṭicca mattikañca paṭicca ākāso parivārito agāraṃ tveva saṅkhaṃ gacchati; evameva kho, āvuso, aṭṭhiñca paṭicca nahāruñca paṭicca maṃsañca paṭicca cammañca paṭicca ākāso parivārito rūpaṃ tveva saṅkhaṃ gacchati.*[12]

> "Friends, just as when space is enclosed by timber and creepers, grass and clay, it comes to be reckoned as 'a house'; even so, when space is enclosed by bones and sinews, flesh and skin, it comes to be reckoned as 'material form.'"

Here the expression *saṅkhaṃ gacchati* stands for a designation as a concept. It is the way something comes to be known. Let us go for another illustration from a sermon by the Buddha himself. It is one that throws a flood of light on some deep aspects of Buddhist philosophy, relating to language, grammar and logic. It comes in the *Poṭṭhapādasutta* of the *Dīgha Nikāya*, where the Buddha is exhorting Citta Hatthisāriputta:

> *Seyyathāpi, Citta, gavā khīraṃ, khīramhā dadhi, dadhimhā navanītaṃ, navanītamhā sappi, sappimhā*

---

[12] M I 190, *MahāHatthipadopamasutta*.

> *sappimaṇḍo. Yasmiṃ samaye khīraṃ hoti, neva tasmiṃ samaye dadhī'ti saṅkhaṃ gacchati, na navanītan'ti saṅkhaṃ gacchati, na sappī'ti saṅkhaṃ gacchati, na sappimaṇḍo'ti saṅkhaṃ gacchati, khīraṃ tveva tasmiṃ samaye saṅkhaṃ gacchati.*[13]
>
> "Just, Citta, as from a cow comes milk, and from milk curds, and from curds butter, and from butter ghee, and from ghee junket. But when it is milk, it is not reckoned as curd or butter or ghee or junket, it is then simply reckoned as milk."

We shall break up the relevant quotation into three parts, for facility of comment. This is the first part giving the introductory simile. The simile itself looks simple enough, though it is suggestive of something deep. The simile is in fact extended to each of the other stages of milk formation, namely curd, butter, ghee, and junket, pointing out that in each case, it is not reckoned otherwise. Now comes the corresponding doctrinal point:

> *Evameva kho, Citta, yasmiṃ samaye oḷāriko attapaṭilābho hoti, neva tasmiṃ samaye manomayo attapaṭilābho'ti saṅkhaṃ gacchati, na arūpo attapaṭilābho'ti saṅkhaṃ gacchati, oḷāriko attapaṭilābho tveva tasmiṃ samaye saṅkhaṃ gacchati.*
>
> "Just so, Citta, when the gross mode of personality is going on, it is not reckoned as 'the mental mode of personality,' nor as 'the formless mode of personality,' it is then simply reckoned as 'the gross mode of personality.'"

---

13 D I 201, *Poṭṭhapādasutta.*

These three modes of personality correspond to the three planes of existence, the sensuous, the form, and the formless. The first refers to the ordinary physical frame, sustained by material food, *kabaḷīkārāhārabhakkho*, enjoying the sense pleasures.[14] At the time a person is in this sensual field, possessing the gross mode of personality, one must not imagine that the mental mode or the formless mode of personality is hidden in him.

This is the type of confusion the ascetics entrenched in a soul theory fell into. They even conceived of self as fivefold, encased in concentric shells. Whereas in the *Taittirīya Upaniṣad* one comes across the *pañcakośa* theory, the reference here is to three states of the self, as gross, mental and formless modes of personality. Out of the five selves known to *Upaniṣadic* philosophy, namely *annamaya, prāṇamaya, saṃjñāmaya, vijñāṇamaya* and *ānandamaya*, only three are mentioned here, in some form or other. The gross mode of personality corresponds to *annamayātman*, the mental mode of personality is equivalent to *saṃjñāmayātman*, while the formless mode of personality stands for *vijñāṇamayātman*.

The correct perspective of understanding this distinction is provided by the milk simile. Suppose someone gets a *jhāna* and attains to a mental mode of personality. He should not imagine that the formless mode of personality is already latent in him. Nor should he think that the former gross mode of personality is still lingering in him. They are just temporary states, to be distinguished like milk and curd. This is the moral the Buddha is trying to drive home.

Now we come to the third part of the quotation, giving the Buddha's conclusion, which is extremely important. *Imā kho, Citta, lokasamaññā lokaniruttiyo lokavohārā lokapaññattiyo, yāhi Tathāgato voharati aparāmasaṃ.* "For all these, Citta, are worldly apparitions, worldly expressions, worldly usages, worldly designa-

---

[14] D I 195, *Poṭṭhapādasutta*.

tions, which the *Tathāgata* makes use of without tenacious grasping."

It is the last word in the quotation, *aparāmasaṃ,* which is extremely important. There is no tenacious grasping. The Buddha uses the language much in the same way as parents make use of a child's homely prattle, for purpose of meditation. He had to present this *Dhamma,* which goes against the current,[15] through the medium of worldly language, with which the worldlings have their transaction in defilements. That is probably the reason why the Buddha at first hesitated to preach this *Dhamma*. He must have wondered how he can convey such a deep *Dhamma* through the terminology, the grammar and the logic of worldlings.

All this shows the immense importance of the *Poṭṭhapādasutta.* If the ordinary worldling presumes that ghee is already inherent in the milk obtained from the cow, he will try to argue it out on the grounds that after all it is milk that becomes ghee. And once it becomes ghee, he might imagine that milk is still to be found in ghee, in some latent form.

As a general statement, this might sound ridiculous. But even great philosophers were unaware of the implications of their theories. That is why the Buddha had to come out with this homely milk simile, to bring them to their senses. Here lies the secret of the soul theory. It carried with it the implication that past and future also exist in the same sense as the present.

The Buddha, on the other hand, uses the verb *atthi*, 'is,' only for what exists in the present. He points out that, whatever is past, should be referred to as *ahosi*, 'was,' and whatever is yet to come, in the future, should be spoken of as *bhavissati*, 'will be.' This is the fundamental principle underlying the *Niruttipathasutta* already quoted. Any departure from it would give rise to such confusions as referred to above.

---

15 *Paṭisotagāmi* at M I 168, *Ariyapariyesanasutta*.

Milk, curd, butter and ghee are merely so many stages in a certain process. The worldlings, however, have put them into watertight compartments, by designating and circumscribing them. They are caught up in the conceptual trap of their own making.

When the philosophers started working out the logical relationship between cause and effect, they tended to regard these two as totally unrelated to each other. Since milk becomes curd, either the two are totally different from each other, or curd must already be latent in milk for it to become curd. This is the kind of dilemma their logic posed for them.

Indian philosophical systems reflect a tendency towards such logical subtleties. They ended up with various extreme views concerning the relation between cause and effect. In a certain school of Indian philosophy, known as *ārambhavāda*, effect is explained as something totally new, unrelated to the cause. Other schools of philosophy, such as *satkāriyavāda* and *satkaraṇavāda*, also arose by confusing this issue. For them, effect is already found hidden in the cause, before it comes out. Yet others took only the cause as real. Such extreme conclusions were the result of forgetting the fact that all these are mere concepts in worldly usage. Here we have a case of getting caught up in a conceptual trap of one's own making.

This confusion regarding the three periods of time, characteristic of such philosophers, could be illustrated with some folktales and fables, which lucidly bring out a deep truth. There is, for instance, the tale of the goose that lays golden eggs, well known to the West. A certain goose used to lay a golden egg everyday. Its owner, out of excessive greed, thought of getting all the as yet ones. He killed the goose and opened it up, only to come to grief. He had wrongly imagined the future to be already existing in the present.

This is the kind of blunder the soul theorists also committed. In the field of philosophy, too, the prolific tendency led to such subtle complications. It is not much different from the proliferations indulged in by the ordinary worldling in his daily life. That is why reckonings born of prolific perception are said to be so overwhelming. One is overwhelmed by one's own reckonings and figurings out, under the influence of prolific perceptions.

An Indian poet once spotted a ruby, shining in the moonlight, and eagerly approached it, enchanted by it, only to find a blood red spittle of beetle. We often come across such humorous stories in literature, showing the pitfalls of prolific conceptualisation.

The introductory story, leading up to the *Dhammapada* verse on the rambling nature of the mind, *dūraṅgamaṃ ekacaraṃ, asarīraṃ guhāsayaṃ*, as recorded in the commentary to the *Dhammapada,* is very illustrative.[16] The pupil of venerable Saṅgharakkhita *Thera*, a nephew of his, indulged in a *papañca* while fanning his teacher. In his imagination, he disrobed, got married, had a child, and was coming in a chariot with his wife and child to see his former teacher. The wife, through carelessness, dropped the child and the chariot run away. So he whipped his wife in a fit of anger, only to realize that he had dealt a blow on his teacher's head with the fan still in his hand. Being an *arahant* with psychic powers, his teacher immediately understood the pupil's state of mind, much to the latter's discomfiture.

A potter in Sanskrit literature smashed his pots in a sort of business *papañca* and was remorseful afterwards. Similarly the proud milk maid in English literature dropped a bucket of milk on her head in a daydream of her rosy future. In all these cases one takes as present something that is to come in the future. This is a serious confusion between the three periods of time. The perception of permanence, characteristic of concepts, lures one away from reality into a world of fantasy, with the result that one is overwhelmed and obsessed by it.

So this is what is meant by *papañcasaññāsaṅkhasamudācāra*. So overwhelming are reckonings born of prolific perception. As we saw above, the word *saṅkhā* is therefore nearer to the idea of reckoning than that of part or portion.

---

16 Dhp 37, *Cittavagga*; Dhp-a I 301.

Tathāgatas are free from such reckonings born of prolific perception, *papañcasaññāsaṅkhā*, because they make use of worldly linguistic usages, conventions and designation, being fully aware of their worldly origin, as if they were using a child's language. When an adult uses a child's language, he is not bound by it. Likewise, the Buddhas and *arahants* do not forget that these are worldly usages. They do not draw any distinction between the relative and the absolute with regard to those concepts. For them, they are merely concepts and designations in worldly usage. That is why the *Tathāgatas* are said to be free from *papañca*, that is to say they are *nippapañca*, whereas the world delights in *papañca.* This fact is clearly expressed in the following verse in the *Dhammapada*:

> *Ākāse va padaṃ natthi*
> *samaṇo natthi bāhire,*
> *papañcābhiratā pajā,*
> *nippapañcā Tathāgatā.*[17]

> "No track is there in the air,
> And no recluse elsewhere,
> This populace delights in prolificity,
> But 'Thus-gone-ones' are non-prolific."

It is because the *Tathāgatas* are non-prolific that *nippapañca* is regarded as one of the epithets of *Nibbāna* in a long list of thirty-three.[18] Like *dukkhūpasama*, quelling of suffering, *papañcavūpasama,* 'quelling of prolificity,' is also recognized as an epithet of *Nibbāna*. It is also referred to as *papañcanirodha*, 'cessation of prolificity.' We come across such references to *Nibbāna* in terms of *papañca* quite often.

---

[17] Dhp 254, *Malavagga.*

[18] S IV 370, *Asaṅkhatasaṃyutta*.

The *Tathāgatas* are free from *papañcasaññāsaṅkhā*, although they make use of worldly concepts and designations. In the *Kalahavivādasutta* we come across the dictum *saññānidānā hi papañcasaṅkhā*,[19] according to which reckonings through prolificity arise from perception. Now the *Tathāgatas* have gone beyond the pale of perception in attaining wisdom. That is why they are free from *papañcasaññāsaṅkhā*, reckonings born of prolific perception.

Such reckonings are the lot of those who grope in the murk of ignorance, under the influence of perception. Since Buddhas and *arahants* are enlightened with wisdom and released from the limitations of perception, they do not entertain such reckonings born of prolific perception. Hence we find the following statement in the *Udāna*: *Tena kho pana samayena Bhagavā attano papañcasaññāsaṅkhāpahānaṃ paccavekkhamāno nisinno hoti.*[20] "And at that time the Exalted One was seated contemplating his own abandonment of reckonings born of prolific perception." The allusion here is to the bliss of emancipation. Quite a meaningful verse also occurs in this particular context:

> *Yassa papañcā ṭhiti ca natthi,*
> *sandānaṃ palighañca vītivatto,*
> *taṃ nittaṇhaṃ muniṃ carantaṃ,*
> *nāvajānāti sadevako pi loko.*[21]

> "To whom there are no proliferations and standstills,
> Who has gone beyond the bond and the deadlock,
> In that craving-free sage, as he fares along,
> The world with its gods sees nothing to decry."

---

19 Sn 874, *Kalahavivādasutta*.

20 Ud 77, *Papañcakhayasutta*.

21 Ud 77, *Papañcakhayasutta*.

The two words *papañca* and *ṭhiti* in juxtaposition highlight the primary sense of *papañca* as a 'rambling' or a 'straying away.' According to the *Nettippakaraṇa*, the idiomatic standstill mentioned here refers to the latencies, *anusaya*.[22] So the rambling *papañcas* and doggedly persisting *anusayas* are no longer there. The two words *sanḍānaṃ* and *palighaṃ* are also metaphorically used in the *Dhamma*. Views, *diṭṭhi*, are the bond, and ignorance, *avijjā*, is the deadlock.[23]

The fact that *papañca* is characteristic of worldly thoughts, connected with the household life, emerges from the following verse in the *Saḷāyatanasaṃyutta* of the *Saṃyutta Nikāya*:

Papañcasaññā itarītarā narā,
papañcayantā upayanti saññino,
manomayaṃ gehasitañca sabbaṃ,
panujja nekkhammasitaṃ irīyati.[24]

"The common run of humanity, impelled by prolific perception,
Approach their objects with rambling thoughts, limited by perception as they are,
Dispelling all what is mind-made and connected with the household,
One moves towards that which is connected with renunciation."

The approach meant here is comparable to the approach of that imaginative poet towards the ruby shining in moonlight, only to discover a spittle of beetle. The last two lines of the verse bring out the correct approach of one who is aiming at *Nibbāna*.

---

[22] Nett 37.

[23] Ud-a 373.

[24] S IV 71, *Adanta-aguttasutta*.

It requires the dispelling of such daydreams connected with the household as entertained by the nephew of Venerable Saṅgharakkhita *Thera*.

Worldlings are in the habit of constructing speculative views by taking too seriously linguistic usage and grammatical structure. All pre-Buddhistic philosophers made such blunders as the confusion between milk and curd. Their blunders were mainly due to two reasons, namely, the persistent latency towards perception and the dogmatic adherence to views. It is precisely these two points that came up in the very first statement of the *Madhupiṇḍikasutta*, discussed in our previous sermon. That is to say, they formed the gist of the Buddha's cursory reply to the *Sakyan* Daṇḍapāṇi's question. For the latter it was a riddle and that is why he raised his eyebrows, wagged his tongue and shook his head. The question was: "What does the recluse assert and what does he proclaim?"[25] The Buddha's reply was: "According to whatever doctrine one does not quarrel or dispute with anyone in the world, such a doctrine do I preach. And due to whatever statements, perceptions do not underlie as latencies, such statements do I proclaim."

This might well appear a strange paradox. But since we have already made some clarification of the two terms *saññā* and *paññā*, we might as well bring up now an excellent quotation to distinguish the difference between these two. It is in fact the last verse in the *Māgandiyasutta* of the *Sutta Nipāta*, the grand finale as it were:

> *Saññāviratassa na santi ganthā,*
> *paññāvimuttassa na santi mohā,*
> *saññañca diṭṭhiñca ye aggahesuṃ,*
> *te ghaṭṭhayantā vicaranti loke.*[26]

---

25 M I 108, *Madhupiṇḍikasutta*.

26 Sn 847, *Māgandiyasutta*.

"To one unattached to percepts no bonds exist,
In one released through wisdom no delusions persist,
But they that cling to percepts and views,
Go about rambling in this world."

In the *Pupphasutta* of the *Khandhasaṃyutta* one comes across the following declaration of the Buddha. *Nāhaṃ, bhikkhave, lokena vivadāmi, loko va mayā vivadati.*[27] "Monks, I do not dispute with the world, it is the world that is disputing with me."

This looks more or less like a contradictory statement, as if one would say 'he is quarrelling with me but I am not quarrelling with him.' However, the truth of the statement lies in the fact that the Buddha did not hold on to any view. Some might think that the Buddha also held on to some view or other. But he was simply using the child's language, for him there was nothing worth holding on to in it.

There is a Canonical episode which is a good illustration of this fact. One of the most well-known among the debates the Buddha had with ascetics of other sects is the debate with Saccaka, the ascetic. An account of it is found in the *CūḷaSaccakasutta* of the *Majjhima Nikāya.* The debate had all the outward appearance of a hot dispute. However, towards the end of it, the Buddha makes the following challenge to Saccaka: "As for you, *Aggivessana,* drops of sweat have come down from your forehead, soaked through your upper robe and reached the ground. But, *Aggivessana*, there is no sweat on my body now." So saying he uncovered his golden-hued body in that assembly, *iti Bhagavā tasmiṃ parisatiṃ suvaṇṇavaṇṇaṃ kāyaṃ vivari.*[28]

Even in the midst of a hot debate, the Buddha had no agitation because he did not adhere to any views. There was for him no

---

[27] S III 138, *Pupphasutta.*

[28] M I 233, *CūḷaSaccakasutta.*

bondage in terms of craving, conceit and views. Even in the thick of a heated debate the Buddha was uniformly calm and cool.

It is the same with regard to perception. Percepts do not persist as a latency in him. We spoke of name-and-form as an image or a reflection. Buddhas do not have the delusion arising out of name-and-form, since they have comprehended it as a self-image. There is a verse in the *Sabhiyasutta* of the *Sutta Nipāta* which puts across this idea:

> *Anuvicca papañca nāmarūpaṃ,*
> *ajjhattaṃ bahiddhā ca rogamūlaṃ,*
> *sabbarogamūlabandhanā pamutto,*
> *anuvidito tādi pavuccate tathattā.*[29]

> "Having understood name-and-form, which is a product of prolificity,
> And which is the root of all malady within and without,
> He is released from bondage to the root of all maladies,
> That Such-like-one is truly known as 'the one who has understood.'"

Name-and-form is a product of *papañca*, the worldling's prolificity. We spoke of the reflection of a gem in a pond and the image of a dog on a plank across the stream.[30] One's grasp on one's world of name-and-form is something similar. Now as for the Buddha, he has truly comprehended the nature of name-and-form. Whatever maladies, complications and malignant conditions there are within beings and around them, the root cause of all that malady is this *papañca nāmarūpa*. To be free from it is to be 'such.' He is the one who has really understood.

---

[29] Sn 530, *Sabhiyasutta*.

[30] See sermons 6 and 7 (dog simile) and sermon 9 (gem simile).

If we are to say something in particular about the latency of perception, we have to pay special attention to the first discourse in the *Majjhima Nikāya*. The advice usually given to one who picks up the *Majjhima Nikāya* these days is to skip the very first *sutta*. Why? Because it is not easy to understand it. Even the monks to whom it was preached could not understand it and were displeased. 'It is too deep for us, leave it alone.'

But it must be pointed out that such an advice is not much different from asking one to learn a language without studying the alphabet. This is because the first discourse of the *Majjhima Nikāya*, namely the *Mūlapariyāyasutta*, enshrines an extremely vital first principle in the entire field of Buddhist philosophy. Just as much as the first discourse of the *Dīgha Nikāya,* namely the *Brahmajālasutta*, is of great relevance to the question of views, even so the *Mūlapariyāyasutta* is extremely important for its relevance to the question of perception.

Now what is the basic theme of this discourse? There is a certain pattern in the way objects occur to the mind and are apperceived. This discourse lays bare that elementary pattern. The Buddha opens this discourse with the declaration, *sabbadhammamūlapariyāyaṃ vo, bhikkhave, desessāmi,*[31] "Monks, I shall preach to you the basic pattern of behaviour of all mind objects."

In a nutshell, the discourse deals with twenty-four concepts, representative of concepts in the world. These are fitted into a schema to illustrate the attitude of four types of persons towards them.

The twenty-four concepts mentioned in the *sutta* are *paṭhavi, āpo, tejo, vāyo, bhūta, deva, Pajāpati, Brahma, Ābhassara, Subhakinha, Vehapphala, abhibhū, ākāsānañcāyatanaṃ, viññāṇañcāyatanaṃ, ākiñcaññāyatanaṃ, nevasaññānāsaññāyatanaṃ, diṭṭhaṃ, sutaṃ, mutaṃ, viññātaṃ, ekattaṃ, nānattaṃ, sabbaṃ, Nibbānaṃ*. "Earth, water, fire, air, beings, gods, *Pajāpati*,

---

[31] M I 1, *Mūlapariyāyasutta*.

Brahma, the *Abhassara Brahmas*, the *Subhakinha Brahmas,* the *Vehapphala Brahmas,* the overlord, the realm of infinite space, the realm of infinite consciousness, the realm of nothingness, the realm of neither-perception-nor-non-perception, the seen, the heard, the sensed, the cognised, unity, diversity, all, *Nibbāna*."

The discourse describes the differences of attitude in four types of persons with regard to each of these concepts. The four persons are:

1) An untaught ordinary person, who has no regard for the Noble Ones and is unskilled in their *Dhamma*, *assutavā puthujjana*.

2) A monk who is in higher training, whose mind has not yet reached the goal and who is aspiring to the supreme security from bondage, *bhikkhu sekho appattamānaso.*

3) An *arahant* with taints destroyed who has lived the holy life, done what has to be done, laid down the burden, reached the goal, destroyed the fetters of existence and who is completely liberated through final knowledge, *arahaṃ khīṇāsavo*.

4) The *Tathāgata*, accomplished and fully enlightened, *Tathāgato arahaṃ sammāsambuddho*.

Out of these, the second category comprises the Stream-winner, the Once-returner and the Non-returner. Though there are four types, according to the analysis of their attitudes, the last two can be regarded as one type, since their attitudes to those concepts are the same. So we might as well speak of three kinds of attitudes. Let us now try to understand the difference between them.

What is the world-view of the untaught ordinary person, the worldling? The Buddha describes it as follows:

> *Paṭhaviṃ paṭhavito sañjānāti. Paṭhaviṃ paṭhavito saññatvā paṭhaviṃ maññati, paṭhaviyā maññati, paṭhavito*

> *maññati, 'paṭhaviṃ me'ti maññati, paṭhaviṃ abhinandati. Taṃ kissa hetu? Apariññātaṃ tassā'ti vadāmi.*
>
> "He perceives earth as 'earth.' Having perceived earth as 'earth,' he imagines 'earth' as such, he imagines 'on the earth,' he imagines 'from the earth,' he imagines 'earth is mine,' he delights in earth. Why is that? I say that it is because he has not fully comprehended it."

The untaught ordinary person can do no better than to perceive earth as 'earth,' since he is simply groping in the dark. So he perceives earth as 'earth' and goes on imagining, for which the word used here is *maññati*, methinks. One usually methinks when a simile or a metaphor occurs, as a figure of speech. But here it is something more than that. Here it refers to an indulgence in a deluded mode of thinking under the influence of craving, conceit and views. Perceiving earth as 'earth,' he imagines earth to be substantially 'earth.'

Then he resorts to inflection, to make it flexible or amenable to his methinking. 'On the earth,' 'from the earth,' 'earth is mine,' are so many subtle ways of methinking, with which he finally finds delight in the very concept of earth. The reason for all this is the fact that he has not fully comprehended it.

Then comes the world-view of the monk who is in higher training, that is, the *sekha. Paṭhaviṃ paṭhavito abhijānāti. Paṭhaviṃ paṭhavito abhiññāya paṭhaviṃ mā maññi, paṭhaviyā mā maññi, paṭhavito mā maññi, 'paṭhaviṃ me'ti mā maññi, paṭhaviṃ mābhinandi. Taṃ kissa hetu? Pariññeyyaṃ tassā'ti vadāmi.*

"He understands through higher knowledge earth as 'earth.' Having known through higher knowledge earth as 'earth,' let him not imagine 'earth' as such, let him not imagine 'on the earth,' let him not imagine 'from the earth,' let him not imagine 'earth is mine,' let him not delight in earth. Why is that? I say it is because it should be well comprehended by him." As for the monk who is in higher training, he does not merely perceive, but understands through higher knowledge.

Here we are against a peculiar expression, which is rather problematic, that is, *mā maññi*. The commentary simply glosses over with the words *maññatī'ti maññi*, taking it to mean the same as *maññati*, "imagines."[32] Its only explanation for the use of this peculiar expression in this context is that the *sekha*, or the one in higher training, has already done away with *diṭṭhimaññanā* or imagining in terms of views, though he still has imaginings through craving and conceit. So, for the commentary, *mā maññi* is a sort of mild recognition of residual imagining, a dilly-dally phrase. But this interpretation is not at all convincing.

Obviously enough the particle *mā* has a prohibitive sense here, and *mā maññi* means 'let one not imagine,' or 'let one not entertain imaginings,' *maññanā*. A clear instance of the use of this expression in this sense is found at the end of the *Samiddhisutta*, discussed in an earlier sermon.[33] Venerable Samiddhi answered Venerable Sāriputta's catechism creditably and the latter acknowledged it with a "well-done," *sādhu sādhu*, but cautioned him not to be proud of it, *tena ca mā maññi*, "but do not be vain on account of it."[34]

The use of the prohibitive particle with reference to the world-view of the monk in higher training is quite apt, as he has to train himself in overcoming the tendency to go on imagining. For him it is a step of training towards full comprehension. That is why the Buddha concludes with the words "Why is that? I say it is because it should be well comprehended by him."

---

[32] Ps I 41.

[33] See sermon 9.

[34] A IV 386, *Samiddhisutta*.

Nibbāna Sermon 13

Namo tassa Bhagavato Arahato Sammāsambuddhassa
Namo tassa Bhagavato Arahato Sammāsambuddhassa
Namo tassa Bhagavato Arahato Sammāsambuddhassa

Etaṃ santaṃ, etaṃ paṇītaṃ, yadidaṃ sabbasaṅkhārasamatho sabbūpadhipaṭinissaggo taṇhakkhayo virāgo nirodho nibbānaṃ.[1]

"This is peaceful, this is excellent, namely the stilling of all preparations, the relinquishment of all assets, the destruction of craving, detachment, cessation, extinction."

With the permission of the Most Venerable Great Preceptor and the assembly of the venerable meditative monks.

This is the thirteenth sermon in the series of sermons on *Nibbāna*. In our last sermon we attempted an exposition under the topic *sabbadhammamūlapariyāya*, "the basic pattern of behaviour of all mind objects," which constitutes the theme of the very first *sutta* of the *Majjhima Nikāya*, namely the *Mūlapariyāyasutta*.[2]

We happened to mention that the discourse describes three different attitudes regarding twenty-four concepts such as earth, water, fire and air. We could however discuss only two of them the other day, namely the world view, or the attitude of the untaught ordinary person, and the attitude of the noble one, who is in higher training.

---

1 M I 436, *MahāMālunkyasutta*.

2 M I 1, *Mūlapariyāyasutta*.

So today, to begin with, let us bring up the third type of attitude given in the discourse, that is, the attitude of *arahants* and that of the *Tathāgata*, both being similar. It is described in these words:

> *Paṭhaviṃ paṭhavito abhijānāti, paṭhaviṃ paṭhavito abhiññāya paṭhaviṃ na maññati, paṭhaviyā na maññati, paṭhavito na maññati, 'paṭhaviṃ me'ti na maññati, paṭhaviṃ nābhinandati. Taṃ kissa hetu? 'Pariññātaṃ tassā'ti vadāmi.*

> "The *arahant* (as well as the *Tathāgata*) understands through higher knowledge earth as 'earth,' having understood through higher knowledge earth as 'earth,' he does not imagine earth to be 'earth,' he does not imagine 'on the earth,' he does not imagine 'from the earth,' he does not imagine 'earth is mine,' he does not delight in earth. Why is that? I say, it is because it has been well comprehended by him."

Let us now try to compare and contrast these three attitudes, so that we can understand them in greater detail. The attitude of the untaught ordinary person in regard to any of the twenty-four concepts like earth, water, fire, air (the twenty-four cited being illustrations), is so oriented that he perceives it as such.

For instance in the case of earth, he perceives a real earth, that is, takes it as earth per se. It may sometimes be only a block of ice, but because it is hard to the touch, he grasps it as 'earth.' Thus the ordinary person, the worldling, relies only on perception in his pursuit of knowledge. Having perceived earth as 'earth,' he imagines it to be 'earth.' The peculiarity of *maññanā*, or 'me'-thinking, is that it is an imagining in terms of 'I' and 'mine.'

So he first imagines it as 'earth,' then he imagines 'on the earth,' 'from the earth,' 'earth is mine' and delights in the earth. Here we find various flexional forms known to grammar.

As a matter of fact, grammar itself is a product of the worldlings for purposes of transaction in ideas bound up with defilements. Its purpose is to enable beings, who are overcome by the personality view, to communicate with their like-minded fellow beings. Grammar, therefore, is something that caters to their needs. As such, it embodies certain misconceptions, some of which have been highlighted in this context.

For instance, *paṭhaviṃ maññati* could be interpreted as an attempt to imagine an earth – as a full-fledged noun or substantive. It is conceived as something substantial. By *paṭhaviyā maññāti*, "he imagines 'on the earth,'" the locative case is implied; while '*paṭhaviṃ me'ti maññati*, "he imagines 'earth is mine,'" is an instance of the genitive case, expressing the idea of possession.

Due to such imaginings, a reality is attributed to the concept of 'earth' and its existence is taken for granted. In other words, these various forms of imaginings go to confirm the notion already aroused by the concept of 'earth.' Once it is confirmed one can delight in it, *paṭhaviṃ abhinandati*. This, then, is the worldview of the untaught ordinary person.

The other day we mentioned that the monk who is in higher training understands through higher knowledge, not through perception, earth as 'earth.' Though it is a higher level of understanding, he is not totally free from imaginings. That is why certain peculiar expressions are used in connection with him, such as *paṭaviṃ mā maññi, paṭhaviyā mā maññi, paṭhavito mā maññi, 'paṭhaviṃ me'ti mā maññi, paṭhaviṃ mā abhinandi.*

Here we have to call in question the commentarial explanation. According to the commentary, this peculiar expression had to be used as a dilly-dally phrase, because the monk in higher training could not be said to imagine or not imagine.[3] But it is clear enough that the particle *mā* in this context is used in its prohibitive sense. *Mā maññi* means "do not imagine!" and *mā abhinandi* means "do not delight!"

---

[3] Ps I 41.

What is significant about the *sekha*, the monk in higher training, is that he is in a stage of voluntary training. In fact, the word *sekha* literally means a "learner." That is to say, he has obtained a certain degree of higher understanding but has not attained as yet full comprehension.

It is precisely for that reason that the section about him is summed up by the statement: *Taṃ kissa hetu? Pariññeyyaṃ tassā'ti vadāmi.* "Why is that? Because, I say, that it should be comprehended by him." Since he has yet to comprehend it, he is following that course of higher training. The particle *mā* is therefore a pointer to that effect. For example, *mā maññi,* "do not imagine!" and *mā abhi nandi,* "do not delight!"

In other words, the monk in higher training cannot help using the grammatical structure in usage among the worldlings and as his latencies are not extinct as yet, he has to practise a certain amount of restraint. By constant employment of mindfulness and wisdom he makes an attempt to be immune to the influence of the worldling's grammatical structure.

There is a possibility that he would be carried away by the implications of such concepts as earth, water, fire and air, in his communications with the world regarding them. So he strives to proceed towards full comprehension with the help of the higher understanding already won, keeping mindfulness and wisdom before him. That is the voluntary training implied here.

The monk in higher training is called *attagutto*, in the sense that he tries to guard himself.[4] Such phrases like *mā maññi* indicate that voluntary training in guarding himself. Here we had to add something more to the commentarial explanation. So this is the situation with the monk in higher training.

Now as to the *arahant* and the *Tathāgata*, the world views of both are essentially the same. That is to say, they both have a higher knowledge as well as a full comprehension with regard to

---

[4] A III 6, *Kāmasutta*; see also Dhp 379, *Bhikkhuvagga*.

the concept of earth, for instance. *Pariññātaṃ tassā'ti vadāmi*, "I say it has been comprehended by him."

As such, they are not carried away by the implications of the worldlings' grammatical structure. They make use of the worldly usage much in the same way as parents do when they are speaking in their child's language. They are not swept away by it. There is no inner entanglement in the form of imagining. There is no attachment, entanglement and involvement by way of craving, conceit and view, in regard to those concepts.

All this goes to show the immense importance of the *Mūlapariyāyasutta*. One can understand why this *sutta* came to be counted as the first among the *suttas* of the *Majjhima Nikāya*. It is as if this *sutta* was intended to serve as the alphabet in deciphering the words used by the Buddha in his sermons delivered in discursive style. As a matter of fact the *Majjhima Nikāya* in particular is a text abounding in deep *suttas*. This way we can understand why both higher knowledge and full comprehension are essential.

We have shown above that this discourse bears some relation to the grammatical structure. Probably due to a lack of recognition of this relationship between the modes of imagining and the grammatical structure, the commentators were confronted with a problem while commenting upon this discourse.

Such phrases as *paṭhaviṃ maññati* and *paṭhaviyā maññati* occur all over this discourse in referring to various ways of imagining. The commentator, however, always makes it a point to interpret these ways of imagining with reference to craving, conceit and views. So when he comes to the phrase *mā abhinandi*, he finds it to be superfluous. That is why Venerable Buddhaghosa treats it as a repetition and poses a possible question as follows:

'Paṭhaviṃ maññatī'ti' eteneva etasmiṃ atthe siddhe kasmā evaṃ vuttanti ce. Avicāritaṃ etaṃ porāṇehi. Ayaṃ pana me attano mati, desanāvilāsato vā ādīnavadassanato vā.[5]

---

5 Ps I 28.

Now this is how the commentator poses his own problem: When the phrase *paṭhaviṃ maññati* by itself fulfills the purpose, why is it that an additional phrase like *paṭhaviṃ abhinandati* is brought in? That is to say, if the imagining already implies craving, conceit and views, what is the justification for the concluding phrase *paṭhaviṃ abhinandati*, "he delights in earth," since craving already implies a form of delighting?

So he takes it as a repetition and seeks for a justification. He confesses that the ancients have not handed down an explanation and offers his own personal opinion on it, *ayaṃ pana me attano mati,* "but then this is my own opinion."

And what does his own explanation amount to? *Desanāvilāsato vā ādīnavadassanato vā*, "either as a particular style in preaching, or by way of showing the perils of the ways of imagining." He treats it as yet another way of preaching peculiar to the Buddha, or else as an attempt to emphasize the perils of imagining.

However, going by the explanation we have already given above, relating these modes of imagining to the structure of grammar, we can come to a conclusion as to why the phrase *mā abhinandi* was brought in. The reason is that each of those concepts crystallized into a real thing as a result of imagining, based on the framework of grammar. It received real object status in the world of imagination. Once its object status got confirmed, one can certainly delight in it. It became a thing in truth and fact. The purpose of these ways of imagining is to mould it into a thing.

Let us go deeper into this problem. There is, for instance, a certain recurrent passage in the discourses on the subject of sense restraint.[6] The gist of that passage amounts to this: A person with defilements takes in signs and features through all the six sense doors, inclusive of the mind. Due to that grasping at signs and features, various kinds of influxes are said to flow in, according to the passages outlining the practice of sense restraint. From this we

---

[6] E.g. D I 70, *Sāmaññaphalasutta*.

can well infer that the role of *maññanā*, or imagining, is to grasp at signs with regard to the objects of the mind.

That is to say, the mind apperceives its object as 'something,' *dhammasaññā*. The word *dhamma* in the opening sentence of this *sutta, sabbadhammamūlapariyāyaṃ vo, bhikkhave, desessāmi*, means a 'thing,' since everything is an object of the mind in the last analysis.

Paṭhaviṃ maññati, "He imagines earth as earth," is suggestive of a grasping at the sign in regard to objects of the mind. Thinking in such terms as *paṭhaviyā maññati, paṭhavito maññāti*, and '*paṭhaviṃ me'ti maññati*, "He imagines 'on the earth,' he imagines 'from the earth,' he imagines 'earth is mine,'" are like the corroborative features that go to confirm that sign already grasped.

The two terms *nimitta,* sign, and *anuvyañjana*, feature, in the context of sense restraint have to be understood in this way. Now the purpose of a *nimitta*, or sign, is to give a hazy idea like 'this may be so.' It receives confirmation with the help of corroborative features, *anuvyañjana*, all the features that are accessory to the sign. The corroboration comes, for instance, in this manner: 'This goes well with this, this accords with this, therefore the sign I took is right.' So even on the basis of instructions on sense restraint, we can understand the special significance of this *maññanā*, or 'me'-thinking.

The reason for the occurrence of these different ways of me-thinking can also be understood. In this discourse the Buddha is presenting a certain philosophy of the grammatical structure. The structure of grammar is a contrivance for conducting the worldlings' thought process, characterised by the perception of permanence, as well as for communication of ideas arising out of that process.

The grammatical structure invests words with life, as it were. This mode of hypostasizing is revealed in the nouns and substantives implying such notions as 'in it,' 'by it' and 'from it.' The last of the flexional forms, the vocative case, *he paṭhavi*, "hey earth," effectively illustrates this hypostasizing character of grammar. It is even capable of infusing life into the concept of 'earth' and arousing it with the words "hey earth."

In an earlier sermon we had occasion to refer to a legend in which a tiger was reconstituted and resurrected out of its skeletal remains.[7] The structure of grammar seems to be capable of a similar feat. The *Mūlapariyāyasutta* gives us an illustration of this fact.

It is because of the obsessional character of this *maññanā*, or me-thinking, that the Buddha has presented this *Mūlapariyāya-sutta* to the world as the basic pattern or paradigm representing three types of world views, or the world views of three types of persons.

This discourse deals with the untaught ordinary person, who is obsessed by this grammatical structure, the disciple in higher training, who is trying to free himself from its grip, and the emancipated one, completely free from it, at the same time giving their respective world views as well.

The other day we enumerated the list of twenty-four concepts, presented in that discourse. Out of these concepts, we have to pay special attention to the fact that *Nibbāna* is counted as the last, since it happens to be the theme of all our sermons.

Regarding this concept of *Nibbāna* too, the worldling is generally tempted to entertain some kind of *maññanā*, or me-thinking. Even some philosophers are prone to that habit. They indulge in some sort of prolific conceptualisation and me-thinking on the basis of such conventional usages as 'in *Nibbāna*,' 'from *Nibbāna*,' 'on reaching *Nibbāna*' and 'my *Nibbāna*.' By hypostasizing *Nibbāna* they develop a substance view, even of this concept, just as in the case of *paṭhavi*, or earth. Let us now try to determine whether this is justifiable.

The primary sense of the word *Nibbāna* is 'extinction,' or 'extinguishment.' We have already discussed this point with reference

---

[7] See sermon 11.

to such contexts as *Aggivacchagottasutta.*[8] In that discourse the Buddha explained the term *Nibbāna* to the wandering ascetic Vacchagotta with the help of a simile of the extinction of a fire. Simply because a fire is said to go out, one should not try to trace it, wondering where it has gone. The term *Nibbāna* is essentially a verbal noun. We also came across the phrase *nibbuto tveva saṅkhaṃ gacchati*, "it is reckoned as 'extinguished.'"[9]

As we have already pointed out in a previous sermon, *saṅkhā*, *samaññā* and *paññatti*, 'reckoning,' 'appellation' and 'designation' are more or less synonymous.[10] *Saṅkhaṃ gacchati* only means "comes to be reckoned." *Nibbāna* is therefore some sort of reckoning, an appellation or designation. The word *Nibbāna*, according to the *Aggivacchagottasutta*, is a designation or a concept.

But the commentator takes much pains to prove that the *Nibbāna* mentioned at the end of the list in the *Mūlapariyāyasutta* refers not to our orthodox *Nibbāna*, but to a concept of *Nibbāna* upheld by heretics.[11] The commentator, it seems, is at pains to salvage our *Nibbāna*, but his attempt is at odds with the trend of this discourse, because the *sekha*, or the monk in higher training, has no need to train himself in refraining from delighting in any heretical *Nibbāna*. So here too, the reference is to our orthodox *Nibbāna*.

Presumably the commentator could not understand why the *arahants* do not delight in *Nibbāna*. For instance, in the section on the *Tathāgata* one reads: *Nibbānaṃ nābhinandati. Taṃ kissa hetu? Nandi dukkhassa mūlan'ti iti viditvā, bhavā jāti, bhūtassa jarāmaraṇaṃ.* "He does not delight in *Nibbāna*. Why so? Because

---

[8] See sermon 1.

[9] M I 487, *Aggivacchagottasutta*.

[10] See sermon 12.

[11] Ps I 38.

he knows that delighting is the root of suffering, and from becoming comes birth and to the one become there is decay-and-death."

It seems, then, that the *Tathāgata* does not delight in *Nibbāna*, because delighting is the root of suffering. Now *nandi* is a form of grasping, *upādāna*, impelled by craving. It is sometimes expressly called an *upādāna*: *Yā vedanāsu nandi tadupādānaṃ*, "Whatever delighting there is in feeling, that is a grasping."[12] Where there is delighting, there is a grasping. Where there is grasping, there is *bhava*, becoming or existence. From becoming comes birth, and to the one who has thus come to be there is decay-and-death.

It is true that we project the concept of *Nibbāna* as an objective to aim at in our training. But if we grasp it like the concept of earth and start indulging in me-thinkings or imaginings about it, we would never be able to realize it. Why? Because what we have here is an extraordinary path leading to an emancipation from all concepts, *nissāya nissāya oghassa nittharaṇā*, "crossing over the flood with relative dependence."[13]

Whatever is necessary is made use of, but there is no grasping in terms of craving, conceits and views. That is why even with reference to the *Tathāgata* the phrase *Nibbānaṃ nābhinandati*, "he does not delight in *Nibbāna*," occurs in this discourse.

One might ask: 'What is wrong in delighting in *Nibbāna*?' But then we might recall a pithy dialogue already quoted in an earlier sermon.[14] A deity comes and accosts the Buddha: "Do you rejoice, recluse?" And the Buddha responds: "On getting what, friend?" Then the deity asks: "Well then, recluse, do you grieve?" And the Buddha retorts: "On losing what, friend?" The deity now mildly remarks: "So then, recluse, you neither rejoice nor grieve!" And the Buddha confirms it with the assent: "That is so, friend."[15]

---

[12] M I 266, *MahāTaṇhāsaṅkhayasutta*.

[13] M II 265, *Āneñjasappāyasutta*.

[14] See sermon 2.

[15] S I 54, *Kakudhasutta*.

This then is the attitude of the Buddha and the *arahants* to the concept of *Nibbāna*. There is nothing to delight in it, only equanimity is there.

Seen in this perspective, the word *Nibbāna* mentioned in the *Mūlapariyāyasutta* need not be taken as referring to a concept of *Nibbāna* current among heretics. The reference here is to our own orthodox *Nibbāna* concept. But the attitude towards it must surely be changed in the course of treading the path to it.

If, on the contrary, one grasps it tenaciously and takes it to be substantial, presuming that the word is a full-fledged noun, and goes on to argue it out on the basis of logic and proliferate on it conceptually, it will no longer be our *Nibbāna*. There one slips into wrong view. One would never be able to extricate oneself from wrong view that way. Here then is an issue of crucial importance.

Many philosophers start their exposition with an implicit acceptance of conditionality. But when they come to the subject of *Nibbāna*, they have recourse to some kind of instrumentality. "On reaching *Nibbāna*, lust and delight are abandoned."[16] Commentators resort to such explanations under the influence of *maññanā*. They seem to imply that *Nibbāna* is instrumental in quenching the fires of defilement. To say that the fires of defilements are quenched by *Nibbāna*, or on arriving at it, is to get involved in a circular argument. It is itself an outcome of *papañca*, or conceptual prolificity, and betrays an enslavement to the syntax.

When one says 'the river flows,' it does not mean that there is a river quite apart from the act of flowing. Likewise the idiom 'it rains' should not be taken to imply that there is something that rains. It is only a turn of speech, fulfilling a certain requirement of the grammatical structure.

---

16 Vibh-a 53.

On an earlier occasion we happened to discuss some very important aspects of the *Poṭṭhapādasutta*.[17] We saw how the Buddha presented a philosophy of language, which seems so extraordinary even to modern thinkers. This *Mūlapariyāyasutta* also brings out a similar attitude to the linguistic medium.

Such elements of a language as nouns and verbs reflect the worldling's mode of thinking. As in the case of a child's imagination, a noun appears as a must. So it has to rain for there to be rain. The implicit verbal sense becomes obscured, or else it is ignored. A periphrastic usage receives acceptance. So the rain rains, and the river flows. A natural phenomenon becomes mystified and hypostasized.

Anthropomorphism is a characteristic of the pre-historic man's philosophy of life. Wherever there was an activity, he imagined some form of life. This animistic trend of thought is evident even in the relation between the noun and the verb. The noun has adjectives as attributes and the verb has adverbs to go with it. Particles fall in between, and there we have what is called grammar. If one imagines that the grammar of language must necessarily conform to the grammar of nature, one falls into a grievous error.

Now the commentators also seem to have fallen into such an error in their elaborate exegesis on *Nibbāna*, due to a lack of understanding of this philosophy of language. That is why the *Mūlapariyāyasutta* now finds itself relegated, though it is at the head of the *suttas* of the *Majjhima Nikāya*.

It is in the nature of concepts that nouns are invested with a certain amount of permanence. Even a verbal noun, once it is formed, gets a degree of permanence more or less superimposed on it. When one says 'the river flows,' one somehow tends to forget the flowing nature of the so-called river. This is the result of the perception of permanence.

---

[17] See sermon 12.

As a matter of fact, perception as such carries with it the notion of permanence, as we mentioned in an earlier sermon.[18] To perceive is to grasp a sign. One can grasp a sign only where one imagines some degree of permanence.

The purpose of perception is not only to recognize for oneself, but also to make it known to others. The Buddha has pointed out that there is a very close relationship between recognition and communication. This fact is expressly stated by the Buddha in the following quotation from the Sixes of the *Aṅguttara Nikāya*:

Vohāravepakkaṃ ahaṃ, bhikkhave, saññaṃ vadāmi. Yathā yathā naṃ sañjānāti, tathā tathā voharati, evaṃ saññī ahosin'ti. "Monks, I say that perception has linguistic usage as its result. In whatever way one perceives, so one speaks out about it, saying: 'I was of such a perception.'"[19]

The word *vepakka* is a derivative from the word *vipāka*, which in the context of *kamma*, or ethically significant action, generally means the result of that action. In this context, however, its primary sense is evident, that is, as some sort of a ripening. In other words, what this quotation implies is that perception ripens or matures into verbal usage or convention.

So here we see the connection between *saññā*, perception, and *saṅkhā*, reckoning. This throws more light on our earlier explanation of the last line of a verse in the *Kalahavivādasutta*, namely *saññānidānā hi papañcasaṅkhā*, "for reckonings born of prolificity have perception as their source."[20]

So now we are in a better position to appreciate the statement that linguistic usages, reckonings and designations are the outcome of perception. All this goes to show that an insight into the philosophy of language is essential for a proper understanding of this *Dhamma*. This is the moral behind the *Mūlapariyāyasutta*.

---

18 See sermons 9 and 12.

19 A III 413, *Nibbedhikasutta*.

20 Sn 874, *Kalahavivādasutta*; see sermon 11.

Beings are usually dominated by these reckonings, appellations and designations, because the perception of permanence is inherent in them. It is extremely difficult for one to escape it. Once the set of such terms as milk, curd and butter comes into vogue, the relation between them becomes an insoluble problem even for the great philosophers.

Since we have been talking about the concept of *Nibbāna* so much, one might ask: 'So then, *Nibbāna* is not an absolute, *paramattha*?' It is not a *paramattha* in the sense of an absolute. It is a *paramattha* only in the sense that it is the highest good, *parama attha*. This is the sense in which the word was used in the discourses,[21] though it has different connotations now. As exemplified by such quotations as *āraddhaviriyo paramatthapattiyā*,[22] "with steadfast energy for the attainment of the highest good," the *suttas* speak of *Nibbāna* as the highest good to be attained.

In later Buddhist thought, however, the word *paramattha* came to acquire absolutist connotations, due to which some important discourses of the Buddha on the question of worldly appellations, worldly expressions and worldly designations fell into disuse. This led to an attitude of dwelling in the scaffolding, improvised just for the purpose of constructing a building.

As a postscript to our exposition of the *Mūlapariyāyasutta* we may add the following important note: This particular discourse is distinguished from all other discourses in respect of one significant feature. That is, the concluding statement to the effect that the monks who listened to the sermon were not pleased by it.

Generally we find at the end of a discourse a more or less thematic sentence like *attamanā te bhikkhū Bhagavato bhāsitaṃ abhinanduṃ*, "those monks were pleased and they rejoiced in the words of the Exalted One."[23] But in this *sutta* we find the peculiar

---

[21] E.g. at S 219, *Munisutta*; and Th 748, *TelakāniTheragāthā*.

[22] Sn 68, *Khaggavisāṇasutta*.

[23] E.g. at M I 12, *Sabbāsavasutta*.

ending *idaṃ avoca Bhagavā, na te bhikkhū Bhagavato bhāsitaṃ abhinanduṃ*, "the Exalted One said this, but those monks did not rejoice in the words of the Exalted One."[24]

Commentators seem to have interpreted this attitude as an index to the abstruseness of the discourse.[25] This is probably why this discourse came to be neglected in the course of time. But on the basis of the exposition we have attempted, we might advance a different interpretation of the attitude of those monks. The declaration that none of the concepts, including that of *Nibbāna*, should be egoistically imagined, could have caused displeasure in monks, then as now. So much, then, for the *Mūlapariyāyasutta*.

The Buddha has pointed out that this *maññanā*, or egoistic imagining, or me-thinking, is an extremely subtle bond of *Māra*. A discourse which highlights this fact comes in the *Saṃyutta Nikāya* under the title *Yavakalāpisutta*.[26] In this discourse the Buddha brings out this fact with the help of a parable. It concerns the battle between gods and demons, which is a theme that comes up quite often in the discourses.

In a war between gods and demons, the gods are victorious and the demons are defeated. The gods bind Vepacitti, the king of the demons, in a fivefold bondage, that is, hands and feet and neck, and bring him before Sakka, the king of the gods.

This bondage has a strange mechanism about it. When Vepacitti thinks 'gods are righteous, demons are unrighteous, I will go to the *deva* world,' he immediately finds himself free from that bondage and capable of enjoying the heavenly pleasures of the five senses. But as soon as he slips into the thought 'gods are unrighteous, demons are righteous, I will go back to the *asura* world,' he finds himself divested of the heavenly pleasures and bound again by the fivefold bonds.

---

24 M I 6, *Mūlapariyāyasutta*.

25 Ps I 56.

26 S IV 201, *Yavakalāpisutta*.

After introducing this parable, the Buddha comes out with a deep disquisition of *Dhamma* for which it serves as a simile:

> *Evaṃ sukhumaṃ kho, bhikkhave, Vepacittibandhanaṃ. Tato sukhumataraṃ Mārabandhanaṃ. Maññamāno kho, bhikkhave, baddho Mārassa, amaññamāno mutto pāpimato. Asmī'ti, bhikkhave, maññitaṃ etaṃ, 'ayaṃ ahaṃ asmī'ti maññitaṃ etaṃ, 'bhavissan'ti maññitaṃ etaṃ, 'na bhavissan'ti maññitaṃ etaṃ, 'rūpī bhavissan'ti maññitaṃ etaṃ, 'arūpī bhavissan'ti maññitaṃ etaṃ, 'saññī bhavissan'ti maññitaṃ etaṃ, 'asaññī bhavissan'ti maññitaṃ etaṃ, 'nevasaññīnāsaññī bhavissan'ti maññitaṃ etaṃ. Maññitaṃ, bhikkhave, rogo, maññitaṃ gaṇḍo, maññitaṃ sallaṃ. Tasmātiha, bhikkhave, 'amaññamānena cetasā viharissāmā'ti evañhi vo, bhikkhave, sikkhitabbaṃ.*

> "So subtle, monks, is the bondage of Vepacitti. But more subtle still is the bondage of *Māra*. Imagining, monks, one is bound by *Māra*, not imagining one is freed from the Evil One. 'Am,' monks, is an imagining, 'this am I' is an imagining, 'I shall be' is an imagining, 'I shall not be' is an imagining, 'I shall be one with form' is an imagining, 'I shall be formless' is an imagining, 'I shall be percipient' is an imagining, 'I shall be non-percipient' is an imagining, 'I shall be neither-percipient-nor-non-percipient' is an imagining. Imagining, monks, is a disease, imagining is an abscess, imagining is a barb, therefore, monks, should you tell yourselves: 'We shall dwell with a mind free from imaginings, thus should you train yourselves.'"

First of all, let us try to get at the meaning of this exhortation. The opening sentence is an allusion to the simile given above. It says that the bondage in which Vepacitti finds himself is of a subtle nature, that is to say, it is a bondage connected with his thoughts. Its very mechanism is dependent on his thoughts.

But then the Buddha declares that the bondage of *Māra* is even subtler. And what is this bondage of *Māra*? "Imagining, monks, one is bound by *Māra*, not imagining one is freed from that Evil One." Then comes a list of nine different ways of imaginings.

In the same discourse the Buddha goes on to qualify each of these imaginings with four significant terms, namely *iñjitaṃ*, agitation, *phanditaṃ*, palpitation, *papañcitaṃ*, proliferation, and *mānagataṃ*, conceit.

Iñjitaṃ is an indication that these forms of imaginings are the outcome of craving, since *ejā* is a synonym for *taṇhā*, or craving.

Phanditaṃ is an allusion to the fickleness of the mind, as for instance conveyed by the first line of a verse in the *Dhammapada*, *phandanaṃ capalaṃ cittaṃ*, "the mind, palpitating and fickle."[27] The fickle nature of the mind brings out those imaginings.

They are also the products of proliferation, *papañcita*. We have already discussed the meaning of the term *papañca*.[28] We happened to point out that it is a sort of straying away from the proper path.

Mānagataṃ is suggestive of a measuring. *Asmi*, or 'am,' is the most elementary standard of measurement. It is the peg from which all measurements take their direction. As we pointed out in an earlier sermon, the grammatical structure of language is based on this peg 'am.'[29]

In connection with the three persons, first person, second person and third person, we happened to mention that as soon as one grants 'I am,' a 'here' is born. It is only after a 'here' is born, that a 'there' and a 'yonder' come to be. The first person gives rise to the second and the third person, to complete the basic framework for grammar.

---

[27] Dhp 33, *Cittavagga*.

[28] See sermons 11 and 12.

[29] See sermon 10.

So *asmi*, or 'am,' is itself a product of proliferation. In fact, the deviation from the proper path, implied by the proliferation in *papañca*, is a result of these multifarious imaginings.

It is in the nature of these imaginings that as soon as an imagining or a me-thinking occurs, a thing is born as a matter of course. And with the birth of a thing as 'something,' impermanence takes over. That is to say, it comes under the sway of impermanence. This is a very strange phenomenon. It is only after becoming a 'something' that it can become 'another thing.' *Aññathābhāva*, or otherwiseness, implies a change from one state to another. A change of state already presupposes some state or other, and that is what is called a 'thing.'

Now where does a 'thing' arise? It arises in the mind. As soon as something gets hold of the mind, that thing gets infected with the germ of impermanence.

The modes of imagining listed above reveal a double bind. There is no freedom either way. Whether one imagines 'I shall be with form' or 'I shall be formless,' one is in a dichotomy. It is the same with the two ways of imagining 'I shall be percipient,' 'I shall be non-percipient.'

We had occasion to refer to this kind of dichotomy while explaining the significance of quite a number of discourses. The root of all this duality is the thought 'am.'

The following two verses from the *Dvayatānupassanāsutta* throw light on some subtle aspects of *maññanā*, or imagining:

Yena yena hi maññanti,
tato taṃ hoti aññathā,
taṃ hi tassa musā hoti,
mosadhammaṃ hi ittaraṃ.

Amosadhammaṃ Nibbānaṃ,
tad ariyā saccato vidū,
te ve saccābhisamayā,
nicchātā parinibbutā.

"In whatever way they imagine,
Thereby it turns otherwise,
That itself is the falsity
Of this puerile deceptive thing.

"*Nibbāna* is unfalsifying in its nature,
That they understood as the truth,
And indeed by the higher understanding of that truth
They have become hungerless and fully appeased."[30]

The first verse makes it clear that imagining is at the root of *aññathābhāva*, or otherwiseness, in so far as it creates a thing out of nothing. As soon as a thing is conceived in the mind by imagining, the germ of otherwiseness or change enters into it at its very conception.

So a thing is born only to become another thing, due to the otherwiseness in nature. To grasp a thing tenaciously is to exist with it, and birth, decay and death are the inexorable vicissitudes that go with it.

The second verse says that *Nibbāna* is known as the truth, because it is of an unfalsifying nature. Those who have understood it are free from the hunger of craving. The word *parinibbuta* in this context does not mean that those who have realized the truth have passed away. It only conveys the idea of full appeasement or a quenching of that hunger.

Why is *Nibbāna* regarded as unfalsifying? Because there is no 'thing' in it. It is so long as there is a thing that all the distress and misery follow. *Nibbāna* is called *animitta*, or the signless, precisely because there is no-thing in it.

Because it is signless, it is unestablished, *appaṇihita*. Only where there is an establishment can there be a dislodgement. Since it is not liable to dislodgement or disintegration, it is unshakeable.

---

30 Sn 757-758, *Dvayatānupassanāsutta*.

It is called *akuppā cetovimutti*, unshakeable deliverance of the mind,[31] because of its unshaken and stable nature. Due to the absence of craving there is no directional aspiration, or *paṇidhi*.

Similarly *suññata*, or voidness, is a term implying that there is no essence in *Nibbāna* in the substantial sense in which the worldlings use that term. As mentioned in the *MahāSāropama-sutta*, deliverance itself is the essence.[32] Apart from that, there is nothing essential or substantial in *Nibbāna*. In short, there is no thing to become otherwise in *Nibbāna*.

On an earlier occasion, too, we had to mention the fact that there is quite a lot of confusion in this concern.[33] *Saṅkhata*, the compounded, is supposed to be a thing. And *asaṅkhata*, or the uncompounded, is also a thing. The compounded is an impermanent thing, while the uncompounded is a permanent thing. The compounded is fraught with suffering, and the uncompounded is blissful. The compounded is not self, but the uncompounded is . . . . At this point the line of argument breaks off.

Some of those who attempt this kind of explanation find themselves in a quandary due to their lack of understanding of the issues involved. The two verses quoted above are therefore highly significant.

Because of *maññanā*, worldlings tend to grasp, hold on and adhere to mind-objects. The Buddha has presented these concepts just for the purpose of crossing over the flood, *desitā nissāya nissāya oghassa nittharaṇā*, "The process of crossing over the flood with relative dependence has been preached."[34] All the *dhammas* that have been preached are for a practical purpose, based on an understanding of their relative value, and not for

---

31 E.g. at D III 273, *Dasuttarasutta.*

32 M I 197, *MahāSāropamasutta.*

33 See sermon 2.

34 M II 265, *Āneñjasappāyasutta.*

grasping tenaciously, as illustrated by such discourses like the *Rathavinītasutta* and the *Alagaddūpamasutta*.[35]

Let alone other concepts, not even *Nibbāna* as a concept is to be grasped. To grasp the concept of *Nibbāna* is to slip into an error. So from the couplet quoted above we clearly understand how subtle this *maññanā* is and why it is called an extremely subtle bondage of *Māra*.

It might be recalled that while discussing the significance of the *Brahmanimantanikasutta* we mentioned that the non-manifestative consciousness described in that discourse does not partake of the earthiness of earth.[36] That is to say, it is not under the sway of the earth-quality of earth.

In fact as many as thirteen out of the twenty-four concepts mentioned in the *Mūlapariyāyasutta* come up again in the *Brahmanimantanikasutta*. The implication therefore is that the non-manifestative consciousness is not subject to the influence of any of those concepts. It does not take any of those concepts as substantial or essential, and that is why it is beyond their power.

For the same reason it is called the non-manifestative consciousness. Consciousness as a rule takes hold of some object or other. This consciousness, however, is called non-manifestative in the sense that it is devoid of the nature of grasping any such object. It finds no object worthy of grasping.

What we have discussed so far could perhaps be better appreciated in the light of another important *sutta* in the *Majjhima Nikāya*, namely the *Cūḷataṇhāsaṅkhayasutta*. A key to the moral behind this discourse is to be found in the following dictum occurring in it: *sabbe dhammā nālaṃ abhinivesāya*, "nothing is worth entering into dogmatically."[37]

---

35 M I 145, *Rathavinītasutta*; M I 130, *Alagaddūpamasutta*.

36 See sermon 8; M I 329, *Brahmanimantanikasutta*.

37 M I 251, *CūḷaTaṇhāsaṅkhayasutta*.

The word *abhinivesa*, suggestive of dogmatic adherence, literally means "entering into." Now based on this idea we can bring in a relevant metaphor.

We happened to mention earlier that as far as concepts are concerned, the *arahants* have no dogmatic adherence. Let us take, for instance, the concept of 'a house.' *Arahants* also enter a house, but they do not enter into the concept of 'a house.' This statement might appear rather odd, but what we mean is that one can enter a house without entering into the concept of 'a house.'

Now leaving this as something of a riddle, let us try to analyse a certain fairytale-like episode in the *Cūḷataṇhāsaṅkhayasutta*, somewhat as an interlude.

The main theme of the *Cūḷataṇhāsaṅkhayasutta* is as follows: Once Sakka, the king of the gods, came to see the Buddha when he was staying at Pubbārāma and asked the question: 'How does a monk attain deliverance by the complete destruction of craving?' The quintessence of the Buddha's brief reply to that question is the above mentioned dictum, *sabbe dhammā nālaṃ abhinivesāya*, "nothing is worth entering into dogmatically."

Sakka rejoiced in this sermon approvingly and left. Venerable MahāMoggallāna, who was seated near the Buddha at that time, had the inquisitive thought: 'Did Sakka rejoice in this sermon having understood it, or did he rejoice without understanding it?' Being curious to find this out he vanished from Pubbārāma and appeared in the Tāvatiṃsa heaven as quickly as a strong man might stretch out his bent arm and bend back his outstretched arm.

At that time Sakka was enjoying heavenly music. On seeing Venerable MahāMoggallāna coming at a distance he stopped the music and welcomed the latter, saying: 'Come good sir Moggallāna, welcome good sir Moggallāna! It is a long time, good sir Moggallāna, since you found an opportunity to come here.'

He offered a high seat to Venerable MahāMoggallāna and took a low seat at one side. Then Venerable MahāMoggallāna asked Sakka what sort of a sermon the Buddha had preached to him on his recent visit, saying that he himself is curious on listening to it.

Sakka's reply was: 'Good sir Moggallāna, we are so busy, we have so much to do, not only with our own business, but also with the business of other gods of Tāvatiṃsa. So it is not easy for us to remember such *Dhamma* discussions.' Then Sakka goes on to relate some other episode, which to him seems more important: 'After winning the war against the *asuras*, I had the Vejayanti palace built. Would you like to see it, good sir Moggallāna?'

Probably as a part of etiquette, binding on a visitor, Venerable MahāMoggallāna agreed and Sakka conducted him around the Vejayanti palace in the company of his friend, king Vessavaṇa. It was a wonderful palace with hundreds of towers. Sakka's maids, seeing Venerable MahāMoggallāna coming in the distance, were embarrassed out of modest respect and went into their rooms. Sakka was taking Venerable MahāMoggallāna around, saying: 'See, good sir, how lovely this palace is.'

Venerable MahāMoggallāna also courteously responded, saying that it is a fitting gift for his past merit. But then he thought of arousing a sense of urgency in Sakka, seeing: how negligent he has become now. And what did he do? He shook the Vejayanti palace with the point of his toe, using his supernormal power.

Since Sakka had 'entered into' the Vejayanti palace with his craving, conceit and views, he also was thoroughly shaken, along with the palace. That is to say, a sense of urgency was aroused in him, so much so that he remembered the sermon the Buddha had preached to him.

It was then that Venerable MahāMoggallāna asked Sakka pointedly: 'How did the Exalted One state to you in brief the deliverance through the destruction of craving?' Sakka came out with the full account, creditably.

So after all it seems that the Venerable MahāMoggallāna took all this trouble to drive home into Sakka the moral of the sermon *sabbe dhammā nālaṃ abhinivesāya*, "nothing is worth clinging onto."

If one goes through this discourse ignoring the deeper aspects of it, it appears merely as a fairytale. Even as those heavenly maidens entered their rooms, Sakka also had entered into this Vejayanti palace of his own creation, while showing his distinguished visitor around, like a rich man these days after building his mansion.

So from this we can see the nature of these worldly concepts. For instance, in the case of the concept of 'a house,' entering the house physically does not necessarily mean that one is 'in it.' Only if one has entered into the concept of a house is he 'in it.'

Let us take a simply analogy. Little children sometimes build a little hut, out of fun, with a few sticks and shady leaves. They might even invite their mother for the house-warming. When the mother creeps into the improvised hut, she does not seriously entertain the concept of 'a house' in it, as the children would do.

It is the same in the case of Buddhas and *arahants*. To the Emancipated Ones, who have fully understood and comprehended the true meaning of concepts like 'house,' 'mansion' and 'palace,' the sand castles of adults appear no better than the playthings of little children. We have to grant it, therefore, that *Tathāgatas*, or Such-like Ones, cannot help making use of concepts in worldly usage.

As a matter of fact, once a certain deity even raised the question whether the emancipated *arahant* monks, when they use such expressions as 'I speak' and 'they speak to me,' do so out of conceit. The Buddha's reply was:

Yo hoti bhikkhu arahaṃ katāvī,
khīṇāsavo antimadehadhārī,
'ahaṃ vadāmī'ti pi so vadeyya,
'mamaṃ vadantī'ti pi so vadeyya
loke samaññaṃ kusalo viditvā,
vohāramattena so vohareyyā.

"That monk, who is an *arahant,* who has finished his
task,
Whose influxes are extinct and who bears his final
body,
Might still say 'I speak,'
He might also say 'they speak to me,'

> Being skilful, knowing the world's parlance,
> He uses such terms merely as a convention."[38]

In the case of an *arahant*, who has accomplished his task and is influx-free, a concept like 'house,' 'mansion,' or 'palace' has no influence by way of craving, conceit and views. He might say 'I speak' or 'I preach,' he might even say 'they speak to me,' but since he has understood the nature of worldly parlance, he uses such expressions as mere turns of speech. Therefore the Buddhas and *arahants*, though they may enter a house, do not entertain the concept of 'a house' in it.

Some might think that in order to destroy the concept of 'a house,' one has to break up the tiles and bricks into atoms. But that is not the way to deliverance. One has to understand according to the law of dependent arising that not only is a house dependent on tiles and bricks, but the tiles and bricks are themselves dependent on a house. Very often philosophers forget about the principle of relativity involved here.

Tiles and bricks are dependent on a house. This is a point worth considering. One might think that a house is made up of tiles and bricks, but tiles and bricks themselves come to be because of a house. There is a mutual relationship between them.

If one raises the question: 'What is a tile?,' the answer will be: 'It is an item used for building the roof of a house.' Likewise a brick is an item used in building a wall. This shows the relativity between a house and a tile as well as between a house and a brick. So there is no need to get down to an atomistic analysis like nuclear physicists. Wisdom is something that enables one to see this relativity penetratively, then and there.

Today we happened to discuss some deep sections of the *Dhamma*, particularly on the subject of *maññanā*. A reappraisal of some of the deep *suttas* preached by the Buddha, now relegated

---

38 S I 14, *Arahantasutta*.

into the background as those dealing with conventional truth, will be greatly helpful in dispelling the obsessions created by *maññanā*. What the *Mūlapariyāyasutta* offers in this respect is of utmost importance.

In fact, the Buddha never used a language totally different from the language of the worldlings. Now, for instance, chemists make use of a certain system of symbolic formulas in their laboratories, but back at home they revert to another set of symbols. However, both are symbols. There is no need to discriminate between them as higher or lower, so long as they serve the purpose at hand.

Therefore it is not proper to relegate some sermons as discursive or conventional in style. Always it is a case of using concepts in worldly parlance. In the laboratory one uses a particular set of symbols, but on returning home he uses another. In the same way, it is not possible to earmark a particular bundle of concepts as absolute and unchangeable.

As stated in the *Poṭṭhapādasutta*, already discussed, all these concepts are worldly appellations, worldly expressions, worldly usages, worldly designations, which the *Tathāgata* makes use of without tenacious grasping.[39] However philosophical or technical the terminology may be, the *arahants* make use of it without grasping it tenaciously.

What is of importance is the function it fulfills. We should make use of the conceptual scaffolding only for the purpose of putting up the building. As the building comes up, the scaffolding has to leave. It has to be dismantled. If one simply clings onto the scaffolding, the building would never come up.

---

[39] D I 202, *Poṭṭhapādasutta*.

Nibbāna Sermon 14

Namo tassa Bhagavato Arahato Sammāsambuddhassa
Namo tassa Bhagavato Arahato Sammāsambuddhassa
Namo tassa Bhagavato Arahato Sammāsambuddhassa

Etaṃ santaṃ, etaṃ paṇītaṃ, yadidaṃ sabbasaṅkhāra-samatho sabbūpadhipaṭinissaggo taṇhakkhayo virāgo nirodho nibbānaṃ.[1]

"This is peaceful, this is excellent, namely the stilling of all preparations, the relinquishment of all assets, the destruction of craving, detachment, cessation, extinction."

With the permission of the Most Venerable Great Preceptor and the assembly of the venerable meditative monks.

This is the fourteenth sermon in the series of sermons on *Nibbāna*. In our last sermon we gave a description of the forms of imaginings or methinkings, which the Buddha had compared to an extremely subtle bondage of *Māra*. The *Yavakalāpisutta* of the *Saḷāyatanasaṃyutta* in the *Saṃyutta Nikāya* has shown us that all kinds of thoughts concerning existence that stem from this subtle conceit 'am,' *asmimāna*, are mere imaginings or methinkings, and that they are called a bondage of *Māra*, because they have the power to keep beings shackled to existence.[2]

We have seen how they follow a dichotomy, even like the dilemma posed by the fivefold bondage of Vepacitti, the king of

---

1 M I 436, *MahāMālunkyasutta.*

2 S IV 201, *Yavakalāpisutta.*

demons. Whether one thinks 'I shall be' or 'I shall not be,' one is in bondage to *Māra*. Whether one thinks 'I shall be percipient' or 'I shall be non-percipient,' or 'I shall be neither-percipient-nor-non-percipient,' one is still in bondage to *Māra*.

There is a dichotomy involved here. The fact that these imaginings, which follow a dichotomy, must be transcended completely, as well as the way to transcend them, has been preached by the Buddha to Venerable Pukkusāti in the *Dhātuvibhaṅgasutta* of the *Majjhima Nikāya*.

There is a pithy passage, forming the grand finale of this discourse, in which the Buddha gives a resume. We propose to quote this passage at the very outset as it scintillates with a majestic fervour of the *Dhamma*:

> *Yatthaṭṭhitaṃ maññussavā nappavattanti, maññussave kho pana nappavattamāne muni santo ti vuccatīti, iti kho pan'etaṃ vuttaṃ. Kiñ c'etaṃ paṭicca vuttaṃ?*
>
> *Asmīti bhikkhu maññitam etaṃ, ayam aham asmīti maññitam etaṃ, bhavissan'ti maññitam etaṃ, na bhavissan'ti maññitam etaṃ, rūpī bhavissan'ti maññitam etaṃ, arūpī bhavissan'ti maññitam etaṃ, saññī bhavissan'ti maññitam etaṃ, asaññī bhavissan'ti maññitam etaṃ, nevasaññīnāsaññī bhavissan'ti maññitam etaṃ.*
>
> *Maññitaṃ, bhikkhu, rogo, maññitaṃ gaṇḍo, maññitaṃ sallaṃ. Sabbamaññitānaṃ tveva, bhikkhu, samatikkamā muni santo ti vuccati.*
>
> *Muni kho pana, bhikkhu, santo na jāyati na jiyyati na miyyati na kuppati na piheti. Tam pi'ssa bhikkhu natthi yena jāyetha, ajāyamāno kiṃ jiyyissati, ajiyyamāno kiṃ miyyissati, amiyyamāno kiṃ kuppissati, akuppamāno kissa pihessati?*

Yatthaṭṭhitaṃ maññussavā nappavattanti, maññussave kho pana nappavattamāne muni santo ti vuccatīti, iti yaṃ taṃ vuttaṃ, idam etaṃ paṭicca vuttaṃ.[3]

In the *Dhātuvibhaṅgasutta* we find the Buddha presenting some points as the theme and gradually developing it, analysing, clarifying, and expatiating, as the discourse proceeds. The opening sentence in the above paragraph is a quotation of a part of that original statement of the Buddha, which forms the theme. Here is the rendering:

"'Steadied whereon the tides of imaginings no longer occur in him, and when the tides of imaginings occur no more in him, he is called a sage stilled,' so it was said. And with reference to what was this said?

"'Am,' monk, is something imagined; 'I am this' is something imagined; 'I shall be' is something imagined; 'I shall not be' is something imagined; 'I shall be possessed of form' is something imagined; 'I shall be formless' is something imagined; 'I shall be percipient' is something imagined; 'I shall be non-percipient' is something imagined; 'I shall be neither-percipient-nor-non-percipient' is something imagined.

"The imagined is a disease, the imagined is an abscess, the imagined is a dart. It is with the surmounting of all what is imagined, monk, that a sage is called 'stilled.'

"The sage who is stilled is not born, nor does he age, nor does he die, nor is he shaken, and he has no longing. Even that is not in him whereby he might be born. Not being

---

3 M III 246, *Dhātuvibhaṅgasutta*.

> born, how shall he age? Not aging, how shall he die? Not dying, how shall he be shaken? Being unshaken, what shall he long for?
>
> "So it was with reference to this, that it was said 'steadied whereon the tides of imaginings no longer occur in him, and when the tides of imagining occur no more in him, he is called a sage stilled.'"

All this goes to show how relevant the question of imaginings is to the path leading to *Nibbāna*. This pithy passage, which brings the discourse to a climax, portrays how the sage is at peace when his mind is released by stemming the tides of imaginings. He attains release from birth, decay and death, here and now, because he has realized the cessation of existence in this very world.

It is in this light that we have to interpret the above statement "even that is not in him whereby he might be born." Dependent on existence is birth. Due to whatever postulate of existence one can speak of a 'birth,' even that existence is not in him. Not being born, how can he age? How can he grow old or decay? This is because of the implicit interrelation between conditions.

Here we can flash back to our analogy of a tree, mentioned earlier.[4] In order to explain the mutual interrelation between the concepts of birth, decay and death, we brought up a simile, which however is not canonical. That is to say, supposing there is some kind of a tree, the buds, the leaves, the flowers, the fruits and the wood of which could be sold for making one's livelihood.

If five men trading in those items respectively are made to line up at some particular stage in the growth of this tree and asked whether the tree is too young or too old, the answers given might differ according to the individual standpoint grasped in each case.

---

[4] See sermon 4.

It turns out to be a difference of viewpoint. For instance, the man who makes his living by selling the buds would reply that the tree is too old when the buds turn into leaves. Similarly, when it is the season for the leaves to fall and the flowers to bloom, one who trades in leaves might say that the tree is too old. And when flowers turn into fruits, the florist's viewpoint would be similar. In this way one can understand how this concept changes according to what one grasps – that there is an implicit relativity about it.

Now, as for this sage, he has given up everything that he had grasped. Grasping has been given up completely. Imagining, too, has been abandoned. Hence, not being 'born,' how shall he age? The sage has no postulate of existence. Since there is no existence, there is no 'birth.' Because there is no birth, there is no decay.

It is a well known fact that the term *jarā* implies both growth and decay. It is after setting a limit that we speak of a process of 'decay,' after 'growth.' This limit, however, varies according to our individual standpoint grasped – according to our point of view. That is what we have tried to illustrate by this analogy.

Then we have the statement "not aging, how shall he die?" Since decay is an approach to death, where there is no decay, there is no death. The fact that there is no death we have already seen in our exposition of the significance of the verses quoted above from the *Adhimutta Theragāthā*.[5] When the bandits got round to kill the Venerable Adhimutta, he declared:

> *Na me hoti ahosin'ti,*
> *bhavissan'ti na hoti me,*
> *saṅkhārā vibhavissanti,*
> *tattha kā paridevanā?*[6]

---

[5] See sermon 8.

[6] Th 715, *Adhimutta Theragāthā*.

"It does not occur to me 'I was,'
Nor does it occur to me 'I shall be,'
Mere preparations will get destroyed,
What is there to lament?"

This declaration exemplifies the above statement. When all graspings are given up, there is no 'decay' or 'death.'

Amiyyamāno kiṃ kuppissati, "not dying, how shall he be shaken?" The verb *kuppati* does not necessarily mean "getting annoyed." Here it means to be "shaken up" or "moved." When one holds on to a standpoint, one gets shaken up if someone else tries to dislodge him from that standpoint.

The deliverance in *Nibbāna* is called *akuppā cetovimutti*, the unshakeable deliverance of the mind.[7] All other deliverances of the mind, known to the world, are shakeable, *kuppa*. They are unsteady. They shake before the pain of death. Only *Nibbāna* is called *akuppā cetovimutti*, the unshakeable deliverance of the mind.

So this peaceful sage, the *arahant*, established in that concentration of the fruit of *arahant*-hood, *arahatta phalasamādhi*, which is known as the influx-free deliverance of the mind, *anāsavā cetovimutti*, and is endowed with the wisdom proper to *arahant*-hood, *paññāvimutti*, "deliverance through wisdom," is unshaken before death. His mind remains unshaken. That is why the *arahant Thera* Venerable Adhimutta fearlessly made the above declaration to the bandits.

Now as to the significance of the Buddha's statement *amiyyamāno kiṃ kuppissati, akuppamāno kissa pihessati*, "not dying, how shall he be shaken, and being unshaken, what shall he long for?" When there is no shock, no agitation or trembling, what does one long for? *Pihā* means longing, desiring for something or other.

---

[7] E.g. at D III 273, *Dasuttarasutta.*

In this context it refers to that longing which arises at the moment of death in one who has not destroyed craving.

It is as a consequence of that longing that he enters some form of existence, according to his *kamma*. That longing is not there in this sage, for the simple reason that he is unshaken before death. He has nothing to look forward to. No desires or longings. *Akuppamāno kissa pihessati*, "being unshaken, what shall he long for?"

It is obvious, therefore, that the concepts of birth, decay and death become meaningless to this sage. That is precisely why he is at peace, having transcended all imaginings.

All this goes to show, that *Nibbāna* is a state beyond decay and death. We can clearly understand from this discourse why *Nibbāna* is known as a decayless, deathless state, realizable in this very world. That sage has conquered decay and death here and now, because he has realized the cessation of existence, here and now.

This is something extremely wonderful about the *arahant*. He realizes the cessation of existence in his attainment to the fruit of *arahant*-hood. How does he come to realize the cessation of existence? Craving is extinct in him, hence there is no grasping. Where there is no grasping, there is no existence. Because there is no existence, birth, decay and death, along with sorrow and lamentation, cease altogether.

From the foregoing we could well infer that all those concepts like birth, decay, death, sorrow, lamentation, pain, grief and despair, come about as a result of a heap of pervert perceptions, pervert thoughts and pervert views, based on the conceit of an existence, the conceit 'am.'

These three kinds of perversions known as *saññāvipallāsa*, *cittavipallāsa* and *diṭṭhivipallāsa* give rise to a mass of concepts of an imaginary nature.[8] The entire mass of suffering, summed up by

---

[8] The *vipallāsas* occur at A II 52, *Vipallāsasutta*.

the terms birth, decay, death, sorrow, lamentation, pain, grief and despair, are basically of a mental origin.

For an illustration of this fact, we can go back to our analogy of winding some strands into a rope, mentioned earlier.[9] We pointed out that in the case of some strands that are being mistakenly wound in the same direction, it is the grasp in the middle that gives at least a semblance of a rope to it. So long as there is no such grasping, the strands do not become knotty or tense, as they go round and round. It is only when someone grasps it in the middle that the strands begin to get winded up, knotty and tense. What is called existence, or becoming, *bhava*, follows the same norm.

True to the law of impermanence, everything in the world changes. But there is something innocent in this change. Impermanence is innocuous in itself. We say it is innocuous because it means no harm to anyone. It is simply the nature of this world, the suchness, the norm. It can do us harm only when we grasp, just as in the case of that quasi-rope.

The tenseness between winding and unwinding, arising out of that grasp in the middle, is comparable to what is called *bhavasaṅkhāra*, "preparations for existence." *Saṅkhārā*, or preparations, are said to be dependent on *avijjā*, or ignorance.

Now we can form an idea of the relationship between these two even from this analogy of the rope. The grasp in the middle creates two ends, giving rise to a dilemma. In the case of existence, too, grasping leads to an antinomian conflict. To become a thing, is to disintegrate into another thing.

On a previous occasion we happened to discuss the significance of the term *maññanā*, me-thinking or imagining, with reference to the verse *yena yena hi maññati, tato taṃ hoti aññathā.*[10] *Maññanā* itself gives rise to a 'thing,' which from its very inception goes on disintegrating into another thing.

---

[9] See sermon 8.

[10] See sermon 2; Ud 32, *Lokasutta.*

Just as much as grasping leads to the concept of two ends, to become a thing is to start changing into another thing, that is, it comes under the sway of the law of impermanence. illustrations of this norm are sometimes to be met with in the discourses, but their significance is often ignored.

The idea of the two ends and the middle sometimes finds expression in references to an 'above,' 'below' and 'across in the middle,' *uddhaṃ, adho, tiriyaṃ majjhe*; or in the terms 'before,' 'behind' and 'middle,' *pure, pacchā, majjhe*. Such references deal with some deep aspects of the *Dhamma*, relating to *Nibbāna*.

As a good illustration, we may take up the following two verses from the *Mettagūmāṇavapucchā* in the *Pārāyanavagga* of the *Sutta Nipāta*:

> *Yaṃ kiñci sampajānāsi,*
> *uddhaṃ adho tiriyaṃ cāpi majjhe,*
> *etesu nandiñca nivesanañca*
> *panujja viññāṇaṃ bhave na tiṭṭhe.*
>
> *Evaṃ vihārī sato appamatto,*
> *bhikkhu caraṃ hitvā mamāyitāni,*
> *jātijaraṃ sokapariddavañca*
> *idh'eva vidvā pajaheyya dukkhaṃ.*[11]
>
> "Whatever you may know to be
> Above, below and across in the middle,
> Dispel the delight and the tendency to dwell in them,
> Then your consciousness will not remain in existence.
>
> A monk, endowed with understanding,
> Thus dwelling mindful and heedful,
> As he fares along giving up all possessions,

---

[11] Sn 1055-1056, *Mettagūmāṇavapucchā.*

Would abandon even here and now
Birth, decay, sorrow, lamentation and suffering."

The word *idh'eva* occurring in the second verse is highly significant, in that it means the abandonment of all those things here and now, not leaving it for an existence to come.

In the *MahāViyūhasutta* of the *Sutta Nipāta* also a similar emphasis is laid on this idea of 'here and now.' About the *arahant* it is said that he has no death or birth here and now – *cutūpapāto idha yassa natthi*, "to whom, even here, there is no death or birth."[12] In this very world he has transcended them by making those two concepts meaningless.

The word *nivesanaṃ*, occurring in the first verse, is also significant. It means "dwelling." In consciousness there is a tendency to 'dwell in.' That is why in some contexts it is said that form is the abode or dwelling place of consciousness, *rūpadhātu kho, gahapati, viññāṇassa oko*, "the form element, householder, is the abode of consciousness."[13] The terms *oka, niketa* and *nivesana* are synonymous, meaning "abode," "home," or "dwelling place."

The nature of consciousness in general is to abide or dwell in. That non-manifestative consciousness, *anidassana viññāṇa*, however, has got rid of the tendency to abide or dwell in.

Now we can revert to the passage in the *Dhatuvibhaṅgasutta*, which speaks of an occurrence of tides of imaginings. The passage actually begins with the words *yatthaṭṭhitaṃ maññussavā nappavattanti*, "steadied where-on the tides of imaginings occur no more in him." The idea behind this occurrence of tides of imaginings is quite often represented by the concept of *āsava*, influx. Sensuality, *kāma*, existence, *bhava*, views, *diṭṭhi* and ignorance, *avijjā*, are referred to as "influxes," *āsavā*, or "floods," *oghā*.

---

12 Sn 902, *MahāViyūhasutta*.

13 S III 9, *Hāliddikānisutta*.

These are the four kinds of *samsāric* habits that continuously flow into the minds of beings.

The above mentioned *sutta* passage refers to a place steadied whereon the tides of imaginings do not occur or flow in, a place that is free from their 'influence.' This is none other than *Nibbāna*, for which one of the epithets used is *dīpa*, or island.[14]

Since *Nibbāna* is called an island, some might take it literally to mean some sort of a place in this world. In fact, this is the general concept of *Nibbāna* some are prone to uphold in their interpretation of *Nibbāna*.

But why it is called an island is clearly explained for us by a discourse in the *Pārāyanavagga* of the *Sutta Nipāta*, namely the *Kappamāṇavapucchā*. In this *sutta*, the Brahmin youth Kappa poses the following question to the Buddha:

> *Majjhe sarasmiṃ tiṭṭhataṃ*
> *oghe jāte mahabbhaye*
> *jarāmaccuparetānaṃ*
> *dīpaṃ pabrūhi, mārisa.*
> *Tvañca me dīpam akkhāhi*
> *yathayidaṃ nāparaṃ siyā.*[15]

> "To them that stand midstream,
> When the frightful floods flow forth,
> To them in decay and death forlorn,
> An island, sire, may you proclaim.
> An island which none else excels,
> Yea, such an isle, pray tell me sire."

And this is the Buddha's reply to it:

---

[14] S IV 372, *Asaṅkhatasaṃyutta*.

[15] Sn 1092, *Kappamāṇavapucchā*.

Akiñcanaṃ anādānaṃ
etaṃ dīpaṃ anāparaṃ
'nibbānam' iti naṃ brūmi
jarāmaccuparikkhayaṃ.[16]

"Owning naught, grasping naught,
The isle is this, none else besides,
Nibbāna – that is how I call that isle,
Wherein Decay is decayed and Death is dead."

The Buddha's reply makes it clear that the term *Nibbāna* stands for the extinction of craving and grasping. The ideal of owning naught and grasping naught is itself *Nibbāna*, and nothing else. If the term had any other connotation, the Buddha would have mentioned it in this context.

It is indubitably clear, then, that the epithet *dīpaṃ*, or island, has to be understood in a deeper sense when it refers to *Nibbāna*. It is that owning nothing and grasping nothing, that puts an end to decay and death.

Though we have yet to finish the discussion of the *Dhatuvibhaṅgasutta*, the stage is already set now to understand the significance of a certain brief discourse in the *Udāna*, which is very often quoted in discussions on *Nibbāna*. For facility of understanding, we shall take it up now, as it somehow fits into the context:

Atthi, bhikkhave, ajātaṃ abhūtaṃ akataṃ asaṅkhataṃ. No ce taṃ, bhikkhave, abhavissa ajātaṃ abhūtaṃ akataṃ asaṅkhataṃ, nayidha jātassa bhūtassa katassa saṅkhatassa nissaraṇaṃ paññāyetha. Yasmā ca kho, bhikkhave,

---

[16] Sn 1094, *Kappamāṇavapucchā.*

> *atthi ajātaṃ abhūtaṃ akataṃ asaṅkhataṃ, tasmā jātassa bhūtassa katassa saṅkhatassa nissaraṇaṃ paññāyati.*[17]
>
> "Monks, there is a not-born, a not-become, a not-made, a not-compounded. Monks, if that not-born, not-become, not-made, not-compounded were not, there would be no stepping out here from what is born, become, made and compounded. But since, monks, there is a not-born, a not-become, a not-made, a not-compounded, therefore there is a stepping out from what is born, become, made and compounded."

The terms *ajātaṃ*, not-born, *abhūtaṃ*, not-become, *akataṃ*, not-made, and *asaṅkhataṃ*, not-compounded, are all epithets for *Nibbāna*. The Buddha declares that if not for this not-born, not-become, not-made, not-compounded, there would be no possibility of stepping out or release here, that is, in this very world, from the born, the become, the made and the compounded.

The second half of the passage rhetorically reiterates and emphasises the same fact. Now as to the significance of this profound declaration of the Buddha, we may point out that the terms not-born, not-become, not-made, not-compounded, suggest the emancipation of the *arahant*'s mind from birth, becoming and preparations, *saṅkhārā*. They refer to the cessation of birth, becoming and preparations realized by the *arahant*. So then the significance of these terms is purely psychological.

But the commentator, the Venerable Dhammapāla, pays little attention to the word *idha*, "here," in this passage, which needs to be emphasized. The fact that there is a possibility here and now, of stepping out from the state of being born, become, made and compounded, surely deserves emphasis, since, until then, release

---

17 Ud 80, *Tatiyanibbānapaṭisaṃyuttasutta.*

from decay and death was thought to be possible only in another dimension of existence, that is, after death.

The prospect of stepping out from decay and death here and now in this very world has to be asserted for its novelty, which is why the declaration opens with the word *atthi*, "there is." However, most of the scholars who tried to interpret this passage in their discussion on *Nibbāna*, instead of laying stress on the word *idha*, "here," emphasize the opening word *atthi*, "there is," to prove that *Nibbāna* is some form of reality absolutely existing somewhere.

As that passage from the *Dhatuvibhaṅgasutta* on *maññanā*, which we discussed, has shown us, the terms *ajātaṃ abhūtaṃ akataṃ* and *asaṅkhataṃ* have to be understood in a deeper sense.

Existence is a conceit deep rooted in the mind, which gives rise to a heap of pervert notions. Its cessation, therefore, has also to be accomplished in the mind and by the mind. This is the gist of the Buddha's exhortation.

Let us now come back to the *Dhatuvibhaṅgasutta* to discuss another facet of it. We started our discussion with the grand finale of that discourse, because of its relevance to the question of *maññanā*. However, as a matter of fact, this discourse preached by the Buddha to the Venerable Pukkusāti is an exposition of a systematic path of practice for the emancipation of the mind from imaginings or *maññanā*.

The discourse begins with the declaration *chadhāturo ayaṃ, bhikkhu, puriso*, "monk, man as such is a combination of six elements."[18] The worldling thinks that a being, *satta* (Sanskrit *sattva*), exists at a higher level of reality than inanimate objects.

Now what did the Buddha do to explode this concept of a being in his discourse to Venerable Pukkusāti? He literally thrashed out that concept, by breaking up this 'man' into his basic elements and defining him as a bundle of six elements, namely earth, water, fire, air, space and consciousness.

---

[18] M III 239, *Dhātuvibhaṅgasutta*.

As the discourse proceeds, he explains in an extremely lucid manner how one can detach one's mind from each of these elements. We happened to mention at the very outset that the depth of the *Dhamma* has to be seen through lucidity and not through complicated over-drawings. In fact, this discourse exhibits such lucidity.

The meditation subject of elements, which grew in complexity at the hands of later Buddhist philosophers, who took to atomistic analysis of a speculative sort, is presented here in this *Dhatu-vibhaṅgasutta* with a refreshing clarity and lucidity. Here it is explained in such a way that one can directly experience it.

For instance in describing the earth element, the Buddha gives as examples of the internal earth element such parts of the body as head hairs, body hairs, nails and teeth. Because the external earth element hardly needs illustration, nothing in particular has been mentioned as to that aspect. Anyone can easily understand what is meant by it. There is no attempt at atomistic analysis.

However, the Buddha draws special attention to a certain first principle of great significance:

> *Yā c'eva kho pana ajjhattikā paṭhavīdhātu, yā ca bāhirā paṭhavīdhātu, paṭhavīdhātur ev'esā. Taṃ n'etaṃ mama, n'eso ham asmi, na me so attā ti evam etaṃ yathābhūtaṃ sammappaññāya daṭṭhabbaṃ. Evam etaṃ yathābhūtaṃ sammappaññāya disvā paṭhavīdhātuyā nibbindati, paṭhavīdhātuyā cittaṃ virājeti.*[19]

> "That which is the internal earth element, and that which is the external earth element, they are both just the earth element itself. And that should be seen as it is with right wisdom, thus: 'this is not mine,' 'I am not this,' 'this is not my self.' Having seen thus with right wisdom as it is, he

---

[19] M III 240, *Dhātuvibhaṅgasutta*.

becomes dejected with the earth element, he detaches his mind from the earth element."

It is this first principle that is truly important and not any kind of atomic theory. This resolution of the internal/external conflict has in it the secret of stopping the *saṃsāric* vortex of reiterated becoming, *saṃsāravaṭṭa*. It is due to the very discrimination between an 'internal' and an 'external' that this *saṃsāric* vortex is kept going.

Now in the case of a vortex, what is found inside and outside is simply water. But all the same there is such a vehement speed and activity and a volley of changes going on there. So it is the case with this 'man.' What is found in his body is the earth element. What is to be found outside is also the earth element. And yet, the ordinary person sees quite a wide disparity between the two. Why is that? That is because of the illusory nature of consciousness.

We have devoted a number of sermons to explain the relationship between consciousness and name-and-form. We happened to speak of name-and-form as a reflection or a self-image.[20] Even as one who comes before a mirror, on seeing his reflection on it, would say: 'this is mine,' 'this am I,' 'this is my self,' the worldling is in the habit of entertaining cravings, conceits and views.

In fact the purpose of cravings, conceits and views is to reinforce the distinction between an internal and an external. Already when one says 'this is mine,' one discriminates between the 'this' and 'I,' taking them to be separate realities. 'This am I' and 'this is my self' betray the same tacit assumption.

Just as by looking at a mirror one may like or dislike the image appearing on it, these three points of view give rise to various pervert notions. All this because of the perpetuation of the distinction between an internal and an external, which is the situation with the ordinary worldling.

---

[20] See sermons 6 and 7.

Since cravings, conceits and views thus reinforce the dichotomy between an internal and an external, the Buddha has upheld this principle underlying the meditation on the four elements, to resolve this conflict.

The fact that with the resolution of this conflict between the internal and the external concerning the four elements the mind becomes emancipated is put across to us in the following verse in the *Tālapuṭa Theragāthā*:

Kadā nu kaṭṭhe ca tiṇe latā ca
khandhe ime 'haṃ amite ca dhamme
ajjhattikān' eva ca bāhirāni ca
samaṃ tuleyyaṃ, tad idaṃ kadā me?[21]

This verse gives expression to Venerable Tālapuṭa *Thera*'s aspiration to become an *arahant*. It says:

"When shall I weigh as equal all these
Limitless things both internal and external,
Twigs, grass, creepers and these aggregates,
O! when shall that be for me?"

It is at the stage of *arahant*-hood that the internal and the external appear alike. That is precisely why the Venerable Adhimutta *Thera*, whom we quoted earlier, uttered the lines:

Tiṇakaṭṭhasamaṃ lokaṃ,
yadā paññāya passati.[22]

"When one sees through wisdom,
The world to be comparable to grass and twigs."

---

21 Th 1101, *Tālapuṭa Theragāthā.*

22 Th 717, *Adhimutta Theragāthā,* see sermon 8.

The comparison is between the internal world of the five aggregates, or this conscious body, and the inanimate objects outside.

Just as in the case of the four elements earth, water, fire and air, the Buddha pointed out a way of liberating one's mind from the space element with the help of similar illustrations. In explaining the space element, too, he gave easily intelligible examples.

The internal space element is explained in terms of some apertures in the body that are well known, namely those in the ears, nose and the mouth.[23] Apart from such instances, he did not speak of any microscopic space element, as in scientific explanations, probably because it is irrelevant. Such an analysis is irrelevant for this kind of reflection.

Here we have to bear in mind the fact that perception as such is a mirage.[24] However far one may go on analysing, form and space are relative to each other like a picture and its background. A picture is viewed against its background, which is relative to it. So also are these two concepts of form and space. Consciousness provides the frame work for the entire picture.

By way of clarification we may allude to the pre-Buddhistic attempts of Yogins to solve this problem, solely through the method of serenity, *samatha*, ignoring the method of insight, *vipassanā*. The procedure they followed was somewhat on these lines:

They would first of all surmount the concept of form or matter through the first four mental absorptions, or *jhānas*. Then as they inclined towards the formless, what confronted them first was space. A very appropriate illustration in this context would be the method of removing the sign of the *kasiṇa* and attending to the space left by that removal as 'infinite' or 'boundless,' in order to arouse the base of infinity of space.[25]

---

23 M III 244, *Dhātuvibhaṅgasutta*.

24 S III 141, *Pheṇapiṇḍūpamasutta*.

25 Vism 327.

This mode of contemplation of space betrays the fact that space is also something made up, or prepared, *saṅkhata*. Whatever is prepared, *saṅkhata*, is thought out and mind-made, *abhisaṅkhataṃ abhisañcetayitaṃ*.

The Buddha proclaimed that there is only one *asaṅkhata*, unprepared, that is *Nibbāna*.[26] But later philosophers confounded the issue by taking space also to be *asaṅkhata*.[27] They seem to have ignored its relation to the mind in regarding causes and conditions as purely external things.

Here we see the relativity between form and space. Like the picture and its background, form and space stand relative to each other. All this is presented to us by attention, *manasikārasambhavā sabbe dhammā*,[28] "all things originate from attention."

Some of the later speculations about the nature of the space element are not in consonance with the basic principles outlined in the *Dhamma*. Such confusion arose probably due to a lack of understanding of the term *asaṅkhata*.

Now if we are to say something more about this particular discourse, what remains after detaching one's mind from these five elements, namely earth, water, fire, air and space, is a consciousness that is extremely pure.

The basic function of consciousness is discrimination. It distinguishes between the bitter and the sweet, for instance, to say: 'this is bitter,' 'this is sweet.' Or else it distinguishes between the pleasant, the unpleasant and the neutral with regard to feelings: 'this is pleasant,' 'this is unpleasant,' 'this is neither-unpleasant-nor-pleasant.'

Now that the five elements earth, water, fire, air and space, which create discrete objects as the outward manifestations of consciousness, have been totally removed, the residual function of

---

26 Cf. *Asaṅkhatasaṃyutta*, S IV 359-373.

27 Mil 268.

28 A IV 338, *Kiṃmūlakasutta*.

consciousness amounts to a discrimination between the three grades of feelings.

The sage who has arrived at this stage of progress on the path to *Nibbāna* takes the next step by observing these three kinds of feelings, pleasant, unpleasant and neither-unpleasant-nor-pleasant, as they arise and cease dependent on specific contacts, thereby gradually bringing the mind to equanimity.

He brings his mind to a stage of radiant equanimity. But even this equanimity he does not grasp by way of me-thinking or imagining. The phrase used in this connection is *visaṃyutto naṃ vedeti*, "being detached he experiences it."[29] There is a detachment, an aloofness, even in going through those sensations. This is clearly expressed in that context.

For instance, in the case of a pleasant feeling, it is said: *aniccā ti pajānāti, anajjhositā ti pajānāti, anabhinanditā ti pajānāti*, "he understands it to be impermanent, he understands it to be uninvolved, he understands it to be unrejoiced." With the understanding of impermanence, conceit goes down. The non-involvement does away with the views. The absence of rejoicing suggests the extinction of craving.

So the attainment of *arahant*-hood is in effect the cessation of that consciousness itself. That consciousness is divested of its most primary function of discriminating between the three grades of feeling, pleasant, unpleasant and neither-unpleasant-nor-pleasant.

The term *visaṃyutto* connotes disjunction, suggestive of dispassion and detachment. In this way, the *Dhatuvibhaṅgasutta* clearly brings out the relevance of the question of *maññanā* to the path leading to *Nibbāna*.

In some contexts, this practice of desisting from me-thinking or imagining is called *atammayatā*, non-identification. This is the

---

[29] M III 244, *Dhātuvibhaṅgasutta*.

term used by the Buddha throughout the *Sappurisasutta* of the *Majjhima Nikāya*. For instance we read there:

Sappuriso ca kho, bhikkhave, iti paṭisañcikkhati: nevasaññā-nāsaññāyatanasamāpattiyā pi kho atammayatā vuttā Bhagavatā. Yena yena hi maññanti, tato taṃ hoti aññathā ti.[30]

"The good man reflects thus: the principle of non-identification has been recommended by the Buddha even with regard to the attainment of the sphere of neither-perception-nor-non-perception thus: in whatever way they imagine about it, thereby it turns otherwise." The 'good man' referred to here is the noble disciple on the supramundane path.

This term *tammaya* needs to be clarified in order to understand the significance of this statement. It is derived from *tad maya*, literally "made of that" or "of that stuff." It is on a par with such terms as *sovaṇṇamaya*, golden, and *rajatamaya*, silvery.

When one has cravings, conceits and views about something, he practically becomes one with it due to that very grasping. In other words, he identifies himself with it. That is why the person who has imaginings about the sphere of neither-perception-nor-non-perception, which he has attained, thinks 'I am one who has attained the sphere of neither-perception-nor-non-perception.'

He thereby has conceit, which is a defilement in itself. As a result, when he loses his mastery of that attainment, he becomes disconcerted. It is for that reason that the Buddha had enjoined that one should cultivate the attitude of *atammayatā*, or non-identification, even with regard to the attainment of the sphere of neither-perception-nor-non-perception.

The *arahant* is called *atammayo* in the sense that he does not identify himself with anything. An *arahant* cannot be identified with what he appears to possess. This is well expressed by the following verse in the *Devadūtavagga* of the *Aṅguttara Nikāya*:

---

30 M III 44, *Sappurisasutta*.

Pasayha Māraṃ abhibhuyya antakaṃ
yo ca phusī jātikkhayaṃ padhānavā
sa tādiso lokavidū sumedho
sabbesu dhammesu atammayo muni.[31]

"That ardent sage who has touched the extinction of birth,
Having overpowered *Māra* and conquered the Ender,
That Such-like one, the wise sage, the knower of the world,
Is aloof in regard to all phenomena."

The idea of this aloofness can be presented in another way, that is as detachment from the seen, the heard, the sensed and the cognized, *diṭṭha, suta, muta, viññāta*. One of the most important *suttas* that merits discussion in this respect is the *Bāhiyasutta* in the *Bodhivagga* of the *Udāna*. It is generally acclaimed as an extremely profound discourse.

The ascetic Bāhiya Dārucīriya came all the way from far off Suppāraka to see the Buddha. When he reached Jetavana monastery at Sāvatthi, he heard that the Buddha had just left on his alms-round. Due to his extreme eagerness, he ran behind the Buddha and, on meeting him, fell prostrate before him and begged: "May the Exalted One preach to me the *Dhamma.*"

The Buddha, however, seemed not so responsive, when he remarked: "Now it is untimely, Bāhiya, we are on our alms-round." Some might be puzzled by this attitude of the Buddha. But most probably it is one of those skilful means of the Buddha, suggestive of his great compassion and wisdom. It served to tone down the over enthusiastic haste of Bāhiya and to arouse a reverential respect for the *Dhamma* in him.

---

[31] A I 150, *Ādhipateyyasutta*.

Bāhiya repeated his request for the second time, adding: "I do not know whether there will be a danger to the Exalted One's life or to my own life." For the second time the Buddha refused.

It was when Bāhiya made his request for the third time that the Buddha acceded to it by giving a terse discourse, *saṅkhitta Dhammadesanā*, of extraordinary depth. The exhortation, brief and deep as it is, was quite apt, since Bāhiya Dārucīriya belonged to that rare category of persons with quick understanding, *khippā-bhiññā*:[32]

> *Tasmātiha te, Bāhiya, evaṃ sikkhitabbaṃ: diṭṭhe diṭṭhamattaṃ bhavissati, sute sutamattaṃ bhavissati, mute mutamattaṃ bhavissati, viññāte viññātamattaṃ bhavissati. Evaṃ hi te, Bāhiya,, sikkhitabbaṃ.*
>
> *Yato kho te, Bāhiya, diṭṭhe diṭṭhamattaṃ bhavissati, sute sutamattaṃ bhavissati, mute mutamattaṃ bhavissati, viññāte viññātamattaṃ bhavissati, tato tvaṃ Bāhiya na tena. Yato tvaṃ Bāhiya na tena, tato tvaṃ Bāhiya na tattha. Yato tvaṃ Bāhiya na tattha, tato tvaṃ Bāhiya nev'idha na huraṃ na ubhayamantarena. Es'ev'anto dukkhassa.*[33]

No sooner had the Buddha finished his exhortation, the ascetic Bāhiya attained *arahant*-hood then and there. Let us now try to unravel the meaning of this abstruse discourse.

The discourse starts off abruptly, as if it had been wrested from the Buddha by Bāhiya's repeated requests. *Tasmātiha, Bāhiya, evaṃ sikkhitabbaṃ*, "Well then, Bāhiya, you had better train yourself thus." And what is that training?

---

[32] A I 24, *Etadaggavagga*.

[33] Ud 8, *Bāhiyasutta*.

"In the seen there will be just the seen, in the heard there will be just the heard, in the sensed there will be just the sensed, in the cognized there will be just the cognized. Thus, Bāhiya, should you train yourself."

It is as if the Buddha had addressed the ascetic Bāhiya in the terminology of the *Ariyans* and established him on the path to *Nibbāna*. Here the term *muta*, or "sensed," stands for whatever is experienced through the tongue, the nose, and the body.

The basic principle in this training seems to be the discipline to stop short at bare awareness, *diṭṭhe diṭṭhamattaṃ, sute sutamattaṃ*, etc. The latter half of the discourse seems to indicate what happens when one goes through that training. The entire discourse is a presentation of the triple training of morality, concentration and wisdom in a nutshell.

"And when to you, Bāhiya, there will be in the seen just the seen, in the heard just the heard, in the sensed just the sensed, in the cognized just the cognized, then, Bāhiya, you are not by it. And when you are not by it, you are not in it. And when, Bāhiya, you are not in it, then, Bāhiya, you are neither here, nor there, nor in between. This itself is the end of suffering."

As a literal translation this appears cryptic enough to demand an explanation. Let us first of all give a few clues to unravel the puzzle.

The terms "by it," *tena*, and "in it," *tattha*, are rather elliptical. Though unexpressed, they seem to imply the relevance of *maññanā* to the whole problem.

As we happened to mention earlier, imaginings or methinkings by way of craving, conceit and views, lead to an identification, for which the term used is *tammayatā*. Such an identification makes one unsteady, for when the thing identified with is shaken, one also gets shaken up.

This kind of imagining 'in terms of' is indicated by the elliptical *tena*, for we get a clear proof of it in the following two lines from the *Jarāsutta* in the *Aṭṭhakavagga* of the *Sutta Nipāta*:

Dhono na hi tena maññati
yad idaṃ diṭṭhasutaṃ mutesu vā.[34]

Dhona is a term for the *arahant* as one who has "shaken off" all defilements. So these lines could be rendered as follows:

"The *arahant*, the one who has shaken off,
Does not imagine 'in terms of'
Whatever is seen, heard and sensed."

34 Sn 813, *Jarāsutta*.

Nibbāna Sermon 15

Namo tassa Bhagavato Arahato Sammāsambuddhassa
Namo tassa Bhagavato Arahato Sammāsambuddhassa
Namo tassa Bhagavato Arahato Sammāsambuddhassa

Etaṃ santaṃ, etaṃ paṇītaṃ, yadidaṃ sabbasaṅkhārasamatho sabbūpadhipaṭinissaggo taṇhakkhayo virāgo nirodho nibbānaṃ.[1]

"This is peaceful, this is excellent, namely the stilling of all preparations, the relinquishment of all assets, the destruction of craving, detachment, cessation, extinction."

With the permission of the Most Venerable Great Preceptor and the assembly of the venerable meditative monks.

This is the fifteenth sermon in the series of sermons on *Nibbāna*. Towards the end of our last sermon we happened to quote a brief exhortation on *Dhamma* from the *Udāna*, which enabled the ascetic *Bāhiya Dārucīriya* to liberate his mind from imaginings and attain the state of non-identification, *atammayatā*, or *arahant*-hood. In order to attempt an exposition of that exhortation of the Buddha, which was pithy enough to bring about instantaneous *arahant*-hood, let us refresh our memory of that brief discourse to Bāhiya:

> *Tasmātiha te, Bāhiya, evaṃ sikkhitabbaṃ: diṭṭhe diṭṭhamattaṃ bhavissati, sute sutamattaṃ bhavissati, mute*

---

[1] M I 436, *MahāMālunkyasutta*.

mutamattaṃ bhavissati, viññāte viññātamattaṃ bhavissati. Evaṃ hi te, Bāhiya, sikkhitabbaṃ.

Yato kho te, Bāhiya, diṭṭhe diṭṭhamattaṃ bhavissati, sute sutamattaṃ bhavissati, mute mutamattaṃ bhavissati, viññāte viññātamattaṃ bhavissati, tato tvaṃ Bāhiya na tena. Yato tvaṃ Bāhiya na tena, tato tvaṃ Bāhiya na tattha. Yato tvaṃ Bāhiya na tattha, tato tvaṃ Bāhiya nev'idha na huraṃ na ubhayamantarena. Es'ev'anto dukkhassa.[2]

"Well, then, Bāhiya, you had better train yourself thus: In the seen there will be just the seen, in the heard there will be just the heard, in the sensed there will be just the sensed, in the cognized there will be just the cognized. Thus, Bāhiya, should you train yourself.

"And when to you, Bāhiya, there will be in the seen just the seen, in the heard just the heard, in the sensed just the sensed, in the cognized just the cognized, then, Bāhiya, you will not be by it. And when, Bāhiya, you are not by it, then, Bāhiya, you are not in it. And when, Bāhiya, you are not in it, then, Bāhiya, you are neither here nor there nor in between. This, itself, is the end of suffering."

As a clue to an exegesis of this discourse, we made an attempt, the other day, to unravel the meaning of the two puzzling terms in the text, namely, *na tena* and *na tattha*. These two terms are apparently unrelated to the context. To get at their significance, we brought up a quotation of two lines from the *Jarāsutta* of the *Aṭṭhakavagga* of the *Sutta Nipāta*:

---

[2] Ud 8, *Bāhiyasutta*.

Dhono na hi tena maññati
yadidaṃ diṭṭhasutaṃ mutesu vā.[3]

Dhona is a term for the *arahant* in the sense that he has "shaken off" the dust of defilements. So then, these two lines imply that the *arahant* does not imagine thereby, namely *yadidaṃ*, in terms of whatever is seen, heard or sensed. These two lines are, as it were, a random exegesis of our riddle terms in the *Bāhiyasutta*.

The first line itself gives the clue to the rather elliptical term *na tena*, which carries no verb with it. Our quotation makes it clear that the implication is *maññanā*, or imagining. *Dhono na hi tena maññati*, the *arahant* does not imagine 'by it' or 'thereby.'

Although the *Bāhiyasutta* makes no mention of the word *maññanā*, this particular expression seems to suggest that what is implied here is a form of imagining. By way of further proof we may allude to another quotation, which we had to bring up several times: *Yena yena hi maññanti, tato taṃ hoti aññathā.*[4] "In whatever terms they imagine it, thereby it turns otherwise." We came across another expression, which has a similar connotation: *tena ca mā maññi,* "do not be vain thereby."[5]

The first thing we can infer, therefore, from the above quoted two lines of the verse, is that what is to be understood by the elliptical expression *na tena* in the *Bāhiyasutta* is the idea of imagining, or in short, *na tena maññati*, "does not imagine thereby."

Secondly, as to what precisely is implied by the word *tena*, or "by it," can also be easily inferred from those two lines. In fact, the second line beginning with the word *yadidaṃ*, which means "namely" or "that is," looks like a commentary on the first line

---

3 Sn 813, *Jarāsutta*.

4 Sn 757, *Dvayatānupassanāsutta*; see sermon 13.

5 A IV 386, *Samiddhisutta*; see sermon 12.

itself. The *dhono*, or the *arahant*, does not imagine 'thereby,' namely by whatever is seen, heard and sensed.

The verse in question mentions only the three terms *diṭṭha, suta* and *muta*, whereas the *Bāhiyasutta* has as its framework the four terms *diṭṭha, suta, muta* and *viññata*. Since what precedes the term *na tena* in the *Bāhiyasutta* is the fourfold premise beginning with *diṭṭhe diṭṭhamattaṃ bhavissati*, "when to you, Bāhiya, there will be in the seen just the seen," it stands to reason that what the Buddha meant by the term *na tena* is the attitude of not thinking 'in terms of' whatever is seen, heard, sensed or cognized. That is to say, not imagining 'thereby.'

This same attitude of not imagining 'thereby' is what is upheld in the *Mūlapariyāyasutta*, which we discussed at length on a previous occasion.[6] There we explained the word *maññanā*, "me-thinking," "imagining," taking as a paradigm the first term *paṭhavi*, occurring in the list of twenty-four terms given there. Among the twenty-four terms, we find mentioned the four relevant to our present problem, namely *diṭṭha, suta, muta* and *viññāta*.[7]

We are now used to the general schema of the *Mūlapariyāya-sutta*, concerning the attitude of the three categories of persons mentioned there. Let us, for instance, take up what is said in that context with regard to the *sekha*, or the monk in higher training.

Paṭhaviṃ paṭhavito abhiññāya paṭhaviṃ mā maññi, paṭhaviyā mā maññi, paṭhavito mā maññi, paṭhaviṃ me ti mā maññi, paṭhaviṃ mā abhinandi.

This is how the attitude of the *sekha* is described with regard to *paṭhavi*, or earth. Suppose we substitute *diṭṭha*, or the seen, in place of *paṭhavi*. This is what we should get:

Diṭṭhaṃ diṭṭhato abhiññāya diṭṭhaṃ mā maññi, diṭṭhasmiṃ mā maññi, diṭṭhato mā maññi, diṭṭhaṃ me ti mā maññi, diṭṭhaṃ mā abhinandi.

---

[6] See sermons 12 and 13.

[7] M I 3, *Mūlapariyāyasutta*.

What the *sekha* has before him is a step of training, and this is how he has to train in respect of the four things, the seen, the heard, the sensed and the cognized. He should not imagine in terms of them.

For instance, he understands through higher knowledge, and not through the ordinary perception of the worldling, the seen as 'seen.' Having thus understood it, he has to train in not imagining the seen as a thing, by objectifying it. *Diṭṭhaṃ mā maññi*, let him not imagine a 'seen.' Also, let him not imagine 'in the seen,' or 'from the seen.' We have already pointed out the relationship between these imaginings and the grammatical structure.[8]

This objectification of the seen gives rise to acquisitive tendencies, to imagine the seen as 'mine.' *Diṭṭhaṃ me ti mā maññi,* let him not imagine 'I have seen' or 'I have a seen.'

This acquisition has something congratulatory about it. It leads to some sort of joy, so the monk in higher training has to combat that too. *Diṭṭhaṃ mā abhinandi*, let him not delight in the seen.

It seems, then, that the Buddha has addressed the ascetic Bāhiya Dārucīriya in the language of the *ariyans*, for the very first instruction given to him was "in the seen there will be just the seen." So highly developed in wisdom and quick witted was Bāhiya[9] that the Buddha promptly asked him to stop short at the seen, by understanding that in the seen there is just the seen.

Not to have imaginings or me-thinkings about the seen is therefore the way to stop short at just the seen. If one does not stop short at just the seen, but goes on imagining in terms of 'in the seen,' 'from the seen,' etc., as already stated, one will end up with an identification, or *tammayatā*.

In our last sermon we brought up the term *tammayatā*. When one starts imagining in such terms about something, one tends to become one with it, *tammayo*, even as things made out of gold and

---

8 See sermon 13.

9 According to A I 24 *Bāhiya* was outstanding for his *khippābhiññā*.

silver are called golden, *suvaṇṇamaya*, and silvery, *rajatamaya*. It is as if one who grasps a gem becomes its owner and if anything happens to the gem he is affected by it. To possess a gem is to be possessed by it.

When one gets attached and becomes involved and entangled in the seen through craving, conceit and views, by imagining egoistically, the result is identification, *tammayatā*, literally "of-thatness."

In this present context, however, the Buddha puts Bāhiya Dārucīriya on the path to non-identification, or *atammayatā*. That is to say, he advises Bāhiya not to indulge in such imaginings. That attitude leads to non-identification and detachment. When one has no attachments, involvements and entanglements regarding the seen, one does not have the notion of being in the seen.

Once we spoke about a children's hut into which the mother was invited.[10] When she crept into that plaything of a hut, she did not seriously entertain the thought of being 'in' it. Similarly if one does not indulge in imaginings, one has no notion of being 'in' the seen.

This, then, is the significance of the words *na tattha*, "not in it." *Yato tvaṃ Bāhiya na tena, tato tvaṃ Bāhiya na tattha.* "When, Bāhiya, you are not by it, then, Bāhiya, you are not in it." That is to say, when for instance Bāhiya does not imagine 'by the seen,' he is not 'in the seen.' Likewise, he is not in the heard, sensed or cognized. From this we can deduce the meaning of what follows.

Yato tvaṃ Bāhiya na tattha, tato tvaṃ Bāhiya nev'idha na huraṃ na ubhayamantarena. At whatever moment you neither *imagine* 'by the seen' nor entertain the notion of being 'in the seen,' which is tantamount to projecting an 'I' into the seen, then you are neither here nor there nor in between.

In a number of earlier sermons we have sufficiently explained the significance of the two ends and the middle as well as the

---

[10] See sermon 13.

above, the below and the across in the middle. What do they signify?

As we happened to point out on an earlier occasion, it is by driving the peg of the conceit 'am' that a world is measured out, construed or postulated.[11] We also pointed out that the grammatical structure springs up along with it. That is to say, together with the notion 'am' there arises a 'here.' 'Here' am I, he is 'there' and you are 'yon' or in front of me. This is the basic ground plan for the grammatical structure, known to grammar as the first person, the second person and the third person.

A world comes to be measured out and a grammatical structure springs up. This, in fact, is the origin of proliferation, or *papañca*. So it is the freedom from that proliferation that is meant by the expression *nev'idha na huraṃ na ubhayamantarena*, "neither here nor there nor between the two." The notion of one's being in the world, or the bifurcation as 'I' and 'the world,' is no longer there. *Es'ev'anto dukkhassa*, this, then, is the end of suffering, *Nibbāna*.

The fundamental first principles underlying this short exhortation of the Buddha could thus be inferred to some extent. We could perhaps elicit something more regarding the significance of the four key terms in question.

In the section of the fours in the *Aṅguttara Nikāya* we come across four modes of noble usages, *cattāro ariya vohārā*,[12] namely:

1) *diṭṭhe diṭṭhavāditā,*

2) *sute sutavāditā,*

3) *mute mutavāditā,*

4) *viññāte viññātavāditā.*

---

[11] See sermon 10.

[12] A II 246, *Catutthavohārasutta*.

These four are:

1) Asserting the fact of having seen in regard to the seen,
2) Asserting the fact of having heard in regard to the heard,
3) Asserting the fact of having sensed in regard to the sensed,
4) Asserting the fact of having cognized in regard to the cognized.

Generally speaking, these four noble usages stand for the principle of truthfulness. In some discourses, as well as in the *Vinayapiṭaka*, these terms are used in that sense. They are the criteria of the veracity of a statement in general, not so much in a deep sense.

However, there are different levels of truth. In fact, truthfulness is a question of giving evidence that runs parallel with one's level of experience. At higher levels of experience or realization, the evidence one gives also changes accordingly.

The episode of Venerable MahāTissa *Thera* is a case in view.[13] When he met a certain woman on his way, who displayed her teeth in a wily giggle, he simply grasped the sign of her teeth. He did not totally refrain from grasping a sign, but took it as an illustration of his meditation subject. Later, when that woman's husband, searching for her, came up to him and asked whether he had seen a woman, he replied that all he saw was a skeleton. Now that is a certain level of experience.

Similarly the concept of truthfulness is something that changes with levels of experience. There are various degrees of truth, based on realization. The highest among them is called *paramasacca*.[14] As to what that is, the *Dhātuvibhaṅgasutta* itself provides the *answer* in the following statement of the Buddha.

---

[13] Vism 21.

[14] The term occurs e.g. at M I 480, *Tevijjavacchagottasutta*; at M II 173, *Cankīsutta*; and at A II 115, *Patodasutta*.

Etañhi, bhikkhu, paramaṃ ariyasaccaṃ yadidaṃ amosa-dhammaṃ Nibbānaṃ.[15] "Monk, this is the highest noble truth, namely *Nibbāna*, that is of a non-falsifying nature." All other truths are falsified when the corresponding level of experience is transcended. But *Nibbāna* is the highest truth, since it can never be falsified by anything beyond it.

The fact that it is possible to give evidence by this highest level of experience comes to light in the *Chabbisodhanasutta* of the *Majjhima Nikāya*. In this discourse we find the Buddha instructing the monks as to how they should interrogate a fellow monk who claims to have attained *arahant*-hood. The interrogation has to follow certain criteria, one of which concerns the four standpoints *diṭṭha, suta, muta* and *viññāta*, the seen, the heard, the sensed and the cognized.

What sort of answer a monk who rightly claims to *arahant*-hood would give is also stated thereby the Buddha. It runs as follows: *Diṭṭhe kho ahaṃ, āvuso, anupāyo anapāyo anissito appaṭibaddho vippamutto visaṃyutto vimariyādikatena cetasā viharāmi.*[16]

Here, then, is the highest mode of giving evidence in the court of Reality as an *arahant*. "Friends, with regard to the seen, I dwell unattracted, unrepelled, independent, uninvolved, released, unshackled, with a mind free from barriers."

He is unattracted, *anupāyo*, by lust and unrepelled, *anapāyo*, by hate. He is not dependent, *anissito*, on cravings, conceits and views. He is not involved, *appaṭibaddho*, with desires and attachments and is released, *vippamutto*, from defilements. He is no longer shackled, *visaṃyutto*, by fetters and his mind is free from barriers.

What these barriers are, we can easily infer. They are the bifurcations such as the internal and the external, *ajjhatta bahiddhā*,

---

15 M III 245, *Dhātuvibhaṅgasutta*.

16 M III 29, *Chabbisodhanasutta*.

which are so basic to what is called existence, *bhava*. Where there are barriers, there are also attach-ments, aversions and conflicts. Where there is a fence, there is defence and offence.

So the *arahant* dwells with a mind unpartitioned and barrierless, *vimariyādikatena cetasā*. To be able to make such a statement is the highest standard of giving evidence in regard to the four noble usages.

It is also noteworthy that in the *Bāhiyasutta* the Buddha has presented the triple training of higher morality, higher concentration and higher wisdom, *adhisīla, adhicitta* and *adhipaññā*, through these four noble usages. The commentary, too, accepts this fact.[17] But this is a point that might need clarification. How are we to distinguish between morality, concentration and wisdom in this brief exhortation?

Now how does the exhortation begin? It opens with the words *tasmātiha te, Bāhiya, evaṃ sikkhitabbaṃ*, "well then, Bāhiya, you should train yourself thus." This is an indication that the Buddha introduced him to a course of training, and this is the preliminary training: *Diṭṭhe diṭṭhamattaṃ bhavissati, sute sutamattaṃ bhavissati, mute mutamattaṃ bhavissati, viññāte viññātamattaṃ bhavissati.* "In the seen there will be just the seen, in the heard there will be just the heard, in the sensed there will be just the sensed, in the cognized there will be just the cognized."

What is hinted at by this initial instruction is the training in higher morality, *adhisīlasikkhā*. The most important aspect of this training is the morality of sense-restraint, *indriya saṃvara sīla*. The first principles of sense-restraint are already implicit in this brief instruction.

If one stops short at just the seen in regard to the seen, one does not grasp a sign in it, or dwell on its details. There is no sorting out as 'this is good,' 'this is bad.' That itself conduces to sense-restraint. So we may conclude that the relevance of this brief

---

[17] Ud-a 90.

instruction to the morality of sense-restraint is in its enjoining the abstention from grasping a sign or dwelling on the details. That is what pertains to the training in higher morality, *adhisīlasikkha.*

Let us see how it also serves the purpose of training in higher concentration. To stop at just the seen in the seen is to refrain from discursive thought, which is the way to abandon mental hindrances. It is discursive thought that brings hindrances in its train. So here we have what is relevant to the training in higher concentration as well.

Then what about higher wisdom, *adhipaññā*? Something more specific has to be said in this concern. What precisely is to be understood by higher wisdom in this context? It is actually the freedom from imaginings, *maññanā*, and proliferation, *papañca.*

If one stops short at just the seen in the seen, such ramifications as mentioned in discourses like the *Mūlapariyāyasutta* do not come in at all. The tendency to objectify the seen and to proliferate it as 'in it,' 'from it' and 'it is mine' receives no sanction. This course of training is helpful for the emancipation of the mind from imaginings and proliferations.

The Buddha has compared the six sense-bases, that is eye, ear, nose, tongue, body and mind, to a deserted village.[18] *Suññaṃ idaṃ attena vā attaniyena vā.* "This is void of a self or anything belonging to a self." All these sense-bases are devoid of a self or anything belonging to a self. Therefore they are comparable to a deserted village, a village from which all inhabitants have fled.

The dictum 'in the seen there will be just the seen' is an advice conducive to the attitude of regarding the six sense-bases as a deserted village. This is what pertains to higher wisdom in the Buddha's exhortation.

Papañca, or prolific conceptualisation, is a process of transaction with whatever is seen, heard, sensed, etc. So here there is no process of such transaction. Also, when one trains oneself accord-

---

[18] S IV 174, *Āsīvisasutta.*

ing to the instruction, "in the seen there will be just the seen, in the heard there will be just the heard, in the sensed there will be just the sensed, in the cognized there will be just the cognized," that identification implied by the term *tammayatā* will no longer be there.

Egotism, the conceit 'am' and all what prompts conceptual proliferation will come to an end. This kind of training uproots the peg of the conceit 'am,' thereby bringing about the cessation of prolific conceptualisation, the cessation of becoming and the cessation of suffering.

We can therefore conclude that the entire triple training is enshrined in this exhortation. What happens as a result of this training is indicated by the riddle like terms *na tena, na tattha, nev'idha na huraṃ na ubhayamantarena*.

When the wisdom of the ascetic Bāhiya Dārucīriya had sufficiently matured by following the triple course of training, the Buddha gave the hint necessary for realization of that cessation of becoming, which is *Nibbāna*, in the following words: "Then, Bāhiya, you will not be by it. And when, Bāhiya, you are not by it, then, Bāhiya, you are not in it. And when, Bāhiya, you are not in it, then, Bāhiya, you are neither here nor there nor in between. This, itself, is the end of suffering."

This sermon, therefore, is one that succinctly presents the quintessence of the *Saddhamma*. It is said that the mind of the ascetic Bāhiya Dārucīriya was released from all influxes immediately on hearing this exhortation.

Now let us come back to the sequence of events in the story as mentioned in the *Udāna*. It was after the Buddha had already set out on his alms round that this sermon was almost wrenched from him with much insistence. When it had proved its worth, the Buddha continued with his alms round. Just then a cow with a young calf gored the *arahant* Bāhiya Dārucīriya to death.

While returning from his alms round with a group of monks, the Buddha saw the corpse of the *arahant* Bāhiya. He asked those monks to take the dead body on a bed and cremate it. He even told them to build a cairn enshrining his relics, saying: "Monks, a co-celibate of yours has passed away."

Those monks, having carried out the instructions, came back and reported to the Buddha. Then they raised the question: "Where has he gone after death, what is his after death state?" The Buddha replied: "Monks, Bāhiya Dārucīriya was wise, he lived up to the norm of the *Dhamma*, he did not harass me with questions on *Dhamma*. Monks, Bāhiya Dārucīriya has attained *Parinibbāna*."

In conclusion, the Buddha uttered the following verse of uplift:

Yattha āpo ca paṭhavī,
tejo vāyo na gādhati,
na tattha sukkā jotanti,
ādicco nappakāsati,
na tattha candimā bhāti,
tamo tattha na vijjati.
Yadā ca attanāvedi,
muni monena brāhmaṇo,
atha rūpā arūpā ca,
sukhadukkhā pamuccati.[19]

On the face of it, the verse seems to imply something like this:

"Where water, earth, fire and air
Do not find a footing,
There the stars do not shine,
And the sun spreads not its lustre,
The moon does not appear resplendent there,
And no darkness is to be found there.
When the sage, the brahmin with wisdom,
Understands by himself,

---

[19] Ud 9, *Bāhiyasutta*.

Then is he freed from form and formless,
And from pleasure and pain as well."

The commentary to the *Udāna*, *Paramatthadīpanī*, gives a strange interpretation to this verse. It interprets the verse as a description of the destination of the *arahant* Bāhiya Dārucīriya after he attained *Parinibbāna*, the place he went to.[20] Even the term *Nibbānagati* is used in that connection, the 'place' one goes to in attaining *Parinibbāna*. That place, according to the commentary, is not easily understood by worldlings. Its characteristics are said to be the following:

The four elements, earth, water, fire and air, are not there. No sun, or moon, or stars are there. The reason why the four elements are negated is supposed to be the fact that there is nothing that is compounded in the uncompounded *Nibbāna* element, into which the *arahant* passes away.

Since no sun, or moon, or stars are there in that mysterious place, one might wonder why there is no darkness either. The commentator tries to forestall the objection by stating that it is precisely because one might think that there should be darkness when those luminaries are not there, that the Buddha emphatically negates it. So the commentarial interpretation apparently leads us to the conclusion that there is no darkness in the *Nibbāna* element, even though no sun or moon or stars are there.

The line of interpretation we have followed throughout this series of sermons allows us to depart from this commentarial trend. That place where earth, water, fire and air do not find a footing is not where the *arahant* Bāhiya Dārucīriya had 'gone' when he passed away. The commentator seems to have construed this verse as a reply the Buddha gave to the question raised by those monks. Their question was: "Where has he gone after death, what is his after death state?" They were curious about his borne.

---

[20] Ud-a 98.

But when we carefully examine the context, it becomes clear that they raised that question because they did not know that the corpse they cremated was that of an *arahant*. Had they known it, they would not have even asked that question. That is precisely the reason for the Buddha's declaration that Bāhiya attained *Parinibbāna*, a fact he had not disclosed before. He added that Bāhiya followed the path of *Dhamma* without harassing him with questions and attained *Parinibbāna*.

Now that is the answer proper. To reveal the fact that Bāhiya attained *Parinibbāna* is to answer the question put by those inquisitive monks. Obviously they knew enough of the *Dhamma* to understand then, that their question about the borne and destiny of Venerable Bāhiya was totally irrelevant.

So then the verse uttered by the Buddha in conclusion was something extra. It was only a joyous utterance, a verse of uplift, coming as a grand finale to the whole episode.

Such verses of uplift are often to be met with in the *Udāna*. As we already mentioned, the verses in the *Udāna* have to be interpreted very carefully, because they go far beyond the implications of the story concerned.[21] They invite us to take a plunge into the ocean of *Dhamma*. Just one verse is enough. The text is small but deep. The verse in question is such a spontaneous utterance of joy. It is not the answer to the question 'where did he go?'

Well, in that case, what are we to understand by the word *yattha*, "where"? We have already given a clue to it in our seventh sermon with reference to that non-manifestative consciousness, *anidassana viññāṇa*. What the Buddha describes in this verse, is not the place where the Venerable *arahant* Bāhiya went after his demise, but the non-manifestative consciousness he had realized here and now, in his concentration of the fruit of *arahant*-hood, or *arahattaphalasamādhi*.

Let us hark back to the four lines quoted in the *Kevaḍḍhasutta*:

---

21 See sermon 1.

Viññāṇaṃ anidassanaṃ,
anantaṃ sabbato pabhaṃ,
ettha āpo ca paṭhavī,
tejo vāyo na gādhati.[22]

"Consciousness which is non-manifestative,
Endless, lustrous on all sides,
It is here that water, earth,
Fire and air no footing find."

The first two lines of the verse in the *Bāhiyasutta*, beginning with the correlative *yattha*, "where," find an answer in the last two lines quoted above from the *Kevaḍḍhasutta*. What is referred to as "it is here," is obviously the non-manifestative consciousness mentioned in the first two lines. That problematic place indicated by the word *yattha*, "where," in the *Bāhiyasutta*, is none other than this non-manifestative consciousness.

We had occasion to explain at length in what sense earth, water, fire and air find no footing in that consciousness. The ghostly elements do not haunt that consciousness. That much is clear. But how are we to understand the enigmatic reference to the sun, the moon and the stars? It is said that the stars do not shine in that non-manifestative consciousness, the sun does not spread its lustre and the moon does not appear resplendent in it, nor is there any darkness. How are we to construe all this?

Briefly stated, the Buddha's declaration amounts to the revelation that the sun, the moon and the stars fade away before the superior radiance of the non-manifestative consciousness, which is infinite and lustrous on all sides.

How a lesser radiance fades away before a superior one, we have already explained with *reference* to the cinema in a number

---

[22] D I 223, *Kevaḍḍhasutta*.

of earlier sermons.[23] To sum up, the attention of the audience in a cinema is directed to the narrow beam of light falling on the screen. The audience, or the spectators, are seeing the scenes making up the film show with the help of that beam of light and the thick darkness around.

This second factor is also very important. Scenes appear not simply because of the beam of light. The thickness of the darkness around is also instrumental in it. This fact is revealed when the cinema hall is fully lit up. If the cinema hall is suddenly illuminated, either by the opening of doors and windows or by some electrical device, the scenes falling on the screen fade away as if they were erased. The beam of light, which was earlier there, becomes dim before the superior light. The lesser lustre is superseded by a greater lustre.

We might sometimes be found fault with for harping on this cinema simile, on the ground that it impinges on the precept concerning abstinence from enjoying dramatic performances, song and music. But let us consider whether this cinema is something confined to a cinema hall.

In the open air theatre of the world before us, a similar phenomenon of supersedence is occurring. In the twilight glow of the evening the twinkling stars enable us to faintly figure out the objects around us, despite the growing darkness. Then the moon comes up. Now what happens to the twinkling little stars? They fade away, their lustre being superseded by that of the moon.

Then we begin to enjoy the charming scenes before us in the serene moonlit night. The night passes off. The daylight gleam of the sun comes up. What happens then? The soft radiance of the moon wanes before the majestic lustre of the sun. The moon gets superseded and fades away. Full of confidence we are now watching the multitude of technicoloured scenes in this massive

---

23 See sermons 5, 7 and 9.

theatre of the world. In broad daylight, when sunshine is there, we have no doubt about our vision of objects around us.

But now let us suppose that the extraneous defilements in the mind of a noble disciple, treading the noble eightfold path, get dispelled, allowing its intrinsic lustre of wisdom to shine forth. What happens then? The stars, the moon and the sun get superseded by that light of wisdom. Even the forms that one had seen by twilight, moonlight and sunlight fade away and pale into insignificance. The umbra of form and the penumbra of the formless get fully erased.

In the previous sermon we happened to mention that form and space are related to each other, like the picture and its background. Now all this is happening in the firmament, which forms the background. We could enjoy the scenes of the world cinema, because of that darkness. The twilight, the moonlight and the sunlight are but various levels of that darkness.

The worldling thinks that one who has eyes must surely see if there is sunshine. He cannot think of anything beyond it. But the Buddha has declared that there is something more radiant than the radiance of the sun. *Natthi paññāsamā ābhā*, "there is no radiance comparable to wisdom."[24]

Let us hark back to a declaration by the Buddha we had already quoted in a previous sermon:

> *Catasso imā, bhikkhave, pabhā. Katamā catasso? Candappabhā, sūriyappabhā, aggippabhā, paññappabhā, imā kho, bhikkhave, catasso pabhā. Etadaggaṃ, bhikkhave, imāsaṃ catunnaṃ pabhānaṃ, yad idaṃ paññappabhā.*[25]
>
> "Monks, there are these four lustres. What four? The lustre of the moon, the lustre of the sun, the lustre of fire, the

---

[24] S I 6, *Natthiputtasamasutta*.

[25] A II 139, *Pabhāsutta*; see sermon 7.

> lustre of wisdom. These, monks, are the four lustres. This, monks, is the highest among these four lustres, namely the lustre of wisdom."

So, then, we can now understand why the form and the formless fade away. This wisdom has a penetrative quality, for which reason it is called *nibbedhikā paññā*.[26] When one sees forms, one sees them together with their shadows. The fact that one sees shadows there, is itself proof that darkness has not been fully dispelled. If light comes from all directions, there is no shadow at all. If that light is of a penetrative nature, not even form will be manifest there.

Now it is mainly due to what is called 'form' and 'form-less,' *rūpa/arūpa*, that the worldling experiences pleasure and pain in a world that distinguishes between a 'pleasure' and a 'pain.'

Though we have departed from the commentarial path of exegesis, we are now in a position to interpret the cryptic verse in the *Bāhiyasutta* perhaps more meaningfully. Let us now recall the verse in question:

> *Yattha āpo ca paṭhavī,*
> *tejo vāyo na gādhati,*
> *na tattha sukkā jotanti,*
> *ādicco nappakāsati,*
> *na tattha candimā bhāti,*
> *tamo tattha na vijjati.*
> *Yadā ca attanāvedi,*
> *muni monena brāhmaṇo,*
> *atha rūpā arūpā ca,*
> *sukhadukkhā pamuccati.*[27]

---

[26] E.g. S II 45, *Bhikkhusutta*; or A II 178, *Ummaggasutta*.

[27] Ud 9, *Bāhiyasutta*.

The verse can be fully explained along the lines of interpretation we have adopted. By way of further proof of the inadequacy of the commentarial explanation of the references to the sun, the moon and the stars in this verse, we may draw attention to the following points.

According to the commentary the verse is supposed to express that there are no sun, moon or stars in that mysterious place called *anupādisesa Nibbānadhātu*, which is incomprehensible to worldlings. We may, however, point out that the verbs used in the verse in this connection do not convey the sense that the sun, the moon and the stars are simply nonexistent there. They have something more to say.

For instance, with regard to the stars it is said that there the stars do not shine, *na tattha sukkā jotanti*. If in truth and fact stars are not there, some other verb like *na dissanti*, "are not seen," or *na vijjanti*, "do not exist," could have been used.

With reference to the sun and the moon, also, similar verbs could have been employed. But what we actually find here, are verbs expressive of spreading light, shining, or appearing beautiful: *Na tattha sukkā jotanti,* "there the stars do not shine"; *ādicco nappakāsati,* "the sun spreads not its lustre"; *na tattha candimā bhāti,* "the moon does not appear resplendent there."

These are not mere prosaic statements. The verse in question is a joyous utterance, *Udānagāthā*, of extraordinary depth. There is nothing recondite about it.

In our earlier assessment of the commentarial interpretation we happened to lay special stress on the words 'even though.' We are now going to explain the significance of that emphasis. For the commentary, the line *tamo tattha na vijjati,* "no darkness is to be found there," is a big riddle. The sun, the moon and the stars are not there. Even though they are not there, presumably, no darkness is to be found there.

However, when we consider the law of superseding, we have already mentioned, we are compelled to give a totally different interpretation. The sun, the moon and the stars are not manifest, precisely because of the light of that non-manifestative consciousness. As it is lustrous on all sides, *sabbato pabha*, there is no darkness there and luminaries like the stars, the sun and the moon do not shine there.

This verse of uplift thus reveals a wealth of information relevant to our topic. Not only the exhortation to Bāhiya, but this verse also throws a flood of light on the subject of *Nibbāna*.

That extraordinary place, which the commentary often identifies with the term *anupādisesa Nibbānadhātu*, is this mind of ours. It is in order to indicate the luminosity of this mind that the Buddha used those peculiar expressions in this verse of uplift.

What actually happens in the attainment to the fruit of *arahant*-hood? The worldling discerns the world around him with the help of six narrow beams of light, namely the six sense-bases. When the superior lustre of wisdom arises, those six sense-bases go down. This cessation of the six sense-bases could also be referred to as the cessation of name-and-form, *nāmarūpanirodha*, or the cessation of consciousness, *viññāṇanirodha*.

The cessation of the six sense-bases does not mean that one does not see anything. What one sees then is voidness. It is an in-'sight.' He gives expression to it with the words *suñño loko*, "void is the world." What it means is that all the sense-objects, which the worldling grasps as real and truly existing, get penetrated through with wisdom and become non-manifest.

If we are to add something more to this interpretation of the *Bāhiyasutta* by way of review, we may say that this discourse illustrates the six qualities of the *Dhamma*, namely *svākkhāto*, well proclaimed, *sandiṭṭhiko*, visible here and now, *akāliko*, timeless, *ehipassiko*, inviting to come and see, *opanayiko*, leading onward and *paccattaṃ veditabbo viññūhi*, to be realized by the wise each one by himself. These six qualities are wonderfully exemplified by this discourse.

In a previous sermon we had occasion to bring up a simile of a dewdrop, dazzling in the morning sunshine.[28] The task of seeing the spectrum of rainbow colours through a tiny dew drop hanging from a creeper or a leaf is one that calls for a high degree of mindfulness. Simply by standing or sitting with one's face towards the rising sun, one will not be able to catch a glimpse of the brilliant spectrum of rainbow colours through the dewdrop. It requires a particular viewpoint. Only when one focuses on that viewpoint, can one see it.

So it is with the spectrum of the six qualities of the *Dhamma*. Here, too, the correct viewpoint is a must, and that is right view. Reflection on the meaning of deep discourses helps one to straighten up right view.

Where right view is lacking, morality inclines towards dogmatic attachment to rituals, *sīlabbataparāmāsa*. Concentration turns out to be wrong concentration, *micchā samādhi*.

Like the one who sits facing the sun, one might be looking in the direction of the *Dhamma*, but right view is not something one inherits by merely going to refuge to the Buddha. It has to be developed with effort and proper attention. View is something that has to be straightened up. For *diṭṭhujukamma*, the act of straightening up one's view is reckoned as one of the ten skilful deeds, *kusalakamma*.

So however long one may sit with folded legs, gazing at the Buddha sun, one might not be able to see the six rainbow colours of the *Dhamma*. One may be short of just one-hundredth of an inch as the proper adjustment for right view. Yet it is a must. Once that adjustment is made, one immediately, then and there, *tavad'eva*, catches a glimpse of the spectrum of the *Dhamma* that the Buddha has proclaimed.

We have stressed the importance of right view in particular, because many are grappling with a self-created problem, concern-

---

[28] See sermon 9.

ing the proper alignment between the triple training and the right view of the noble eightfold path.

Now as to the triple training, morality, concentration and wisdom, we find wisdom mentioned last. It seems, then, that we have to perfect morality first, then develop concentration, and only lastly wisdom. One need not think of wisdom before that. But when we come to the noble eightfold path, we find a different order of values. Here right view takes precedence. As a matter of fact, in the *Mahācattārīsakasutta* of the *Majjhima Nikāya* we find the Buddha repeatedly declaring emphatically *tatra, bhikkhave, sammā diṭṭhi pubbaṅgamā*, "monks, therein right view takes precedence."[29] Even in a context where the subject is morality, we find a similar statement. So how are we to resolve this issue?

In the noble eightfold path, pride of place is given to right view, which is representative of the wisdom group. As the well-known definition goes, right view and right thoughts belong to the wisdom group; right speech, right action and right livelihood come under the morality group; and right effort, right mindfulness and right concentration belong to the concentration group.

So in this way, in the noble eightfold path, wisdom comes first, then morality and lastly concentration. But in the context of these three groups, firstly comes morality, secondly concentration and lastly wisdom, Here, too, the answer given by the *arahant*-nun Venerable Dhammadinnā to the lay disciple Visākha comes to our aid.

The lay disciple Visākha poses the following question to Venerable Dhammadinnā: *Ariyena nu kho ayye aṭṭhaṅgikena maggena tayo khandhā saṅgahitā, udāhu tīhi khandhehi ariyo aṭṭhaṅgiko maggo saṅgahito?* "Good lady, are the three groups morality, concentration and wisdom, included by the noble

---

[29] M III 71, *Mahācattārīsakasutta.*

eightfold path, or is the noble eightfold path included by the three groups?"[30]

Even at that time there may have been some who raised such questions. That is probably the reason for such a query. Then the *arahant*-nun Dhammadinnā answers: *Na kho āvuso Visākha ariyena aṭṭhaṅgikena maggena tayo khandhā saṅgahitā, tīhi ca kho āvuso Visākha khandhehi ariyo aṭṭhaṅgiko maggo saṅgahito.* "Friend Visākha, it is not that the threefold training is included by the noble eightfold path, but the noble eightfold path is included by the threefold training."

Since this appears to be something of a tangle, let us try to illustrate the position with some other kind of tangle. Suppose someone is trying to climb up a long rope, made up of three strands. As he climbs up, his fingertips might come now in contact with the first strand, now with the second and now with the third. He is not worried about the order of the three strands, so long as they are well knit. One can safely climb up, holding onto the three strands, only when they are firmly wound up into a sturdy rope.

All these questions seem to have arisen due to an attitude of taking too seriously the numerical order of things. To the noble disciple climbing up the rope of the noble eightfold path, there need not be any confusion between the numerical order of the triple training and that of the noble eightfold path. But if someone taking the cue from the order of the triple training neglects right view or ignores its prime import, he might end up confused.

All in all, we are now in a position to correctly assess the deep significance of the *Bāhiyasutta*. Here we have the quintessence of the entire *Saddhamma*. We are not confronted with heaps of perceptual data, which we are told today are essential requisites for admission into the 'city' of *Nibbāna*.

For the ordinary worldling, amassing a particular set of percepts or concepts seems a qualification for entering *Nibbāna*. But what

---

[30] M I 301, *CūḷaVedallasutta*.

we have here, is a way of liberating the mind even from latencies to percepts, cf. *saññā nānusenti*, *Madhupiṇḍikasutta*, "perceptions do not lie latent."[31] There is no heaping up anew.

What are called "extraneous taints," *āgantukā upakkilesā*,[32] are not confined to the well known defilements in the world. They include all the rust and dust we have been collecting throughout this long *saṃsāra*, with the help of the influxes, *āsavā*. They include even the heap of percepts which the world calls 'knowledge.' Even numerals are part of it.

The Buddha has briefly expressed here the mode of practice for disabusing the mind from all such taints. Therefore there is no reason for underestimating the value of this discourse, by calling it *vohāra desanā*, conventional teaching. This discourse in the *Udāna* is one that is truly 'up'-lifting. It indeed deserves a paean of joy.

---

31 M I 108, *Madhupiṇḍikasutta*.

32 A I 10, *Accharāsaṅghātavagga*.

Nibbāna Sermon 16

Namo tassa Bhagavato Arahato Sammāsambuddhassa
Namo tassa Bhagavato Arahato Sammāsambuddhassa
Namo tassa Bhagavato Arahato Sammāsambuddhassa

Etaṃ santaṃ, etaṃ paṇītaṃ, yadidaṃ sabbasaṅkhārasamatho sabbūpadhipaṭinissaggo taṇhakkhayo virāgo nirodho nibbānaṃ.[1]

"This is peaceful, this is excellent, namely the stilling of all preparations, the relinquishment of all assets, the destruction of craving, detachment, cessation, extinction."

With the permission of the Most Venerable Great Preceptor and the assembly of the venerable meditative monks.

This is the sixteenth sermon in the series of sermons on *Nibbāna*. In the course of our discussion of the *Bāhiyasutta* in our last sermon, we drew attention to the wide gap that exists between the sensory experience of the worldling and that experience the *arahant* gets through the eye of wisdom. It is the same gap that obtains between the two terms *papañca* and *nippapañca*. In sensory experience, which is based on worldly expressions, worldly usages and worldly concepts, there is a discrimination between a thing to be grasped and the one who grasps, or, in other words, a subject-object relationship.

There is always a bifurcation, a dichotomy, in the case of sensory perception. If there is a seen, there has to be something seen and

[1] M I 436, *MahāMālunkyasutta*.

the one who sees. That is the logic. In the *Bāhiyasutta*, beginning with 'in the seen there will be just the seen,' the Buddha proclaimed to the ascetic Bāhiya a brief exhortation on *Dhamma* which enables one to transcend the above narrow viewpoint and attain the state of non-proliferation or *nippapañca*.

There is nothing to see, no one to see, only 'a seen' is there. The cause of all these conceptual proliferation, or *papañca*, in the world is contact. The *arahants* understood this by their insight into the fact that the seen, the heard, the sensed and the cognized are simply so many collocations of conditions which come together for a moment due to contact, only to break up and get dispersed the next moment.

What is called the seen, the heard, the sensed and the cognized are for the worldling so many 'things.' But to the wisdom eye of the *arahants* they appear as mere conglomerations of conditions, dependent on contact, which momentarily come together and then get dispersed. This insight into the dependence on contact, *phassam paṭicca,* is the very essence of the law of dependent arising, *paṭicca samuppāda*. It is equivalent to seeing the law of dependent arising itself.

In order to transcend the narrow point of view limited to the bases of sense contact or the six sense spheres and realize the state of *Nibbāna* indicated by the words *viññāṇaṃ anidassanaṃ, anantaṃ sabbato pabhaṃ,*[2] "consciousness which is non-manifestative, endless, lustrous on all sides," one has to see the cessation of contact.

In a certain discourse in the *Mucalindavagga* of the *Udāna*, the Buddha has declared in a verse of uplift that the cessation of contact comes about only by doing away with that which brings about contact. The wandering ascetics of other sects grew jealous of the Buddha and his congregation of monks, because of their own loss of gain and honour, and began to hurl abuse on monks in

---

[2] D I 223, *Kevaḍḍhasutta.*

the village and in the forest. A group of monks came and reported this to the Buddha. The Buddha's response to it was only a paean of joy. *Udāna* actually means a spontaneous utterance of joy, and the verse he uttered was such a one. But it embodied an instruction on *Dhamma* and a norm of *Dhamma* as well:

Gāme araññe sukhadukkhaphuṭṭho,
nev'attato no parato dahetha,
phusanti phassā upadhiṃ paṭicca,
Nirūpadhiṃ kena phuseyyum phassā.[3]

In the first two lines we get an instruction:

"Touched by pain in village or in forest,
Think not in terms of oneself or others,"

The reason for it is given in the norm of *Dhamma* which follows:

"Touches can touch one, because of assets,
How can touches touch him, who is asset-less?"

This is all what the Buddha uttered. From this we can glean another aspect of the significance of the terms *sabbūpadhipaṭinissagga*, relinquishment of all assets, and *nirupadhi*, the asset-less, used with reference to *Nibbāna*.

In a number of previous sermons we happened to explain the concept of *upadhi* to some extent, as and when the terms *upadhi* and *paṭinissagga* came up.[4] To refresh our memory, we may summarize all that now. What is the concept of *upadhi*, or "assets," recognized by the world?

---

[3] Ud 12, *Sakkārasutta*.

[4] See sermon 8.

Whatever that bolsters up the ego, be it gold, silver, pearls, gems, money, house and property, deposits and assets. All these are reckoned as *upadhi* in general. But when considered from the point of view of *Dhamma*, *upadhi* in a deeper sense stands for this fivefold grasping groups, *pañcupādānakkhandha*.

Upādānakkhandha literally means "groups of grasping." Groups of grasping do not necessarily imply that there are material objects to be grasped. But the worldling, overcome by that triple proliferation of cravings, conceits and views, and carried away by the worldly conventions, imagines those groups of grasping as things grasped and deposited. The concept of *upadhi* as assets has arisen as a result of this tendency to think of groups of grasping as things grasped and deposited. So it turns out to be a question of viewpoint.

Cravings, conceits and views prompt one to look upon all what one has grasped so far and what one hopes to grasp in the future as things one is grasping right now. One thinks of them as things deposited in a safe. The worldlings are holding on to such a mass of assets.

Nibbāna is the relinquishment of all such assets, accumulated in the mind. In order to relinquish these assets there must be some kind of understanding – an enlightenment. The vanity of all these assets has to be seen through by the light of wisdom. It is only by seeing their vanity that the assets are relinquished. In fact it is not so much a deliberate giving up of assets, as a sequential liquidation.

In a previous sermon we gave an illustration of the situation that precipitates relinquishment. Let us bring it up again. We found the cinema quite helpful as an illustration. In explaining the phenomenon of relinquishment of assets with reference to the cinema, we described how the assets accumulated in the minds of the audience, that is, the assets proper to the cinema world woven around the story that is filmed, are automatically abandoned when the cinema hall gets lit up.[5] Then one understands the illusory nature of what has been going on. It is that understanding, that enlightenment, which precipitates the giving up or relinquishment of assets.

To go a step further in this illustration, when lights came on the *saṅkhāras* or preparations pertaining to the film show got exposed for what they are. In fact, *saṅkhāra* is a word that has associations with the dramatic tradition in its relation to the acting of actors and actresses down to their make-up, which is so artificial and spurious.

When the cinema hall gets lit up all of a sudden, one who has been enjoying the film show is momentarily thrown out of the cinema world, because those preparations are pacified or nullified, *sabba saṅkhārasamatho*. As a consequence of it, the heap of experiences which he had hitherto regarded as real and genuine, lose their sanction. Those assets get liquidated or relinquished, *sabbūpadhipaṭinissagga*. In their absence, that craving necessary for the appreciation or enjoyment of the scenes to come becomes extinct, *taṇhakkhayo*. When craving is gone, the floridity of the scenes to come also fades away, *virāga*. With that fading away or decolouration, the film show ceases for the person concerned, *nirodha*, though technically the movie is going on. Because of that cessation all the fires of defilements proper to the cinema world, with which he was burning, get extinguished, *Nibbāna*.

So here we have the full gamut of the cinema simile as an illustration for *Nibbāna*. This kind of awakening in the cinema world gives us a clue to the fact that the assets, *upadhi*, are relinquished through an understanding born of enlightenment in the light of wisdom. This in fact is something that should be deeply ingrained in our minds. Therefore we shall endeavour to give some more illustrations to that effect.

---

5 See sermons 5, 7, 9, 11, 15.

In our everyday life, too, we sometimes see and hear of instances where assets get relinquished due to understanding. Someone heaps up a huge bundle of currency notes of the highest denomination, deposits it in his safe and keeps watch and ward over it day and night. One fine morning he wakes up to hear that for some reason or other that currency note has been fully devalued by law the previous night. How does he look upon the wads of notes in his safe now? For him, it is now a mere heap of papers. The craving, conceit and view he had earlier in regard to the notes are completely gone. The bank notes are no longer valid. He might as well make a bonfire of it. So this is some sort of relinquishment of assets in the world, however temporary it may be.

Another person gets a sudden transfer and is getting ready to leave for his new station. His immovable assets he is forced to leave behind, but his movable assets he hurriedly gathers up to take with him. The vehicle has already come and is tooting impatiently, signalling delay. It is well past time, but his 'preparations' are not finished. Time-pressed, in hot haste, he is running here and there. At last, when he can delay no longer, he grabs the utmost he can take and darts to the door step. Just then, he wakes up. It was only a dream! The transfer came in a dream. No real vehicle, no real preparation, only a panting for nothing!

So here we have an 'awakening' peculiar to the dream world. This is an instance of letting go of assets connected with a dream. We go through such experiences quite often. Of course, we take it for granted that when we pass from the dream world to the real world, the assets proper to the dream world drop off. But are we sure that in leaving the dream world we are entering a real world? Is awakening from a dream a true awakening when considered from the point of view of the *Dhamma*? Do we actually open our eyes, when we awaken from a dream?

Terms like *Buddha*, *bodhi* and *sambodhi* convey the sense of awakening as well as understanding. Sometimes in the *Dhamma* the emphasis is on the sense of awakening. Here then is a kind of awakening.

Expressions like *dhammacakkhu*, "Dhamma-eye," *paññā-cakkhu*, "Wisdom-eye," and *cakkhuṃ udapādi*, "the eye arose," bespeak of an arising of some sort of an eye. We already have eyes, but an eye is said to arise. All this goes to show that in the context of *Nibbāna*, where we are concerned with the deeper aspects of the *Dhamma*, the awakening from a dream is not a true awakening. It is only a passage from one dream world to another.

But let us see how the concept of *upadhi*, or assets, goes deeper. What lies before us is the dream of *saṃsāra*. In order to awaken from this dream, we have to understand somehow the vanity of all assets connected with the dream that is *saṃsāra*. The fact that this understanding also comes through some illumination we have already explained the other day in our discussion of the paean of joy at the end of the *Bāhiyasutta*.[6] As we pointed out then, the world of the six sense-bases which the worldlings regard as 'their world,' when examined against the background of that *Udāna* verse reveals itself to be no more than six narrow beams of light, appearing through a solidly thick curtain, namely the darkness of delusion.

We happened to mention the other day that the sun, the moon and the stars shine precisely because of the presence of darkness. In the non-manifestative consciousness which is infinite and lustrous all round, *viññāṇaṃ anidassanaṃ, anantaṃ sabbato pabhaṃ*, sun, moon and stars are not manifest, because there is absolutely no darkness for them to shine forth. Even the formless, which is the penumbra of form, disappears in that penetrative lustre of wisdom.

So the relinquishment of all assets, *Nibbāna*, is not like the other temporary awakenings already mentioned. Those three instances of awakening are of a temporary nature. The awakening in the cinema world is extremely short lived. That film fan, although he became disenchanted with the scenes because of the

---

6 Ud 9, *Bāhiyasutta*; see sermon 15.

unexpected sudden illumination of the cinema hall, when it is dark again, influxes of sensuality, existence and ignorance so overwhelm him that he gets engrossed in the cinema world as before.

The case of the devalued currency note is also like that. Though the cravings, conceits and views about the devalued note are gone, one still runs after notes that are valid. As for the awakening from a dream, we all know that it is temporary. When again we go to sleep, we have dreams.

But the awakening in *Nibbāna* is not of such a temporary character. Why? Because all the influxes that lead one into the *saṃsāric* slumber with its dreams of recurrent births are made extinct in the light of that perfect knowledge of realization. That is why the term *āsavakkhaya*, extinction of influxes, is used in the discourses as an epithet of *Nibbāna*. The *arahants* accomplish this feat in the concentration on the fruit of *arahant*-hood, *arahattaphalasamādhi*.

Though there are enough instances of references to this *arahattaphalasamādhi* in the discourses, they are very often interpreted differently. As we have already seen in the context of that verse of uplift in the *Bāhiyasutta*, some discourses alluding to the nature of an *arahant*'s mind have been misinterpreted, so much so that there is a lot of confusion in regard to the concept of *Nibbāna*. As a matter of fact, that concentration peculiar to an *arahant* is of an extraordinary type. It baffles the worldling's powers of understanding. This can well be inferred from the following verse of the *Ratanasutta*:

Yaṃ Buddhaseṭṭho parivaṇṇayī suciṃ,
samādhim ānantarikaññam āhu,
samādhinā tena samo na vijjati,

idampi Dhamme ratanaṃ paṇītaṃ,
etena saccena suvatthi hotu.[7]

"That pure concentration, which the Supremely
Awakened One extolled,
That concentration which the Noble Ones call
'immediate' (*ānantarika*),
There is no concentration comparable to it,
This is the excellent jewel nature of the *Dhamma,*
By the power of this truth may there be well-being."

This incomparable and extraordinary concentration has given rise to many problems concerning the concept of *Nibbāna*. The extraordinariness of this concentration of the *arahant* is to some extent connected with the term *ānantarika*, referred to above. Now let us turn our attention to the significance of this term.

The verse says that the concentration of the *arahant* is also known as *ānantarika*. The term *ānantarika* is suggestive of an extraordinary aspect of the realization of *Nibbāna*. Immediately after the extinction of the defilements through the knowledge of the path of *arahant*-hood one realizes *Nibbāna*, the cessation of existence or the cessation of the six sense-bases. As we mentioned earlier, it is as if the results are out as soon as one has written for an examination.[8] One need not wait for the results. Realization is immediate.

There is a special term to denote this experience of realization, namely, *aññā*. It is a highly significant term, derived from *ājānāti*, "to know fully." *Aññā* is "full comprehension."

The concentration of the fruit of *arahant*-hood is also called *aññāphalasamādhi* and *aññāvimokkha*. *Aññā* carries with it a high degree of importance. We come across in the *Sutta* terminology a

---

7 Sn 226, *Ratanasutta*.

8 See sermon 1.

number of terms derived from the root *ñā*, "to know," namely *saññā, viññāṇa, paññā, ñāṇa, abhiññā, pariññā, aññā*. *Saññā* is "perception," *viññāṇa* is, radically, "discriminative knowledge," *paññā* is "distinctive knowledge," *ñāṇa* is "knowledge" as such, *abhiññā* is "specialized knowledge," *pariññā* is "comprehensive knowledge," *aññā* is that "final knowledge" of certitude through realization. The high degree of importance attached to *aññā* is revealed by the following two verses in the *Itivuttaka*:

Sekhassa sikkhamānassa
ujumaggānusārino
khayasmiṃ paṭhamaṃ ñāṇaṃ
tato aññā anantarā.

Tato aññā vimuttassa,
ñāṇaṃ ve hoti tādino
akuppā me vimuttīti
bhavasaṃyojanakkhaye.[9]

"To the disciple in higher training, as he fares along
Training according to the straight path,
There arises first the knowledge of extinction,
And then immediately the final knowledge of certitude.

"And to that steadfast such-like-one,
Thus released by final knowledge of certitude,
There arises the thought: 'Unshakeable is my
deliverance,'
Upon the destruction of fetters of existence."

It is evident from these two verses that the realization referred to is in many ways final and complete. In point of fact, these two verses

---

[9] It 53, *Indriyasutta*.

have been presented by the Buddha in this context by way of defining three things relevant to the realization of *Nibbāna*. These three are called faculties, *indriya*. They are:

1) *anaññātaññāssāmīt'indriya*

2) *aññindriya*

3) *aññātāvindriya*

The term *aññā* is implicit even in the faculty called *anaññātaññāssāmīt'indriya*. *Anaññātaññāssāmi* means "I shall know what has not been fully known." This is the definition of what in the verse is referred to as *khayasmiṃ paṭhamaṃ ñāṇaṃ*, "first there is the knowledge of extinction." The knowledge of the extinction of the defilements is called *anaññātaññāssāmīt'indriya* in this context. The words *tato aññā anantarā*, "and then immediately the final knowledge of certitude," refer to that faculty of final knowledge, or *aññindriya*. The knowledge that prompts the conviction "unshakeable is my deliverance" is the knowledge and vision of deliverance, which is defined as *aññātāvindriya*. It refers to one who is endowed with the final knowledge of certitude.

The difference between *aññindriya* and *aññātāvindriya* is a subtle one. For instance, the expression *bhuttāvī pavārito*, one has finished eating and made a sign of refusal, decisively shows that one has had one's fill.[10] Similarly, it is that *aññātāvindriya* (note the past active participle), which prompts the words "unshakeable is my deliverance," *akuppā me vimutti*.[11] The knowledge and vision of deliverance is reassuring to that extent.

As the above quoted verse from the *Ratanasutta* makes it clear, this unique and extraordinary concentration has been extolled by the Buddha in various discourses. But for some reason or other,

---

10 Vin IV 82, *Pācittiya* 35.

11 E.g. M I 167, *Ariyapariyesanasutta*.

the commentators have simply glossed over references to it, though they sometimes expatiate on a particle of mere grammatical interest. Let us now take up for comment a few such discourses.

In the section of the Elevens in the *Aṅguttara Nikāya* there comes a discourse called *Sandhasutta*. There the Buddha gives to Venerable Sandha a description of a level of concentration characteristic of an excellent thoroughbred of a man. It is a strange type of concentration. One who has that concentration is described as follows:

> *So neva paṭhaviṃ nissāya jhāyati, na āpaṃ nissāya jhāyati, na tejaṃ nissāya jhāyati, na vāyaṃ nissāya jhāyati, na ākāsānañcāyatanaṃ nissāya jhāyati, na viññāṇañcāyatanaṃ nissāya jhāyati, na ākiñcaññāyatanaṃ nissāya jhāyati, na nevasaññānāsaññāyatanaṃ nissāya jhāyati, na idhalokaṃ nissāya jhāyati, na para-lokaṃ nissāya jhāyati, yam p'idaṃ diṭṭhaṃ sutaṃ mutaṃ viññātaṃ pattaṃ pariyesitaṃ anuvicaritaṃ manasā, tam pi nissāya na jhāyati, jhāyati ca pana.*
>
> *Evaṃ jhāyiṃ ca pana, Sandha, bhadraṃ purisājānīyaṃ saindā devā sabrahmakā sapajapatikā ārakā 'va namassanti:*
>
> > *Namo te purisājañña,*
> > *namo te purisuttama,*
> > *yassa te nābhijānāma,*
> > *yampi nissāya jhāyasi.*[12]

In this discourse, the Buddha gives, as an illustration, the musing of a thoroughbred of a horse, which we shall drop for brevity's

---

[12] A V 324, *Sandhasutta.*

sake. The musing of an excellent thoroughbred of a man is described as follows:

> "He muses not dependent on earth, water, fire, air, the sphere of infinite space, the sphere of infinite consciousness, the sphere of nothingness, the sphere of neither-perception-nor-non-perception, he muses not dependent on this world or on the world beyond, whatever is seen, heard, sensed, cognized, attained, sought after, traversed by the mind, dependent on all that he muses not – and yet he does muse.
>
> "Moreover, Sandha, to him thus musing the *devas* with Indra, with Brahmā and with Pajāpati even from afar bow down, saying:
>
>> 'Homage to you, O thoroughbred of a man,
>> Homage to you, O most excellent of men,
>> For what it is on which you go on musing,
>> We are at a loss to comprehend.'"

Though all possible objects of concentration are negated, the Buddha affirms that he does muse. Venerable Sandha, out of curiosity inquires: "But then how, Lord, does that thoroughbred of a man muse?" The Buddha explains that while in that state of concentration, the perception of earth in earth, for instance, is gone for him, *pathaviyā pathavīsaññā vibhūtā hoti*. So also in the case of other objects of the senses, such as water, fire, air, down to whatever is seen, heard, sensed, cognized, attained, sought after and traversed by the mind.

The verb *vibhūtā*, repeatedly used in this connection, is however differently interpreted in the commentary. It is paraphrased by *pākaṭā*, which means "clearly manifest."[13] This interpretation seems to distort the meaning of the entire passage.

It is true that in certain contexts *vibhūta* and *avibhūta* are taken to mean "manifest" and "unmanifest," since *vibhava* is a word which seems to have undergone some semantic development. However, its primary sense is sufficiently evident in the *Sutta* terminology. For instance, the twin term *bhava/vibhava* stands for "existence" and "non-existence." In this context, too, *vibhūta* seems to have a negative sense, rather than the sense of being manifest. Hence our rendering: "T... he perception of earth is gone for him."

It is obvious enough by the recurrent negative particle in the first part of the *Sutta* (*neva paṭhaviṃ nissāya jhāyati, na āpaṃ nissāya jhāyati*, etc.) that all those perceptions are negated and not affirmed as manifest. The commentator seems to have missed the true import of the *Sutta* when he interprets *vibhūta* to mean 'manifest.'

If further proof is required, we may quote instances where the word *vibhūta* is used in the *Suttas* to convey such senses as "gone," "departed" or "transcended." In one of the verses we happened to quote earlier from the *Kalahavivādasutta*, there was the question posed: *Kismiṃ vibhūte na phusanti phassā?*[14] "When what is not there, do touches not touch?" The verse that follows gives the answer: *Rūpe vibhūte na phusanti phassā.*[15] "When form is not there, touches do not touch." In this context, too, *vibhūta* implies absence.

A clearer instance comes in the *Posālamāṇavapucchā* of the *Pārāyanavagga* in the *Sutta Nipāta*, namely the term *vibhūta-rūpasaññissa*, occurring in one of the verses there.[16] The canonical

---

[13] Mp V 80.

[14] Sn 871, *Kalahavivādasutta*; see sermon 11.

[15] Sn 872, *Kalahavivādasutta*.

[16] Sn 1113, *Posālamāṇavapucchā*.

commentary *Cūḷaniddesa*, which the commentator often draws upon, also paraphrases the term with the words *vigatā, atikkantā, samatikkantā, vītivattā,*[17] "gone, transcended, fully transcended, and superseded."

So the word *vibhūta* in the passage in question definitely implies the absence of all those perceptions in that concentration. This, then, is a unique concentration. It has none of the objects which the worldlings usually associate with a level of concentration.

We come across a number of instances in the discourses, in which the Buddha and some other monks have been interrogated on the nature of this extraordinary concentration. Sometimes even Venerable Ānanda is seen to confront the Buddha with a question on this point. In a discourse included in the section of the Elevens in the *Aṅguttara Nikāya*, Venerable Ānanda questions on the possibility of attaining to such a concentration with an air of wonderment:

> *Siyā nu kho, bhante, bhikkhuno tathārūpo samādhipaṭilābho yathā neva pathaviyaṃ pathavīsaññī assa, na āpasmiṃ āposaññī assa, na tejasmiṃ tejosaññī assa, na vāyasmiṃ vāyosaññī assa, na ākāsānañcāyatane ākāsā-nañcāyatanasaññī assa, na viññāṇañcāyatane viññāṇan-cāyatanasaññī assa, na ākiñcaññāyatane ākiñcaññā-yatanasaññī assa, na nevasaññānāsaññāyatane neva-saññānāsaññāyatanasaññī assa, na idhaloke idhaloka-saññī assa, na paraloke paralokasaññī assa, yam p'idaṃ diṭṭhaṃ sutaṃ mutaṃ viññātaṃ pattaṃ pari-yesitaṃ anuvicaritaṃ manasā tatrāpi na saññī assa, saññī ca pana assa?*[18]

---

[17] Nid II 166 (Burm. ed.)

[18] A V 318, *Saññāsutta*.

> "Could there be, Lord, for a monk such an attainment of concentration wherein he will not be conscious (literally 'percipient') of earth in earth, nor of water in water, nor of fire in fire, nor of air in air, nor will he be conscious of the sphere of infinite space in the sphere of infinite space, nor of the sphere of infinite consciousness in the sphere of infinite consciousness, nor of the sphere of nothingness in the sphere of nothingness, nor of the sphere of neither-perception-nor-non-perception in the sphere of neither-perception-nor-non-perception, nor will he be conscious of a this world in this world, nor of a world beyond in a world beyond, whatever is seen, heard, sensed, cognized, attained, sought after, traversed by the mind, even of it he will not be conscious – and yet he will be conscious?"

Whereas the passage quoted earlier began with *so neva pathaviṃ nissāya jhāyati*, "he muses not dependent on earth" and ended with the emphatic assertion *jhāyati ca pana*, "and yet he does muse," here we have a restatement of it in terms of perception, beginning with *neva pathaviyaṃ pathavīsaññī* and ending with *saññī ca pana assa*. The Buddha answers in the affirmative and on being questioned as to how it is possible he gives the following explanation:

> *Idh'Ānanda, bhikkhu, evaṃ saññī hoti: Etaṃ santaṃ, etaṃ paṇītaṃ, yadidaṃ sabbasaṅkhārasamatho sabbūpadhipaṭinissaggo taṇhakkhayo virāgo nirodho nibbānan'ti. Evaṃ kho, Ānanda, siyā bhikkhuno tathārūpo samādhipaṭilābho . . .*

> "Herein, Ānanda, a monk is thus conscious (*evaṃ saññī*): This is peaceful, this is excellent, namely the stilling of all preparations, the relinquishment of all assets, the destruction of craving, detachment, cessation, extinction. It is thus, Ānanda, that there could be for a monk such an attainment of concentration . . ."

This, in fact, is the theme of all our sermons. Venerable Ānanda, of course, rejoiced in the Buddha's words, but approached Venerable Sāriputta also and put forward the same question. Venerable Sāriputta gave the same answer verbatim.

Then Venerable Ānanda gave expression to a joyous approbation: *Acchariyaṃ āvuso, abbhutaṃ āvuso, yatra hi nāma satthu ca sāvakassa ca atthena atthaṃ vyañjanena vyañjanaṃ saṃsandissati samessati na viggahissati, yad idaṃ aggapadasmiṃ.* "Friend, it is wonderful, it is marvelous, that there is perfect conformity between the statements of the teacher and the disciple to the letter and to the spirit without any discord on the question of the highest level of attainment."

These last words, in particular, make it sufficiently clear that this concentration is *arahattaphalasamādhi*, the concentration proper to an *arahant*. Here, then, is the experience of *Nibbāna*, extraordinary and unique.

Quite a number of discourses touch upon this *samādhi*. Let us take up some of the more important references. Venerable Ānanda is seen to pose the same question, rephrased, on yet another occasion. It runs thus:

> *Siyā nu kho, bhante, tathārūpo samādhipaṭilābho yathā na cakkhuṃ manasikareyya, na rūpaṃ manasikareyya, na sotaṃ manasikareyya, na saddaṃ manasikareyya, na ghānaṃ manasikareyya, na gandhaṃ manasikareyya, na jivhaṃ manasikareyya, na rasaṃ manasikareyya, na kāyaṃ manasikareyya, na phoṭṭhabbaṃ manasikareyya, na pathaviṃ manasikareyya, na āpaṃ manasikareyya, na tejaṃ manasikareyya, na vāyaṃ manasikareyya, na ākāsānañcāyatanaṃ manasikareyya, na viññāṇañcāyatanaṃ manasikareyya, na ākiñcaññāyatanaṃ manasikareyya, na nevasaññānāsaññāyatanaṃ manasikareyya, na idhalokaṃ manasikareyya, na paralokaṃ mana-*

> *sikareyya, yam p'idaṃ diṭṭhaṃ sutaṃ mutaṃ viññātaṃ pattaṃ pariyesitaṃ anuvicaritaṃ manasā tam pi na manasikareyya, manasi ca pana kareyya?*[19]

> "Could there be, Lord, for a monk such an attainment of concentration wherein he will not be attending to the eye, nor to form, nor to the ear, nor to sound, nor to the nose, nor to smell, nor to the tongue, nor to taste, nor to the body, nor to touch, nor to earth, nor to water, nor to fire, nor to air, nor to the sphere of infinite space, nor to the sphere of infinite consciousness, nor to the sphere of nothingness, nor to the sphere of neither-perception-nor-non-perception, nor to this world, nor to the world beyond, whatever is seen, heard, sensed, cognized, attained, sought after, traversed by the mind, even to that he will not be attending – and yet he will be attending?"

"There could be such a concentration," says the Buddha, and Venerable Ānanda rejoins with his inquisitive: "How, Lord, could there be?" Then the Buddha gives the following explanation, which tallies with the one earlier given:

> *Idh'Ānanda, bhikkhu evaṃ manasi karoti: Etaṃ santaṃ, etaṃ paṇītaṃ, yadidaṃ sabbasaṅkhārasamatho sabūpadhipaṭinissaggo taṇhakkhayo virāgo nirodho nibbānan'ti. Evaṃ kho, Ānanda, siyā bhikkhuno tathārūpo samādhipaṭilābho . . .*

> "Herein, Ānanda , a monk attends thus: This is peaceful, this is excellent, namely the stilling of all preparations, the relinquishment of all assets, the destruction of craving, de-

---

[19] A V 321, *Manasikārasutta*.

tachment, cessation, extinction. It is thus, Ānanda, that there could be such an attainment of concentration . . ."

In the light of the foregoing discussion, we are now in a position to take up for comment that enigmatic verse of the *Kalahavivādasutta*, which in a previous sermon we left unexplained, giving only a slight hint in the form of a simile:[20]

Na saññasaññī na visaññasaññī,
no pi asaññī na vibhūtasaññī,
evaṃ sametassa vibhoti rūpaṃ,
saññānidānā hi papañcasaṅkhā.[21]

The general trend of this verse seems to imply something like this: The worldlings usually believe that one has to have some form of perception or other. But the one referred to in this verse is not percipient with any such perception, *na saññasaññī*. As if to forestall the question, whether he is then in a swoon, there is the negation *na visaññasaññī*. A possible alternative, like a plane of existence devoid of perception, is also avoided by the emphatic assertion *no pi asaññī*. Yet another possibility, that he has gone beyond perception or rescinded it, is rejected as well with the words *na vibhūtasaññī*.

The third line says that it is to one thus endowed that form ceases to exist, while the last line seems to give an indication as to why it is so: *Saññānidānā hi papañcasaṅkhā*, "for reckonings born of proliferation have perception as their source."

The nature of these reckonings we have already discussed at length. The conclusion here given is that they are rooted in *papañca*. Now the passages we have so far quoted are suggestive

---

20 See sermon 11.

21 Sn 874, *Kalahavivādasutta*.

of such a state of consciousness. Briefly stated, even the emphatic tone characteristic of these discourses is sufficient proof of it.

For instance, in the first discourse we took up for discussion, there is the recurrent phrase *na jhāyati*, "does not muse," with reference to all the possible objects of the senses, but at the end of it all comes the emphatic assertion *jhāyati ca pana*, "nevertheless, he does muse." Similarly the passage dealing with the *saññā* aspect starts with *neva pathaviyaṃ pathavisaññī*, "he is neither conscious (literally 'percipient') of earth in earth," followed by a long list of negations, only to end up with an emphatic *saññī ca pana assa*, "but nevertheless he is conscious." So also in the passage which takes up the attending aspect and winds up with the assertion *manasi ca pana kareyya*, "and yet he will be attending."

All this evidence is a pointer to the fact that we have to interpret the reference to the paradoxical state of consciousness implied by *na saññasaññī na visaññasaññī* etc. in the *Kalahavivādasutta* in the light of that unique concentration of the *arahant* – the *arahattaphalasamādhi*.

This is obvious enough even if we take into consideration the occurrence of the term *papañcasaṅkhā* in the last line of the verse in question. The worldly concepts born of the prolific tendency of the mind are rooted in perception. That is precisely why perception has to be transcended. That is also the reason for our emphasis on the need for freedom from the six sense-bases and from contact. The abandonment of *papañcasaṅkhā* is accomplished at this extraordinary level of concentration.

The immense importance attached to the *arahattaphalasamādhi* comes to light in the passages we have quoted. These discourses are abundant proof of the fact that the Buddha has extolled this *samādhi* in various ways. The verse beginning with *na saññasaññī na visaññasaññī* in particular points to this fact.

On an earlier occasion we gave only a clue to its meaning in the form of an allusion to our simile of the cinema. That is to say, while one is watching a film show, if the cinema hall is fully illuminated all of a sudden, one undergoes such an internal transformation, that it becomes questionable whether he is still seeing the film show. This is because his perception of the film show has undergone a peculiar change. He is no longer conscious of a film show, nor has he put an end to consciousness. It is a strange paradox. His gaze is actually a vacant gaze.

The verse in question expresses such a vacant gaze. When the six sense-bases of the *arahant* cease and the lustre of wisdom comes up, giving the conviction that all assets in the world are empty, the vision in the *arahattaphalasamādhi* is as vacant as that gaze of the man at the cinema. It is neither conscious, nor unconscious, nor non-conscious, nor totally devoid of consciousness. At that level of concentration even this material form is abandoned.

The line in the paean of joy in the *Bāhiyasutta*, which we came across the other day, *atha rūpā arūpā ca, sukhadukkhā pamuccati*,[22] "and then from form and formless and from pleasure and pain is he freed," can be better appreciated in the light of the foregoing discussion. With the relinquishment of all assets, even this body and the experience of a form and of a formless, as well as pleasure and pain, cease altogether due to the cessation of contact. That is why *Nibbāna* is called a bliss devoid of feeling, *avedayita sukha*.[23]

Now as to this vacant gaze, there is much to be said, though one might think that it is not at all worth discussing about. If someone asks us: 'What is the object of the gaze of one with such a vacant gaze,' what shall we say? The vacant gaze is, in fact, not established anywhere (*appatiṭṭham*). It has no existence (*appavattaṃ*) and it is object-less (*anārammaṇaṃ*). Even at the mention of these three terms, *appatiṭṭham, appavattaṃ,* and *anārammaṇaṃ*, some might recall those highly controversial discourses on *Nibbāna*.[24]

Why do we call the vision of the *arahant* a vacant gaze? At the highest point of the development of the three characteristics

---

22 Ud 9, *Bāhiyasutta*; see sermon 15.

23 Ps III 115, *aṭṭhakathā* on the *Bahuvedanīyasutta*.

24 Ud 80, *Paṭhamanibbānapaṭisaṃyuttasutta*.

impermanence, suffering and not-self, that is, through the three deliverances *animitta, appaṇihita* and *suññata*, the "signess," the "undirected" and the "void," the *arahant* is now looking at the object with a penetrative gaze. That is why it is not possible to say what he is looking at. It is a gaze that sees the cessation of the object, a gaze that penetrates the object, as it were.

When the cinema hall is fully illuminated, the mind of the one with that vacant gaze at the film show does not accumulate the stuff that makes up a film. Why? Because all those cinema preparations are now stilled, cinema assets are relinquished and the craving and the passion for the cinema film have gone down, at least temporarily, with the result that the cinema film has 'ceased' for him and he is 'extinguished' within. That is why he is looking on with a vacant gaze. With this illustration one can form an idea about the inner transformation that occurs in the *arahant*.

From the very outset the meditator is concerned with *saṅkhāras*, or preparations. Hence the term *sabbasaṅkhārasamatha*, the stilling of all preparations, comes first. Instead of the arising aspect of preparations, he attends to the cessation aspect, the furthest limit of which is *Nibbāna*. It is for that reason that the term *nirodha* is directly applied to *Nibbāna*.

Simply because we have recapitulated the terms forming the theme of our sermons, some might think that the formula as such is some form of a gross object of the mind. This, in fact, is the root of the misconception prevalent today.

It is true that the Buddha declared that the *arahant* has as his perception, attention and concentration the formula beginning with *etaṃ santaṃ etaṃ paṇītaṃ* etc. But this does not mean that the *arahant* in his *samādhi* goes on reciting the formula as we do at the beginning of every sermon. What it means is that the *arahant* reverts to or re-attains the realization he has already won through the lustre of wisdom, namely the realization of the stilling of all preparations, the relinquishment of all assets, the total abandonment of the five aggregates, the destruction of craving, dispassion, cessation and extinguishment. That is what one has to understand by the saying that the *arahant* attends to *Nibbāna* as his object.

The object is cessation, *nirodha*. Here is something that *Māra* cannot grasp, that leaves him utterly clueless. This is why Venerable Nandiya in the *Nandiyatheragāthā* challenges *Māra* in the following verse:

> *Obhāsajātaṃ phalagaṃ,*
> *cittaṃ yassa abhiṇhaso,*
> *tādisam bhikkhum āsajja*
> *kaṇha dukkhaṃ nigacchasi.*[25]

> "The monk whose mind is always bright,
> And gone to the fruit of *arahant*-hood,
> Should you dare to challenge that monk,
> O Blackie, you only come to grief."

Kaṇha, Blackie, is one of the epithets of *Mara*. Even gods and *Brahmas* are unable to find out the object of the *arahant*'s mind when he is in the *phalasamāpatti*, the attainment to the fruit. *Māra* can never discover it. That is why this attainment is said to leave *Māra* clueless or deluded (*Mārassetaṃ pamohanaṃ*).[26] All this is due to the uniqueness of this level of concentration.

The three deliverances *animitta, appaṇihita* and *suññata*, are indeed extraordinary and the verse *na saññāsaññī* refers to this *arahattaphalasamādhi*, which is signless, undirected and void.

Usually one's vision alights somewhere or picks up some object or other, but here is a range of vision that has no horizon. In general, there is a horizon at the furthest end of our range of vision. Standing by the seaside or in a plain, one gazes upon a horizon where the earth and sky meet. The worldling's range of vision, in general, has such a horizon. But the *arahant*'s range of vision, as here described, has no such horizon. That is why it is

---

25 Th 25, *Nandiyatheragāthā*.

26 Dhp 274, *Maggavagga*.

called *anantaṃ*, endless or infinite. *Viññāṇaṃ anidassanaṃ, anantaṃ sabbato pabhaṃ*, "the non-manifestative consciousness, endless, lustrous on all sides."

That vacant gaze is an 'endless' perception. One who has it cannot be called conscious, *saññī*. Nor can he be called unconscious, *visaññī* – in the worldly sense of the term. Nor is he devoid of consciousness, *asaññī*. Nor has he put an end to consciousness, *vibhūtasaññī*.

Let us now take up two verses which shed a flood of light on the foregoing discussion and help illuminate the meaning of canonical passages that might come up later. The two verses are from the *Arahantavagga* of the *Dhammapada*:

Yesaṃ sannicayo natthi,
ye pariññāta bhojanā,
suññato animitto ca,
vimokkho yesa gocaro,
ākāse va sakuntānaṃ,
gati tesaṃ durannayā.

Yass'āsavā parikkhīṇā,
āhāre ca anissito,
suññato animitto ca,
vimokkho yassa gocaro,
ākāse va sakuntānaṃ,
padaṃ tassa durannayaṃ.[27]

"Those who have no accumulations,
And understood fully the subject of food,
And whose feeding ground
Is the void and the signless,

[27] Dhp 92-93, *Arahantavagga*.

Their track is hard to trace,
Like that of birds in the sky.

"He whose influxes are extinct,
And is unattached to nutriment,
Whose range is the deliverance,
Of the void and the signless,
His path is hard to trace,
Like that of birds in the sky."

The accumulation here meant is not of material things, such as food. It is the accumulation of karma and *upadhi*, assets. The comprehension of food could be taken to imply the comprehension of all four nutriments, namely gross material food, contact, will and consciousness. The feeding ground of such *arahants* is the void and the signless. Hence their track is hard to trace, like that of birds in the sky.

The term *gati*, which we rendered by "track," has been differently interpreted in the commentary. For the commentary *gati* is the place where the *arahant* goes after death, his next borne, so to speak.[28] But taken in conjunction with the simile used, *gati* obviously means the "path," *padaṃ*, taken by the birds in the sky. It is the path they take that cannot be traced, not their destination.

Where the birds have gone could perhaps be traced, with some difficulty. They may have gone to their nests. It is the path they went by that is referred to as *gati* in this context. Just as when birds fly through the sky they do not leave behind any trace of a path, even so in this concentration of the *arahant* there is no object or sign of any continuity.

The second verse gives almost the same idea. It is in singular and speaks of an *arahant* whose influxes are extinct and who is unattached to nutriment. Here, in the simile about the birds in the

---

[28] Dhp-a II 172.

sky, we find the word *padaṃ*, "path," used instead of *gati*, which makes it clear enough that it is not the destiny of the *arahant* that is spoken of.

The commentary, however, interprets both *gati* and *padaṃ* as a reference to the *arahant*'s destiny. There is a tacit assumption of some mysterious *anupādisesa Nibbānadhātu*. But what we have here is a metaphor of considerable depth. The reference is to that unique *samādhi*.

The bird's flight through the air symbolizes the flight of the mind. In the case of others, the path taken by the mind can be traced through the object it takes, but not in this case. The key word that highlights the metaphorical meaning of these verses is *gocaro*. *Gocara* means "pasture." Now, in the case of cattle roaming in their pasture one can trace them by their footsteps, by the path trodden. What about the pasture of the *arahants*?

Of course, they too consume food to maintain their bodies, but their true 'pasture' is the *arahattaphalasamādhi*. As soon as they get an opportunity, they take to this pasture. Once they are well within this pasture, neither gods nor *Brahmas* nor *Māra* can find them. That is why the path taken by the *arahants* in the *phalasamādhi* cannot be traced, like the track of birds in the sky.

We have yet to discuss the subject of *sa-upādisesa* and *anupādisesa Nibbānadhātu*. But even at this point some clarity of understanding might emerge. When the *arahant* passes away, at the last moment of his lifespan, he brings his mind to this *arahattaphalasamādhi*. Then not even *Mara* can trace him. There is no possibility of a rebirth and that is the end of all. It is this 'extinction' that is referred to here.

This extinction is not something one gets in a world beyond. It is a realization here and now, in this world. And the *arahant*, by way of blissful dwelling here and now, enjoys in his everyday life the supreme bliss of *Nibbāna* that he had won through the incomparable deliverances of the mind.

Nibbāna Sermon 17

Namo tassa Bhagavato Arahato Sammāsambuddhassa
Namo tassa Bhagavato Arahato Sammāsambuddhassa
Namo tassa Bhagavato Arahato Sammāsambuddhassa

Etaṃ santaṃ, etaṃ paṇītaṃ, yadidaṃ sabbasaṅkhārasamatho sabbūpadhipaṭinissaggo taṇhakkhayo virāgo nirodho nibbānaṃ.[1]

"This is peaceful, this is excellent, namely the stilling of all preparations, the relinquishment of all assets, the destruction of craving, detachment, cessation, extinction."

With the permission of the Most Venerable Great Preceptor and the assembly of the venerable meditative monks.

This is the seventeenth sermon in the series of sermons on *Nibbāna*. In our last sermon, we tried to analyse some discourses that give us a clue to understand what sort of an experience an *arahant* has in his realization of the cessation of existence in the *arahattaphalasamādhi*.

We happened to mention that the *arahant* sees the cessation of existence with a deeply penetrative vision of the void that may be compared to a gaze that knows no horizon. We also dropped the hint that the non-manifestative consciousness, endless and lustrous on all sides, we had spoken of in an earlier sermon,[2] is an explicit reference to this same experience.

---

1 M I 436, *MahāMālunkyasutta*.

2 See especially sermon 7.

How the *arahant*, ranging in his triple pasture of the signless deliverance, the undirected deliverance and the void deliverance, *animitta vimokkha*, *appaṇihita vimokkha* and *suññata vimokkha*, gets free from the latency to perception, transcends the duality of form and formless, and crosses over this ocean of existence unhindered by *Māra*, has been described in various ways in various discourses.

Let us now take up for discussion in this connection three significant verses that are found in the *Itivuttaka*:

Ye ca rūpūpagā sattā
ye ca arūpaṭṭhāyino,
nirodhaṃ appajānantā
āgantāro punabbhavaṃ.

Ye ca rūpe pariññāya,
arūpesu asaṇṭhitā,
nirodhe ye vimuccanti,
te janā maccuhāyino.

Kāyena amataṃ dhātuṃ,
phusaytivā nirūpadhiṃ,
upadhipaṭinissaggaṃ,
sacchikatvā anāsavo,
deseti sammāsambuddho,
asokaṃ virajaṃ padaṃ.[3]

"Those beings that go to realms of form,
And those who are settled in formless realms,
Not understanding the fact of cessation,
Come back again and again to existence.

---

[3] It 62, *Santatara Sutta*.

"Those who, having comprehended realms of form,
Do not settle in formless realms,
Are released in the experience of cessation,
It is they that are the dispellers of death.

"Having touched with the body the deathless element,
Which is asset-less,
And realized the relinquishment of assets,
Being influx-free, the perfectly enlightened one,
Proclaims the sorrow-less, taintless state."

The meaning of the first verse is clear enough. Those who are in realms of form and formless realms are reborn again and again due to not understanding the fact of cessation.

In the case of the second verse, there is some confusion as to the correct reading. We have mentioned earlier, too, that some of the deep discourses present considerable difficulty in determining what the correct reading is.[4] They have not come down with sufficient clarity. Where the meaning is not clear enough, there is a likelihood for the oral tradition to become corrupt. Here we accepted the reading *asaṇṭhitā*:

Ye ca rūpe pariññāya,
arūpesu asaṇṭhitā,

"Those who, having comprehended realms of form,
Do not settle in formless realms."

But there is the variant reading *susaṇṭhitā*, which gives the meaning "settled well." The two readings contradict each other and so we have a problem here. The commentary accepts the

[4] See sermon 7.

reading *asaṇṭhitā*.[5] We too followed it, for some valid reason and not simply because it accords with the commentary.

However, in several modern editions of the text, the reading *asaṇṭhitā* has been replaced by *susaṇṭhitā*, probably because it seems to make sense, *prima facie*.

But, as we pointed out in this series of sermons, there is the question of the dichotomy between the form and the formless. The formless, or *arūpa*, is like the shadow of form, *rūpa*. therefore, when one comprehends form, one also understands that the formless, too, is not worthwhile settling in. It is in that sense that we brought in the reading *asaṇṭhitā* in this context.

Those who have fully comprehended form, do not depend on the formless either, and it is they that are released in the realization of cessation. They transcend the duality of form and formless and, by directing their minds to the cessation of existence, attain emancipation.

In the last verse it is said that the Buddha realized the relinquishment of assets known as *nirupadhi*, the "asset-less." It also says that he touched the deathless element with the body. In a previous sermon we happened to quote a verse from the *Udāna* which had the conclusive lines:

> *Phusanti phassā upadhiṃ paṭicca,*
> *Nirupadhiṃ kena phuseyyum phassā.*[6]

> "Touches touch one because of assets,
> How can touches touch him who is asset-less?"

According to this verse, it seems that here there is no touch. So what we have stated above might even appear as contradictory. The above verse speaks of a 'touching' of the deathless element

---

[5] It-a II 42.

[6] Ud 12, *Sakkārasutta*; see sermon 16.

with the body. One might ask how one can touch, when there is no touch at all? But here we have an extremely deep idea, almost a paradox.

To be free from touch is in itself the 'touching' of the deathless element.

What we mean to say is that, as far as the fear of death is concerned, here we have the freedom from the pain of death and in fact the freedom from the concept of death itself.

The Buddha and the *arahants*, with the help of that wisdom, while in that *arahattaphalasamādhi* described as *anāsavā cetovimutti paññāvimutti*,[7] or *akuppā cetovimutti*,[8] let go of their entire body and realized the cessation of existence, thereby freeing themselves from touch and feeling. That is why *Nibbāna* is called a bliss devoid of feeling, *avedayita sukha*.[9]

This giving up, this letting go when *Māra* is coming to grab and seize, is a very subtle affair. To give up and let go when *Māra* comes to grab is to touch the deathless, because thereby one is freed from touch and feelings. Here, then, we have a paradox. So subtle is this *Dhamma*!

How does one realize cessation? By attending to the cessation aspect of preparations.

As we have already mentioned, to arise and to cease is of the nature of preparations, and here the attention is on the ceasing aspect. The worldlings in general pay attention to the arising aspect. They can see only that aspect. The Buddhas, on the other hand, have seen the cessation of existence in a subtle way. The culmination of the practice of paying attention to the cessation aspect of preparations is the realization of the cessation of existence.

---

7 This expression occurs e.g. at M I 35, *Ākaṅkheyyasutta*.

8 This expression occurs e.g. at S IV 297, *Godattasutta*.

9 Ps III 115, *aṭṭhakathā* on the *Bahuvedanīyasutta*.

Bhava, or existence, is the domain of *Māra*. How does one escape from the grip of *Māra*? By going beyond his range of vision, that is to say by attending to the cessation of existence, *bhavanirodha*.

All experiences of pleasure and pain are there so long as one is in *bhava*. The *arahant* wins to the freedom from form and formless and from pleasure and pain, as it was said in a verse already quoted:

> *Atha rūpā arūpā ca,*
> *sukhadukkhā pamuccati.*[10]

> "And then from form and formless,
> And from pleasure and pain is he freed."

We explained that verse as a reference to *arahattaphalasamādhi*. Here, too, we are on the same point. The concept of the cessation of existence is indeed very deep. It is so deep that one might wonder whether there is anything worthwhile in *Nibbāna*, if it is equivalent to the cessation of existence.

As a matter of fact, we do come across an important discourse among the Tens of the *Aṅguttara Nikāya*, where *Nibbāna* is explicitly called *bhavanirodha*. It is in the form of a dialogue between Venerable Ānanda and Venerable Sāriputta. As usual, Venerable Ānanda is enquiring about that extraordinary *samādhi*:

> *Siyā nu kho, āvuso Sāriputta, bhikkhuno tathārūpo samādhipaṭilābho yathā neva pathaviyaṃ pathavisaññī assa, na āpasmiṃ āposaññī assa, na tejasmiṃ tejosaññī assa, na vāyasmiṃ vāyosaññī assa, na ākāsānañcāyatane ākāsānañcāyatanasaññī assa, na viññāṇañcāyatane viññāṇancāyatanasaññī assa, na ākiñcaññāyatane ākiñcañ-*

---

[10] Ud 9, *Bāhiyasutta*; see sermon 15.

> *ñāyatanasaññī assa, na nevasaññānāsaññāyatane nevasaññānāsaññāyatanasaññī assa, na idhaloke idhalokasaññī assa, na paraloke paralokasaññī assa – saññī ca pana assa?*[11]
>
> "Could there be, friend Sāriputta, for a monk such an attainment of concentration wherein he will not be conscious of earth in earth, nor of water in water, nor of fire in fire, nor of air in air, nor will he be conscious of the sphere of infinite space in the sphere of infinite space, nor of the sphere of infinite consciousness in the sphere of infinite consciousness, nor of the sphere of nothingness in the sphere of nothingness, nor of the sphere of neither-perception-nor-non-perception in the sphere of neither-perception-nor-non-perception, nor of a this world in this world, nor of a world beyond in a world beyond – and yet he will be conscious?"

Venerable Sāriputta's reply to it is: "There could be, friend Ānanda." Then Venerable Ānanda asks again: "But then, friend Sāriputta, in which manner could there be such an attainment of concentration for a monk?"

At that point Venerable Sāriputta comes out with his own experience, revealing that he himself once attained to such a *samādhi*, when he was at Andhavana in Sāvatthi. Venerable Ānanda, however, is still curious to ascertain what sort of perception he was having, when he was in that *samādhi*. The explanation given by Venerable Sāriputta in response to it, is of utmost importance. It runs:

---

11 A V 8, *Sāriputtasutta*.

> *Bhavanirodho nibbānaṃ, bhavanirodho nibbānan'ti kho me, avuso, aññā'va saññā uppajjati aññā'va saññā nirujjhati.*
>
> *Seyyathāpi, āvuso, sakalikaggissa jhāyamānassa aññā'va acci uppajjati, aññā'va acci nirujjhati, evam eva kho me āvuso bhavanirodho nibbānaṃ, bhavanirodho nibbānam 'ti aññā'va saññā uppajjati aññā'va saññā nirujjhati, bhavanirodho nibbānaṃ saññī ca panāhaṃ, āvuso, tasmiṃ samaye ahosiṃ.*
>
> "One perception arises in me, friend: 'cessation of existence is *Nibbāna*,' 'cessation of existence is *Nibbāna*,' and another perception fades out in me: 'cessation of existence is *Nibbāna*,' 'cessation of existence is *Nibbāna*.'
>
> "Just as, friend, in the case of a twig fire, when it is burning one flame arises and another flame fades out. Even so, friend, one perception arises in me: 'cessation of existence is *Nibbāna*,' 'cessation of existence is *Nibbāna*,' and another perception fades out in me: 'cessation of existence is *Nibbāna*,' 'cessation of existence is *Nibbāna*,' at that time, friend, I was of the perception 'cessation of existence is *Nibbāna*.'"

The true significance of the simile of the twig fire is that Venerable Sāriputta was attending to the cessation aspect of preparations. As we mentioned in connection with the formula *etaṃ santaṃ, etaṃ paṇītaṃ,* "this is peaceful, this is excellent," occurring in a similar context, we are not to conclude that Venerable Sāriputta kept on repeating 'cessation of existence is *Nibbāna*.'

The insight into a flame could be different from a mere sight of a flame. Worldlings in general see only a process of burning in a flame. To the insight meditator it can appear as an intermittent series of extinctions. It is the outcome of a penetrative vision. Just like the flame, which simulates compactness, existence, too, is a product of *saṅkhāras*, or preparations.

The worldling who attends to the arising aspect and ignores the cessation aspect is carried away by the perception of the compact. But the mind, when steadied, is able to see the phenomenon of cessation: *Ṭhitaṃ cittaṃ vippamuttaṃ, vayañcassānupassati,*[12] "The mind steadied and released contemplates its own passing away."

With that steadied mind the *arahant* attends to the cessation of preparations. At its climax, he penetrates the gamut of existence made up of preparations, as in the case of a flame, and goes beyond the clutches of death.

As a comparison for existence, the simile of the flame is quite apt. We happened to point out earlier, that the word *upādāna* can mean "grasping" as well as "fuel."[13] The totality of existence is sometimes referred to as a fire.[14] The fuel for the fire of existence is grasping itself. With the removal of that fuel, one experiences extinction.

The dictum *bhavanirodho nibbānam* clearly shows that *Nibbāna* is the cessation of existence. There is another significant discourse which equates *Nibbāna* to the experience of the cessation of the six sense-bases, *saḷāyatananirodha*. The same experience of realization is viewed from a different angle. We have already shown that the cessation of the six sense-bases, or the six sense-spheres, is also called *Nibbāna.*[15]

The discourse we are now going to take up is one in which the Buddha presented the theme as some sort of a riddle for the monks to work out for themselves:

---

12 A III 379, *Soṇasutta*.

13 See sermon 1.

14 S IV 19, *Ādittasutta*.

15 See sermons 9 and 15.

> *Tasmātiha, bhikkhave, se āyatane veditabbe yattha cakkhuñca nirujjhati rūpasaññā ca virajjati, se āyatane veditabbe yattha sotañca nirujjhati saddasaññā ca virajjati, se āyatane veditabbe yattha ghānañca nirujjhati gandhasaññā ca virajjati, se āyatane veditabbe yattha jivhā ca nirujjhati rasasaññā ca virajjati, se āyatane veditabbe yattha kāyo ca nirujjhati phoṭṭabbasaññā ca virajjati, se āyatane veditabbe yattha mano ca nirujjhati dhammasaññā ca virajjati, se āyatane veditabbe, se āyatane veditabbe.*[16]

> "Therefore, monks, that sphere should be known wherein the eye ceases and perceptions of form fade away, that sphere should be known wherein the ear ceases and perceptions of sound fade away, that sphere should be known wherein the nose ceases and perceptions of smell fade away, that sphere should be known wherein the tongue ceases and perceptions of taste fade away, that sphere should be known wherein the body ceases and perceptions of the tangible fade away, that sphere should be known wherein the mind ceases and perceptions of mind objects fade away, that sphere should be known, that sphere should be known."

There is some peculiarity in the very wording of the passage, when it says, for instance, that the eye ceases, *cakkhuñca nirujjhati* and perceptions of form fade away, *rūpasaññā ca virajjati.* As we once pointed out, the word *virāga*, usually rendered by "detachment," has a nuance equivalent to "fading away" or "decolouration."[17] Here that nuance is clearly evident. When the eye ceases, perceptions of forms fade away.

---

[16] S IV 98, *Kāmaguṇasutta*.

[17] See sermon 5.

The Buddha is enjoining the monks to understand that sphere, not disclosing what it is, in which the eye ceases and perceptions of form fade away, and likewise the ear ceases and perceptions of sound fade away, the nose ceases and perceptions of smell fade away, the tongue ceases and perceptions of taste fade away, the body ceases and perceptions of the tangible fade away, and last of all even the mind ceases and perceptions of mind objects fade away. This last is particularly noteworthy.

Without giving any clue to the meaning of this brief exhortation, the Buddha got up and entered the monastery, leaving the monks perplexed. Wondering how they could get it explained, they approached Venerable Ānanda and begged him to comment at length on what the Buddha had preached in brief. With some modest reluctance, Venerable Ānanda complied, urging that his comment be reported to the Buddha for confirmation. His comments, however, amounted to just one sentence:

> *Saḷāyatananirodhaṃ, kho āvuso, Bhagavatā sandhāya bhāsitaṃ.*
>
> "Friends, it is with reference to the cessation of the six sense-spheres that the Exalted One has preached this sermon."

When those monks approached the Buddha and placed Venerable Ānanda's explanation before him, the Buddha ratified it. Hence it is clear that the term *āyatana* in the above passage refers not to any one of the six sense-spheres, but to *Nibbāna*, which is the cessation of all of them.

The commentator, Venerable Buddhaghosa, too accepts this position in his commentary to the passage in question. *Saḷāyatananirodhan'ti saḷāyatananirodho vuccati nibbānam, tam sandhāya bhāsitan ti attho*, "The cessation of the six sense-spheres, what is called the cessation of the six sense-spheres is *Nibbāna*, the meaning is that the Buddha's sermon is a reference to it."[18]

The passage in question bears testimony to two important facts. Firstly that *Nibbāna* is called the cessation of the six sense-spheres. Secondly that this experience is referred to as an *āyatana*, or a 'sphere.'

The fact that *Nibbāna* is sometimes called *āyatana* is further corroborated by a certain passage in the *Saḷāyatanvibhaṅgasutta*, which defines the term *nekkhammasita domanassa*.[19] In that discourse, which deals with some deeper aspects of the *Dhamma*, the concept of *nekkhammasita domanassa*, or "unhappiness connected with renunciation," is explained as follows:

"If one contemplates with insight wisdom the sense-objects like forms and sounds as impermanent, suffering-fraught and transient, and develops a longing for *Nibbāna*, due to that longing or expectation one might feel an unhappiness. It is such an unhappiness which, however, is superior to an unhappiness connected with the household life, that is called *nekkhammasita domanassa*, or 'unhappiness connected with renunciation.'"

How such an unhappiness may arise in a monk is described in that discourse in the following manner:

> *'Kudāssu nāmāhaṃ tadāyatanaṃ upasampajja viharissāmi yadariyā etarahi āyatanaṃ upasampajja viharanti?' iti anuttaresu vimokkhesu pihaṃ upaṭṭhāpayato uppajjati pihāpaccayā domanassaṃ. Yaṃ evarūpaṃ domanassaṃ idaṃ vuccati nekkhammasitadomanassaṃ.*

> "'O, when shall I attain to and dwell in that sphere to which the Noble Ones now attain and dwell in?' Thus, as

---

[18] Spk II 391.

[19] M III 217, *Saḷāyatanavibhaṅgasutta*.

> he sets up a longing for the incomparable deliverances, there arises an unhappiness due to that longing. It is such an unhappiness that is called unhappiness connected with renunciation."

What are called "incomparable deliverances" are the three doorways to *Nibbāna*, the signless, the undirected and the void. We can therefore conclude that the sphere to which this monk aspires is none other than *Nibbāna*. So here we have a second instance of a reference to *Nibbāna* as a 'sphere' or *āyatana*. Now let us bring up a third:

> *Atthi, bhikkhave, tad āyatanaṃ, yattha n'eva pathavī na āpo na tejo na vāyo na ākāsānañcāyatanaṃ na viññāṇānañcāyatanaṃ na ākiñcaññāyatanaṃ na nevasaññānāsaññāyatanaṃ na ayaṃ loko na paraloko na ubho candimasūriyā. Tatra p'ahaṃ bhikkhave, n'eva āgatiṃ vadāmi na gatiṃ na ṭhitiṃ na cutiṃ na upapattiṃ, appatiṭṭhaṃ appavattaṃ anārammaṇaṃ eva taṃ. Es'ev'anto dukkhassā'ti.*[20]

Incidentally, this happens to be the most controversial passage on *Nibbāna*. Scholars, both ancient and modern, have put forward various interpretations of this much vexed passage. Its riddle-like presentation has posed a challenge to many a philosopher bent on determining what *Nibbāna* is.

This brief discourse comes in the *Udāna* as an inspired utterance of the Buddha on the subject of *Nibbāna*, *Nibbānapaṭisaṃyuttasutta*. To begin with, we shall try to give a somewhat literal translation of the passage:

---

[20] Ud 80, *Paṭhamanibbānapaṭisaṃyuttasutta*.

> "Monks, there is that sphere, wherein there is neither earth, nor water, nor fire, nor air; neither the sphere of infinite space, nor the sphere of infinite consciousness, nor the sphere of nothingness, nor the sphere of neither-perception-nor-non-perception; neither this world nor the world beyond, nor the sun and the moon. There, monks, I say, is no coming, no going, no staying, no passing away and no arising; it is not established, it is not continuing, it has no object. This, itself, is the end of suffering."

Instead of getting down to the commentarial interpretation at the very outset, let us try to understand this discourse on the lines of the interpretation we have so far developed. We have already come across two references to *Nibbāna* as an *āyatana* or a sphere. In the present context, too, the term *āyatana* is an allusion to *arahattaphalasamādhi*. Its significance, therefore, is psychological.

First of all we are told that earth, water, fire and air are not there in that *āyatana*. This is understandable, since in a number of discourses dealing with *anidassana viññāṇa* and *arahattaphalasamādhi* we came across similar statements. It is said that in *anidassana viññāṇa*, or non-manifestative consciousness, earth, water, fire and air do not find a footing. Similarly, when one is in *arahattaphalasamādhi*, one is said to be devoid of the perception of earth in earth, for instance, because he does not attend to it. So the peculiar negative formulation of the above *Udāna* passage is suggestive of the fact that these elements do not exercise any influence on the mind of one who is in *arahattaphalasamādhi*.

The usual interpretation, however, is that it describes some kind of a place or a world devoid of those elements. It is generally believed that the passage in question is a description of the 'sphere' into which the *arahant* passes away, that is, his after death 'state.' This facile explanation is often presented only as a tacit assumption, for fear of being accused of heretical views. But it must be pointed out that the allusion here is to a certain level of experience of the living *arahant*, namely the realization, here and now, of the cessation of existence, *bhavanirodha*.

The four elements have no part to play in that experience. The sphere of infinite space, the sphere of infinite consciousness etc. also do not come in, as we have already shown with reference to a number of discourses. So it is free from both form and formless.

The statement that there is neither this world nor a world beyond could be understood in the light of the phrase, *na idhaloke idhalokasaññī, na paraloke paralokasaññī*, "percipient neither of a this world in this world, nor of a world beyond in a world beyond" that came up in a passage discussed above.

The absence of the moon and the sun, *na ubho candima sūriyā*, in this sphere, is taken as the strongest argument in favour of concluding that *Nibbāna* is some kind of a place, a place where there is no moon or sun.

But as we have explained in the course of our discussion of the term *anidassana viññāṇa*, or non-manifestative consciousness, with the cessation of the six sense-spheres, due to the all lustrous nature of the mind, sun and moon lose their lustre, though the senses are all intact. Their lustre is superseded by the lustre of wisdom. They pale away and fade into insignificance before it. It is in this sense that the moon and the sun are said to be not there in that sphere.

Why there is no coming, no going, no staying, no passing away and no arising, can be understood in the light of what we have observed in earlier sermons on the question of relative concepts. The verbal dichotomy characteristic of worldly concepts is reflected in this reference to a coming and a going etc. The *arahant* in *arahattaphalasamādhi* is free from the limitations imposed by this verbal dichotomy.

The three terms *appatiṭṭhaṃ, appavattaṃ* and *anārammaṇaṃ*, "not established," "not continuing," and "object-less," are suggestive of the three doorways to deliverance. *Appatiṭṭhaṃ* refers to *appaṇihita vimokkha*, "undirected deliverance," which comes through the extirpation of craving. *Appavattaṃ* stands for *suññata vimokkha*, the "void deliverance," which is the negation of continuity. *Anārammaṇaṃ* is clearly enough a reference to *animitta vimokkha*, the "signless deliverance." Not to have an object is to be signless.

The concluding sentence "this itself is the end of suffering" is therefore a clear indication that the end of suffering is reached here and now. It does not mean that the *arahant* gets half of *Nibbāna* here and the other half 'there.'

Our line of interpretation leads to such a conclusion, but of course, in case there are shortcomings in it, we could perhaps improve on it by having recourse to the commentarial interpretation.

Now as to the commentarial interpretation, this is how the *Udāna* commentary explains the points we have discussed:[21] It paraphrases the term *āyatana* by *kāraṇa*, observing that it means reason in this context. Just as much as forms stand in relation of an object to the eye, so the *asaṅkhata dhātu*, or the "unprepared element," is said to be an object to the *arahant*'s mind, and here it is called *āyatana*.

Then the commentary raises the question, why earth, water, fire and air are not there in that *asaṅkhata dhātu*. The four elements are representative of things prepared, *saṅkhata*. There can not be any mingling or juxtaposition between the *saṅkhata* and the *asaṅkhata*. That is why earth, water, fire and air are not supposed to be there, in that *āyatana*.

The question why there are no formless states, like the sphere of infinite space, the sphere of infinite consciousness, the sphere of nothingness, the sphere of neither-perception-nor-non-perception, is similarly explained, while asserting that *Nibbāna* is nevertheless formless.

Since in *Nibbāna* one has transcended the sensuous sphere, *kāmaloka*, the concepts of a this world and a world beyond are

---

[21] Ud-a 389.

said to be irrelevant. As to why the sun and the moon are not there, the commentary gives the following explanation:

"In realms of form there is generally darkness, to dispel which there must be a sun and a moon. But *Nibbāna* is not a realm of form, so how could sun and moon come in?"

Then what about the reference to a coming, a going, a staying, a passing away and an arising? No one comes to *Nibbāna* from anywhere and no one goes out from it, no one stays in it or passes away or reappears in it.

Now all this is mystifying enough. But the commentary goes on to interpret the three terms *appatiṭṭhaṃ, appavattaṃ* and *anārammaṇaṃ* also in the same vein. Only that which has form gets established and *Nibbāna* is formless, therefore it is not established anywhere. *Nibbāna* does not continue, so it is *appavattaṃ*, or non-continuing. Since *Nibbāna* takes no object, it is objectless, *anārammaṇaṃ*. It is as good as saying that, though one may take *Nibbāna* as an object, *Nibbāna* itself takes no object.

So this is what the traditional interpretation amounts to. If there are any shortcomings in our explanation, one is free to go for the commentarial. But it is obvious that there is a lot of confusion in this commentarial trend. Insufficient appreciation of the deep concept of the cessation of existence seems to have caused all this confusion.

More often than otherwise, commentarial interpretations of *Nibbāna* leaves room for some subtle craving for existence, *bhavataṇhā*. It gives a vague idea of a place or a sphere, *āyatana*, which serves as a surrogate destination for the *arahants* after their demise. Though not always explicitly asserted, it is at least tacitly suggested. The description given above is ample proof of this trend. It conjures up a place where there is no sun and no moon, a place that is not a place. Such confounding trends have crept in probably due to the very depth of this *Dhamma*.

Deep indeed is this *Dhamma* and hard to comprehend, as the Buddha once confided in Venerable Sāriputta with a trace of tiredness:

> *Saṅkhittenapi kho ahaṃ, Sāriputta, dhammaṃ deseyyaṃ, vitthārenapi kho ahaṃ, Sāriputta, dhammaṃ deseyyaṃ, saṅkhittenavitthārenapi kho ahaṃ, Sāriputta, dhammaṃ deseyyaṃ, aññātāro ca dullabhā.*[22]
>
> "Whether I were to preach in brief, Sāriputta, or whether I were to preach in detail, Sāriputta, or whether I were to preach both in brief or in detail, Sāriputta, rare are those who understand."

Then Venerable Sāriputta implores the Buddha to preach in brief, in detail and both in brief and in detail, saying that there will be those who understand. In response to it the Buddha gives the following instruction to Venerable Sāriputta:

> *Tasmātiha, Sāriputta, evaṃ sikkhitabbaṃ: 'Imasmiñca saviññāṇake kāye ahaṅkāramamaṅkāramānānusayā na bhavissanti, bahiddhā ca sabbanimittesu ahaṅkāramamaṅkāramānānusayā na bhavissanti, yañca cetovimuttiṃ paññāvimuttiṃ upasampajja viharato ahaṅkāramamaṅkāramānānusayā na honti, tañca cetovimuttiṃ paññāvimuttiṃ upasampajja viharissāmā'ti. Evañhi kho, Sāriputta, sikkhitabbaṃ,*
>
> "If that is so, Sāriputta, you all should train yourselves thus: In this conscious body and in all external signs there shall be no latencies to conceits in terms of I-ing and my-ing, and we will attain to and dwell in that deliverance of the mind and that deliverance through wisdom whereby no such latencies to conceits of I-ing and my-ing will arise. Thus should you all train yourselves!"

---

[22] A I 133, *Sāriputtasutta*.

The Buddha goes on to declare the final outcome of that training:

> *Ayaṃ vuccati, Sāriputta, bhikkhu acchecchi taṇhaṃ vāvattayi saṃyojanaṃ sammā mānābhisamayā antam akāsi dukkhassa.*
>
> "Such a monk, Sāriputta, is called one who has cut off craving, turned back the fetters, and by rightly understanding conceit for what it is, has made an end of suffering."

We find the Buddha summing up his exhortation by quoting two verses from a *Sutta* in the *Pārāyanavagga* of the *Sutta Nipāta*, which he himself had preached to the Brahmin youth Udaya. We may mention in passing that among canonical texts, the *Sutta Nipāta* was held in high esteem so much so that in a number of discourses the Buddha is seen quoting from it, particularly from the two sections *Aṭṭhakavagga* and *Pārāyanavagga*. Now the two verses he quotes in this instance from the *Pārāyanavagga* are as follows:

> *Pahānaṃ kāmacchandānaṃ,*
> *domanassāna cūbhayaṃ,*
> *thīṇassa ca panūdanaṃ,*
> *kukkuccānaṃ nivāraṇaṃ,*
>
> *Upekhāsatisaṃsuddhaṃ,*
> *dhammatakkapurejavaṃ,*
> *aññāvimokhaṃ pabrūmi,*
> *avijjāyappabhedanaṃ.*[23]
>
> "The abandonment of both sensuous perceptions,
> And unpleasant mental states,

---

[23] Sn 1106-1107, *Udayamāṇavapucchā*.

The dispelling of torpidity,
And the warding off of remorse,

"The purity born of equanimity and mindfulness,
With thoughts of *Dhamma* forging ahead,
And blasting ignorance,
This I call the deliverance through full understanding."

This is ample proof of the fact that the *arahattaphalasamādhi* is also called *aññāvimokkha*. Among the Nines of the *Aṅguttara Nikāya* we come across another discourse which throws more light on the subject. Here Venerable Ānanda is addressing a group of monks:

Acchariyaṃ, āvuso, abbhutam, āvuso, yāvañcidaṃ tena Bhagavatā jānatā passatā arahatā sammāsambuddhena sambādhe okāsādhigamo anubuddho sattānaṃ visuddhiyā sokapariddavānaṃ samatikkamāya dukkhadomanassānaṃ atthaṅgamāya ñāyassa adhigamāya nibbānassa sacchikiriyāya.

Tadeva nāma cakkhuṃ bhavissati te rūpā tañcāyatanaṃ no paṭisaṃvedissati. Tadeva nāma sotaṃ bhavissati te saddā tañcāyatanaṃ no paṭisaṃvedissati. Tadeva nāma ghānaṃ bhavissati te gandhā tañcāyatanaṃ no paṭisaṃvedissati. Sā ca nāma jivhā bhavissati te rasā tañcāyatanaṃ no paṭisaṃvedissati. So ca nāma kāyo bhavissati te phoṭṭhabbā tañcāyatanaṃ no paṭisaṃvedissati.[24]

"It is wonderful, friends, it is marvelous, friends, that the Exalted One who knows and sees, that Worthy One, fully enlightened, has discovered an opportunity in obstructing

---

[24] A IV 426, *Ānandasutta*.

circumstances for the purification of beings, for the transcending of sorrow and lamentation, for the ending of pain and unhappiness, for the attainment of the right path, for the realization of *Nibbāna*.

"In as much as that same eye will be there, those forms will be there, but one will not be experiencing the appropriate sense-sphere. That same ear will be there, those sounds will be there, but one will not be experiencing the appropriate sense-sphere. That same nose will be there, those smells will be there, but one will not be experiencing the appropriate sense-sphere. That same tongue will be there, those flavours will be there, but one will not be experiencing the appropriate sense-sphere. That same body will be there, those tangibles will be there, but one will not be experiencing the appropriate sense-sphere."

What is so wonderful and marvelous about this newly discovered opportunity is that, though apparently the senses and their corresponding objects come together, there is no experience of the appropriate spheres of sense contact. When Venerable Ānanda had described this extraordinary level of experience in these words, Venerable Udāyī raised the following question:

Saññīmeva nu kho āvuso Ānanda, tadāyatanaṃ no paṭisaṃvedeti udāhu asaññī?

"Friend, is it the fact that while being conscious one is not experiencing that sphere or is he unconscious at that time?"

Venerable Ānanda affirms that it is while being conscious, *saññīmeva*, that such a thing happens. Venerable Udāyī's cross-question gives us a further clue to the riddle like verse we discussed earlier, beginning with *na sañña saññī na visañña saññī.*

It is indeed puzzling why one does not experience those sense-objects, though one is conscious. As if to drive home the point, Venerable Ānanda relates how he once answered a related question put to him by the nun Jaṭilagāhiyā when he was staying at the Deer Park in Añjanavana in Sāketa. The question was:

> *Yāyaṃ, bhante Ānanda, samādhi na cābhinato na cāpanato na ca sasaṅkhāraniggayhavāritavato, vimuttattā ṭhito, ṭhitattā santusito, santusitattā no paritassati. Ayaṃ, bhante, samādhi kiṃphalo vutto Bhagavatā?*

> "That concentration, Venerable Ānanda, which is neither turned towards nor turned outwards, which is not a vow constrained by preparations, one that is steady because of freedom, contented because of steadiness and not hankering because of contentment, Venerable Sir, with what fruit has the Exalted One associated that concentration?"

The question looks so highly compressed that the key words in it might need some clarification. The two terms *abhinata* and *apanata* are suggestive of lust and hate, as well as introversion and extroversion. This concentration is free from these extreme attitudes. Whereas in ordinary concentration *saṅkhāras*, or preparations, exercise some degree of control as the term *vikkhambhana*, "propping up," "suppression," suggests, here there is no implication of any forcible action as in a vow. Here the steadiness is born of freedom from that very constriction.

Generally, the steadiness characteristic of a level of concentration is not much different from the apparent steadiness of a spinning top. It is the spinning that keeps the top up. But here the very freedom from that spinning has brought about a steadiness of a higher order, which in its turn gives rise to contentment.

The kind of peace and contentment that comes with *samādhi* in general is brittle and irritable. That is why it is sometimes called *kuppa paṭicca santi*, "peace subject to irritability."[25] Here, on the contrary, there is no such irritability.

We can well infer from this that the allusion is to *akuppā ceto-vimutti*, "unshakeable deliverance of the mind." The kind of contentment born of freedom and stability is so perfect that it leaves no room for hankering, *paritassanā*.

However, the main point of the question posed by that nun amounts to this: What sort of a fruit does a *samādhi* of this description entail, according to the words of the Exalted One? After relating the circumstances connected with the above question as a flashback, Venerable Ānanda finally comes out with the answer he had given to the question:

> *Yāyaṃ, bhagini, samādhi na cābhinato na cāpanato na ca sasaṅkhāraniggayhavāritavato, vimuttattā ṭhito, ṭhitattā santusito, santusitattā no paritassati, ayaṃ, bhagini, samādhi aññāphalo vutto Bhagavatā.*

> "Sister, that concentration which is neither turned towards nor turned outwards, which is not a vow constrained by preparations, one that is steady because of freedom, contented because of steadiness and not hankering because of contentment, that concentration, sister, has been declared by the Buddha to have full understanding as its fruit."

Aññā, or full understanding, is one that comes with realization conferring certitude and it is the fruit of the concentration described above. Then, as if coming back to the point, Venerable Ānanda adds: *Evaṃ saññīpi kho, āvuso, tad āyatanaṃ no paṭi-*

---

[25] Sn 784, *Duṭṭhaṭṭhakasutta*.

saṃvedeti. "Being thus conscious, too, friend, one does not experience an appropriate sphere of sense."

So now we have garnered sufficient evidence to substantiate the claims of this extraordinary *arahattaphalasamādhi.* It may also be mentioned that sometimes this realization of the *arahant* is summed up in a sentence like *anāsavaṃ cetovimuttiṃ paññāvimuttiṃ diṭṭheva dhamme sayaṃ abhiññā sacchikatvā upasampajja viharati,*[26] "having realized by himself through higher knowledge here and now the influx-free deliverance of the mind and deliverance through wisdom, he dwells having attained to it."

There is another significant discourse in the section of the Fours in the *Aṅguttara Nikāya* which throws some light on how one should look upon the *arahant* when he is in *arahattaphalasamādhi.* The discourse deals with four types of persons, namely:

1) *anusotagāmī puggalo,* "downstream bound person."
2) *paṭisotagāmī puggalo,* "upstream bound person."
3) *ṭhitatto puggalo,* "stationary person."
4) *tiṇṇo pāragato thale tiṭṭhati brāhmaṇo,* "the Brahmin standing on dry ground having crossed over and gone beyond."[27]

The first type of person indulges in sense pleasures and commits evil deeds and is thus bound downstream in *saṃsāra.* The second type of person refrains from indulgence in sense pleasures and from evil deeds. His upstream struggle is well expressed in the following sentence: *Sahāpi dukkhena sahāpi domanassena assumukhopi rudamāno paripuṇṇaṃ parisuddhaṃ brahmacariyaṃ carati,* "Even with pain, even with displeasure, with tearful

---

[26] E.g. D I 156, *Mahālisutta.*

[27] A II 5, *Anusotasutta.*

face and crying he leads the holy life in its fullness and perfection."

The third type, the stationary, is the non-returner who, after death, goes to the *Brahma* world and puts an end to suffering there, without coming back to this world.

It is the fourth type of person who is said to have crossed over and gone to the farther shore, *tiṇṇo pāragato*, and stands there, *thale tiṭṭhati*. The word *brahmin* is used here as an epithet of an *arahant*. This riddle-like reference to an *arahant* is explained there with the help of the more thematic description *āsavānaṃ khayā anāsavaṃ cetovimuttiṃ paññāvimuttiṃ diṭṭheva dhamme sayaṃ abhiññā sacchikatvā upasampajja viharati*, "with the extinction of influxes he attains to and abides in the influx free deliverance of the mind and deliverance through wisdom."

This brings us to an extremely deep point in our discussion on *Nibbāna*. If the *arahant* in *arahattaphalasamādhi* is supposed to be standing on the farther shore, having gone beyond, what is the position with him when he is taking his meals or preaching in his everyday life? Does he now and then come back to this side?

Whether the *arahant*, having gone to the farther shore, comes back at all is a matter of dispute. The fact that it involves some deeper issues is revealed by some discourses touching on this question.

The last verse of the *Paramaṭṭhakasutta* of the *Sutta Nipāta*, for instance, makes the following observation:

> *Na kappayanti na purekkharonti,*
> *dhammā pi tesaṃ na paṭicchitāse,*
> *na brāhmaṇo sīlavatena neyyo,*
> *pāraṃgato na pacceti tādi.*[28]

---

[28] Sn 803, *Paramaṭṭhakasutta*.

"They, the *arahants*, do not formulate or put forward views,
They do not subscribe to any views,
The true Brahmin is not liable to be led astray by ceremonial rites and ascetic vows,
The Such like One, who has gone to the farther shore, comes not back."

It is the last line that concerns us here. For the *arahant* it uses the term *tādī*, a highly significant term which we came across earlier too. The rather literal rendering "such-like" stands for steadfastness, for the unwavering firmness to stand one's ground. So, the implication is that the *arahant*, once gone beyond, does not come back. The steadfastness associated with the epithet *tādī* is reinforced in one *Dhammapada* verse by bringing in the simile of the firm post at the city gate: *Indakhīlūpamo tādi subbato*,[29] "who is steadfast and well conducted like the pillar at the city gate."

The verse in question, then, points to the conclusion that the steadfast one, the *arahant*, who has attained supramundane freedom, does not come back.

[29] Dhp 95, *Arahantavagga*.

Nibbāna Sermon 18

Namo tassa Bhagavato Arahato Sammāsambuddhassa
Namo tassa Bhagavato Arahato Sammāsambuddhassa
Namo tassa Bhagavato Arahato Sammāsambuddhassa

Etaṃ santaṃ, etaṃ paṇītaṃ, yadidaṃ sabbasaṅkhārasamatho sabbūpadhipaṭinissaggo taṇhakkhayo virāgo nirodho nibbānaṃ.[1]

"This is peaceful, this is excellent, namely the stilling of all preparations, the relinquishment of all assets, the destruction of craving, detachment, cessation, extinction."

With the permission of the Most Venerable Great Preceptor and the assembly of the venerable meditative monks.

This is the eighteenth sermon in the series of sermons on *Nibbāna*. We happened to mention, in our last sermon, that many of the discourses dealing with the subject of *Nibbāna*, have been misinterpreted, due to a lack of appreciation of the fact that the transcendence of the world and crossing over to the farther shore of existence have to be understood in a psychological sense.

The view that the *arahant* at the end of his life enters into an absolutely existing *asaṅkhata dhātu*, or 'unprepared element,' seems to have received acceptance in the commentarial period. In the course of our last sermon, we made it very clear that some of the discourses cited by the commentators in support of that view deal, on the contrary, with some kind of realization the *arahant*

1 M I 436, *MahāMālunkyasutta*.

goes through here and now, in this very life, in this very world – a realization of the cessation of existence, or the cessation of the six sense-spheres.

Even when the Buddha refers to the *arahant* as the Brahmin who, having gone beyond, is standing on the farther shore,[2] he was speaking of the *arahant* who has realized, in this very life, the influx-free deliverance of the mind and deliverance through wisdom, in his concentration of the fruit of *arahant*-hood.

Therefore, on the strength of this evidence, we are compelled to elicit a subtler meaning of the concept of 'this shore' and the 'farther shore' from these discourses dealing with *Nibbāna* than is generally accepted in the world. Our sermon today is especially addressed to that end.

As we mentioned before, if one is keen on getting a solution to the problems relating to *Nibbāna*, the discourses we are now taking up for discussion might reveal the deeper dimensions of that problem. We had to wind up our last sermon while drawing out the implications of the last line in the *Paramaṭṭhakasutta* of the *Sutta Nipāta*: *pāraṃgato na pacceti tādi*.[3] We drew the inference that the steadfast one, the arahant, who is such-like, once gone to the farther shore, does not come back.

We find, however, quite a different idea expressed in a verse of the *Nālakasutta* in the *Sutta Nipāta*. The verse, which was the subject of much controversy among the ancients, runs as follows:

> *Uccāvāca hi paṭipadā,*
> *samaṇena pakāsitā,*
> *na pāraṃ diguṇaṃ yanti,*
> *na idaṃ ekaguṇaṃ mutaṃ.*[4]

---

[2] E.g. It 57, *Dutiyarāgasutta*: *tiṇṇo pāraṃ gato thale tiṭṭhati brāhmaṇo.*

[3] Sn 803, *Paramaṭṭhakasutta.*

[4] Sn 714, *Nālakasutta.*

"High and low are the paths,
Made known by the recluse,
They go not twice to the farther shore,
Nor yet is it to be reckoned a going once."

The last two lines seem to contradict each other. There is no going twice to the farther shore, but still it is not to be conceived as a going once.

Now, as for the first two lines, the high and low paths refer to the modes of practice adopted, according to the grades of understanding in different character types. For instances, the highest grade of person attains *Nibbāna* by an easy path, being quick-witted, *sukhā paṭipadā khippābhiññā*, whereas the lowest grade attains it by a difficult path, being relatively dull-witted, *dukkhā paṭipadā dandhābhiññā*.[5]

The problem lies in the last two lines. The commentary tries to tackle it by interpreting the reference to not going twice to the farther shore, *na pāraṃ diguṇaṃ yanti*, as an assertion that there is no possibility of attaining *Nibbāna* by the same path twice, *ekamaggena dvikkhattuṃ nibbānaṃ na yanti*.[6] The implication is that the supramundane path of a stream-winner, a once-returner or a non-returner arises only once. Why it is not to be conceived as a going once is explained as an acceptance of the norm that requires not less than four supramundane paths to attain *arahant*-hood.

However, a deeper analysis of the verse in question would reveal the fact that it effectively brings up an apparent contradiction. The commentary sidetracks by resolving it into two different problems. The two lines simply reflect two aspects of the same problem.

They go not twice to the farther shore, and this not going twice, *na idaṃ*, is however not to be thought of as a 'going once' either.

---

[5] Cf. e.g. A II 149, *Saṃkhittasutta*.

[6] Pj II 498.

The commentary sidetracks by taking *idaṃ*, 'this,' to mean the farther shore, *pāraṃ*, whereas it comprehends the whole idea of not going twice. Only then is the paradox complete.

In other words, this verse concerns the such-like one, the *arahant*, and not the stream-winner, the once-returner or the non-returner. Here we have an echo of the idea already expressed as the grand finale of the *Paramaṭṭhakasutta*: *pāraṃgato na pacceti tādi*,[7] the such-like one, "gone to the farther shore, comes not back."

It is the last line, however, that remains a puzzle. Why is this 'not going twice,' not to be thought of as a 'going once?' There must be something deep behind this riddle.

Now, for instance, when one says 'I won't go there twice,' it means that he will go only once. When one says 'I won't tell twice,' it follows that he will tell only once. But here we are told that the *arahant* goes not twice, and yet it is not a going once.

The idea behind this riddle is that the influx-free *arahant*, the such-like-one, gone to the farther shore, which is supramundane, does not come back to the mundane. Nevertheless, he apparently comes back to the world and is seen to experience likes and dislikes, pleasures and pains, through the objects of the five senses. From the point of view of the worldling, the *arahant* has come back to the world. This is the crux of the problem.

Why is it not to be conceived of as a going once? Because the *arahant* has the ability to detach himself from the world from time to time and re-attain to that *arahattaphalasamādhi*. It is true that he too experiences the objects of the five external senses, but now and then he brings his mind to dwell in that *arahattaphalasamādhi,* which is like standing on the farther shore.

Here, then, we have an extremely subtle problem. When the *arahant* comes back to the world and is seen experiencing the objects of the five senses, one might of course conclude that he is

---

[7] Sn 803, *Paramaṭṭhakasutta*.

actually 'in the world.' This problematic situation, namely the question how the influx-free *arahant*, gone to the farther shore, comes back and takes in objects through the senses, the Buddha resolves with the help of a simple simile, drawn from nature. For instance, we read in the *Jarāsutta* of the *Sutta Nipāta* the following scintillating lines:

> *Udabindu yathā pi pokkhare,*
> *padume vāri yathā na lippati,*
> *evaṃ muni nopalippati,*
> *yadidaṃ diṭṭhasutammutesu vā.*[8]

> "Like a drop of water on a lotus leaf,
> Or water that taints not the lotus petal,
> So the sage unattached remains,
> In regard to what is seen, heard and sensed."

So the extremely deep problem concerning the relation between the supramundane and the mundane levels of experience, is resolved by the Buddha by bringing in the simile of the lotus petal and the lotus leaf.

Let us take up another instance from the *Māgandiyasutta* of the *Sutta Nipāta*:

> *Yehi vivitto vicareyya loke,*
> *na tāni uggayha vadeyya nāgo,*
> *elambujaṃ kaṇṭakaṃ vārijaṃ yathā,*
> *jalena paṃkena anūpalittaṃ,*
> *evaṃ munī santivādo agiddho,*
> *kāme ca loke ca anūpalitto.*[9]

---

[8] Sn 812, *Jarāsutta.*

[9] Sn 845, *Māgandiyasutta.*

"Detached from whatever views, the *arahant* wanders in
the world,
He would not converse, taking his stand on them,
Even as the white lotus, sprung up in the water,
Yet remains unsmeared by water and mud,
So is the sage, professing peace and free from greed,
Unsmeared by pleasures of sense and things of the world."

Among the Tens of the *Aṅguttara Nikāya* we come across a discourse in which the Buddha answers a question put by Venerable Bāhuna. At that time the Buddha was staying near the pond Gaggara in the city of Campa. Venerable Bāhuna's question was: *Katīhi nu kho, bhante, dhammehi tathāgato nissaṭo visaṃyutto vippamutto vimariyādikatena cetasā viharati?*[10]

"Detached, disengaged and released from how many things does the *Tathāgata* dwell with an unrestricted mind?" The Buddha's answer to the question embodies a simile, aptly taken from the pond, as it were:

> *Dasahi kho, Bāhuna, dhammehi tathāgato nissaṭo visaṃyutto vippamutto vimariyādikatena cetasā viharati. Katamehi dasahi? Rūpena kho, Bāhuna, Tathāgato nissaṭo visaṃyutto vippamutto vimariyādikatena cetasā viharati, vedanāya . . . saññāya . . . saṅkhārehi . . . viññāṇena . . . jātiyā . . . jarāya . . . maraṇena . . . dukkhehi . . . kilesehi kho, Bāhuna, Tathāgato nissaṭo visaṃyutto vippamutto vimariyādikatena cetasā viharati.*

> *Seyyathāpi, Bāhuna, uppalaṃ vā padumaṃ vā puṇḍarīkaṃ vā udake jātaṃ udake saṃvaḍḍhaṃ udakā accugamma tiṭṭhati anupalittaṃ udakena, evam eva kho*

---

[10] A V 151, *Bāhunasutta*.

> *Bāhuna Tathāgato imehi dasahi dhammehi nissaṭo visaṃyutto vippamutto vimariyādikatena cetasā viharati.*
>
> "Detached, disengaged and released from ten things, Bāhuna, does the *Tathāgata* dwell with a mind unrestricted. Which ten? Detached, disengaged and released from form, Bāhuna, does the *Tathāgata* dwell with a mind unrestricted; detached, disengaged and released from feeling . . . from perceptions . . . from preparations . . . from consciousness . . . from birth . . . from decay . . . from death . . . from pains . . . from defilements, Bāhuna, does the *Tathāgata* dwell with a mind unrestricted.
>
> "Just as, Bāhuna, a blue lotus, a red lotus, or a white lotus, born in the water, grown up in the water, rises well above the water and remains unsmeared by water, even so, Bāhuna, does the *Tathāgata* dwell detached, disengaged and released from these ten things with a mind unrestricted."

This discourse, in particular, highlights the transcendence of the *Tathāgata*, though he seems to take in worldly objects through the senses. Even the release from the five aggregates is affirmed.

We might wonder why the *Tathāgata* is said to be free from birth, decay and death, since, as we know, he did grow old and pass away. Birth, decay and death, in this context, do not refer to some future state either. Here and now the *Tathāgata* is free from the concepts of birth, decay and death.

In the course of our discussion of the term *papañca*, we had occasion to illustrate how one can be free from such concepts.[11] If concepts of birth, decay and death drive fear into the minds of worldlings, such is not the case with the *Tathāgata*. He is free

---

[11] See sermon 12.

from such fears and forebodings. He is free from defilements as well.

The discourse seems to affirm that the *Tathāgata* dwells detached from all these ten things. It seems, therefore, that the functioning of the *Tathāgata*'s sense-faculties in his everyday life also should follow a certain extraordinary pattern of detachment and disengagement. In fact, Venerable Sāriputta says something to that effect in the *Saḷāyatanasaṃyutta* of the *Saṃyutta Nikāya*:

Passati Bhagavā cakkhunā rūpaṃ, chandarāgo Bhagavato natthi, suvimuttacitto Bhagavā.[12] "The Exalted One sees forms with the eye, but there is no desire or attachment in him, well freed in mind is the Exalted One."

We come across a similar statement made by the brahmin youth Uttara in the *Brahmāyusutta* of the *Majjhima Nikāya*, after he had closely followed the Buddha for a considerable period to verify the good report of his extraordinary qualities:

Rasapaṭisaṃvedī kho pana so bhavaṃ Gotamo āhāraṃ āhāreti, no rasarāgapaṭisaṃvedī.[13] "Experiencing taste Master Gotama takes his food, but not experiencing any attachment to the taste."

It is indeed something marvelous. The implication is that there is such a degree of detachment with regard to things experienced by the tongue, even when the senses are taking in their objects. One can understand the difference between the mundane and the supramundane, when one reflects on the difference between experiencing taste and experiencing an attachment to taste.

Not only with regard to the objects of the five senses, but even with regard to mind-objects, the emancipated one has a certain degree of detachment. The *arahant* has realized that they are not 'such.' He takes in concepts, and even speaks in terms of 'I' and 'mine,' but knows that they are false concepts, as in the case of a child's language,

---

[12] S IV 164, *Koṭṭhikasutta*.

[13] M II 138, *Brahmāyusutta*.

There is a discourse among the Nines of the *Aṅguttara Nikāya* which seems to assert this fact. It is a discourse preached by Venerable Sāriputta to refute a wrong viewpoint taken by a monk named Chandikāputta:

> *Evaṃ sammā vimuttacittassa kho, āvuso, bhikkhuno bhusā cepi cakkhuviññeyyā rūpā cakkhussa āpāthaṃ āgacchanti, nevassa cittaṃ pariyādiyanti, amissīkatamevassa cittaṃ hoti ṭhitaṃ āneñjappattaṃ, vayaṃ cassānupassati. Bhusā cepi sotaviññeyyā saddā . . . bhūsa cepi ghānaviññeyyā gandhā . . . bhūsa cepi jivhāviññeyyā rasā . . . bhūsa cepi kāyaviññeyyā phoṭṭhabbā . . . bhūsa cepi manoviññeyyā dhammā manassa āpāthaṃ āgacchanti, nevassa cittaṃ pariyādiyanti, amissīkatamevassa cittaṃ hoti ṭhitaṃ āneñjappattaṃ, vayaṃ cassānupassati.*[14]

> "Friend, in the case of a monk who is fully released, even if many forms cognizable by the eye come within the range of vision, they do not overwhelm his mind, his mind remains unalloyed, steady and unmoved, he sees its passing away. Even if many sounds cognizable by the ear come within the range of hearing . . . even if many smells cognizable by the nose . . . even if many tastes cognizable by the tongue . . . even if many tangibles cognizable by the body . . . even if many mind-objects cognizable by the mind come within the range of the mind, they do not overwhelm his mind, his mind remains unalloyed, steady and unmoved, he sees its passing away."

So here we have the ideal of the emancipated mind. Generally, a person unfamiliar with the nature of a lotus leaf or a lotus petal, on

---

[14] A IV 404, *Silāyūpasutta*.

seeing a drop of water on a lotus leaf or a lotus petal would think that the water drop smears them.

Earlier we happened to mention that there is a wide gap between the mundane and the supramundane. Some might think that this refers to a gap in time or in space. In fact it is such a conception that often led to various misinterpretations concerning *Nibbāna*. The supramundane seems so far away from the mundane, so it must be something attainable after death in point of time. Or else it should be far far away in outer space. Such is the impression made in general.

But if we go by the simile of the drop of water on the lotus leaf, the distance between the mundane and the supramundane is the same as that between the lotus leaf and the drop of water on it.

We are still on the problem of the hither shore and the farther shore. The distinction between the mundane and the supramundane brings us to the question of this shore and the other shore.

The *arahant*'s conception of this shore and the other shore differs from that of the worldling in general. If, for instance, a native of this island goes abroad and settles down there, he might even think of a return to his country as a 'going abroad.' Similarly, as far as the emancipated sage is concerned, if he, having gone to the farther shore, does not come back, one might expect him to think of this world as the farther shore.

But it seems the *arahant* has no such distinction. A certain *Dhammapada* verse alludes to the fact that he has transcended this dichotomy:

> *Yassa pāraṃ apāraṃ vā,*
> *pārāpāraṃ na vijjati,*
> *vītaddaraṃ visaṃyuttaṃ,*
> *tam ahaṃ brūmi brāhmaṇaṃ.*[15]

---

[15] Dhp 385, *Brāhmaṇavagga.*

This is a verse we have quoted earlier too, in connection with the question of the verbal dichotomy.[16] *Yassa pāraṃ apāraṃ vā, pārāpāraṃ na vijjati,* "to whom there is neither a farther shore, nor a hither shore, nor both." That is to say, he has no discrimination between the two. *Vītaddaraṃ visaṃyuttaṃ, tam ahaṃ brūmi brāhmaṇaṃ*, "who is free from pangs of sorrow and entanglements, him I call a Brahmin."

This means that the *arahant* is free from the verbal dichotomy, which is of relevance to the worldling. Once gone beyond, the emancipated one has no more use of these concepts. This is where the Buddha's dictum in the raft simile of the *Alagaddūpamasutta* becomes meaningful.

Even the concepts of a 'this shore' and a 'farther shore' are useful only for the purpose of crossing over. If, for instance, the *arahant*, having gone beyond, were to think 'ah, this is my land,' that would be some sort of a grasping. Then there will be an identification, *tammayatā*, not a non-identification, *atammayatā*.

As we had mentioned earlier, there is a strange quality called *atammayatā*, associated with an *arahant*.[17] In connection with the simile of a man who picked up a gem, we have already stated the ordinary norm that prevails in the world:[18] if we possess something – we are possessed by it; if we grasp something – we are caught by it.

This is the moral behind the parable of the gem. It is this conviction, which prompts the *arahant* not to grasp even the farther shore, though he may stand there. 'This shore' and the 'other shore' are concepts, which have a practical value to those who are still on this side.

As it is stated in the *Alagaddūpamasutta*, since there is no boat or bridge to cross over, one has to improvise a raft by putting

---

16 See sermon 5.

17 See sermon 14.

18 See sermon 9.

together grass, twigs, branches and leaves, found on this shore. But after crossing over with its help, he does not carry it with him on his shoulder:

> *Evameva kho, bhikkhave, kullūpamo mayā dhammo desito nittharaṇatthāya no gahaṇatthāya. Kullūpamaṃ vo bhikkhave ājānantehi dhammā pi vo pahātabbā, pag'eva adhammā.*[19]

> "Even so, monks, have I preached to you a *Dhamma* that is comparable to a raft, which is for crossing over and not for grasping. Well knowing the *Dhamma* to be comparable to a raft, you should abandon even the good things, more so the bad things."

One might think that the *arahant* is in the sensuous realm, when, for instance, he partakes of food. But that is not so. Though he attains to the realms of form and formless realms, he does not belong there. He has the ability to attain to those levels of concentration, but he does not grasp them egoistically, true to that norm of *atammayatā*, or non-identification.

This indeed is something extraordinary. Views and opinions about language, dogmatically entertained by the worldlings, lose their attraction for him. This fact is clearly illustrated for us by the *Uragàsutta* of the *Sutta Nipāta*, the significance of which we have already stressed.[20] We happened to mention that there is a refrain, running through all the seventeen verses making up that discourse. The refrain concerns the worn out skin of a snake. The last two lines in each verse, forming the refrain, are:

---

[19] M I 135, *Alagaddūpamasutta.*

[20] See sermon 5.

So bhikkhu jahāti orapāraṃ,
urago jiṇṇamiva tacaṃ purāṇaṃ.[21]

"That monk forsakes the hither and the thither,
Even as the snake its skin that doth wither."

The term *orapāraṃ* is highly significant in this context. *Oraṃ* means "this shore" and *paraṃ* is the "farther shore." The monk, it seems, gives up not only this shore, but the other shore as well, even as the snake sloughs off its worn out skin. That skin has served its purpose, but now it is redundant. So it is sloughed off.

Let us now take up one more verse from the *Uragasutta* which has the same refrain, because of its relevance to the understanding of the term *papañca*. The transcendence of relativity involves freedom from the duality in worldly concepts such as 'good' and 'evil.' The concept of a 'farther shore' stands relative to the concept of a 'hither shore.' The point of these discourses is to indicate that there is a freedom from worldly conceptual proliferations based on duality and relativity. The verse we propose to bring up is:

Yo nāccasārī na paccasārī,
sabbaṃ accagamā imaṃ papañcaṃ,
so bhikkhu jahāti orapāraṃ,
urago jiṇṇamiva tacaṃ purāṇaṃ.[22]

"Who neither overreaches himself nor lags behind,
And has gone beyond all this proliferation,
That monk forsakes the hither and the thither,
Even as the snake its slough that doth wither."

---

21 Sn 1-17 , *Uragasutta.*

22 Sn 8, *Uragasutta.*

This verse is particularly significant in that it brings out some points of interest. The overreaching and lagging behind is an allusion to the verbal dichotomy. In the context of views, for instance, annihilationism is an overreaching and eternalism is a lagging behind. We may give another illustration, easier to understand. Speculation about the future is an overreaching and repentance over the past is a lagging behind. To transcend both these tendencies is to get beyond proliferation, *sabbaṃ accagamā imaṃ papañcaṃ*.

When a banknote is invalidated, cravings, conceits and views bound with it go down. Concepts current in the world, like banknotes in transaction, are reckoned as valid so long as cravings, conceits and views bound with them are there. They are no longer valid when these are gone.

We have defined *papañca* with reference to cravings, conceits and views.[23] Commentaries also speak of *taṇhāpapañca. diṭṭhi-papañca* and *mānapapañca*.[24] By doing away with cravings, conceits and views, one goes beyond all *papañca*.

The term *orapāraṃ*, too, has many connotations. It stands for the duality implicit in such usages as the 'internal' and the 'external,' 'one's own' and 'another's,' as well as 'this shore' and the 'farther shore.' It is compared here to the worn out skin of a snake. It is worn out by transcending the duality characteristic of linguistic usage through wisdom.

Why the Buddha first hesitated to teach this *Dhamma* was the difficulty of making the world understand.[25] Perhaps it was the conviction that the world could easily be misled by those limitations in the linguistic medium.

---

[23] See sermon 12.

[24] E.g. Ps I 183, commenting on M I 40, *Sallekhasutta*: *n'etaṃ mama, n'eso ham asmi, na meso attā ti*.

[25] M I 168, *Ariyapariyesanasutta*.

We make these few observations in order to draw attention to the relativity underlying such terms as 'this shore' and the 'other shore' and to show how *Nibbāna* transcends even that dichotomy.

In this connection, we may take up for comment a highly controversial *sutta* in the *Itivuttaka*, which deals with the two aspects of *Nibbāna* known as *sa-upādisesā Nibbānadhātu* and *anupādisesā Nibbānadhātu*. We propose to quote the entire *sutta*, so as to give a fuller treatment to the subject:

Vuttaṃ hetaṃ Bhagavatā, vuttam arahatā ti me suttaṃ:

Dve-mā, bhikkhave, nibbānadhātuyo. Katame dve? Sa-upadisesā ca nibbānadhātu, anupādisesā ca nibbānadhātu.

Katamā, bhikkhave, sa-upadisesā nibbānadhātu? Idha, bhikkhave, bhikkhu arahaṃ hoti khīṇāsavo vusitavā katakaraṇīyo ohitabhāro anuppattasadattho parikkhīṇabhavasaṃyojano sammadaññāvimutto. Tassa tiṭṭhanteva pañcindriyāni yesaṃ avighātattā manāpāmanāpaṃ paccanubhoti, sukhadukkhaṃ paṭisaṃvediyati. Tassa yo rāgakkhayo dosakkhayo mohakkhayo, ayaṃ vuccati, bhikkhave, sa-upadisesā nibbānadhātu.

Katamā ca, bhikkhave, anupādisesā nibbānadhātu? Idha, bhikkhave, bhikkhu arahaṃ hoti khīṇāsavo vusitavā katakaraṇīyo ohitabhāro anuppattasadattho parikkhīṇabhavasaṃyojano sammadaññāvimutto. Tassa idheva sabbavedayitāni anabhinanditāni sītibhavissanti, ayaṃ vuccati, bhikkhave, anupādisesā nibbānadhātu.

Etam atthaṃ Bhagavā avoca, tatthetaṃ iti vuccati:

Duve imā cakkhumatā pakāsitā,
nibbānadhātū anissitena tādinā,

ekā hi dhātu idha diṭṭhadhammikā,
sa-upadisesā bhavanettisaṅkhayā,
anupādisesā pana samparāyikā,
yamhi nirujjhanti bhavāni sabbaso.

Ye etad-aññāya padaṃ asaṅkhataṃ,
vimuttacittā bhavanettisaṅkhayā,
te dhammasārādhigamā khaye ratā,
pahaṃsu te sabbabhavāni tādino.
Ayampi attho vutto Bhagavatā, iti me sutaṃ.[26]

"This was said by the Exalted One, said by the Worthy One, so have I heard:

'Monks, there are these two *Nibbāna* elements. Which two? The *Nibbāna* element with residual clinging and the *Nibbāna* element without residual clinging.

'And what, monks, is the *Nibbāna* element with residual clinging? Herein, monks, a monk is an *arahant*, with influxes extinct, one who has lived the holy life to the full, done what is to be done, laid down the burden, reached one's goal, fully destroyed the fetters of existence and released with full understanding. His five sense faculties still remain and due to the fact that they are not destroyed, he experiences likes and dislikes, and pleasures and pains. That extirpation of lust, hate and delusion in him, that, monks, is known as the *Nibbāna* element with residual clinging.

'And what, monks, is the *Nibbāna* element without residual clinging? Herein, monks, a monk is an *arahant*, with

[26] It 38, *Nibbānadhātusutta*.

influxes extinct, one who has lived the holy life to the full, done what is to be done, laid down the burden, reached one's goal, fully destroyed the fetters of existence and released with full understanding. In him, here itself, all what is felt will cool off, not being delighted in. This, monks, is the *Nibbāna* element without residual clinging.'

"To this effect the Exalted One spoke and this is the gist handed down as 'thus said':

'These two *Nibbāna* elements have been made known,
By the one with vision, unattached and such,
Of relevance to the here and now is one element,
With residual clinging, yet with tentacles to becoming snapped,
But then that element without residual clinging is of relevance to the hereafter,
For in it surcease all forms of becoming.

'They that comprehend fully this state of the unprepared,
Released in mind with tentacles to becoming snapped,
On winning to the essence of *Dhamma* they take delight in seeing to an end of it all,
So give up they, all forms of becoming, steadfastly such-like as they are.'"

The standard phrase summing up the qualification of an *arahant* occurs in full in the definition of the *sa-upādisesā Nibbānadhātu*. The distinctive feature of this *Nibbāna* element is brought out in the statement that the *arahant*'s five sense faculties are still intact, owing to which he experiences likes and dislikes, and pleasure and pain. However, to the extent that lust, hate and delusion are extinct in him, it is called the *Nibbāna* element with residual clinging.

In the definition of the *Nibbāna* element without residual clinging, the same standard phrase recurs, while its distinctive feature is summed up in just one sentence: *Tassa idheva sabbavedayitāni anabhinanditāni sītibhavissanti*, "in him, here itself, all what is felt will cool off, not being delighted in." It may be noted that the verb is in the future tense and apart from this cooling off, there is no guarantee of a world beyond, as an *asaṅkhata dhātu*, or 'unprepared element,' with no sun, moon or stars in it.

The two verses that follow purport to give a summary of the prose passage. Here it is clearly stated that out of the two *Nibbāna* elements, as they are called, the former pertains to the here and now, *diṭṭhadhammika*, while the latter refers to what comes after death, *samparāyika*. The *Nibbāna* element with residual clinging, *sa-upādisesā Nibbānadhātu*, has as its redeeming feature the assurance that the tentacular craving for becoming is cut off, despite its exposure to likes and dislikes, pleasures and pains, common to the field of the five senses.

As for the *Nibbāna* element without residual clinging, it is definitely stated that in it all forms of existence come to cease. The reason for it is none other than the crucial fact, stated in that single sentence, namely, the cooling off of all what is felt as an inevitable consequence of not being delighted in, *anabhinanditāni*.

Why do they not take delight in what is felt at the moment of passing away? They take delight in something else, and that is: the very destruction of all what is felt, a foretaste of which they have already experienced in their attainment to that unshakeable deliverance of the mind, which is the very pith and essence of the *Dhamma*, *dhammasāra*.

As stated in the *Mahāsāropamasutta* of the *Majjhima Nikāya*, the pith of the *Dhamma* is that deliverance of the mind,[27] and to take delight in the ending of all feelings, *khaye ratā*, is to revert to the *arahattaphalasamādhi* with which the *arahant* is already

---

[27] M I 197, *Mahāsāropamasutta*.

familiar. That is how those such-like ones abandon all forms of existence, *pahaṃsu te sabbabhavāni tādino*.

Let us now try to sort out the problems that are likely to be raised in connection with the interpretation we have given. First and foremost, the two terms *diṭṭhadhammika* and *samparāyika* have to be explained.

A lot of confusion has arisen, due to a misunderstanding of the meaning of these two terms in this particular context. The usual commentarial exegesis on the term *diṭṭhadhammika* amounts to this: *Imasmiṃ attabhāve bhavā vattamānā*,[28] "in this very life, that is, in the present." It seems all right. But then for *samparāyika* the commentary has the following comment: *samparāye khandha-bhedato parabhāge*, "*Samparāya* means after the breaking up of the aggregates." The implication is that it refers to the *arahant*'s after death state.

Are we then to conclude that the *arahant* gets half of his *Nibbāna* here and the other half hereafter? The terms *diṭṭhad-hammika* and *samparāyika*, understood in their ordinary sense, would point to such a conclusion.

But let us not forget that the most distinctive quality of this *Dhamma* is associated with the highly significant phrase, *diṭṭhevadhamme*, "in this very life." It is also conveyed by the expression *sandiṭṭhika akālika*, "here and now" and "timeless."[29] The goal of endeavour, indicated by this *Dhamma*, is one that could be fully realized here and now, in this very life. It is not a piecemeal affair. Granting all that, do we find here something contrary to it, conveyed by the two terms *diṭṭhadhammika* and *samparāyika*? How can we reconcile these two passages?

In the context of *kamma*, the meaning of the two terms in question can easily be understood. For instance, that category of *kamma* known as *diṭṭhadhammavedanīya* refers to those actions

---

[28] It-a I 167.

[29] In the standard formula for recollecting the *Dhamma*, e.g. at D II 93.

which produce their results here and now. *Samparāyika* pertains to what comes after death, as for instance in the phrase *samparāye ca duggati*, an "evil born after death."[30] In the context of *kamma* it is clear enough, then, that the two terms refer to what is experienced in this world and what comes after death, respectively.

Are we justified in applying the same criterion, when it comes to the so-called two elements of *Nibbāna*? Do the *arahants* experience some part of *Nibbāna* here and the rest hereafter?

At this point, we have to admit that the term *diṭṭhadhammika* is associated with *sa-upādisesā Nibbānadhātu* while the term *samparāyika* is taken over to refer to *anupādisesā Nibbānadhātu*. However, the fact that *Nibbāna* is explicitly defined elsewhere as the cessation of existence, *bhavanirodho Nibbānaṃ*,[31] must not be forgotten. If *Nibbāna* is the cessation of existence, there is nothing left for the *arahant* to experience hereafter.

Nibbāna is solely the realization of the cessation of existence or the end of the process of becoming. So there is absolutely no question of a hereafter for the *arahant*. By way of clarification, we have to revert to the primary sense of the term *Nibbāna*. We have made it sufficiently clear that *Nibbāna* means 'extinction' or 'extinguishment,' as of a fire.

All the commentarial jargon, equating *vāna* to *taṇhā*, is utterly irrelevant. If the idea of an extinguishment of a fire is brought in, the whole problem is solved. Think of a blazing fire. If no more firewood is added to it, the flames would subside and the embers would go on smouldering before turning into ashes. This is the norm. Now this is not an analogy we are superimposing on the *Dhamma*. It is only an echo of a canonical simile, picked up from the *Nāgasutta* of the *Aṅguttara Nikāya*. The relevant verse, we are quoting, recurs in the *Udāyi Theragāthā* as well:

---

[30] S I 34, *Maccharisutta*.

[31] A V 9, *Sāriputtasutta*.

Mahāgini pajjalito,
anāhārūpasammati,
aṅgāresu ca santesu,,
nibbuto ti pavuccati.[32]

"As a huge blazing fire, with no more firewood added,
Goes down to reach a state of calm,
Embers smouldering, as they are, could be reckoned,
So long as they last, as almost 'extinguished.'"

Though we opted to render the verse this way, there is a variant reading, which could lead to a different interpretation. As so often happens in the case of deep *suttas*, here too the correct reading is not easily determined. Instead of the phrase *aṅgāresu ca santesu*, attested as it is, many editions go for the variant reading *saṅkhāresūpasantesu*. If that reading is adopted, the verse would have to be rendered as follows:

"As a huge blazing fire, with no more firewood added,
Goes down to reach a state of calm,
When *saṅkhāras* calm down,
One is called 'extinguished.'"

It may be pointed out that this variant reading does not accord with the imagery of the fire presented by the first two lines of the verse. It is probably a scribe's error that has come down, due to the rhythmic similarity between the two phrases *aṅgāresu ca santesu*, and *saṅkhāresūpasantesu.*[33] Between the reciter and the scribe, phrases that have a similar ring and rhythm, could sometimes bring about a textual corruption. Be that as it may, we have opted for the reading *aṅgāresu ca santesu*, because it makes more sense.

---

32 A III 347, *Nāgasutta* and Th 702, *Udāyitheragāthā*.

33 The corresponding verse in the Chinese parallel, *Madhyama Āgama* discourse 118 (Taishō I 608c27), does not mention *saṅkhāra* at all. (Anālayo)

From the particular context in which the verse occurs, it seems that this imagery of the fire is a restatement of the image of the lotus unsmeared by water. Though the embers are still smouldering, to the extent that they are no longer hungering for more fuel and are not emitting flames, they may as well be reckoned as 'extinguished.'

We can draw a parallel between this statement and the definition of *sa-upādisesā Nibbānadhātu* already quoted. As a full-fledged *arahant*, he still experiences likes and dislikes and pleasures and pains, owing to the fact that his five sense-faculties are intact.

The assertion made by the phrase beginning with *tassa tiṭṭhanteva pañcindriyāni yesaṃ avighātattā* . . . , "his five senses do exist, owing to the non-destruction of which . . . ," rather apologetically brings out the limitations of the living *arahant*. It is reminiscent of those smouldering embers in the imagery of the *Nāgasutta*. However, in so far as flames of lust, hate and delusion are quenched in him, it comes to be called *sa-upādisesā Nibbānadhātu*, even as in the case of those smouldering embers.

Craving is aptly called *bhavanetti*,[34] in the sense that it leads to becoming by catching hold of more and more fuel in the form of *upādāna*. When it is under control, the functioning of the sense-faculties do not entail further rebirth. The inevitable residual clinging in the living *arahant* does not precipitate a fresh existence.

This gives us a clue to the understanding of the term *anupādisesa*. The element *upādi* in this term is rather ambiguous. In the *Satipaṭṭhānasutta*, for instance, it is used as the criterion to distinguish the *anāgāmi*, the "non-returner," from the *arahant*, in the statement *diṭṭhevadhamme aññā, sati vā upādisese anāgāmitā*,[35] "either full convincing knowledge of *arahant*-hood

---

[34] A II 1, *Anubuddhasutta*.

[35] M I 62, *Satipaṭṭhānasutta*.

here and now, or the state of non-return in the case of residual clinging."

But when it comes to the distinction between *sa-upādisesa* and *anupādisesa*, the element *upādi* has to be understood in a more radical sense, in association with the word *upādiṇṇa*. This body, as the product of past *kamma*, is the 'grasped' par excellence, which as an organic combination goes on functioning even in the *arahant* until his last moment of life.

Venerable Sāriputta once declared that he neither delighted in death nor delighted in life, *nābhinandāmi maraṇaṃ nābhinandāmi jīvitaṃ.*[36] So the embers go on smouldering until they become ashes. It is when the life-span ends that the embers finally turn to ashes.

The popular interpretation of the term *anupādisesā Nibbānadhātu* leaves room for some absolutist conceptions of an *asaṅkhata dhātu*, unprepared element, as the destiny of the *arahant*. After his *parinibbāna*, he is supposed to enter this particular *Nibbānadhātu*. But here, in this discourse, it is explained in just one sentence: *Tassa idheva, bhikkhave, sabbavedayitāni anabhinanditāni sītibhavissanti,* "In the case of him," (that is the *arahant*), "O! monks, all what is felt, not having been delighted in, will cool off here itself."

This cooling off happens just before death, without igniting another spark of life. When *Māra* comes to grab and seize, the *arahant* lets go. The pain of death with which *Māra* teases his hapless victim and lures him into another existence, becomes ineffective in the case of the *arahant*. As he has already gone through the supramundane experience of deathlessness, in the *arahattaphalasamādhi*, death loses its sting when at last it comes. The influx-free deliverance of the mind and the influx-free deliverance through wisdom enable him to cool down all feelings in a way that baffles *Māra*.

---

36 Th 1001, *Sāriputtatheragāthā*.

So the *arahant* lets go of his body, experiencing ambrosial deathlessness. As in the case of Venerable Dabba Mallaputta, he would sometimes cremate his own body without leaving any ashes.[37] Outwardly it might appear as an act of self-immolation, which indeed is painful. But this is not so. Using his *jhānic* powers, he simply employs the internal fire element to cremate the body he has already discarded.

This, then, is the Buddha's extraordinary solution to the problem of overcoming death, a solution that completely outwits *Māra*.

---

[37] Ud 92, *Paṭhamadabbasutta*.

Nibbāna Sermon 19

Namo tassa Bhagavato Arahato Sammāsambuddhassa
Namo tassa Bhagavato Arahato Sammāsambuddhassa
Namo tassa Bhagavato Arahato Sammāsambuddhassa

Etaṃ santaṃ, etaṃ paṇītaṃ, yadidaṃ sabbasaṅkhārasamatho sabbūpadhipaṭinissaggo taṇhakkhayo virāgo nirodho nibbānaṃ.[1]

"This is peaceful, this is excellent, namely the stilling of all preparations, the relinquishment of all assets, the destruction of craving, detachment, cessation, extinction."

With the permission of the Most Venerable Great Preceptor and the assembly of the venerable meditative monks.

This is the nineteenth sermon in the series of sermons on *Nibbāna*. Towards the end of our last sermon, we started commenting on the two terms *sa-upādisesā Nibbānadhātu* and *anupādisesā Nibbānadhātu*. Our discussion was based on a discourse, which we quoted from the *Itivuttaka*. We also drew attention to a certain analogy found in the discourses, which shows that the two *Nibbāna* elements actually represent two stages of the extinguishment implicit in the term *Nibbāna*.

When no more firewood is added to a blazing fire, flames would subside and the logs of wood already burning go on smouldering as embers. After some time, they too get extinguished and become ashes. With regard to the *arahant*, too, we have to think in terms of this analogy. It can be taken as an illustration of

1 M I 436, *MahāMālunkyasutta*.

the two *Nibbāna* elements. To the extent the living *arahant* is free from fresh graspings, lust, hate and delusions do not flare up. But so long as he has to bear the burden of this organic combination, this physical frame, the *arahant* has to experience certain afflictions and be receptive to likes and dislikes, pleasures and pains.

In spite of all that, mentally he has access to the experience of the extinguishment he has already won. It is in that sense that the *arahant* is said to be in the *Nibbāna* element with residual clinging in his everyday life, while taking in the objects of the five senses.

At the last moment of the *arahant*'s life, even this organic body that had been grasped as *upādiṇṇa* has to be abandoned. It is at that moment, when he is going to detach his mind from the body, that *anupādisesā parinibbānadhātu* comes in. A brief hint to this effect is given in one of the verses occurring in the *Nāgasutta* referred to earlier. The verse runs thus:

Vītarāga vītadoso
vītamoho anāsavo
sarīraṃ vijahaṃ nāgo
parinibbissati anāsavo.[2]

"The one who has abandoned lust,
Hate and delusion and is influx-free,
That elephant of a man, on giving up his body,
Will attain full appeasement, being influx-free."

If we define in brief the two *Nibbāna* elements this way, a more difficult problem confronts us relating to the sense in which they are called *diṭṭhadhammika* and *samparāyika*. *Diṭṭhadhammika* means what pertains to this life and *samparāyika* refers to what comes after death. What is the idea in designating *sa-upādisesā Nibbānadhātu* as *diṭṭhadhammika* and *anupādisesā Nibbānadhātu* as *samparāyika*?

---

[2] A III 347, *Nāgasutta*.

In the context of *kamma*, the meaning of these two terms is easily understood. But when it comes to *Nibbāna*, such an application of the terms would imply two types of *Nibbānic* bliss, one to be experienced here and the other hereafter.

But that kind of explanation would not accord with the spirit of this *Dhamma*, because the Buddha always emphasizes the fact that *Nibbāna* is something to be realized here and now in toto. It is not a piecemeal realization, leaving something for the hereafter. Such terms like *diṭṭhevadhamme*, in this very life, *sandiṭṭhika*, here and now, and *akālika*, timeless, emphasize this aspect of *Nibbāna*.

In the context of *Nibbāna*, these two terms have to be understood as representing two aspects of a perfect realization attainable in this very life. Briefly stated, *anupādisesā Nibbānadhātu* is that which confers the certitude, well in time, that the appeasement experienced by an *arahant* during this life time remains unchanged even at death. To say that there is a possibility of realizing or ascertaining one's state after death might even seem contradictory. How can one realize one's after death state?

We get a clear-cut answer to that question in the following passage in the *Dhātuvibhaṅgasutta* of the *Majjhima Nikāya*:

> *Seyyathāpi, bhikkhu, telañca paṭicca vaṭṭiñca paṭicca telappadīpo jhāyati, tasseva telassa ca vaṭṭiyā ca pariyādānā aññassa ca anupahārā anāhāro nibbāyati, evameva kho, bhikkhu, kāyapariyantikaṃ vedanaṃ vediyamāno 'kāyapariyantikaṃ vedanaṃ vedayāmī'ti pajānati, jīvitapariyantikaṃ vedanaṃ vediyamāno 'jīvitapariyantikaṃ vedanaṃ vedayāmī'ti pajānati, 'kāyassa bhedā paraṃ maraṇā uddhaṃ jīvitapariyādānā idheva sabbavedayitāni anabhinanditāni sītībhavissantī'ti pajānati.*[3]

[3] M III 245, *Dhātuvibhaṅgasutta*.

> "Just as, monk, an oil lamp burns depending on oil and the wick, and when that oil and the wick are used up, if it does not get any more of these, it is extinguished from lack of fuel, even so, monk, when he feels a feeling limited to the body, he understands 'I feel a feeling limited to the body,' when he feels a feeling limited to life, he understands 'I feel a feeling limited to life,' he understands 'on the breaking up of this body, before life becomes extinct, even here itself, all that is felt, not being delighted in, will become cool."

The last sentence is particularly noteworthy in that it refers to an understanding well beforehand that all feelings, not being delighted in, will become cool at death. The futuristic ending signifies an assurance, here and now, as the word idheva, even here itself, clearly brings out. The delighting will not be there, because all craving for a fresh existence is extirpated.

The *arahant* has won this assurance already in his *arahattaphalasamādhi*, in which he experiences the cooling off of all feelings. That is why we find the *arahants* giving expression to their *Nibbānic* bliss in the words *sītibhūto'smi nibbuto*, "gone cool am I, yea, extinguished."[4]

Since for the *arahant* this cooling off of feelings is a matter of experience in this very life, this realization is referred to as *anupādā parinibbāna* in the discourses. Here we seem to have fallen into another track. We opened our discussion with an explanation of what *anupādisesa parinibbāna* is, now we are on *anupādā parinibbāna*. How are we to distinguish between these two?

Anupādisesa parinibbāna comes at the last moment of the *arahant*'s life, when this organic combination of elements, grasped par excellence, *upādiṇṇa*, is discarded for good. But *anupādā parinibbāna* refers to the *arahattaphalasamādhi* as such, for which

[4] Th 298, *Rāhulatheragāthā*.

even other terms like *anupādā vimokkha* are also applied on occasion.[5]

As the term *anupādā parinibbāna* signifies, the *arahant* experiences, even in this very life, that complete extinguishment, *parinibbāna*, in his *arahattaphalasamādhi*. This fact is clearly brought out in the dialogue between Venerable Sāriputta and Venerable Puṇṇa Mantāniputta in the *Rathavinītasutta* of the *Majjhima Nikāya*.

Venerable Sāriputta's exhaustive interrogation ending with *kim atthaṃ carahāvuso, bhagavati brahmacariyaṃ vussati?*,[6] "For the sake of what then, friend, is the holy life lived under the Exalted One?," gets the following conclusive answer from Venerable Puṇṇa Mantāniputta: *anupādāparinibbānatthaṃ kho, āvuso, bhagavati brahmacariyaṃ vussati*, "Friend, it is for the sake of perfect *Nibbāna* without grasping that the holy life is lived under the Exalted One."

As the goal of endeavour, *anupādā parinibbāna* surely does not mean the ending of life. What it implies is the realization of *Nibbāna*. It is that experience of the cooling off of feelings the *arahant* goes through in the *arahattaphalasamādhi*. It is sometimes also called *nirupadhi*, the "asset-less."[7] Here we have a problem of a semantic type. At a later date, even the term *nirupadhisesa* seems to have come into vogue, which is probably a cognate formed after the term *anupādisesa*.[8]

Nowhere in the discourses does one comes across the term *nirupadhisesa parinibbāna*. Only such terms as *nirupadhi*, *nirūpadhiṃ*, *nirupadhi dhammaṃ* are met with. They all refer to that *arahattaphalasamādhi*, as for instance in the following verse, which we had occasion to quote earlier too:

---

[5] E.g. M II 265, *Āneñjasappāyasutta*.

[6] M I 147, *Rathavinītasutta*.

[7] S I 194, *Moggallānasutta*.

[8] Bv-a 252.

Kāyena amataṃ dhātuṃ,
phusayitvā nirūpadhiṃ,
upadhipaṭinissaggaṃ,
sacchikatvā anāsavo,
deseti sammāsambuddho,
asokaṃ virajaṃ padaṃ.[9]

"Having touched with the body,
The deathless element, which is asset-less,
And realized the relinquishment of assets,
Being influx-free, the perfectly enlightened one,
Proclaims the sorrow-less, taintless state."

To proclaim, one has to be alive. Therefore *nirupadhi* is used in the discourses definitely for the *arahattaphalasamādhi*, which is a living experience for the *arahant*. *Anupādā parinibbāna*, *anupādā vimokkha* and *nirupadhi* all refer to that experience of the cooling off of feelings. This fact is clearly revealed by the following two verses in the *Vedanāsaṃyutta* of the *Saṃyutta Nikāya*:

Samāhito sampajāno,
sato Buddhassa sāvako,
vedanā ca pajānāti,
vedanānañca sambhavaṃ.

Yattha cetā nirujjhanti,
maggañca khayagāminaṃ,
vedanānaṃ khayā bhikkhu,
nicchāto parinibbuto.[10]

In this couplet, the experience of the fruit of *arahant*-hood is presented under the heading of feeling. The disciple of the Bud-

---

[9] It 62, *Santatarasutta*, see sermon 17.

[10] S IV 204, *Samādhisutta*.

dha, concentrated, fully aware and mindful, understands feelings, the origin of feelings, and the point at which they surcease and the way leading to their extinction. With the extinction of feelings, that monk is hunger-less and perfectly extinguished. The reference here is to that bliss of *Nibbāna* which is devoid of feeling, *avedayita sukha*.[11] It is hunger-less because it is free from craving.

The perfect extinguishment mentioned here is not to be understood as the death of the *arahant*. In the discourses the term *parinibbuta* is used as such even with reference to the living *arahant*. Only in the commentaries we find a distinction made in this respect. The *parinibbāna* of the living *arahant* is called *kilesaparinibbāna*, the perfect extinguishment of the defilements, while what comes at the last moment of an *arahant*'s life is called *khandhaparinibbāna*, the perfect extinguishment of the groups or aggregates.[12] Such a qualification, however, is not found in the discourses.

The reason for this distinction was probably the semantic development the term *parinibbāna* had undergone in the course of time. The fact that this perfect extinguishment is essentially psychological seems to have been ignored with the passage of time. That is why today, on hearing the word *parinibbāna*, one is immediately reminded of the last moment of the life of the Buddha or of an *arahant*. In the discourses, however, *parinibbāna* is clearly an experience of the living *arahant* in his *arahattaphalasamādhi*.

This fact is clearly borne out by the statement in the *Dhātuvibhaṅgasutta* already quoted: *idheva sabbavedayitāni anabhinanditāni sītībhavissantī'ti pajānati*,[13] "He understands that all what is felt will cool off here itself." It is this very understanding that is essential. It gives the certitude that one can defeat *Māra* at the moment of death through the experience of the cooling off of feelings.

---

11 Ps III 115, *aṭṭhakathā* on the *Bahuvedanīyasutta*.

12 E.g. at Mp I 91.

13 M III 245, *Dhātuvibhaṅgasutta*.

The phrase *jīvitapariyantikaṃ vedanaṃ* refers to the feeling which comes at the termination of one's life. For the *arahant*, the *arahattaphalasamādhi* stands in good stead, particularly at the moment of death. That is why it is called *akuppā cetovimutti*, the unshakeable deliverance of the mind. All other deliverances of the mind get shaken before the pain of death, but not this unshakeable deliverance of the mind, which is the REAL-ization of extinguishment that is available to the *arahant* already in the *arahattaphalasamādhi*, in the experience of the cooling off of feelings. It is this unshakeable deliverance of the mind that the Buddha and the *arahants* resort to at the end of their lives, when *Māra* comes to grab and seize.

So now we can hark back to that verse which comes as the grand finale in the long discourse from the *Itivuttaka* we have already quoted:

> *Ye etad aññāya padaṃ asaṅkhataṃ,*
> *vimuttacittā bhavanettisaṅkhayā,*
> *te dhammasārādhigamā khaye ratā,*
> *pahaṃsu te sabbabhavāni tādino.*[14]

This verse might appear problematic, as it occurs at the end of a passage dealing with the two *Nibbāna* elements. *Ye etad aññāya padaṃ asaṅkhataṃ*, "those who having fully comprehended this unprepared state," *vimuttacittā bhavanettisaṅkhayā*, "are released in mind by the cutting off of tentacles to becoming," *te dhammasārādhigamā khaye ratā*, "taking delight in the extirpation of feelings due to their attainment to the essence of dhamma," that is the unshakeable deliverance of the mind, *pahaṃsu te sabbabhavāni tādino*, "being steadfastly such like, they have given up all forms of becoming."

The last line is an allusion to the experience of the cessation of existence here and now, which in effect is the realization of

[14] It 39, *Nibbānadhātusutta*, see sermon 18.

Nibbāna, true to the definition *bhavanirodho nibbānaṃ*, "cessation of existence is *Nibbāna*."[15] It is that very cessation of existence that is called *asaṅkhata dhātu*, the "unprepared element." If *bhava*, or existence, is to be called *saṅkhata*, the 'prepared,' the cessation of existence has to be designated as *asaṅkhata*, the 'unprepared.' Here lies the difference between the two.

So we have here two aspects of the same unprepared element, designated as *sa-upādisesā parinibbānadhātu* and *anupādisesā parinibbānadhātu*. The mind is free even at the stage of *sa-upādisesa*, to the extent that the smouldering embers do not seek fresh fuel. *Anupādisesa* refers to the final experience of extinguishment. There the relevance of the term *parinibbāna* lies in the fact that at the moment of death the *arahants* direct their minds to this unshakeable deliverance of the mind. This is the 'island' they resort to when *Māra* comes to grab.

The best illustration for all this is the way the Buddha faced death, when the time came for it. Venerable Anuruddha delineates it beautifully in the following two verses:

Nāhu assāsapassāso,
ṭhitacittassa tādino,
anejo santimārabbha,
yaṃ kālamakarī muni.

Asallīnena cittena,
vedanaṃ ajjhavāsayi,
pajjotass'eva nibbānaṃ,
vimokkho cetaso ahu.[16]

"Adverting to whatever peace,
The urgeless sage reached the end of his lifespan,

---

15 A V 9, *Sāriputtasutta*.

16 D II 157, *Mahāparinibbānasutta*.

There were no in-breaths and out-breaths,
For that steadfastly such-like one of firm mind.

"With a mind fully alert,
He bore up the pain,
The deliverance of the mind was like
The extinguishment of a torch."

The allusion here is to the deliverance of the mind. This is a description of how the Buddha attained *parinibbāna*. Though there is a great depth in these two verses, the commentarial exegesis seems to have gone at a tangent at this point. Commenting on the last two lines of the first verse, the commentary observes: *Buddhamuni santiṃ gamissāmīti, santiṃ ārabbha kālamakari*, "the Buddha, the sage, passed away for the sake of that peace with the idea 'I will go to that state of peace.'"[17]

There is some discrepancy in this explanation. Commentators themselves usually give quite a different sense to the word *ārabbha* than the one implicit in this explanation. Here it means "for the sake of." It is for the sake of that peace that the Buddha is said to have passed away.

In such commentaries as *Jātaka-aṭṭhakathā* and *Dhammapada-aṭṭhakathā*, commentators do not use the word *ārabbha* in the introductory episodes in this sense. There it only means "in connection with," indicating the origin of the story, as suggested by the etymological background of the word itself. When for instance it is said that the Buddha preached a particular sermon in connection with Devadatta *Thera*, it does not necessarily mean that it was meant for him.[18] He may not have been there at all, it may be that he was already dead by that time. The term *ārabbha* in such contexts only means that it was in connection with him. It can

---

[17] Sv II 595.

[18] *Devadattaṃ ārabbha* at Dhp-a I 133 and Ja I 142.

refer to a person or an incident, as the point of origin of a particular sermon.

Granted this, we have to explain the verse in question not as an allusion to the fact that the Buddha, the sage, passed away for the sake of that peace with the idea 'I will attain to that state of peace.' It only means that the Buddha, the sage, passed away having brought his mind into that state of peace. In other words, according to the commentary the passing away comes first and the peace later, but according to the *sutta* proper, peace comes first and the passing away later.

There is a crucial point involved in this commentarial divergence. It has the presumption that the Buddha passed away in order to enter into 'that *Nibbāna* element.' This presumption is evident quite often in the commentaries. When hard put to it, the commentaries sometimes concede the *sutta*'s standpoint, but more often than otherwise they follow a line of interpretation that comes dangerously close to an eternalist point of view, regarding *Nibbāna*.

Here too the commentarial exegesis, based on the term *ārabbha*, runs the same risk. On the other hand, as we have pointed out, the reference here is to the fact that the Buddha adverted his mind to that peace well before the onset of death, whereby *Māra*'s attempt is foiled, because feelings are already cooled off. It is here that the unshakeable deliverance of the mind proves its worth.

As a 'real'-ization it is already available to the Buddha and the *arahants* in the *arahattaphalasamādhi*, and when the time comes, they put forward this experience to beat off *Māra*. That is why we find a string of epithets for *Nibbāna*, such as *tāṇaṃ*, *leṇaṃ*, *dīpaṃ*, *saraṇaṃ*, *parāyanaṃ*, *khemaṃ* and *amataṃ*. When faced with death, or the pain of death, it gives 'protection,' *tānaṃ*. It provides shelter, like a 'cave,' *leṇaṃ*. It is the 'island,' *dīpaṃ*, within easy reach. It is the 'refuge,' *saraṇaṃ*, and the 'resort,' *parāyanaṃ*. It is the 'security,' *khemaṃ*, and above all the 'death-less,' *amataṃ*.[19]

---

19 S IV 371, *Asaṅkhatasaṃyutta*.

This deathlessness they experience in this very world, and when death comes, this realization stands them in good stead.

Why Venerable Anuruddha brought in the profane concept of death with the expression *kālamakari* into this verse, describing the Buddha's *parinibbāna*, is also a question that should arrest our attention. This particular expression is generally used in connection with the death of ordinary people. Why did he use this expression in such a hallowed context? It is only to distinguish and demarcate the deliverance of the mind, couched in the phrase *vimokkho cetaso ahu*, from the phenomenon of death itself.

The Buddhas and *arahants* also abandon this body, like other beings. The expression *kālamakari*, "made an end of time," is an allusion to this phenomenon. In fact, it is only the Buddhas and *arahants* who truly make an 'end' of time, being fully aware of it. Therefore the most important revelation made in the last two lines of the first verse, *anejo santimārabbha, yaṃ kālamakarī muni*, is the fact that the Buddha passed away having brought his mind to the peace of *Nibbāna*.

All this goes to prove that an *arahant*, even here and now in this very life, has realized his after death state, which is none other than the birthless cessation of all forms of existence that amounts to deathlessness itself.

In all other religions immortality is something attainable after death. If one brings down the Buddha's *Dhamma* also to that level, by smuggling in the idea of an everlasting *Nibbāna*, it too will suffer the same fate. That would contradict the teachings on impermanence, *aniccatā*, and insubstantiality, *anattatā*.

But here we have an entirely different concept. It is a case of overcoming the critical situation of death by directing one's mind to a concentration that nullifies the power of *Māra*. So it becomes clear that the two terms *sa-upādisesā parinibbānadhātu* and *anupādisesā parinibbānadhātu* stand for two aspects of the same *asaṅkhatadhātu*, or the unprepared element.

As a matter of fact, *arahants* have already directly realized, well in time, their after death state. That is to say, not only have they gone through the experience of extinguishment here and now, but they are also assured of the fact that this extinguishment is irreversible even after death, since all forms of existence come to cease.

This is an innovation, the importance of which can hardly be overestimated. Here the Buddha has transcended even the dichotomy between the two terms *sandiṭṭhika* and *samparāyika*. Generally, the world is inclined to believe that one can be assured only of things pertaining to this life. In fact, the word *sandiṭṭhika* literally means that one can be sure only of things visible here and now. Since one cannot be sure of what comes after death, worldlings are in the habit of investing faith in a particular teacher or in a god.

To give a clearer picture of the principle involved in this statement, let us bring up a simple episode, concerning the general Sīha, included among the Fives of the *Aṅguttara Nikāya*. It happens to centre on *dānakathā*, or talks on liberality. Let it be a soft interlude – after all these abstruse discourses.

Sīha, the general, is a wealthy benefactor, endowed with deep faith in the Buddha. One day he approaches the Buddha and asks the question: *sakkā nu kho, bhante, sandiṭṭhikaṃ dānaphalaṃ paññāpetuṃ?*[20] "Is it possible, Lord, to point out an advantage or fruit of giving visible here and now?"

What prompted the question may have been the usual tendency to associate the benefits of giving with the hereafter. Now the Buddha, in his answer to the question, gave four advantages visible here and now and one advantage to come hereafter. The four fruits of giving visible here and now are stated as follows:

1) *dāyako, sīha, dānapati bahuno janassa piyo hoti manāpo*, "Sīha, a benevolent donor is dear and acceptable to many people."

2) *dāyakaṃ dānapatiṃ santo sappurisā bhajanti*, "Good men of integrity resort to that benevolent donor."

---

20 A III 39, *Sīhasenāpattisutta*.

3) *dāyakassa dānapatino kalyāṇo kittisaddo abbhuggacchati*, "A good report of fame goes in favour of that benevolent donor."

4) *dāyako dānapati yaṃ yadeva parisaṃ upasaṅkamati, yadi khattiyaparisaṃ yadi brāhmaṇaparisaṃ yadi gahapatiparisaṃ yadi samaṇaparisaṃ, visārado va upasaṅkamati amaṅkubhūto*, "Whatever assembly that benevolent donor approaches, be it an assembly of kings, or brahmins, or householders, or recluses, he approaches with self confidence, not crestfallen."

These four fruits or advantages are reckoned as *sandiṭṭhika*, because one can experience them here and now. In addition to these, the Buddha mentions a fifth, probably by way of encouragement, though it is outside the scope of the question:

5) *dāyako, sīha, dānapati kāyassa bhedā paraṃ maraṇā sugatiṃ saggaṃ lokaṃ upapajjati*, "The benevolent donor, Sīha, when his body breaks up after death is reborn in a happy heavenly world."

This is a fruit of giving that pertains to the next world, *samparāyikaṃ dānaphalaṃ*. Then Sīha the general makes a comment, which is directly relevant to our discussion:

> *Yānimāni, bhante, bhagavatā cattāri sandiṭṭhikāni dānaphalāni akkhātāni, nāhaṃ ettha bhagavato saddhāya gacchāmi, ahaṃ petāni jānāmi. Yañca kho maṃ, bhante, bhagavā evamāha 'dāyako, sīha, dānapati kāyassa bhedā paraṃ maraṇā sugatiṃ saggaṃ lokaṃ upapajjatī'ti, etāhaṃ na jānāmi, ettha ca panāhaṃ bhagavato saddhāya gacchāmi.*
>
> "Those four fruits of giving, visible here and now, which the Lord has preached, as for them, I do not believe out of faith in the Exalted One, because I myself know them to

> be so. But that about which the Exalted One said: 'Sīha, a benevolent donor, when the body breaks up after death is reborn in a happy heavenly world,' this I do not know. As to that, however, I believe out of faith in the Exalted One."

Regarding the first four advantages of giving, Sīha says "I do not believe out of faith in the Exalted One, because I myself know them to be so," *nāhaṃ ettha bhagavato saddhāya gacchāmi, ahaṃ petāni jānāmi*. It is because he knows out of his own experience that they are facts that he does not believe out of faith in the Exalted One. There is something deep, worth reflecting upon, in this statement.

Then with regard to the fruit of giving, mentioned last, that is to say the one that concerns the hereafter, *samparāyika*, Sīha confesses that he does not know it as a fact, but that he believes it out of faith in the Exalted One, *etāhaṃ na jānāmi, ettha ca panāhaṃ bhagavato saddhāya gacchāmi*. It is because he does not know, that he believes out of faith in the Exalted One.

Here then we have a good illustration of the first principle we have outlined earlier. Where there is knowledge born of personal experience, there is no need of faith. Faith is displaced by knowledge of realization. It is where one has no such experiential knowledge that faith comes in. That is why Sīha confesses that he has faith in the fifth fruit of giving. With regard to the first four, faith is something redundant for him.

Now that we have clarified for ourselves this first principle, there is a certain interesting riddle verse in the *Dhammapada*, to which we may apply it effectively, not out of a flair for riddles, but because it is relevant to our topic:

> *Assaddho akataññū ca,*
> *sandhicchedo ca yo naro,*

hatāvakāso vantāso,
sa ve uttamaporiso.[21]

This is a verse attributed to the Buddha that comes in the *Arahantavagga* of the *Dhammapada*, which puns upon some words. Such riddle verses follow the pattern of a figure of speech called double entendré, which makes use of ambiguous words. The above verse sounds blasphemous on the first hearing. The Buddha is said to have employed this device to arrest the listener's attention. The surface meaning seems to go against the *Dhamma*, but it provokes deeper reflection.

For instance, *assaddho* means faithless, to be *akataññū* is to be ungrateful, *sandhicchedo* is a term for a housebreaker, *hatāvakāso* is a hopeless case with no opportunities, *vantāso* means greedy of vomit. So the surface meaning amounts to this:

"That faithless ungrateful man,
Who is a housebreaker,
Who is hopeless and greedy of vomit,
He indeed is the man supreme."

For the deeper meaning the words have to be construed differently. *Assaddho* implies that level of penetration into truth at which faith becomes redundant. *Akata*, the unmade, is an epithet for *Nibbāna*, and *akataññū* is one who knows the unmade. *Sandhicchedo* means one who has cut off the connecting links to *saṃsāra*. *Hatāvakāso* refers to that elimination of opportunities for rebirth. *Vantāso* is a term for one who has vomited out desires. The true meaning of the verse, therefore, can be summed up as follows:

"That man who has outgrown faith, as he is a knower of the unmade,

---

21 Dhp 97, *Arahantavagga*.

> Who has sundered all shackles to existence and destroyed all possibilities of rebirth,
> Who has spewed out all desires,
> He indeed is the man supreme."

The description, then, turns out to be that of an *arahant*. *Assaddho* as an epithet for the *arahant* follows the same norm as the epithet *asekho*. *Sekha*, meaning "learner," is a term applied to those who are training for the attainment of *arahant*-hood, from the stream-winner, *sotāpanna*, upwards. Literally, *asekha* could be rendered as "unlearned" or "untrained." But it is certainly not in that sense that an *arahant* is called *asekha*. He is called *asekha* in the sense that he is no longer in need of that training, that is to say, he is an adept. *Assaddho*, too, has to be construed similarly.

As we have mentioned before, the *arahant* has already realized the cessation of existence in his *arahattaphalasamādhi*, thereby securing the knowledge of the unmade, *akata*, or the unprepared, *asaṅkhata*. The term *akataññū* highlights that fact of realization. The most extraordinary and marvelous thing about the realization of *Nibbāna* is that it gives an assurance not only of matters pertaining to this life, *sandiṭṭhika*, but also of what happens after death, *samparāyika* – in other words, the realization of the cessation of existence.

Nibbāna as the realization here and now of the cessation of existence, *bhavanirodho nibbānaṃ*, carries with it the assurance that there is no more existence after death. So there is only one *asaṅkhatadhātu*. The verse we already quoted, too, ends with the words *pahaṃsu te sabbabhavāni tādino*, "those steadfastly such-like ones have given up all forms of existence."[22]

One thing should be clear now. Though there are two *Nibbāna* elements called *sa-upādisesā Nibbānadhātu* and *anupādisesā Nibbānadhātu*, there is no justification whatsoever for taking *anupādisesā Nibbānadhātu* as a place of eternal rest for the

---

[22] It 39, *Nibbānadhātusutta*.

arahants after death – an everlasting immortal state. The deathlessness of *Nibbāna* is to be experienced in this world itself. That is why an *arahant* is said to feast on ambrosial deathlessness, *amataṃ paribhuñjati*, when he is in *arahattaphalasamādhi*. When it is time for death, he brings his mind to this *samādhi*, and it is while he is partaking of ambrosial deathlessness that *Māra* quietly takes away his body.

An *arahant* might even cremate his own body, as if it is another's. Now we are at an extremely deep point in this *Dhamma*. We have to say something in particular about the two terms *saṅkhata* and *asaṅkhata*. In our last sermon, we happened to give a rather unusual explanation of such pair-wise terms like the 'hither shore' and the 'farther shore,' as well as the 'mundane' and the 'supramundane.' The two terms in each pair are generally believed to be far apart and the gap between them is conceived in terms of time and space. But we compared this gap to that between the lotus leaf and the drop of water on it, availing ourselves of a simile offered by the Buddha himself.

The distance between the lotus leaf and the drop of water on it is the same as that between the hither shore and the farther shore, between the mundane and the supramundane. This is no idle sophistry, but a challenge to deeper reflection.

The *Dhammapada* verse we quoted earlier beginning with *yassa pāraṃ apāraṃ vā, pārāpāraṃ na vijjati*,[23] "to whom there is neither a farther shore nor a hither shore nor both," is puzzling enough. But what it says is that the *arahant* has transcended both the hither shore and the farther shore. It is as if he has gone beyond this shore and the other shore as well, that is to say, he has transcended the dichotomy.

We have to say something similar with regard to the two terms *saṅkhata* and *asaṅkhata*. *Saṅkhata*, or the prepared, is like a floral design. This prepared floral design, which is *bhava*, or existence, is made up, as it were, with the help of the glue of craving, the

---

[23] Dhp 385, *Brāhmaṇavagga*; see sermon 18.

tangles of views and the knots of conceits. If one removes the glue, disentangles the tangles and unties the knots, the *saṅkhata*, or the prepared, itself becomes *asaṅkhata*, the unprepared, then and there. The same floral design, which was the *saṅkhata*, has now become the *asaṅkhata*. This itself is the cessation of existence, *bhavanirodho*. When one can persuade oneself to think of *Nibbāna* as an extinguishment, the term *parinibbāna* can well be understood as 'perfect extinguishment.'

The *parinibbāna* of the *arahant* Dabba Mallaputta is recorded in the *Udāna* as a special occasion on which the Buddha uttered a paean of joy. Venerable Dabba Mallaputta was an *arahant*, gifted with marvelous psychic powers, specializing in miracles performed by mastering the fire element, *tejo dhātu*. His *parinibbāna*, too, was a marvel in itself.

When he found himself at the end of his lifespan, he approached the Buddha and informed him of it, as if begging permission, with the words: *parinibbāna kālo me dāni, sugata*,[24] "it is time for me to attain *parinibbāna*, O well-gone one." And the Buddha too gave permission with the words: *yassa dāni tvaṃ, Dabba, kālaṃ maññasi*, "Dabba, you may do that for which the time is fit."

As soon as the Buddha uttered these words, Venerable Dabba Mallaputta rose from his seat, worshipped the Buddha, circumambulated him, went up into the sky and, sitting cross-legged, aroused the concentration of the fire element and, rising from it, attained *parinibbāna*. As his body thus miraculously self-cremated burnt in the sky, it left no ashes or soot.

This was something significant that fits in with the definition of *Nibbāna* so far given. That is probably why the Buddha is said to have uttered a special verse of uplift or paean of joy at this extinguishment, which was perfect in every sense:

Abhedi kāyo, nirodhi saññā,
vedanā sītirahaṃsu sabbā,

---

[24] Ud 92, *Paṭhamadabbasutta*.

vūpasamiṃsu saṅkhārā,
viññānaṃ attham agamā.

"Body broke up, perceptions ceased,
All feelings cooled off,
Preparations calmed down,
Consciousness came to an end."

This event was of such a great importance that, though it occurred at Veḷuvana *ārāma* in Rājagaha, the Buddha related the event to the congregation of monks when he returned to Sāvatthī. It was not an incidental mention in reply to a particular question, but a special peroration recounting the event and commemorating it with the following two *Udāna* verses, which so aptly constitute the grand finale to our *Udāna* text:

Ayoghanahatass'eva,
jalato jātavedaso,
anupubbūpasantassa,
yathā na ñāyate gati.

Evaṃ sammāvimuttānaṃ,
kāmabandhoghatārinaṃ,
paññāpetuṃ gatī n'atthi,
pattānaṃ acalaṃ sukhaṃ.[25]

"Just as in the case of a fire,
Blazing like a block of iron in point of compactness,
When it gradually calms down,
No path it goes by can be traced.

"Even so of those who are well released,

---

[25] Ud 93, *Dutiyadabbasutta*.

Who have crossed over the floods of shackles of sensuality,
And reached Bliss Unshaken,
There is no path to be pointed out."

We have deviated from the commentarial interpretation in our rendering of the first two lines of the verse. The commentary gives two alternative meanings, probably because it is in doubt as to the correct one. Firstly it brings in the idea of a bronze vessel that is being beaten at the forge with an iron hammer, giving the option that the gradual subsidence mentioned in the verse may apply either to the flames or to the reverberations of sound arising out of it.[26] Secondly, as a 'some say so' view, *kecidvāda*, it gives an alternative meaning, connected with the ball of iron beaten at the forge.

In our rendering, however, we had to follow a completely different line of interpretation, taking the expression *ayoghanahatassa* as a comparison, *ayoghanahatassa + iva*, for the blazing fire, *jalato jātavedaso*. On seeing a fire that is ablaze, one gets a notion of compactness, as on seeing a red hot block of solid iron.

In the *Dhammapada* verse beginning with *seyyo ayogulo bhutto, tatto aggisikhūpamo,*[27] "better to swallow a red hot iron ball, that resembles a flame of fire," a cognate simile is employed somewhat differently. There the ball of iron is compared to a flame of fire. Here the flame of fire is compared to a block of iron.

All in all, it is highly significant that the Buddha uttered three verses of uplift in connection with the *parinibbāna* of the *arahant* Venerable Dabba Mallaputta. The most important point that emerges from this discussion is that *Nibbāna* is essentially an extinction or extinguishment.

An extinguished fire goes nowhere. In the case of other *arahants*, who were cremated after their *parinibbāna*, there is a

---

26 Ud-a 435.

27 Dhp 308, *Nirayavagga*.

leftover as ashes for one to perpetuate at least the memory of their existence. But here Venerable Dabba Mallaputta, as if to drive a point home, through his psychic powers based on the fire element, saw to it that neither ashes nor soot will mar his perfect extinguishment in the eyes of the world. That is why the Buddha celebrated it with these special utterances of joy.

So then the cessation of existence is itself *Nibbāna*. There is no everlasting immortal *Nibbāna* awaiting the *arahants* at their *parinibbāna*.

That kind of argument the commentaries sometimes put forward is now and then advanced by modern day writers and preachers, too, in their explanations. When it comes to *Nibbāna*, they resort to two pet parables of recent origin, the parable of the tortoise and the parable of the frog.

In the former, a tortoise goes down into the water and the fishes ask him where he came from. The tortoise replies that he came from land. In order to determine what sort of a thing land is, the fishes go on asking the tortoise a number of questions based on various qualities of water. To each question the tortoise has to reply in the negative, since land has none of the qualities of water.

The parable of the frog is much the same. When it gets into water it has to say 'no no' to every question put by the toad, still unfamiliar with land. To make the parables convincing, those negative answers, the 'no-nos,' are compared to the strings of negative terms that are found in the *sutta* passages dealing with the *arahattaphalasamādhi*, which we have already quoted.

For instance, to prove their point those writers and teachers would resort to the famous *Udāna* passage beginning with:

> *'Atthi, bhikkhave, tad āyatanaṃ, yattha n'eva pathavī na āpo na tejo na vāyo na ākāsānañcāyatanaṃ na viññāṇānañcāyatanaṃ na ākiñcaññāyatanaṃ na neva-*

> *saññānāsaññāyatanaṃ na ayaṃ loko na paraloko na ubho candimasūriyā . . .*'[28]
>
> "There is, monks, that sphere, in which there is neither earth, nor water, nor fire, nor air; neither the sphere of infinite space, nor the sphere of infinite consciousness, nor the sphere of nothingness, nor the sphere of neither-perception-nor-non-perception; neither this world nor the world beyond, nor the sun and the moon . . . "

But we have reasonably pointed out that those passages do not in any way refer to a non-descript realm into which the *arahants* enter after their demise, a realm that the tortoise and the frog cannot describe. Such facile explanations contradict the deeper teachings on the cessation of existence, dependent arising and not self. They create a lot of misconceptions regarding *Nibbāna* as the ultimate aim.

The purpose of all those arguments is to assert that *Nibbāna* is definitely not an annihilation. The ideal of an everlasting *Nibbāna* is held out in order to obviate nihilistic notions. But the Buddha himself has declared that when he is preaching about the cessation of existence, those who held on to eternalist views wrongly accused him for being an annihilationist, who teaches about the annihilation, destruction and non-existence of a truly existing being, *sato satassa ucchedaṃ vināsaṃ vibhavaṃ paññāpeti.*[29]

On such occasions, the Buddha did not in any way incline towards eternalism in order to defend himself. He did not put forward the idea of an everlasting *Nibbāna* to counter the accusation. Instead, he drew attention to the three signata and the four noble truths and solved the whole problem. He maintained that the charge is groundless and utterly misconceived, and concluded with the memorable declaration: *pubbe cāhaṃ, bhikkhave, etarahi ca*

---

28 Ud 80, *Paṭhamanibbānapaṭisaṃyuttasutta*, see sermon 17.

29 M I 140, *Alagaddūpamasutta.*

dukkhañceva paññāpemi, dukkhassa ca nirodhaṃ, "formerly as well as now, I point out only a suffering and a cessation of that suffering."

Even the term *tathāgata*, according to him, is not to be conceived as a self. It is only a mass of suffering that has come down through *saṃsāra*, due to ignorance. The so-called existence, *bhava*, is an outcome of grasping, *upādāna*. When grasping ceases, existence comes to an end. That itself is the cessation of existence, *bhavanirodha*, which is *Nibbāna*.

As the term *anupādā parinibbāna* suggests, there is no grasping in the experience of the cessation of existence. It is only when one is grasping something that he can be identified with it, or reckoned by it. When one lets go of everything, he goes beyond reckoning. Of course, even the commentaries sometimes use the expression *apaññattikabhāvaṃ gatā*,[30] "gone to the state beyond designation" with regard to the *parinibbāna* of *arahants*.

Nevertheless, they tacitly grant a destination, which in their opinion defies definition. Such vague arguments are riddled with contradictions. They obfuscate the deeper issues of the *Dhamma*, relating to *paṭicca samuppāda* and *anattā*, and seek to perpetuate personality view by slanting towards eternalism.

It is to highlight some extremely subtle aspects of the problem of *Nibbāna* that we brought out all these arguments today.

---

[30] Sv II 635.

Nibbāna Sermon 20

Namo tassa Bhagavato Arahato Sammāsambuddhassa
Namo tassa Bhagavato Arahato Sammāsambuddhassa
Namo tassa Bhagavato Arahato Sammāsambuddhassa

Etaṃ santaṃ, etaṃ paṇītaṃ, yadidaṃ sabbasaṅkhārasamatho sabbūpadhipaṭinissaggo taṇhakkhayo virāgo nirodho nibbānaṃ.[1]

"This is peaceful, this is excellent, namely the stilling of all preparations, the relinquishment of all assets, the destruction of craving, detachment, cessation, extinction."

With the permission of the Most Venerable Great Preceptor and the assembly of the venerable meditative monks.

This is the twentieth sermon in the series of sermons on *Nibbāna*. In our last sermon we described, as something of a marvel in the attainment of *Nibbāna*, the very possibility of realizing, in this very life, as *diṭṭhadhammika*, one's after death state, which is *samparāyika*. The phrase *diṭṭheva dhamme sayaṃ abhiññā sacchikatvā*, "having realized here and now by one's own higher knowledge,"[2] occurs so often in the discourses because the emancipated one ascertains his after death state as if by seeing with his own eyes.

Natthi dāni punabbhavo, "there is no re-becoming now,"[3] *khīṇā jāti*, "extinct is birth,"[4] are some of the joyous utterances of the

---

1 M I 436, *MahāMālunkyasutta.*

2 E.g. at M I 35, *Ākaṅkheyyasutta.*

3 E.g. at M I 167, *Ariyapariyesanasutta.*

Buddha and the *arahants*, which were inspired by the realization of the cessation of existence in this very life. Through that realization itself, they experience a bliss devoid of feeling, which is called "the cooling off of feelings." That is why *Nibbāna* as such is known as *avedayita sukha*, a "bliss devoid of feeling."[5]

At the end of their lives, at the moment when death approaches, those emancipated ones, the *arahants*, put forward their unshakeable deliverance of the mind, *akuppā cetomivutti* (which remains unshaken even in the face of death), and become deathless well before their death, not after it.

On many an occasion the Buddha has spoken highly of this unshakeable deliverance of the mind, describing it as the supreme bliss, the supreme knowledge and the supreme freedom from death. For instance, among the Sixes of the *Aṅguttara Nikāya*, we come across the following two verses:

Tassa sammā vimuttassa,
ñāṇaṃ ce hoti tādino,
'akuppā me vimuttī'ti,
bhavasaṃyojanakkhaye.

Etaṃ kho paramaṃ ñāṇaṃ,
etaṃ sukhamanuttaraṃ,
asokaṃ virajaṃ khemaṃ,
etaṃ ānaṇyamuttamaṃ.[6]

"To that such like one, who is fully released,
There arises the knowledge:
'Unshakeable is my deliverance,'
Upon his extinction of fetters to existence.

---

[4] E.g. at M I 23, *Bhayabheravasutta*.

[5] Ps III 115, *aṭṭhakathā* on the *Bahuvedanīyasutta*.

[6] A III 354, *Iṇasutta*.

"This is the highest knowledge,
This is the unsurpassed bliss,
This sorrow-less, taintless security,
Is the supreme debtless-ness."

Arahants are said to be debtless in regard to the four requisites offered by the laity out of faith, but when *Nibbāna* is regarded as a debtless-ness, it seems to imply something deeper.

Saṃsāra or reiterated existence is itself a debt, which one can never pay off. When one comes to think of *kamma* and its result, it is a debt that keeps on gathering an interminable interest, which can never be paid off. But even from this debt the *arahants* have won freedom by destroying the seeds of *kamma*, by rendering them infertile. They are made ineffective beyond this life, as there is no rebirth. The meaningful line of the *Ratanasutta*, *khīṇaṃ purāṇaṃ, navaṃ natthi sambhavaṃ*,[7] "whatever is old is extinct and there is no arising anew," has to be understood in that sense. The karmic debt is paid off and there is no fresh incurring.

All this is in praise of that unshakeable deliverance of the mind. It is a kind of extraordinary knowledge, almost unimaginable, a 'real'-ization of one's own after death state.

In almost all serious discussions on *Nibbāna*, the subtlest moot point turns out to be the question of the after death state of the emancipated one. A brief answer, the Buddha had given to this question, we already brought up in our last sermon, by quoting the two concluding verses of the *Udāna*, with which that collection of inspired utterances ends with a note of exceptional grandeur. Let us recall them:

Ayoghanahatass'eva,
jalato jātavedaso,
anupubbūpasantassa,
yathā na ñāyate gati.

---

7 Sn 235, *Ratanasutta.*

Evaṃ sammāvimuttānaṃ,
kāmabandhoghatārinaṃ,
paññāpetuṃ gati natthi,
pattānaṃ acalaṃ sukhaṃ.[8]

"Just as in the case of a fire,
Blazing like a block of iron in point of compactness,
When it gradually calms down,
No path it goes by can be traced.

"Even so, of those who are well released,
Who have crossed over the flux of shackles of sensuality,
And reached bliss unshaken,
There is no path to be pointed out."

The last two lines are particularly significant. There is no path to be pointed out of those who have reached bliss unshaken. *Acalaṃ sukhaṃ*, or "unshakeable bliss," is none other than that unshakeable deliverance of the mind. *Akuppa* means "unassailable" or "unshakeable." Clearly enough, what the verse says is that after their death the emancipated ones leave no trace of a path gone by, even as the flames of a raging fire.

The flame may appear as something really existing due to the perception of the compact, *ghanasaññā*, but when it goes down and disappears, no one can say that it went in such and such a direction.

Though this is the obvious meaning, some try to attribute quite a different meaning to the verse in question. The line *paññāpetuṃ gati n'atthi*, "there is no path to be pointed out," is interpreted even by the commentators (who take the word *gati* to mean some state of existence) as an assertion that, although such a bourne

---

[8] Ud 93, *Dutiyadabbasutta*.

cannot be pointed out, the *arahants* pass away into some nondescript realm.

This kind of interpretation is prompted by an apprehension of the charge of annihilation. A clear instance of this tendency is revealed in the commentary to the following verse in the *Dhammapada*:

Ahiṃsakā ye munayo,
niccaṃ kāyena saṃvutā,
te yanti accutaṃ ṭhānaṃ,
yattha gantvā na socare.[9]

"Innocent are the sages,
That are ever restrained in body,
They go to that state unshaken,
Wherein they grieve no more."

The commentator, in paraphrasing, brings in the word *sassataṃ*, "eternal," for *accutaṃ*, thereby giving the idea that the *arahants* go to an eternal place of rest.[10] Because the verb *yanti*, "go," occurs there, he must have thought that this state unshaken, *accutaṃ*, is something attainable after death. But we can give another instance in support of our explanation of the term *accutaṃ*. The following verse in the *Hemakamāṇavapucchā* of the *Pārāyanavagga* in the *Sutta Nipāta* clearly shows what this *accutaṃ* is:

Idha diṭṭhasutamutaviññātesu,
piyarūpesu Hemaka,

---

9 Dhp 225, *Kodhavagga*.

10 Dhp-a III 321.

chandarāgavinodanaṃ,
nibbānapadaṃ accutaṃ.[11]

"The dispelling here in this world of desire and lust,
In pleasurable things,
Seen, heard, sensed and cognized,
Is *Nibbāna* itself, O Hemaka."

This is further proof of the fact that there is no eternal immortal rest awaiting the *arahants* after their demise. The reason for such a postulate is probably the fear of falling into the annihilationist view. Why this chronic fear? To the worldlings overcome by craving for existence any teaching that leads to the cessation of existence appears dreadful.

That is why they put forward two new parables, following the same commentarial trend. The other day we mentioned about those two parables, the parable of the tortoise and the parable of the frog.[12] When the fish and the toad living in water ask what sort of a thing land is, the tortoise and the frog are forced to say 'no, no' to every question they put. Likewise the Buddha, so it is argued, was forced to give a string of negative terms in his discourses on *Nibbāna*.

But we have pointed out that this argument is fallacious and that those discourses have to be interpreted differently. The theme that runs through such discourses is none other than the cessation of existence.

In the *Alagaddūpama Sutta* of the *Majjhima Nikāya* the Buddha declares in unmistakeable terms that some recluses and brahmins, on hearing him preaching the *Dhamma* for the cessation of existence, wrongly accuse him with the charge of being an annihilationist, *sato sattassa ucchedaṃ vināsaṃ vibhavaṃ*

---

[11] Sn 1086, *Hemakamāṇavapucchā*.

[12] See sermon 19.

paññāpeti, "he is showing the way to the annihilation, destruction and non-existence of a truly existing being."[13]

He clearly states that some even grieve and lament and fall into despair, complaining *ucchijjissāmi nāma su, vinassissāmi nāma su, na su nāma bhavissāmi*, "so it seems I shall be annihilated, so it seems I shall perish, so it seems I shall be no more."[14]

Even during the lifetime of the Buddha there were various debates and controversies regarding the after death state of the emancipated person among recluses and brahmins. They were of the opinion that the after death state of the emancipated one in any particular religious system has to be explained according to a fourfold logic, or tetralemma. A paradigm of that tetralemma occurs quite often in the discourses. It consists of the following four propositions:

1) *hoti tathāgato paraṃ maraṇā,* "The *Tathāgata* exists after death."
2) *na hoti tathāgato paraṃ maraṇā,* "The *Tathāgata* does not exist after death."
3) *hoti ca na ca hoti tathāgato paraṃ maraṇā,* "The *Tathāgata* both exists and does not exist after death."
4) *n'eva hoti na na hoti tathāgato paraṃ maraṇā,* "The *Tathāgata* neither exists nor does not exist after death."[15]

This four-cornered logic purports to round up the four possible alternatives in any situation, or four possible answers to any question. The dilemma is fairly well known, where one is caught up between two alternatives. The tetralemma, with its four

---

13 M I 140, *Alagaddūpamasutta.*

14 M I 137, *Alagaddūpamasutta.*

15 E.g. at M I 484, *Aggivacchagottasutta.*

alternatives, is supposed to exhaust the universe of discourse in a way that one cannot afford to ignore it.

When it comes to a standpoint regarding a particular issue, one is compelled to say 'yes' or 'no,' or at least to assert both standpoints or negate them altogether. The contemporary recluses and brahmins held on to the view that the *Tathāgata*'s after death state has to be predicated in accordance with the four-cornered logic.

When we hear the term *Tathāgata*, we are immediately reminded of the Buddha. But for the contemporary society, it was a sort of technical term with a broader meaning. Those recluses and brahmins used the term *Tathāgata* to designate the perfected individual in any religious system, whose qualifications were summed up in the thematic phrase *uttamapuriso*, *paramapuriso*, *paramapattipatto*,[16] "the highest person, the supreme person, the one who has attained the supreme state."

This fact is clearly borne out by the *Kutūhalasālāsutta* in the *Avyākata Saṃyutta* of the *Saṃyutta Nikāya*. In that discourse we find the wandering ascetic Vacchagotta coming to the Buddha with the following report:

> "Recently there was a meeting of recluses, brahmins and wandering ascetics in the debating hall. In that assembly, the following chance talk arose: 'Now there is this teacher, Pūraṇa Kassapa, who is widely acclaimed and who has a large following. When an ordinary disciple of his passes away, he predicates his destiny. So also in the case of a disciple who has attained the highest state of perfection in his religious system. Other well known teachers like Makkhali Gosāla, Nigaṇṭha Nātaputta, Sañjaya Belaṭṭhiputta, Pakudha Kaccāyana and Ajita Kesakambali do the same. They all declare categorically the after death state of both types of their disciples.

---

[16] S III 116, *Anurādhasutta.*

"'But as for this ascetic Gotama, who also is a teacher widely acclaimed with a large following, the position is that he clearly declares the after death state of an ordinary disciple of his, but in the case of a disciple who has attained the highest state of perfection, he does not predicate his destiny according to the above mentioned tetralemma. Instead he makes such a declaration about him as the following:

"*Acchecchi taṇhaṃ, vāvattayi saññojanaṃ, sammā mānābhisamayā antam akāsi dukkhassa,*[17] 'He cut off craving, disjoined the fetter and, by rightly understanding conceit for what it is, made an end of suffering.'"

Vacchagotta concludes this account with the confession that he himself was perplexed and was in doubt as to how the *Dhamma* of the recluse Gotama has to be understood. The Buddha grants that Vacchagotta's doubt is reasonable, with the words *alañhi te, Vaccha, kaṅkhituṃ, alaṃ vicikicchituṃ, kaṅkhaniye ca pana te ṭhāne vicikicchā uppannā*, "It behooves you to doubt, Vaccha, it behooves you to be perplexed, for doubt has arisen in you on a dubious point."

Then the Buddha comes out with the correct standpoint in order to dispel Vacchagotta's doubt. *Sa-upādānassa kvāhaṃ, Vaccha, upapattiṃ paññāpemi, no anupādānassa*, "It is for one with grasping, Vaccha, that I declare there is an occurrence of birth, not for one without grasping."

He gives the following simile by way of illustration. *Seyyathāpi, Vaccha, aggi sa-upādāno jalati no anupādāno, evam eva kvāhaṃ, Vaccha, sa-upādānassa upapattiṃ paññāpemi, no anupādānassa*, "Just as a fire burns when it has fuel to grasp and not when it has no fuel, even so, Vaccha, I declare that there is an occurrence of birth for one with grasping, not for one without grasping."

---

[17] S IV 399, *Kutūhalasālāsutta*.

As we have mentioned before, the word *upādāna* has two meanings, it means both grasping as well as fuel. In fact fuel is just what the fire 'grasps.' Just as the fire depends on grasping in the form of fuel, so also the individual depends on grasping for his rebirth.

Within the context of this analogy, Vacchagotta now raises a question that has some deeper implications: *Yasmiṃ pana, bho Gotama, samaye acci vātena khittā dūrampi gacchati, imassa pana bhavaṃ Gotamo kim upādānasmiṃ paññāpeti*, "Master Gotama, at the time when a flame flung by the wind goes even far, what does Master Gotama declare to be its object of grasping or fuel?"

The Buddha's answer to that question is: *Yasmiṃ kho, Vaccha, samaye acci vātena khittā dūrampi gacchati, tamahaṃ vātupādānaṃ vadāmi; vāto hissa, Vaccha, tasmiṃ samaye upādānaṃ hoti*, "At the time, Vaccha, when a flame flung by the wind goes even far, that, I say, has wind as its object of grasping. Vaccha, at that time wind itself serves as the object of grasping."

Now this is only an analogy. Vaccha raises the question proper only at this point: *Yasmiñca pana, bho Gotama, samaye imañca kāyaṃ nikkhipati satto ca aññataraṃ kāyam anuppatto hoti, imassa pana bhavaṃ Gotamo kim upādānasmiṃ paññāpeti*, "At the time, Master Gotama, when a being lays down this body and has reached a certain body, what does Master Gotama declare to be a grasping in his case?"

The Buddha replies: *Yasmiñca pana, Vaccha, samaye imañca kāyaṃ nikkhipati satto ca aññataraṃ kāyam anuppatto hoti, tam ahaṃ taṇhupādānaṃ vadāmi; taṇhā hissa, Vaccha, tasmiṃ samaye upādānaṃ hoti,* "At the time, Vaccha, when a being lays down this body and has reached a certain body, I say, he has craving as his grasping. At that time, Vaccha, it is craving that serves as a grasping for him."

With this sentence the discourse ends abruptly, but there is an intricate point in the two sections quoted above. In these two sections, we have adopted the reading *anuppatto*, "has reached," as more plausible in rendering the phrase *aññataraṃ kāyam anuppatto*, "has reached a certain body."[18] The commentary, however, seeks to justify the reading *anupapanno*, "is not reborn," which gives quite an opposite sense, with the following explanation *cutikkhaṇeyeva paṭisandhicittassa anuppannattā anuppanno hoti*,[19] "since at the death moment itself, the rebirth consciousness has not yet arisen, he is said to be not yet reborn."

Some editors doubt whether the correct reading should be *anuppatto*.[20] The doubt seems reasonable enough, for even syntactically, *anuppatto* can be shown to fit into the context better than *anuppanno*. The word *aññataraṃ* provides us with the criterion. It has a selective sense, like "a certain," and carries definite positive implications. To express something negative a word like *aññaṃ*, "another," has to be used instead of the selective *aññataraṃ*, "a certain."

On the other hand, the suggested reading *anuppatto* avoids those syntactical difficulties. A being lays down this body and has reached a certain body. Even the simile given as an illustration is in favour of our interpretation. The original question of Vaccha about the flame flung by the wind, reminds us of the way a forest fire, for instance, spreads from one tree to another tree some distance away. It is the wind that pushes the flame for it to catch hold of the other tree.

The commentarial explanation, however, envisages the situation in which a being lays down this body and is not yet reborn in another body. It is in the interim that craving is supposed to be the grasping or a fuel. Some scholars have exploited this commentari-

---

18 This suggestion finds support in the Chinese parallel to the *Kutūhalasālāsutta*, *Saṃyukta Āgama* discourse 957 (Taishō II 244b2), which speaks of the being that has passed away as availing himself of a mind-made body. (Anālayo)

19 Spk III 114.

20 Feer, L. (ed.): *Saṃyutta Nikāya*, PTS 1990 (1894), p 400 n 2.

al explanation to postulate a theory of *antarābhava*, or interim existence, prior to rebirth proper.

Our interpretation, based on the reading *anuppatto*, rules out even the possibility of an *antarābhava*. Obviously enough, Vacchagotta's question is simple and straightforward. He is curious to know what sort of a grasping connects up the being that lays down the body and the being that arises in another body. That is to say, how the apparent gap could be bridged.

The answer given by the Buddha fully accords with the analogy envisaged by the premise. Just as the wind does the work of grasping in the case of the flame, so craving itself, at the moment of death, fulfills the function of grasping for a being to reach another body. That is precisely why craving is called *bhavanetti*, "the guide in becoming."[21] Like a promontory, it juts out into the ocean of *saṃsāra*. When it comes to rebirth, it is craving that bridges the apparent gap. It is the invisible combustible fuel that keeps the raging *saṃsāric* forest fire alive.

All in all, what transpired at the debating hall (*Kutūhalasālā*) reveals one important fact, namely that the Buddha's reluctance to give a categorical answer regarding the after death state of the emancipated one in his dispensation had aroused the curiosity of those recluses and brahmins. That is why they kept on discussing the subject at length.

However, it was not the fact that he had refused to make any comment at all on this point. Only, that the comment he had made appeared so strange to them, as we may well infer from Vacchagotta's report of the discussion at the debating hall.

The Buddha's comment on the subject, which they had quoted, was not based on the tetralemma. It was a completely new formulation. *Acchecchi taṇhaṃ, vāvattayi saññojanaṃ, sammā mānābhisamayā antam akāsi dukkhassa*, "He cut off craving, disjoined the fetter and, by rightly understanding conceit for what it is, made an end of suffering."

---

[21] E.g. S III 190, *Bhavanettisutta*.

This then, is the correct answer, and not any one of the four corners of the tetralemma. This brief formula is of paramount importance. When craving is cut off, the 'guide-in-becoming,' which is responsible for rebirth, is done away with. It is as if the fetter binding to another existence has been unhooked. The term *bhavasaṃyojanakkhaya*, "destruction of the fetter to existence," we came across earlier, conveys the same sense.[22]

The phrase *sammā mānābhisamaya* is also highly significant. With the dispelling of ignorance, the conceit 'am,' *asmimāna*, is seen for what it is. It disappears when exposed to the light of understanding and that is the end of suffering as well. The concluding phrase *antam akāsi dukkhassa*, "made an end of suffering," is conclusive enough. The problem that was there all the time was the problem of suffering, so the end of suffering means the end of the whole problem.

In the *Aggivacchagottasutta* of the *Majjhima Nikāya* the Buddha's response to the question of the after death state of the *arahant* comes to light in greater detail. The question is presented there in the form of the tetralemma, beginning with *hoti tathāgato paraṃ maraṇā*.[23]

While all the other recluses and brahmins held that the answer should necessarily take the form of one of the four alternatives, the Buddha put them all aside, *ṭhapitāni*, rejected them, *patikkhittāni*, refused to state his view categorically in terms of them, *avyākatāni*. This attitude of the Buddha puzzled not only the ascetics of other sects, but even some of the monks like Māluṅkyāputta. In very strong terms, Māluṅkyāputta challenged the Buddha to give a categorical answer or else confess his ignorance.[24]

As a matter of fact there are altogether ten such questions, which the Buddha laid aside, rejected and refused to answer

---

[22] It 53, *Indriyasutta*; see sermon 16.

[23] M I 484, *Aggivacchagottasutta*.

[24] M I 427, *CūḷaMāluṅkyāputtasutta*.

categorically. The first six take the form of three dilemmas, while the last four constitute the tetralemma already mentioned. Since an examination of those three dilemmas would reveal some important facts, we shall briefly discuss their significance as well. The three sets of views are stated thematically as follows:

1) *sassato loko*, "The world is eternal."
2) *asassato loko*, "The world is not eternal."
3) *antavā loko*, "The world is finite."
4) *anantavā loko*, "The world is infinite."
5) *taṃ jīvaṃ taṃ sarīraṃ*, "The soul and the body are the same."
6) *aññaṃ jīvaṃ aññaṃ sarīraṃ*, "The soul is one thing and the body another."

These three dilemmas, together with the tetralemma, are known as *abyākatavatthūni*, the ten undetermined points.[25] Various recluses and brahmins, as well as king Pasenadi Kosala, posed these ten questions to the Buddha, hoping to get categorical answers.

Why the Buddha laid them aside is a problem to many scholars. Some, like Māluṅkyāputta, would put it down to agnosticism. Others would claim that the Buddha laid them aside because they are irrelevant to the immediate problem of deliverance, though he could have answered them. That section of opinion go by the *Siṃsapāvanasutta* in the *Saccasaṃyutta* of the *Saṃyutta Nikāya*.[26]

Once while dwelling in a *siṃsapā* grove, the Buddha took up some *siṃsapā* leaves in his hands and asked the monks: "What do you think, monks, which is more, these leaves in my hand or those in the *siṃsapā* grove?" The monks reply that the leaves in the hand are few and those in the *siṃsapā* grove are greater in number. Then the Buddha makes a declaration to the following effect:

---

25 The expression *abyākatavatthu* occurs e.g. at A IV 68, *Abyākatasutta*.

26 S V 437, *Sīsapāvanasutta*.

"Even so, monks, what I have understood through higher knowledge and not taught you is far more than what I have taught you."

If we rely on this simile, we would have to grant that the questions are answerable in principle, but that the Buddha preferred to avoid them because they are not relevant. But this is not the reason either.

All these ten questions are based on wrong premises. To take them seriously and answer them would be to grant the validity of those premises. The dilemmas and the tetralemma seek arbitrarily to corner anyone who tries to answer them. The Buddha refused to be cornered that way.

The first two alternatives, presented in the form of a dilemma, are *sassato loko*, "the world is eternal," and *asassato loko*, "the world is not eternal." This is an attempt to determine the world in temporal terms. The next set of alternatives seeks to determine the world in spatial terms.

Why did the Buddha refuse to answer these questions on time and space? It is because the concept of 'the world' has been given quite a new definition in this dispensation.

Whenever the Buddha redefined a word in common usage, he introduced it with the phrase *ariyassa vinaye*, "in the discipline of the noble ones."

We have already mentioned on an earlier occasion that according to the discipline of the noble ones, 'the world' is said to have arisen in the six sense-spheres, *chasu loko samuppanno.*[27] In short, the world is redefined in terms of the six spheres of sense. This is so fundamentally important that in the *Saḷāyatanasaṃyutta* of the *Saṃyutta Nikāya* the theme comes up again and again.

For instance, in the *Samiddhisutta* Venerable Samiddhi poses the following question to the Buddha: *'Loko, loko'ti, bhante, vuccati. Kittāvatā nu kho, bhante, loko vā assa lokapaññatti vā?*[28]

---

[27] S I 41, *Lokasutta*; see sermon 4.

[28] S IV 39, *Samiddhisutta.*

"'The world, the world,' so it is said Venerable sir, but how far, Venerable sir, does this world or the concept of the world go?"

The Buddha gives the following answer: *Yattha kho, Samiddhi, atthi cakkhu, atthi rūpā, atthi cakkhuviññāṇaṃ, atthi cakkhuviññāṇaviññātabbā dhammā, atthi tattha loko vā lokapaññatti vā,* "Where there is the eye, Samiddhi, where there are forms, where there is eye-consciousness, where there are things cognizable by eye-consciousness, there exists the world or the concept of the world."

A similar statement is made with regard to the other spheres of sense, including the mind. That, according to the Buddha, is where the world exists. Then he makes a declaration concerning the converse: *Yattha ca kho, Samiddhi, natthi cakkhu, natthi rūpā, natthi cakkhuviññāṇaṃ, natthi cakkhuviññāṇaviññātabbā dhammā, natthi tattha loko vā lokapaññatti vā*, "Where there is no eye, Samiddhi, where there are no forms, where there is no eye-consciousness, where there are no things cognizable by eye-consciousness, there the world does not exist, nor any concept of the world."

From this we can well infer that any attempt to determine whether there is an end of the world, either in temporal terms or in spatial terms, is misguided. It is the outcome of a wrong view, for there is a world so long as there are the six spheres of sense. That is why the Buddha consistently refused to answer those questions regarding the world.

There are a number of definitions of the world given by the Buddha. We shall cite two of them. A certain monk directly asked the Buddha to give a definition of the world: *'Loko, loko'ti bhante, vuccati. Kittāvatā nu kho, bhante, loko'ti vuccati?* "'The world, the world,' so it is said. In what respect, Venerable sir, is it called a world?" Then the Buddha makes the following significant declaration:

> *Lujjatī'ti kho, bhikkhu, tasmā loko'ti vuccati. Kiñca lujjati? Cakkhu kho, bhikkhu, lujjati, rūpā lujjanti, cakkhuviññāṇaṃ lujjati, cakkhusamphasso lujjati, yampidaṃ cakkhusamphassapaccayā uppajjati vedayitaṃ sukhaṃ vā*

> *dukkhaṃ vā adukkhamasukhaṃ vā tampi lujjati. Lujjatī'ti kho, bhikkhu, tasmā loko'ti vuccati.*[29]
>
> "It is disintegrating, monk, that is why it is called 'the world.' And what is disintegrating? The eye, monk, is disintegrating, forms are disintegrating, eye-consciousness is disintegrating, eye-contact is disintegrating, and whatever feeling that arises dependent on eye-contact, be it pleasant, or painful, or neither-pleasant-nor-painful, that too is disintegrating. It is disintegrating, monk, that is why it is called 'the world.'"

Here the Buddha is redefining the concept of the world, punning on the verb *lujjati*, which means to "break up" or "disintegrate." To bring about a radical change in outlook, in accordance with the *Dhamma*, the Buddha would sometimes introduce a new etymology in preference to the old. This definition of 'the world' is to the same effect.

Venerable Ānanda, too, raises the same question, soliciting a redefinition for the well-known concept of the world, and the Buddha responds with the following answer: *Yaṃ kho, Ānanda, palokadhammaṃ, ayaṃ vuccati ariyassa vinaye loko.*[30] "Whatever, Ānanda, is subject to disintegration that is called 'the world' in the noble one's discipline."

He even goes on to substantiate his statement at length:

> *Kiñca, Ānanda, palokadhammaṃ? Cakkhuṃ kho, Ānanda, palokadhammaṃ, rūpā palokadhammā, cakkhuviññāṇaṃ palokadhammaṃ, cakkhusamphasso palokadhammo, yampidaṃ cakkhusamphassapaccayā uppajjati vedayitaṃ sukhaṃ vā dukkhaṃ vā adukkhamasukhaṃ vā tampi palo-*

---

29 S IV 52, *Lokapañhāsutta*.

30 S IV 53, *Palokadhammasutta*.

> *kadhammaṃ. Yaṃ kho, Ānanda, palokadhammaṃ, ayaṃ vuccati ariyassa vinaye loko.*
>
> "And what, Ānanda, is subject to disintegration? The eye, Ānanda, is subject to disintegration, forms are subject to disintegration, eye-consciousness is subject to disintegration, eye-contact is subject to disintegration, and whatever feeling that arises dependent on eye-contact, be it pleasant, or painful, or neither-pleasant-nor-painful, that too is subject to disintegration. Whatever is subject to disintegration, Ānanda, is called 'the world' in the noble one's discipline."

In this instance, the play upon the word *loka* is vividly apt in that it brings out the transcendence of the world. If the world by definition is regarded as transient, it cannot be conceived substantially as a unit. How then can an eternity or infinity be predicated about it? If all the so-called things in the world, listed above, are all the time disintegrating, any unitary concept of the world is fallacious.

Had the Buddha answered those misconceived questions, he would thereby concede to the wrong concept of the world current among other religious groups. So then we can understand why the Buddha refused to answer the first four questions.

Now let us examine the next dilemma, *taṃ jīvaṃ taṃ sarīraṃ, aññaṃ jīvaṃ aññaṃ sarīraṃ*, "the soul and the body are the same, the soul is one thing and the body another." To these questions also, the other religionists insisted on a categorical answer, either 'yes' or 'no.'

There is a 'catch' in the way these questions are framed. The Buddha refused to get caught to them. These two questions are of the type that clever lawyers put to a respondent these days. They would sometimes insist strictly on a 'yes' or 'no' as answer and ask a question like 'have you now given up drinking?' If the respondent happens to be a teetotaler, he would be in a quandary, since both answers tend to create a wrong impression.

So also in the case of these two alternatives, "the soul and the body are the same, the soul is one thing and the body another."

Either way there is a presumption of a soul, which the Buddha did not subscribe to. The Buddha had unequivocally declared that the idea of soul is the outcome of an utterly foolish view, *kevalo paripūro bāladhammo*.[31] That is why the Buddha rejected both standpoints.

A similar 'catch,' a similar misconception, underlies the tetralemma concerning the after death state of the *Tathāgata*. It should be already clear to some extent by what we have discussed so far.

For the Buddha, the term *Tathāgata* had a different connotation than what it meant for those of other sects. The latter adhered to the view that both the ordinary disciple as well as the perfected individual in their systems of thought had a soul of some description or other.

The Buddha never subscribed to such a view. On the other hand, he invested the term *Tathāgata* with an extremely deep and subtle meaning. His definition of the term will emerge from the *Aggivacchagottasutta*, which we propose to discuss now.

In this discourse we find the wandering ascetic Vacchagotta trying to get a categorical answer to the questionnaire, putting each of the questions with legal precision one by one, as a lawyer would at the courts of law.

Kiṃ nu kho, bho Gotamo, 'sassato loko, idam eva saccaṃ, mogham aññan'ti, evaṃ diṭṭhi bhavaṃ Gotamo?[32] "Now, Master Gotama, 'the world is eternal, this only is true, all else is false,' are you of this view, Master Gotama?" The Buddha replies: *Na kho ahaṃ, Vaccha, evaṃ diṭṭhi*, "No, Vaccha, I am not of this view."

Then Vacchagotta puts the opposite standpoint, which too the Buddha answers in the negative. To all the ten questions the Buddha answers 'no,' thereby rejecting the questionnaire in toto. Then Vacchagotta asks why, on seeing what danger, the Buddha refuses to hold any of those views. The Buddha gives the following explanation:

---

[31] M I 138, *Alagaddūpamasutta*.

[32] M I 484, *Aggivacchagottasutta*.

> *'Sassato loko'ti kho, Vaccha, diṭṭhigatam etaṃ diṭṭhigahanaṃ diṭṭhikantāraṃ diṭṭhivisūkaṃ diṭṭhivipphanditaṃ diṭṭhisaṃyojanaṃ sadukkhaṃ savighātaṃ sa-upāyāsaṃ sapariḷāhaṃ, na nibbidāya na virāgāya na nirodhāya na upasamāya na abhiññāya na sambodhāya na nibbānāya saṃvattati.*
>
> "Vaccha, this speculative view that the world is eternal is a jungle of views, a desert of views, a distortion of views, an aberration of views, a fetter of views, it is fraught with suffering, with vexation, with despair, with delirium, it does not lead to disenchantment, to dispassion, to cessation, to tranquility, to higher knowledge, to enlightenment, to *Nibbāna*." So with regard to the other nine views.

Now here we find both the above-mentioned reasons. Not only the fact that these questions are not relevant to the attainment of *Nibbāna*, but also the fact that there is something wrong in the very statement of the problems. What are the dangers that he sees in holding any of these views?

Every one of them is just a speculative view, *diṭṭhigataṃ*, a jungle of views, *diṭṭhigahanaṃ*, an arid desert of views, *diṭṭhikantāraṃ*, a mimicry or a distortion of views, *diṭṭhivisūkaṃ*, an aberration of views, *diṭṭhivipphanditaṃ*, a fetter of views, *diṭṭhisaṃyojanaṃ*. They bring about suffering, *sadukkhaṃ*, vexation, *savighātaṃ*, despair, *sa-upāyāsaṃ*, delirium, *sapariḷāhaṃ*. They do not conduce to disenchantment, *na nibbidāya*, to dispassion, *na virāgāya*, to cessation, *na nirodhāya*, to tranquility, *na upasamāya*, to higher knowledge, *na abhiññāya*, to enlightenment, *na sambodhāya*, to extinguishment, *na nibbānāya*.

From this declaration it is obvious that these questions are ill founded and misconceived. They are a welter of false views, so much so that the Buddha even declares that these questions simply do not exist for the noble disciple, who has heard the *Dhamma*. They occur as real problems only to the untaught worldling. Why is that?

Whoever has a deep understanding of the four noble truths would not even raise these questions. This declaration should be enough for one to understand why the Buddha refused to answer them.

Explaining that it is because of these dangers that he rejects them in toto, the Buddha now makes clear what his own stance is. Instead of holding any of those speculative views, he has seen for himself the rise, *samudaya*, and fall, *atthagama*, of the five aggregates as a matter of direct experience, thereby getting rid of all 'I'-ing and 'my'-ing and latencies to conceits, winning ultimate release.

Even after this explanation Vacchagotta resorts to the fourfold logic to satisfy his curiosity about the after death state of the monk thus released in mind. *Evaṃ vimuttacitto pana, bho Gotamo, bhikkhu kuhiṃ uppajjati?* "When a monk is thus released in mind, Master Gotama, where is he reborn?" The Buddha replies: *Uppajjatī'ti kho, Vaccha, na upeti*, "To say that he is reborn, Vaccha, falls short of a reply."

Then Vacchagotta asks: *Tena hi, bho Gotama, na uppajjati?* "If that is so, Master Gotama, is he not reborn?" – *Na uppajjatī'ti kho, Vaccha, na upeti*, "To say that he is not reborn, Vaccha, falls short of a reply."

Tena hi, bho Gotama, uppajjati ca na ca uppajjati? "If that is so, Master Gotama, is he both reborn and is not reborn?" – *Uppajjati ca na ca uppajjatī'ti kho, Vaccha, na upeti*, "To say that he is both reborn and is not reborn, Vaccha, falls short of a reply."

Tena hi, bho Gotama, neva uppajjati na na uppajjati? "If that is so, Master Gotama, is he neither reborn nor is not reborn?" – *Neva uppajjati na na uppajjatī'ti kho, Vaccha, na upeti*, "To say that he is neither reborn nor is not reborn, Vaccha, falls short of a reply."

At this unexpected response of the Buddha to his four questions, Vacchagotta confesses that he is fully confused and bewildered. The Buddha grants that his confusion and bewilderment are understandable, since this *Dhamma* is so deep and subtle that it cannot be plumbed by logic, *atakkāvacaro*.

However, in order to give him a clue to understand the *Dhamma* point of view, he gives an illustration in the form of a catechism.

Taṃ kiṃ maññasi, Vaccha, sace te purato aggi jaleyya, jāneyyāsi tvaṃ 'ayaṃ me purato aggi jalatī'ti? "What do you think, Vaccha, suppose a fire were burning before you, would you know 'this fire is burning before me?'" – *Sace me, bho Gotama, purato aggi jaleyya, jāneyyāhaṃ 'ayaṃ me purato aggi jalatī'ti.* "If, Master Gotama, a fire were burning before me, I would know 'this fire is burning before me.'"

Sace pana taṃ, Vaccha, evaṃ puccheyya 'yo te ayaṃ purato aggi jalati, ayaṃ aggi kiṃ paṭicca jalatī'ti, evaṃ puṭṭho tvaṃ, Vaccha, kinti byākareyyāsi? "If someone were to ask you, Vaccha, 'what does this fire that is burning before you burns in dependence on,' being asked thus, Vaccha, what would you answer?" – *Evaṃ puṭṭho ahaṃ, bho Gotama, evaṃ byākareyyaṃ 'yo me ayaṃ purato aggi jalati, ayaṃ aggi tiṇakaṭṭhupādānaṃ paṭicca jalatī'ti.* "Being asked thus, Master Gotama, I would answer 'this fire burning before me burns in dependence on grass and sticks.'"

Sace te, Vaccha, purato so aggi nibbāyeyya, jāneyyāsi tvaṃ 'ayaṃ me purato aggi nibbuto'ti? "If that fire before you were to be extinguished, Vaccha, would you know 'this fire before me has been extinguished?'" – *Sace me, bho Gotamo, purato so aggi nibbāyeyya, jāneyyāhaṃ 'ayaṃ me purato aggi nibbuto'ti.* "If that fire before me were to be extinguished, Master Gotama, I would know 'this fire before me has been extinguished.'"

Sace pana taṃ, Vaccha, evaṃ puccheyya 'yo te ayaṃ purato aggi nibbuto, so aggi ito katamaṃ disaṃ gato, puratthimaṃ vā dakkhiṇaṃ vā pacchimaṃ vā uttaraṃ vā'ti, evaṃ puṭṭho tvaṃ, Vaccha, kinti byākareyyāsi? "If someone were to ask you, Vaccha, when that fire before you were extinguished, 'to which direction did it go, to the east, the west, the north or the south,' being asked thus, what would you answer?" – *Na upeti, bho Gotama, yañhi so, bho Gotama, aggi tiṇakaṭṭhupādānaṃ paṭicca jalati, tassa ca pariyādānā aññassa ca anupahārā anāhāro nibbuto tveva saṅkhaṃ gacchati.* "That wouldn't do as a reply, Master Gotama, for that fire burnt in dependence on its fuel of grass and sticks. That being used up and not getting any more fuel, being without fuel, it is reckoned as extinguished."

At this point a very important expression comes up, which we happened to discuss earlier too, namely *saṅkhaṃ gacchati*.[33] It means "to be reckoned," or "to be known as," or "to be designated." So the correct mode of designation in this case is to say that the fire is reckoned as 'extinguished,' and not to say that it has gone somewhere.

If one takes mean advantage of the expression 'fire has gone out' and insists on locating it, it will only be a misuse or an abuse of linguistic usage. It reveals a pervert tendency to misunderstand and misinterpret. Therefore, all that can be said by way of predicating such a situation, is *nibbuto tveva saṅkhaṃ gacchati*, "it is reckoned as 'extinguished.'"

Now comes a well-timed declaration in which the Buddha, starting right from where Vacchagotta leaves off, brings the whole discussion to a climactic end:

> *Evameva kho, Vaccha, yena rūpena tathāgataṃ paññāpayamāno paññāpeyya, taṃ rūpaṃ tathāgatassa pahīnaṃ ucchinnamūlaṃ tālāvatthukataṃ anabhāvakataṃ āyatiṃ anuppādadhammaṃ. Rūpasaṅkhavimutto kho, Vaccha, tathāgato, gambhīro appameyyo duppariyogāho, seyyathāpi mahāsamuddo. Uppajjatī'ti na upeti, na uppajjatī'ti na upeti, uppajjati ca na ca uppajjatī'ti na upeti, neva uppajjati na na uppajjatī'ti na upeti.*

> "Even so, Vaccha, that form by which one designating the *Tathāgata* might designate him, that has been abandoned by him, cut off at the root, made like an uprooted palm tree, made non-existent and incapable of arising again. The *Tathāgata* is free from reckoning in terms of form, Vaccha, he is deep, immeasurable and hard to fathom, like the great ocean. To say that he is reborn falls short of a reply, to say that he is not reborn falls short of a reply, to say

[33] See sermons 1, 12 and 13.

> that he is both reborn and is not reborn falls short of a reply, to say that he is neither reborn nor is not reborn falls short of a reply."

This declaration, which a fully convinced Vacchagotta now wholeheartedly hailed and compared to the very heartwood of a *Sāla* tree, enshrines an extremely profound norm of *Dhamma*.

It was when Vacchagotta had granted the fact that it is improper to ask in which direction an extinguished fire has gone, and that the only proper linguistic usage is simply to say that 'it is extinguished,' that the Buddha came out with this profound pronouncement concerning the five aggregates.

In the case of the *Tathāgata*, the aggregate of form, for instance, is abandoned, *pahīnaṃ*, cut off at the root, *ucchinnamūlaṃ*, made like an uprooted palm tree divested from its site, *tālāvatthukataṃ*, made non-existent, *anabhavakataṃ*, and incapable of arising again, *āyatiṃ anuppādadhammaṃ*.

Thereby the *Tathāgata* becomes free from reckoning in terms of form, *rūpasaṅkhāvimutto kho tathāgato*. Due to this very freedom, he becomes deep, immeasurable and unfathomable like the great ocean. Therefore he cannot be said to be reborn, or not to be reborn, or both or neither. The abandonment of form, referred to above, comes about not by death or destruction, but by the abandonment of craving.

The fact that by the abandonment of craving itself, form is abandoned, or eradicated, comes to light from the following quotation from the *Rādhasaṃyutta* of the *Saṃyutta Nikāya*:

> *Rūpe kho, Rādha, yo chando yo rāgo yā nandī yā taṇhā, taṃ pajahatha. Evaṃ taṃ rūpaṃ pahīnaṃ bhavissati ucchinnamūlaṃ tālāvatthukataṃ anabhāvakataṃ āyatiṃ anuppādadhammaṃ.*[34]

---

[34] S III 193, *Chandarāgasutta*.

> "Rādha, you give up that desire, that lust, that delight, that craving for form. It is thus that form comes to be abandoned, cut off at the root, made like an uprooted palm tree, made non-existent and incapable of arising again."

Worldlings are under the impression that an *arahant*'s five aggregates of grasping get destroyed at death. But according to this declaration, an *arahant* is like an uprooted palm tree. A palm tree uprooted but left standing, divested of its site, might appear as a real palm tree to one who sees it from a distance. Similarly, an untaught worldling thinks that there is a being or person in truth and fact when he hears the term *Tathāgata*, even in this context too.

This is the insinuation underlying the above quoted pronouncement. It has some profound implications, but time does not permit us to go into them today.

Nibbāna Sermon 21

Namo tassa Bhagavato Arahato Sammāsambuddhassa
Namo tassa Bhagavato Arahato Sammāsambuddhassa
Namo tassa Bhagavato Arahato Sammāsambuddhassa

Etaṃ santaṃ, etaṃ paṇītaṃ, yadidaṃ sabbasaṅkhārasamatho sabbūpadhipaṭinissaggo taṇhakkhayo virāgo nirodho nibbānaṃ.[1]

"This is peaceful, this is excellent, namely the stilling of all preparations, the relinquishment of all assets, the destruction of craving, detachment, cessation, extinction."

With the permission of the Most Venerable Great Preceptor and the assembly of the venerable meditative monks.

This is the twenty-first sermon in the series of sermons on *Nibbāna*. The other day we discussed, to some extent, the ten questions known as the "ten indeterminate points," *dasa avyākatavatthūni*, which the Buddha laid aside, refusing to give a categorical answer as "yes" or "no." We pointed out, that the reason why he refused to answer them was the fact that they were founded on some wrong views, some wrong assumptions. To give categorical answers to such questions would amount to an assertion of those views. So he refrained from giving clear-cut answers to any of those questions.

Already from our last sermon, it should be clear, to some extent, how the eternalist and annihilationist views peep through them. The tetralemma on the after death state of the *Tathāgata*, which is

[1] M I 436, *MahāMālunkyasutta*.

directly relevant to our theme, also presupposes the validity of those two extreme views. Had the Buddha given a categorical answer, he too would be committing himself to the presumptions underlying them.

The middle path he promulgated to the world is one that transcended both those extremes. It is not a piecemeal compromise between them. He could have presented a halfway solution by taking up one or the other of the last two standpoints, namely "the *Tathāgata* both exists and does not exist after death," or "the *Tathāgata* neither exists nor does not exist after death." But instead of stooping to that position, he rejected the questionnaire in toto.

On the other hand, he brought in a completely new mode of analysis, illustrative of the law of dependent arising underlying the doctrine of the four noble truths, in order to expose the fallacy of those questions.

The other day we happened to mention the conclusive answer given by the Buddha to the question raised by the wandering ascetic Vacchagotta in the *Aggivacchagottasutta* of the *Majjhima Nikāya*, concerning the after death state of the *Tathāgata*. But we had no time to discuss it at length. Therefore let us take it up again.

When the wandering ascetic Vacchagotta had granted the incongruity of any statement to the effect that the extinguished fire has gone in such and such a direction, and the fact that the term *Nibbāna* is only a reckoning or a turn of speech, the Buddha follows it up with the conclusion:

> *Evameva kho, Vaccha, yena rūpena tathāgataṃ paññāpayamāno paññāpeyya, taṃ rūpaṃ tathāgatassa pahīnaṃ ucchinnamūlaṃ tālāvatthukataṃ anabhāvakataṃ āyatiṃ anuppādadhammaṃ. Rūpasaṅkhāvimutto kho, Vaccha, tathāgato, gambhīro appameyyo duppariyogāho, seyyathāpi mahāsamuddo. Uppajjatī'ti na upeti, na uppa-*

jjatī'ti na upeti, uppajjati ca na ca uppajjatī'ti na upeti, neva uppajjati na na uppajjatī'ti na upeti.[2]

"Even so, Vaccha, that form by which one designating the *Tathāgata* might designate him, that has been abandoned by him, cut off at the root, made like an uprooted palm tree, made non-existent and incapable of arising again. The *Tathāgata* is free from reckoning in terms of form, Vaccha, he is deep, immeasurable and hard to fathom, like the great ocean. To say that he is reborn falls short of a reply, to say that he is not re-born falls short of a reply, to say that he is both reborn and is not reborn falls short of a reply, to say that he is neither reborn nor is not reborn falls short of a reply."

As in the case of the aggregate of form, so also with regard to the aggregates of feeling, perception, preparations and consciousness, that is to say, in regard to all the five aggregates of grasping, the Buddha made this particular declaration. From this it is clear, that in this dispensation the *Tathāgata* cannot be reckoned in terms of any one of the five aggregates.

The similes reveal to us the state of the *Tathāgata* – the simile of the uprooted tree, for instance. On seeing a palm tree uprooted, but somehow left standing, one would mistake it for a growing palm tree. The worldling has a similar notion of the *Tathāgata*. This simile of the tree reminds us of the *Isidattatheragāthā*, which has an allusion to it:

Pañcakkhandhā pariññātā,
tiṭṭhanti chinnamūlakā,

---

[2] M I 487, *Aggivacchagottasutta*.

dukkhakkhayo anuppatto,
patto me āsavakkhayo.[3]

"Five aggregates, now fully understood,
Just stand, cut off at their root,
Reached is suffering's end,
Extinct for me are influxes."

On reaching arahant-hood, one finds oneself in this strange situation. The occurrence of the word *saṅkhā* in this connection is particularly significant. This word came up in our discussion of the term papañca in the contexts *papañcasaṅkhā* and *papañcasaññāsaṅkhā.*[4] There we had much to say about the word. It is synonymous with *samaññā*, "appellation," and *paññatti*, "designation." Reckoning, appellation and designation are synonymous to a great extent. So the concluding statement of the Buddha, already quoted, makes it clear that the *Tathāgata* cannot be reckoned or designated in terms of form, though he has form, he cannot be reckoned by feeling, though he experiences feeling, nor can he be reckoned by, or identified with, the aggregates of perceptions, preparations or consciousness.

Now in order to make a reckoning, or a designation, there has to be a duality, a dichotomy. We had occasion to touch upon this normative tendency to dichotomize. By way of illustration we may refer to the fact that even the price of an article can be reckoned, so long as there is a vortex between supply and demand. There has to be some kind of vortex between two things, for there to be a designation. A vortex, or *vaṭṭa*, is an alternation between two things, a cyclic interrelation. A designation can come in only so long as there is such a cyclic process. Now the *Tathāgata* is free from this duality.

---

[3] Th 120, *Isidattatheragāthā.*

[4] See sermon 12.

We have pointed out that the dichotomy between consciousness and name-and-form is the *saṃsāric* vortex. Let us refresh our memory of this vortex by alluding to a quotation from the *Udāna* which we brought up on an earlier occasion:

Chinnaṃ vaṭṭaṃ na vattati,
es' ev' anto dukkhassa.[5]

"The whirlpool cut off whirls no more.
This, even this, is suffering's end."

This, in fact, is a reference to the *arahant.* The vortex is between consciousness and name-and-form. By letting go of name-and-form, and realizing the state of a non-manifestative consciousness, the *arahant* has, in this very life, realized the cessation of existence, which amounts to a cessation of suffering as well. Though he continues to live on, he does not grasp any of those aggregates tenaciously. His consciousness does not get attached to name-and-form. That is why it is said that the vortex turns no more.

To highlight this figure of the vortex, we can bring up another significant quotation from the *Upādānaparivaṭṭasutta* and the *Sattaṭṭhānasutta* of the *Saṃyutta Nikāya.*

Ye suvimuttā te kevalino, ye kevalino vaṭṭaṃ tesaṃ n'atthi paññāpanāya.[6] "Those who are fully released, are truly alone, and for them who are truly alone, there is no whirling round for purposes of designation."

This statement might sound rather queer. The term *kevalī* occurs not only in the *Saṃyutta Nikāya*, but in the *Sutta Nipāta* as well, with reference to the *arahant.* The commentary to the *Sutta Nipāta*, *Paramatthajotikā*, gives the following definition to the term when it comes up in the *Kasibhāradvāja Sutta: sab-*

---

5 Ud 75, *DutiyaLakuṇṭakabhaddiyasutta*, see sermon 2.

6 S III 59, *Upādānaparivaṭṭasutta* and S III 63, *Sattaṭṭhānasutta.*

baguṇaparipuṇṇaṃ sabbayogavisaṃyuttaṃ vā.[7] According to the commentator, this term is used for the arahant in the sense that he is perfect in all virtues, or else that he is released from all bonds.

But going by the implications of the word *vaṭṭa*, associated with it, we may say that the term has a deeper meaning. From the point of view of etymology, the word *kevalī* is suggestive of singularity, full integration, aloofness and solitude. We spoke of a letting go of name-and-form. The non-manifestative consciousness, released from name-and-form, is indeed symbolic of the *arahant*'s singularity, wholeness, aloofness and solitude.

In the following verse from the *Dhammapada*, which we had quoted earlier too, this release from name-and-form is well depicted:

> *Kodhaṃ jahe vippajaheyya mānaṃ,*
> *saṃyojanaṃ sabbam atikkameyya,*
> *taṃ nāmarūpasmim asajjamānaṃ,*
> *akiñcanaṃ nānupatanti dukkhā.*[8]

> "Let one put wrath away and conceit abandon,
> And get well beyond all fetters as well,
> That one, untrammelled by name-and-form,
> With naught as his own, no pains befall."

We came across another significant reference to the same effect in the *Māghasutta* of the *Sutta Nipāta*:

> *Ye ve asattā vicaranti loke,*
> *akiñcanā kevalino yatattā,*

---

[7] Pj II 152, commenting on Sn 82, *Kasibhāradvājasutta*.

[8] Dhp 221, *Kodhavagga*, see sermon 9.

kālena tesu havyaṃ pavecche,
yo brāhmaṇo puññapekho yajetha.[9]

"They who wander unattached in the world,
Owning naught, aloof, restrained,
To them in time, let the brahmin offer,
That oblation, if merit be his aim."

This verse also makes it clear, that a freedom from ownings and attachments is implicit in the term *kevalī.* It has connotations of full integration and aloofness. The term *kevala*, therefore, is suggestive of the state of release from that vortex.

If, for instance, a vortex in the ocean comes to cease, can one ask where the vortex has gone? It will be like asking where the extinguished fire has gone. One might say that the vortex has 'joined' the ocean. But that, too, would not be a proper statement to make. From the very outset what in fact was there was the great ocean, so one cannot say that the vortex has gone somewhere, nor can one say that it is not gone. It is also incorrect to say that it has joined the ocean. A cessation of a vortex gives rise to such a problematic situation. So is this state called *kevalī.* What, in short, does it amount to? **The vortex has now become the great ocean itself. That is the significance of the comparison of the emancipated one to the great ocean.**

The commentators do not seem to have paid sufficient attention to the implications of this simile. But when one thinks of the relation between the vortex and the ocean, it is as if the *arahant* has become one with the ocean. But this is only a turn of speech.

In reality, the vortex is merely a certain pervert state of the ocean itself. That perversion is now no more. It has ceased. It is because of that perversion that there was a manifestation of suffering. **The cessation of suffering could therefore be com-**

---

9 Sn 490, *Māghasutta.*

pared to the cessation of the vortex, leaving only the great ocean as it is.

Only so long as there is a whirling vortex can we point out a 'here' and a 'there.' In the vast ocean, boundless as it is, where there is a vortex, or an eddy, we can point it out with a 'here' or a 'there.' Even so, in the case of the *saṃsāric* individual, as long as the whirling round is going on in the form of the vortex, there is a possibility of designation or appellation as 'so-and-so.' But once the vortex has ceased, there is actually nothing to identify with, for purposes of designation. The most one can say about it, is to refer to it as the place where a vortex has ceased.

Such is the case with the *Tathāgata* too. Freedom from the duality is for him release from the vortex itself. We have explained on a previous occasion how a vortex comes to be.[10] A current of water, trying to go against the mainstream, when its attempt is foiled, in clashing with the mainstream, gets thrown off and pushed back, but turns round to go whirling and whirling as a whirlpool. This is not the norm. This is something abnormal. Here is a perversion resulting from an attempt to do the impossible. This is how a thing called 'a vortex' comes to be.

The condition of the *saṃsāric* being is somewhat similar. What we are taught as the four 'perversions' in the *Dhamma*, describe these four pervert attitudes of a *saṃsāric* being:

1) Perceiving permanence in the impermanent.
2) Perceiving pleasure in the painful.
3) Perceiving beauty in the foul.
4) Perceiving a self in the not-self.

The *saṃsāric* individual tries to forge ahead in existence, misled by these four pervert views. The result of that attempt is the vortex

---

[10] See sermon 3.

between consciousness and name-and-form, a recurrent process of whirling round and round.

Because of this process of whirling round, as in a vortex, there is an unreality about this world. What for us appears as the true and real state of the world, the Buddha declares to be false and unreal. We have already quoted on an earlier occasion the verse from the *Dvayatānupassanāsutta* of the *Sutta Nipāta*, which clearly illustrates this point:

> *Anattani attamāniṃ,*
> *passa lokaṃ sadevakaṃ,*
> *niviṭṭhaṃ nāmarūpasmiṃ,*
> *idaṃ saccan'ti maññati.*[11]

> "Just see the world, with all its gods,
> Fancying a self where none exists,
> Entrenched in name-and-form it holds
> The conceit that this is real."

What the world entrenched in name-and-form takes to be real, it seems is unreal, according to this verse. This idea is reinforced by the following refrain-like phrase in the *Uragasutta* of the *Sutta Nipāta*: *Sabbaṃ vitatham idan'ti ñatvā loke*,[12] "Knowing that everything in this world is not 'such.'"

We have referred to the special significance of the *Uragasutta* on several occasions.[13] That discourse enjoins a giving up of everything, like the sloughing off of a worn-out skin by a serpent. Now a serpent sheds its worn-out skin by understanding that it is no longer the real skin. Similarly, one has to understand that everything in the world is not 'such.' *Tathā* is "such." Whatever is 'as-it-is,' is *yathābhūta*. To be 'as-it-is,' is to be 'such.' What is

---

[11] Sn 756, *Dvayatānupassanāsutta*, see sermon 6.

[12] Sn 9, *Uragasutta*.

[13] See sermons 5 and 18.

not 'as-it-is,' is *ayathā* or *vitatha*, "unsuch" or "not such," that is to say, unreal.

It seems, therefore, that the vortex whirling between consciousness and name-and-form, in the case of *saṃsāric* beings, is something not 'such.' It is not the true state of affairs in the world. To be free from this aberration, this unreal state of duality, is to be an *arahant*.

The three unskilful mental states of greed, hate and delusion are the outcome of this duality itself. So long as the whirling goes on, there is friction manifesting itself, sometimes as greed and sometimes as hate. Delusion impels and propels both. It is just one current of water that goes whirling round and round, bringing about friction and conflict. This interplay between consciousness and name-and-form is actually a pervert state, abnormal and unreal. To be a *Tathāgata* is a return to reality and suchness, from this unreal, unsuch, pervert state.

We happened to mention earlier that the term *Tathāgata* was already current among ascetics of other sects. But it is not in the same sense that the Buddha used this term. For those of other sects, the term *Tathāgata* carried with it the prejudice of a soul or a self, even if it purported to represent the ideal of emancipation.

But in this dispensation, the *Tathāgata* is defined differently. *Tathā,* "even so," "thus," is the correlative of *yathā*, "just as," "in whatever way." **At whatever moment it becomes possible to say that 'as is the ocean, so is the vortex now,' then, it is the state of *tathāgata.***

The vortex originated by deviating from the course of the main-stream of the ocean. But if an individual, literally so-called, gave up such pervert attitudes, as seeing permanence in what is impermanent, if he got rid of the four perversions by the knowledge and insight into things as-they-are, then he comes to be known as a *Tathāgata*.

He is a "thus gone," in the sense that, as is the norm of the world, 'thus' he is now. There is also an alternative explanation possible, etymologically. *Tathatā* is a term for the law of dependent arising.[14] It means "thusness" or "suchness." This particular term, so integral to the understanding of the significance of *paṭicca samuppāda*, or "dependent arising," is almost relegated to the limbo in our tradition.

Tathāgata could therefore be alternatively explained as a return to that 'thusness' or 'suchness,' by comprehending it fully. In this sense, the derivation of the term could be explained analytically as *tatha + āgata*. Commentators, too, sometimes go for this etymology, though not exactly in this sense.[15]

According to this idea of a return to the true state of suchness, we may say that there is neither an increase nor a decrease in the ocean, when a vortex ceases. Why? Because what was found both inside the vortex and outside of it was simply water. So is the case with the *saṃsāric* individual.

What we have to say from here onwards, regarding this *saṃsāric* individual, is directly relevant to meditation. As we mentioned on an earlier occasion, the four elements, earth, water, fire and air, are to be found both internally and externally. In the *MahāHatthipadopama Sutta* of the *Majjhima Nikāya* we come across a way of reflection that leads to insight in the following instruction:

> *Yā c' eva kho pana ajjhattikā paṭhavidhātu, yā ca bāhirā paṭhavidhātu, paṭhavidhātu ev' esā. Taṃ n' etaṃ mama, n' eso 'haṃ asmi, na meso attā 'ti evam etaṃ yathābhūtaṃ sammappaññāya daṭṭhabbaṃ.*[16]
>
> "Now whatever earth element that is internal, and whatever earth element that is external, both are simply earth el-

---

[14] S II 26, *Paccayasutta*.

[15] Sv I 62: *tathalakkhaṇaṃ āgatoti tathāgato*.

[16] M I 185, *MahāHatthipadopamasutta*.

> ement. That should be seen as it is with right wisdom thus: 'this is not mine, this I am not, this is not my self.'"

The implication is that this so-called individual, or person, is in fact a vortex, formed out of the same kind of primary elements that obtain outside of it. So then, the whole idea of an individual or a person is a mere perversion. The notion of individuality in *saṃsāric* beings is comparable to the apparent individuality of a vortex. It is only a pretence. That is why it is called *asmimāna*, the "conceit 'am.'" In truth and fact, it is only a conceit.

This should be clear when one reflects on how the pure air gets caught up into this vortex as an in-breath, only to be ejected after a while as a foul out-breath. Portions of primary elements, predominating in earth and water, get involved with this vortex as food and drink, to make a few rounds within, only to be exuded as dirty excreta and urine. This way, one can understand the fact that what is actually there is only a certain delimitation or measuring as 'internal' and 'external.'

What sustains this process of measuring or reckoning is the duality – the notion that there are two things. So then, the supreme deliverance in this dispensation is release from this duality. Release from this duality is at the same time release from greed and hate.

Ignorance is a sort of going round, in a winding pattern, as in the case of a coil. Each round seems so different from the previous one, a peculiar novelty arising out of the forgetting or ignoring trait, characteristic of ignorance.

However much one suffers in one life cycle, when one starts another life cycle with a new birth, one is in a new world, in a new form of existence. The sufferings in the previous life cycle are almost forgotten. The vast cycle of *saṃsāra*, this endless faring round in time and space, is like a vortex.

The vortical interplay between consciousness and name-and-form has the same background of ignorance. In fact, it is like the seed of the entire process. A disease is diagnosed by the characteristics of the germ. Even so, the Buddha pointed out, that the basic principle underlying the *saṃsāric* vortex is traceable to the vortical interplay between consciousness and name-and-form, going on within our minds.

This germinal vortex, between consciousness and name-and-form, is an extremely subtle one that eludes the limitations of both time and space. This, indeed, is the timeless principle inherent in the law of *paṭicca samuppāda*, or "dependent arising." Therefore, the solution to the whole problem lies in the understanding of this law of dependent arising.

We have mentioned on a previous occasion that the *saṅkhata*, or the "prepared," becomes *asaṅkhata*, or the "unprepared," by the very understanding of the 'prepared' nature of the *saṅkhata*.[17] The reason is that the prepared appears to be 'so,' due to the lack of understanding of its composite and prepared nature. This might well appear a riddle.

The faring round in *saṃsāra* is the result of ignorance. That is why final deliverance is said to be brought about by wisdom in this dispensation. All in all, one extremely important fact emerges from this discussion, namely the fact that the etymology attributed to the term Tathāgata by the Buddha is highly significant.

It effectively explains why he refused to answer the tetralemma concerning the after death state of the *Tathāgata*. When a vortex has ceased, it is problematic whether it has gone somewhere or joined the great ocean. Similarly, there is a problem of identity in the case of a *Tathāgata*, even when he is living. This simile of the ocean gives us a clue to a certain much-vexed riddle-like discourse on *Nibbāna*.

Many of those scholars, who put forward views on *Nibbāna* with an eternalist bias, count on the *Pahārādasutta* found among the Eights of the *Aṅguttara Nikāya*.[18] In fact, that discourse occurs in the *Vinaya Cūḷavagga* and in the *Udāna* as well.[19] In the *Pahārādasutta*, the Buddha gives a sustained simile, explaining

---

[17] See sermon 19.

[18] A IV 197, *Pahārādasutta*.

[19] Vin II 237 and Ud 53, *Uposathasutta*.

eight marvelous qualities of this dispensation to the *asura* king Pahārāda, by comparing them to eight marvels of the great ocean. The fifth marvelous quality is stated as follows:

> *Seyyathāpi, Pahārāda, yā kāci loke savantiyo mahāsamuddam appenti, yā kāci antalikkhā dhārā papatanti, na tena mahāsamuddassa ūnattaṃ vā pūrattaṃ vā paññāyati, evam eva kho, Pahārāda, bahū ce pi bhikkhū anupādisesāya nibbānadhātuyā parinibbāyanti, na tena nibbānadhātuyā ūnattaṃ vā pūrattaṃ va paññāyati.*[20]

> "Just as, Pahārāda, however many rivers of the world may flow into the great ocean and however much torrential downpours may fall on it from the sky, no decrease or increase is apparent in the great ocean, even so, Pahārāda, although many monks may attain *parinibbāna* in the *Nibbāna* element without residual clinging, thereby no decrease or increase is apparent in the *Nibbāna* element."

Quite a number of scholars draw upon this passage when they put forward the view that *arahants*, after their death, find some place of refuge which never gets overcrowded. It is a ridiculous idea, utterly misconceived. It is incompatible with this *Dhamma*, which rejects both eternalist and annihilationist views. Such ideas seem to have been put forward due to a lack of appreciation of the metaphorical significance of this particular discourse and a disregard for the implications of this comparison of the arahant to the great ocean, in point of his suchness or *tathatā*.

In the light of these facts, we have to conclude that *Nibbāna* is actually the truth, and that *saṃsāra* is a mere perversion. That is why the *Dvayatānupassanāsutta*, from which we have quoted earlier too, is fundamentally important. It says that what the world

---

20 A IV 202, *Pahārādasutta*.

takes as the truth, that the *ariyans* have seen with wisdom as untruth:

Yaṃ pare sukhato āhu,
tad ariyā āhu dukkhato,
yaṃ pare dukkhato āhu,
tad ariyā sukhato vidū.[21]

"What others may call bliss,
That the ariyans make known as pain.
What others may call pain,
That the *ariyans* have known to be bliss."

And it effectively concludes:

Passa dhammaṃ durājānaṃ,
sampamūḷh' ettha aviddasū.

"Behold a norm, so hard to grasp,
Baffled herein are ignorant ones."

The truth of this profound declaration by the Buddha could be seen in these deeper dimensions of the meaning of *tathatā*. By way of further clarification of what we have already stated about the *Tathāgata* and the mode of answering those questions about his after death state, we may now take up the *Anurādhasutta* of the *Saṃyutta Nikāya*, which is of paramount importance in this issue.

According to this discourse, when the Buddha was once dwelling in the gabled hall in Vesalī, a monk named Anurādha was living in a hut in a jungle close by. One day he was confronted with a situation, which shows that even a forest dwelling monk cannot afford to ignore questions like this. A group of wandering

---

21 Sn 762, *Dvayatānupassanāsutta*.

ascetics of other sects approached him and, seated in front of him, made this pronouncement, as if to see his response:

> *Yo so, āvuso Anurādha, tathāgato uttamapuriso paramapuriso paramapattipatto, taṃ tathāgataṃ imesu catūsu ṭhānesu paññāpayamāno paññāpeti: 'Hoti tathāgato paraṃ maraṇā'ti vā 'na hoti tathāgato paraṃ maraṇā'ti vā 'hoti ca na ca hoti tathāgato paraṃ maraṇā'ti vā 'neva hoti na na hoti tathāgato paraṃ maraṇā'ti vā.*[22]

> "Friend Anurādha, as to that *Tathāgata*, the highest person, the supreme person, the one who has attained the supreme state, in designating him one does so in terms of these four propositions: 'the *Tathāgata* exists after death,' 'the *Tathāgata* does not exist after death,' 'the *Tathāgata* both exists and does not exist after death,' 'the *Tathāgata* neither exists nor does not exist after death.'"

What those ascetics of other sects wanted to convey, was that the state of the *Tathāgata* after death could be predicated only by one of these four propositions, constituting the tetralemma. But then Venerable Anurādha made the following declaration, as if to repudiate that view:

> *Yo so, āvuso, tathāgato uttamapuriso paramapuriso paramapattipatto, taṃ tathāgataṃ aññatr'imehi catūhi ṭhānehi paññāpayamāno paññāpeti.*

> "Friends, as to that *Tathāgata*, the highest person, the supreme person, the one who has attained the supreme state, in designating him one does so apart from these four propositions."

---

[22] S III 116 and S IV 380, *Anurādhasutta*.

As soon as he made this statement, those ascetics of other sects made the derogatory remark: "This must be either a new-comer to the Order, just gone forth, or a foolish incompetent elder." With this insult, they got up and left, and Venerable Anurādha fell to thinking: "If those wandering ascetics of other sects should question me further, how should I answer them creditably, so as to state what has been said by the Exalted One, and not to misrepresent him. How should I explain in keeping with the norm of *Dhamma*, so that there will be no justifiable occasion for impeachment." With this doubt in mind, he approached the Buddha and related the whole episode. The Buddha, however, instead of giving a short answer, led Venerable Anurādha step by step to an understanding of the *Dhamma*, catechetically, by a wonderfully graded path. First of all, he convinced Venerable Anurādha of the three characteristics of existence:

'Taṃ kiṃ maññasi, Anurādha, rūpaṃ niccaṃ vā aniccaṃ vā'ti?'
'Aniccaṃ bhante.'

'Yaṃ panāniccaṃ dukkhaṃ vā taṃ sukhaṃ vā'ti?'
'Dukkhaṃ bhante.'

'Yaṃ panāniccaṃ dukkhaṃ vipariṇāmadhammaṃ kallaṃ nu taṃ samanupassituṃ: 'etaṃ mama, eso 'ham asmi, eso me attā'ti?'
'No h'etaṃ bhante.'

"What do you think, Anurādha, is form permanent or impermanent?"
"Impermanent, venerable sir."

"Is what is impermanent suffering or happiness?"
"Suffering, venerable sir."

"Is what is impermanent, suffering, and subject to change, fit to be regarded thus: 'This is mine, this am I, this is my self?'"

"No indeed, venerable sir."

So also with regard to the other aggregates, the Buddha guided Venerable Anurādha to the correct standpoint of the *Dhamma*, in this case by three steps, and this is the first step. He put aside the problem of the *Tathāgata* for a moment and highlighted the characteristic of not-self out of the three signata, thereby convincing Anurādha that what is impermanent, suffering and subject to change, is not fit to be regarded as self. Now comes the second step, which is, more or less, a reflection leading to insight:

Tasmā ti ha, Anurādha, yaṃ kiñci rūpam atītānāgatapaccuppannam ajjhattaṃ vā bahiddhā vā oḷārikaṃ vā sukhumaṃ vā hīnaṃ vā paṇītaṃ vā, yaṃ dūre santike vā, sabbaṃ rūpaṃ 'n' etaṃ mama, n' eso 'ham asmi, na meso attā'ti evam etaṃ yathābhūtaṃ sammappaññāya daṭṭhabbaṃ. Yā kāci vedanā atītānāgatapaccuppannā . . . yā kāci saññā . . . ye keci saṅkhāra . . . yaṃ kiñci viññāṇaṃ atītānāgatapaccuppannam ajjhattaṃ vā bahiddhā vā oḷārikaṃ vā sukhumaṃ vā hīnaṃ vā paṇītaṃ vā, yaṃ dūre santike vā, sabbaṃ viññāṇaṃ 'n' etaṃ mama, n' eso 'ham asmi, na meso attā'ti evam etaṃ yathābhūtaṃ sammappaññāya daṭṭhabbaṃ.

Evaṃ passaṃ, Anurādha, sutavā ariyasāvako rūpasmim pi nibbindati, vedanāya pi nibbindati, saññāya pi nibbindati, saṅkhāresu pi nibbindati, viññāṇasmim pi nibbindati. Nibbindaṃ virajjati, virāgā vimuccati, vimuttasmiṃ vimuttam iti ñāṇaṃ hoti: 'khīṇā jāti vusitaṃ brahmacariyaṃ, kataṃ karaṇīyaṃ, nāparam itthattāyā'ti pajānāti.

"Therefore, Anurādha, any kind of form whatsoever, whether past, future or present, internal or external, gross or subtle, inferior or superior, far or near, all form should be seen as it really is, with right wisdom thus: 'This is not mine, this I am not, this is not my self.' Any kind of feeling whatsoever, whether past, future or present . . . any kind of perception . . . any kind of preparations . . . any kind of consciousness whatsoever, whether past, future or present, internal or external, gross or subtle, inferior or superior, far or near, all consciousness should be seen as it really is, with right wisdom thus: 'This is not mine, this I am not, this is not my self.'

"Seeing thus, Anurādha, the instructed noble disciple gets disgusted of form, gets disgusted of feeling, gets disgusted of perception, gets disgusted of preparations, gets disgusted of consciousness. With disgust, he becomes dispassionate, through dispassion his mind is liberated, when it is liberated, there comes the knowledge 'it is liberated' and he understands: 'Extinct is birth, lived is the holy life, done is what is to be done, there is no more of this state of being.'"

Here the Buddha is presenting a mode of reflection that culminates in *arahant*-hood. If one is prepared to accept the not-self standpoint, then what one has to do, is to see with right wisdom all the five aggregates as not-self in a most comprehensive manner. This is the second step.

Now, as the third step, the Buddha sharply addresses a series of questions to Venerable Anurādha, to judge how he would determine the relation of the *Tathāgata*, or the emancipated one, to the five aggregates:

"What do you think, Anurādha, do you regard form as the *Tathāgata*?"

"No, venerable sir."

"Do you regard feeling . . . perception . . . preparations . . . consciousness as the *Tathāgata*?"

"No, venerable sir."

"What do you think, Anurādha, do you regard the *Tathāgata* as in form?"
"No, venerable sir."

"Do you regard the *Tathāgata* as apart from form?"
"No, venerable sir."

"Do you regard the *Tathāgata* as in feeling?"
"No, venerable sir."

"Do you regard the *Tathāgata* as apart from feeling?"
"No, venerable sir."

"Do you regard the *Tathāgata* as in perception?"
"No, venerable sir."

"Do you regard the *Tathāgata*as apart from perception?"
"No, venerable sir."

"Do you regard the *Tathāgata* as in preparations?"
"No, venerable sir."

"Do you regard the *Tathāgata* as apart from preparations?"
"No, venerable sir."

"Do you regard the *Tathāgata* as in consciousness?"
"No, venerable sir."

"Do you regard the *Tathāgata* as apart from consciousness?"
"No, venerable sir."

"What do you think, Anurādha, do you regard the *Tathāgata* as one who is without form, without feeling, without perception, without preparations, without consciousness?"
"No, venerable sir."

When Venerable Anurādha gives negative answers to all these four modes of questions, the Buddha draws the inevitable conclusion that accords with the *Dhamma*:

> *'Ettha ca te, Anurādha, diṭṭheva dhamme saccato thetato tathāgate anupalabbhiyamāne, kallaṃ nu te taṃ veyyākaraṇaṃ: 'Yo so, āvuso, tathāgato uttamapuriso paramapuriso paramapattipatto, taṃ tathāgataṃ aññatr'imehi catūhi ṭhānehi paññāpayamāno paññāpeti?'' 'No hetaṃ bhante.'*
>
> "So then, Anurādha, when for you a *Tathāgata* is not to be found in truth and fact here in this very life, is it fitting for you to declare, as you did: 'Friends, as to the *Tathāgata*, the highest person, the supreme person, the one who has attained the supreme state, in designating him one does so apart from these four propositions?'" "No, venerable sir."

This conclusion, namely that the *Tathāgata* is not to be found in truth and fact even in this very life, is one that drives terror into many who are steeped in the craving for existence. But this, it seems, is the upshot of the catechism. The rebuke of the wandering ascetics is justifiable, because the tetralemma exhausts the universe of discourse and there is no way out.

The Buddha's reproof of Anurādha amounts to an admission that even here and now the *Tathāgata* does not exist in truth and fact, not to speak of his condition hereafter. When Anurādha accepts this position, the Buddha expresses his approbation with the words:

Sādhu, sādhu, Anurādha, pubbe cāham Anurādha etarahi ca dukkhañceva paññāpemi dukkhassa ca nirodhaṃ. "Good, good, Anurādha, formerly as well as now I make known just suffering and the cessation of suffering."

This declaration makes it clear that the four noble truths are the teaching proper and that terms like *Tathāgata*, *satta* and *pugala* are mere concepts. No doubt, this is a disconcerting revelation. So let us see, whether there is any possibility of salvaging the *Tathāgata*.

Now there is the word *upalabbhati* occurring in this context, which is supposed to be rather ambiguous. In fact, some prefer to render it in such a way as to mean the *Tathāgata* does exist, only that he cannot be traced.

Tathāgata, it seems, exists in truth and fact, though one cannot find him. This is the way they get round the difficulty. But then, let us examine some of the contexts in which the word occurs, to see whether there is a case for such an interpretation.

A clear-cut instance of the usage of this expression comes in the *Vajirā Sutta* of the *Saṃyutta Nikāya*. The *arahant* nun Vajirā addresses the following challenge to *Māra:*

> *Kinnu 'satto'ti paccesi,*
> *Māra diṭṭhigatannu te,*
> *suddhasaṅkhārapuñjo, yaṃ,*
> *nayidha sattūpalabbhati.*[23]

> "What do you mean by a 'being,' O Māra,
> Isn't it a bigoted view, on your part?
> This is purely a heap of preparations, mind you,
> No being is to be found here at all."

The context as well as the tone makes it clear that the word *upalabbhati* definitely means "not to be found," not that there is a being but one cannot find it.

We may take up another instance from the *Purābhedasutta* of the *Sutta Nipāta*, where the theme is the *arahant*:

> *Na tassa puttā pasavo vā,*
> *khettaṃ vatthuṃ na vijjati,*

---

[23] S I 135, *Vajirāsutta.*

attaṃ vāpi nirattaṃ vā
na tasmim upalabbhati.[24]

"Not for him are sons and cattle,
He has no field or site to build,
In him there is not to be found
Anything that is grasped or given up."

The words *attaṃ* and *nirattaṃ* are suggestive of the dichotomy from which the *arahant* is free. The context unmistakeably proves that the expression *na upalabbhati* means "not to be found."

All this goes to show that the Buddha set aside the four questions forming the tetralemma not because they are irrelevant from the point of view of *Nibbāna*, despite the fact that he could have answered them. That is to say, not that he could not, but that he would not. How can one say that the question of an *arahant*'s after death state is totally irrelevant? So that is not the reason.

The reason is that the questions are misleading. Those who posed these questions had the presumption that the word *Tathāgata* implied a truly existing being or a person. But the Buddha pointed out that the concept of a being or a person is fallacious.

Though it is fallacious, for the worldling living in an illusory unreal world, it has its place as a relative reality. Due to the very fact that it is grasped, it is binding on him. Therefore, when a worldling uses such terms as 'I' and 'mine,' or a 'being' and a 'person,' it is not a mere way of expression. It is a level of reality proper to the worldling's scale of values.

But for the *arahants*, who have reached the state of suchness, it is a mere concept. In fact, it becomes a mere concept in the context of the simile of the vortex and the ocean. That is to say, in the case of the *arahants*, their five aggregates resemble the flotsam and jetsam on the surface waters of a vortex already ceased at its depth.

---

[24] Sn 858, *Purābhedasutta*.

On seeing the Buddha and the *arahants*, one might still say, as a way of saying, 'here is the Buddha,' 'here are the *arahants*.' For the Buddha, the concept of a 'being' is something incompatible with his teaching from beginning to end. But for the nonce he had to use it, as is evident from many a discourse.

The expression *aṭṭha ariyapuggalā*, "the eight noble persons," includes the *arahant* as well. Similarly in such contexts as the *Aggappasādasutta*, the term *satta* is used indiscriminately, giving way to conventional usage:

> *Yāvatā, bhikkhave, sattā apadā va dipadā vā catuppadā vā bahuppadā vā rūpino vā arūpino vā saññino vā asaññino vā nevasaññināsaññino vā, tathāgato tesaṃ aggamakkhāyati arahaṃ sammāsambuddho.*[25]

> "Monks, whatever kinds of beings there be, whether footless or two-footed, or four-footed, or many footed, with form or formless, percipient or non-percipient, or neither-percipient-nor-non-percipient, among them the *Tathāgata*, worthy and fully awakened, is called supreme."

Although the term *satta* occurs there, it is only by way of worldly parlance. In truth and fact, however, there is no 'being' as such. In a previous sermon we happened to mention a new etymology given by the Buddha to the term *loka,* or "world." [26] In the same way, he advanced a new etymology for the term *satta*. As mentioned in the *Rādhasaṃyutta* of the *Saṃyutta Nikāya*, Venerable Rādha once posed the following question to the Buddha:

---

[25] A II 34, *Aggappasādasutta*.

[26] See sermon 20.

> *'Satto, satto'ti, bhante, vuccati. Kittāvatā nu kho, bhante, 'satto'ti vuccati?*[27]
>
> "Venerable sir, it is said 'a being,' 'a being.' To what extent can one be called 'a being?'"

Then the Buddha explains:

> *Rūpe . . . vedanāya . . . saññāya . . . saṅkhāresu . . . viññāṇe kho, Rādha, yo chando yo rāgo yā nandī yā taṇhā, tatra satto, tatra visatto, tasmā 'satto'ti vuccati.*
>
> "Rādha, that desire, that lust, that delight, that craving in form . . . feeling . . . perception . . . preparations . . . consciousness, with which one is attached and thoroughly attached to it, therefore is one called a 'being.'"

Here the Buddha is punning on the word *satta*, which has two meanings, a 'being' and 'the one attached.' The etymology attributed to that word by the Buddha brings out in sharp relief the attachment as well, whereas in his redefinition of the term *loka*, he followed an etymology that stressed the disintegrating nature of the world.[28]

Satto visatto, tasmā 'satto'ti vuccati, "Attached, thoroughly attached, therefore is one called a 'being.'" Having given this new definition, the Buddha follows it up with a scintillating simile:

> "Suppose, Rādha, some little boys and girls are playing with sand castles. So long as their lust, desire, love, thirst, passion and craving for those things have not gone away, they remain fond of them, they play with them, treat them as their property and call them their own. But when,

---

[27] S III 190, *Sattasutta*.

[28] S IV 52, *Lokapañhāsutta*.

> Rādha, those little boys and girls have outgrown that lust, desire, love, thirst, passion and craving for those sand castles, they scatter them with their hands and feet, demolish them, dismantle them and render them unplayable."

Now comes the Buddha's admonition, based on this simile:

> *Evam eva kho, Rādha, tumhe rūpaṃ . . . vedanaṃ . . . saññaṃ . . . saṅkhāre . . . viññāṇaṃ vikiratha vidhamatha viddhaṃsetha vikīḷanikaṃ karotha taṇhakkhayāya paṭipajjatha.*

> "Even so, Rādha, you all should scatter form . . . feeling . . . perception . . . preparations . . . consciousness, demolish it, dismantle it and render it unplayable. Practice for the destruction of craving."

And then he winds up with that highly significant conclusive remark: *Taṇhakkhayo hi, Rādha, nibbānaṃ.* "For, the destruction of craving, Rādha, is *Nibbāna*."

Nibbāna Sermon 22

Namo tassa Bhagavato Arahato Sammāsambuddhassa
Namo tassa Bhagavato Arahato Sammāsambuddhassa
Namo tassa Bhagavato Arahato Sammāsambuddhassa

Etaṃ santaṃ, etaṃ paṇītaṃ, yadidaṃ sabbasaṅkhārasamatho sabbūpadhipaṭinissaggo taṇhakkhayo virāgo nirodho nibbānaṃ.[1]

"This is peaceful, this is excellent, namely the stilling of all preparations, the relinquishment of all assets, the destruction of craving, detachment, cessation, extinction."

With the permission of the Most Venerable Great Preceptor and the assembly of the venerable meditative monks.

This is the twenty-second sermon in the series of sermons on *Nibbāna*. We made an attempt, in our last sermon, to explain that the comparison of the emancipated one in this dispensation to the great ocean has a particularly deep significance. We reverted to the simile of the vortex by way of explanation. Release from the *saṃsāric* vortex, or the breach of the vortex of *saṃsāra*, is comparable to the cessation of a whirlpool. It is equivalent to the stoppage of the whirlpool of *saṃsāra*.

Generally, what is known as a vortex or a whirlpool, is a certain pervert, unusual or abnormal activity, which sustains a pretence of an individual existence in the great ocean with a drilling and churning as its centre. It is an aberration, functioning according to a duality, maintaining a notion of two things. As long as it exists,

---

1 M I 436, *MahāMālunkyasutta*.

there is the dichotomy between a 'here' and a 'there,' oneself and another. A vortex reflects a conflict between an 'internal' and an 'external' – a 'tangle within' and a 'tangle without.' The cessation of the vortex is the freedom from that duality. It is a solitude born of full integration.

We happened to discuss the meaning of the term *kevalī* in our last sermon. The cessation of a vortex is at once the resolution of the conflict between an internal and an external, of the tangle within and without. When a vortex ceases, all those conflicts subside and a state of peace prevails. What remains is the boundless great ocean, with no delimitations of a 'here' and a 'there.' As is the great ocean, so is the vortex now.

This suchness itself indicates the stoppage, the cessation or the subsidence of the vortex. There is no longer any possibility of pointing out a 'here' and a 'there' in the case of a vortex that has ceased. Its 'thusness' or 'suchness' amounts to an acceptance of the reality of the great ocean. That 'thus-gone' vortex, or the vortex that has now become 'such,' is in every respect worthy of being called *tathāgata*.

The term *tādī* is also semantically related to this suchness. The *tathāgata* is sometimes referred to as *tādī* or *tādiso*, "such-like." The 'such-like' quality of the *tathāgata* is associated with his unshakeable deliverance of the mind. His mind remains unshaken before the eight worldly vicissitudes.

Why the Buddha refused to give an answer to the tetralemma concerning the after death state of the *tathāgata*, should be clear to a great extent by those *sutta* quotations we brought up in our last sermon. Since the quotation *diṭṭheva dhamme saccato thetato tathāgate anupalabbhiyamāne*,[2] "when a *tathāgata* is not to be found in truth and fact here in this very life," leads to the inference that a *tathāgata* is not to be found in reality even while he is alive, we were forced to conclude that the question 'what happens to the *tathāgata* after his death?' is utterly meaningless.

---

[2] S III 118 and S IV 384, *Anurādhasutta*.

It is also obvious from the conclusive statement, *pubbe cāhaṃ etarahi ca dukkhañceva paññāpemi dukkhassa ca nirodhaṃ* – "formerly as well as now I make known just suffering and the cessation of suffering" – that the Buddha, in answering this question, completely put aside such conventional terms like 'being' and 'person,' and solved the problem on the basis of the four noble truths, which highlight the pure quintessence of the *Dhamma* as it is.

We have to go a little deeper into this question of conventional terms like 'being' and 'person,' because the statement that the *tathāgata* does not exist in truth and fact is likely to drive fear into the minds of the generality of people. In our last sermon, we gave a clue to an understanding of the sense in which this statement is made, when we quoted an extraordinary new etymology, the Buddha had advanced, for the term *satta* in the *Rādhasaṃyutta*:

Rūpe kho, Rādha, yo chando yo rāgo yā nandī yā taṇhā, tatra satto, tatra visatto, tasmā 'satto'ti vuccati.[3] "Rādha, that desire, that lust, that delight, that craving in form with which one is attached and thoroughly attached, therefore is one called a 'being.'"

Here the Buddha has punned on the word *satta*, to give a new orientation to its meaning, that is, *rūpe satto visatto*, "attached and thoroughly attached to form."

From prehistoric times, the word *satta* was associated with the idea of some primordial essence called *sat*, which carried with it notions of permanent existence in the world. As derivatives from the present participle *sant* and *sat*, we get the two words *satya* and *sattva* in Sanskrit. *Satya* means "truth," or what is "true." *Sattva* means a "being" or the "state of being." We might even take *sattva* as the place from which there is a positive response or an affirmation of a state of being.

Due to the semantic affinity between *satya*, "truth," and *sattva*, "being," an absolute reality had been granted to the term *sattva*

---

3 S III 190, *Sattasutta*.

from ancient times. But according to the new etymology advanced by the Buddha, the term *sattva* is given only a relative reality within limits, that is to say, it is 'real' only in a limited and a relative sense. The above quotation from the *Rādhasaṃyutta* makes it clear that a being exists only so long as there is that desire, lust, delight and craving in the five aggregates.

Alternatively, when there is no desire, or lust, or delight, or craving for any of the five aggregates, there is no 'being.' That is why we say that it is real only in a limited and relative sense.

When a thing is dependent on another thing, it is relative and for that very reason it has a limited applicability and is not absolute. Here, in this case, the dependence is on desire or attachment. As long as there is desire or attachment, there is a 'being,' and when it is not there, there is no 'being.' So from this we can well infer that the *tathāgata* is not a 'being' by virtue of the very definition he had given to the term *satta*.

The other day, we briefly quoted a certain simile from the *Rādhasutta* itself, but could not explain it sufficiently. The Buddha gives this simile just after advancing the above new definition:

> "Suppose, Rādha, some little boys and girls are playing with sandcastles. So long as their lust, desire, love, thirst, passion and craving for those things have not gone away, they remain fond of them, they play with them, treat them as their property and call them their own. But when, Rādha, those little boys and girls have outgrown that lust, desire, love, thirst, passion and craving for those sandcastles, they scatter them with their hands and feet, demolish them, dismantle them and render them unplayable."

When we reflect upon the meaning of this simile from the point of view of *Dhamma*, it seems that for those little boys and girls, sandcastles were real things, as long as they had ignorance and craving with regard to them. When they grew wiser and outgrew craving, those sandcastles became unreal. That is why they destroyed them.

The untaught worldling is in a similar situation. So long as he is attached to these five aggregates and has not comprehended their impermanent, suffering-fraught and not-self nature, they are real for him. He is bound by his own grasping.

The reality of the law of *kamma*, of merit and demerit, follows from that very grasping. The dictum *upādānapaccayā bhavo*, "dependent on grasping is existence," becomes meaningful in this context. There is an existence because there is grasping. But at whatever point of time wisdom dawned and craving faded away, all those things tend to become unreal and there is not even a 'being,' as there is no real 'state of being.'

This mode of exposition receives support from the *Kaccāyanagottasutta* of the *Saṃyutta Nikāya*. The way the Buddha has defined right view in that discourse is highly significant. We have already discussed this *sutta* on an earlier occasion.[4] Suffice it to remind ourselves of the basic maxim:

> *'Dukkham eva uppajjamānaṃ uppajjati, dukkhaṃ nirujjhamānaṃ nirujjhatī'ti na kaṅkhati na vicikicchati aparappaccayā ñāṇam ev' assa ettha hoti. Ettāvatā kho, Kaccāyana, sammā diṭṭhi hoti.*[5]

> "It is only suffering that arises and suffering that ceases. Understanding thus, one does not doubt, one does not waver, and there is in him only the knowledge that is not dependent on another. It is in so far, Kaccāyana, that one has right view."

What is called *aparappaccayā ñāṇa* is that knowledge of realization by oneself for which one is not dependent on another. The noble disciple wins to such a knowledge of realization in regard to this fact, namely, that it is only a question of suffering and its

---

[4] See sermon 4.

[5] S II 17, *Kaccāyanagottasutta*.

cessation. The right view mentioned in this context is the supramundane right view, and not that right view which takes *kamma* as one's own, *kammassakatā sammā diṭṭhi*, implying notions of 'I' and 'mine.'

This supramundane right view brings out the norm of *Dhamma* as it is. Being unable to understand this norm of *Dhamma*, contemporary ascetics and brahmins, and even some monks themselves, accused the Buddha of being an annihilationist. They brought up groundless allegations. There was also the opposite reaction of seeking refuge in a form of eternalism, through fear of being branded as annihilationists.

Sometimes the Buddha answered those wrong accusations in unmistakeable terms. We come across such an instance in the *Alagaddūpama Sutta*. First of all the Buddha qualifies the emancipated one in his dispensation with the terms *ariyo pannaddhajo pannabhāro visaṃyutto.*[6] Once the conceit 'am,' *asmimāna*, is abandoned, this noble one is called *pannaddhajo*, "one who has put down the flag of conceit." He has "laid down the burden," *pannabhāro*, and is "disjoined," *visaṃyutto*, from the fetters of existence. About this emancipated one, he now makes the following declaration:

> *Evaṃ vimuttacittaṃ kho, bhikkhave, bhikkhuṃ sa-indā devā sa-pajāpatikā sa-brahmakā anvesaṃ nādhigacchanti: idaṃ nissitaṃ tathāgatassa viññāṇan'ti. Taṃ kissa hetu? Diṭṭhe vāhaṃ, bhikkhave, dhamme tathāgato ananuvejjo'ti vadāmi.*
>
> *Evaṃvādiṃ kho maṃ, bhikkhave, evam akkhāyiṃ eke samaṇabrāhmaṇā asatā tucchā musā abhūtena abbhācikkhanti: venayiko samaṇo Gotamo, sato sattassa ucchedaṃ vināsaṃ vibhavaṃ paññāpeti.*

---

[6] M I 139, *Alagaddūpamasutta.*

> "A monk, thus released in mind, O! monks, gods including Indra, Pajāpati and Brahmā, are unable to trace in their search to be able to say of him: 'the consciousness of this thus-gone-one is dependent on this. And why is that so? Monks, I say, even here and now the *Tathāgata* is not to be found.
>
> "When I say thus, when I teach thus, some recluses and brahmins wrongly and falsely accuse me with the following unfounded allegation: 'recluse Gotama is an annihilationist, he lays down an annihilation, a destruction and non-existence of a truly existing being.'"

As in the *Anurādha Sutta*, here too the Buddha concludes with the highly significant statement of his stance, *pubbe cāhaṃ etarahi ca dukkhañceva paññāpemi dukkhassa ca nirodhaṃ*, "Formerly as well as now I make known just suffering and the cessation of suffering."

Though the statements in the suttas follow this trend, it seems that the commentator himself was scared to bring out the correct position in his commentary. The fact that he sets out with some trepidation is clear enough from the way he tackles the term *tathāgata* in his commentary to the above discourse in the *Majjhima Nikāya*. In commenting on the word *tathāgatassa* in the relevant context, he makes the following observation:

Tathāgatassā'ti ettha satto pi tathāgato'ti adhippeto, uttamapuggalo khīṇāsavo pi.[7] "*Tathāgata*'s, herein, a being also is meant by the term *tathāgata*, as well as the highest person, the influx-free arahant."

Just as he gives two meanings to the word *tathāgata*, Venerable Buddhaghosa attributes two meanings to the word *ananuvejjo* as well:

---

[7] Ps II 117.

Ananuvejjo'ti asaṃvijjamāno vā avindeyyo vā. Tathāgato'ti hi satte gahite asaṃvijjamāno'ti attho vaṭṭati, khīṇāsave gahite avindeyyo'ti attho vaṭṭati. "*Ananuvejjo* – 'non-existing' or 'untraceable.' When by the word *tathāgata* a being is meant, the sense 'non existing' is fitting; and when the influx-free one is meant, the sense 'untraceable' is fitting."

According to this exegesis, the term *tathāgata* in contexts where it means a 'being' is to be understood as non-existing, *asamvijjamāno*, which is equivalent in sense to the expression *anupalabbhiyamāne*, discussed above. On the other hand, the other sense attributed to it is *avindeyyo*, which somehow grants the existence but suggests that it is 'untraceable.' In other words, the *Tathāgata* exists, but he cannot be traced or found out.

The commentator opines that the term in question has to be understood in two different senses, according to contexts. In order to substantiate his view, the commentator attributes the following apocryphal explanation to the Buddha:

> *Bhikkhave, ahaṃ diṭṭheva dhamme dharamānakaṃ yeva khīṇāsavaṃ viññāṇavasena indādīhi avindiyaṃ vadāmi. Na hi sa-indā devā sa-brahmakā sa-pajāpatikā anvesantāpi khīṇāsavassa vipassanācittaṃ vā maggacittaṃ vā phalacittaṃ vā, idaṃ nāma ārammaṇaṃ nissāya vattatī'ti jānituṃ sakkonti. Te appaṭisandhikassa parinibbutassa kiṃ jānissanti?*

> "Monks, I say that even here and now the influx-free one, while he is alive, is untraceable by Indra and others in regard to his consciousness. Gods, including Indra, Brahmā and Pajāpati are indeed unable in their search to find out either the insight consciousness, or the path consciousness, or the fruition consciousness, to be able to say: 'it is dependent on this object.' How then could they find out the consciousness of one who has attained *parinibbāna* with no possibility of conception?"

Presumably, the argument is that, since the consciousness of the *arahant* is untraceable by the gods while he is alive, it is all the more difficult for them to find it out when he has attained *parinibbāna*. That is to say, the *arahant* somehow exists, even after his *parinibbāna*, only that he cannot be traced. It is obvious from this commentarial trend that the commentator finds himself on the horns of a dilemma, because of his inability to grasp an extremely deep dimension of linguistic usage. The Buddha's forceful and candid declaration was too much for him. Probably, he demurred out of excessive faith, but his stance is not in accordance with the *Dhamma*. It falls short of right view.

Let us now recapitulate the correct position in the light of the above *sutta* passage. The Buddha declares at the very outset that the emancipated monk undergoes a significant change by virtue of the fact that he has abandoned the conceit 'am.' That *Tathāgata*, that emancipated monk, who has put down the flag of conceit, laid down the burden of the five aggregates, and won release from the fetters to existence, defies definition and eludes categorization. Why is that?

As we pointed out earlier, the word *asmi* constitutes the very basis of the entire grammatical structure.[8] *Asmi*, or "am," is the basic peg, which stands for the first person. The second person and the third person come later. So *asmi* is basic to the grammatical structure. When this basic peg is uprooted, the emancipated monk reaches that state of freedom from the vortex. There is no dichotomy to sustain a vortex, no two teams to keep up the vortical interplay. Where there is no turning round, there is no room for designation, and this is the implication of the phrase *vaṭṭaṃ tesaṃ n'atthi paññāpanāya*, which we happened to quote on a previous occasion.[9] For the *arahants* there is no vortex whereby to designate.

---

[8] See sermons 10 and 13.

[9] M I 141, *Alagaddūpamasutta*; see sermon 2 and sermon 21.

That is why the *Tathāgata*, in this very life, is said to have transcended the state of a 'being.' Only as a way of speaking in terms of worldly parlance one cannot help referring to him as a 'being.' But in truth and fact, his position is otherwise.

Going by worldly usage, one might indiscriminately think of applying the four propositions of the tetralemma to the *Tathāgata* as well. But it is precisely in this context that the questioner's presumptions are fully exposed. The fact that he has misconceived the implications of the terms *satta* and *Tathāgata* is best revealed by the very question whether the *Tathāgata* exists after his death. It shows that he presumes the *Tathāgata* to be existing in truth and fact, and if so, he has either to go on existing or be annihilated after death. Here, then, we have an extremely deep dimension of linguistic usage.

The commentary says that gods and *Brahmās* cannot find the *Tathāgata* in point of his consciousness. The *Tathāgata* defies definition due to his abandonment of proliferations of cravings, conceits and views. Cravings, conceits and views, which bring in attachments, bindings and entanglements to justify the usage of terms like *satta*, 'being,' and *puggala*, 'person,' are extinct in the *Tathāgata*. That is why he is beyond reckoning.

In the *Brahmajāla Sutta* of the *Dīgha Nikāya* the Buddha makes the following declaration about himself, after refuting the sixty-two views, catching them all in one super-net:

> *Ucchinnabhavanettiko, bhikkhave, tathāgatassa kāyo tiṭṭhati. Yav'assa kāyo ṭhassati tāva naṃ dakkhinti devamanussā. Kāyassa bhedā uddhaṃ jīvitapariyādānā na naṃ dakkhinti devamanussā.*[10]

> "Monks, the *Tathāgata*'s body stands with its leading factor in becoming cut off at the root. As long as his body stands, gods and men will see him. With the breaking up

---

[10] D I 46, *Brahmajālasutta*.

of his body, after the extinction of his life, gods and men will not see him."

And then he follows up this promulgation with a simile:

> *Seyyathā pi, bhikkhave, ambapiṇḍiyā vaṇṭacchinnāya yāni kānici ambāni vaṇṭūpanibandhanāni, sabbāni tāni tad anvayāni bhavanti, evam eva kho, bhikkhave, ucchinnabhavanettiko tathāgatassa kāyo tiṭṭhati. Yav'assa kāyo ṭhassati tāva naṃ dakkhinti devamanussā. Kāyassa bhedā uddhaṃ jīvitapariyādānā na naṃ dakkhinti devamanussā.*
>
> "Just as, monks, in the case of a bunch of mangoes, when its stalk is cut off, whatever mangoes that were connected with the stalk would all of them be likewise cut off, even so, monks, stands the *Tathāgata*'s body with its leading factor in becoming cut off at the root. As long as his body stands, gods and men will see him. With the breaking up of his body, after the extinction of his life, gods and men will not see him."

The simile employed serves to bring out the fact that the *Tathāgata*'s body stands with its leading factor in becoming eradicated. Here it is said that gods and men see the *Tathāgata* while he is alive. But the implications of this statement should be understood within the context of the similes given.

The reference here is to a tree uprooted, one that simply stands cut off at the root. In regard to each aggregate of the Buddha and other emancipated ones, it is clearly stated that it is cut off at the root, *ucchinnamūlo*, that it is like a palm tree divested of its site, *tālāvatthukato*.[11]

In the case of a palm tree, deprived of its natural site but still left standing, anyone seeing it from afar would mistake it for an

---

[11] M I 139, *Alagaddūpamasutta*.

actual tree that is growing. It is the same idea that emerges from the simile of the bunch of mangoes. The *Tathāgata* is comparable to a bunch of mangoes with its stalk cut off.

What then is meant by the statement that gods and men see him? Their seeing is limited to the seeing of his body. For many, the concept of seeing the *Tathāgata* is just this seeing of his physical body. Of course, we do not find in this discourse any prediction that we can see him after five-thousand years.

Whatever it may be, here we seem to have some deep idea underlying this discourse. An extremely important clue to a correct understanding of this *Dhamma*, one that helps to straighten up right view, lies beneath this problem of the Buddha's refusal to answer the tetralemma concerning the *Tathāgata*. This fact comes to light in the *Yamaka Sutta* of the *Khandhasaṃyutta*.

A monk named Yamaka conceived the evil view, the distorted view, *tathāhaṃ bhagavatā dhammaṃ desitaṃ ājānāmi, yathā khīṇāsavo bhikkhu kāyassa bhedā ucchijjati vinassati, na hoti paraṃ maraṇā.*[12] "As I understand the Dhamma taught by the Exalted One, an influx-free monk, with the breaking up of his body, is annihilated and perishes, he does not exist after death."

He went about saying that the Buddha had declared that the emancipated monk is annihilated at death. Other monks, on hearing this, tried their best to dispel his wrong view, saying that the Buddha had never declared so, but it was in vain. At last they approached Venerable Sāriputta and begged him to handle the situation.

Then Venerable Sāriputta came there, and after ascertaining the fact, proceeded to dispel Venerable Yamaka's wrong view by getting him to answer a series of questions. The first set of questions happened to be identical with the one the Buddha had put forward in Venerable Anurādha's case, namely a catechism on the three characteristics. We have already quoted it step by step,

---

[12] S III 109, *Yamakasutta.*

for facility of understanding.[13] Suffice it to mention, in brief, that it served to convince Venerable Yamaka of the fact that whatever is impermanent, suffering and subject to change, is not fit to be looked upon as 'this is mine, this am I, and this is my self.'

The first step, therefore, consisted in emphasizing the not self characteristic through a catechism on the three signata. The next step was to get Venerable Yamaka to reflect on this not self characteristic in eleven ways, according to the standard formula:

> *Tasmātiha, āvuso Yamaka, yaṃ kiñci rūpaṃ atītānāgatapaccuppannaṃ ajjhattaṃ vā bahiddhā vā oḷārikaṃ va sukhumaṃ vā hīnaṃ vā panītaṃ vā yaṃ dūre santike vā, sabbaṃ rūpaṃ n'etaṃ mama n'eso 'ham asmi, na me so attā'ti evam etaṃ yathābhūtaṃ sammāpaññāya daṭṭhabbaṃ. Ya kāci vedanā . . . ya kāci saññā . . . ye keci saṅkhāra . . . yaṃ kiñci viññāṇaṃ atītānāgatapaccuppannaṃ ajjhattaṃ vā bahiddhā vā oḷārikaṃ va sukhumaṃ vā hīnaṃ vā panītaṃ vā yaṃ dūre santike vā, sabbaṃ viññāṇaṃ n'etaṃ mama n'eso 'ham asmi, na me so attā'ti evam etaṃ yathābhūtaṃ sammāpaññāya daṭṭhabbaṃ.*
>
> *Evaṃ passaṃ, āvuso Yamaka, sutavā ariyasāvako rūpasmiṃ nibbindati, vedanāya nibbindati, saññāya nibbindati, saṅkhāresu nibbindati, viññāṇasmiṃ nibbindati. Nibbindam virajjati, virāgā vimuccati, vimuttasmiṃ vimuttam iti ñāṇaṃ hoti. Khīṇā jāti vusitaṃ brahmacariyaṃ kataṃ karaṇīyaṃ nāparaṃ itthattāyā'ti pajānāti.*
>
> "Therefore, friend Yamaka, any kind of form whatsoever, whether past, future or present, internal or external, gross or subtle, inferior or superior, far or near, all form must be seen as it really is with right wisdom thus: 'this is not mine, this I am not, this is not my self.' Any kind of feel-

---

13 See sermon 21.

> ing whatsoever . . . any kind of perception whatsoever . . . any kind of preparations whatsoever . . . any kind of consciousness whatsoever, whether past, future or present, internal or external, gross or subtle, inferior or superior, far or near, all consciousness must be seen as it really is with right wisdom thus: 'this is not mine, this I am not, this is not my self.'"
>
> "Seeing thus, friend Yamaka, the instructed noble disciple gets disgusted of form, gets disgusted of feeling, gets disgusted of perception, gets disgusted of preparations, gets disgusted of consciousness. Being disgusted, he becomes dispassionate, through dispassion his mind is liberated. When it is liberated, there comes the knowledge 'it is liberated' and he understands: 'extinct is birth, lived is the holy life, done is what had to be done, there is no more of this state of being.'"

As the third step in his interrogation of Venerable Yamaka, Venerable Sāriputta poses the same questions which the Buddha addressed to Venerable Anurādha:

> "What do you think, friend Yamaka, do you regard form as the *Tathāgata*?"
> "No, friend."
>
> "Do you regard feeling . . . perception . . . preparations . . . consciousness as the *Tathāgata*?"
> "No, friend."
>
> "What do you think, friend Yamaka, do you regard the *Tathāgata* as in form?"
> "No, friend."
>
> "Do you regard the *Tathāgata* as apart from form?"
> "No, friend."

"Do you regard the *Tathāgata* as in feeling?"
"No, friend."

"Do you regard the *Tathāgata* as apart from feeling?"
"No, friend."

"Do you regard the *Tathāgata* as in perception?"
"No, friend."

"Do you regard the *Tathāgata* as apart from perception?"
"No, friend."

"Do you regard the *Tathāgata* as in preparations?"
"No, friend."

"Do you regard the *Tathāgata* as apart from preparations?"
"No, friend."

"Do you regard the *Tathāgata* as in consciousness?"
"No, friend."

"Do you regard the *Tathāgata* as apart from consciousness?"
"No, friend."

"What do you think, friend Yamaka, do you regard form, feeling, perception, preparations and consciousness as constituting the *Tathāgata*?"
"No, friend."

"What do you think, friend Yamaka, do you regard the Tathāgata as one who is devoid of form, feeling, perception, preparations and consciousness?"
"No, friend."

It was at this juncture that Venerable Sāriputta puts this conclusive question to Venerable Yamaka in order to drive the crucial point home:

> "But then, friend Yamaka, now that for you a *Tathāgata* is not to be found in truth and fact here in this very life, is it proper for you to declare: 'As I understand *Dhamma* taught by the Exalted One, an influx-free monk is annihilated and destroyed when the body breaks up and does not exist after death?'"

At last, Venerable Yamaka confesses, "Formerly, friend Sāriputta, I did hold that evil view, ignorant as I was. But now that I have heard this Dhamma sermon of the Venerable Sāriputta, I have given up that evil view and have gained an understanding of the Dhamma."

As if to get a confirmation of Venerable Yamaka's present stance, Venerable Sāriputta continues: "If, friend Yamaka, they were to ask you the question: 'Friend Yamaka, as to that monk, the influx-free *arahant*, what happens to him with the breaking up of the body after death?' Being asked thus, what would you answer?"

"If they were to ask me that question, friend Sāriputta, I would answer in this way: Friends, form is impermanent, what is impermanent is suffering, what is suffering has ceased and passed away. Feeling . . . perception . . . preparations . . . consciousness is impermanent, what is impermanent is suffering, what is suffering has ceased and passed away. Thus questioned, I would answer in such a way." Be it noted that, in this conclusive answer, there is no mention whatsoever of a *Tathāgata*, a *satta*, or a *puggala*.

Now at this reply, Venerable Sāriputta expresses his approbation: "Good, good, friend Yamaka, well then, friend Yamaka, I will bring up a simile for you that you may grasp this meaning all the more clearly:

> "Suppose, friend Yamaka, there was a householder or a householder's son, prosperous, with much wealth and property, protected by a bodyguard. Then some man

> would come by who wished to ruin him, to harm him, to imperil him, to deprive him of life. And it would occur to that man: 'This householder or householder's son is prosperous, with much wealth and property, he has his bodyguard, it is not easy to deprive him of his life by force. What if I were to get close to him and take his life?'
>
> "Then he would approach that householder or householder's son and say to him: 'Would you take me on as a servant, sir?' Then the householder or householder's son would take him on as a servant. The man would serve him, rising up before him, going to bed after him, being at his beck and call, pleasing in his conduct, endearing in his speech. The householder or householder's son would regard him as a friend, an intimate friend, and would place trust in him. But once the man has ascertained that the householder or householder's son has trust in him, he waits for an opportunity to find him alone and kills him with a sharp knife."

Now this is the simile. Based on this deep simile, Venerable Sāriputta puts the following questions to Venerable Yamaka to see whether he has grasped the moral behind it:

> "What do you think, friend Yamaka, when that man approached that householder or householder's son and said to him 'would you take me on as a servant, sir?,' wasn't he a murderer even then, though the householder or householder's son did not know him as 'my murderer?' And when the man was serving him, rising up before him and going to bed after him, being at his beck and call, pleasing in his conduct and endearing in his speech, wasn't he a murderer then too, though the householder or householder's son did not know him as 'my murderer?' And when the man, finding him alone, took his life with a sharp knife, wasn't he a murderer then too, though the other did not know him as 'my murderer?'"

Venerable Yamaka answers "yes, friend," by way of assent to all these matter-of-fact questions. It was then, that Venerable Sāriputta comes out with the full significance of this simile, portraying the uninstructed worldling in the same light as that naively unsuspecting and ignorant householder or householder's son:

> "So too, friend Yamaka, the uninstructed worldling, who has no regard for the noble ones, and is unskilled and undisciplined in their *Dhamma*, who has no regard for good men and is unskilled and undisciplined in their *Dhamma*, regards form as self, or self as possessing form, or form as in self, or self as in form. He regards feeling as self . . . perception as self . . . preparations as self . . . consciousness as self . . .
>
> "He does not understand, as it really is, impermanent form as 'impermanent form,' impermanent feeling as 'impermanent feeling,' impermanent perception as 'impermanent perception,' impermanent preparations as 'impermanent preparations,' impermanent consciousness as 'impermanent consciousness.'
>
> "He does not understand, as it really is, painful form as 'painful form,' painful feeling as 'painful feeling,' painful perception as 'painful perception,' painful preparations as 'painful preparations,' painful consciousness as 'painful consciousness.'
>
> "He does not understand, as it really is, selfless form as 'selfless form,' selfless feeling as 'selfless feeling,' selfless perception as 'selfless perception,' selfless preparations as 'selfless preparations,' selfless consciousness as 'selfless consciousness.'
>
> "He does not understand, as it really is, prepared form as 'prepared form,' prepared feeling as 'prepared feeling,' prepared perception as 'prepared perception,' prepared

preparations as 'prepared preparations,' prepared consciousness as 'prepared consciousness.'

"He does not understand, as it really is, murderous form as 'murderous form,' murderous feeling as 'murderous feeling,' murderous perception as 'murderous perception,' murderous preparations as 'murderous preparations,' murderous consciousness as 'murderous consciousness.'"

This, then, is what the attitude of the uninstructed worldling amounts to. Venerable Sāriputta now goes on to describe the consequences of such an attitude for the worldling:

So rūpaṃ upeti upādiyati adhiṭṭhāti 'attā me'ti, vedanaṃ . . . saññaṃ . . . saṅkhāre . . . viññāṇaṃ upeti upādiyati adhiṭṭhāti 'attā me'ti. Tassime pañcupādānakkhandhā upetā upādiṇṇā dīgharattaṃ ahitāya dukkhāya saṃvattanti.

"He becomes committed to form, grasps it and takes a stand upon it as 'my self.' He becomes committed to feeling . . . to perception . . . to preparations . . . to consciousness, grasps it and takes a stand upon it as 'my self.' These five aggregates of grasping, to which he becomes committed, and which he grasps, lead to his harm and suffering for a long time."

Then Venerable Sāriputta contrasts it with the standpoint of the instructed disciple:

"But, friend, the instructed noble disciple, who has regard for the noble ones, who is skilled and disciplined in their *Dhamma*, who has regard for good men and is skilled and disciplined in their *Dhamma*, does not regard form as self, or self as possessing form, or form as in self, or self as in form. He does not regard feeling as self . . . perception as self . . . preparations as self . . . consciousness as self, or self as possessing consciousness, or consciousness as in self, or self as in consciousness.

"He understands, as it really is, impermanent form as 'impermanent form,' impermanent feeling as 'impermanent feeling,' impermanent perception as 'impermanent perception,' impermanent preparations as 'impermanent preparations,' impermanent consciousness as 'impermanent consciousness.'

"He understands, as it really is, painful form as 'painful form,' painful feeling as 'painful feeling,' painful perception as 'painful perception,' painful preparations as 'painful preparations,' painful consciousness as 'painful consciousness.'

"He understands, as it really is, selfless form as 'selfless form,' selfless feeling as 'selfless feeling,' selfless perception as 'selfless perception,' selfless preparations as 'selfless preparations,' selfless consciousness as 'selfless consciousness.'

"He understands, as it really is, prepared form as 'prepared form,' prepared feeling as 'prepared feeling,' prepared perception as 'prepared perception,' prepared preparations as 'prepared preparations,' prepared consciousness as 'prepared consciousness.'

"He understands, as it really is, murderous form as 'murderous form,' murderous feeling as 'murderous feeling,' murderous perception as 'murderous perception,' murderous preparations as 'murderous preparations,' murderous consciousness as 'murderous consciousness.'

"He does not become committed to form, does not grasp it, does not take a stand upon it as 'my self.' He does not become committed to feeling . . . to perception . . . to

> preparations . . . to consciousness, does not grasp it, does not take a stand upon it as 'my self.' These five aggregates of grasping, to which he does not become committed, which he does not grasp, lead to his welfare and happiness for a long time."

What Venerable Sāriputta wanted to prove, was the fact that every one of the five aggregates is a murderer, though the worldlings, ignorant of the true state of affairs, pride themselves on each of them, saying 'this is mine, this am I and this is my self.' As the grand finale of this instructive discourse comes the following wonderful declaration by Venerable Yamaka:

> "Such things do happen, friend Sāriputta, to those venerable ones who have sympathetic and benevolent fellow monks in the holy life, like you, to admonish and instruct, so much so that, on hearing this *Dhamma* sermon of the Venerable Sāriputta, my mind is liberated from the influxes by non-grasping."

This might sound extremely strange in this age of scepticism regarding such intrinsic qualities of the *Dhamma* like *sandiṭṭhika*, "visible here and now," *akālika*, "timeless," and *ehipassika*, "inviting to come and see." But all the same we have to grant the fact that this discourse, which begins with a Venerable Yamaka who is bigoted with such a virulent evil view, which even his fellow monks found it difficult to dispel, concludes, as we saw, with this grand finale of a Venerable Yamaka joyfully declaring his attainment of *arahant*-hood.

This episode bears testimony to the fact that the tetralemma concerning the *Tathāgata*'s after death state has beneath it an extremely valuable criterion, proper to this *Dhamma*. There are some who are even scared to discuss this topic, perhaps due to unbalanced faith – faith unwarranted by wisdom. The tetralemma, however, reveals on analysis a wealth of valuable *Dhamma* material that goes to purify one's right view. That is why the Venerable Yamaka ended up as an *arahant*.

So this discourse, also, is further proof of the fact that the Buddha's solution to the problem of the indeterminate points actually took the form of a disquisition on voidness. Such expositions fall into the category called *suññatapaṭisaṃyuttā suttantā*, "discourses dealing with voidness." This category of discourses avoids the conventional worldly usages, such as *satta*, "being," and *puggala*, "person," and highlights the teachings on the four noble truths, which bring out the nature of things 'as they are.'

Generally, such discourses instill fear into the minds of worldlings, so much so that even during the Buddha's time there were those recorded instances of misconstruing and misinterpretation. It is in this light that we have to appreciate the Buddha's prediction that in the future there will be monks who would not like to listen or lend ear to those deep and profound discourses of the Buddha, pertaining to the supramundane and dealing with the void:

> *Puna ca paraṃ, bhikkhave, bhavissanti bhikkhū anāgatamaddhānaṃ abhāvitakāya abhāvitasīlā abhāvitacittā abhāvitapaññā, te abhāvitakāyā samānā abhāvitasīlā abhāvitacittā abhāvitapaññā ye te suttantā tathāgatabhāsitā gambhīrā gambhīratthā lokuttarā suññatāpaṭisaṃyuttā, tesu bhaññamānesu na sussūsanti, na sotaṃ odahissanti, na aññācittaṃ upaṭṭhapessanti, na ca te dhamme uggahetabbaṃ pariyāpuṇitabbaṃ maññissanti.*[14]

> "And moreover, monks, there will be in the future those monks who, being undeveloped in bodily conduct, being undeveloped in morality, being undeveloped in concentration, being undeveloped in wisdom, would not like to listen, to lend ear or to make an attempt to understand and deem it fit to learn when those discourses preached by the *Tathāgata*, which are deep, profound in meaning, supramundane and dealing with the void, are being recited."

---

[14] A III 107, *Tatiyaanāgatabhayasutta*; cf. also S II 267, *Āṇisutta*.

This brings us to an extremely deep dimension of this *Dhamma*. By way of clarification, we may allude to a kind of exorcism practiced by some traditional devil dancers. At the end of an all-night session of devil dancing, the mediating priest goes round, exorcising the spirits from the house with fistfuls of a highly inflammable incense powder. Blazing flames arise, as he sprinkles that powder onto the lighted torch, directing the flames at every nook and corner of the house. Some onlookers even get scared that he is trying to set the house on fire. But actually no harm is done.

Well, the Buddha, too, as the mediating priest of the three realms, had to conduct a similar exorcising ritual over linguistic conventions, aiming at some words in particular. It is true that he made use of conventional language in order to convey his teaching. But his *Dhamma* proper was one that transcended logic, *atakkāvacaro*.[15]

It happened to be a *Dhamma* that soared well above the limitations of grammar and logic, and analytically exposed their very structure. The marvel of the *Dhamma* is in its very inaccessibility to logic. That is why it defied the four-cornered logic of the tetralemma. It refused to be cornered and went beyond the concepts of a 'being' or a 'self.' The *saṃsāric* vortex was breached and concepts themselves were transcended.

Now this is the exorcism the Buddha had to carry out. He smoked out the term *attā*, "self," so dear to the whole world. Of course, he could not help making use of that word as such. In fact there is an entire chapter in the *Dhammapada* entitled *Attavagga*.[16] But it must be emphasized that the term in that context does not refer to a permanent self. It stands for 'oneself.' Some who mistakenly rendered it as 'self,' ended up in difficulties. Take for instance the following verse:

---

15 M I 167, *Ariyapariyesanasutta*.

16 Dhp 157-166 make up the 12th chapter of Dhp, the *Attavagga*.

Attā hi attano nātho,
ko hi nātho paro siyā,
attanā hi sudantena,
nāthaṃ labhati dullabhaṃ.[17]

"Oneself, indeed, is one's own saviour,
What other saviour could there be?
Even in oneself, disciplined well,
One finds that saviour, so hard to find."

Those who render the above verse literally, with a self-bias, would get stuck when confronted with the following verse in the *Bālavagga*, the "Chapter of the Fool":

Puttā m'atthi, dhanam m'atthi,
iti bālo vihaññati,
attā hi attano n'atthi,
kuto puttā, kuto dhanaṃ?[18]

"'Sons I have, wealth I have,'
So the fool is vexed,
Even oneself is not one's own,
Where then are sons, where is wealth?"

Whereas the former verse says *attā hi attano nātho*, here we find the statement *attā hi attano n'atthi*. If one ignores the reflexive sense and translates the former line with something like "self is the lord of self," one will be at a loss to translate the seemingly contradictory statement "even self is not owned by self."

At times, the Buddha had to be incisive in regard to some words, which the worldlings are prone to misunderstand and misinterpret. We have already discussed at length the significance

[17] Dhp 160, *Attavagga*.

[18] Dhp 62, *Bālavagga*.

of such terms as *satta* and *tathāgata*, with reference to their etymological background. *Sakkāyadiṭṭhi*, or "personality view," masquerades even behind the term *tathāgata*, and that is why they raise such ill-founded questions. That is also why one is averse to penetrate into the meanings of these deep discourses.

Like the term *tathāgata*, the term *loka* also had insinuations of a self-bias. The Buddha, as we saw, performed the same ritual of exorcism to smoke out those insinuations. His definition of the 'world' with reference to the six sense-bases is a corrective to that erroneous concept.[19]

Among the indeterminate points, too, we find questions relating to the nature of the world, such as *sassato loko – asassato loko*, "the world is eternal – the world is not eternal," and *antavā loko – anantavā loko*, "the world is finite – the world is infinite."[20] In all such contexts, the questioner had the prejudice of the conventional concept of the world. The commentaries refer to it as *cakkavāḷaloka*, the common concept of "world system." [21] But the Buddha advanced a profound definition of the concept of the world with reference to the six bases of sense-contact.

In this connection, we come across a highly significant discourse in the *Saḷāyatanavagga* of the *Saṃyutta Nikāya*. There we find the Buddha making the following declaration to the monks:

> *Nāhaṃ, bhikkhave, gamanena lokassa antaṃ ñātayyaṃ, daṭṭhayyaṃ, patteyyan'ti vadāmi. Na ca panāhaṃ, bhikkhave, appatvā lokassa antaṃ dukkhassa antakiriyaṃ vadāmi.*[22]

---

[19] S I 41, *Lokasutta*, see also sermon 4; S IV 39, *Samiddhisutta*, see also sermon 20.

[20] E.g. at M I 426, *MahāMālunkyasutta*.

[21] Spk I 116.

[22] S IV 93, *Lokakāmaguṇasutta*.

> "Monks, I do not say that by traveling one can come to know or see or reach the end of the world. Nor do I say that without reaching the end of the world one can put an end to suffering."

After this riddle-like pronouncement, the Buddha gets up and retires to the monastery. We came across this kind of problematic situation earlier too. Most probably this is a device of the Buddha as the teacher to give his disciples an opportunity to train in the art of analytical exposition of the *Dhamma*. After the Buddha had left, those monks, perplexed by this terse and tantalizing declaration, approached Venerable Ānanda and begged him to expound its meaning at length. With some modest hesitation, as usual, Venerable Ānanda agreed and came out with the way he himself understood the significance of the Buddha's declaration in the following words:

> *Yena kho, āvuso, lokasmiṃ lokasaññī hoti lokamānī, ayaṃ vuccati ariyassa vinaye loko. Kena c'āvuso lokasmiṃ lokasaññī hoti lokamānī?*
>
> *Cakkhunā kho, āvuso, lokasmiṃ lokasaññī hoti lokamānī, sotena . . . ghānena . . . jivhāya . . . kāyena . . . manena kho, āvuso, lokasmiṃ lokasaññī hoti lokamānī. Yena kho, āvuso, lokasmiṃ lokasaññī hoti lokamānī, ayaṃ vuccati ariyassa vinaye loko.*
>
> "Friends, that by which one has a perception of the world and a conceit of the world, that in this discipline of the noble ones is called 'the world.' By what, friends, has one a perception of the world and a conceit of the world?
>
> "By the eye, friends, one has a perception of the world and a conceit of the world, by the ear . . . by the nose . . . by the tongue . . . by the body . . . by the mind, friends one has a perception of the world and a conceit of the world. That, friends, by which one has a perception of the world

> and a conceit of the world, that in this discipline of the noble ones is called 'the world.'"

It seems, then, that the definition of the world in the discipline of the noble ones is one that accords with radical attention, *yoniso manasikāra*, whereas the concept of the world as upheld in those indeterminate points is born of wrong attention, *ayoniso manasikāra*. In the present age, too, scientists, when they speak of an 'end of the world,' entertain presumptions based on wrong attention.

When those monks who listened to Venerable Ānanda's exposition reported it to the Buddha, he fully endorsed it. This definition, therefore, is as authentic as the word of the Buddha himself and conclusive enough. It is on the basis of the six sense-bases that the world has a perception of the 'world' and a conceit of the 'world.'

The conceit here meant is not pride as such, but the measuring characteristic of worldly concepts. For instance, there is this basic scale of measuring length: the inch, the span, the foot, the cubit and the fathom. These measurements presuppose this body to be a measuring rod. In fact, all scales of measurement, in some way or other, relate to one or the other of the six sense-bases. That is why the above definition of the world is on the side of radical attention.

The worldling's concept of the world, conventionally so called, is the product of wrong or non-radical attention. It is unreal to the extent that it is founded on the notion of the compact, *ghanasaññā*. The existence of the world, as a whole, follows the norm of arising and ceasing. It is by ignoring this norm that the notion of the compact receives acceptance.

Two persons are watching a magic kettle on display at a science exhibition. Water is endlessly flowing from the magic kettle to a basin. One is waiting until the kettle gets empty, while the other waits to see the basin overflowing. Neither of their wishes is fulfilled. Why? Because a hidden tube conducts the water in the basin back again to the kettle. So the magic kettle never gets emptied and the basin never overflows. This is the secret of the magic kettle.

The world also is such a magic kettle. Gigantic world systems contract and expand in cyclic fashion. In the ancient term for world systems, *cakkavāḷa*, this cyclic nature is already insinuated. Taken in a broader sense, the existence or continuity of the world is cyclic, as indicated by the two terms *saṃvaṭṭa* and *vivaṭṭa*, "contraction" and "expansion." In both these terms, the significant word *vaṭṭa*, suggestive of "turning round," is seen to occur. It is as good as saying "rise and fall," *udayabbaya*.

When one world system gets destroyed, another world system gets crystallized, as it were. We hear of *Brahmā* mansions emerging.[23] So the existence of the world is a continuous process of arising and ceasing. It is in a cycle. How can one find a point of beginning in a cycle? Can one speak of it as 'eternal' or 'non-eternal?' The question as a whole is fallacious.

On the other hand the Buddha's definition of the term *loka*, based on the etymology *lujjati, palujjatī'ti loko*, is quite apt and meaningful.[24] The world is all the time in a process of disintegration. It is by ignoring this disintegrating nature and by overemphasizing the arising aspect that the ordinary uninstructed worldling speaks of a 'world' as it is conventionally understood. The world is afflicted by this process of arising and passing away in every moment of its existence.

It is to be found in our breathing, too. Our entire body vibrates to the rhythm of this rise and fall. That is why the Buddha offered us a redefinition of the world. According to the terminology of the noble ones, the world is to be redefined with reference to the six bases of sense-contact. This includes mind and mind-objects as well. In fact, the range of the six bases of sense-contact is all comprehending. Nothing falls outside of it.

---

[23] D I 17, *Brahmajālasutta*.

[24] S IV 52, *Lokapañhāsutta*, see sermon 20.

Nibbāna Sermon 23

Namo tassa Bhagavato Arahato Sammāsambuddhassa
Namo tassa Bhagavato Arahato Sammāsambuddhassa
Namo tassa Bhagavato Arahato Sammāsambuddhassa

Etaṃ santaṃ, etaṃ paṇītaṃ, yadidaṃ sabbasaṅkhārasamatho sabbūpadhipaṭinissaggo taṇhakkhayo virāgo nirodho nibbānaṃ.[1]

"This is peaceful, this is excellent, namely the stilling of all preparations, the relinquishment of all assets, the destruction of craving, detachment, cessation, extinction."

With the permission of the Most Venerable Great Preceptor and the assembly of the venerable meditative monks.

This is the twenty-third sermon in the series of sermons on *Nibbāna*. The other day, we brought up quotations to prove that *Nibbāna*, as the cessation of becoming, carries no implications of a nihilist or annihilationist view because the *Tathāgata* has transcended the concept of a being.

It became evident, from those quotations, that to assert with an eternalist bias, the proposition that the *Tathāgata* exists after death, simply because he is referred to as a being, or a person, in the discourses, is contrary to the spirit of the *Dhamma*. The fact that the *arahant*, who has done away with the latencies to conceits of 'I' and 'mine,' still continues to use even the words 'I' and 'mine,' only as a concession to worldly conventions and common

---

[1] M I 436, *MahāMālunkyasutta*.

parlance, came to light from the *Arahantasutta* of the *Saṃyutta Nikāya*, quoted on an earlier occasion.

To remind ourselves of the relevant section of that quotation, we may hark back to the following lines:

> *'Ahaṃ vadāmī'ti pi so vadeyya,*
> *'Mamaṃ vadantī'ti pi so vadeyya,*
> *Loke samaññaṃ kusalo viditvā,*
> *Vohāramattena so vohareyya.*[2]

> "He might still say: 'I speak,'
> He might also say: 'They speak to me,'
> Being skilful in knowing the worldly parlance,
> He uses such terms merely as a convention."

The philosophy of voidness that emerges from those discourses which declare that in reality there is no *Tathāgata*, we compared to the blazing flames arising from the fistfuls of a highly inflammable incense powder at the end of an all-night's ceremony of devil dancing. Generally this fire ordeal is horrifying to the onlookers. The Buddha also had to stage a similar fire ordeal in the *Dhammayāga*, or the "*Dhamma*-sacrifice," he administered to exorcize the malignant personality view, *sakkāyadiṭṭhi*,ingrained in the minds of worldlings.

Of course there is no explicit reference to such a fire ordeal in the discourses. However, we do come across a word somewhat suggestive of this kind of exorcism. The word *vidhūpeti*, derived from the word *dhūpa*, "incense," is suggestive of "fumigating" or "smoking out." For instance, we find the following verse in the *Bodhivagga* of the *Udāna* with reference to the stages of reflection on the law of dependent arising, in direct and reverse order, that the Buddha had gone through just after his enlightenment:

---

[2] S I 14, *Arahantasutta*, see sermon 13.

Yadā have pātubhavanti dhammā,
Ātāpino jhāyato brāhmaṇassa,
Vidhūpayaṃ tiṭṭhati Mārasenaṃ,
Suriyo 'va obhāsayam antalikkhaṃ.[3]

"When *dhammas* manifest themselves,
To the resolutely meditating Brahmin,
He stands fumigating the hordes of *Māra*,
Like the sun irradiating the firmament."

The dispelling of the hordes of *Māra* is rather suggestive of a smoking out. In some other discourses, this verb *vidhūpeti* is found contrasted with *sandhūpeti*. The meaning of both these verbs, which have the *dhūpa* element in common, is not quite clear. It is likely that the two words imply two functions of the ritual associated with incense. While some fragrant kinds of incense are used for propitiating benevolent spirits, certain caustic types are utilized for exorcising evil spirits.

For instance in the *Khajjanīyasutta* of the *Saṃyutta Nikāya*, with reference to the noble disciple, the phrase *vidhūpeti na sandhūpeti* occurs.[4] Since the implicit reference is again to the hordes of *Māra*, the phrase could be rendered as "he exorcises and does not propitiate."

The ordinary worldling's mode of recognition of the *Tathāgata* is comparable to the recognition of a vortex that has already ceased with the help of the flotsam and jetsam lightly floating around it. Even after the vortex has ceased, flotsam and jetsam could still go on rotating, giving the wrong impression that the vortex is still there. If one understands that the vortex has actually ceased deep down at its centre, and that what remains there, now, is the great ocean, undifferentiated and unique, one can get rid of

---

3 Ud 3, *Bodhivagga*.

4 S III 89, *Khajjanīyasutta*.

the unfounded fear arising from the statement that there is no *Tathāgata* in truth and fact.

The cessation of the puny centre of the whirlpool is equivalent to inheriting an expansive great ocean. It is where a vortex ceases that the great ocean prevails unhindered. To give up the limitations of a vortex, is to inherit the limitless ocean. The irony arising from these statements is already implicit in the term *arahant*. We use this term with reference to the Buddha as well as the *arahants*. Though the commentators later attributed various other meanings to the term, the basic sense is "to be worthy of gifts." In fact, it is being worthy of receiving everything.

It is by giving up all that one becomes worthy of all. Here too, we have a paradox. To become an *arahant* is to let go of everything. Craving has to be fully abandoned. It is when all desires are gone, when everything is given up, that one becomes worthy of receiving everything. This is the deeper side of the significance of the term *arahant*.

There are six modes of measuring in accordance with the conceit 'am,' *asmimāna*. What is known as *saḷāyatana*, or the six sense-bases, comprise the six scales of measurement, asserting the conceit 'am.' At whatever point of time the measuring, evaluating and assessing done by the six sense-bases, such as the eye, ear, nose etc., ceases, the person concerned thereby becomes immeasurable, invaluable and boundless. It is here that the simile of the vortex and the ocean becomes meaningful. So the only way of becoming immeasurable and boundless is to abandon all those scales of measurement. This might sound extremely strange.

With the cessation of a vortex, the attention of one who has been looking at it turns towards the depth, immeasurability and boundlessness of the great ocean. This line of reflection might even enable one to get a glimpse of an unworldly beauty in this philosophy of the void, which drives an unfounded fear into the minds of the worldlings.

We do get positive proof of this fact in such sections of the *Dhammapada* as those entitled The Flowers, The Worthy, The Buddha, and The Brahmin, as well as in a number of discourses in the *Sutta Nipāta*, where we come across marvelously scintillating verses. This is understandable, since the dawn of that wisdom which sees the voidness of a self and of everything belonging to a self, and the attainment of the fruits of the path in the light of that wisdom, marks the efflorescence as well as the fruition of the *saṃsāric* existence of a being.

This idea comes up, for instance, in the section on flowers in the *Dhammapada*:

Yathā saṅkāradhānasmiṃ,
Ujjhitasmiṃ mahāpathe,
Padumaṃ tattha jāyetha,
Sucigandhaṃ manoramaṃ.

Evaṃ saṅkārabhūtesu,
andhabhūte puthujjane,
atirocati paññāya,
sammāsambuddhasāvako.[5]

"As on top of a rubbish heap,
Dumped by the highway side,
There blossoms forth a lotus,
Pure in fragrance and charming.

"So amidst the worldlings blind,
The Fully Awakened One's disciple,
Outshines them in marked contrast,
In point of wisdom bright."

So, then, the *arahant* is that charming lotus, arising out of the cesspool of *saṃsāra*. Surely there cannot be anything frightful about it. There is nothing to get scared about this prospect.

---

[5] Dhp 58-59, *Pupphavagga*.

In our last sermon we quoted from a discourse that gives some new definitions and new concepts of the world.[6] We brought up two statements from the *Lokakāmaguṇasutta* (No. 1) of the *Saḷāyatanavagga* in the *Saṃyutta Nikāya*. The first statement is somewhat riddle-like. There the Buddha addresses the monks and declares:

> *Nāhaṃ, bhikkhave, gamanena lokassa antaṃ ñātayyaṃ, daṭṭhayyaṃ, pattayyan'ti vadāmi. Na ca panāhaṃ, bhikkhave, appatvā lokassa antaṃ dukkhassa antakiriyaṃ vadāmi.*[7]

> "Monks, I do not say that by traveling one can come to know or see or reach the end of the world. Nor do I say that without reaching the end of the world one can put an end to suffering."

We also mentioned, the other day, the explanation given by Venerable Ānanda to this cryptic statement at the request of those monks who approached him to get it clarified. That explanation embodies the definition given by the Buddha to the term world. It is not the common concept of the world.

> *Yena kho, āvuso, lokasmiṃ lokasaññī hoti lokamānī, ayaṃ vuccati ariyassa vinaye loko. Kena c'āvuso lokasmiṃ lokasaññī hoti lokamānī?*

> *Cakkhunā kho, āvuso, lokasmiṃ lokasaññī hoti lokamānī, sotena . . . ghānena . . . jivhāya . . . kāyena . . . manena kho, āvuso, lokasmiṃ lokasaññī hoti lokamānī. Yena kho, āvuso, lokasmiṃ lokasaññī hoti lokamānī, ayaṃ vuccati ariyassa vinaye loko.*

---

[6] See sermon 22.

[7] S IV 93, *Lokakāmaguṇasutta*.

> "Friends, that by which one has a perception of the world and has a conceit of the world, that in this discipline of the Noble Ones is called 'the world.' By what, friends, has one a perception of the world and a conceit of the world?
>
> "By the eye, friends, one has a perception of the world and a conceit of the world, by the ear . . . by the nose . . . by the tongue . . . by the body . . . by the mind . . . That, friends, by which one has a perception of the world and a conceit of the world, that in this discipline of the Noble Ones is called 'the world.'"

That with which the world is measured, that itself is called 'the world.' The above-mentioned measuring rods, namely the eye, the ear, the nose, the tongue, the body and the mind, give us a conceit of the world and a perception of the world. Apart from these six there is no way of knowing a world. All theories about the world are founded on these six sense-bases.

By way of a simple illustration, we alluded to the fact that in the absence of any standard measuring rod, we resort to the primordial scales based on this physical frame of ours, such as the inch, the span, the foot and the fathom. The subtlest scale of measurement, however, is that based on the mind. It is in this mode of measuring and reckoning that concepts and designations play their part. But the Buddha's philosophy of the void goes against all these mental modes. His exorcism by the vision of the void fumigates all concepts and designations.

The six sense-bases are therefore so many scales of measurement. It is with the help of these that the world is measured. So the above definition of the world brings out the "prepared," *saṅkhata*, nature of the world. It is a thought-construct.

This does not amount to a negation of the role of materiality. All we mean to say is that the concept of the world is actually an outcome of these six sense bases. To that extent it is something prepared, a thought-construct.

While discussing the ten indeterminate points on a previous occasion, we happened to mention that the first four among them concern the world:[8]

1) "The world is eternal."
2) "The world is not eternal."
3) "The world is finite."
4) "The world is infinite."

What those theorists meant by the term world in this context is none other than that prepared world which is constructed by the six sense-bases. That is to say, it is just the concept of the world.

However, they were not aware of the fact that their concept of the world is a thought-construct, because they had no insight into the law of dependent arising. They did not understand that these are mere preparations. The fallacy involved here, that is, the inability to understand that their concept of the world is the outcome of wrong attention, we illustrated by the simile of the magic kettle.

In an exhibition a magic kettle is displayed from which water keeps on flowing into a basin. One curious onlooker is waiting to see the kettle empty, while the other is waiting to see the basin overflowing. Both are unaware of the fact that a hidden tube conveys the water back again to the kettle, unseen through the same flow of water.

The ordinary concept of the world carries with it the same fallacy. The worldlings under the sway of defilements, which thrive on the perception of the compact, *ghanasaññā*, have the habit of grasping everything. The ordinary man of the world, fully overcome by craving and grasping, entertains a perception of permanence since he has no insight. That is why he regards the world as

---

[8] See sermon 20.

a unit due to his perception of the compact, as he takes cognizance only of the arising aspect, ignoring the decaying aspect.

Whether such a world is eternal or not, is the point at issue in the case of the first set of questions mentioned above, while the next set poses the dilemma whether it is finite or infinite. What is at the root of all those ill-conceived notions, is the premise that it is possible to posit an absolute existence or an absolute non-existence. In other words, the two extreme views 'everything exists' and 'nothing exists.'

The unique norm of dependent arising, which the Buddha discovered, dismisses both those extreme views. It is set forth in the *Kaccāyanagottasutta* of the *Nidānasaṃyutta* in the *Saṃyutta Nikāya*, which we have quoted earlier too.[9] We shall, however, bring up again the relevant section to elucidate this point:

> *Dvayanissito khvāyaṃ, Kaccāyana, loko yebhuyyena: atthitañceva natthitañca. Lokasamudayaṃ kho, Kaccāyana, yathābhūtaṃ sammappaññāya passato yā loke natthitā sā na hoti. Lokanirodhaṃ kho, Kaccāyana, yathābhūtaṃ sammappaññāya passato yā loke atthitā sā na hoti.*[10]
>
> "This world, Kaccāyana, for the most part, bases its views on two things: on existence and non-existence. Now, Kaccāyana, to one who with right wisdom sees the arising of the world as it is, the view of non-existence regarding the world does not occur. And to one who with right wisdom sees the cessation of the world as it really is, the view of existence regarding the world does not occur."

This is where our simile of the magic kettle becomes meaningful. Had both onlookers understood that the magic kettle is getting filled at the same time it gets emptied, and that the basin also gets

---

9 See sermons 4 and 22.

10 S II 17, *Kaccāyanagottasutta*.

filled while it is being emptied, they would not have the curiosity to go on looking at it.

In contradistinction to both these viewpoints, the law of dependent arising promulgated by the Buddha transcends them by penetrating into the concept as such. The Buddha explained the arising of the world in terms of the twelve factors, beginning with "dependent on ignorance, preparations," precisely because it cannot be presented in one word.

Usually, the formula of dependent arising is summed up with the words *ayaṃ dukkhasamudayo*, "this is the arising of suffering," or with the more conclusive statement *evam etassa kevalassa dukkhakkhandhassa samudayo hoti*, "thus is the arising of this entire mass of suffering."

There are also instances of explaining the arising of the world through the principle underlying the norm of dependent arising. The world arises in the six sense-bases. It is at the same time the arising of suffering. The arising of suffering is almost synonymous with the arising of the world.

The law of dependent arising is an explanation of the way a concept of the world comes about. This is an extremely subtle point. Since the concept of the world is a product of wrong reflection, it is *saṅkhata*, or "prepared." It is like something imagined. The *saṅkhata*, or the "prepared," has a certain circularity about it.

In fact, the two dilemmas mentioned above involve the question of time and space. The question whether the world is eternal or not eternal concerns time, whereas the question whether the world is finite or infinite relates to space. Both time and space involve a circularity. The furthest limit of the forenoon is the nearest limit of the afternoon, and the furthest limit of the afternoon is the nearest limit of the forenoon. This is how the cycle of the day turns round. Where the forenoon ends is the afternoon, where the afternoon ends is the forenoon.

A similar time cycle is to be found even in one moment. Rise and fall occur as a cycle even within a single moment. The same process goes on within an aeon. That is why an aeon is said to have the two aspects called *saṃvatta*, "contraction," and *vivaṭṭa*, "expansion." World systems go on contracting and expanding. The so-called existence of the world is a continuous process of contraction and expansion. Therefore it is impossible to find any beginning or end. The very question of a first beginning is ill conceived. It is like an attempt to find a starting point in a cycle. It is a problem that cannot be solved by speculation.

Because of the cyclic nature of existence, rise and fall is characteristic of every single moment. It is by ignoring the decaying aspect inherent in one moment that wrong reflection gives rise to the inference that there must be an absolute end of the world.

Because the visible world gets destroyed, one conceives of an absolute end of the world. But when one world system gets destroyed, another world system gets crystallized somewhere else. Speculative views and standpoints about the universe, current among the worldlings, are of such a misleading nature that any reasoning based on them leads to a circularity of argument as is evident from the *Lokāyatikābrāhmaṇāsutta* among the Nines of the *Aṅguttara Nikāya*.

This discourse is about two *Lokāyatikābrāhmins*. The term *Lokāyatika* is a derivative from *lokāyata*, which signifies a branch of knowledge dealing with the length and breadth of the world, perhaps a prototype of modern science, though it relied more on logic than on experiment. The two Brahmins were probably students of such a branch of learning. One day they came to the Buddha and posed this question:

> "Sire Gotama, now there is this teacher Pūraṇa Kassapa who claims omniscience, saying that he sees everything and has knowledge and vision of everything while walking or standing, whether asleep or awake. With these claims to omniscience, he makes the following declaration:

> "*Ahaṃ anantena ñāṇena anantaṃ lokaṃ jānaṃ passaṃ vihārāmi.*[11] 'I dwell knowing and seeing an infinite world with an infinite knowledge.'
>
> "But then there is this teacher Nigaṇṭha Nāthaputta who also has similar claims to omniscience, but declares: *Ahaṃ antavantena ñāṇena antavantaṃ lokaṃ jānaṃ passaṃ vihārāmi.* 'I dwell knowing and seeing a finite world with a finite knowledge.'"

Then the two Brahmins ask the Buddha which of these two teachers claiming omniscience in such contradictory terms is correct. But the Buddha's reply was: *Alaṃ brāhmaṇā, tiṭṭhat' etaṃ . . . Dhammaṃ vo desissāmi*, "Enough, brahmins, let that question be . . . I shall preach to you the *Dhamma*."

The expression used here is suggestive of the fact that the question belongs to the category of unexplained points. Terms like *ṭhapita*, "left aside," and *ṭhapanīya*, "should be left aside," are used with reference to indeterminate points.

Why did the Buddha leave the question aside? We can guess the reason, though it is not stated as such. Now the standpoint of Pūraṇa Kassapa is: "I dwell knowing and seeing an infinite world with an infinite knowledge." One can question the validity of his claim with the objection: you see an infinite world, because your knowledge is not finite, that is to say, incomplete. If it is complete, there must be an end. Therefore, going by the sense of incompleteness in the word *anantaṃ*, one can refute the former view. Why you see the world as infinite is because your knowledge lacks finality.

Nigaṇṭha Nāthaputta, on the other hand, is asserting that he sees a finite world with a finite knowledge. But the followers of Pūraṇa Kassapa can raise the objection: you are seeing the world as finite because your knowledge is limited. Your knowledge has an end,

---

11 A IV 428, *Lokāyatikābrāhmaṇāsutta*.

that is why you see a finite world. So here, too, we have a circle, or rather a circularity of argument. The two terms *anta* and *ananata* are ambiguous. That must be the reason why the Buddha rejected the two standpoints in question.

Then he declares: "I shall preach to you the *Dhamma*," and brings up as a simile an illustration which could be summed up as follows. Four persons endowed with the highest ability to walk, the highest speed and the widest stride possible, stand in the four directions. Their speed is that of an arrow and their stride is as wide as the distance between the eastern ocean and the western ocean. Each of them tells himself: 'I will reach the end of the world by walking' and goes on walking for hundred years, that being his full lifespan, resting just for eating, drinking, defecating, urinating and giving way to sleep or fatigue, only to die on the way without reaching the end of the world.

'But why so?,' asks the Buddha rhetorically and gives the following explanation. "I do not say, O! Brahmins, that the end of the world can be known, seen or reached by this sort of running. Nor do I say that there is an ending of suffering without reaching the end of the world." Then he declares: "Brahmins, it is these five strands of sense pleasures that in the Noble One's discipline are called 'the world.'"

In this particular context, the Buddha calls these five kinds of sense-pleasures 'the world' according to the Noble One's terminology. This does not contradict the earlier definition of the world in terms of the six sense-bases, for it is by means of these six sense-bases that one enjoys the five strands of sense-pleasures. However, as an art of preaching, the Buddha defines the world in terms of the five strands of sense-pleasures in this context.

Then he goes on to proclaim the way of transcending this world of the five sense pleasures in terms of *jhānic* attainments. When one attains to the first *jhāna*, one is already far removed from that world of the five sense-pleasures. But about him, the Buddha makes the following pronouncement: *Aham pi, brāhmaṇā, evaṃ vadāmi: 'ayam pi lokapariyāpanno, ayam pi anissaṭo lokamhā'ti*, "And I too, O! Brahmins, say this: 'This one, too, is included in the world, this one, too, has not stepped out of the world.'"

The Buddha makes the same pronouncement with regard to those who attain to the other jhānic levels. But finally he comes to the last step with these words:

> *Puna ca paraṃ, brāhmaṇā, bhikkhu sabbaso nevasaññānāsaññāyatanaṃ samatikkama saññāvedayitanirodhaṃ upasampajja viharati, paññāya c' assa disvā āsavā parikkhīṇā honti. Ayaṃ vuccati, brāhmaṇā, bhikkhu lokassa antam āgamma lokassa ante viharati tiṇṇo loke visattikaṃ.*
>
> "But then, O! Brahmins, a monk, having completely transcended the sphere of neither-perception-nor-non-perception, attains to and abides in the cessation of perceptions and feelings, and in him, having seen with wisdom, the influxes are made extinct. This one, O! Brahmins, is known as one who, on reaching the end of the world, is dwelling at its very end, having crossed over the agglutinative craving."

Going by these discourses, one might conclude that the cessation of perceptions and feelings is actually *Nibbāna* itself. But the most important part of the above quotation is the statement *paññāya c' assa disvā āsavā parikkhīṇā honti*, "having seen with wisdom, the influxes are made extinct in him." While in the attainment of the cessation of perceptions and feelings, all preparations subside and it is on rising from it that all influxes are made extinct by the vision of wisdom.

This fact comes to light in the following answer of Venerable Dhammadiṇṇā *Therī* to the question raised by the lay-follower Visākha, her former husband, in the *Cūḷavedalla Sutta*:

> *Saññāvedayitanirodhasamāpattiyā vuṭṭhitaṃ, kho āvuso Visākha, bhikkhuṃ tayo phassā phusanti: suññato phasso, animitta phasso, appaṇihito phasso.*[12]
>
> "Friend Visākha, when a monk has emerged from the attainment of the cessation of perceptions and feelings, three kinds of contact touch him: voidness contact, signless contact, desireless contact."

On this point, the commentary too, gives the explanation *suññatā nāma phalasamāpatti,*[13] "'voidness' means the attainment of the fruit of *arahant*-hood."

In answer to another question, Venerable Dhammadiṇṇā *Therī* says, *Saññāvedayitanirodhasamāpattiyā vuṭṭhitassa, kho āvuso Visākha, bhikkhuno vivekaninnaṃ cittaṃ hoti vivekapoṇaṃ vivekapabbhāraṃ*, "Friend Visākha, when a monk has emerged from the attainment of the cessation of perceptions and feelings, his mind inclines to seclusion, slants to seclusion, tends to seclusion."

Here the commentary explains *nibbānaṃ viveko nāma*, "what is called seclusion is *Nibbāna*." So it is on emerging from the attainment of the cessation of perceptions and feelings, that is in the *arahattaphalasamādhi*, references to which we have cited earlier,[14] that *Nibbāna* is realized. It is then that one actually sees the end of the world.

So from this we can well infer that in advancing a new definition of the world, in introducing a new concept of the world, the Buddha was not trying to sidetrack the moot point of the worldlings by bringing in something totally irrelevant. He was simply rejecting for some sound reason the worldlings' concept of the world, which is born of wrong reflection, and illustrating the

---

12 M I 302, *Cūḷavedallasutta.*

13 Ps II 367.

14 See sermons 16 and 17.

correct measuring rod, the true criterion of judgement regarding the origin of the concept of the world according to radical reflection.

Out of all the discourses dealing with the question of the end of the world and the end of suffering, perhaps the most significant is the *Rohitassa Sutta*, which is found in the *Sagāthakasaṃyutta* of the *Saṃyutta Nikāya*, as well as in the section of the Fours in the *Aṅguttara Nikāya*. Once when the Buddha was staying at the Jetavana monastery at Sāvatthī, a deity named Rohitassa visited him in the night and asked the following question: "Where Lord one does not get born, nor grow old, nor die, nor pass away, nor get reborn, is one able, Lord, by traveling to come to know that end of the world or to see it or to get there?"

The Buddha replies: "Where, friend, one does not get born, nor grow old, nor die, nor pass away, nor get reborn, that end of the world, I say, one is not able by traveling to come to know or to see or to arrive at."

When the Buddha gave this brief answer, the deity Rohitassa praised him with the following words of approbation: *Acchariyaṃ bhante, abbhutaṃ bhante, yāva subhāsitam idaṃ bhagavatā,*[15] "It is wonderful, Lord, it is marvelous, Lord, how well it is said by the Exalted One."

Why did he express his approbation? Because he had already realized the truth of the Buddha's statement by his own experience. Then he goes on to relate the whole story of his past life:

> "In times past, Lord, I was a seer, Rohitassa by name, son of Bhoja, gifted so that I could fly through the air, and so swift, Lord, was my speed that I could fly just as quickly as a master of archery, well-trained, expert, proficient, a past master in his art, armed with a strong bow, could without difficulty send a light arrow far past the area coloured by a palm tree's shadow; and so great, Lord, was

---

15 S I 61 and A II 49 *Rohitassasutta*.

my stride that I could step from the eastern to the western ocean. In me, Lord, arose such a wish as this: 'I will arrive at the end of the world by walking.' And though such, Lord, was my speed and such my stride, and though with a lifespan of a century, living for a hundred years, I walked continuously for hundred years, except for the times spent in eating, drinking, chewing or tasting, or in answering calls of nature, and the time I gave to way to sleep or fatigue, yet I died on the way, without reaching the end of the world. Wonderful is it, O! Lord, marvelous is it, Lord, how well it is said by the Exalted One:

"Where, friend, one does not get born, nor grow old, nor die, nor pass away, nor get reborn, that end of the world, I say, one is not able by traveling to come to know or to see or to arrive at."

It is at this point, that the Buddha comes out with a momentous declaration, while granting Rohitassa's approbation:

Yattha kho, āvuso, na jāyati na jīyati na mīyati na cavati na upapajjati, nāhaṃ taṃ 'gamanena lokassa antaṃ ñāteyyaṃ daṭṭheyyaṃ patteyyan'ti vadāmi. Na cāhaṃ, āvuso, appatvā lokassa antaṃ dukkhassantakiriyaṃ vadāmi. Api c'āhaṃ, āvuso, imasmiṃ yeva byāmamatte kaḷevare sasaññimhi samanake lokañca paññāpemi lokasamudayañca lokanirodhañca lokanirodhagāminiñca paṭipadaṃ.

"Where, friend, one does not get born, nor grow old, nor die, nor pass away, nor get reborn, that end of the world, I say, one is not able by traveling to come to know or to see or to arrive at. But neither do I say, friend, that without having reached the end of the world there could be an ending of suffering. It is in this very fathom-long physical frame with its perceptions and mind, that I declare lies the world, the arising of the world, the cessation of the world, and the path leading to the cessation of the world."

This momentous declaration, which is comparable to a fearless lion's roar that puts all religious and philosophical systems to flight, has been misinterpreted by some who have not grasped its true significance. They say that according to this discourse the cessation of the world is not here and that only the other three are to be found in this fathom-long body.

Such misinterpretations are the result of taking seriously various far-fetched speculations of later origin about *Nibbāna*. According to them, *Nibbāna* is some mysterious non-descript place of rest for the *arahants* after their demise. One who goes by that kind of speculation is not ready to accept the Buddha's declaration that it is in this very fathom-long body with its perceptions and mind that a cessation of the world can be realized.

The commentary in this context simply observes that the four noble truths are to be found not in grass and twigs outside, but in this body consisting of the four elements.[16] It has nothing more to add. A certain modern scholar has rightly pointed out that the commentator has missed a great opportunity for exegesis.[17] The reason for the commentator's lack of interest, in the case of such a discourse of paramount importance, is probably his predilection for these later speculations on *Nibbāna*.

All what we have so far stated in explaining the significance of discourses dealing with the subject of *Nibbāna*, could even be treated as a fitting commentary to the *Rohitassasutta*.

The point of relevance is the couple of words *sasaññimhi samanake*, occurring in the discourse in question. This fathom-long physical frame is here associated with perceptions and mind. The expression used by the Buddha in this context is full of significance.

---

[16] Spk I 118 and Mp III 89.

[17] Mrs. Rhys Davids: The Book of the Kindred Sayings, PTS 1979, p 86 n 3.

As we saw above, Venerable Ānanda defines the term 'world' as follows: *yena kho, āvuso, lokasmiṃ lokasaññī hoti lokamānī, ayaṃ vuccati ariyassa vinaye loko.* "Friends, that by which one has a perception of the world and has a conceit of the world that in the discipline of the Noble Ones is called 'the world.'" The conceit of the world is a form of measuring with the mind. So the two words *sasaññimhi samanake* are suggestive of the concept of the world in the Noble Ones' discipline.

While discussing the significance of *arahattaphalasamāpatti*, also known as *aññāphalasamādhi*, and *aññāvimokkha*, we had occasion to bring up such quotations as the following:

> *Siyā nu kho, bhante, bhikkhuno tathārūpo samādhipaṭilābho yathā neva paṭhaviyaṃ paṭhavīsaññī assa, na āpasmiṃ āposaññī assa, na tejasmiṃ tejosaññī assa, na vāyasmiṃ vāyosaññī assa, na ākāsānañcāyatane ākāsānañcāyatanasaññī assa, na viññāṇañcāyatane viññāṇancāyatanasaññī assa, na ākiñcaññāyatane ākiñcaññāyatanasaññī assa, na nevasaññānāsaññāyatane nevasaññānāsaññāyatanasaññī assa, na idhaloke idhalokasaññī assa, na paraloke paralokasaññī assa, yam p'idaṃ diṭṭhaṃ sutaṃ mutaṃ viññātaṃ pattaṃ pariyesitaṃ anuvicaritaṃ manasā tatrāpi na saññī assa, saññī ca pana assa?*[18]
>
> "Could there be, Lord, for a monk such an attainment of concentration wherein he will not be conscious (literally: 'percipient') of earth in earth, nor of water in water, nor of fire in fire, nor of air in air, nor will he be conscious of the sphere of infinite space in the sphere of infinite space, nor of the sphere of infinite consciousness in the sphere of infinite consciousness, nor of the sphere of nothingness in the sphere of nothingness, nor of the sphere of neither-

---

[18] A V 318, *Saññāsutta*, see also sermon 16.

> perception-nor-non-perception in the sphere of neither-perception-nor-non-perception, nor will he be conscious of a this world in this world, nor of a world beyond in a world beyond, whatever is seen, heard, sensed, cognized, attained, sought after, traversed by the mind, even of that he will not be conscious – and yet he will be conscious?"

The *arahattaphalasamādhi* is so extraordinary that while in it one has no perception of earth, water, fire and air, or of this world, or of the other world, of whatever is seen, heard, sensed and cognized, but one is all the same percipient or conscious, *saññī ca pana assa.*

To the question: 'Of what is he percipient?,' *kiṃ saññī?*, once Venerable Sāriputta gave the answer that the perception is of *Nibbāna* as the cessation of existence, *bhavanirodho nibbānaṃ.*[19]

In another discourse that we happened to quote, the mode of questioning has the following sequence: "Could there be, Lord, for a monk such an attainment of concentration wherein he will not be attending to the eye, nor to form, nor to the ear, nor to sound," etc., but ends with the riddle like phrase, "and yet he will be attending," *manasi ca pana kareyya.*[20]

When the Buddha grants the possibility of such a concentration, Venerable Ānanda rejoins with an inquisitive "how could there be, Lord?," and the Buddha explains that what a monk attends to while in that attainment could be summed up in the stereotyped phrase:

Etaṃ santaṃ, etaṃ paṇītaṃ, yadidaṃ sabbasaṅkhārasamatho sabbūpadhipaṭinissaggo taṇhakkhayo virāgo nirodho nibbānaṃ, "This is peaceful, this is excellent, namely the stilling of all preparations, the relinquishment of all assets, the destruction of craving, detachment, cessation, extinction."

---

[19] A V 9, *Sāriputtasutta*, see also sermon 17.

[20] A V 321, *Manasikārasutta*, see also sermon 16

It is *Nibbāna*, then, that one attends to while in that attainment. So we find even the terms "perception," *saññā*, and "attention," *manasikāra*, being used in the context of *arahattaphalasamāpatti*, or "attainment to the fruit of *arahant*-hood."

Therefore, *Nibbāna* is not an experience as dry as a log of wood, but a state of serene awareness of its true significance. It is a transcendence of the world by realization of its cessation. That is why the two words *sasaññimhi samanake*, "with its perceptions and mind," have been used to qualify, *kaḷevare*, "physical frame," or "body," in the momentous declaration.

We also came across some instances in the discourses where the Buddha calls the cessation of the six sense-spheres itself *Nibbāna*. The most notable instance is perhaps the *Kāmaguṇasutta* we had already quoted.[21] As we saw, even its presentation is rather enigmatic. It runs:

> *Tasmātiha, bhikkhave, se āyatane veditabbe yattha cakkhuñca nirujjhati rūpasaññā ca virajjati, se āyatane veditabbe yattha sotañca nirujjhati saddasaññā ca virajjati, se āyatane veditabbe yattha ghānañca nirujjhati gandhasaññā ca virajjati, se āyatane veditabbe yattha jivhā ca nirujjhati rasasaññā ca virajjati, se āyatane veditabbe yattha kāyo ca nirujjhati phoṭṭabbasaññā ca virajjati, se āyatane veditabbe yattha mano ca nirujjhati dhammasaññā ca virajjati, se āyatane veditabbe.*[22]
>
> "Therefore, monks, that sphere should be known wherein the eye ceases and the perception of forms fades away, the ear ceases and the perception of sounds fades away, the nose ceases and the perception of smells fades away, the tongue ceases and the perception of tastes fades away, the body ceases and the perception of tangibles fades away,

---

21 See sermon 17.

22 S IV 98, *Kāmaguṇasutta*.

the mind ceases and the perception of ideas fades away, that sphere should be known."

Venerable Ānanda, commenting on this riddle-like sermon of the Buddha, concludes that the Buddha is here referring to the cessation of the six sense-spheres, *saḷāyatananirodhaṃ, āvuso, Bhagavatā sandhāya bhāsitaṃ.* "Friends, it is with reference to the cessation of the six sense-spheres that the Exalted One has preached this sermon." The cessation of the six sense-spheres is *Nibbāna*.

All this goes to show that the concept of a world is the product of the six sense-spheres. Those six measuring rods have measured out a world for us.

Since the world is built up by the six sense-spheres, it has also to cease by the cessation of those six sense-spheres. That is why *Nibbāna* is defined as the cessation of the six sense-spheres, *saḷāyatananirodho Nibbānaṃ.* All those measuring rods and scales lose their applicability with the cessation of the six sense-spheres.

How can there be an experience of cessation of the six sense-spheres? The cessation here meant is actually the cessation of the spheres of contact. A sphere of contact presupposes a duality. Contact is always between two things, between eye and forms, for instance. It is because of a contact between two things that one entertains a perception of permanence in those two things. Dependent on that contact, feelings and perceptions arise, creating a visual world. The visual world of the humans differs from that of animals. Some things that are visible to animals are not visible to humans. That is due to the constitution of the eye-faculty. It is the same with regard to the ear-faculty. These are the measuring rods and scales which build up a world.

Now this world, which is a product of the spheres of sense-contact, is a world of *papañca*, or "proliferation." *Nibbāna* is called *nippapañca* because it transcends this proliferation, puts an end to proliferation. The end of proliferation is at the same time the end of the six sense-spheres.

There is a discourse in the section of the Fours in the *Aṅguttara Nikāya* which clearly brings out this fact. There we find Venerable

Mahākoṭṭhita putting a question to Venerable Sāriputta on this point. Venerable Mahākoṭṭhita and Venerable Sāriputta are often found discussing intricate points in the *Dhamma*, not because they are in doubt, but in order to clarify matters for us. They are thrashing out problems for our sake. In this particular instance, Venerable Mahākoṭṭhita puts the following question to Venerable Sāriputta:

Channaṃ, āvuso, phassāyatanānaṃ asesavirāganirodhā atth'aññaṃ kiñci?[23] "Friend, with the remainderless fading away and cessation of the six spheres of sense-contact, is there something left?"

Venerable Sāriputta's response was: *Mā hevaṃ āvuso*, "Do not say so, friend." Venerable Mahākoṭṭhita follows it up with three other possible alternatives, all of which Venerable Sāriputta dismisses with the same curt reply. The three alternatives are:

Channaṃ, āvuso, phassāyatanānaṃ asesavirāganirodhā natth' aññaṃ kiñci? "Friend, with the remainderless fading away and cessation of the six spheres of sense-contact, is there nothing left?"

Channaṃ, āvuso, phassāyatanānaṃ asesavirāganirodhā atthi ca natthi ca aññaṃ kiñci? "Friend, with the remainderless fading away and cessation of the six spheres of sense-contact, is it the case that there is and is not something left?"

Channaṃ, āvuso, phassāyatanānaṃ asesavirāganirodhā nev'atthi no natth'aññaṃ kiñci? "Friend, with the remainderless fading away and cessation of the six spheres of sense-contact, is it the case that there neither is nor is not something left?"

The mode of questioning takes the form of a tetralemma and Venerable Sāriputta dismisses all the four alternatives as inapplicable. Then Venerable Mahākoṭṭhita asks why all these four questions were ruled out, and Venerable Sāriputta explains:

> *'Channaṃ, āvuso, phassāyatanānaṃ asesavirāganirodhā atth' aññaṃ kiñcī'ti, iti vadaṃ appapañcaṃ papañceti.*

---

[23] A II 161, *Mahākoṭṭhitasutta.*

'Channaṃ, āvuso, phassāyatanānaṃ asesavirāganirodhā natth'aññaṃ kiñcī'ti, iti vadaṃ appapañcaṃ papañceti. 'Channaṃ, āvuso, phassāyatanānaṃ asesavirāganirodhā atthi ca natthi ca aññaṃ kiñcī'ti, iti vadaṃ appapañcaṃ papañceti. 'Channaṃ, āvuso, phassāyatanānaṃ asesavirāganirodhā nev'atthi no natth'aññaṃ kiñcī'ti, iti vadaṃ appapañcaṃ papañceti.

Yāvatā, āvuso, channaṃ phassāyatanānaṃ gati tāvatā papañcassa gati, yāvatā papañcassa gati tāvatā channaṃ phassāyatanānaṃ gati. Channaṃ, āvuso, phassāyatanānaṃ asesavirāganirodhā papañcanirodho papañcavūpasamo.

"Friend, he who says: 'With the remainderless fading away and cessation of the six spheres of sense-contact, there is something left' is conceptually proliferating what should not be proliferated conceptually. Friend, he who says: 'With the remainderless fading away and cessation of the six spheres of sense-contact, there is nothing left' is conceptually proliferating what should not be proliferated conceptually. Friend, he who says: 'With the remainderless fading away and cessation of the six spheres of sense-contact, there is and is not something left' is conceptually proliferating what should not be proliferated conceptually. Friend, he who says: 'With the remainderless fading away and cessation of the six spheres of sense-contact, there neither is nor is not something left' is conceptually proliferating what should not be proliferated conceptually.

"Friend, whatever is the range of the six spheres of sense-contact, that itself is the range of conceptual proliferation, and whatever is the range of conceptual proliferation, that itself is the range of the six spheres of sense-contact. By the remainderless fading away and cessation of the six spheres of sense-contact, there comes to be the cessation and appeasement of conceptual proliferation."

The commentator gives the following explanation to the expression *atth' aññaṃ kiñci*, "is there something left?": '*tato paraṃ koci appamattako pi kileso atthī'ti pucchati*.[24] According to him, Venerable Mahākoṭṭhita is asking whether there is even a little defilement left after the cessation of the six spheres of sense-contact. But the question is obviously not about the remaining defilements, in which case even a categorical negative could have been the correct answer. The question here is about the very usage of the expressions 'is' and 'is not.'

With the cessation of the six spheres of sense-contact all four propositions of the tetralemma, based on the two standpoints 'is' and 'is not,' lose their applicability. They are rejected in toto. Here the *papañca*, or "conceptual proliferation," implied, is the very discrimination between 'is' and 'is not.'

The entire world is built up on the two concepts 'is' and 'is not.' Being unaware of the *saṅkhata*, or "prepared," nature of these concepts, we are accustomed to say 'this is' as occasion demands. This recording machine before us 'is there.' So also are the things which we presume to exist. We ourselves do exist, do we not? One could say 'I am.'

Out of the two rapid processes going on within us every moment, namely arising and passing away, we are most of the time dwelling on the side of arising. The two concepts 'is' and 'is not' are structured on the six spheres of sense-contact. Not only 'is' and 'is not,' but also the entire logical structure connecting these two postulates is founded on these six spheres. Here, then, we see the fistfuls of inflammable incense powder the Buddha had directed towards language and logic, setting all that ablaze.

What this discourse highlights is the fact that by the very cessation of the six spheres of sense-contact the cessation of conceptual proliferation is brought about. With reference to speculative views, particularly to those wrong views that were put aside as unex-

---

[24] Mp III 150.

plained points, the Buddha uses the term *diṭṭhipariḷāha*, "delirium of views."[25] *Pariḷāha* means "delirious fever."

Patients in delirium cry out for water. The worldlings, in general, are in high delirium. Even such teachers like Pūraṇa Kassapa and Nigaṇṭha Nātaputta, who were trying to solve these speculative problems about the world by logic, were also in delirium. Their views, based on wrong reflections, were mere hallucinations. They kept on raising such questions, because they had no insight into the nature of *saṅkhāras*, or "preparations."

The worldlings spend their whole lifetime running in search of the world's end. All that is *papañca*, conceptual proliferation. In fact, the term *papañca* is so pervasive in its gamut of meaning that it encompasses the entire world. Usually, the term is glossed over by explaining it with reference to *taṇhā*, *māna* and *diṭṭhi*, bringing in craving, conceits and views as illustrations of *papañca*. But that does not amount to an explanation proper. It is only a definition in extension by giving three instances of *papañca*. To rattle off the three instances is not a fit answer to the question 'what is *papañca*.'

The primary significance of *papañca* is traceable to the linguistic medium. We have already shown how the network of grammar spreads as soon as the peg 'am' is driven down to earth, as it were.[26] The reality in the first person in grammar beckons a second and a third person to complete the picture. In logic, too, a similar legerdemain takes place. The interminable questions of identity and difference lead the logician up the garden path.

The 'world' is precariously perched on a fictitious network of grammar and logic.

It is as a solution to all this that the Buddha came out with the extraordinary prospect of a cessation of the six spheres of sense-contact. This, then, is a level of experience realizable here and

---

[25] A II 11, *Yogasutta*.

[26] See sermons 13 and 15.

now. That is why the Buddha declared that the world is in this very fathom-long body with its perceptions and mind.

Now as to the questions about the world, we have already pointed out that there is a circularity involved. Though one cannot find an end in something of a cyclic nature, there is still a solution possible. There is only one solution, that is, to break the cycle. That is what the term *vaṭṭupaccheda* means. One can breach the cycle. The cycle cannot be discovered by traveling. It is not out there, but in this very stream of consciousness within us. We have already described it as the vortex between consciousness and name-and-form. An allusion to the breach of the vortex is found in the following verse, which we have already discussed in connection with *Nibbāna*:

Viññāṇaṃ anidassanaṃ,
anantaṃ sabbato pabhaṃ,
ettha āpo ca paṭhavī,
tejo vāyo na gādhati.

Ettha dīghañca rassañca,
aṇuṃ thūlaṃ subhāsubhaṃ,
ettha nāmañca rūpañca,
asesaṃ uparujjhati,
viññāṇassa nirodhena,
etth'etaṃ uparujjhati.[27]

"Consciousness, which is non-manifestative,
Endless, lustrous on all sides,
Here it is that earth and water,
Fire and air no footing find.

"Here it is that long and short,
Fine and coarse, pleasant, unpleasant,

[27] D I 223, *Kevaḍḍhasutta*, see also sermon 6.

And Name-and-form are cut off without exception,
When consciousness has surceased,
These are held in check herein."

Here one can see how name-and-form are cut off. *Viññāṇaṃ anidassanaṃ, anantaṃ sabbato pabhaṃ*, "Consciousness, which is non-manifestative, infinite and lustrous on all sides." In this consciousness even the four great primaries earth, water, fire and air, do not find a footing. *Cakkavāla*, or a world-system, is supposed to be made up of these four primary elements. Even the term *cakkavāla* implies something cyclic. The world is a product of these primary elements, but these are not there in that non-manifestative consciousness.

Such relative distinctions as long and short, subtle and gross, have no place in it. Name-and-form cease there, leaving no residue. Like an expert physician, who treats the germ of a disease and immunizes the patient, the Buddha effected a breach in the *saṃsāric* vortex by concentrating on its epicycle within this fathom-long body.

The ever recurrent process of mutual interrelation between consciousness and name-and-form forming the epicycle of the *saṃsāric* vortex was breached. With the cessation of consciousness comes the cessation of name-and-form. With the cessation of name-and-form comes the cessation of consciousness. That is the dictum of the *Naḷakalāpīsutta*.[28] Out of the two bundles of reeds left standing, supporting each other, when one is drawn the other falls down. Even so, with the cessation of consciousness comes the cessation of name-and-form. With the cessation of name-and-form comes the cessation of consciousness. That is how the Buddha solved this problem.

---

[28] S II 114, *Naḷakalāpīsutta*, see also sermon 3.

Nibbāna Sermon 24

Namo tassa Bhagavato Arahato Sammāsambuddhassa
Namo tassa Bhagavato Arahato Sammāsambuddhassa
Namo tassa Bhagavato Arahato Sammāsambuddhassa

Etaṃ santaṃ, etaṃ paṇītaṃ, yadidaṃ sabbasaṅkhārasamatho sabbūpadhipaṭinissaggo taṇhakkhayo virāgo nirodho nibbānaṃ.[1]

"This is peaceful, this is excellent, namely the stilling of all preparations, the relinquishment of all assets, the destruction of craving, detachment, cessation, extinction."

With the permission of the Most Venerable Great Preceptor and the assembly of the venerable meditative monks.

This is the twenty-fourth sermon in the series of sermons on *Nibbāna*. In our last sermon, we brought up a quotation from the *Rohitassa Sutta*, which enshrines a momentous declaration by the Buddha to the effect that the world, the arising of the world, the cessation of the world, and the path leading to the cessation of the world, could be pointed out with reference to this same body with its perceptions and mind.[2]

The six sense-spheres, or the six bases of sense-contact, with which we acquaint ourselves with the world as it is conventionally understood and measured out, are themselves called 'the world' according to the Noble One's terminology.[3] Therefore, one can

1 M I 436, *MahāMālunkyasutta*.

2 S I 62 and A II 50 *Rohitassasutta*; see sermon 23.

3 S IV 95, *Lokakāmaguṇasutta*.

declare in accordance with the *Dhamma*, that the very cessation of those six sense-spheres is the cessation of the world. It is this state of the cessation of the world that is known as *asaṅkhata dhātu*, or the "unprepared element." That unprepared state, described in discourses on *Nibbāna* in such terms as *atthi, bhikkhave, ajātaṃ abhūtaṃ akataṃ asaṃkataṃ*,[4] "monks, there is an unborn, an unbecome, an unmade, an unprepared," is this cessation of the six spheres of sense, which is the end of that prepared world.

So, then, this particular world's end, the end of the world as defined here, is not a destination to be reached by traveling. The sage Rohitassa walked for hundred years in search of this world's end at a speed of a flying arrow, but he failed to discover the world's end. Why? It is because he took 'the world' along with him in his journey to see its end. Since this six-based body with its perceptions and mind is itself the world, he was taking the world with him in his exploration. That is why he had to die on the way without seeing the end of the world.

That end of the world, which one cannot see or reach by traveling, the Buddha pointed out in the very cessation of the six sense-spheres. This fact comes to light in the discourses dealing with *Nibbāna* in the *Pāṭaligāmiyavagga* of the *Udāna*, which we had already discussed.[5] For instance, in the first discourse on *Nibbāna*, beginning with the words *atthi, bhikkhave, tad āyatanaṃ*, "there is, monks, that sphere," we find towards the end the following statement:

Tatra p'ahaṃ, bhikkhave, n'eva āgatiṃ vadāmi na gatiṃ na ṭhitiṃ na cutiṃ na upapattiṃ, appatiṭṭhaṃ appavattaṃ anārammaṇaṃ eva taṃ, es' ev' anto dukkhassa.[6]

In that particular state, described as a 'sphere,' in which there is neither earth, nor water, nor fire, nor air, etc., "I say, there is neither a coming, nor a going, nor a standing, nor a passing away,

---

[4] Ud 80, *Pāṭaligāmiyavagga*.

[5] See sermon 7.

[6] Ud 80, *Pāṭaligāmiyavagga*.

nor a being reborn; that state which is unestablished, non-continuing and objectless, is itself the end of suffering." So, then, this journey's end, the journey's end that cannot be reached by journeying, the Buddha pointed out in the cessation of the six sense-spheres.

We come across the following passage in the fourth discourse on *Nibbāna* in the *Pāṭaligāmiyavagga* of the *Udāna*:

> *Nissitassa calitaṃ, anissitassa calitaṃ n' atthi, calite asati passaddhi, passaddhiyā sati nati no hoti, natiyā asati āgatigati na hoti, āgatigatiyā asati cutūpapāto na hoti, cutūpapāte asati n' ev' idha na huraṃ na ubhayamantare, es' ev' anto dukkhassa.*[7]

> "To the attached there is wavering, to the unattached there is no wavering; wavering not being, there is calm; calm being, there is no inclination; inclination not being, there is no coming and going; coming and going not being, there is no passing away or reappearing; when there is no passing away or reappearing, there is neither a 'here,' nor a 'there,' nor anything between the two – this is the end of suffering."

It is in such profound terms, that the Buddha described the end of the world. One cannot see it by journeying. It can be seen only by wisdom. In fact, even the very concept of 'going' has to be transcended in order to see it.

So, it seems, Rohitassa carried the world with him in his journey to see the end of the world. He made another blunder. He was going in search of a place where there is no death, in order to escape death. Even that, the Buddha had declared, is not possible to see or reach by traveling.

---

[7] Ud 81, *Pāṭaligāmiyavagga*.

Rohitassa took *Māra* along with him in his journey to find a place where there is no death. Why do we say so? In the *Rādhasaṃyutta* of the *Saṃyutta Nikāya* we find Venerable Rādha putting the following question to the Buddha:

'Māro, māro'ti, bhante, vuccati, kittāvatā nu kho, bhante, 'māro'ti vuccati?[8] "*Māra, Māra*, they say, venerable sir, to what extent is *Māra* called as such?"

Now this is how the Buddha answers the question:

> *Rūpe kho, Rādha, sati Māro vā assa māretā vā yo vā pana mīyati. Tasmātiha tvaṃ, Rādha, rūpaṃ 'Māro'ti passa, 'māretā'ti passa, 'mīyatī'ti passa, 'rogo'ti passa, 'gaṇḍo'ti passa, 'sallan'ti passa, 'aghan'ti passa, 'aghabhūtan'ti passa. Ye nam evaṃ passanti te sammā passanti.*
>
> "Where there is form, Rādha, there would be a *Māra*, or one who kills, or one who dies. Therefore, Rādha, in this context you look upon form as '*Māra*,' as 'one who kills,' as 'one who dies,' as a disease, as a boil, as a dart, as a misery, as a wretchedness. They that look upon thus are those that see rightly."

As in the case of form, so also in regard to feeling, perception, preparations and consciousness, the same mode of seeing rightly is recommended. So, in this context, each of the five aggregates is looked upon as a *Māra*, from the point of view of the *Dhamma*. That is why we say that Rohitassa went in search of a deathless place taking death along with him.

From this definition it is clear that so long as one grasps with craving the aggregates of form, feeling, perception, preparations and consciousness, there is a *Māra*, a killer, and one who dies. Therefore it is, that by giving up the five aggregates one is freed

---

[8] S III 189, *Mārosutta*.

from *Māra*, is liberated from death and attains the deathless state. That is why we said that the *arahant* has attained the deathless state, here and now, in this world itself.[9] The principle involved here we have already stated while discussing the law of dependent arising.[10]

Let us remind ourselves of the relevant section of a verse in the *Bhadrāvudhamāṇavappucchā* of the *Pārāyanavagga* of the *Sutta Nipāta*:

> *Yaṃ yaṃ hi lokasmiṃ upādiyanti,*
> *ten' eva Māro anveti jantuṃ.*[11]

> "Whatever thing they grasp in this world,
> By that itself *Māra* pursues a man."

Because of grasping, there is becoming or existence and with it birth, decay and death, etc., follow suit, all due to craving. That is the deep idea behind the Buddha's definition of the five grasping groups in terms of *Māra*.

In fact, these six sense-spheres, the six bases, are within the jurisdiction of *Māra*. This is evident from *Māra*'s own words in the *Kassakasutta* of the *Sagāthakavagga* of the *Saṃyutta Nikāya*.

Once, when the Buddha was admonishing the monks with a sermon on *Nibbāna*, it occurred to *Māra*, the Evil One: "Now this recluse Gotama is admonishing the monks and the monks are listening attentively. I must go and blind their eye of wisdom." With this evil intention, he came there in the guise of a farmer, carrying a plough on his shoulder, a goad in his hand, with dishevelled hair and muddy feet, and asked the Buddha: "Recluse, did you see my oxen?" Then the Buddha retorted: "What is the use of oxen for you, Evil One?" *Māra* understood that the Buddha had

---

[9] See sermon 14.

[10] See sermon 3.

[11] Sn 1103, *Bhadrāvudhamāṇavappucchā*.

recognized him and came out with the following boast of his superiority:

> *Mam eva, samaṇa, cakkhu, mama rūpā, mama cakkhusamphassaviññāṇāyatanaṃ, kuhiṃ me, samaṇa, gantvā mokkhasi?*[12]
>
> *Mam eva, samaṇa, sotaṃ . . . Mam eva, samaṇa, ghānaṃ . . . Mam eva, samaṇa, jivhā . . . Mam eva, samaṇa, kāyo . . .*
>
> *Mam eva, samaṇa, mano, mama dhammā, mama manosamphassaviññāṇāyatanaṃ, kuhiṃ me, samaṇa, gantvā mokkhasi?*
>
> "Mine, O recluse, is the eye, mine are the forms and mine the sphere of eye-contact, where will you, recluse, go to escape me?
>
> "Mine, O recluse, is the ear . . . Mine, O recluse, is the nose . . . Mine, O recluse, is the tongue . . . Mine, O recluse, is the body . . .
>
> "Mine, O recluse, is the mind, mine are the mind-objects and mine the sphere of mind-contact, where will you, recluse, go to escape me?"

Now this is how the Buddha responded to that challenge:

> *Taveva, pāpima, cakkhu, tava rūpā, tava cakkhusamphassaviññāṇāyatanaṃ, yattha ca kho, pāpima, n' atthi cakkhu, n' atthi rūpā, n' atthi cakkhusamphassaviññāṇāyatanaṃ, agati tava tattha pāpima.*

---

[12] S I 115, *Kassakasutta.*

> *Taveva, pāpima, sotaṃ . . . Taveva, pāpima, ghāṇaṃ . . . Taveva, pāpima, jivhaṃ . . . Taveva, pāpima, kāyaṃ . . .*
>
> *Taveva, pāpima, mano, tava dhammā, tava manosamphassaviññāṇāyatanaṃ, yattha ca kho, pāpima, n' atthi mano, n' atthi dhammā, n' atthi manosamphassa-viññāṇāyatanaṃ, agati tava tattha pāpima.*
>
> "Yours, O Evil One, is the eye, yours are the forms and yours the sphere of eye-contact, but where there is no eye, no forms and no sphere of eye-contact, there you cannot go, Evil One.
>
> "Yours, Evil One, is the ear . . . Yours, Evil One, is the nose . . . Yours, Evil One, is the tongue . . . Yours, Evil One, is the body . . .
>
> "Yours, Evil One, is the mind, yours are the mind-objects and yours the sphere of mind-contact, but where there is no mind, no mind-objects and no sphere of mind-contact, there you cannot go, Evil One."

From the Buddha's reprisal to *Māra*'s challenge, we can well infer that there indeed is a place to which *Māra* has no access. That is none other than the cessation of the six sense-spheres. Since it is something realizable, it is referred to as a 'sphere' in such contexts as, for instance, in the discourse on *Nibbāna* beginning with the words *atthi, bhikkhave, tad āyatanaṃ*,[13] "there is, monks, that sphere," etc.

It is this same cessation of the six sense-spheres that is referred to as *papañcanirodha* and *papañcavūpasama*, cessation or appeasement of conceptual proliferation. In the *Mahākoṭṭhitasutta* we discussed in our previous sermon, we found Venerable

[13] Ud 80, *Pāṭaligāmiyavagga*.

Sāriputta making the following conclusive statement to the same effect:

Channaṃ, āvuso, phassāyatanānaṃ asesavirāganirodhā papañcanirodho papañcavūpasamo,[14] "Friend, by the remainderless fading away and cessation of the six spheres of sense-contact, there comes to be the cessation and appeasement of conceptual proliferation."

That itself is the non-prolific state. All concepts of 'going,' 'coming,' 'being born,' 'growing old' and 'dying,' are to be found in the prolific. They simply do not exist in the non-prolific. That is why it is inaccessible to *Māra*. In it, neither the sense-bases, such as the eye, ear and nose, nor their respective objects are to be found. So it is clear that the cessation of the six sense-spheres is that state of release from *Māra*, attainable here and now.

All the six sense-spheres are built up on the perception of permanence. Therefore, the realization of their cessation is possible only through the perception of impermanence. The contemplation of impermanence is the path to its realization.

An extremely subtle contemplation on impermanence, that can bring about the cessation of the six sense-spheres, is to be found in the *Dvayamsutta* number two of the *Saḷāyatanavagga* of the *Saṃyutta Nikāya*. *Dvayaṃ* means a dyad. There are two discourses by that name, and this is the second. A strikingly deep vision of consciousness unfolds itself in this discourse as follows:

> *Dvayaṃ, bhikkhave, paṭicca viññāṇaṃ sambhoti. Kathañca, bhikkhave, dvayaṃ paṭicca viññāṇaṃ sambhoti? Cakkhuñca paṭicca rūpe ca uppajjati cakkhuviññāṇaṃ. Cakkhu aniccaṃ vipariṇāmi aññathābhāvi. Rūpā aniccā vipariṇāmino aññathābhāvino. Itthetaṃ dvayaṃ calañceva vyayañca aniccaṃ vipariṇāmi aññathābhāvi.*

---

[14] A II 162, *Mahākoṭṭhitasutta*; see sermon 23.

> *Cakkhuviññāṇaṃ aniccaṃ vipariṇāmi aññathābhāvi. Yo pi hetu yo pi paccayo cakkhuviññāṇassa uppādāya, so pi hetu so pi paccayo anicco vipariṇāmī aññathābhāvī. Aniccaṃ kho pana, bhikkhave, paccayaṃ paṭicca uppannaṃ cakkhuviññāṇaṃ, kuto niccaṃ bhavissati?*
>
> *Yā kho, bhikkhave, imesaṃ tiṇṇaṃ dhammānaṃ saṅgati sannipāto samavāyo, ayaṃ vuccati, bhikkhave, cakkhusamphasso. Cakkhusamphasso pi anicco vipariṇāmī aññathābhāvī. Yo pi hetu yo pi paccayo cakkhusamphassassa uppādāya, so pi hetu so pi paccayo anicco vipariṇāmī aññathābhāvī. Aniccaṃ kho pana, bhikkhave, paccayaṃ paṭicca uppanno cakkhusamphasso, kuto nicco bhavissati?*
>
> *Phuṭṭho, bhikkhave, vedeti, phuṭṭho ceteti, phuṭṭho sañjānāti. Itthete pi dhammā calā ceva vayā ca aniccā vipariṇāmino aññathābhāvino.*[15]

Even by listening to it, one can easily guess that there is a string of terms giving the idea of impermanence. Let us now try to translate it:

> "Dependent on a dyad, monks, consciousness comes to be. How is it, monks, that consciousness comes to be dependent on a dyad? Depending on eye and forms arises eye-consciousness. Eye is impermanent, changing, becoming otherwise. Forms are impermanent, changing, becoming otherwise. Thus this dyad is unstable, evanescent, impermanent, changing, becoming otherwise.
>
> "Eye-consciousness is impermanent, changing, becoming otherwise. Whatever cause and condition there is for the

---

15 S IV 67, *Dutiyadvayamsutta*.

> arising of eye-consciousness, that cause, that condition, too, is impermanent, changing and becoming otherwise. How can eye-consciousness, arisen in dependence on an impermanent condition, be permanent, monks?
>
> "That concurrence, that meeting, that togetherness of these three things, monks, is called eye-contact. Even the eye-contact, monks is impermanent, changing, becoming otherwise. Whatever cause and condition there is for the arising of eye-contact, that cause and condition, too, is impermanent, changing and becoming otherwise. How can eye-contact, arisen in dependence on an impermanent condition, be permanent, monks?
>
> "Contacted, monks, one feels, contacted one intends, contacted one perceives. Thus these things, too, are unstable, evanescent, impermanent, changing and becoming otherwise."

The *Sutta* proceeds in this way, stressing the impermanence of the other sense-spheres as well, the ear, the nose, the tongue, the body and the mind. The entire discourse vibrates with the tone of impermanence.

It is the law of dependent arising that the Buddha presents here with reference to the six sense-spheres. In other words, how the world gets built up. It is not founded on stable existing things, but on what is impermanent, unstable and changing, whose nature is to become otherwise. This is how the entire perception of the world is built up. Its foundation is always crumbling, changing and transforming.

Generally, in the discourse dealing with the question of sense-restraint, one comes across the phrase *na nimittaggāhi nānuvyañjanaggāhī*, "he doesn't grasp a sign nor does he dwell on its details."[16] The tendency to grasp a sign in regard to the objects of the six senses is the result of the perception of permanence. Due to the perception of permanence, there is a grasping of signs, and due to that grasping of signs, influxes flow in. Proliferations through craving, conceits and views get heaped up. This is how our world is constructed. This is the way the aggregates of attachment get accumulated. On the other hand, the contemplation of impermanence that leads to the signless concentration is helpful in freeing the mind from these signs.

The reflection on an object can be of two types. Where there is a perception of permanence, the tendency is to grasp the object tenaciously and hang on to it. This pervert tendency is known as *parāmasana*. It is impelled by the triple proliferations of craving, conceits and views. Under its influence one is carried away by prolific perceptions, *papañcasaññā*, and is kept under the sway of worldly concepts and designations born of prolific perceptions, *papañcasaññāsaṅkhā*.

On the contrary, the perception of impermanence fosters a detached and observant attitude in reflection, which is known as *sammasana*. It is that healthy attitude which progressively leads to the liberation of the mind from the influence of signs, and attenuates the prolific tendencies to craving, conceits and views. This kind of reflection is the harbinger of insight. Contemplation of impermanence on these lines effectively puts an end to this entire mass of *saṃsāric* suffering, as is evident from the following powerful declaration by the Buddha in the *Khandhasaṃyutta*:

> *Aniccasañña, bhikkhave, bhāvitā bahulīkatā sabbaṃ kāmarāgaṃ pariyādiyati, sabbaṃ rūparāgaṃ pariyādiyati, sabbaṃ bhavarāgaṃ pariyādiyati, sabbaṃ avijjaṃ*

16 E.g. in D I 70, *Sāmaññaphalasutta*.

> *pariyādiyati, sabbaṃ asmimānaṃ pariyādiyati samūhanati.*[17]
>
> "The perception of impermanence, monks, when developed and intensively practised, extirpates all sensual lust, extirpates all lust for forms, extirpates all lust for existence, extirpates all ignorance and extirpates and eradicates the conceit 'am.'"

The contemplation of impermanence, therefore, strikes at the very root of this entire mass of *saṃsāric* suffering. The discourse on the dyad, quoted above, amply illustrates this fact. The recurrent terms like *cala*, "unstable," and *vaya*, "evanescent," in the passage, indicate that the entire superstructure of sensory knowledge is founded on certain pervert attitudes. An imperceptible impermanence underlies it.

In a number of sermons we had to bring up the simile of the motion picture. The simile is not our own, but only a modernization of a canonical simile used by the Buddha himself. The point of divergence was the question the Buddha had addressed to the monks in the *Gaddulasutta*.

Diṭṭhaṃ vo, bhikkhave, caraṇaṃ nāma cittaṃ?[18] "Monks, have you seen a picture called a movie?" The monks answer in the affirmative, and so the Buddha proceeds:

Tampi kho, bhikkhave, caraṇaṃ nāma cittaṃ citteneva cintitaṃ. Tena pi kho, bhikkhave, caraṇena cittena cittaññeva cittataraṃ. "Monks, that picture called a movie is something thought out by the mind. But the thought itself, monks, is even more picturesque than that picture."

To say that it is more picturesque is to suggest its variegated character. Thought is intrinsically variegated. We have no idea what sort of a motion picture was there at that time, but the

---

[17] S III 155, *Aniccasaññāsutta*.

[18] S III 150, *Gaddulasutta*; see also sermons 5 and 6.

modern day movie has a way of concealing impermanence by the rapidity of projections of the series of pictures on the screen. The rapidity itself gives an impression of permanence, which is a perversion, *vipallāsa*.

The movie is enjoyable because of this perversion. Due to the perception of permanence, there is a grasping of signs, and in the wake of it influxes flow in, giving rise to proliferation, due to which one is overwhelmed by reckonings born of prolific conceptualization, *papañcasaññāsaṅkhā*. That is how one enjoys a film show. All this comes about as a result of ignorance, or lack of awareness of the cinematographic tricks concealing the fleeting, vibrating and evanescent nature of the scenes on the screen.

Though we resort to such artificial illustrations, by way of a simile, the Buddha declares that actually it is impossible to give a fitting simile to illustrate the rapidity of a thought process. Once he proclaimed: *Upamā pi na sukarā yāva lahuparivattaṃ cittaṃ*,[19] "It is not easy even to give a simile to show how rapidly thought changes."

Sometimes the Buddha resorts to double entendre to bring out piquantly some deep idea. He puns on the word *citta*, "thought" or "picture," in order to suggest the 'picturesque' or variegated nature of thought, when he asserts that thought is more picturesque, *cittatara*, than the picture. We can see that it is quite reasonable in the light of the *Dvayamsutta*. It is this series of picturesque formations that gives us a perception of permanence, which in turn is instrumental in creating a world before our eyes.

Our eye changes every split second. It is quivering, vibrating and transient. So also are the forms. But there is a malignantly pervert idea, ingrained in *saṃsāric* beings, known as the perception of permanence in the impermanent, *anicce niccasaññā*, which prevents them from seeing the inherent transience of eye and forms. That is how the six spheres of sense create a world before us.

---

[19] A I 10, *Paṇihita-acchavagga*.

It is the substructure of this sense-created world that the Buddha has revealed to us in this particular discourse on impermanence. The substructure, on analysis, reveals a duality, *dvayaṃ, bhikkhave, paṭicca viññāṇaṃ sambhoti*, "dependent on a dyad, monks, arises consciousness."

Consciousness is not something substantial and absolute, like the so-called soul. That is precisely the point of divergence for Buddhism, when compared with those religious systems which rely on soul theories.

In the *Dhamma* there is mention of six consciousnesses, as *cakkhuviññāṇa*, *sotaviññāṇa*, *ghānaviññāṇa*, *jivhāviññāṇa*, *kāyaviññāṇa* and *manoviññāṇa*, eye-, ear-, nose-, tongue-, body- and mind-consciousness. Every one of these consciousnesses is based on a dyad. Just as in the case of eye-consciousness we are given the formula beginning with *cakkhuñca paṭicca rūpe ca*, "dependent on eye and forms," so with regard to ear-consciousness we get *sotañca paṭicca sadde ca*, "dependent on ear and sounds," and so on. Even when we come to mind-consciousness, the theme is the same, *manañca paṭicca dhamme ca*, "dependent on mind and mind-objects." Mind also is vibrating, changing and transforming with extreme rapidity every moment. So are the objects of the mind.

The entire world is structured on these vibrant, transient and evanescent basic elements. That is the burden of this powerful discourse of the Buddha. Therefore, if someone developed the contemplation of impermanence to the highest degree and brought his mind to the signless state, having started from the sign itself, it goes without saying that he has realized the cessation of the world. That is, the experience of *Nibbāna*.

It is, at the same time, the cessation of proliferation, *papañcanirodha*. Prolific conceptualization is founded on the perception of permanence, whereby one comes under the sway of reckonings born of prolific perceptions, *papañcasaññāsaṅkhā*. Proliferation creates things, giving rise to the antinomian conflict. Duality masquerades behind it.

It is by mistaking the impermanent eye and the impermanent forms as permanent that the whole confusion has come about. One imagines the eye and forms as permanent and thereby becomes blind to their momentary change and transience. The glue of craving and intoxicating influxes create a facade of a real world before him. That is the world we touch with our hands and see with our eyes. All this exposes the insubstantial nature of this world.

The products of the six sense-bases can be summed up by the four terms *diṭṭha*, *suta*, *muta* and *viññāta*, things seen, heard, sensed and cognized. The *Dvayamsutta* brings to light the fact that all these four are insubstantial and coreless. Due to this very fact, the *Tathāgata* who realized the cessation of the six sense-bases, was confronted with the stupendous problem of mediating with the world that could not even imagine the frightful prospect of a cessation of the six sense-bases. That is to say, when he reached the state of non-proliferation, *nippapañca*, by experiencing the cessation of the world through the cessation of the six sense-bases, the *Tathāgata* had to grapple with the serious problem of truth and falsehood in mediating with the world.

There is an extremely important discourse connected with the idea of the void, *suññatāpaṭisaṃyutta*, which echoes this epistemological crisis, in the section of the Fours in the *Aṅguttara Nikāya*, entitled *Kāḷakārāmasutta*. This *Kāḷakārāmasutta* was preached by the Buddha to the congregation of monks at the Kāḷaka monastery in the city of Sāketa. The discourse, though brief, is one that is extremely deep in its presentation of the idea of the void.

Before getting down to an exposition of this discourse, by way of sketching its historical background, we may mention a few things. Apart from the mention of the venue, nothing much could be gleaned from the discourse itself as to how it was inspired. The commentaries, however, relate the episode of Cūḷasubhaddhā, daughter of Anāthapiṇḍika, to explain the context in which the discourse was preached.

Cūḷasubhaddhā, who was a stream-winner, *sotāpannā*, was given in marriage to the son of the millionaire Kāḷaka of Sāketa, a devout follower of Nigaṇṭha Nātaputta. Cūḷasubhaddhā managed to convert Kāḷaka by inviting the Buddha to Sāketa and getting him to listen to the *Dhamma.* After his conversion, he built a monastery in his park and offered it to the Buddha.

The commentary says that a group of five-hundred newly ordained monks of Sāketa gathered in this Kāḷaka monastery and were speaking in praise of the Buddha, marveling at his extraordinary feat of converting the millionaire and the inhabitants of Sāketa. It was at this juncture that the Buddha came and addressed this deep discourse to those monks. According to the commentary, the discourse was so profound that at five points of the sermon the earth shook miraculously and at the end of the sermon all the five-hundred monks who listened to it attained *arahant*-hood.

It is chronicled in the history of Buddhism that, during the great missionary movement initiated by the emperor Asoka, Venerable Mahārakkhita was sent to convert the country of the Yonakas. The very first sermon he preached there was based on this *Kāḷakārāmasutta*, on hearing which thirty-seven-thousand attained fruits of the noble path. If the identification of the Yonakas with the Greeks is correct, the choice of this deeply philosophical discourse is understandable.

According to the chronicles and the commentaries, another significant occasion in which the *Kāḷakārāmasutta* served as a theme was when Kālabuddharakkhita *Thera* gave an all-night sermon on the dark night of the new-moon *Poya* day, seated under the black *Timbaru* tree at Cetiya Pabbata in Sri Lanka. King Saddhātissa was also present in the audience.

The fact that this discourse was held in high esteem is evident from its historical background. As in the case of many other deep discourses, here too we are faced with the problem of variant readings. Even the commentator is at a loss to conclude and editors go their own way. We have to wade through the variant readings to make some sense out of the discourse as it is handed down. Let us now take up the relevant portions of this abstruse discourse:

> *Yaṃ, bhikkhave, sadevakassa lokassa samārakassa sabrahmakassa sassamaṇabrāhmaṇiyā pajāya sade-*

vamanussāya diṭṭhaṃ sutaṃ mutaṃ viññātaṃ pattaṃ pariyesitaṃ anuvicaritaṃ manasā, tam ahaṃ jānāmi.

Yaṃ, bhikkhave, sadevakassa lokassa samārakassa sabrahmakassa sassamaṇabrāhmaṇiyā pajāya sadevamanussāya diṭṭhaṃ sutaṃ mutaṃ viññātaṃ pattaṃ pariyesitaṃ anuvicaritaṃ manasā, tam ahaṃ abhaññāsiṃ. Taṃ tathāgatasssa viditaṃ, taṃ tathāgato na upaṭṭhāsi.

Yaṃ, bhikkhave, sadevakassa lokassa samārakassa sabrahmakassa sassamaṇabrāhmaṇiyā pajāya sadevamanussāya diṭṭhaṃ sutaṃ mutaṃ viññātaṃ pattaṃ pariyesitaṃ anuvicaritaṃ manasā, tam ahaṃ 'na jānāmī'ti vadeyyaṃ, taṃ mama assa musā, tam ahaṃ 'jānāmi ca na ca jānāmī'ti vadeyyaṃ, taṃ p' assa tādisam eva, tam ahaṃ 'neva jānāmi na na jānāmī'ti vadeyyaṃ, taṃ mama assa kali.

Iti kho, bhikkhave, tathāgato diṭṭhā daṭṭhabbaṃ diṭṭhaṃ na maññati, adiṭṭhaṃ na maññati, daṭṭhabbaṃ na maññati, daṭṭhāraṃ na maññati. Sutā sotabbaṃ sutaṃ na maññati, asutaṃ na maññati, sotabbaṃ na maññati, sotāraṃ na maññati. Mutā motabbaṃ mutaṃ na maññati, amutaṃ na maññati, motabbaṃ na maññati, motāraṃ na maññati. Viññātā viññātabbaṃ viññātaṃ na maññati, aviññātaṃ na maññati, viññātabbaṃ na maññati, viññātāraṃ na maññati.

Iti kho, bhikkhave, tathāgato diṭṭha-suta-muta-viññātabbesu dhammesu tādī, yeva tādī tamhā ca pana tādimhā añño tādī uttaritarovā paṇītataro vā n' atthī'ti vadāmi.

> *Yaṃ kiñci diṭṭhaṃ va sutaṃ mutaṃ vā,*
> *ajjhositaṃ saccamutaṃ paresaṃ,*
> *na tesu tādī saya saṃvutesu,*
> *saccaṃ musā vā pi paraṃ daheyyaṃ.*

Etañca sallaṃ paṭigacca disvā,
ajjhositā yattha pajā visattā,
jānāmi passāmi tath' eva etaṃ,
ajjhositaṃ n' atthi tathāgatānaṃ.[20]

"Monks, whatsoever in the world, with its gods, *Māras* and *Brahmas*, among the progeny consisting of recluses and Brahmins, gods and men, whatsoever is seen, heard, sensed, cognized, thought after and pondered over by the mind, all that do I know.

"Monks, whatsoever in the world, with its gods, *Māras* and *Brahmas*, among the progeny consisting of recluses and Brahmins, gods and men, whatsoever is seen, heard, sensed, cognized, thought after and pondered over by the mind, that have I fully understood. All that is known to the *Tathāgata*, but the *Tathāgata* has not taken his stand upon it.

"If I were to say, monks, whatsoever in the world, with its gods, *Māras* and *Brahmas*, among the progeny consisting of recluses and Brahmins, gods and men, whatsoever is seen, heard, sensed, cognized, thought after and pondered over by the mind, all that I do not know, it would be a falsehood in me. If I were to say I both know it and know it not, that too would be a falsehood in me. If I were to say I neither know it nor am ignorant of it, it would be a fault in me.

"Thus, monks, a *Tathāgata* does not imagine a visible thing as apart from seeing, he does not imagine an unseen, he does not imagine a thing worth seeing, he does not imagine a seer. He does not imagine an audible thing as apart

---

20 A II 25, *Kāḷakārāmasutta*.

from hearing, he does not imagine an unheard, he does not imagine a thing worth hearing, he does not imagine a hearer. He does not imagine a thing to be sensed as apart from sensation, he does not imagine an unsensed, he does not imagine a thing worth sensing, he does not imagine one who senses. He does not imagine a cognizable thing as apart from cognition, he does not imagine an uncognized, he does not imagine a thing worth cognizing, he does not imagine one who cognizes.

"Thus, monks, the *Tathāgata*, being such in regard to all phenomena, seen, heard, sensed and cognized, is such. Moreover than he who is such there is none other higher or more excellent, I declare.

"Whatever is seen, heard, sensed,
Or clung to and esteemed as truth by other folk,
Midst those who are entrenched in their own views,
Being such, I hold none as true or false.

"This barb I beheld well in advance,
Whereon mankind is hooked, impaled,
I know, I see, 'tis verily so,
No such clinging for the *Tathāgatas*."

In the first statement the Buddha declares that he knows, *tam ahaṃ jānāmi*, whatever is seen, heard, sensed, cognized, thought after and pondered over by all beings in the world, and that is the sum total of the knowledge acquired through the six sense-bases.

In the second statement he affirms that the knowledge he has is of a higher order, *tam ahaṃ abhaññāsiṃ*, that amounts to an understanding, *taṃ tathāgatasssa viditaṃ*, by virtue of which he does not take his stand upon it, he has no stance, *taṃ tathāgato na upaṭṭhāsi*.

The third statement flows from this detached perspective. It is to the effect that the *Tathāgata* cannot disclaim knowledge, despite his detached attitude, as it would be tantamount to prevarication in the eyes of the world, *taṃ mama assa musā*.

The fourth statement highlights the same incongruity, because the *Tathāgata* placed in this awkward situation cannot compromise by both claiming and disclaiming knowledge at the same time, *tam ahaṃ 'jānāmi ca na ca jānāmī'ti vadeyyaṃ, taṃ p' assa tādisam eva*.

As the fifth statement makes it clear, the *Tathāgata* does not deem it fit to wriggle out by neither claiming nor disclaiming knowledge of sense-data.

Then comes the declaration as to how the *Tathāgata* treats this body of sensory knowledge of the worldling. "Thus, monks, a *Tathāgata* does not imagine a visible thing as apart from the seen," *iti kho, bhikkhave, tathāgato diṭṭhā daṭṭhabbaṃ diṭṭhaṃ na maññati*.

We have come across the terms *diṭṭha*, *suta*, *muta*, *viññāta* quite often, for instance in our discussion of the *Bāhiyasutta* in the context *diṭṭhe diṭṭhamattaṃ bhavissati, sute sutamattaṃ bhavissati, mute mutamattaṃ bhavissati, viññāte viññātamattaṃ bhavissati*, "In the seen there will be just the seen, in the heard there will be just the heard, in the sensed there will be just the sensed, in the cognized there will be just the cognized."[21]

In common parlance, the word 'seen' connotes something seen. But here we have something more radical, avoiding substantialist insinuations. It is just the seen in the seen, implied by *diṭṭha*, in this context too. The *Tathāgata* takes it just as a seen, without imagining that there is something substantial worthwhile seeing, as apart from it, *diṭṭhā daṭṭhabbaṃ diṭṭhaṃ na maññati*.

We are already familiar with the term *maññanā*, having discussed it in such discourses as the *Mūlapariyāyasutta* and the *Bāhiyasutta*.[22] It stands for imaginings, prompted by cravings, conceits and views. The *Tathāgata* is free from such imaginings.

---

[21] Ud 8, *Bāhiyasutta*, see sermon 14.

[22] See sermons 12 to 15.

He does not imagine a thing worthwhile seeing apart from the seen, nor does he imagine an unseen, *adiṭṭhaṃ na maññati*. The phenomenon of seeing is not denied.

The phrase *daṭṭhabbaṃ na maññati* conveys the idea that the *Tathāgata* does not imagine that there is something worth seeing, that there is something essential in it. *Daṭṭhāraṃ na maññati*, he does not imagine a seer or one who sees. He does not project an agent into the phenomenon by taking seriously the subject-object relationship.

With regard to the heard, *suta*, the sensed, *muta*, and the cognized, *viññāta*, too, the *Tathāgata* has no such imaginings. Then, in summing up it is said: *Iti kho, bhikkhave, tathāgato diṭṭha-suta-muta-viññātabbesu dhammesu tādi, yeva tādi*, "Thus, monks, the Tathāgata, being such in regard to all phenomena, seen, heard, sensed and cognized, is 'such.'"

The term *tādī*, too, came up in a number of our earlier sermons.[23] We rendered it by "such." It stands for the quality of steadfastness of the *arahant* in remaining unshaken by the eight worldly vicissitudes. His mainstay, in this respect, is *atammayatā*, or non-identification. He is such because he does not grasp any of those things as 'mine.' So he is 'such' in regard to whatever is seen, heard, sensed and cognized. There is no one who is higher or more excellent than this such-like-one in point of suchness. Then comes a couplet of verses, presenting the gist of the sermon.

Our rendering of the sermon is in need of further explication. Though it gives a general idea, some words and phrases in the original have far reaching implications. The basic idea behind the series of declarations made is the extraordinary change of attitude towards the question of speculative views, which marks off the *Tathāgata* from all his contemporaries. He took a completely different turn, transcending the extremes of eternalism and annihilationism. This difference of attitude is revealed by the riddle like statements in the first part of the discourse. One gets the

---

[23] See sermons 17 and 22.

impression that the *Tathāgata* was confronted with a problematic situation of the highest order.

The first statement is to the effect that the *Tathāgata* knows whatever in the world with its gods, *Māras* and *Brahmas*, among the progeny consisting of recluses and Brahmins, gods and men, is seen, heard, sensed, cognized, thought after and pondered over by the mind.

The second statement asserts that the *Tathāgata* has a higher understanding of all that. All the same, he takes no stance in regard to whatever is seen, heard, sensed and cognized.

This might appear as a riddle. Usually when one has a higher understanding of something, one is inclined to take one's stand upon it. But here we have a denial. The discourse bears some resemblance to the tetralemma we had discussed earlier.[24] But there seems to be a difference here, in the formulation of the first proposition of the tetralemma.

Normally the first proposition amounts to an unqualified assertion of the affirmative standpoint. In this case, however, we find the statement that the *Tathāgata* not only knows all what the world knows, but that he has a higher understanding of it, *abhaññāsiṃ*. It is precisely because he has a higher understanding that he takes no stance in regard to it.

This might appear problematic, but let us remind ourselves of the two levels of understanding mentioned in the *Mūlapariyāya-sutta*, discussed earlier, namely *sañjānāti* and *abhijānāti*. As an instance of the first level of understanding, we get the following passage in that discourse in regard to the untaught ordinary person, *assutavā puthujjano*:

> *Paṭhaviṃ paṭhavito sañjānāti. Paṭhaviṃ paṭhavito saññatvā paṭhaviṃ maññati, paṭhaviyā maññati, paṭhavito*

---

[24] See sermon 20.

> *maññati, 'paṭhaviṃ me'ti maññati, paṭhaviṃ abhinandati.*[25]
>
> "He perceives earth as 'earth.' Having perceived earth as 'earth,' he imagines 'earth' as such, he imagines 'on the earth,' he imagines 'from the earth,' he imagines 'earth is mine,' he delights in earth."

The untaught ordinary person has a perceptual knowledge of earth, *sañjānāti*. That, too, is a level of knowledge. It is in fact the lowest grade of knowing. The untaught ordinary person can do no better than perceive earth as earth.

Having perceived earth as earth, he takes it seriously by its face value and goes on imagining by way of craving, conceit and views, granting it object-status. He imposes the grammatical superstructure on it. He imagines 'on the earth,' he imagines 'from the earth,' he imagines 'earth is mine,' he delights in earth. This, then, is the lowest grade of knowledge.

On the other hand, about the *Tathāgata*'s level of understanding, the *Mūlapariyāyasutta* has the following description:

> *Paṭhaviṃ paṭhavito abhijānāti, paṭhaviṃ paṭhavito abhiññāya paṭhaviṃ na maññati, paṭhaviyā na maññati, paṭhavito na maññati, 'paṭhaviṃ me'ti na maññati, paṭhaviṃ nābhinandati.*
>
> "He understands through higher knowledge earth as 'earth,' having understood through higher knowledge earth as 'earth,' he does not imagine earth to be 'earth,' he does not imagine 'on the earth,' he does not imagine 'from the earth,' he does not imagine 'earth is mine,' he does not delight in earth."

---

25 M I 1, *Mūlapariyāyasutta*.

The *Tathāgata*, who has a higher knowledge of earth, as suggested by the word *abhijānāti*, does not entertain imaginings by taking earth at its face value. He is not carried away by the grammatical structure to imagine in such terms as 'on the earth' and 'from the earth.'

In the present context, too, the same distinction in grades of knowledge is evident. Firstly, the *Tathāgata* says: "All that do I know, that have I fully understood. All that is known to the *Tathāgata*." It is precisely because of this full understanding that he has not taken his stand upon it. He has no stance in regard to all that. This is the gist of the first paragraph of the discourse, which sounds more or less a paradox. It is because of this apparently queer state of affairs that the *Tathāgata* had to confess that it would be a falsehood on his part to say: "All that I do not know."

If someone asks whether it is because he does not know that he takes no stance, he cannot say: "Yes." As a matter of fact, it is precisely because he has understood that he takes no stance. But the worldlings are of the opinion that knowledge of a thing entitles one to assert it dogmatically.

To say "I both know it and know it not" or "I neither know it nor am ignorant of it" would also be mistaken by the world as a prevarication or equivocation. The first paragraph of the discourse has to be understood in this light.

The commentary has it that the earth shook at five points in the discourse. According to it the three significant terms *jānāmi*, *abbhaññāsiṃ* and *viditaṃ*, "I know," "I have fully understood," all that is "known" to the *Tathāgata* represent a plane of omniscience, *sabbaññutabhūmi*, peculiar to a Buddha.[26] Even at the end of this proclamation of omniscience, it is said the earth shook as a mark of approbation.

Then the phrase *na upaṭṭhāsi*, "does not take his stand upon it," is interpreted by the commentary as indicating the plane of the influx-free one, *khīṇāsavabhūmi*. Why the *Tathāgata* has no

---

26 Mp III 38.

stance in regard to sensory data is said to be due to his freedom from influxes. He does not grasp them by way of craving, conceit and views. He does not take his stand upon things seen, heard, sensed and cognized. He has no inclination or clinging towards them.

Nibbāna Sermon 25

Namo tassa Bhagavato Arahato Sammāsambuddhassa
Namo tassa Bhagavato Arahato Sammāsambuddhassa
Namo tassa Bhagavato Arahato Sammāsambuddhassa

Etaṃ santaṃ, etaṃ paṇītaṃ, yadidaṃ sabbasaṅkhārasamatho sabbūpadhipaṭinissaggo taṇhakkhayo virāgo nirodho nibbānaṃ.[1]

"This is peaceful, this is excellent, namely the stilling of all preparations, the relinquishment of all assets, the destruction of craving, detachment, cessation, extinction."

With the permission of the Most Venerable Great Preceptor and the assembly of the venerable meditative monks.

This is the twenty-fifth sermon in the series of sermons on Nibbāna. The other day we made an attempt to understand, in the light of the *Kāḷakārāmasutta*, the enlightened attitude of the *Tathāgata*, who has realized the cessation of the six bases of sense-contact, towards the view-points of the worldlings, who find themselves confined within those six bases.

In that discourse, the Buddha declared with the words *tam ahaṃ jānāmi*, "[all] that do I know,"[2] the fact that he has understood all what the world with its gods, *Māras* and *Brahmas*, and the progeny consisting of recluses and Brahmins, gods and men, have seen, heard, sensed, cognized, thought after and pondered over by the mind.

---

1 M I 436, *MahāMālunkyasutta*.

2 A II 25, *Kāḷakārāmasutta*.

By his next assertion *tam ahaṃ abbhaññāsiṃ*, the Buddha proclaimed that he not only knows all that, but knows it thoroughly in some special way. With the words *taṃ tathāgatassa viditaṃ*, he declares that by virtue of this special knowledge he has understood all what the world claims to know. Despite this special knowledge and understanding, the *Tathāgata* takes no stance and has no inclination or partiality towards those sensory data, as is evident from the expression *taṃ tathāgato na upaṭṭhāsi*.

Worldings in general are in the habit of asserting dogmatically 'I know, I see, it is verily so,' *jānāmi passāmi tath' eva etaṃ*,[3] when they have a special knowledge or understanding of something or other. But according to this discourse, it seems that the Buddha takes no stance and has no inclination or partiality towards those sensory data, precisely because he has a special knowledge and understanding with regard to them. This fact is highlighted by the concluding summary verses, particularly by the lines:

Jānāmi passāmi tath' eva etaṃ,
ajjhositaṃ n' atthi tathāgatānaṃ.

"I know, I see, 'tis verily so.
No such clinging for the *Tathāgatas*."

In order to explain this strange difference of attitude, we quoted the other day two significant terms from the *Mūlapariyāyasutta* of the *Majjhima Nikāya*, namely *sañjānāti* and *abhijānāti*. They represent two levels of knowledge in the context of that particular discourse.

Sañjānāti stands for perceptual knowledge, whereas *abhijānāti* conveys the idea of some special understanding of a higher order. The level of knowledge implied by the term *sañjānāti* is that which characterizes the ordinary worldling's world view. He is deluded by the mirage-like perception in his view of the world and

[3] Sn 908, *MahāViyūhasutta*.

goes on imagining, *maññanā*, a real world enslaved to the patterns of the grammatical structure.

But the *Tathāgata* has penetrated into the true nature of those seens, heards, sensed and the like, with his extraordinary level of higher knowledge, *abhiññā*, yielding full comprehension. Therefore, he does not take his stand upon any of them. He has no stance to justify the usage of the term *upaṭṭhāsi*, since he does not entertain imaginings, *maññanā*.

What is called *maññanā* is the imagining in egoistic terms, imparting reality to illusory things. It is this principle of refraining from vain imaginings that is indicated by the term *na upaṭṭhāsi*, "does not take his stand upon."

Tathāgatas have no clinging or entanglement, *ajjhositaṃ*, precisely because they entertain no imaginings. In regard to things seen, heard, etc. the *Tathāgatas* have no clinging, binding or entanglement by way of craving, conceit and views, respectively.

We happened to mention the other day that those peculiar declarations, with which the *Kāḷakārāmasutta* opens, bear some resemblance to the tetralemma discussed in our treatment of the undetermined points.[4]

The set of four alternative propositions concerning the *Tathāgata*'s after death state may be cited as a paradigm for the tetralemma:

1) *Hoti tathāgato paraṃ maraṇā*, "The *Tathāgata* exists after death."
2) *na hoti tathāgato paraṃ maraṇā*, "The *Tathāgata* does not exist after death."
3) *hoti ca na ca hoti tathāgato paraṃ maraṇā*, "The *Tathāgata* both exists and does not exist after death."

---

[4] See esp. sermon 20.

4) *n'eva hoti na na hoti tathāgato paraṃ maraṇā*, "The *Tathāgata* neither exists nor does not exist after death."[5]

The declarations found in this discourse bear some affinity to the above-mentioned tetralemma. However, we find here the Buddha making the first declaration in several stages. Firstly, he makes the statement that whatever is seen, heard, sensed, and cognized, thought after and pondered over by all beings in the world, that he knows.

In the second statement he affirms that he has a higher knowledge of all that. Then comes a sentence which reaffirms that the *Tathāgata* has understood, but ends with the statement "the *Tathāgata* does not take his stand upon it."

Generally, when confronted with the tetralemma, the Buddha summarily dismisses all the four alternative propositions. But here the peculiarity is in not dismissing the first proposition at once. He declares that he knows, that he has a higher knowledge, and that he has understood all that.

Apparently he is affirming the first proposition, granting the validity of sensory data. But then comes the concluding statement to the effect that he does not take his stand upon them, *na upaṭṭhāsi*, which amounts to a negation.

The secret behind this peculiar presentation will emerge when we bring up the proper similes and parables. Till then, what can be gleaned from the context is that the *Tathāgata* has no stance, not because he is ignorant, but due to the very fact that he knows full well and has understood the nature of the sum total of sensory data.

The worldlings are prone to think that it is when convincing knowledge is lacking that one has no such stance. But the Buddha declares here that he takes no stance in regard to what is seen, heard, sensed etc., precisely because he has a special understanding, a penetrative knowledge of the essence-lessness of the data obtained through the six sense-bases.

---

[5] E.g. at M I 484, *Aggivacchagottasutta*.

So it seems, in this context too, we have the negation of the first alternative, as is usual in the case of a tetralemma, only that the negation is expressed here in a very peculiar way. Let us now take up the second declaration:

> *Yaṃ, bhikkhave, sadevakassa lokassa samārakassa sa-brahmakassa sassamaṇabrāhmaṇiyā pajāya sade-vamanussāya diṭṭhaṃ sutaṃ mutaṃ viññātaṃ pattaṃ pariyesitaṃ anuvicaritaṃ manasā, tam ahaṃ 'na jānāmī'ti vadeyyaṃ, taṃ mama assa musā.*

> "If I were to say, monks, whatsoever in the world, with its gods, *Māras* and *Brahmas*, among the progeny consisting of recluses and Brahmins, gods and men, whatsoever is seen, heard, sensed, and cognized, thought after and pondered over by the mind, all that I do not know, it would be a falsehood in me."

There is a difference of opinion as to the correct reading of this second declaration. Deep *suttas* often present difficulties in determining the exact reading, and this is especially the case with the *Kāḷakārāmasutta*.

In this instance, the commentary has followed the reading *tam ahaṃ 'jānāmī'ti vadeyyaṃ, taṃ mama assa musā*, "if I were to say 'that I know,' it would be a falsehood in me." But as we have pointed out earlier, this reading is not meaningful.[6] That is probably why the *Chaṭṭhasaṅgītipiṭaka* edition has followed the variant reading *tam ahaṃ 'na jānāmī'ti vadeyyaṃ*, "if I were to say 'that I do not know.'" This departure from the commentarial tradition seems justifiable, since the Buddha has already declared that he knows all that.

It stands to reason, therefore, that in the second declaration he makes it clear that to say 'I do not know' would be a contradiction, a falsehood. But why this clarification?

---

[6] See sermon 24.

Generally the worldlings expect one to unequivocally assert and take one's stand upon one's viewpoint in categorical terms, as expressed by the dictum *idam eva saccaṃ, mogham aññaṃ*, "this alone is true, all else is false."[7] Failure to do so is recognized as a lack of knowledge or precision. The second declaration is meant to forestall such an objection, since the first declaration ends with the clause *taṃ tathāgato na upaṭṭhāsi*, "but the *Tathāgata* has not taken his stand upon it." So it amounts to a statement like 'it is not because I do not know that I take no stance.' In the same strain, we can explain the declarations that follow.

It seems, then, that the second declaration *tam ahaṃ 'na jānāmī'ti vadeyyaṃ, taṃ mama assa musā*, "if I were to say, 'all that I do not know,' it would be a falsehood in me," amounts to the second alternative of the tetralemma.

The next declaration follows the same trend. To quote the relevant portion, *tam ahaṃ 'jānāmi ca na ca jānāmī'ti vadeyyaṃ, taṃ p' assa tādisam eva*, "if I were to say 'I both know it and do not know it,' that too would be a falsehood in me."

In regard to the aforesaid seens, heards, sensed etc., if I were to say that I know, I do not know, or even a combination of both those statements as 'I both know and do not know,' it would be a falsehood on my part. Why? Because the world is accustomed to put down such a vacillation to a lack of certitude. To say 'I both know it and know it not' looks like a confession of partial knowledge, since it can mean knowledge and ignorance going fifty-fifty. So the Buddha says, in this instance, too, that it would likewise be a falsehood, *taṃ p' assa tādisam eva*.

Now we come to the fourth statement. The Buddha declares, "if I were to say 'I neither know it, nor am ignorant of it,' it would be a fault in me," *tam ahaṃ 'neva jānāmi na na jānāmī'ti vadeyyaṃ, taṃ mama assa kali*.

We can understand that position, too. Generally the worldlings think that a refusal to make a categorical statement is either due to partial knowledge, or to an attitude of wriggling out. In fact, this

---

[7] E.g. at M I 484, *Aggivacchagottasutta*.

attitude of wriggling out had already assumed the status of a philosophy in itself in Sañjaya Belaṭṭhiputta, a contemporary of the Buddha.

When he was interrogated, he would respond with such a series of negations like "I do not say it is, I do not say it is thus, I do not say it is otherwise, nor do I say it is neither," etc.[8] The attempt here is to evade the issue by a sort of 'eel-wriggling.' That school of philosophy, which resorted to such an evasive legerdemain, came to be known as *amarā-vikkhepa-vāda*. The Buddha refuses to subscribe to such tactical sophistry by rejecting the fourth alternative 'I neither know it, nor am ignorant of it.'

Here, then, we have the same tetralemma, presented in a different guise. It smacks of a riddle that the Buddha was confronted with – the riddle of coming to terms with worldly parlance. As we have already mentioned, the commentary analyses the main theme of the discourse into five planes. It also records that the earth shook at five points of the discourse, that is, at the end of the proclamation for each plane.[9]

According to the commentary, the first plane is the plane of omniscience, *sabbaññutabhūmi*. The phrases representative of that plane are said to be *tam ahaṃ jānāmi*, "that I know," *tam aham abbhaññāsiṃ*, "that have I fully understood," and *taṃ tathāgatassa viditaṃ*, "that is known to the *Tathāgata*."

Then comes the plane of the influx-free one, *khīṇāsavabhūmi*, represented by the section ending with the phrase *na upaṭṭhāsi*, "does not take his stand upon it." It is so called because that phrase brings out the characteristic of not taking a stance by way of cravings, conceits and views in the case of an influx-free one.

The three phrases *taṃ mama assa musā*, "it would be a falsehood on my part," *taṃ p' assa tādisam eva*, "likewise, that too would be a falsehood in me," and *taṃ mama assa kali*, "it would be a fault in me," are interpreted by the commentary as represent-

---

8 D I 58, *Sāmaññaphalasutta*.

9 Mp III 38.

ing the third plane of truth, *saccabhūmi*. We have now dealt with that, too.

What comes next as the fourth plane is the deepest of all. The commentary calls it the plane of the void, *suññatābhūmi*. It is with good reason that it is so called. The paragraph that follows is said to represent that plane; it runs:

> *Iti kho, bhikkhave, tathāgato diṭṭhā daṭṭhabbaṃ diṭṭhaṃ na maññati, adiṭṭhaṃ na maññati, daṭṭhabbaṃ na maññati, daṭṭhāraṃ na maññati. Sutā sotabbaṃ sutaṃ na maññati, asutaṃ na maññati, sotabbaṃ na maññati, sotāraṃ na maññati. Mutā motabbaṃ mutaṃ na maññati, amutaṃ na maññati, motabbaṃ na maññati, motāraṃ na maññati. Viññātā viññātabbaṃ viññātaṃ na maññati, aviññātaṃ na maññati, viññātabbaṃ na maññati, viññātāraṃ na maññati.*

Here, too, we are confronted with the question of variant readings. To begin with, here we have given the phrase *diṭṭhā daṭṭhabbaṃ diṭṭhaṃ*, whereas the commentary takes it as *daṭṭhā daṭṭhabbaṃ diṭṭhaṃ*. According to the commentary, *daṭṭhā* is a hypothetical variant of the absolutive form *disvā*, for it paraphrases *'daṭṭhā daṭṭhabban'ti disvā daṭṭhabbaṃ*,[10] that is, "*daṭṭhā daṭṭhabbaṃ* stands for *disvā daṭṭhabbaṃ*." So the whole sentence in question is said to convey the sense "having seen, he does not imagine a seen worth seeing." But the variant reading *diṭṭha* is granted, though the commentator prefers the reading *daṭṭha* as it is suggestive of an absolutive *dṛṣṭvā*.

Taking the cue from this commentarial preference, the Burmese *Chaṭṭhasaṅgīti* edition goes a step further in substituting *sutvā*, *mutvā* and *viññatvā* rather arbitrarily to give an absolutive twist to the three phrases that follow as *sutvā sotabbaṃ sutaṃ*, *mutvā motabbaṃ mutaṃ*, and *viññatvā viññātabbaṃ viññātaṃ*. Probably

---

[10] Mp III 39.

the editors thought that in this context the terms *diṭṭha*, *suta*, *muta* and *viññāta* could not be interpreted as they are.

But we may point out that, in keeping with the line of interpretation we have followed so far, these three terms may be said to stand for an extremely deep dimension of this discourse, dealing with the void. The other day we simply gave a sketch of a possible rendering.

The statement *diṭṭhā daṭṭhabbaṃ diṭṭhaṃ na maññati* has to be interpreted as an assertion that the *Tathāgata* "does not imagine a sight worthwhile seeing as apart from the seen," that there is nothing substantial in the seen. So also the other statements, *sutā sotabbaṃ sutaṃ na maññati*, "does not imagine a worthwhile hearing apart from the heard"; *mutā motabbaṃ mutaṃ na maññati*, "does not imagine a worthwhile sensing apart from the sensed"; *viññātā viññātabbaṃ viññātaṃ na maññati*, "does not imagine a worthwhile cognition apart from the cognized."

In case our interpretation still appears problematic, we may hark back to the *Bāhiyasutta* we have already explained at length.[11] The philosophy behind the Buddha's exhortation to the ascetic Bāhiya could be summed up in the words *diṭṭhe diṭṭhamattaṃ bhavissati, sute sutamattaṃ bhavissati, mute mutamattaṃ bhavissati, viññāte viññātamattaṃ bhavissati*,[12] "In the seen there will be just the seen, in the heard there will be just the heard, in the sensed there will be just the sensed, in the cognized there will be just the cognized."

What is meant is that one has to stop at just the seen, without discursively imagining that there is some-'thing' seen, some-'thing' substantial behind the seen. Similarly in regard to the heard, one has to take it as just a heard, not some-'thing' heard.

In the case of the phrase *diṭṭhā daṭṭhabbaṃ diṭṭhaṃ na maññati*, the word *diṭṭhā*, being in the ablative case, we may render it as "does not imagine a sight worthwhile seeing 'as apart from' the

---

[11] See sermon 15.

[12] Ud 8, *Bāhiyasutta*.

seen." By way of further clarification of this point, we may revert to the simile of the dog on the plank, which we gave in our explanation of *nāma-rūpa*.[13] The simile, of course, is not canonical, but of fable origin.

When a dog, while crossing a stream, stops halfway on the plank and starts wagging its tail and peeping curiously down, the reason is the sight of its own image in the water. It imagines a dog there, a 'water-dog.' The dog thinks that there is something worthwhile seeing, apart from the seen.

It is unaware of the fact that it is seeing what it sees because it is looking. It thinks that it is looking because there is something out there to be seen. The moment it realizes that it is seeing because it is looking, it will stop looking at its own image in the water.

We have here a very subtle point in the law of dependent arising, one that is integral to the analysis of name-and-form. So, then, due to the very ignorance of the fact that it is seeing because it is looking, the dog imagines another dog, there, in the water. What is called *maññanā* is an imagining of that sort.

No such imagining is there in the *Tathāgata*, *diṭṭhā daṭṭhabbaṃ diṭṭhaṃ na maññati*, "he does not imagine a sight worth seeing as apart from the seen." In short, for him the seen is the be all and the end all of it.

The seen is dependently arisen. It comes about due to a collocation of conditions, apart from which it has no existence per se. Every instance of looking down at the water is a fresh experience and every time an image of the dog in the water and of another looking at it is created. The dog is seeing its own image. Everything is dependently arisen, *phassapaccayā*, says the *Brahmajālasutta*, "dependent on contact."[14]

Here there is something really deep. It is because of the personality-view, *sakkāyadiṭṭhi*, that the world is carried away by this illusion. One goes on looking saying that one is doing so as there

---

[13] See sermon 6.

[14] D I 42, *Brahmajālasutta*.

is something to be seen. But the seen is there because of the looking.

This, then, is the moral behind the statement *diṭṭhā daṭṭhabbaṃ diṭṭhaṃ na maññati*, "does not imagine a seen worthwhile seeing as apart from the seen itself." This is the dictum implicit in the *Bāhiyasutta*, too, which could be illustrated by the simile of the dog on the plank. The *Tathāgata* does not imagine a sight as existing apart from the bare act of seeing.

If further illustrations are needed, let us take the case of hearing music from a distance. One imagines a thing called 'music' and with the idea of listening to the same music goes to the place where the music is going on. One is not aware of the fact that at each step in that direction one is hearing a different music. Why? Because one is ignorant of the law of dependent arising. Just as in the former case the dog seen is dependent on the dog looking, here too, the auditory consciousness of a music is the outcome of a dependence between ear and sound.

So, deluded as he is, he goes to the music hall to listen better to the same music. He will realize the extent of his delusion if he happens to put his ear to the musical instrument. When he does so, he will hear not a music, but a set of crude vibrations. But this is what is going on in the world. The world is steeped in the delusion of imagining that it is the same music one is hearing, though at each step in that direction the music changes. This is due to the fact that it is dependently arisen. Actually, there is no person hearing, but only a state of affairs dependent on the ear and sound, a conditioned arising dependent on contact. In the present textual context, the terms *diṭṭha*, *suta*, *muta* and *viññāta*, seen, heard, sensed and cognized, have to be understood in this light.

So this is how the phrase *diṭṭhā daṭṭhabbaṃ diṭṭhaṃ na maññati* has to be interpreted. But the commentary does not seem to have appreciated the relevance of this paragraph to the Buddha's teachings on voidness. While commenting on *diṭṭhaṃ na maññati* it expatiates *'ahaṃ mahājanena diṭṭhameva passāmī'ti taṇhāmānadiṭṭhīhi na maññati*. According to it, what is meant is that the *Tathāgata* does not imagine by way of cravings, conceits and views that he is seeing just what the common people have seen. This is an oversimplification, a rather shallow interpretation.

The next phrase, *adiṭṭhaṃ na maññati*, is similarly explained, *'adiṭṭhaṃ na maññatī'ti 'ahaṃ mahājanena adiṭṭhameva etaṃ passāmī'ti evampi taṇhādihi maññanāhi na maññati*, "he does not imagine an unseen" means that the *Tathāgata* does not imagine by way of imaginings through craving etc. that he is seeing something unseen by the common people. The commentary, it seems, has gone at a tangent, bypassing the deeper sense.

We have already explained the deeper significance of the phrase, *diṭṭhaṃ na maññati*, "does not imagine a seen." Now what does *adiṭṭhaṃ na maññati* mean?

In terms of our simile of the dog on the plank, *diṭṭhaṃ na maññati* means that the *Tathāgata* does not imagine a dog in the water. *Adiṭṭhaṃ na maññati* could therefore mean that the *Tathāgata* does not imagine that the dog has not seen. Why he does not treat it as an unseen should be clear from that declaration we had already cited, ending with *tam ahaṃ 'na jānāmī'ti vadeyyaṃ, taṃ mama assa musā*, "if I were to say 'that I do not know,' it would be a falsehood in me."

The fact of seeing is not denied, though what is seen is not taken as a dog, but only as an image of one, that is dependently arisen. Since the understanding of it as a dependently arisen phenomenon is there, the *Tathāgata* does not imagine an unseen either, *adiṭṭhaṃ na maññati.*

The phrase *daṭṭhabbaṃ na maññati*, is also explicable in the light of the foregoing discussion. Now, the dog on the plank keeps on looking down at the water again and again because it thinks that there is something worthwhile seeing in the water. Such a delusion is not there in the *Tathāgata*. He knows that at each turn it is a phenomenon of a seen dependently arisen, dependent on contact, *phassapaccayā.*

Every time it happens, it is a fresh sight, a new preparation, *saṅkhāra*. So there is nothing to look for in it. Only a looking is there, nothing worth looking at. Only a seeing is there, nothing to be seen. Apart from the bare act of hearing, there is nothing to be heard. It is the wrong view of a self that gives a notion of substantiality. The above phrase, therefore, is suggestive of insubstantiality, essencelessness, and voidness.

Music is just a word. By taking seriously the concept behind that word, one imagines a thing called 'music.' The pandemonium created by a number of musical instruments is subsumed under the word 'music.' Then one goes all the way to listen to it. The same state of affairs prevails in the case of the seen. It is because the *Tathāgata* has understood this fact that he does not imagine a thing worth seeing or hearing. The same applies to the other sensory data.

Then comes the phrase *daṭṭhāraṃ na maññati*, "does not imagine a seer." Here we have the direct expression of voidness – the voidness of a self or anything belonging to a self. Now that dog on the plank has not understood the fact that there is a mutual relationship between the looking dog and the seen dog. It is because of the looking dog that the seen dog is seen. There is a conditioned relationship between the two.

In other words, dependent on eye and forms arises eye-consciousness, *cakkhuñca paṭicca rūpe ca uppajjati cakkhu-viññāṇaṃ.*[15] The mere presence of the eye is not enough for eye consciousness to arise, but dependent on eye and forms, arises eye-consciousness.

Though stated simply, it has a depth that is not easy to fathom. To say that it is dependent on eye and form is to admit that it is dependently arisen. The law of dependent arising is already implicated. There is therefore no seer, apart from the phenomenon of seeing, according to the *Tathāgata*. He does not imagine a seer, *daṭṭhāraṃ na maññati*. For the worldling, the bare act of seeing carries with it a perception of 'one who sees.' He has a notion of a self and something belonging to a self.

The same teaching is found in the *Bāhiyasutta*. After instructing Bāhiya to stop at just the seen, the heard, the sensed and the cognized, the Buddha goes on to outline the end result of that training:

---

15 E.g. M I 111, *Madhupiṇḍikasutta*.

> *Yato kho te, Bāhiya, diṭṭhe diṭṭhamattaṃ bhavissati, sute sutamattaṃ bhavissati, mute mutamattaṃ bhavissati, viññāte viññātamattaṃ bhavissati, tato tvaṃ Bāhiya na tena. Yato tvaṃ Bāhiya na tena, tato tvaṃ Bāhiya na tattha. Yato tvaṃ Bāhiya na tattha, tato tvaṃ Bāhiya nev' idha na huraṃ na ubhayamantarena. Es' ev' anto dukkhassa.*[16]

> "And when to you, Bāhiya, there will be in the seen just the seen, in the heard just the heard, in the sensed just the sensed, in the cognized just the cognized, then, Bāhiya, you are not by it. And when, Bāhiya, you are not by it, then, Bāhiya, you are not in it. And when, Bāhiya, you are not in it, then, Bāhiya, you are neither here nor there nor in between. This, itself, is the end of suffering."

That is to say, when, Bāhiya, you have gone through that training of stopping at just the seen, the heard, the sensed and the cognized, then you would not be imagining in terms of them. The algebraic-like expressions *na tena* and *na tattha* have to be understood as forms of egoistic imagining, *maññanā.*

When you do not imagine in terms of them, you would not be in them. There would be no involvement in regard to them. In the case of that music, for instance, you would not be in the orchestra. The egoistic imagining, implicating involvement with the music, presupposes a hearer, *sotaraṃ*, dwelling in the orchestra.

"When, Bāhiya, you do not dwell in it," *yato tvaṃ Bāhiya na tattha*, "then, Bāhiya, you are neither here, nor there, nor in between the two," *tato tvaṃ Bāhiya nev' idha na huraṃ na ubhayamantarena*. This itself is the end of suffering. In other words, you would have realized voidness, *suññatā*. The expressions *daṭṭhāraṃ na maññati*, "does not imagine a seer"; *sotāraṃ na maññati*, "does not imagine a hearer"; *motāraṃ na maññati*, "does not imagine a sensor"; and *viññātāraṃ na maññati*,

---

16 Ud 8, *Bāhiyasutta*.

"does not imagine a knower," have to be understood in this light. The *Tathāgata* does not even imagine a thinker apart from thought. This is the plane of the void, *suññatābhūmi*, the perfect realization of the corelessness or essencelessness of the seen, the heard, the sensed and the cognized.

The very absence of *maññanā*, or "egoistic imagining," is to be understood by *suññatābhūmi*, or "the plane of the void." The worldling takes seriously the subject-object relationship in the grammatical structure, as it seems the simplest explanation of phenomena. Because there is something to be seen, there is someone who sees. Because there is someone who sees, there is something to be seen.

There is a duality between these two. To understand the law of dependent arising is to be free from this duality. It is the ability to see a concatenation of conditions, a conglomeration of causal factors – an assemblage instead of a bifurcation.

The way of the worldlings, however, is to follow the subject-object relationship, a naive acceptance of the grammatical structure, which is the easiest mode of communication of ideas. They are misled by it to take seriously such notions as 'one who sees' and a 'thing seen,' 'one who hears' and a 'thing heard,' but the *Tathāgata* is free from that delusion. Now we come to the fifth section of the discourse, known as *tādibhūmi*, the "plane of the such." It runs:

> *Iti kho, bhikkhave, tathāgato diṭṭha-suta-muta-viññātabbesu dhammesu tādī yeva tādī, tamhā ca pana tādimhā añño tādī uttaritaro vā paṇītataro vā n' atthī'ti vadāmi.*
>
> "Thus, monks, the *Tathāgata*, being such in regard to all phenomena, seen, heard, sensed and cognized, is such. Moreover than he who is such there is none other higher or more excellent, I declare."

The most difficult word, here, is *tādī*. We have already explained it to some extent. It can be rendered by "such" or "thus." The commentary explains it by the phrase *tāditā nāma ekasadisatā*,[17] "suchness means to be always alike."

By way of illustration, the commentary states *Tathāgato ca yādiso lābhādīsu, tādisova alābhādīsu*, "as he is in regard to gain, etc., so is the *Tathāgata* in regard to loss, etc." The allusion here is to the eight worldly vicissitudes, gain/loss, fame/ill-fame, praise/blame, and pleasure/pain.[18]

But this explanation is rather misleading, as it ignores a certain deep dimension of the meaning of the term *tādī*. When it is said "as he is in regard to gain, so is he in regard to loss," one can ask: 'How is he in regard to gain?' This is imprecise as a meaning.

However, the commentator happens to quote from the *Mahāniddesa* another explanation, which is more to the point. It is briefly stated as *iṭṭhāniṭṭhe tādī*, "such in regard to the desirable and the undesirable"; and explained as *lābhepi tādī, alābhepi tādī, yasepi tādī,*[19] *ayasepi tādī, nindāyapi tādī, pasaṃsāyapi tādī, sukhepi tādī, dukkhepi tādī*, "he is such in gain as well as in loss, he is such in fame as well as in ill-fame . . ." etc. That is the correct explanation. Instead of saying "as he is in gain, so is he in loss," we have here a continuous suchness in regard to all vicissitudes. He is such in gain as well as in loss, he is such in fame as well as in ill-fame, he is such in praise as well as in blame, he is such in pleasure as well as in pain.

The reason for this suchness we have explained on an earlier occasion.[20] In one sense, the term *tādī* stands for the understanding of the norm called *tathatā*. The other implication is the abstinence from the tendency towards identification or acquisition, meant by *tammayatā*. This exemplary trait is called *atammayatā*. This is an extremely important term, occurring in the discourses, which, however, has fallen into neglect at present.

---

[17] Mp III 40.

[18] A IV 157, *Paṭhamalokadhammasutta*.

[19] Nid II 459.

[20] See sermon 21.

In the case of music, for instance, *tammayatā* would imply an attachment to it that amounts to an identification with it. *Tammayo* means "made of that," as in *suvaṇṇamaya*, "made of gold," and *rajatamaya*, "made of silver." To be free from this *tammayatā*, is to be *tādī*, "such," that is to say, not to be of that stuff, *atammayatā*. The attitude of not leaning on or grasping is meant by it.

The quality of being *tādī*, or "such," is often rendered by "firmness," "steadfastness," and "immovability." Generally, one associates firmness, immovability or stability with holding on or leaning on. But here we have just the contrary. Not to hold on to anything, is to be 'such.' This suchness has a flexibility of a higher order, or an adaptability. The adaptability characteristic of the sage who lives on *piṇḍapāta*, or alms-food, is highlighted in the following verse:

Alatthaṃ yadidaṃ sādhu,
nālatthaṃ kusalām iti,
ubhayeneva so tādī,
rukkhaṃ va upanivattati.[21]

"Suppose I got it, well and good,
Suppose I didn't get, that's fine too,
In both circumstances he is such,
And comes back [like one who walks up to a] tree."

This kind of adaptability and resilience is also implied by the term *tādī*. Though the term is sometimes rendered by the word "steadfast," it does not stand for any rigidity. Instead, it carries implications of a non-rigid resilience.

This is a wonderful quality in *Tathāgatas* and *arahants*. We may compare it to a revolving swing in a children's playground. One who is seated in a revolving swing has nothing to get upset about falling headlong when the swing goes up. The seats are hung in such a way that they also turn with the revolving motion of the

21 Sn 712, *Nālakasutta*.

swing. Had they been rigidly fixed, one seated there would fall off the seat when it goes up. It is that kind of resilience that is characteristic of the quality of *tāditā*, or "suchness." This is how we have to understand the famous lines in the *Mahāmaṅgalasutta*:

> *Phuṭṭhassa lokadhammehi,*
> *cittam yassa na kampati,*[22]
>
> "Whose mind remains unshaken,
> When touched by worldly vicissitudes."

This quality of being unshaken, this immovability, is the result of not grasping. It comes when there is no tenacious clinging. It is to one who rests on or leans on something that there is dislodgement or instability.

Now I am leaning on the wall, if someone does damage to the wall, I would get shaken.That is what is suggested by the axiom *nissitassa calitaṃ, anissitassa calitaṃ n'atthi*, "to one who is attached, there is dislodgement, to the one detached, there is no dislodgement."[23] The worldling, on the other hand, thinks that to lean on or to rely on something is the mark of stability.

So it seems that the term *tādī* has an extraordinary dimension of meaning. In this particular context, however, the suchness spoken of does not concern the eight worldly vicissitudes like gain and loss. Here it carries a special nuance as is evident from the statement:

Iti kho, bhikkhave, tathāgato diṭṭha-suta-muta-viññātabbesu dhammesu tādī yeva tādī. "Thus, monks, the *Tathāgata*, being such in regard to all phenomena, seen, heard, sensed and cognized, is such."

The suchness here meant is about the views adhered to by the worldlings. In regard to things seen, heard, sensed and cognized,

---

[22] Sn 268, *Mahāmaṅgalasutta*.

[23] Ud 81, *Catutthanibbānapaṭisaṃyuttasutta*.

the worldlings go on asserting dogmatically *idam eva saccaṃ, mogham aññaṃ*, "this alone is true, all else is false." But the *Tathāgata* has no such dogmatic involvement. He only analytically exposes them for what they are.

As we tried to illustrate by the simile of the dog on the plank, the *Tathāgata* simply penetrates into their dependently arisen nature and declares that all those views are dependent on contact, *phassapaccayā*. That is the *tādī* quality meant here. If we are to understand the plane of suchness, *tādībhūmi*, in a deeper sense, this is how we have to appreciate its significance. Now we come to the couplet forming the grand finale to the *Kāḷakārāmasutta*:

Yaṃ kiñci diṭṭhaṃ va sutaṃ mutaṃ vā,
ajjhositaṃ saccamutaṃ paresaṃ,
na tesu tādī sayasaṃvutesu,
saccaṃ musā vā pi paraṃ daheyyaṃ.

Etañca sallaṃ paṭigacca disvā,
ajjhositā yattha pajā visattā,
jānāmi passāmi tath' eva etaṃ,
ajjhositaṃ n' atthi tathāgatānaṃ.

In the first verse, we have the difficult term *sayasaṃvutesu*, which we rendered by "amidst those who are entrenched in their own views." The term carries insinuations of philosophical inbreeding, which often accounts for dogmatic adherence to views. The *Tathāgata* declares that he does not hold as true or false any of the concepts of individual truths based on what is seen, heard, sensed and cognized by others, because of his suchness. Being such, he does not categorically label any of those views as true or false. He penetrates into and analyses the psychological background of all those dogmatic views and understands them as such.

In the final verse, he declares that he has seen well in advance "the barb on which mankind is hooked impaled." The barb is none other than the dogmatic assertion, 'I know, I see, it is verily so.' Having seen this barb, well in advance, the *Tathāgata* entertains no dogmatic involvement of that sort.

The precise meaning of some words and phrases here is a matter of controversy. A discussion of them might throw more light on their deeper nuances. The most difficult term seems to be *sayasaṃvuta*. The commentary gives the following explanation:

'Sayasaṃvutesu'ti 'sayameva saṃvaritvā piyāyitvā gahitagahaṇesu diṭṭhigatikesū'ti attho. Diṭṭhigatikā hi 'sayaṃ saṃvutā'ti vuccanti.[24] "*Sayasaṃvutesu* means among those dogmatic view-holders, who have grasped those views, having recollected them and cherished them. Dogmatic view-holders are called *sayasaṃvuta*."

According to the commentary, the term *sayasaṃvuta* refers to persons who hold dogmatic views. But we interpreted it as a reference to such views themselves.

By way of clarification, we may allude to some discourses in the *Aṭṭhakavagga* of the *Sutta Nipāta*, which bring up a wealth of material to substantiate the salient points in the *Kāḷakārāmasutta*, while throwing more light on the particular term in question. The chapter called *Aṭṭhakavagga* in the *Sutta Nipāta* in particular embodies a deep analysis of the controversies among contemporary dogmatists.

Let us, first of all, take up for comment some verses that throw more light on the meaning of the term *sayasaṃvuta* from the *Cūḷaviyūhasutta*. That discourse unfolds itself in the form of question and answer. The commentary explains, that this medium of dialogue was adopted by the Buddha to resolve the clash of philosophical moot points current in the society, and that the interlocutor is a replica of the Buddha himself, created by his psychic power.[25] Be that as it may, the relevant question for the present context is presented as follows:

Kasmā nu saccāni vadanti nānā,
pavādiyāse kusalā vadānā,

---

[24] Mp III 41.

[25] Pj II 554

saccāni su tāni bahūni nānā,
udāhu te takkam anussaranti.[26]

"Why do they proclaim various truths,
Claiming to be experts each in his field,
Are there several and various truths,
Or do they merely follow logical consistency?"

The Buddha's reply to it is as follows.

Na h'eva saccāni bahūni nānā,
aññatra saññāya niccāni loke,
takkañ ca diṭṭhīsu pakappayitvā,
'saccaṃ musā'ti dvayadhammam āhu.

"There are no several and various truths,
That are permanent in the world, apart from perception,
It is by manipulating logic in speculative views,
That they speak of two things called 'truth and falsehood.'"

There is no plurality in the concept of truth, apart from the perception based on which they declare various speculative views. It seems that the Buddha grants the possibility of various levels of perception as a truth for all times, though he does not accept a plurality of truths, arising out of a variety of speculative views based on them.

He understands the psychology of logic, having seen penetratively the perceptual background of each and every view. He accepts as a psychological fact that such and such a perception could precipitate such and such a view. Therefore, in a limited or relative sense, they are 'true.'

The dichotomy between truth and falsehood has arisen in the world due to a manipulation of logic on individual viewpoints.

---

[26] Sn 885, *CūḷaViyūhasutta.*

This fact comes up for further comment in the *Mahāviyūhasutta* that follows:

> *Sakaṃ hi dhammaṃ paripuṇṇam āhu,*
> *aññasssa dhammaṃ pana hīnaṃ āhu,*
> *evam pi viggayha vivādiyanti,*
> *sakaṃ sakaṃ sammutim āhu sacaṃ.*[27]

This verse describes how debating parties go on clashing with each other. They call their own system of thought perfect, and the other system of thought inferior. Thus they quarrel and dispute. Their own individual viewpoint they assert as true. The phrase *sakaṃ sakaṃ sammutim*, "each his own viewpoint," is somewhat suggestive of *sayasaṃvutesu*, the problematic term in the *Kāḷakārāmasutta*.

Yet another verse from the *Pasūrasutta* in the *Aṭṭhakavagga* exposes the biases and prejudices underlying these individual truths:

> *'Idh' eva suddhi' iti vādiyanti,*
> *nāññesu dhammesu visuddhim āhu,*
> *yaṃ nissitā tattha subhaṃ vadānā,*
> *paccekasaccesu puthū niviṭṭhā.*[28]

> "'Here in this system is purity,' they assert polemically,
> They are not prepared to grant purity in other systems of thought,
> Whatever view they lean on, that they speak in praise of,
> They are severally entrenched in their own individual truths."

---

[27] Sn 905, *MahāViyūhasutta*.

[28] Sn 824, *Pasūrasutta*.

The last line is particularly relevant, as it brings up the concept of *paccekasacca*. To be a *Paccekabuddha* means to be enlightened for oneself. So the term *paccekasacca* can mean "truth for oneself." Those who hold conflicting views go on debating entrenched each in his own concept of truth.

The three expressions *pacekasacca, sakaṃ sakaṃ sammutim* and *sayasaṃvutesu* convey more or less the same idea. The words *tesu sayasaṃvutesu* refer to those narrow viewpoints to which they are individually confined, or remain closeted in. The *Tathāgata* does not hold as true or false any of those views limited by the self-bias.

Another lapse in the commentary to the *Kāḷakārāmasutta* is its comment on the phrase *paraṃ daheyyaṃ*. It takes the word *paraṃ* in the sense of "supreme," *uttamaṃ katvā*, whereas in this context it means "the other." Here, too, we may count on the following two lines of the *Cūḷaviyūhasutta* of the *Sutta Nipāta* in support of our interpretation:

> *Yen' eva 'bālo'ti paraṃ dahāti,*
> *tenātumānaṃ 'kusalo'ti cāha.*[29]

> "That by which one dubs the other a fool,
> By that itself one calls oneself an expert."

From this it is clear that the phrase *paraṃ dahāti* means "dubs another." The last two lines of the *Kāḷakārāmasutta* are of utmost importance:

> *Jānāmi passāmi tath' eva etaṃ,*
> *ajjhositaṃ n' atthi tathāgatānaṃ.*

> "I know I see, it is verily so,
> No such clinging for the *Tathāgatas*."

---

[29] Sn 888, *CūḷaViyūhasutta*.

Worldlings dogmatically grasp the data heaped up by their six sense-bases, but the *Tathāgatas* have no such entanglements in regard to sensory knowledge. Why so? It is because they have seen the cessation of the six sense-bases.

By way of illustration, we may compare this seeing of the cessation of the six sense-bases to an exposure of the inner mechanism of a high-speed engine by removing the bonnet. In the *Dvayamsutta*, from which we quoted in our last sermon, the Buddha showed us the functioning of the gigantic machine called the six-fold sense-base, its vibrations, revolutions, beats and running gears. The discourse analyses the mechanism in such words as:

> *Cakkhu aniccaṃ vipariṇāmi aññathābhāvi. Rūpā aniccā vipariṇāmino aññathābhāvino. Itthetaṃ dvayaṃ calañceva vyayañca aniccaṃ vipariṇāmi aññathābhāvi.*[30]

> "Eye is impermanent, changing, becoming otherwise. Forms are impermanent, changing, becoming otherwise. Thus this dyad is unstable, evanescent, impermanent, changing, becoming otherwise."

The discourse proceeds in this vein and concludes with the words:

> *Phuṭṭho, bhikkhave, vedeti, phuṭṭho ceteti, phuṭṭho sañjānāti. Itthete pi dhammā calā ceva vayā ca aniccā vipariṇāmino aññathābhāvino.*

> "Contacted, monks, one feels, contacted one intends, contacted one perceives. Thus these things, too, are unstable, evanescent, impermanent, changing and becoming otherwise."

---

[30] S IV 67, *Dutiyadvayamsutta*.

The concluding reference is to the products of the six sense-bases. Feelings, intentions and perceptions, arising due to contact, are also unstable, evanescent, impermanent, changing and becoming otherwise.

The sum total of percepts is indicated by the words *diṭṭha*, *suta*, *muta* and *viññāta*. The totality of percepts are made up or 'prepared,' *saṅkhata*. The term *saṅkhata* has nuances suggestive of 'production.' If we take the six-fold sense-base as a high-speed machine, productive of perceptions, the Buddha has revealed to us the workings of its intricate machinery. Each and every part of this machine is unstable, evanescent, impermanent, changing and becoming otherwise.

The Buddha understood the made up or prepared nature, *saṅkhata*, of all these, as well as the preparations, *saṅkhārā*, that go into it. That is why the Buddha has no dogmatic involvement in regard to the products of this machine, the totality of all what is seen, heard, sensed and cognized, *diṭṭha*, *suta*, *muta*, *viññāta*. None of them is substantial. They are essenceless and insubstantial. There is nothing worthwhile grasping here as apart from the activities or preparations that are dynamic in themselves.

So far we have tried to understand the state of affairs with reference to this discourse. But now let us take up a canonical simile that facilitates our understanding. The Buddha has compared consciousness to a magic show in the *Pheṇapiṇḍūpamasutta* of the *Khandhasaṃyutta* we had already cited:[31]

> *Pheṇapiṇḍūpamaṃ rūpaṃ,*
> *vedanā bubbuḷūpamā,*
> *marīcikūpamā saññā,*
> *saṅkhārā kadalūpamā,*
> *māyūpamañca viññāṇaṃ,*
> *dīpitādiccabandhunā.*

---

[31] S III 142, *Pheṇapiṇḍūpamasutta*, see sermon 11

"Form is like a mass of foam,
And feeling but an airy bubble,
Perception is like a mirage,
And formations a banana trunk,
Consciousness is a magic show [a juggler's trick entire],
[All these similes] were made known by the kinsman of
the sun."

As a matter of fact, the verse itself is a mnemonic summary of a certain sermon delivered by the Buddha. According to it, the Buddha, the kinsman of the sun, has compared form to a mass of foam, feeling to a water bubble, perception to a mirage, preparations to a banana trunk, and consciousness to a magic show.

What is of relevance to us here is the comparison of consciousness to a magic show. The simile of the magic show is presented in that *sutta* in the following words:

Seyyathāpi, bhikkhave, māyākāro vā māyākārantevāsī vā cātummahāpathe māyaṃ vidaṃseyya. Tam enaṃ cakkhumā puriso passeyya nijjhāyeyya yoniso upaparikkheyya. Tassa taṃ passato nijjhāyato yoniso upaparikkhato rittakaññeva khāyeyya tucchakaññeva khāyeyya asārakaññeva khāyeyya. Kiñhi siyā, bhikkhave, māyāya sāro?

Evam eva kho, bhikkhave, yaṃ kiñci viññāṇaṃ atītānāgatapaccuppannaṃ, ajjhattaṃ vā bahiddhā vā, oḷārikaṃ vā sukhumaṃ vā, hīnaṃ vā paṇītaṃ vā, yaṃ dūre santike vā, taṃ bhikkhu passati nijjhāyati yoniso upaparikkhati. Tassa taṃ passato nijjhāyato yoniso upaparikkhato rittakaññeva khāyati tucchakaññeva khāyati asārakaññeva khāyati. Kiñhi siyā, bhikkhave, viññāṇe sāro?

"Suppose, monks, a magician or a magician's apprentice should hold a magic show at the four crossroads and a keen-sighted man should see it, ponder over it and reflect on it radically. Even as he sees it, ponders over it and reflects on it radically, he would find it empty, he would find it hollow, he would find it void of essence. What essence, monks, could there be in a magic show?

"Even so, monks, whatever consciousness – be it past, future or present, in oneself or external, gross or subtle, inferior or superior, far or near – a monk sees it, ponders over it and reflects on it radically. And even as he sees it, ponders over it and reflects on it radically, he would find it empty; he would find it hollow; he would find it void of essence. What essence monks, could there be in a consciousness? . . ."

Form is like a mass of foam
And feeling – but an airy bubble.
Perception is like a mirage
And formations a plantain tree.

Consciousness is a magic-show,
A juggler's trick entire,
All these similes were made known
By the 'Kinsman-of-the-Sun."[32]

---

[32] S.III.142. Cp. The central verse of the *Diamond Sutra*. (Bh. Isidatta)

Sadhu! Sadhu! Sadhu!

By the Same Author

- Concept and Reality in Early Buddhist Thought, BPS1970
- Samyutta Nikaya – An anthology, Part II, Wheel Series No. 183/185, BPS 1972
- Ideal Solitude – Wheel No. 188, BPS 1973
- The Magic of the Mind, BPS 1974
- Uttaritara Hudekalawa – Damsak No. 172/173 – BPS 1990
- Towards Calm and Insight – Free Distribution 1991
- Vidasun Upades ("Insight Instruction"), Free Distribution 1996
- Nivane Niveema (Nibbana Sermons – The Mind Stilled), Free Distribution since 1997
- From Topsy-turvydom to wisdom – volume 1 (Essays written for "beyondthenet.net"), Free Distribution 1998
- Pahan Kanuwa Dharma Deshana – ("Sermons given at the forest hermitage of Pahan Kanuwa"), Vol.1 for free distribution 1999
- Seeing Through, Free Distribution 1999
- Hitaka Mahima, Free Distribution 1999
- Nivane Niveema – Library Edition – Part I, 2000
- Hita thanima, 2000
- Pahan Kanuwa Dharma Desana, Vol. 2

- Towards a better world – Translation of Lowada Sangarawa, 2000
- Pavatma ha navatama, 2001
- Athi Hati Dakma, 2001
- Pahan Kanuwa Dharma Deshana, Vol. III. 2002
- Kaya Anuwa Giya Sihiya ("Mindfulness of the Body"), 2001
- Divi Katare Sanda Andura, 2001
- Pahan Kanuwa Dharma Deshana, Vol. I, 2003
- Nibbana – The Mind Stilled – Vol. I, 2003
- Abinikmana, 2003
- Hitaka Mahima II, 2003
- Nibbana and the Fire Simile, 2009

For more information about Ven. K. Ñāṇananda's writings and meditation methods as developed by Ven. Ñāṇārāma and Ven. Ñāṇananda visit us at:

www.nibbanam.com

Appendix

The Heretic Sage

A Dhamma-Interview with Ven. Bhikkhu K. Ñānananda by Ven. Bhikkhu Yogananda

Potgulgal Hermitage,
Devalegama, Sri Lanka 2009

How does a bhikkhu know the ford? Here a bhikkhu goes from time to time to such bhikkhus who have learned much, who are well versed in the tradition, who maintain the Dhamma, the Discipline, and the Codes, and he enquires and asks questions of them thus: 'How is this, venerable sir? What is the meaning of this?' These venerable ones reveal to him what has not been revealed, clarify what is not clear, and remove his doubts about numerous things that give rise to doubt. That is how a bhikkhu knows the ford.

–Mahāgopālaka Sutta (MN 33)

THE HERETIC SAGE (PART 1)

Bhante Ñāṇananda is not the monk I thought he would be. He is much more. As I recall my first meeting with him in his small cave kuti, the first word that crosses my mind is "innocent". For a senior monk who has been in the order for more than 40 years, he is disarmingly simple, unpretentious and friendly. Childlike even. But you would not get that impression from his classics *Concept and Reality in Early Buddhist Thought* and *The Magic of the Mind.*

I was introduced to his writings by my friend Ven. Sumana, an English monk. It was Bhante Ñāṇananda's *Nibbāna – The Mind Stilled* collection that I first read. Later I would go through *The Magic of the Mind*, which I would find both enchanting and baffling at the same time. It would take me even longer to take up *Concept and Reality*. All of them would leave a lasting impression on me, and define the way I interpret the Dhamma. But not before completely misconceiving what he was saying, engage in a lengthy correspondence with him, and finally meet him only to learn that I was miserably wrong on many things all that time. And it would be a meeting I'll always remember.

I was a staunch 'Ñāṇavirist' until that meeting, so for me *Nibbāna – The Mind Stilled* was more or less a commentary on *Notes on Dhamma* by Ven. Ñāṇavira Thera. Sure enough there were some passages here and there that took some effort to beat into submission, but language is a flexible medium and the mind is infinitely creative. On the few occasions when that problem could not be easily shrugged off, I resorted to considering Bhante Ñāṇananda the scholar who needed to bow in front of the experience of Ven. Ñāṇavira.

The first *vassa* in 2009 was a time when my understanding of the Dhamma went through some changes. I noted those thoughts down, and sent some of it to Bhante Ñāṇananda for review. A particularly long letter that ran into more than 50 pages took two months for a reply. Bhante thought it would take an equally long letter to explain the matters, which he was not in a position to write: he had just returned from a two-month stay in the hospital. Instead, he invited me to visit him in his monastery and stay a few days. Which created a few problems, because Ven. Katukurunde Ñāṇananda Thera is an outcast.

His critical analysis of Buddhist texts and the unwillingness to adhere to the commentarial tradition has made Bhante Ñāṇananda a radical and a heretic. He probably knew what he was getting into from the very beginning. In the introduction to *Concept and Reality*, written in 1969, he states:

It is feared that the novelty of some of our interpretations will draw two types of extreme reaction. One the one hand, it might give rise to a total antipathy towards the critical analysis of doctrinal points as attempted here. On the other, it might engender an unreasonable distrust leading to a sweeping condemnation of the commentaries as a whole. This work has failed in its purpose if its critical scrutiny of the occasional shortcomings in the commentarial literature makes anyone forget his indebtedness to the commentaries for his knowledge of the Dhamma.[1]

Over the years he would become less apologetic and more straightforward in his assertions, but his criticisms would always remain subtle, his delightful sarcasm barely noticed unless approached with the necessary background knowledge and the attention they deserve. For example, criticising the*Ābhidhammika* atomism and the commentarial *sabhāva* (own-essence) doctrine, he says:

An insight meditator, too, goes through a similar experience when he contemplates on name-and-form, seeing the four elements as empty and void of essence, which will give him at least an iota of the conviction that this drama of existence is empty and insubstantial. He will realize that, as in the case of the dumb show, he is involved with things that do not really exist. [...] Seeing the reciprocal relationship between name-and-form, he is disinclined to dabble in concepts or gulp down a dose of prescriptions. [...] What is essential here, is the very understanding of essencelessness. If one sits down to draw up lists of concepts and prescribe them, it would only lead to a mental constipation.[2]

It is in his latest booklet *Nibbana and the Fire Simile* that I found him being the most direct:

There is a flush of Buddhist literature thriving in the West which attempts to interpret this fire simile in the light of the Vedic myth that the extinguished fire 'goes into hiding'. Though the Buddha succeeded in convincing the Brahmin interlocutors of the dependently arisen nature of the fire by the reductio-ad-absurdum method, these scholars seem to be impervious to his arguments. What is worse, misinterpretations have even sought refuge in blatant mistranslations of sacred texts. [...]

The term 'extinction' is anathema to the West in general. Perhaps as a euphemism, 'extinguishment' might be 'passable'. But rather than playing with the 'fire-simile' it is better to accept the obvious conclusions, willy nilly.[3]

To appreciate the rebelliousness of these passages and many others like it, one needs to understand the context in which they were written. The monastic Sangha in general is quite dogmatic and traditionalist, not entirely welcoming of challenging views. When the Nibbāna sermons were delivered at the Nissarana Vanaya, Bhante Ñāṇananda had the backing of his teacher, the illustrious Elder Ven. Matara Sri Ñāṇārāma Mahathera, who not only allowed him the freedom but invited and encouraged him to express his radical views. Even then he was criticized by many of his colleagues. Those views were a main reason that led to Bhante Ñāṇananda's departure from the Nissarana Vanaya after the death of Ven. Ñāṇārāma. He left on his own accord, and set up a small monastery in Devalegama: Pothgulgala Aranya. It was there that I first met him in November last year.

It is late in the evening that I arrive, and Bhante Ñāṇananda is out visiting a doctor, something that was becoming more frequent as his asthma was getting worse. After he returns at around 10 pm, I'm taken to his small cave kuti by his student Ven. Damita. I'm surprised to see how frail and almost fragile Bhante Ñāṇananda is. I introduce myself; he slaps his head and laughs, and asks: "How did you manage to escape?"

The next day, after *piṇḍapāta* I went to visit him in his kuti. He warmly welcomes me. I pull out his last reply to my letters in which he provided some points to ponder on, and start asking him for clarifications on each of the points. As I sit there on the floor listening to his thoroughly informative commentary, some of my cherished views get blasted to bits.

Answering a question dealing with the structure of experience, Bhante Ñāṇananda quotes the Hemakamāṇavapucchā of the Sutta Nipāta (from memory, of course), and uses the simile of the plaintain trunk to illustrate the way knowledge of experience is gained.

"It's a beautiful sutta, where Hemaka explains the reason why he gained faith in the Buddha.

Ye me pubbe viyākaṃsu
Huraṃ gotama sāsanaṃ,
Iccāsi iti bhavissati
Sabbaṃ taṃ itihitihaṃ
Sabbaṃ taṃ takkavaḍḍhanaṃ
Nāhaṃ tattha abhiramiṃ.
Tvañ ca me dhammam akkhāhi taṅhā nigghātanaṃ muni,
Yaṃ viditvā sato caraṃ tare loke visattikaṃ.

Those in the past who explained their teachings to me outside Gotama's dispensation said "so it was and so it will be". All that is "so and so" talk; all that promoted speculation. I did not delight in them. And you, O Sage, do expound to me the teaching of destruction of craving, knowing which faring mindfully I shall cross over the clinging in the world.

"Those verses cut to the heart of the problem. They show the value of this *akālika* Dhamma. *Taṇhā* is something that is here and now, and it is *taṇhakkhayo* that is Nibbāna.

"Now, the simile of the plaintain trunk comes in here. At the end, all of this is just a heap of *saṇkhāra*–s – preparations, which the Buddha has equated to a plaintain trunk. It is not necessary to roll the sheaths to realize the pithlessness of it; one just needs to take the sword of *paññā* and cut through. From the cross section itself one realizes. Actually that is what is meant by understanding *paṭiccasamuppāda*, not memorizing the 12 links. The Dhamma is *akālika*because of the principle."

In his letter Bhante has mentioned the importance of understanding the difference between *vijānāti* and *pajānāti* when it comes to discussing *viññāṇa*. I ask for an elaboration.

"This is something that tends to get overlooked. There are many words that share the *ñā* root in the texts: *sañjānāti, vijānāti, pajānāti, abhijānāti, parijānāti, ājānāti*. There may be more. It is with a reason that there are these differences between them.

"It is commonly known that the root *ñā* stands for 'knowledge'. Why is it said'*vijānāti'* when it could have easily been said '*jānāti*'? Most translations just use 'knows'. But *vijānāti* means 'discriminatively knows'. What is the main job of*viññāṇa*? We can clarify from the Mahāvedalla Sutta. There we get the phrases*yaṃ sañjānāti taṃ vijānāti* and *yaṃ vijānāti taṃ pajānāti*. 'What one perceives, that one discriminates' and 'what one discriminates, that one knows'.

"From the examples that follow that phrase we can understand the *jānana*level of each. For *sañjānāti*: *Nīlakampi sañjānāti, pītakampi sañjānāti, lohitakampi sañjānāti, odātampi sañjānāti* – using colours. When someone is coming from a distance, all we see is just some blob of colour. When he comes closer we separate him from the others: 'oh, he is this person, not the other'. When we know deeply, at *pajānāti* level, all is the same, just the four elements, but let's leave that aside for the moment.

"What are the examples given for *vijānāti*? There are two; the first is *sukhan'ti pi vijānāti, dukkhan'ti pi vijānāti, adukkhamasukhan'ti pi vijānāti*. This clearly shows that*vijānana* is unique to living beings, not found in trees and rocks. The first level of*viññāṇa* is in discriminating between different feelings. For instance, in the Mahānidāna Sutta we find the Buddha asking Ven. Ananda Thera whether there would be any self notion where there is no feeling. The answer is 'no'. That shows that feeling is fundamental. So what is there in feeling? Bifurcation, which is the most fundamental delusion."

He pauses to say how glad he is that there is no need to use 'footnotes' when talking to me. I'm glad I did the homework. If you want to find Bhante Ñāṇananda in his zone, do the necessary preparatory studies, and be willing to put up with copious amounts of Pāḷi, not all of which would be translated.

But then he asks "Do you remember the other example for *vijānāti*?" I don't.

"There is a second example for *vijānāti* from the Khajjanīya Sutta: *ambilampi vijānāti, tittakampi vijānāti, kaṭukampi vijānāti, madhurakampi vijānāti, khārikampi vijānāti, akhārikampi vijānāti, loṇikampi vijānāti, aloṇikampi vijānāti* — different tastes. Do you see any difference between knowing colours and knowing tastes?"

I mumble my ignorance.

"With taste the discrimination is explicit. When we taste something, it takes a while to decide whether its sweet or sour or salty. Some foods we can't easily categorize by taste, like the *Nelli* fruit. But it is not essential to go that far: what is important is to remember that discriminating between different feeling tones is the main function of *viññāṇa*.

"A unique feature of *paṭiccasamuppāda* is the way one result becomes the cause for another. One pulls the other in.

When we take a pair of items in*paṭiccasamuppāda*, one member is also a member in the next pair. The very question whether *saññā* and *viññāṇa* are the same or different reeks of absolutism, an attempt to separate them into water-tight compartments. But their connectedness is pointed out in the Sutta with *yaṃ sañjānāti taṃ vijānāti, yaṃ vijānāti taṃ pajānāti*. This doesn't mean all three are the same either. The nuances are important.

"The difference between *viññāṇa* and *paññā* is explained as *paññā bhāvetabbā, viññāṇaṃ pariññeyyaṃ*: *paññā* is to be developed, *viññāṇa* is to be understood. When *paññā* is fulfilled, *viññāṇa* is fully comprehended. As in the magic show: to see through the magic is to miss the show."

The last sentence is a reference to Bhante Ñāṇananda's short masterpiece*The Magic of the Mind*.

"In the floodlights of *paññā* there is no room for the shadows of *viññāṇa*. The delusion of self love reflects a world, so there's the two: an I and a world. Reflections on the eye, reflections on the ear, reflections on the mind: taking these reflections that fall on the senses as true, the materialists go looking for a world out there. When the Buddha called all of that a mere illusion, he meant all, including concepts. That's why it is said *sabba dhammakkhayaṃpatto vimutto upadhisaṅkhaye*.[4] Mind and dhammas is the last resort of delusion."

This is one of the most controversial of Bhante Ñāṇananda's views. *The Magic of the Mind* discusses this topic at length. He has been called an idealist and an illusionist because of it; he rejects both accusations. Being a Ñāṇavirist at the time, this 'illusionist' interpretation was something I too found difficult to accept, especially in light of Ven. Ñāṇavira's explicit and vehement rejection of the notion of māyā as a hindu concept shared by the Mahayanists.

"It is *viññāṇa* that discriminates between a sense and an object. The *Ābhidhammikas* are stuck thinking that even when all else falls apart *mano viññāṇa*remains. It is like we separating a flowing river in to parts, naming them, and then putting the parts back together to create a river. I remember something Dr. W.S. Karunaratne said: 'the grammar of nature does not correspond to the grammar of language'. That's a nice saying. This is beautifully illustrated in thePoṭṭhapāda Sutta. We separate the flux of existence in to parts, with *papañca-saññā-saṇkhā*. Those *saṇkhā*s are mere suggestions. They can only nudge us toward a certain direction. We cannot *understand* reality using them.

"Words have a limited capacity. It is okay to use them as long as one realizes their limitations. One who realizes their limitations would not be limited by them. The Poṭṭhapāda Sutta ends with *imā kho Citta lokasamaññā lokaniruttiyo lokavohārā lokapaññattiyo, yāhi Tathāgato voharati, aparāmasaṃ*. We must be so grateful to the ancient bhāṇakas: it would have been such a loss if that last word was forgotten. *Aparāmasaṃ* – not grasping. That's where the whole secret lies."

And then he laughs his delightful laugh, as if all that should have been obvious in the first place.

NOTES

1. Ñāṇananda. K. (1997) [1971], *Concept and Reality in Early Buddhist Thought*, Buddhist Publication Society, p. VI.
2. ^ Ñāṇananda, Katukurunde, Bhikkhu (2004), *Nibbāna – The Mind Stilled, Vol. II*, Dharma Grantha Mudrana Bharaya, p. 183.
3. ^ Ñāṇananda, Katukurunde, Bhikkhu (2010), *Nibbāna and the Fire Simile*, Dharma Grantha Mudrana Bharaya, p. 26.
4. ^ Sn 992

THE HERETIC SAGE (PART 2)

There is hardly any teaching that has given rise to more internal disputes among Buddhists than *paṭiccasamuppāda*. My next question is based on a comment by Bhante Ñāṇananda, which considers*paṭiccasamuppāda* as the golden mean between *atthitā* (existence) and *natthitā*(non-existence), replacing them with *samudaya* (arising) and *vaya* (passing away).

"Everyone knows that the middle way is the noble eightfold path. Everyone knows that the first sermon was the Dhammacakkappavattana Sutta. But if for some reason Āḷārakālāma or Uddaka Rāmaputta were alive, what we would have as the Dhammacakkappavattana would be something short like the Bāhiya Sutta, because they were facing a duality of a different nature.

"The five ascetics were given a teaching based on the ethical middle path, avoiding the two extremes of *kāmasukhallikānuyoga* and *attakilamathānuyoga*. But the middle path of right view is found in the Kaccānagotta Sutta, beautifully used by Ven. Nāgārjuna. When the Theravadins got engrossed with the Abhidhamma they forgot about it. The Mādhyamikas were alert enough to give it the attention it deserved.

"Extremism is found not only in ethics, but also in various kinds of views. The duality of *asti* and *nāsti* has a long history. I don't have much knowledge in the Vedas, but I remember in Ṛg Veda, in the Nāsādīya Sūkta,[1] you get the beautiful phrase *nāsadāsīn no sadāsīt tadānīṃ*. They were speculating about the beginnings: did existence come from non-existence or vice-versa.

"All those kinds of dualities, be it *asti/nāsti* or *sabbaṃ ekattaṃ/sabbaṃ puthuttaṃ* etc. were rejected by the Buddha: *majjhena Tathāgato Dhammaṃ deseti*– he taught the Dhamma *by the middle*. It's not just the middle path. It's not a mixture of 50% of each. We usually think that the middle is between two ends. It's a rejection of both ends and an introduction of a novel standpoint. Again, I remember Dr. W.S. Karunaratne saying how *paṭiccasamuppāda*, both as a philosophy and as a word, was novel to Indian thinking. There were other *vāda*-s such as *Adhiccasamuppāda* and *Issaranimmāna*, but not *paṭiccasamuppāda*, and it is not a *vāda*.

"The 'parroting' method of *paṭiccasamuppāda* involves dishing out the 12 terms, and even then, the *paṭiloma* is often forgotten. But the important thing is the principle, embedded in *'asmiṃ sati...'*, as seen in many Suttas. There again, I also made a mistake inadvertently when translating: in early editions of *The Magic of the Mind* I used 'this/that' following the standard English translations. That's completely wrong. It should be 'this/this'.

"In the formula we must take two elements that make a pair and analyse the conditionality between them. 'That' implies something outside the pair, which is misleading. *Paṭiccasamuppāda* is to be seen among the elements in a pair. The trick is in the middle; there's no point in holding on to the ends. And even that middle needs to be let go of, not grasped.

"When introducing *paṭiccasamuppāda* we first get the principle: *imasmiṃ sati idaṃ hoti, imassuppādā idaṃ uppajjati...* and then *yadidaṃ* – the word *yadidaṃ*clearly shows that what follows is an illustration. And then the well known 12 elements are given. But how is it in the *paṭiloma*? *Avijjaya tu eva* – there's an emphasis, as if to say: yes, the arising of suffering is a fact, it is the nature of the world, but it doesn't end there; from the fading away of that same ignorance this suffering could be made to cease. That is why we can't categorically say that any of these things exist or not. It entirely depends on *upādāna*. It is *upādāna*that decides between existence and non-existence. When there is no *upādāna* you get *anupādā parinibbāna*, right then and there. And that is why the Dhamma is*akālika*."

The impossibility of making categorical statements about existence was discussed extensively in Bhante Ñāṇananda's *The Magic of the Mind*, and he reminds me again about the importance of the Kālakārāma Sutta which provided the basis for that book. He quickly adds that the Buddha's stand is not something like that of his contemporary sceptic agnostic Sañjaya Bellaṭṭhiputta, the so-called eel-wriggler; rather, the situation is beyond what could be expressed through the linguistic medium. It can only be known individually: *paccattaṃ veditabbo.*

His interpretation of *paṭiccasamuppāda*, which dramatically deviates from the traditional exegesis, has earned Bhante Ñāṇananda a few vehement critics. He amusedly mentions a recent letter sent by a monk where he was accused of 'being a disgrace to the Theriya tradition'. This criticism, no doubt coming from a Theravāda dogmatist, is understandable seeing how accommodating Bhante Ñāṇananda is when it comes to teachings traditionally considered Mahāyāna, hence taboo for any self-respecting Theravādin. However, if one delves deeper, one would see that he is only trying to stay as close as possible to early Buddhist teachings.

"I didn't quote from the Mahāyāna texts in the Nibbāna sermons," he says, "because there was no need. All that was needed was already found in the Suttas. Teachers like Nāgārjuna brought to light what was already there but was hidden from view. Unfortunately his later followers turned it in to a *vāda*."

He goes on to quote two of his favourite verses from Ven. Nāgārjuna'sMūlamādhyamakakārikā (as usual, from memory):

Śūnyatā sarva-dṛṣṭīnaṃ proktā niḥsaranaṃ jinaiḥ,
yeṣāṃ śūnyatā-dṛṣtis tān asādhyān babhāṣire [MK 13.8]
The Victorious Ones have declared that emptiness is the relinquishing of all views. Those who are possessed of the view of emptiness are said to be incorrigible.

Sarva-dṛṣti-prahāṇāya yaḥ saddharmam adeśayat,
anukampam upādāya taṃ namasyāmi gautamaṃ [MK 26.30]
I reverently bow to Gautama who, out of compassion, has taught the doctrine in order to relinquish all views.

Bhante doesn't bother translating the verses; the ones provided above are by David Kalupahana.

"When I first read the Kārikā I too was doubting Ven. Nāgārjuna's sanity" he laughs. "But the work needs to be understood in the context. He was taking a jab at the Sarvāstivādins. To be honest, even the others deserve the rebuke, although they now try to get away by using Sarvāstivāda as an excuse. How skilled Ven. Nāgārjuna must have been, to compose those verses so elegantly and filling them with so much meaning, like the Dhammapada verses. It's quite amazing. This has been rightly understood by Prof. Kalupahana."

Prof. David J. Kalupahana is an eminent Sri Lankan scholar who stirred up another controversy when he portrayed Ven. Nāgārjuna as a reformist trying to resurrect early Buddhist teachings. He had been a lecturer during Bhante Ñāṇananda's university days as a layman at Peradeniya.

"If there is no substance in anything, what is left is emptiness. But many people are afraid of words. Like *śūnyatā*. They want to protect their four." With that 'irreverent' comment about the four *paramattha dhamma*-s of the Abhidhamma, Bhante Ñāṇananda breaks into amused laughter.

"If one does not approach the commentarial literature with a critical eye, one would be trapped. Unfortunately many are. In fact, I had to remove a few pages from the manuscript of *Concept and Reality* on Ven. Nyanaponika's request".

I'm disappointed to hear that, as *Concept and Reality* had already become my favourite commentary on the Buddhist teachings. There are some delightfully understated criticisms of the traditional views in the book, and I wonder what we have lost in the editorial process at the hands of Ven. Nyanaponika Thera, an undoubtedly very learned yet quite conservative scholar. When I express my dismay, Bhante Ñāṇananda adds that now he tends to agree with Ven. Nyanaponika.

"I did it unwillingly, but later on I also thought it may have been too much as it was my first book. Perhaps what is left is quite enough. The message still gets through. Some of that I could restate in the Nibbāna sermons as I had the backing of my teacher."

This teacher is Ven. Matara Sri Ñāṇārāma Mahathera, then abbot of the Nissarana Vanaya and an illustrious elder of the Sri Lankan forest tradition. I ask Bhante what the response of the Sangha was when those controversial sermons were delivered.

"Apart from a very few, the others didn't really understand. Some went around criticising, calling me a heretic. Fortunately it didn't get out of hand thanks to the teacher. But then some others like Ven. Khemānanda were very appreciative."

Our discussion moves on to Ven. Ñāṇavīra Thera. I wonder what influence this radical monk had on Bhante Ñāṇananda, but I can't muster enough courage to ask directly. So I just let him speak on his views.

"It is true, Ven. Ñāṇavīra made a start. But I think he went to an extreme in his criticisms, until his followers were dropping even the useful things. And he failed to make the necessary distinctions between *saupādisesa* and *anupādisesa*Nibbāna elements. That led to an idealized view of the noble disciple. And now there is a lineage of 'Ñāṇavīrists' who fail to see anything beyond Ven. Ñāṇavīra's views. They are simply idolizing him."

I was one of them until I started a correspondence with Bhante Ñāṇananda, so I know the way of thinking.

To end the discussion I pick up the thorniest of issues. I ask: "What is a 'thing'? Is it completely imaginary, or is it something made by the mind using the ingredients 'out there'?" A straightforward answer to that rather extremist question would make Bhante Ñāṇananda's position clear on the gamut of views.

"I'm sure you have read Ven. Bhikkhu Bodhi's translation of the Saṃyutta Nikāya. You must have come across the Pheṇapindūpama Sutta. In the notes you'll see Ven. Bodhi explaining that although the lump is illusory, the ingredients aren't. It is worse when it comes to the magic show. He says that only the magic is not real; the magician's appurtenances are. This is a distortion of the simile given by the Buddha. We must appreciate the great work done by Ven. Bodhi, but it is unfortunate that he is bound by the commentarial tradition.

"What is considered the 'truth' is relative to each individual. Each person gives evidence in the court of reality based on his own level of experience. For example, parents often give false explanations to their little children. But these are true to the kids. When asked, the kid will tell what his parents told him. It's true for the child, but not for us. In the famous commentarial story about Ven. Tissa Thera we find him seeing a woman as a skeleton, and saying so when asked by her husband. The venerable was closer to the truth.

"When we transcend one level of truth, the new level becomes what is true for us. The previous one is now false. What one experiences may not be what is experienced by the world in general, but that may well be truer. But how do we reach the ultimate truth? This is beautifully explained in the Dhātuvibhaṇga Sutta: *Taṃ saccaṃ, yaṃ amosadhammaṃ nibbānaṃ.* And from the Dvayatānupassanā Sutta: *amosadhammaṃ nibbānaṃ tad ariyā saccato vidū*. It is Nibbāna that is of non-falsifying nature, where there is no 'thing'. Nibbāna is the highest truth because there is no other truth to transcend it.

"The Buddha called himself the first chick in this era to break out of the egg of ignorance. All these wonderful things we do such as space travel all happen inside this *saḷāyatana* shell. If *paṭiccasamuppāda* is presented properly, perhaps a few more chicks would be able to break through today.

"Ven. Nāgārjuna was right: at the end, all is empty. We are not willing to accept that existence is a perversion. Existence is suffering precisely because it is a perversion."

It may not be a categorical answer, and it probably isn't possible to give one. But I will bring this issue up again later.

We have been talking for more than an hour, and it is time for Bhante's meal. I end the discussion, looking forward to another one in the evening.

NOTES

1. ^ Ṛgveda: sūkta 10.129 (English translation)

THE HERETIC SAGE (PART 3)

In the traditional exegesis, *pancupādānakkhandhā* (five aggregates of clinging) and *nāma-rūpa* (name-and-form) are used interchangeably, implying that these two are the same. As Ven. Ñāṇavīra Thera also pointed out in his *Notes on Dhamma*, this is a dubious interpretation that does not find explicit support in the Suttas. I ask Bhante Ñāṇananda how we should understand the connection between *pancupādānakkhandha* and *nāma-rūpa*.

"It is quite common to hear that these two are the same: that *rūpa-upādānakkhandha* is the same as the *rūpa* in *nama-rūpa*, and the other four aggregates are *nāma*. That is like trying to measure distance in kilograms – a confusion.

"In that beautiful seminar in a moonlit night recorded in the Mahāpuṇṇama Sutta, it is made quite clear that *viññāna* cannot be a part of *nāma*. One venerable asks *"Ko hetu ko paccayo rūpakkhandhassa paññāpanāya?"* and so on — what is the cause for the designation of each aggregate? And the Buddha answers that it is the four great elements that give rise to the designation of an aggregate of form. For *vedanā, saññā* and *saṅkhāra*, it is *phassa* – contact. But for *viññāna*, the cause is *nāma-rūpa*.

"We are used to explaining *paṭiccasamuppāda* in the form of the standard 12 links starting from avijjā. However, always trying to put *avijjā* at the lead in exegesis led to misinterpretations of certain Suttas. For example, commenting on the Mahānidāna Sutta, Ven. Buddhaghosa Thera brings in the so-called three-life interpretation whereas there is nothing missing from the Sutta itself. As I tried to explain in *The*

Magic of the Mind, it is from the preparations that are done in the darkness of ignorance that the duality of *viññāna* and*nāma-rūpa* arise.

"And what is that duality? The same duality seen by the dog on a plank over water." Bhante Ñāṇananda is referring to a simile he has often used in Dhamma discussions:

A dog is crossing a plank over a stream. Half way through it looks in to the water and sees another dog there. It wags its tail and the other responds. It snarls and the other reacts. It looks away to ignore, but when it looks again the water dog is still there looking on.

The view of an existing self is also due to such an unwise attention. "I think therefore I am" is the resulting wrong conclusion. Neither narcissistic love nor masochistic hate can solve the problem. Ignoring with a cynical sneer is to evade the problem. Therefore one has to thrash-down this problem of the elusive self image to the basic confrontation between consciousness and name and form.

– "Reflect Rightly on the Reflection", *From Topsy-turvydom to Wisdom*

"*Nāma-rūpa* is a deception. It is unreal. But in the illusion of *viññāna*, wherever you look, it is there. Whatever it may be, whether it's a sight or a sound or a thought, it is just *vedanā, saññā, cetanā, phassa, manasikāra*. But here again there is a common misinterpretation: when listing the *nāma-dhamma*–s, some start from *phassa, vedanā,...* They put *phassa* to the front. But *phassa* has to be at the back."

He says the above in Sinhala, where the word for 'back' is '*passa*'. The pun is lost in translation. As for putting *phassa* first, it is often seen in the Abhidhamma literature when listing the *cetasika*–s.

"They say so because in *paṭiccasamuppāda, phassa* comes before *vedanā*. That doesn't apply here. In the Suttas, such as the Sammādiṭṭhi Sutta, the ordering is never in that form. The Buddha and the Arahats were not mistaken; *logically*one can have phassa first, but *psychologically* it is *vedanā* that is primary. It is through *vedanā* that one recognizes the four great elements, not through*phassa*. The self notion hinges on *vedanā*. That is why it deserves to be the first.

"So one develops a *saññā* according to *vedanā*, based on which one has *cetanā*, at which point the 'personality' is taken for granted. This creates the duality necessary for *phassa*. *Manasikāra* is at the end, somewhat like *ekaggatā*, unifying them all: *manasikāra sambhavā sabbe dhammā* – all things arise from attention.

"With *vedanā*, the self notion 'awakens', although here it is more like dreaming. Or like a blind man groping in the dark. The blind man reacts only to the feeling of bumping on to something. That is why Ven. Ananda Thera replied to the Buddha that it is not possible to have any self notion when there is no *vedanā*.*Taṇhā* arises from *vedanā*.

"So where does *pañcupādānakkhandha* come in? *Pañcupādānakkhandhā is the final result of the constant tussle between viññāṇa and nāma-rūpa*. This is made clear in theMahāsaḷāyatanika Sutta. What is gathered from the six *viññāṇa*–s, at the end, are filtered down to things grasped as "these are my forms, these are my feelings, these are my perceptions, ...

"You might remember how the Buddha explained the designation ofa*khandha*, in the Mahāpuṇṇama Sutta: *atītānāgatapaccuppannaṃ ajjhattaṃ vā bahiddhā vā oḷārikaṃ vā sukhumaṃ vā hīnaṃ vā paṇītaṃ vā yaṃ dūre santike vā* (past, future, present, internal or external, gross or subtle, inferior or superior, far or near). That's the demarcation of the heap."

One of the main themes of Bhante Ñāṇananda's classic *The Magic of the Mind* is the illusory nature of *viññāṇa*. Earlier we discussed some of the nuances involved in differentiating between *viññāṇa* and *paññā*, and now the discussion moves on to the relationship between *viññāṇa* and *nāma-rūpa*.

"It's a pity that many Buddhists still cannot accept that the goal of this practice is the cessation of *viññāṇa*. It is a suffering; the simile for *viññāṇâhāra* is being beaten by a spear 300 times a day. The darkness of *avijjā* creates the background for it. As I pointed out with the similes of the cinema and the magic show, these things can only happen as long as there is darkness. All this is just an illusion, a drama. In fact, the oldest meaning of *saṅkhāra* is found in that context of a stage show.

"The connection between *viññāṇa* and *nāma-rūpa* can be illustrated with a childish simile: it is like a dog chasing its own tail. The modern Rohitassas who try to overcome a world as seen through *viññāna* are no different. They chase after what the Buddha dismissed as an illusion. There is nothing to go chasing after here; all that needs to be done is to stay where one is, and to realize that it is merely a shadow. When the darkness of *avijjā* is dispelled, *saṅkhāra*-s are stilled. The game is over.

"*Viññāṇa* and *nāma-rūpa* revolve around each other at an indescribable speed. That's why it was told to Ven. Sāti that it is wrong to say *"viññāṇaṃ sandhāvati saṃsarati anaññaṃ"* (it is this same *viññāṇa* that runs and wanders, not another). If only the Ābhidhammikas realized that *parivatta* in *lahuparivattaṃ cittaṃ* means 'revolving': *viññāṇa paccayā nāmarūpaṃ, nāmarūpa paccayā viññāṇaṃ.*

"The Gāthās in the Sagāthaka Vagga, although often not given enough attention, are very deep. I stopped the Nibbāna series at sermon number 33, but what I had planned for 34, although never delivered, was based on that beautiful verse from the Nimokkha Sutta:

Nandībhavaparikkhayā saññāviññāṇasaṅkhayā,
Vedanānaṃ nirodhā upasamā evaṃ khvāhaṃ āvuso jānāmi
Sattānaṃ nimokkhaṃ pamokkhaṃ vivekan'ti. [SN 1.2]

When delight and existence are exhausted
When perception and consciousness are both destroyed
When feelings cease and are appeased – thus, O friend,
Do I know, for them that live
Deliverance, freedom, detachment.

– *Translation by Bhante Ñāṇananda:* Saṃyutta Nikāya – An Anthology

"In all other religions, *viññāṇa* was taken as a unit, and worse, as the soul. It is taught that even if everything else is impermanent, this isn't. And it is taught as that which reaches *Brahmā*. But the Buddha pointed out that it is a mere illusion. It can't exist on its own.

"That brings us to a nice point. What is the simile used by Ven. Sariputta Thera to illustrate the *aññamaññapaccayatā* (interdependence) of *viññāṇa* and*nāma-rūpa*?"

"The simile of the two bundles of bamboo reeds" I reply.

"Why is that? Couldn't he have chosen something better, some wood with pith – say, two bundles of Sāla wood? See how penetrative they are even in their use of similes. The Pāḷi for bamboo reed is *tacasāra. Taca* means skin or peel, so *tacasāra* means that which has just the skin for its pith. The thing taken by the world as being full of pith is summarily dismissed by Ven. Sariputta Thera. It's not a unit either, but a bundle.

"I'm reminded of something Ven. Ñāṇavīra said: 'all consciousness is self consciousness.' That is quite right. Occasionally he came up with brilliant insights like that which shook the establishment. He was one who wasn't afraid to point out these misinterpretations. It is unfortunate that he was rather extremist in other areas.

"The whole notion of the so-called *antarābhava* depends on the belief that*viññāṇa* 'goes' on its own. The Buddha's explanation of the wandering of*viññāṇa* is not like that of the Upanishads where the simile of the leech is used.[1]According to the Dhamma *viññāṇa* and *nāma-rūpa* are in a state of whirling or turning around.

"The wandering of the mind is not like that of physical things. It's a circuitous journey of a mind and its object. With the taking up of one object by a mind, a sort of whirling begins; when one end is lost from grasp, the other end is taken up: *itthabāvaññathābhāvaṃ saṃsāraṃ n'ātivattati* – this-ness and otherwise-ness, that's all there is in *saṃsāra*. Our minds keep wandering away but keep coming back to this *upādinna*. Who likes to let go of it, to die? It always comes back to that which is held dearly. At the last moment, when Māra comes to snatch it away, one does not want to give it up, so there is a contest: the struggle for life. The Buddha asked us to just give it up.

"Think of any kind of existence, and you will see that it depends on grasping. There is no 'thing' that exists on its own. Here again, I'm reminded of something Dr. W.S.

Karunaratne said: 'Existence has got to be relative; there is no absolute existence.' But the world thinks of unitary things existing on their own. They ask, 'why, even when I don't look at this thing, doesn't it continue existing'? But really there is only a *diṭṭha*, a seen. There is only a *suta*, a heard. But the moment we think of a seen 'thing', a heard 'thing', we are trapped. We create things with*maññanā*, ideation.

"The problem with 'things' is solved in the Bāhiya Sutta: there are only *diṭṭha, suta, muta, viññāta*, nothing else. That is the theme in the Kālakārāma Sutta too. As long as one does *maññanā* about these, one would be deluded."

Here we seem to have encountered a more thorough answer to my earlier question about the 'reality of things', and it is quite clear that Bhante Ñāṇananda has quite a different view from the standard Theravadin interpretation which is closer to naïve realism. It is also opposed to Ven. Ñāṇavīra Thera's explanations, and readers who are familiar with *Clearing the Path* would notice that Bhante Ñāṇananda's interpretation is close to Sister Vajira's earlier views. It is easy to see why Bhante is sometimes accused of being a *viññāṇavādin*by those who are less willing to consider the subtleties involved.

"But how is *viññāṇa* made to cease?" Bhante adds, discussing the final goal of Buddhist practice. "*Viññāṇa* has the nature to reflect, and what it reflects is*nāma-rūpa*. One is attached to the reflection because one doesn't know that it is a reflection. But when the knowledge arises, attachment drops. In many instances where *paññā* is discussed, we find the words *paṭivedha* and *ativijjha*, meaning 'penetration'. The view is replaced by a vision."

Bhante then quotes from his own *Concept and Reality*:
For the Arahant ... all concepts have become transparent to such a degree in that all-encompassing vision, that their boundaries together with their umbra and penumbra have yielded to the radiance of wisdom. This, then, is the significance of the word *anantaṃ* (endless, infinite). Thus the paradoxically detached gaze of the contemplative sage as he looks through the concepts is one which has no object (*ārammaṇa*) as the point of focus for the worldling to iden-

tify it with. It is a gaze that is neither conscious nor non-conscious (*na saññī assa, saññī ca pana assa*), neither attentive nor non-attentive (*na manasikareyya, manasi ca pana kareyya*), neither fixed nor not fixed (*na jhāyati, jhāyati ca pana*) – a gaze that knows no horizon.

NOTES

1. ^ E.g.: "And just as a leech moving on a blade of grass reaches its end, takes hold of another and draws itself together towards it, so does the self, after throwing off this body, that is to say, after making it unconscious, take hold of another support and draw itself together towards it." [Bṛhadāraṇyaka Upaniṣad 4.4.3] – From *The Upanishads – A New Translation* by Swami Nikhilananda

THE HERETIC SAGE (PART 4)

The following is a minimally edited transcript of Bhante Ñāṇananda's comments on the Neyyattha Sutta, which seems to have been the seed out of which the Two Truths doctrine has been developed.

"We come across this in the Aṅguttara Nikāya: *nītattha sutta* and *neyyattha sutta.Nīta*, taken as it is, means you are led to it. *Neyya* means you have to be led. So *nīta*means you are already at the meaning; you don't have to reinterpret it. Whatever is supposed to be the *nīta* in the Buddha word, you have to take it 'as such'. Now, it is different when it comes to *neyyattha*: in that case you have to understand it in the context of the Dhamma; you can't take it as it appears.

"It is from this distinction that *sammuti / paramattha* and *samvṛti/paramārtha* (in Buddhist Sanskrit) have been developed. And also this is the reason I think the Nettippakaraṇa and Petakopadesa were composed, as guides to the commentator. Because it is the job of the commentator to explain a sutta, and *how* it should be explained is a problem. There are occasions when the Buddha used*loka samaññā loka nirutti* (worldly conventions, worldly parlance) as they are, according to the context. And on some occasions, especially to monks, he would say something very deep, which you have to take as it is.

"The traditional interpretation, as you get in the commentaries, is very simple: it says *neyyattha* would be such suttas where the ordinary concepts of beings etc. come in, but *nītattha* is where you get *anicca, dukkha, anattā*. That's a very simple definition of it.

"Among the discourses, there are some, like the Bāhiya Sutta, where you don't have to reintroduce anything in to it. But the people will have to introduce something to understand them – that's the whole trouble. A case which came to my attention was that sutta in the Saṃyutta Nikāya, the case of Moliyaphagguna, where, step by step, the Buddha had to correct even the question of Moliyaphagguna.[1] *Ko nu kho bhante phusati?* — it goes like that: 'who, lord, does touch?' [The Buddha replies:] 'I don't say like that. If I did, then you can ask me like that. The correct question should be: *Kim paccayā?*'

"So the *paccaya* terminology is actually the *nītattha*, if I may say so. But you can't talk with *paccaya* always. In fact, I remember some people who tried to avoid the 'I' concept altogether in conversations, using such phrases as 'this*pañcakkhandha*'. But that's only artificial.

"This I may say is a challenge to understand the discourses. Because you always have to ask yourself: what are the *nītattha* suttas and what are the *neyyattha* suttas? Without a criterion to decide, you are in a fix. But if you start on your own, I think you could take instances where the Buddha is talking about the four noble truths, as well as *paticcasamuppāda*.

"This is an instance where we see the difference between the grammar of nature and the grammar of language. You have to give way to the grammar of language if you're to talk. Because if you are to explain, you have to make compromises with language, as we say 'it rains' or *'devo vassatu'*. Otherwise there is something lacking. The subject, the object and then the adjectives and adverbs and the sentence structure – these are deciding our thinking. The logicians are bound by it. That is why the Dhamma is *atakkāvacara*. That again is a challenge: what is meant by *atakkāvacara*?

"Logic has to distinguish one from the other. It is again a logical question when they ask: *saññā* and *vedanā* – are they completely different, or are they the same thing? That is the way logic would put it. There's no half way between. Even that they tried to cover: I'm not very familiar with logic but what is already apparent in the canon is the tetralemma. The question of contradiction comes in: either it has to be this or the other. But there are these grey areas.

"All these problems come up because, first of all, we break reality – the flux of life – in to pieces. We differentiate between a 'thing' and its colour: the colour is an adjective; the object is something else. So we create problems for ourselves. But then the Buddha had to convey a message – and in fact I make it a point to say, why the Buddha hesitated to teach was not out of jealousy or any other reason, but the problem was how to present this doctrine in an intelligible way to people. I may say that only the Buddha had that ability. Though it is again an unsolved problem, about the *Pacceka Buddha*-s, it seems, if ever they remain silent, hence called 'silent' Buddhas, it is because they could not, unlike the Buddha, bring these two truths in to alignment.

"Already in the Kalakārāma Sutta you see how deep the problem is. But the Buddha could explain it sufficiently for one to start practicing. And once you start practicing, then, as in the Cūlahatthipadopama Sutta, you are walking the Dhamma-way, and you'll realize by yourself. You go and see. Now, even though the Dhamma says *ehipassika*, we don't want to go; we want to stay where we are and go through logic to understand the Dhamma. That is the problem with the scholars.

"The Buddha's Dhamma was an invitation. If you start the practice, the rest you will know by yourself. The map can't be the same as the journey. No map is complete by itself; it may use colours and signs etc. but it is never complete. So is the Dhamma. Much of it, the Buddha left unexplained. That is probably why the people are now complaining that there is no methodology here and that something is lacking in the Dhamma. But you can't be spoon-fed.

"It is because the Buddha has given sufficient advice that some could realize even by just listening. They didn't merely listen: they listened with rapt attention. Like in Ven. Bāhiya's case, they were not leading idle lives. Their plaything was *jhāna*. So it was easy for the Buddha to make them understand, as they had a sharp receptive apparatus. They only needed *saddhā*. Without *saddhā, with logic* if you're hoping to understand, you're gravely mistaken.

"So now, getting down to the type of suttas we have, at a glance, perhaps, Bāhiya sutta is a clear cut case, although those who want something objective, with a substantialist view, would find something lacking there. And also, for instance, when the Buddha answered the accusations of the Brahmins, and when we come to the ten indeterminate points, that perhaps is something like*nītattha*. The Buddha is put to that point where He can't agree any longer to the convention. Because He used conventional words, people made it an excuse to glean advantage from it. That is the case with Nibbāna: the fire going out.

"If the fire 'goes out' some think you should be able to go and locate where it is. Some scholars in the West also follow the same Hindu way where they think when the fire goes out it stays in some ineffable state. When it comes to such points of absurdity the Buddha had to correct them. Otherwise the Buddha would, for all practical purposes, use the convention. Even to Bāhiya He said 'This is our *pinḍapāta* time', as if there's some strict time for *pinḍapāta*. As if His whole life is for *pinḍapāta*. 'We have to go on pinḍapāta, don't come and question us'! But when it comes to the Dhamma: 'in the seen, just the seen, in the heard, just the heard.' When Bāhiya could master and muster sufficient Samādhi he had built up in the past, when he was sufficiently calmed down, then the Buddha gave the real thing.

"There are also other occasions, for instance in the Saṃyutta Nikāya, where you find the verses:

Ahaṃ vadāmīti pi so vadeyya
Mamaṃ vadantīti pi so vadeyya,
Loke samaññaṃ kusalo viditvā
Vohāramattena so vohareyyā'ti. [SN 1.25]

That monk still might use such words as "I,"
Still perchance might say: "They call this mine."
Well aware of common worldly speech,
He would speak conforming to such use. (*Source*)

"So every time the Buddha says 'I'm going' and so on, you should not think that He's contradicted His own *anattā* doctrine.

"*Nītattha* could also be in such cases like in the Alagaddūpama Sutta where the brahmins are repremanded for false accusations. The Buddha comes out with the statement: *Pubbe c'āhaṃ bhikkhave etarahi ca dukkhañceva paññāpemi dukkhassa ca nirodhaṃ* – that is the best criterion to decide on which side you are. 'All formerly and now, I merely say that there is suffering' – there is no *one* suffering, whether it's a *puggala* or person or individual – all this rot comes in because of not knowing that the Buddha's message is also part and parcel of language.

"For all practical purposes, the Buddha's words are enough. But for those who do not practice, but who are armchair critics, there is so much contradiction in the Buddha's words. Sometimes He says there is *dukkha* only, and sometimes He says you are suffering. This is also the reason why there is such a mess in the interpretations of the *kamma* doctrine also. In *sammādiṭṭhi,* we may say there's the 'lower' *sammādiṭṭhi* and the 'higher' *sammādiṭṭhi.*[2] The *dasa-vatthuka sammādiṭṭhi* is *kammassakatā.* When a person takes *kamma* as his own, he's bound by it. You are bound by your own grasping. Then it's a fact that you're going to these various realms etc.: dependent on *avijjā* there is *saṅkhāra.* Such people have to be judged by their own standards.

"By the way, I may also say, now that we are on the point: if you're translating the Dhammapada, it is wrong according to my understanding to translate the*attavagga* as the chapter on *Self.* It should be *oneself.* Otherwise, as Radhakrishnan finds it, you are on the side of attā. But it is 'oneself': reflexive. If you understand that as self there's a contradiction between *attāhi attano natthi* and*attāhi attano natho.* But these are just *loke samaññā.*

"Similarly in the Poṭṭhapāda Sutta, now and then the Buddha had to come out, especially in the last words of the sutta – they are very powerful: *imā kho citta loka samaññā... yāhi tathāgato voharati, aparāmasaṃ* ("Citta, these are the world's designations, the world's expressions, the world's ways of speaking, the world's descriptions, with which the Tathagata expresses himself but without grasping to them.") I remember reading *The Meaning of Meaning* by Ogden and Richards; there they quoted from the Poṭṭhapāda Sutta. They understood that there's something very deep in that simile about milk, curd, butter etc. Though they didn't get everything, they knew the Buddha was nearer the truth about semantics.

"But now we think that where there's a word there should be something. It's the *thing* that's causing all the trouble. There's just a flux of life, a functioning, but no agent in it. But the language requires both. That is why we have to say 'it rains', leaving the room for someone to ask 'what is this 'it'?'. The fire goes out: where has it 'gone'? The Buddha from time to time had to show the absurdity of such questions. In such contexts you come across the *nītattha*."

NOTES

1. ^ SN 12.12 (excerpt below)
2. ^ "And what is right view? Right view, I tell you, is of two sorts: There is right view with effluents, siding with merit, resulting in the acquisitions; and there is noble right view, without effluents, transcendent, a factor of the path." [MN 117]

ADDENDUM FOR NOTE 1

[...]

"Who, now, Lord, exercises contact?"

"Not a fit question", said the Exalted One. "I am not saying (someone) exercises contact. If I were saying so, the question would be a fit one. But I am not saying so. And I not saying so, if anyone were to ask this: 'Conditioned, now, by what, Lord, is contact?', this were a fit question. And the fit answer there, would be: 'Conditioned by the sixfold sense-sphere, is contact, conditioned by contact is feeling'." [...]

– Translation by Bhante Ñāṇananda: Saṃyutta Nikāya – An Anthology

THE HERETIC SAGE (PART 5)

The final part of the Mahāhatthipadopama Sutta contains an interesting analysis by Ven. Sāriputta Thera which sheds light on the connection between *saḷāyatana* and *pañcupādānakkhandha*. I had carelessly commented on this section by reading the English translation without referring to the Pāḷi, and in his reply to my notes Bhante Ñāṇananda pointed out an important distinction I had failed to make.

Ven. Ñāṇamoli's translation of the relevant section reads as follows:

If, friends, internally the eye is intact but no external forms come into its range, and there is no corresponding [conscious] engagement, then there is no manifestation of the corresponding section of consciousness. [MLDB (2009) p. 283]

'Corresponding [conscious] engagement' is Ven. Ñāṇamoli's rendering of *tajjo samannāhāra*. I had taken this to be identical to *manasikāra* (attention), influenced by Ven. Ñāṇavīra Thera's writings. In my interview, I ask Bhante Ñāṇananda for an explanation on the difference between the two.

"Earlier we pointed out how, in a discussion that may be categorized as*nītattha*, the Buddha corrected Ven. Moliyaphagguna's questions which implied an agent behind action. He rephrased them with the *paccaya* terminology. Similarly, when we say *manasikāra*, some may tend to think of an agent behind the attention. But Ven. Sāriputta Thera takes a different approach here when explaining the arising of *viññāṇa*.

"He discusses three possibilities:

1. The eye is not 'broken' – it is functional. External forms don't come to the vicinity. And *Tajjo samannāhāra*, whatever that may be, is not present. Then, there's no eye consciousness.

"Here, we have to be specific about *viññāṇa*. Again, I'm reminded of something Dr. W.S. Karunaratne said: "There is no *'the viññāṇa'*; it is always *'a viññāṇa'*. Everything has to be concrete – there is no abstract consciousness." But people think that consciousness exists on its own, and this has given rise to various theories. Ven. Ñāṇavīra Thera also pointed this out when he said "*paṭiccasamuppāda* is *viññāṇa*".[1] I may not agree with everything he said, but here he did reveal an important matter. The reciprocal relationship betweenviññāṇa and *nāma-rūpa* is the vortex of existence, and it is the heart of*paṭiccasamuppāda*.

2. The eye is not broken, and external forms do come to the vicinity. But *tajjo samannāhāra* is absent. Then, there is no eye-consciousness.

3. The eye is not broken, external forms come to the vicinity, and there is *tajjo samannāhāra*. Then, there is eye-consciousness.

"The word *tajjo* comes from *tat + ja*. *Tat* means 'that [itself]'. It is the root of such important words as *tādī* and *tammaya*. So tatja means 'arisen out of that itself'. What is *samannāhāra*? You might remember that, in the Caṅkī Sutta, the Buddha happens to see the Kāpaṭhika Brahmin youth. There we find the word*upasaṃharati* along with *samannāhāra*,[2] referring to a sort of focusing that may have not been planned – a chance meeting of eye to eye. *Samannāhāra* (*āharati* = brings) refers to a certain 'bringing together'.

"So *tajjo samannāhāra* points to the fact that this 'bringing together' of the necessary factors for the arising of consciousness is inherent to the situation itself. It is unique to the situation, and does not come from within a person or from the outside. It is not exerted by oneself or an external agent: some thought that there is an *ātman* inside who is in charge, while others said that it is a God that injects consciousness into the man. Letting go of all these extremes, Ven. Sāriputta Thera pointed out the crucial role of *tajjo samannāhāra* with his analysis of the three possibilities."

And then Bhante falls silent, and looks on with a smile.

After a few moments, he asks: "What do you hear?"

There is a bird singing in the distance.

"Did it start singing only now?"

It probably had started earlier (and now that I am listening to the tapes as I transcribe this, I know that it had started many minutes earlier).

"It must have been singing all this while, but only now..." I say.

"Only now...?"

"Only now did the attention went there."

"*There* you have *tajjo samannāhāra*! So is it only because of the sound of the bird that you heard it? Didn't you hear it only after I stopped talking? There could be other reasons too: had there been louder noises, you may not have heard it. So we see that it is circumstantial. That is why we mentioned in our writings:*everything is circumstantial; nothing is substantial*."

Please allow me to interject here and add that the last sentence would remain something that I'll always cherish from these interviews. Not only because of the simple profundity of the statement or the nice little practical experiment that led up to it, but also because of the gentle kindness in the way it was uttered.

"The attention that is present in a situation is to be understood as having arisen out of the circumstances. If there is anything of value in the Paṭṭhāna, that would be here, in its analysis of the 24 causes. I can't say for certain, but it may well be an attempt at systematising the general concept mentioned in this sutta: how a thought is connected to another. Since it is impossible to explain this mechanism by breaking it apart with words, Ven. Sāriputta Thera says it is circumstantial – unique to the situation itself.

"It is because of this nature of the Buddhadhamma that the later Indian philosophers called it a *saṅghātavāda* – pluralism, or a theory of aggregates, where the causes are not limited to one or two or none. So my silence *paṭicca*, the sound of the bird *paṭicca*, absence of other sounds *paṭicca* etc. there was the arising of a different ear-consciousness.

"It is alright to refer to *tajjo samannāhāra* as *manasikāra* as long as we make it clear that the process is impersonal. We may also bring in the Kiṃ Mūlaka Sutta[3] here. Unfortunately my explanation of it in *The Magic of the Mind*, in the chapter 'Essence of Concepts', was not accepted even by Ven. Nyanaponika. In the sutta we find the statement *manasikāra sambhavā sabbe dhammā* (born of attention are all things). The commentary limits the discussion just to skillful states, which is a very narrow way of looking at it. Be it *sammā* or *micchā*, there the Buddha is pointing out the general principle.

"It is probably because of the importance of the principle discussed that the Buddha brought up the subject without being prompted by anyone. It is as if He declared it because the world would not hear or realize it otherwise. The sutta is a wonderful revelation about what we take as a 'thing'. It is not something existing on its own in the world but a result of many psychological causes. But when we say that, we are accused of being *viññāṇavādins* and *suññatavādins*.

"One has to ask: why did the Buddha say *'manopubbaṇgamā dhammā, manoseṭṭhā manomayā'* (Mind precedes all dhammas. Mind is their chief; they are all mind-wrought – Dhp 1)? One has to admit that the Dhamma is *mano-mūlika*. But again, the mind is just one of the senses. What we have here is just a self-created problem. We discussed how existence is a perversion. The arising of dhammas is also the arising of *dukkha*. Not realizing this, some go looking for the truth among 'things'.

"The search goes on because of delusion, and it is fruitless because they are chasing illusions. Dhammas, things, are all fabricated. They are all relative. They are all results of *maññanā* (ideation). Just as those who were entrenched in self-view saw the Buddha as a nihilist, those who are entrenched in materialism cannot grasp the Buddhist philosophy which puts the mind first."

Here I ask a recurring question, probably because I still can't bring myself to accept the already given answers due to my own materialistic tendencies (of those days): what would one see if one looks at the world 'objectively' – if such a thing were possible? Perhaps this is another way of asking what one sees in the*arahattaphala samādhi*.

"*Suññatā*" comes the quick reply.

"Whether people accept it or not, the truth is emptiness. We need not go far: it is already there in the three words *animitta, appaṇihita* and *suññata*. One has to go from *nimitta* (sign) to *animitta* (signless), with the help of signs. The culmination of*paṇidhi* (resolve) is *appaṇihita* (undirected). 'Thingness' gives way to emptiness.

"Imagine there were a large box here, with a label saying that the contents weigh 1000kg. If I were to ask you to move it, you'd object saying that it is too heavy for one person to handle. Let's say I somehow coax you to try. When you try to lift, it comes off almost without effort – there's no bottom to the box! The 1000kg sign was deceiving you. That's why the realization of the Dhamma is equated to laying down of a burden.

"To realize emptiness, one has to know what one is aiming at. *Yad'anuseti, tad'anumīyati, yad'anumīyati, tena saṇkhaṃ gacchati* (If one has an underlying tendency towards something, then one is measured in accordance with it. If one is measured in accordance with something, then one is reckoned in terms of it. [SN 22.36]). As long as there is *anusaya* there would be measuring, giving rise to the concept of 'things'. Elimination of *anusaya* is like the bottom of the box giving way. After that, anyone can lift it."

COLOPHON

This is part 5 of a series on Ven. Katukurunde Ñāṇananda Thera. In November 2009 I had the opportunity to stay at his monastery for a few days and have several long conversations with him. The articles are based on the recordings of these discussions.

NOTES

1. ^ ... any exemplification of *paṭiccasamuppāda* in the sphere of experience can be re-stated in the form of the fundamental exemplification of*paṭiccasamuppāda* in the sphere of experience, which is, as it must be, that beginning with *viññāṇa*.
Thus, *viññāṇa* and *paṭiccasamuppāda* are one.
– Ven. Ñāṇavīra Thera, *Notes on Dhamma*, "A Note on Paṭiccasamuppāda", para. 20
2. ^ *Atha kho kāpaṭhikassa māṇavassa etadahosi: 'yadā me samaṇo gotamo cakkhunā cakkhuṃ* ***upasaṃharissati****, athāhaṃ samaṇaṃ gotamaṃ pañhaṃ pucchissāmī'ti. Atha kho bhagavā kāpaṭhikassa māṇavassa cetasā cetoparivitakkamaññāya yena kāpaṭhiko māṇavo tena cakkhūni* ***upasaṃhāsi****. Atha kho kāpaṭhikassa māṇavassa etadahosi: '****samannāharati*** *kho maṃ samaṇo gotamo, yannūnāhaṃ samaṇaṃ gotamaṃ pañhaṃ puccheyyanti.* [MII p. 169 (PTS)]
Then the thought occurred to Kāpaṭhika the youth, "When Gotama the contemplative meets my gaze with his, I will ask him a question." And so the Blessed One, encompassing Kāpaṭhika's awareness with his awareness, met his gaze. Kāpaṭhika thought, "Gotama the contemplative has turned to me. Suppose I ask him a question." [MN 95]
3. ^ [...] Rooted in desire (or interest) friends, are all things; born of attention are all things; arising from contact are all things; converging on feelings are all things; headed by concentration are all things; dominated by mindfulness are all things; surmountable by wisdom are all things; yielding deliverance as essence are all things; merging in the Deathless are all things; terminating in Nibbana are all things. [Excerpted from AN 8.83]
– Translation by Bhante Ñāṇananda (*The Magic of the Mind*)

Sadhu! Sadhu! Sadhu!

8654487R1

Made in the USA
Lexington, KY
19 February 2011